EVENT MANAGE-MENT

FOR TOURISM, CULTURAL, BUSINESS AND SPORTING EVENTS

EDITION 5

EVENT MANAGE-MENT

LYNN VAN DER WAGEN
LAUREN WHITE

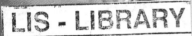
✺ CENGAGE

Australia • Brazil • Mexico • Singapore • United Kingdom • United States

Event Management: For tourism, cultural, business and
sporting events
5th Edition
Lynn van der Wagen
Lauren White

Publishing manager: Dorothy Chiu
Publishing editor: Chee Ng
Developmental editor: Lydia Crisp/Rhiannon Bowen
Project editor: Sutha Surenddar
Cover design: Chris Starr (MakeWork)
Text design: Norma van Rees
Editor: Paul Smitz/Julie Wicks
Proofreader: Jamie Anderson
Permissions/Photo researcher: Wendy Duncan
Project Designer: Emma Alsweiler
Typeset by MPS Ltd

Any URLs contained in this publication were checked for
currency during the production process. Note, however, that
the publisher cannot vouch for the ongoing currency of URLs.

The previous edition was published by Pearson, Van der
Wagen & White, Events Management 4e.

Acknowledgements

Every effort has been made to track and acknowledge
copyright. However, if any infringement has occurred, the
publishers tender their apologies and invite the copyright
holder to contact them.

For product information and technology assistance,
in Australia call **1300 790 853**;
in New Zealand call **0800 449 725**

For permission to use material from this text or product, please email
aust.permissions@cengage.com

National Library of Australia Cataloguing-in-Publication Data

Creator: Lynn van der Wagen, author.
Title: Event Management: For tourism, cultural, business
and sporting events/Lynn van der Wagen and Lauren white
Edition: 5th edition
ISBN: 9780170394451 (paperback)
Notes: Includes index.
Subjects: Event Management.
Other Creators/Contributors:
Lauren White, author.

Cengage Learning Australia
Level 7, 80 Dorcas Street
South Melbourne, Victoria Australia 3205

Cengage Learning New Zealand
Unit 4B Rosedale Office Park
331 Rosedale Road, Albany, North Shore 0632, NZ

For learning solutions, visit **cengage.com.au**

Printed in China by China Translation & Printing Services.
1 2 3 4 5 6 7 22 21 20 19 18

BRIEF CONTENTS

CONTENTS

Guide to the text

As you read this text you will find a number of features in every chapter to enhance your study of Event management and help you understand how the theory is applied in the real world.

CHAPTER OPENING FEATURES

1

SOURCE AND USE INFORMATION ON THE EVENTS INDUSTRY

OVERVIEW

This chapter will provide an overview of the event industry, covering the scope of the many different types of events. It will also highlight relationships with other sectors, such as tourism, hospitality, sports, business and the community.

As the industry is so dynamic, it is essential to keep up to date with current and emerging information, particularly in the areas of technology, laws, regulations and ethical issues. The event industry evolves very quickly, and the focus of this chapter is on researching information and maintaining currency.

LEARNING OBJECTIVES

On completion of this chapter, you will be able to:

1. source and interpret relevant industry information identifying key products and services in order to assist with operational duties and enhance the quality of work performance
2. source and use compliance information – that is, laws and regulations that apply to events – and ensure that ethical issues are considered
3. keep up to date with technological changes that impact on event planning and execution, including online and virtual components
4. monitor current trends and issues and share this information with colleagues.

NEW: Identify the key concepts that the chapter will cover with the **Learning Objectives** and **Overview** at the start of each chapter.

FEATURES WITHIN CHAPTERS

INDUSTRY VIEWPOINT

Consumers advised to beware when buying concert tickets

NSW Fair Trading Minister Matthew Mason-Cox is encouraging consumers who are planning to purchase concert tickets to buy from reputable ticketing agencies, as complaints surge.

Gain an insight into how Event Management theories relate to the real world through the **Industry Viewpoint** at the beginning of each chapter.

EXAMPLE

TICKETING DEBACLE LEAVES RICKY MARTIN FANS FURIOUS

Ricky Martin treated Townsville to the Australian premiere of his global One World Tour at the weekend, giving his adoring fans the type of show that's rarely seen in the city. Saucy dancers, polished routines and a high-energy performance left Townsville fans at his two sold-out shows screaming for more.

Analyse practical applications of concepts through the real-world **Examples**.

Discuss the press release below by answering the following question from the viewpoint of the police, the event organiser and the individual concerned: Who has responsibility for managing the safety of drug users at festivals?

EXTENSION ACTIVITY

DRUG CHARGES AT MUSIC FESTIVAL FORTITUDE VALLEY

Police have charged more than 120 people during an outdoor music festival on December 6 and 7 in Fortitude Valley, Brisbane. A total of 123 people were arrested and charged with 127 offences

Research how theoretical concepts have been used in practice through the **Extension Activity** boxes.

END-OF-CHAPTER FEATURES

At the end of each chapter you'll find several tools
to help you to review, practise and extend your
knowledge of the key learning objectives.

Summary

In this chapter we have reviewed the stages of event registration. Hopefully, the key message of this chapter is understood to be 'attention to detail'. An athlete with the wrong timing device, a graduate without a certificate, a new citizen given the wrong information about a ceremony – all are examples of the things that can go wrong at important times for event attendees. People can also arrive late and be confused, needing direction and reassurance, as getting around some of the larger events is confounding. Thus, the role of anyone working at the point of registration is to provide a good first impression and give clear directions and instructions.

Key terms

Accreditation	Process of issuing access to specific event zones or areas
Event program	The line-up of speakers or entertainers at an event
Indemnity	Exemption from liability for damages
RFID	Radio frequency identification chip or transponder
Trade show	A trade show is designed to sell products, mainly to retailers

Review your understanding of the key chapter topics with the **Summary** and **Key terms** recap.

REVIEW YOUR KNOWLEDGE

1   What is a budget?
2   What are the different types of budgets?
3   Why are budgets important for a business?
4   What are some of the important factors you would consider before allocating budget resources?

APPLY YOUR KNOWLEDGE

Using the following budget, and actual figures, calculate the variances for each item. Suggest ways in which profitability can be improved in relation to managing expenses.

Test your knowledge and consolidate your learning through the **Review your knowledge** and **Apply your knowledge** questions.

CASE STUDY

STUDENT RAVE PARTY

A group of university students decided to hold a rave party up in some nearby mountains one December and advertised it on Facebook. Three bands attended the three-day party and there was 24-hour music. One young girl described it as a living hell, although why she stayed is unfathomable: 'The dance area was in a valley, and to get a drink of water you had to climb a steep hill. Even then, the water was dirty and brown. The toilets were so far away that nobody bothered to use them. The music pounded all night and the floor vibrated so you couldn't sleep. My friend was unwell and there was no medical help. The organisers didn't have a clue. They just wanted to make a fast buck'.

QUESTIONS

1   What are some of the things that could go wrong, or have gone wrong, at similar events?
2   List three ways in which the organisers' arrangements were unsatisfactory.
3   List three ways in which the event could have been improved.
4   This event was described to the authorities as a cultural festival. Do you think this was accurate?
5   The legal compliance issues of such an event will be covered in a later chapter. However, investigate the concept of 'duty of care' and summarise your understanding of it.

Analyse in-depth **Case studies** that present issues in context and ask you to make your own decisions.

Guide to the online resources

FOR THE INSTRUCTOR

Cengage Learning is pleased to provide you with a selection of resources that will help you prepare your lectures and assessments. These teaching tools are accessible via cengage.com.au/instructors for Australia or cengage.co.nz/instructors for New Zealand.

MAPPING GRID

The **Mapping grid** is a simple grid that shows how the content of this book relates to the units of competency needed to complete the Diploma of Event Management SIT50316.

SOLUTIONS MANUAL

The **Solutions manual** provides detailed solutions to the questions at the end of each chapter in the text.

WORD-BASED TEST BANK

This bank of questions has been developed in conjunction with the text for creating quizzes, tests and exams for your students. Deliver these though your LMS and in your classroom.

POWERPOINT™ PRESENTATIONS

Use the chapter-by-chapter **PowerPoint slides** to enhance your lecture presentations and handouts by reinforcing the key principles of your subject.

ARTWORK FROM THE TEXT

Add the **digital files** of graphs, tables, pictures and flow charts into your course management system, use them in student handouts, or copy them into your lecture presentations.

FOR THE STUDENT

Visit the **Event Management** companion website. You'll find:

- flashcards
- glossary
- more tools to help you excel in your studies

PREFACE

As a professional field of practice, event management requires sophisticated skills in strategic planning, risk analysis, marketing, budgeting, cash flow planning and human resource management. There are chapters on all these topics and many others in this book. Indeed, more and more public events are appointing professionally trained staff to senior positions. The project nature of events, as well as the range of risks they carry (including financial risk), means that skilled and knowledgeable management staff are required. In fact, many major projects in today's corporate world are one-off events requiring these skills.

The knowledge and skills gained in the study of event management can be used in diverse contexts. Event management covers a wide range of interest areas, including business, sport and the arts. Most significantly, governments and local councils are developing policies and procedures supported by legislation, making legal compliance and risk management important responsibilities for the professional event manager.

The appendix to this book is provided by the City of Greater Geelong. This comprehensive guide, which is accompanied by more tools and templates online, is extremely helpful for anyone planning an event. Similar guidelines are available from other government bodies on subjects such as the safety of mass gatherings, food hygiene, traffic management and so on. The websites listed at the end of each chapter link to many of these very helpful sites.

Students emerge from this field of study with business and project management skills of the highest order, ready to face any business challenge. They can confidently apply for a wide range of positions (few of them titled 'event manager') for which this type of training has prepared them. Indeed, recognising the project orientation and customer responsiveness of most modern organisations, students can be confident that they are developing skills for the future. Many events are also community focused and this has particular appeal for many entrants to the area. The tourism impact of events is increasingly attracting the interest of governments seeking to maximise domestic and international tourism revenues. All of these trends are contributing towards the development of events management as a professional practice.

About this book

This is the fifth edition of the popular text Event Management. The wide range of events illustrated in this edition demonstrates the diverse range of events that managers may encounter during their careers. Examples are provided for tourism, cultural, business and sporting events, to name a few, with the primary focus being on the project orientation of work in this field. Given that we are moving towards an 'experience economy', an understanding of events as projects is highly relevant to many areas of the modern workplace. The knowledge and skills outlined in the book cover key areas of event services, event planning, on-site operations, concepts and bids, compliance, marketing, finance, workforce planning and event implementation.

This text is closely aligned with the nationally recognized Diploma of Event Management. Numerous pedagogical features are included including chapter openings (quotes from the industry), examples and illustrations. The chapters include engagement activities for discussion and debate. At the end of each chapter there are assessment activities requiring understanding, application and analysis of case studies. Web links to useful industry resources will be valuable. A glossary of terms is included at the end of the book.

The final chapter covers the biggest challenges facing an event manager, that being planning infrastructure and services for a council approved event. The Appendix provides a summative assessment and guidelines from government and industry to guide readers. These include the very helpful event planning guidelines provided by Geelong City Council, part one being reproduced in the text with links to more detailed planning guidelines such as traffic management also available online.

Guide to resources

References made to third party resources can be followed using weblinks provided.

Event planning guides (e.g. Geelong City Council) and exhibition manuals (e.g. Perth Convention and Exhibition Centre) are available with permission.

The blog on wordpress provides currency: https://lynnvanderwagen.wordpress.com/

Guide to instructor resources

1   Powerpoints are provided for each chapter
2   Model answers and marking guides are provided for end of chapter assessments
3   Multiple choice questions are provided for each chapter
4   The above assessments are mapped to the competency unit
5   A photo library is also provided for instructors

ABOUT THE AUTHORS

Dr Lynn Van der Wagen is Head Teacher of Tourism and Events at TAFE NSW, Northern Sydney. She coordinates the delivery of the Bachelor of Event and Tourism Management (which is delivered in partnership with Canberra University). Lynn played a key role in the team that trained the 100 000-strong workforce for the 2000 Sydney Olympic Games. Her enthusiasm for the mega-event evolved into roles with the Beijing Olympic Games, Shanghai Expo and London Olympic Games.

Awarded a NSW Premier's Teacher Scholarship in 2014, Lynn conducted extensive research in China (home of the world's largest trade exhibition, the Canton fair) and Singapore in order to look at new trends, in particular the ICT skills required by event managers of the future.

Lauren White has extensive experience in corporate communications. She has a degree in Communications from the University of Technology Sydney (UTS) and has managed public relations campaigns which have included media events. She has volunteered for the Rugby World Cup, experiencing the media component of that event. As trends in new media, social networking and experiential marketing have important implications for event managers of the future, the experience she brings is highly relevant in the new edition.

ACKNOWLEDGEMENTS

We would like to thank the many people and organisations acknowledged throughout the book who made invaluable contributions by providing case studies, diagrams, photographs and discussion material. Several people provided professional support in the writing of this book, including Ron Beeldman, Anitra Walker, Robyn Spencer, Lesley Guthrie, Warwick Hamilton and Mike Hammond. Staging Connections has supplied several images and several event and government organisations have provided information and illustrations.

This text is based on the Tourism, Travel and Hospitality Training Package, produced by the Commonwealth Department of Education and Training. It comprises nationally endorsed standards and qualifications for assessing and recognising people's skills. In order to accurately reflect the nationally agreed guidelines, a number of headings, paragraphs and lists from the training package have been integrated into the text, and the author hereby acknowledges the use of this copyright material.

The authors and Cengage Learning would also like to thank the following reviewers for their incisive and helpful feedback:

- Leighanne Campbell – Prime Learning
- Patrea D'Antonio – Northern Sydney Institute of TAFE
- Julie Edwards – Sejumi Institute
- Jeremy Glover – Swinburne TAFE
- Eugene Gomes – Polytechnic West
- Paraic Kavanagh – North Coast Institute of TAFE
- Isabell Kormos – Gordon Institute of TAFE
- Paul Newburn – Evolution Hospitality Institute
- Peter Seabrook – Northern Sydney Institute of TAFE

We would also like to acknowledge Lynn Van der Wagen's *Hospitality Management* (third edition), which has provided useful content for a number of chapters of this book.

It has been a pleasure working on this edition with the highly professional team at Cengage. And to loyal readers, students everywhere, thank you for your feedback. May all your events be successful!

Lynn Van der Wagen and Lauren White

1

EVENT SERVICES

1 SOURCE AND USE INFORMATION ON THE EVENTS INDUSTRY

OVERVIEW

This chapter will provide an overview of the event industry, covering the scope of the many different types of events. It will also highlight relationships with other sectors, such as tourism, hospitality, sports, business and the community.

As the industry is so dynamic, it is essential to keep up to date with current and emerging information, particularly in the areas of technology, laws, regulations and ethical issues. The event industry evolves very quickly, and the focus of this chapter is on researching information and maintaining currency.

LEARNING OBJECTIVES

On completion of this chapter, you will be able to:

1. source and interpret relevant industry information identifying key products and services in order to assist with operational duties and enhance the quality of work performance

2. source and use compliance information – that is, laws and regulations that apply to events – and ensure that ethical issues are considered

3. keep up to date with technological changes that impact on event planning and execution, including online and virtual components

4. monitor current trends and issues and share this information with colleagues.

INDUSTRY VIEWPOINT

Lost paradise: Escape the norm for an adventure amongst nature

Lost Paradise is a music, arts, yoga, performance, food and camping experience like no other. Kindred spirits commune together for three days on the sacred grounds of Glenworth Valley, New South Wales to explore and discover new music, indulge in delicious dining, interact with visual and performance art outside a traditional setting, and celebrate life in all its technicolour glory.

Placed in an amazing setting within a valley on ancient land known to local Indigenous Elders as 'Paradise Lost', it showcases a brilliant line-up, secret hideaways and glittering late night discos, an inspirational art and performance repertoire, spoken word and debate, a magnificent Carnival parade, culinary feasts, restorative massage, a variety of Yoga to indulge the body, mind and soul, and much, much more. It appeals to both fans of electronic music as to nature lovers, to families with young kids as to the 30 somethings that like the finer things in life, to foodies as to folkies, funksters as to late night revellers. There is something at Lost Paradise for everyone.

Source: Lost Paradise (2016). https://lostparadise.com.au/experiences-activities

INTRODUCTION

Similar in many respects to California's Coachella, Lost Paradise, held in NSW's Glenworth Valley, provides a wide variety of experiences and offers on-site camping. It is a new event – the first Lost Paradise was held in 2015. Coachella, which was founded in 1999, is reported to be one of the most profitable music festivals in the United States (Faughder, 2016). It features many genres of music across several stages and also includes art installations and sculptures. Coachella is now so popular that the festival is held on consecutive three-day weekends with the same line-up.

The first Woodstock Festival was held in 1969 in New York State. It attracted nearly 500 000 people, causing massive traffic jams across miles of highway. Only 200 000 people were expected. None of the required infrastructure was in place and the muddy festival grounds were described as a disaster.

Lost in Paradise

These events illustrate the complexity of event planning, particularly when the site has to be built from the ground up. The audience at all these types of events are generally very tolerant of emerging operational problems, such as at Glastonbury in 2016, where the mud was described as the worst ever at the event.

While events can have positive as well as negative social impacts, increasingly, governments want to attract events to their States, Territories and other regions due to the economic benefits associated with increased tourism. Getz and Page (2016b) point out that event tourism as a concept was established only a few decades ago and they describe the growth of event tourism since then as 'spectacular'.

Many charity events are sustainable from a social point of view; the Cancer Council's Daffodil Day is one such example. Movember is a more recent Australian innovation started by a group of men who agreed to grow a moustache for 30 days. This foundation raised $579 million for research in its first ten years. Not many new charitable events achieve such traction in a short period of time as there are many cause-related events competing for public attention. All events, including fashion, music and fundraising events, are influenced by contemporary trends and have to work hard to remain sustainable in the long term. Events also play an important role in local communities, maintaining heritage, supporting schools, providing entertainment, and keeping people connected.

EXTENSION ACTIVITY

Watch the YouTube video at https://youtu.be/4MwJjiVh9bE or search online for 'Glastonbury mud'. Investigate news articles on the topic of problems that occurred at the 2016 festival. What were the two biggest operational problems for the organisers of this popular festival?

The aim of this book is to assist you in your training to become an event manager of the highest calibre. Many of us have observed events, most of us have participated in events, but few of us have managed events. As an event manager, you are there to do far more than just observe, and you are definitely not there as a participant. You are there to ensure the smooth running of the event, to minimise the risks and to maximise the enjoyment of the event audience. The demands placed on an event manager are far greater than you would expect. The career path for a successful event manager does not involve running a party which turns into a riot, something that has happened on several occasions in Australia, involving police and damage bills in the hundreds of thousands of dollars.

Many events carry a significant risk to the safety of participants. Accidents and injuries sustained at soccer matches and music festivals, for example, are sometimes fatal. Concerns for safety are paramount and risk assessment forms a major part of any event proposal. Qualifications and experience in risk management, covering all facets of event organisation, are essential for the modern event manager, as is the ability to identify all legal compliance issues.

Financial risk is also an important concern of the event manager. Events are generally extremely expensive, with high expenditure required over a very short period of time, and there are far higher levels of uncertainty about revenue and profit than there are in relation to the average business.

In the case of voluntary and charitable events, of which there are many in every community, the risk is that the time invested by individuals will be wasted and their objectives will not be achieved.

Finally, one of the most important things about an event is that it is often a highlight of a person's life. This is not to be taken lightly. A significant birthday, a wedding or a christening is so important to the main participants that nothing must go wrong. If something does go wrong, it cannot always be easily rectified. A wedding at which the power fails due to overloading of the electrical supply cannot be repeated. The offer to 'Come back again at our expense' just doesn't work! The event manager therefore carries overall responsibility for ensuring that the event, however large or small, is a success, as there is often only one chance to get it right.

Based on what we have discussed so far, events are characterised by the following:

- They are often 'once in a lifetime' experiences for the participants.
- They are generally expensive to stage.
- They usually take place over a short time span.
- They require careful planning.
- They often take place once only. (However, many events are held annually, often at the same time every year.)
- They carry a high level of risk, including financial and safety risk.
- There is often a lot at stake for those involved, including the event management team.

This last characteristic is crucial, since every performer, whether they are an athlete or an entertainer, wants to deliver their best performance. The bride wants the day to be perfect in every way. The marketing manager and the design team want the new product to be seen in the best possible light. Consider for a moment how much easier it is to run a restaurant, where you spread your risk over a number of days and a number of customers, than it is to run a one-off, big-budget product launch – particularly if the launch has 500 key industry players and the media in attendance, and is taking place at a unique location with unusual demands regarding logistics, lighting, sound and special effects.

Having pointed out the level of demand on the event manager and thus the possible downside of the profession, it is important also to point out that the event industry is one in which people (the event audience) tend to have the time of their lives. Making this possible and sharing this with them is extremely gratifying. The work is demanding, exciting and challenging, requiring a fine balance between task management and people management. The team needs to be both organised and flexible. Events can be unpredictable and do require quick thinking, based on a sound knowledge of procedures and options. Decision making is one of the most important skills of the event manager, and those with first-class analytical skills are highly sought after by most industries.

Professor Donald Getz and Stephen Page (2016a), well-known writers in the field of event management, define special events from two perspectives, that of the customer and that of the event manager, as follows:

Festival crowd

- A special event is a one-time or infrequently occurring event outside normal programs or activities of the sponsoring or organising body.
- To the customer or guest, a special event is an opportunity for a leisure, social or cultural experience outside the normal range of choices or beyond everyday experience (p. 16).

Another well-known author, Dr J. Goldblatt (2010), defines a special event as 'that which is different from a normal day of living' (p. 6).

In this book, the emphasis is on a wide range of events, including 'special events', as defined above, and more common events such as sporting events, meetings, parties, carnivals and prize-giving ceremonies, which may not meet the definition 'outside the normal range of choices'.

SOURCE AND INTERPRET RELEVANT INDUSTRY INFORMATION

Internationally, there is fierce competition for the staging of major and mega events. Countries compete against each other for the right to hold the next Olympic Games, Rugby World Cup, FIFA World Cup and World Expo. In this competitive environment, Australia battles it out with other countries, such as France, Brazil and China. Australian cities also compete against each other for major sporting events, such as motor racing and major entertainment events. In the conference exhibition area, there are convention centres in all capital cities vying for business. Aside from the prestige that some of these events bring to a country or city, the wider social and economic impacts of staging such events is often the key reason why the competition is so fierce. As this chapter will show, events play a vital role in profiling a country as an attractive tourism destination, and event tourism contributes significantly to a country's economy. While this is hard to quantify, we know that event-related tourism is an important export for Australia.

Staying in touch with event industry trends is therefore essential, and this is done by researching event industry information using the following sources:

* discussions with experienced industry personnel
* industry accreditation operators
* industry associations and organisations
* industry journals, reference books and seminars
* online sources
* libraries and media
* networking with colleagues and suppliers
* documents issued by government regulators which describe laws relevant to the events industry
* training courses
* unions.

In conducting this research, one can stay up to date with the economic and social significance of the industry, as well as career opportunities and quality assurance initiatives. The area of most relevance to most event managers is legislative compliance, and following this, risk management, which is the process by which 'reasonable' risks are anticipated and treated. By investigating problems that have arisen at past events, the rationale for these regulations and processes becomes clear.

Event industry structure

Within the events arena, there are several key organisations and businesses which collectively describe the scope and structure of the industry and the potential career paths that exist within it.

Government agencies

Many government agencies take responsibility for managing large events, such as the City of Sydney, which runs the annual New Year's Eve fireworks event. On a smaller scale, many local councils run Australia Day celebrations and other community festivals. Figure 1.1 illustrates the three levels of government that may be involved in staging an event, depending on its size and the relevant legislation.

Governments operate at the federal, State/Territory and local levels. Organisers of smaller events work mainly with the relevant council, while organisers of major sporting, arts or business events might work nationally with federal and State/Territory bodies.

FIGURE 1.1 Levels of government involvement

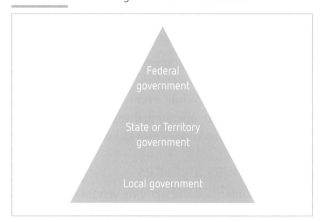

Event organisations

In the case of some major events, specific organisations are formed, such as the Adelaide Festival Corporation, which was set up to run the Adelaide Festival. This corporation also manages another biennial event, the Adelaide Festival of Ideas (FOI), which is held in the year following the Adelaide Festival. There are also many event organisations that sit within the government framework, such as Events Geelong and Events ACT.

Council-run food and wine and sustainability festival

Promoters

Promoters have a crucial part to play in the organisation and staging of certain major events. Chugg Entertainment, for example, is recognised globally as one of Australia's leading tour promoters and works with some of the biggest names in music. Founded in 2000 by music industry pioneer Michael Chugg, Chugg Entertainment has toured hundreds of major international acts, including Dolly Parton, Coldplay, Radiohead, Elton John, Pearl Jam, Robbie Williams, Florence + the Machine and many more. In general, promoters are responsible for staging the performance and they are also called entertainment promoters.

Event service providers

Event services such as catering, cleaning and waste disposal are highly specialised, and so too is event security. These services are generally provided by specialist organisations such as Spotless Catering and Hospitality, Clean Event (a division of Spotless) and ACES (Australian Concert and Entertainment Security). In addition to providing staffing solutions, ACES conducts a risk assessment as a service to the event organiser. Management services can also be provided by businesses specialising in this area, including party planners and wedding consultants.

Event suppliers

Party and equipment hire companies can provide anything from chair covers to scaffolding. Stage equipment, lighting, sound systems, stages, props and seating are all supplied by event suppliers. While event suppliers generally provide these more tangible items, they also contribute operational support such as information technology and catering. They are also known as 'service providers'.

Venues and sites

Conference and wedding venues likewise provide a range of services that support the delivery of an event, including catering, bar service, cleaning and security. In some cases, the client hires the venue as a blank canvas and plans all aspects of the event. A venue is usually a built environment, such as a banquet room or sports centre, whereas a site is generally an outdoor space, such as a park, at which an event is held. A **greenfield site** refers to a site that has no buildings or other infrastructure, and all equipment needs to be brought in, including portaloos, kitchens, stages and seating. The most famous greenfield site for an event was the farm on which Woodstock was held in 1969.

> **Greenfield site**
> Site that has no buildings or other infrastructure, and where all equipment needs to be brought in

Non-specialist and in-house event producers

In addition to the above specialist organisations, many events are staged in-house by companies (for example, a large bank might run a product update for its clients). Corporate events include those run internally (such as staff training and awards nights) and those run externally. Often, the external events have a marketing focus and may include trade shows, product launches and publicity stunts.

Many smaller private events are also organised informally by friends and family who may or may not call on some of the specialists mentioned for one or more facets of the organisation.

As these examples illustrate, there is a great deal of overlap between the above agencies, organisations and businesses.

Crossover industries

Several allied and crossover industries work alongside the event industry, including organisations involved in tourism, hospitality, arts and culture, sports and recreation. This is illustrated in Figure 1.2, in which all of the industries represented are set within a legal and business environment. This diagram sketches the structure and functions in a simplified way for an industry that is diverse and complex.

FIGURE 1.2 Relationships within the event industry

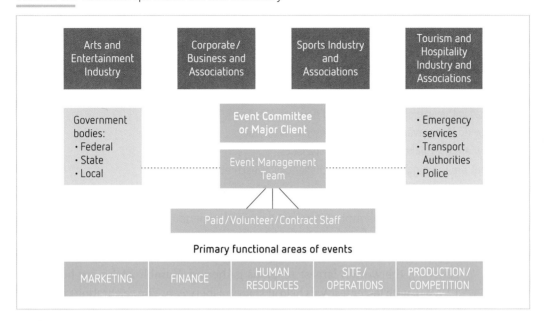

Event classification

There are a number of ways in which events can be classified: in terms of the *size* of the audience, the organiser's *motivation* for running the event (raising money, selling products, providing entertainment), or in terms of the *event characteristics*, including the *profile of the event audience*. Events can also be *public* (open to everyone) or *private*. Private events are usually by invitation only; however, distribution of information about the event can sometimes lead to gatecrashers turning up. Another simple way to differentiate events is between those where *profit* is the motive versus those which are *not-for-profit*, such as charitable events.

Size

The largest events are called **mega events** and these are generally targeted at international markets. The Olympic Games, Commonwealth Games, FIFA World Cup and the Super Bowl are good examples. The Super Bowl, for which in 1967 there were 30 000 tickets unsold, now sells out before the tickets have been printed and attracts 100 000 visitors to the host city. It is televised to an audience of 800 million and adds US$300 million to the local economy.

> **Mega events**
> Large-scale, internationally broadcast events of global interest, with significant economic impacts

All such events have a specific yield in terms of increased tourism, media coverage and economic impact. While some cities are continuing to meet a legacy of debt after hosting an Olympic Games, Sydney was fortunate in meeting its budget due to a last-minute surge in ticket and merchandise sales, returning $10 million to taxpayers. However, as with all events of this size, it is difficult to calculate the costs accurately with so many stakeholders (mainly government) involved. The budget for the 2004 Athens Olympic Games did not include a new tram network and a suburban railway line, which were both funded by the European Union's Third Community Support Framework.

EXTENSION ACTIVITY

Research the following festivals online and put your answers into a comparative table:

- Kumbh Mela, India
- Glastonbury Festival, UK
- Summerfest, USA
- Oktoberfest, Germany
- Carnival, Brazil

1   What is the size of the festival and how often is it held?
2   How do these events differ? List key characteristics.
3   How are they alike? List key characteristics.
4   What are the biggest operational challenges of each event?

While the size of the Olympic Games in terms of expenditure, sponsorship, economic impact and worldwide audience would undoubtedly put it in the category of mega event, it is worth comparing its size with, for example, that of the Kumbh Mela ('Grand Pitcher Festival'), the world's largest religious gathering. Kumbh Melas are held every 12 years, with lesser festivals held at stages in-between. The celebrations comprise the largest religious gatherings of people in the world, with estimates of up to 120 million people attending, 30 million in a single day.

Hallmark events are designed to increase the appeal of a specific tourism destination or region. The Tamworth Country Music Festival, the Melbourne Cup and Floriade in Canberra are all examples of tourist destinations in Australia achieving market positioning for both domestic and international tourism markets through their annual events. The Edinburgh Military Tattoo and the Rio Carnival are international festivals with significant event tourism impact. In fact, Edinburgh has 16 key festivals that form the basis of its event tourism calendar. These events and their host cities become inseparable in the minds of consumers.

> **Hallmark events**
> Designed to gain prominence in the tourism market, helping with destination branding and marketing
>
> **Major events**
> Regular or one-off events that generate significant economic, social and cultural benefits, and so are often supported by governments

Events that attract significant local interest and a large number of participants, as well as generating significant tourism revenue, are known as **major events**. The National Multicultural Festival in Canberra and Chinese New Year celebrations fit into this category, as do many of the hallmark events described earlier. The three-week Chinese New Year festival in Sydney includes market stalls, food stalls, exhibitions, street entertainment, parades and dragon boat races. Friends and relatives of members of the local Chinese community often visit at this time. According to Destination NSW (2016), the Vivid Festival injects $110 million into the State's economy.

A visitor scans the list of exhibitors at an international expo

Most events, however, fall into the category of **minor events**, and it is here that most event managers gain their experience. Almost every town and city in Australia runs annual events. For example, the Broome area promotes the Pearl Festival, the Battle of Broome and the Mango Festival. In addition to annual events, there are many one-off events, including historical, cultural, musical and dance performances. Meetings, parties, celebrations, award ceremonies, sporting finals, and many other community and social events also fit into this category.

> **Minor events**
> Smaller-scale events generally involving domestic or local audiences

Motives for running events

Business events are generally commercially motivated. They include meetings, incentives, conferences and exhibitions. This sector was previously known as **MICE** and continues to be labelled as such in many countries. There is a great deal of international competition for the business event dollar as the average daily expenditure of business visitors exceeds that of other tourists.

> **MICE**
> Meetings, incentives, conferences and exhibitions

Table 1.1 shows some of the business events staged in Australia's major cities. From this, it is clear that there are competitive pressures between the major convention and exhibition centres, particularly between Melbourne and Sydney. Asian destinations also compete with Australia's convention centres. The bidding and planning processes for some of these events can take up to 10 years. The economic impacts of business events are most important, thus providing the impetus for government support of this sector.

TABLE 1.1 Business events

BUSINESS EVENT	CITY
Australasian Weeds Conference	Perth
Asia-Oceania Conference on Obesity	Adelaide
International Astronautical Congress	Adelaide
World Congress of Melanoma	Brisbane
World Wide Web Conference	Perth
International Bar Association Conference	Sydney
Australasian Society for Infectious Diseases	Gold Coast

Festivals Australia is a government funding program designed to assist the presentation of arts and cultural activities at Australian regional and community festivals. The emphasis is on supporting new projects, which add to the quality and diversity of the arts and cultural programming. For the purposes of this program, a festival is 'a regular public celebration that is organised by members of the community, has clear, strong and broad-based community support, and involves public outcomes such as performances, exhibitions/displays, film screenings, etc.' (Australian Government Department of Communication and the Arts, 2017). Table 1.2 describes the major arts festivals held in the capital cities. Festivals such as these have important social impacts, profiling the arts in many forms.

TABLE 1.2 Festival calendar

MONTH	FESTIVAL
January	Each year, the **Sydney Festival** offers a rich and diverse program spanning all art forms, including dance, theatre, music, visual arts, film, forums and large-scale free outdoor events. For three weeks in January, the festival hosts around 80 events involving upwards of 500 artists from Australia and abroad. In any given year, it makes use of most of the main theatres across the breadth of the city and also has a commitment to the presentation of quality, large-scale outdoor events.
February	The **National Multicultural Festival** is held in Canberra over two weeks and features the very best in local, national and international music, dance, food and creative arts. Festival favourites include the Food and Dance Spectacular, the Greek Glendi, Carnivale, the International Concert and the Pacific Islander Showcase. The Festival Fringe complements the mainstream festival, providing a full-on week of zany entertainment.
February	The **Perth International Arts Festival** is the oldest annual international multi-arts festival in the southern hemisphere and is Western Australia's premier cultural event. The first Perth Festival was held in 1953. It has come a long way since then and now offers the people of Western Australia some of the best international and contemporary drama, theatre, music, film, visual arts, street arts, literature, comedy and free community events. Other events on the program include the Western Australian Indigenous Arts Showcase (WAIAS), involving Indigenous singers and songwriters, musicians, actors and comedians from all over Australia's largest State.
March	The **Adelaide Festival** has created a strong tradition of innovation since 1960, inspiring celebration and presenting diverse art from across Australia and around the world. Held in the warm South Australian autumn in every 'even' year, it is a large-scale multi-arts event of extraordinary richness and diversity.
March	Tasmania's flagship celebration of island arts and culture, **Ten Days on the Island**, boasts a multitude of events at 50 locations across the island. Events and activities range across all types of music, dance, visual arts, theatre, literature, food and film. Individual artists and companies come from all corners of the globe, and a number of local artists also take part.
August	The **Darwin Festival** is an acknowledgement of the city's uniqueness, celebrating its multicultural community, youthful energy and tropical climate. The cultural program provides a feast of local, national and international performances to excite, inspire and entertain. It includes opera, cabaret, dance, music, film, comedy, the visual arts and workshops – incorporating music and dance from Indigenous, Indonesian and Pacific island communities. There is also a strong visual arts component, with traditional landowners guiding visitors through the many galleries exhibiting Indigenous art.
September	The **Brisbane Festival** is Brisbane's foremost international multi-arts festival, offering an outstanding program of theatre, dance, music, opera, multimedia and free community events for the residents of Brisbane and its visitors. Held every two years, it endeavours to include the entire community in its program of activities by having intellectual rigour, international artistic credibility and an extremely broad grassroots support base.
October	The **Melbourne International Arts Festival** has a reputation for presenting unique international and Australian events in the fields of dance, theatre, music, visual arts and multimedia. Free and outdoor events are held over 17 days each October.

As Table 1.2 shows, these festivals are fairly evenly spread across the year, as it is pointless to compete on the domestic tourism calendar.

Charities usually run events on the basis that any funds raised in excess of operating costs are allocated to the charitable cause. In contrast, music producers who bring big-name artists to the country or who run large annual music events are clearly motivated by profit. Neither can afford to run at a loss if the event or business is to be sustained.

Event impacts

From the above, it is clear that the key motivations for running events are *economic* (including profit making and flow-on effects to the wider economy), *social* (the main impact of celebrations of cultural, historical, religious or social significance) and *political* (major and mega events may have a political impact, in addition to their social and economic impacts); see Figure 1.3. For example, it was said that the Olympic Games in Beijing put China on the world stage as a modern economy.

FIGURE 1.3 Impact of events

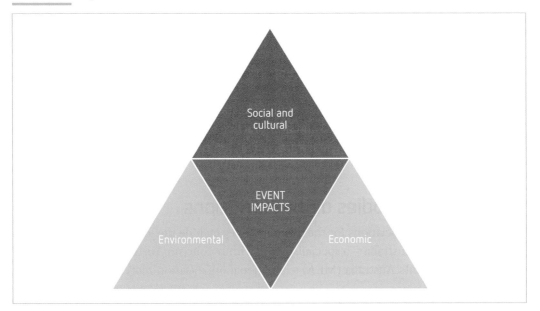

Likewise, the Edinburgh Festival – not just one festival but 10, including the Fringe Festival. Collectively, they are the jewels in the crown of Scotland's cultural scene, attracting hundreds of thousands of visitors and pumping millions of pounds into the nation's economy every year. Only the Olympics and the World Cup exceed the number of tickets sold for Edinburgh's festival events.

Events such as the Australian Open Tennis Championships and the Melbourne Cup also have economic benefits, mainly through increases in domestic tourism and the multiplier effect. Tourism and events create jobs in the tertiary sector, and they also encourage growth in the primary and secondary sectors of industry. This is what is known as the **multiplier effect,** which in its simplest form is how many times money spent by a tourist circulates through a country's economy. Money spent at an event, attraction, restaurant or hotel helps to create jobs directly, but it also creates jobs indirectly elsewhere in the economy. The restaurant, for example, has to buy food from local farmers, who may spend some of this money on other items. The demand for local products increases as tourists buy food, petrol, merchandise and souvenirs, which increases secondary employment. The multiplier effect continues until the money eventually 'leaks' from the economy through imports – the purchase of goods from other countries.

> **Multiplier effect**
> Describes how money spent by event organisers and visitors circulates through the economy

Triple bottom line
Economic, social and environmental impacts

When researchers talk about the **triple bottom line** they are referring to economic, social and environmental impacts. Impacts can be both positive and negative. Examples of negative impacts include:

- gatecrashing, drug use at music events, drunken behaviour, parking inconvenience to locals (social impacts)
- cost to taxpayers in provision of infrastructure and services such as policing (economic impact)
- displacement of 'normal' visitors; for example, at World Youth Day (social and economic impacts)
- white elephants: new arenas and stadiums not being used enough (economic impact)
- ill-defined careers due to the nature of the event industry and oversupply of graduates (social impacts)
- waste, damage to environment, noise and so on (environmental impacts).

There are, of course, many positive impacts, which is why events are supported and funded by many government agencies.

The International Organization for Standardization's (ISO) 20121 Event Sustainability Management System offers guidance and best practice to help manage an event and control its social, economic and environmental impact. This international standard will be discussed in more detail in Chapter 16.

Event industry bodies and associations

Support bodies and associations for the event industry include the following:

- Business Events Australia – a specialist team within Tourism Australia
- Meetings & Events Australia (MEA) – a national organisation representing members of the industry
- Events Industry Association (EIA) – represents the events industry in Western Australia
- Exhibition & Event Association of Australasia (EEAA) – the peak association for the exhibition and event industry
- Regional Arts Australia (RAA) – the key national body representing the broad, complex interests and concerns of those working with and for the arts in regional, rural and remote Australia
- Northern Territory Major Events Company – identifies and attracts major sporting and cultural events which have the potential to benefit the Northern Territory by providing substantial economic and social benefits.

Many other organisations fund and support events as well, including governmental bodies at the federal, State/Territory and regional levels.

Event categories

Event categories help to explain the diversity of the industry and the scope of employment within it:

- conference
- symposium
- exhibition
- festival
- promotional event

- show (e.g. agricultural)
- sporting event
- parade
- cultural celebration
- trade and consumer show
- social event
- private and public event
- corporate event
- charitable or fundraising event.

When differentiating events, it is useful to look at the following variables:

- purpose and objectives of the event (e.g. fundraising, product promotion)
- scope of the event (e.g. single or multiple venues, road show)
- nature of the audience (e.g. businesspeople, leisure tourists, locals)
- marketing and distribution channels (e.g. online ticket sales, part of tourism product promotion such as Visit Melbourne, free entry/gold coin contribution at the gate)
- key stakeholders (for major and hallmark events, it is likely that government bodies will be key stakeholders)
- key elements of staging (e.g. competition, display, parade, exhibition, conference).

Figure 1.4 illustrates these criteria using the Byron Bay Bluesfest as an example. As you can see, this event has clearly articulated aims and objectives, and its position on sustainability is described in detail on the website, which also describes the audience and infrastructure required for the festival.

FIGURE 1.4 Differentiating events, using Byron Bay Bluesfest as an example

AIMS AND OBJECTIVES	SCOPE	AUDIENCE	MARKETING AND DISTRIBUTION	KEY STAKEHOLDERS	KEY STAGING ELEMENTS
• Building institutional sustainability and management capacity • A culturally relevant festival • A festival that respects, transforms and grows local community • A zero-waste festival • A carbon-neutral festival • A festival site that is a functioning, healthy, natural ecosystem	• Began in 1990 • Over 200 artists in a 5-day period • One of Australia's most acclaimed and respected festivals • Has won many awards	• With a crowd of 6000 when it began in 1990, Bluesfest now attracts an audience of over 100 000 • Bluesfest prides itself on being an all-ages family event, with female attendances being slightly greater than males, and approximately 30 per cent of its audience being local	• Bluesfest website • Membership • Ticket sales, Ticketek • Ticket sales, other venues • Twitter • Myspace • Facebook	• Byron Shire Council • Charities • Sponsors • 1000 VIPs and guests • 50 festival staff • 100 stallholders and staff • Other contractors • Performers	• Permanent site at Tyagarah Tea Tree Farm • Camping • Temporary stages • Lighting and sound • Catering and waste • Security, fencing

Source: Based on information from Byron Bay Bluesfest (2017). www.bluesfest.com.au

SOURCE AND USE COMPLIANCE INFORMATION

Legal issues will be discussed in detail in Chapter 17. Here, we will briefly look at duty of care, safety, workplace health and safety (WHS), risk management and insurance, as risks are higher for the event industry than for many other industries. To manage an event that meets legal compliance and regulatory requirements, one first needs to understand which of these apply to a specific event. The following are a starting point; however, these may change, so staying up to date is essential. By searching for information using Google's advanced search function and narrowing the results to the site or domain *.gov.au*, you will find the most useful and recent material.

Legal issues

Duty of care is the responsibility shown by organisations to all people attending an event, whether they are staff, visitors or contractors on-site. This responsibility is covered more specifically under WHS legislation in chapters 9 and 18, which look closely at workplace health and safety, and establishing policies and procedures that must be implemented in all workplaces. Risk management is an approach used to identify potential risks, analyse and evaluate them, and implement risk treatments. Some treatments are preventative, such as the use of barriers and barricades or police on horseback, while other treatments apply when risks cannot be prevented; for example, first-aid emergencies. Insurance, in the form of public liability insurance, is compulsory for all event venues, organisations and contractors in case of an accident involving a member of the public. Workers compensation insurance is also compulsory for all employers.

It is obligatory to ensure that where licences are required, they are validated and up to date. In the events business, this includes licences for rigging, forklift operation and use of fireworks.

EXTENSION ACTIVITY

What is a rave party and which aspects of such parties are potentially illegal? Research three serious incidents that have arisen at rave parties. Discuss the balance of responsibility between the event organisers and the participants, including those who are under-age. Use a table to highlight the key points. Are there ethical as well as legal issues?

Liaison and approval from local government

There are a number of local government Acts and regulations that may apply to the event. These vary considerably from one area to another. Detailed guidelines are provided by some councils, whereas others are more informal. The size of the event determines to a large extent the detail required in the submission, since smaller events tend to have low impact on the community.

An event organiser may need to meet different requirements even if the event has been held in another council area with approval. Likewise, if the event covers more than one jurisdiction, more than one proposal may need to be submitted.

A development application for permanent structures is generally required. This links to the local environment plan (LEP), which is the community's vision for the future of the area. Application for the use of premises and property for entertainment may be necessary. Plans for erecting temporary structures will need to be developed and an application made to the relevant council. Approvals are required by most councils for:

- using loudspeakers or amplifiers in public spaces
- installing amusement devices
- charging fees for singing or providing entertainment in public places
- using a building or structure for entertainment (change of approval classification).

Of course, councils are most interested in the cleaning programs planned for during and after the event. They also demand that the site or venue be returned to the same condition it was in prior to the event, and their key priority is to maintain the lifestyle of local residents and support businesses.

Other relevant Acts and regulations cover clean air, clean water and noise, falling under the banner of environmental protection. Noise is a particularly troublesome problem for festivals and events since by their very nature they attract crowds. Entertainment events are particularly loud, so it is essential to check noise limitations in terms of decibels and the times during which music is permitted. Discharge of sewage, oil and other waste into water systems is illegal and the waterways are protected by a number of Acts across the States and Territories.

Industrial law

Industrial law regulates the relationships between employers and employees and covers many aspects of employment, such as minimum wages, wage agreements, annual leave entitlements, union membership and so on. In particular, equal employment opportunity (EEO) laws cover discrimination and harassment, the main provision being equal treatment regarding job-related benefits.

Privacy law and consumer protection

Consumer protection law ensures that clients 'get what they pay for'. Complaints arising in the event industry might include event cancellation, overbooking, changes to the line-up, or simply a failure to deliver on the promises made. Australian consumer law guarantees a consumer's rights when they buy goods and services. Privacy legislation requires that any personal information about individuals is protected, in particular prohibiting the use or sale of personal information to other organisations for marketing purposes.

Quality assurance

There are several ways in which event organisations can demonstrate their credibility to clients; for example, by being accredited by an industry association such as Meetings & Events Australia, Restaurant and Catering Australia, and Professional Conference Organisers. Compliance can also be demonstrated by certification marks such as for HACCP (hazard analysis and critical control points, relating to food safety).

Ethical issues

Ethical industry practices may relate to:

- procedures for payment of commissions
- bookings at venues
- confidentiality of contracts, personnel and performers

- overbooking
- subcontractors not meeting standards
- exploitation of volunteers
- pricing and scalping
- providing free entry
- tolerating unsociable behaviour.

When running events for under-18s, the control of unsociable behaviour is vitally important. Many schoolies week destinations have put in place a broad series of risk management strategies to keep celebrating teenagers as safe as possible.

A search of the Internet using the words 'ticket fiasco' will result in examples of ticketing problems at events, notable ones being the Edinburgh Fringe Festival in 2009 and Byron Bay's cancelled Maitreya Festival in 2016. The Australian Consumer Law website (listed at the end of the chapter) has a dedicated page on music festivals, which was provided in response to many complaints relating to ticketing. Cancellation is a primary concern for the audience. Getting ticketing right is crucial, particularly where there are lots of young people in attendance, as party rage can erupt when ticket holders are barred from entering a venue because it has reached capacity due to overselling.

The careful appointment of contractors, ideally through an objective tendering and reference checking process, is also advised.

The International Special Events Society (ISES) adheres to the following code of ethics, which is a useful guide for event managers:

- Promote and encourage the highest level of ethics within the profession of the special events industry while maintaining the highest standards of professional conduct.
- Strive for excellence in all aspects of our profession by performing consistently at or above acceptable industry standards.
- Use only legal and ethical means in all industry negotiations and activities.
- Protect the public against fraud and unfair practices and promote all practices which bring credit to the profession.
- Maintain adequate and appropriate insurance coverage for all business activities.
- Maintain industry standards of safety and sanitation.
- Provide truthful and accurate information with respect to the performance of duties.
- Use a written contract stating all changes, services, products, performance expectations and other essential information.

Many event industry associations, including those mentioned earlier in this chapter, have accreditation schemes with similar codes for ethical dealing, covering many aspects of professional behaviour.

SOURCE AND USE INFORMATION ON EVENTS TECHNOLOGY

The event industry is similar to tourism in that most event products (tickets) are purchased online through an e-commerce option. Indeed, it could be argued that the anticipatory build-up to an event, which involves frequent visits to the event website to study the program, is part of the final fleeting marketing product. Thus, the design and maintenance of the event's website and mobile app is vitally important, as it is here that the consumer looks for the event line-up or the history of competition.

In addition to e-commerce, advances in technology allow many other activities to be carried out online. For example, event planners, including brides, can plan online the size of the function, the menus and the layout of the venue, and even develop a budget prior to contacting a salesperson.

Technology

Technological advances are also evident in audio and video production, with larger and larger screens, better vision and remote conferencing being offered. Security systems are becoming increasingly complex, and even banquet chefs employ computerised cooking and refrigeration processes.

The main technology solutions used by the industry include:

- project planning software (Gantt charts and PERT charts are used for critical path analysis)
- venue booking systems (for leasing and contracting venues and services)
- audience reservation and registration systems (used for concert ticketing, conference bookings, races and competitions)
- identification and accreditation systems (to capture data about individuals attending exhibitions or race officials working in the field of play)
- employee records and police checks
- security systems (for managing assets, checking inventory, and monitoring crowd movements)
- CAD (computer-aided design) systems (for designing stages, stands and venues)
- timing and scoring systems
- broadcasting systems (e.g. big-screen replays and closed-circuit viewing for judging)
- communications systems (e.g. radios).

Given the wide range of applications used at a major event, a sophisticated IT team is needed for the installation of computer networks, customisation of software, and integration of the tasks performed by the software packages.

Social media

It is widely acknowledged that social media can support events in a wide variety of ways, and this concept of shared interest has extended as far as the notion of *crowdfunding* for some events. Primarily, social media enables the audience to interact with the event, sending and receiving tweets from performers and watching updates and commentary. Experiential marketing can be supported by events that raise brand values and awareness through social media strategies.

Interactivity and legacy

A key change is interactivity. In the post-television world, the Internet enables a user to visit an event numerous times beforehand, gamble, play related games, acquire information, and interact in various ways with the event before it begins. During the event, content can be

FIGURE 1.5 Timeline for engaging the audience

provided in a variety of ways, including live streaming, statistics, replays and interviews. After the event, content can be made available as required. The event organiser (or marketer) is thus connected to the audience in a two-way relationship before, during and after the event, as shown in Figure 1.5.

UPDATE PERSONAL AND ORGANISATIONAL KNOWLEDGE OF THE EVENTS INDUSTRY

There are many ways to update event industry knowledge; for example, through supplier websites and the media. One important resource is the online publication of event planning guides by government organisations. These detailed outlines for planning and proposal development are exceptionally useful, as too are the extensive guidelines on event safety, risk management and emergency planning.

Wood chopping competition at an agricultural show

There are many opportunities to visit and observe events and to participate in industry seminars and training courses. Membership of industry associations such as the MEA can provide opportunities for professional development and informal networking. Industry journals, all available online, are another important source of current information.

By staying up to date with industry trends, you can take advantage of new technologies, keep abreast of legislative changes, and monitor consumer trends. Legal issues that concern professionals working in the industry, such as public liability, duty of care, licensing, risk management, and WHS, are all newsworthy, with case studies emerging in the media almost daily.

Staying up to date can be done by:

- reading newspapers
- attending industry seminars
- participating in training seminars
- upgrading and extending qualifications
- joining relevant associations
- participating in industry association activities
- networking with colleagues
- reading industry journals
- subscribing to industry magazines (e.g. *micenet*)
- Internet research.

When researching the event industry, it is important to note the overlap with other academic fields of study, including leisure studies, tourism studies, hospitality studies, sports management, arts and cultural management. In their text, Getz and Page (2016a) cover theory, research and policy for planned events. Developing a detailed understanding of the social and economic context of the event industry is helpful for both study and career planning, with this book being invaluable.

As mentioned earlier, careers in the event business are extremely varied, though few have the title 'Event Manager'. Conventions, exhibitions, sports competitions, product launches, charity gala dinners, incentive tours and music performances all come under the umbrella of event management. The skills required are largely in the area of project management, covering the full range of traditional business skills, but applied in a more challenging, dynamic and deadline-driven environment. Continuing research and reading will enable you to develop a better understanding of this evolving professional field and the many players involved, ranging from government to business to community groups.

As this chapter has illustrated, the event industry is dynamic and responsive to social trends and legislative changes. Staying current with these trends is essential for the event manager and for anyone planning a career in this field.

Summary

This chapter has highlighted the important role played by events, particularly in relation to economic and social benefits to communities. Business events, in particular, have been singled out by governments due to the significant role they play in boosting tourism revenues. This is also the case for sporting events, large and small. And the area of arts and entertainment is clearly of interest to the younger demographic, with music festivals becoming increasingly popular. The importance of safety is indicated by the level of attention paid to compliance with legislation and regulation. The planning and monitoring of safety is undertaken using risk management as a tool. The deaths of young people at music festivals in recent years have prompted increasing concern among government bodies and event organisations, with many preventative measures being implemented. For all these reasons, it is important for all those working in this exciting industry to keep up to date with trends and developments.

Key terms

Greenfield site	Site that has no buildings or other infrastructure, and where all equipment needs to be brought in
Hallmark events	Designed to gain prominence in the tourism market, helping with destination branding and marketing
Major events	Regular or one-off events that generate significant economic, social and cultural benefits, and so are often supported by governments
Mega events	Large-scale, internationally broadcast events of global interest, with significant economic impacts

MICE	Meetings, incentives, conferences and exhibitions
Minor events	Smaller-scale events generally involving domestic or local audiences
Multiplier effect	Describes how money spent by event organisers and visitors circulates through the economy
Triple bottom line	Economic, social and environmental impacts

REVIEW YOUR KNOWLEDGE

1 The economic, social and environmental impacts of events can be both positive and negative. Give examples of both positive and negative impacts, using three specific events for analysis.
2 Describe how new technologies have impacted on one sector of the event industry, such as sport or music.
3 Explain why regional areas are keen to host events.
4 Describe five key ways in which the negative impacts of events can be managed effectively by councils and other government agencies. Source only government sites for this research.
5 Explain the nature of the event industry and associated overlapping industries by means of a diagram.

APPLY YOUR KNOWLEDGE

Investigate two events (ideally two that are quite different) and describe them in detail. You might like to do your research on the Internet, starting with one of the State or Territory tourism websites such as **www.destinationnsw.com.au** or **www.melbournecb.com.au**, or you could visit your local council. In this activity, you need to compare the two events and link your findings to three current industry trends. Discuss your findings with colleagues and forecast the top trends for festivals and events over the next decade.

CASE STUDY

STUDENT RAVE PARTY

A group of university students decided to hold a rave party up in some nearby mountains one December and advertised it on Facebook. Three bands attended the three-day party and there was 24-hour music. One young girl described it as a living hell, although why she stayed is unfathomable: 'The dance area was in a valley, and to get a drink of water you had to climb a steep hill. Even then, the water was dirty and brown. The toilets were so far away that nobody bothered to use them. The music pounded all night and the floor vibrated so you couldn't sleep. My friend was unwell and there was no medical help. The organisers didn't have a clue. They just wanted to make a fast buck'.

QUESTIONS

1 What are some of the things that could go wrong, or have gone wrong, at similar events?
2 List three ways in which the organisers' arrangements were unsatisfactory.
3 List three ways in which the event could have been improved.
4 This event was described to the authorities as a cultural festival. Do you think this was accurate?
5 The legal compliance issues of such an event will be covered in a later chapter. However, investigate the concept of 'duty of care' and summarise your understanding of it.

The Victorian Health Department has a 'code of practice for running safer music festivals' online and this will be very helpful with this case study — you can search for it at www2.health.vic.gov.au

Online resources

Visit http://login.cengagebrain.com and search for this book to access the study tools that come with your textbook.

References

Australian Government Department of Communication and the Arts (2017). Festivals Australia. www.arts.gov.au/funding-and-support/festivals-australia

Destination NSW (2016). Vivid Sydney injects $110 million into the NSW economy. 9 September. www.destinationnsw.com.au/news-and-media/media-releases/vivid-sydney-injects-110-million-nsw-economy

Faughder, Ryan (2016). Coachella by the numbers: A breakdown of the festival's $700-million impact. *Los Angeles Times*, 22 April. http://www.latimes.com/entertainment/envelope/cotown/la-et-ct-coachella-economy-by-the-numbers-20160420-story.html

Getz, D., & Page, S. J. (2016a). *Event Studies: Theory, Research and Policy for Planned Events*. London: Routledge.

Getz, D., & Page, S. J. (2016b). Progress and prospects for event tourism research. *Tourism Management*, 52, 593–631.

Goldblatt, J. J. (2010). *Special Events: A New Generation and the Next Frontier* (vol. 13). Hoboken, NJ: John Wiley & Sons.

Websites

Association of Australian Convention Bureaux (AACB), www.aacb.org.au

Australian Consumer Law (music festivals), http://consumerlaw.gov.au/musicfestivals

Business Events Australia, www.businessevents.australia.com

Business Events Council of Australia (BECA), www.businesseventscouncil.org.au

Code of practice for running safer music festivals and events, https://www2.health.vic.gov.au

Events Industry Association (WA), www.eia.com.au

Exhibition & Event Association of Australasia, www.eeaa.com.au

Festivals Australia, www.arts.gov.au/funding-and-support/festivals-australia

Meetings & Events Australia, www.meetingsevents.com.au

Professional Conference Organisers Association, www.pco.asn.au

2

ENHANCE CUSTOMER SERVICE EXPERIENCES

OVERVIEW

This chapter will highlight the importance of enhanced customer service and positive communication. The event environment is particularly challenging in that there are limited opportunities for extended customer contact at the front line of a festival or sporting competition. In contrast, important relationships are developed with clients booking corporate events, couples planning weddings and sponsors making significant financial contributions to events. Stress contributes to communication breakdown at busy times when crowds are arriving or the event program is delayed. Dealing well with disaster is often the hallmark of a talented event manager.

LEARNING OBJECTIVES

On completion of this chapter, you will be able to:

1. provide a quality service experience by determining customer needs and preferences
2. proactively respond to difficult service situations, taking immediate action to address any issues
3. resolve customer complaints by deciding on optimal solutions but taking organisational constraints into account
4. develop customer relationships in order to build repeat business and customer loyalty.

INDUSTRY VIEWPOINT

Cancellation and rescheduling events

While attending an entertainment event should be an exciting activity, consumers will quickly become frustrated if they are unaware of the terms and conditions which apply when buying a ticket. This can particularly be true when dealing with disreputable ticket sellers. The Live Performance Ticketing Code of Practice is a voluntary scheme which aims to protect consumers in the live performance industry.

'You have a right to a refund if the Event to which you purchased a Ticket from an Authorised Seller is cancelled prior to the Event. When an Event is cancelled, the Member should make reasonable endeavours to advise you as soon as practicable. Your contact details are generally obtained at the point of sale for this purpose.

If you paid for your Tickets by credit card, the value of the Tickets, plus any additional fees and charges, should be automatically credited back to your card. If you purchased your Tickets by cash, voucher or other non-traceable means, you will need to apply for a refund from the point of purchase in a timely manner.

You have a right to a refund if the Event to which you purchased a Ticket from an Authorised Seller is rescheduled prior to the Event (and you cannot or do not wish to attend the rescheduled Event).

If you are unable or unwilling to attend the Event on the rescheduled date, you should apply for a refund in a timely manner. Where possible, you should apply for a refund from the point of purchase not more than five working days after the announcement of the rescheduled date, and in any event before the rescheduled Event takes place.'

Source: Live Performance Australia, Ticketing Code of Practice. Sixth Edition 2016, p10. http://liveperformance.com.au/sites/liveperformance.com.au/files/resources/lpa_ticketing_cop_consumer_code_final_20151104.pdf <accessed 12/12/2017>

INTRODUCTION

As this article illustrates, consumers are protected if an event is cancelled or rescheduled. For the event manager, things do not always go smoothly. Contingency planning is the process of identifying what could go wrong and developing plans to deal with the situation if it arises. This includes delays due to traffic issues, staff shortages, severe weather or systems failure. Planning for these possibilities is one way to minimise service problems. Indeed, this is foundational for service planning at the execution stage of the event, on the day or week in which it is implemented.

The following operational plans will be presented in later chapters and illustrate how customer service can be enhanced in the event environment, with frontline staff becoming involved in complaints or outright conflict:

- crowd control barriers to ensure that queues are orderly
- effective signage at a level where the audience can easily read directions
- adequate provision of toilet facilities

- security measures to ensure that disruption by badly behaved fans is dealt with quickly
- well-planned menus so that food service is efficient.

These measures are a few of the ways in which the event organiser can pre-empt problems and ensure that staff do not have to deal with irate visitors or event participants.

Long queues at the entry point create a poor first impression

PROVIDE A QUALITY SERVICE EXPERIENCE

External customers
Users of the end product or service of an organisation

Internal customers
Another department or service provider working to deliver the final product or service to the external customer

In general terms, there are several touchpoints for quality service for the event customer. These include booking, transport, arrival, seating, food and beverage, security and other service interactions. The task facing most event organisers is to manage the flow of services to customers effectively so that the overall experience is seamless for the customer. This is despite the fact that these steps may involve services provided by various entities such as the ticketing agency, traffic authority, venue management or security contractor. Additionally, most of the food and beverage served at events is supplied by concessions; that is fast-food outlets and bars run by independent operators.

EXTENSION ACTIVITY

When the audience leaves an event that has been really successful, such as a great sports match or a fabulous music festival, they are likely to thank security staff as they stream out the gates. Who do you think most deserves this feedback among the range of service providers who have contributed to the staging of the event?

People in an audience or joggers participating in a fun run are **external customers**. They are the final recipient of the service – this is illustrated in Figure 2.1. When talking about customer service, however, we need to think about **internal customers** as well. All the various groups that work together to stage the event are reliant on each other for support and service too. For example, if the security agency is understaffed and bag searches are slow, then volunteers might bear the brunt of the frustration of the arriving audience, particularly if the show has already started. If the hotel loading dock is blocked by bins, then the audiovisual team can't offload their equipment in time to set up. Thus, internally there are many different stakeholders all contributing to the customers' experience. Planning effectively and communicating clearly are both part of the process of event planning. On the day of the event, all members of the workforce – paid staff, contractors/service providers and volunteers – need to work together to provide a seamless experience. That said, this is extremely difficult given the short duration of most events and the impact of large crowds.

FIGURE 2.1 The event experience is provided by the whole workforce

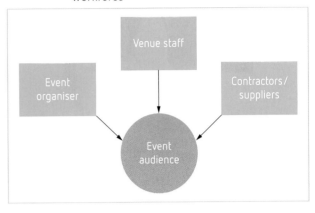

Customer needs and expectations

Individual customers have different needs. They attend events based on those needs, and their expectations are developed according to the advertising and other promotions they have seen. Even if an event has been portrayed accurately, all customers will have different perceptions of it, depending on their cultural or social backgrounds. Staff must then ensure that these needs are met, even if they are not within their own area of responsibility, by exceeding expectations wherever possible. Providing information and promoting other services that are available are excellent ways of meeting unrecognised needs.

Event customers include the audience, visitors, delegates, fans, participants, clients and guests. Some event customers spend less than $100 on their tickets and others spend over $1000 on a conference and hotel package. According to Easy Weddings website, the average Australian wedding now costs $30 000 (Easy Weddings, 2017). In fact, IBISworld (2016) reports that weddings are a $4.31 billion industry in Australia. In this situation, the customer is spending a significant amount of money and the client relationship is extremely important. Once again, the team that produces the reception is diverse, including the wedding planner, venue manager, chef, wait staff, decorator, DJ, photographer and florist, not to mention those looking after the ceremonial aspects of the wedding. The bridal party, including parents, are also notorious for issuing conflicting instructions. In Chapter 7, we will look in detail at contractual relationships and the important specifications that form part of the quote, adding clarity to the products and services designed to meet the expectations of the clients.

Customers can become very frustrated if they have to actively seek out information. Most prefer that the necessary information is offered to them by attentive staff. Every customer sees his or her needs as the most urgent. In practice, customers' needs have to be prioritised to some extent. Emergency and risk situations (such as accidents or gas leaks) need to be investigated immediately. This may involve escalating the issue to a higher level and involving other people.

Shutterstock.com/oliveromg

Bride with wedding planner

Products and services

Products and services are not easily differentiated. The easiest way to think about this is to think of products as the tangible, visible part of what the customer buys, and services as the intangible, invisible aspects. In the event industry context, the tangible aspects might include the décor, lighting, and food and beverages. The service component is the registration process, food service and entertainment. Evidently there is no clear line between these two areas, and in fact many organisations simply refer to the 'product', fully incorporating the idea of service.

Events go further than simply providing products and services. They provide an experience with an emotional impact. Pine and Gilmore (1999, 2011) introduced the idea of the experience economy in a book titled *The Experience Economy: Work Is Theatre & Every Business a Stage*. Already one can see the synergies between marketing and event management, and this will be discussed in more detail in later chapters. Shobeiri (2016), for example, labels commercial experiences as Enhanced, Tradition-Breaker, Variety-Adder and New Horizons experiences, and categorises them as lifetime and once-in-life. He goes on to suggest that these theoretical client categories can be applied to brand development.

In summary, event industry professionals whose overall goal is to provide and enhance the customer experience in traditional ways in the arts or in business may be called upon in future to design experiences as marketing initiatives. Already, the idea of a shopping experience is widely discussed as an antidote to online sales. Examples of experiential marketing include the campaigns by Red Bull, Vans and Samsung which can be reviewed by following the link '10 very cool examples of experiential marketing' that's provided at the end of the chapter.

EXTENSION ACTIVITY

Watch 'Millennials and the rise of the "experience economy"' (https://youtu.be/YFN2vcBuGyQ). Explain how a dining experience or shopping experience, one that is quite out of the ordinary, can lead to the likelihood that the customer will return.

Selling products and services

Some service staff are very reluctant to sell. What they don't realise is that customers want to be given information, as they want to try new things. For example, a customer might welcome a suggestion to try a new format for an annual meeting, especially if it were described in an interesting way.

There are several types of selling, and these are described below.

Top-down selling

In this type of selling, you offer the highest price and quality first, moving down the scale until you establish the customer's needs.

Bottom-up selling

Once the customer has been told the lowest price available and what will be provided, you can work your way up the scale, offering better products and services. Hot rather than cold lunches, breakout sessions in smaller rooms, and innovative lighting design could all be offered once the basics have been agreed to.

Suggestive selling

With this method, the product and service features are sold to the customer. Flavours and textures, freshness and preparation method, colour and presentation of food items are some of the features that would help a customer to choose an item on a menu. Taste testing is even more effective. Outlook, price, convenience and spaciousness will assist in selling a banquet room.

Cross-selling

In addition to the basic service or product being sold, there may be other associated products of interest to the customer. Overnight accommodation for party guests, a shuttle bus to take everyone home, and a limo for the birthday girl are some examples. This is also known as lateral selling.

Benefit selling

This approach involves selling benefits to the customer. For example, an early check-in to the hotel the night before an awards night would allow a group to enjoy some tourism experiences during the day, thus enhancing the whole experience. Providing a guide/translator to an international exhibition visitor would certainly prove beneficial.

Informational selling

Where the salesperson is very knowledgeable, they are likely to be viewed by the customer as highly credible. A customer will take the advice of an event planner who has all the facts and prices at their fingertips, rather than from one who immediately starts searching for information online. Providing testimonials and photographs of past events is another convincing sales strategy.

Special needs and requests

A final suggestion for improved communication is to offer choices in order to narrow down the possibilities: 'Would you like … or …?' is a good strategy when dealing with customers who are unfamiliar with the options. Then ask which option the customer prefers, ideally while showing them a brochure.

As already mentioned, in many cultures around the world, the word 'No' is not often used. For example, in some countries, if you explain something to someone and then ask them if they understand you, they will always answer 'Yes'. To say 'No' would mean that you had not communicated clearly. Therefore, to be polite and avoid embarrassment, the person will say 'Yes'. In many cultures, it is also rude to refuse food. Once again, offering a choice will enable the person to select as much or as little as they please. For this reason, buffets have proved very popular with international tourists.

Here are some other tips for effective cross-cultural communication:

- Avoid double negatives. ('You can't go on the tour if you haven't booked a ticket in advance.')
- Use simple English words.
- Be logical in your explanations.
- Use short sentences and simple sentence structures.
- Use pictures or symbols.
- Show or demonstrate what you are trying to convey.
- Give only the key information.
- Avoid jargon and idioms.

Teamwork

As this chapter has already demonstrated, the event workforce is diverse, ranging from ice-cream sellers to traffic controllers. As there are so many service providers involved, it is often hard to follow reporting relationships, and for this reason flexibility is vital. For example, a volunteer might be given instructions by a security officer. In such situations, teamwork is essential.

For teams to be effective, they require the full participation of members and agreement on common goals. Every member of the workforce should demonstrate the following work team skills:

- contribute ideas
- help others
- give feedback
- check understanding
- ask questions
- respect differences
- follow procedures
- share leadership
- agree on goals.

Contribute ideas

Feedback from staff has been identified as an essential component of any event service environment. Individual employees must be able to contribute ideas and communicate them clearly at briefings and debriefings.

Help others

In any work team, some members will be more experienced than others, some members will be more knowledgeable, and some members will be more skilled. Working cooperatively means assisting one another to develop and harness individual strengths.

Give feedback

One key role of a team member is to provide feedback to colleagues. People respond particularly well to positive feedback, which is most useful when it is specific. For example, you might describe what a person did that was helpful and why it was helpful. Positive feedback sounds something like, 'When you … it was good because …'

When conflict develops in a group, it is sometimes difficult to confront the person concerned. But as with positive feedback, negative feedback should be specific. If it is vague ('You're useless!'), it will not be effective. Negative feedback can be given in the following way: 'When you … then … If you could … then …' As an example, you might say, 'When you interrupt me, then I feel that my view is not important and I get annoyed. If you could wait until I have finished speaking …'

Check understanding

Paraphrasing is a useful tool for checking understanding. It involves repeating the gist of what someone has said; for example, 'You are saying that operations management have logistics working on this?' In this way, you show that you are listening attentively and at the same time you are checking your understanding. This is one of the most powerful communication strategies that can be used with other staff and with customers.

Ask questions

Questions can help to clarify goals. 'Why do we need to talk about that issue when surely we need more information first?' is a helpful question to keep the group on track. Questions can be closed (looking for 'Yes' and 'No' answers) or open, such as the one above where a full answer is required.

Respect differences

Much of this text has been about differences, those between individuals and those between groups. In an event context, a full consensus may not be reached in all situations. Where this is the case, differences need to be respected and worked through to achieve mutually agreed goals.

Follow procedures

Structure is useful in any group discussion. Timing should be agreed beforehand, as should the topics to be discussed. Decisions should be recorded so that the individuals in the group can check their understanding. The 'standing meeting' in which members of the event team are not allowed to sit down ensures that most topics are dealt with quickly. Only traditional businesses can afford to sit everyone around the table with coffee and cakes for long meetings!

Share leadership

Team members all have different skills, and to some extent everyone is capable of leading from time to time. This is certainly a requirement in an event workplace, where shiftwork and staff turnover mean that a team's composition changes regularly. Taking the initiative and showing leadership is a key attribute for all team members.

Agree on goals

The final characteristic of an effective work team is the ability to reach agreement on team goals. Teams that achieve their goals become very cohesive (consider, for example, the sporting team that wins games). For this reason, goals have to be realistic and achievable, taking into account the skills of the members.

The model for successful communication presented in this book is based on a deep understanding of individual differences and a positive attitude towards communicating effectively. This is illustrated in Figure 2.2, which summarises the following key points:

* Attentive and responsive customer service is good customer service in any environment.
* Cohesive work teams are groups that work towards shared goals.
* Checking for understanding and obtaining feedback are the core skills required for effective communication.
* An open-minded attitude towards people, their individual differences and their needs underpins the above three points.

FIGURE 2.2 Components of good service underpinned by teamwork

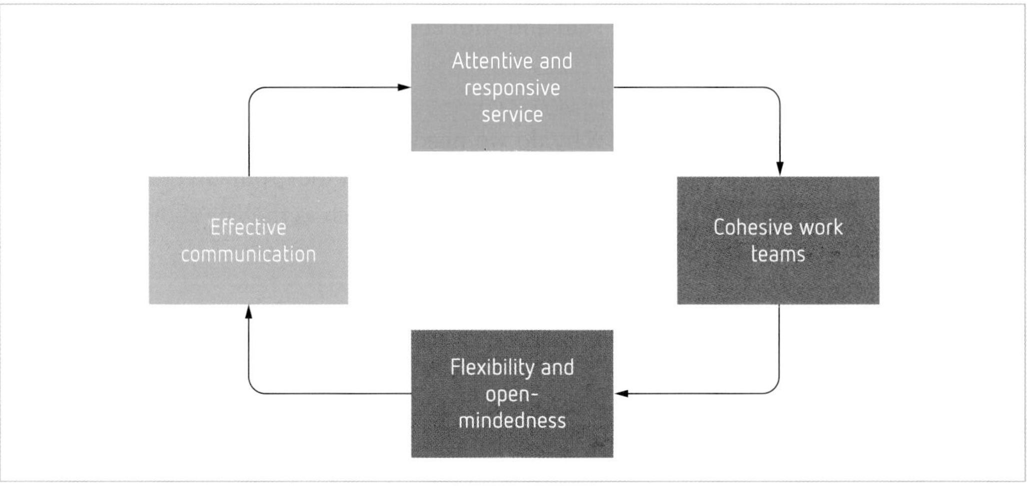

Dealing with conflict in the team

When a conflict situation develops within the team, it needs to be dealt with promptly and effectively. The following guidelines are useful in resolving conflict in the event environment.

Identify the conflict situation

Early identification of a developing conflict can lead to a quick resolution. Being sensitive to this possibility is also helpful in maintaining team spirit. Situations in which the personal safety of customers or colleagues is threatened need particularly urgent attention.

Understand the causes of the conflict

As mentioned earlier, listening is one of the most effective ways of fully understanding a conflict situation and the causes underpinning it, but it is also essential to take a neutral position until the investigation has been concluded. All parties need to be treated with respect and asked for their ideas on potential solutions.

Take charge of the conflict situation

When a situation is serious, it needs to be handled confidentially and discreetly, and this might involve moving to a quiet area to discuss it. Recommending a positive outcome as the goal is usually appreciated by everyone involved in the situation. Successful resolution of a conflict or a complaint can lead to closer working relationships and more satisfied customers.

Escalate the situation

In serious situations, the issue must be escalated promptly. For example, a situation involving a drug-affected or violent person is beyond a volunteer's capacity to resolve. Recognising such situations and following correct procedures is essential.

If you were working at an event as a volunteer and one of your team was constantly leaving her post and disappearing to sleep under a tree, who would you speak to first and why?

EXTENSION ACTIVITY

PROACTIVELY RESPOND TO DIFFICULT SERVICE SITUATIONS

Being proactive can help you avoid any number of problems. A customer who is responded to immediately and has their problem acknowledged will most likely respond well to your intervention. Many issues that arise relate to factors outside your control, such as extreme heat, and sometimes the customer simply wants to share their concerns. Listening is the first step in effective problem solving.

Identify problems

In the previous section, the problems associated with conflict within the workforce or work team were discussed. In this section, the focus is on customer problems and complaints, and their resolution.

Some problems that customers might face are minor, such as:

- poor line of sight due to pillars
- sound spill from other stages
- queues
- lack of shade
- long distances to walk

Other problems are significant, such as:

- delays to the scheduled headline performance
- change of race route due to weather issues

- loss of data so that everyone has to register again
- crowd problems and long queues at entry gate after a game has started
- spectator collapsing
- fights and unruly behaviour.

It is clear that many of these are problems that are out of anyone's control, certainly in respect to frontline staff.

Listening is arguably the most important communication skill for anyone in a frontline event role. Careful listening can cut down the amount of information you need to find. In fact, much time can be saved by asking questions and listening attentively.

The technique of asking open questions is the first step to finding out the extent of the problem. Another useful technique is paraphrasing. By repeating parts of the message, the customer feels that understanding is being reached.

To sum up, listening can become more active if you:

- use attentive body language
- make positive noises and give feedback
- repeat parts of the sender's message
- ask open-ended questions.

Indeed, many situations can be resolved through effective and attentive listening and follow-up action. Where solutions are possible, organisational constraints have to be considered. For example, if the person cannot see well, what is the policy regarding moving him or her to a vacant seat near the front? What is the policy regarding sitting in the aisles, putting up umbrellas or standing up? Policies and procedures are set up to assist staff in dealing with this type of issue. Ushers are used to dealing with these situations firmly, but in rare situations they have to resort to calling management or security.

Act proactively

Briefings and debriefings are commonplace in the event business. The event briefing brings together all the service providers so that everyone understands the running order and the different responsibilities. Volunteers in particular find the briefing extremely useful as they are then able to pass on important and current information to the event audience. The briefing provides an opportunity to act proactively, thus avoiding at least some of the potential problems that may arise.

For an awards night, for example, the briefing would include the event organiser, the MC, the stage manager, the audiovisual team, the chef and the banquet manager. The meal service needs to be synchronised with the awards presentations so that speeches are not drowned out by a chorus of cutlery.

RESOLVE CUSTOMER COMPLAINTS

Assessing the impact of a complaint is the first step in a hectic, fast-paced environment. Some situations present more risk than others for satisfaction or safety. A risk management approach is the foundation for managing safety, and the same principles can be applied to customer problems and complaints. For example, a visitor to an event wants to go into the

VIP area and can prove that he works for the media. This situation is different to one where the visitor tries to get into the athlete zone on a flimsy pretext.

The risk management approach will be elaborated on in later chapters. For the time being, the general concept is to evaluate potential consequences associated with solutions.

There are simple steps to follow for complaint handling, as described below, though in the heat of a complex situation they can be easily forgotten.

Use questioning techniques

Finding out what is wrong is the most effective way of improving the quality of the products or services provided to customers. Complaints and suggestions should be welcomed: 'Thank you for bringing that to my attention'. Listening with full attention is what the client expects and this will go a long way towards ameliorating the situation. Using empathy and active listening (repeating the key content of the message) is recommended.

Assess the impact on the customer

The seriousness of the situation needs to be evaluated from the customer's viewpoint. A missing instrument is a serious concern for a band about to play. A change to the line-up, however, is something over which you have no control – all you can do is reiterate the reasons why the change has occurred (if you have the information) or restate the current situation and apologise.

Take responsibility

Using 'I' indicates that you are personally involved in finding a solution, even if you can only 'own' the problem to the extent that you will be taking the issue to the next level; for example, 'I will contact security for you to see if anyone has handed it in'.

Determine options

In most problem or complaint situations there are several solutions and these are constrained by policies and procedures. For example, for access to given areas, a particular lanyard may be required. Preventing children from entering operational areas is necessary for their safety and parents need to be advised of this, first clearly and then perhaps more strongly, by indicating the self-evident safety risk. Children sitting on the stairs in an auditorium may be moved because it is against the fire safety regulations. Some members of the audience have special techniques for obtaining better seating, such as by complaining about the people nearby. Often it is a thinly disguised strategy against the policy for seating arrangements. In less formal situations it may be quite possible to move the patron.

Avoid escalation

If all of the above steps have been followed and the options explored and discussed, the complaint generally will be resolved. Sometimes the complaint is sufficiently serious for it to be referred to a more senior staff member for resolution. This should be done personally, not simply through stonewalling by saying, 'You have to see the manager about that'.

In serious situations where a patron is risking the safety of others, the problem does need to be escalated for security to step in.

Turn complaints into satisfaction

Social media feedback is doubly good if it involves problem resolution. Many satisfied customers will post their stories online and this is very effective publicity. At the very least, customers will tell someone else if their issue has been dealt with effectively.

Follow-up

Finally, a follow-up call or email will leave the impression that the company really cares.

EXTENSION ACTIVITY

Fake ticketing websites and email scams can mislead you into believing that you are buying legitimate event tickets. But the seller has to be authorised to resell tickets – many terms and conditions of purchase preclude resale and punters may be refused entry. How would you react if you were refused entry to a festival when carrying a ticket given to you by a friend? How would you expect the festival staff to deal with the situation?

DEVELOP CUSTOMER RELATIONSHIPS

For legal and other reasons, including quality management, it is important to document any issues and the steps taken to resolve them. A follow-up process of checking that all matters have been satisfactorily resolved is a valuable final step. In the hectic environment of a music festival, for example, a small problem can lead to a bigger one, such as a freshwater supply running out. The event operations manager aims to provide good service and to keep the audience comfortable and above all safe. Codes of practice for running safer music festivals and events recommend free drinking water and chill-out areas. Additionally, first aid and emergency services providers play an important role in managing the safety of music fans. This means that they need to work with the audience so that people do not hesitate to seek help; they need to circulate and offer support. This was exemplified at the 2011 Roskilde festival, where the psychological aspects of crowd safety were evident (see the weblink 'Event safety and crowd management' at the end of the chapter).

Obtaining feedback is done in a variety of ways. Informal feedback is usually harnessed by frontline event staff, but there are various ways to establish the level of satisfaction of the event audience, including formal and structured approaches. Ways of getting feedback include:

* observation (queues, for example)
* formal surveys
* focus groups
* casual discussion
* interviews.

This feedback closes the loop, ensuring that subsequent days of the event program run more successfully or that subsequent events are planned more effectively.

Benefits of using customer feedback

The recurring theme throughout this chapter has been how to understand customer needs and perceptions and how they make decisions. Rather than trying to speculate about customers who may walk through the door, event managers need to learn instead from the ones who are there, or who have been there.

Seeking feedback, with open-ended questions, is the most effective way of improving and modifying service to meet customers' expectations and unanticipated needs. An organisation that encourages staff to request feedback, and which harnesses that feedback for the dynamic process of change, is an organisation that has a competitive edge.

A number of benefits, as outlined below, result from good communication in the event workplace, not least of which is the achievement of a more satisfying experience for the guests and for the staff who serve them.

Time saved

When clients are given specific information, rather than huge amounts of unnecessary information, everyone saves time. Selling should not produce information overload; selling should provide exactly what the customer is looking for. Questioning is a key communication skill and it should be utilised to establish this.

Fewer mistakes

If careful listening is part of the interaction with the client, and the information is checked, fewer mistakes are likely to occur. In the event industry in particular, one small mistake can have dreadful repercussions. This has occurred at football events where the ticket checkpoints have been opened during a crowd surge, thus filling parts of the stadium beyond capacity.

Accurate expectations

If clients or guests are given accurate information, they will have accurate expectations. If, for example, it is possible that a garden party will have to be held indoors if the weather is bad, guests should be informed of this and told what to expect. This is particularly relevant to outdoor weddings.

Increased customer satisfaction

If customers' needs are fulfilled, they are likely to be satisfied with their experiences. If value is added to good, positive and professional service throughout the whole process, this will lead to even higher levels of customer satisfaction.

Increased employee morale

Working in an environment where things go smoothly (most of the time) and where both staff and customers are enjoying themselves, is a decided pleasure and immensely rewarding. This is the attraction that the industry has for its employees.

Promote repeat business

In some situations, the problem cannot be satisfactorily resolved and the best one can do is offer the customer another ticket or some inducement to come again. In general terms, it is essential to follow up satisfied customers too and encourage them to return, even without an inducement such as a discount. An email with several images of the successful event is a simple way to develop the client relationship.

Maintain customer profiles

Ticketing and registration software is very useful for developing customer profiles. Harnessed with these details, an exhibition company can provide invaluable marketing advice to exhibitors. In all sectors of the event industry, the data obtained about customers is extremely useful, even to the extent of transport planning for the next event.

Provide tailored products

Finally, good use of client or customer data can enable the event organisation to provide tailored products. Demographic details about the event audience can, for example, encourage a sponsor when this profile matches their marketing initiatives. An analysis of special food requests is useful for subsequent events. If customers ask the same question at the information desk all the time, this is a signal to improve the website information or signage.

Summary

This chapter has discussed the principles and benefits of enhanced customer service. Unlike a traditional business (such as a café) where customer loyalty develops over time, an event business caters to visitors who are engaged for only a short, intense period. Added to this is the challenge of a diverse workforce comprising staff, volunteers, emergency services and other service providers. The development of clear policies and procedures beforehand will help immensely, and there is no substitute for daily briefings to cover issues that can be resolved on an ongoing basis. Of course, there are longer-term relationships with corporate clients and events that run regularly, weekly or annually. In these situations, particular attention needs to be paid to the negotiation and management of the agreed contract and the specifications identified by the client. This will lead to more harmonious relationships and client satisfaction. This topic will be covered in more detail in Chapter 7.

Key terms

External customers   Users of the end product or service of an organisation

Internal customers   Another department or service provider working to deliver the final product or service to the external customer

REVIEW YOUR KNOWLEDGE

1 Explain the difference between internal and external customers in the event environment.

2 Sometimes, people planning big birthdays and weddings approach a consultant only to find that they simply look things up on the Internet and do not provide any value. How can an event consultant such as a party planner or wedding coordinator add value to the customer relationship?

3 From the perspective of a salesperson, explain how top-down, bottom-up and benefit selling work, using an example in each case.

4 What are the particular challenges for customer service in an event environment? In your response, focus on the composition of the workforce at a food and wine festival.

5 What are the steps involved in resolving complaints or dealing with problems?

APPLY YOUR KNOWLEDGE

1 Ticketing issues can be problematic. Research this topic by finding a case study of customers complaining about event tickets. Explain the recourse that customers have if they are unhappy.

2 The terms and conditions associated with tickets for music festivals usually include guidelines for audience behaviour and provide the basis for intervention when there are complaints. Give three examples.

3 Preventative aspects of event planning can go a long way towards proactively solving problems. Using the potential issues associated with queuing, discuss two ways in which effective planning can be helpful.

4 A mother is unhappy with the styling of the room for her daughter's 18th birthday party, and the event starts in three hours. What, if any, solutions are possible? What are the possible organisational constraints in making last-minute changes to décor?

CASE STUDY

The awards night for the top sales staff of Indigo Cosmetics was to be held in the banquet room of a five-star hotel. Booking the venue and planning the event was the responsibility of Maggie Turlton, the public relations manager for the company. In the process of planning the event, she worked with the hotel's catering manager, Mike Malone, and until a few hours before the event she was quite happy with the arrangements.

When she arrived two hours before the banquet for 600 people and the ceremony for 10 award-winning salespeople, Maggie's phone was running hot. Her top five problems were as follows:

• Mike Malone had delegated operational responsibility to Helen Chen, who was the banquet manager on duty. While helpful, Helen was confused about some of the plans and seemed to be late setting up the tables, as the previous client had only just packed up.

• The presentation slides were on a USB that had been left behind in the Indigo office, and the hotel's wi-fi kept dropping out so Maggie couldn't download the slides from her email account. The AV guy, Phil, was like a cat on a hot tin roof — he wanted to rehearse the presentation sequence beforehand and was very anxious.

• A separate room had been promised, in which to set up the trophies and assemble the nominees before the event, and interview the winners after they had won their categories. Maggie had assumed that the technical people understood that cameras and sound equipment would need to be used in this room. But on arrival, she found that nothing had been set up for this purpose. In addition, several nominees had arrived early and were hanging about.

- Ten calls on Maggie's mobile phone were from guests who wanted to change their meal requests, which involved vegetarian, vegan and nut allergy issues.
- The Asia-Pacific marketing manager for Indigo Cosmetics had just arrived from Singapore and was checking in downstairs.

Draw a diagram to show all the people involved. Note that Indigo Cosmetics is the client for the services provided by the hotel. Different aspects of organising the event are the responsibility of the client (Indigo Cosmetics) and the service providers (hotel and AV company).

Analyse each of the situations described and make a priority list for Maggie. Then explain how you would prioritise the issues that have arisen and how you would deal with each of them.

Online resources

Visit http://login.cengagebrain.com and search for this book to access the study tools that come with your textbook.

References

Easy Weddings (2017). How much does the average Australian wedding cost? www.easyweddings.com.au/articles/much-average-australian-wedding-cost

IBISworld (2016). Bridal stores in Australia: Market research report. December. www.ibisworld.com.au/industry/bridal-stores.html

Pine, B. J., & Gilmore, J. H. (1999). *The Experience Economy: Work Is Theatre & Every Business a Stage*. Boston: Harvard Business Press.

Pine, B. J., & Gilmore, J. H. (2011). *The Experience Economy*. Boston: Harvard Business Press.

Shobeiri, S. (2016). Positioning of commercial experiences in the experience economy. *The Marketing Review*, 16(1), 78 – 91.

Websites

10 very cool examples of experiential marketing, https://econsultancy.com/blog/65230-10-very-cool-examples-of-experiential-marketing/

Event industry trends, www.bizbash.com

Event safety and crowd management (YouTube), https://youtu.be/NwpR4xCGS8Q

Ticket scalping is an offence in Queensland, www.qld.gov.au/law/your-rights/consumer-rights-complaints-and-scams/buying-products-and-services/buying-services/music-festivals-and-concerts/

Ticketing code of practice, www.liveperformance.com.au/ticketing_code_practice

COORDINATE ON-SITE EVENT REGISTRATIONS

3

OVERVIEW

This chapter will describe the key steps involved in coordinating event registrations. Attention to detail is required in this area as even the smallest error can cause confusion or loss of valuable client data. Preparing for registrations, including a careful set-up arrangement, is the first priority. The registration area is located at the entrance to every exhibition, conference or sporting contest and it therefore provides the first impression for visitors. This will be a negative one if there are queues that aren't managed well. Customer service in the form of effective communication ensures that delegates, exhibition visitors and/or athletes are all primed for the event.

LEARNING OBJECTIVES

On completion of this chapter, you will be able to:

1. prepare on-site registration materials and equipment prior to the event and confirm arrangements with the venue

2. set up the registration area, checking that equipment is working correctly, including hardware and registration software

3. process on-site registrations after welcoming attendees, resolve any discrepancies, and process payments.

INDUSTRY VIEWPOINT

Gatecrashers can disturb many types of events, sparking violence, distributing drugs or simply eating and drinking all the food and alcohol. When I worked as a banquet manager I remember a 'gang' of old ladies who would gatecrash the luncheon banquets, queuing up with all the delegates and scooping food into their handbags. Of course they were completely noticeable to the staff, standing out in their floral dresses among the suited delegates. We felt sorry for them but after a couple of incidents security had to be called. Monitoring conference delegates becomes more difficult as the days progress; by day three many have lost their badges/lanyards or they have simply left them in their hotel rooms. In these situations it is also unclear whose responsibility it is to closely monitor the people present, the venue [banquet staff] or the client booking the conference. In my role as an hotelier there are also financial issues. The price quoted to the client hosting the event is based on certain numbers – these can't afford to be rubbery! Our clients often find it hard to understand that the chef can't respond instantly to changes in menu, special requests or numbers of attendees.

Hotel manager

Event program
The line-up of speakers or entertainers at an event

Trade show
A trade show is designed to sell products, mainly to retailers

INTRODUCTION

When we talk about event registrations, business meetings and conferences spring to mind. For these events, registration is about meeting delegates at arrival, giving them personalised badges or lanyards, and updating them with key information. This is often provided in the form of a satchel containing the **event program** or schedule, but these days much of this information may be available on a mobile app which lists the speakers and conference sessions. Indeed, an app may also allow for the selection of breakout sessions and external activities such as tours, or enable participants to interact with speakers and with each other. Later in this chapter, there will be more discussion regarding the role of software packages in managing registrations.

The second major type of business event is the exhibition. Some exhibitions are called **trade shows** in that they only invite and admit buyers, not the general public. Examples include trade shows for farm equipment, wholesale furniture or automotive parts. In many cases, a conference and an exhibition will be linked together, such as a clean energy conference and an accompanying exhibition.

The largest trade show in the world is the Canton Trade Fair. Run in three phases annually in Guangzhou, China, the scale of the event is extraordinary. In 2017 there were

Getty Images / kasto80

Conferences are often broken up into different sessions

over 60 000 booths for exhibitors and 196 000 visiting buyers, leading to a total turnover of over US$30 billion (China Import and Export Fair, 2017).

Trade shows can involve many exhibitors

Many other exhibitions are open to the public, including fishing and boating expos, baby and children's expos, and indoor and outdoor home renovation shows.

Registrations are most challenging when athletes, swimmers and other sportspeople are involved. Many of these events are set up in age groups or heats. For some categories of marathon, the runners need to demonstrate specific time/distance achievements to enter a particular category; this is also known as seeded and priority starts. Many marathons have elite athletes running at the front of the pack, with others entering in categories such as 'junior dash' or 'wheelchair half-marathon'. Corporate teams also need to be catered for in sporting events such as marathons and triathlons.

In summary, on-site registration or ticketing is involved in all of the following event types:

- business and corporate events such as conferences and meetings
- community events such as multicultural festivals
- entertainment and leisure events, including shows such as at outdoor cinemas
- exhibitions, expositions and fairs
- festivals of all types, music being the most common
- fundraising charity dinners and the like
- government and civic events, including those on Australia Day
- marketing, including product launches
- sports competitions and fun runs
- private events such as weddings.

PREPARE ON-SITE REGISTRATION MATERIALS

The most obvious requirement for event registration is the attendee list that shows invitees and their status, such as 'confirmed' and 'paid'. For a graduation ceremony, for example, one would expect the RSVP list to show who will be coming to the event, although this is not always the case. Some people do not advise that they are attending but turn up anyway. Others advise that they are coming but do not turn up after all. This makes the registration process critical and time-consuming.

What can go wrong at graduation? One student took her parents to a town hall all dressed up and proudly pumped, only to find that her name was not called during the ceremony, even though it was in the graduation booklet. The family was most upset.

In another situation, the winner of a talent show was announced incorrectly and the MC was obliged to reverse her statement, causing absolute mayhem. It was not her fault – cards had been prepared for both finalists and she had been handed the wrong one.

How can these problems be avoided?

EXTENSION ACTIVITY

The registration desk at an exhibition

Accreditation

Accreditation limits access to various parts of an event site. At a music festival, for example, only people wearing the correct lanyard are allowed backstage. Lanyards are commonly used to display badges, tickets or ID cards for identification where security is required. When the accreditation system is specifically designed, various zones are created and codes or colours allocated to them. As you can imagine, the Olympic Games has one of the most complex accreditation systems of any event, which is essential for security reasons. At major events, it is quite common for staff to undergo police security checks and have a photo ID on the lanyard.

Once the system is in place, it is then necessary to post a security guard or volunteer at each entry to a zone. Tact and patience are required as many people try to breach the system, insisting on access to places for which they do not have the appropriate accreditation. The media often have one of the highest levels of accreditation, enabling them, for example, to take photographs at the front or back of the stage.

> **Accreditation**
> Process of issuing access to specific event zones or areas

FIGURE 3.1 Data applications for sporting events

Registration process online

↓

Issue of timing device at the race start

↓

↓

Timing recorded

↓

Certificate of participation issued

Prepare materials

The different materials required for registration depend on the type of event and the level of online or office-based registration that has already been done. For most conference attendees, the software will show all their details, and all that remains is to confirm their attendance and distribute name badges.

In other situations, such as a swimming race, participants might simply turn up on the day, in which case they are required to fill in all the forms and the data is entered on the spot. This implies the use of computers even at a beach. Time-recording devices have to be issued and matched to the attendee on the database. Timing systems generally use **RFID** (radio frequency identification) chip race-timing products. This is attached to the ankle, shoelaces or a numbered bib. The athlete's time is registered as they cross the start and then the finish line (see Figure 3.1).

This type of technology is also useful to exhibitors, as a visitor to a stand can be 'clocked' as they come near and show interest in the product. In the past, an exchange of business cards was necessary to identify expo visitors with purchase intentions or at least a clear interest in specific products.

RFID
Radio frequency identification chip or transponder

Computers are thus required for the registration area, and this implies an electrical supply and in most cases wi-fi accessibility. The following materials are also needed:

- lanyards, bibs or badges
- RFID devices as described above
- attendee kits (e.g. promotional satchels, programs, site maps)
- cash float for anyone registering and paying at the last minute
- EFTPOS payment devices
- receipts
- banners and posters, directional signage
- stationery
- vouchers (lunch) or tickets.

Software for registration and accreditation

There are many different event and venue management software packages that cover the whole planning process, including registration. Ungerboeck, for example, provides a range of modules linked to a single, cloud-based database which builds on existing customer data over time. As Figure 3.2 shows, these units handle online registrations, marketing campaigns, mobile event apps, presenter management, online payment and reporting.

Registration software in general, such as EventsPro, can enable the performance of a wide range of tasks using integrated websites, including:

- client inquiries
- showing availability
- venue/room/event bookings
- catering and beverage requirements
- staffing requirements
- equipment set-up
- invoice and receipt creation and tracking
- contracts and deposits
- client event history
- client communication history
- business analysis
- booking and resource conflict checking
- event schedule promotion
- room utilisation
- automatic reminders
- tracking of suppliers and orders
- attendee management
- letter templates and mail merges
- exports to various accounting packages
- basically, all of your event, finance and management reporting needs.

FIGURE 3.2 Ungerboeck for Conferences & Events – conference management software

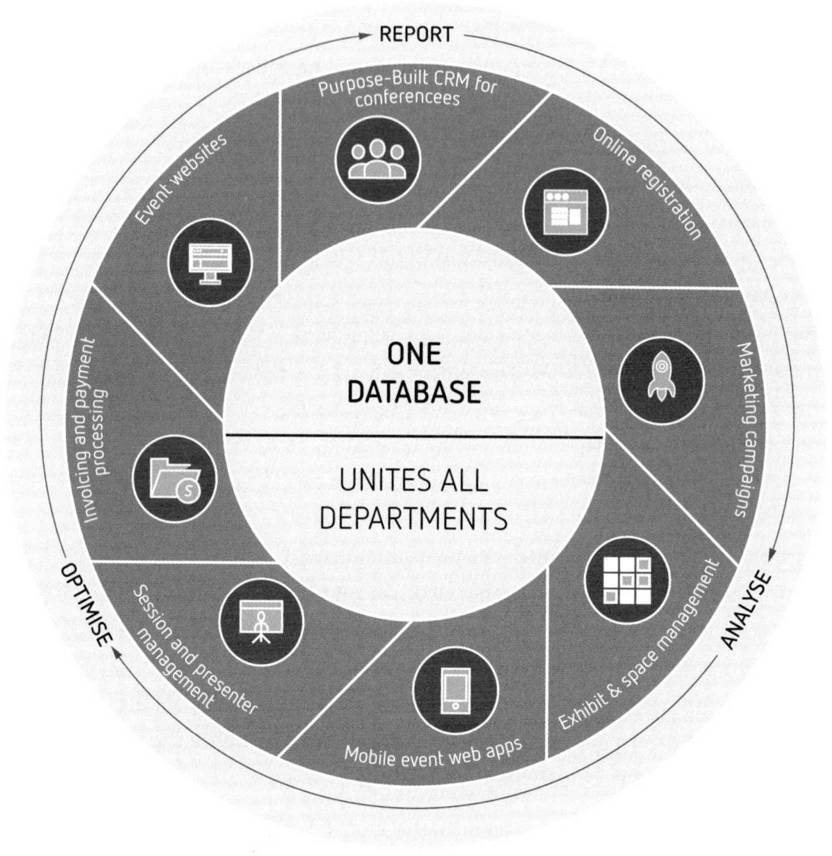

REPORT

Purpose-Built CRM for conferencees

Event websites

Online registration

Marketing campaigns

ONE DATABASE

UNITES ALL DEPARTMENTS

Invoicing and payment processing

OPTIMISE

Session and presenter management

Mobile event web apps

Exhibit & space management

ANALYSE

Source: Ungerboeck Software International (2017). Ungerboeck for conferences. https://ungerboeck.com/event-products/ungerboeck-for-conferences

As this list shows, the software does more than just register participants; it assists from initial promotion right through to billing and settlement. Furthermore, it offers a methodical way of managing client data to avoid duplication of efforts across systems. The tracking and reminder features are extremely valuable in event planning.

For smaller, informal events such as weddings, it is possible to use a spreadsheet to manage the invitation list and RSVPs. Even in this case, free downloads of Excel spreadsheets are available.

Prepare for the unexpected

One of the most common problems for organisers is the unexpected guest. A wedding reception, for example, has carefully placed name tags at each table, often the result of many weeks of deliberation regarding who will sit where. 'Yeah, we said it would be difficult to come with a brand-new baby, but here we are' is likely to send everyone into panic mode about seating and food. Awards nights present similar problems. Some people can arrive late or be absent, leaving tables half-empty and food wasted.

When it became evident that an award recipient at one event was in a wheelchair, the banquet manager decided to put this person and her guests at a back table so that service personnel could get around the other tables more easily. How can better planning prevent this situation from arising?

Hint: Think about questions that should be asked as part of the pre-event-registration process to avoid problems with seating and food.

Another issue is the guest who arrives but has not paid and says, 'The cheque is in the mail', or something similar. In other cases, an expected attendee sends a substitute, which is problematic when it comes to corporate functions.

Here are other situations which might arise that need careful handing:

- the person who turns up after declining
- gatecrashers
- people with special diets who have not advised the organisers in advance
- complaints about seating arrangements because guests simply feel out of favour and want to move places
- paparazzi
- a breach of confidentiality by staff involving the media
- the person who tries to access a zone for which they are not accredited (e.g. backstage).

Below, we discuss other issues associated with accessibility and ticketing terms and conditions.

Accessibility issues

Accessibility is an issue for many attendees, including those who are in wheelchairs, have difficulty walking, have a sight or hearing disability, or are accompanied by children and/ or prams. Special access ramps may be necessary, for instance, which are also useful for organisers who may need to bring unwieldy items onto the site. It is usually the registration staff who field any requests for information about accessibility.

Doshi et al. (2014) provide a checklist to help make meetings accessible to people with disabilities. The checklist is divided into sections related to event planning, venue accessibility, venue staff, invitations/registrations, greeting people with a disability, actions during the event, and suggestions for effective presenters. These will be discussed in more detail in later chapters on event planning. For the moment, it is important to note that the reception desk should be at a height that is accessible for people who use wheelchairs. Also, any text should be presented in readable formats, such as on devices that can be accessed by specialist software. Note that PDF documents cannot be accessed by people who use screen-reading technology.

Terms and conditions

Chapter 2 dealt with problem solving and conflict management in general terms. With regard to admission to an event at the time of registration or ticket collection, a key aspect of staff training relates to the event's terms and conditions. Generally listed on a website at the time of booking or featured on the back of a ticket, these are the rules that apply to the event. A copy of the terms and conditions should be on hand in case a staff member has to refer to them.

Terms and conditions will address such things as:

- tickets not being refundable
- payment methods
- right of admission reserved
- items not admitted
- entry search
- change of line-up
- ticket substitution
- valid forms of identification
- severe weather.

TICKETING DEBACLE LEAVES RICKY MARTIN FANS FURIOUS

Ricky Martin treated Townsville to the Australian premiere of his global One World Tour at the weekend, giving his adoring fans the type of show that's rarely seen in the city. Saucy dancers, polished routines and a high-energy performance left Townsville fans at his two sold-out shows screaming for more.

The star was genuinely excited to be in Townsville, playing to a large crowd of adoring fans, most of whom had never seen him live before. 'That's what it is all about', he said to his fans of getting to play in a new city. 'I want you to forget about all the issues you have at home, or the issues in the world … I am not leaving this stage until you are happy.'

Fans were warmed up for the main event by Australian star Delta Goodrem, who has joined her The Voice Australia co-star on tour.

Ticketing issues put a dampener on Martin's Townsville launch, with dozens of fans left disappointed or without seats. Some forked out big money for premium seating only to be allocated bleacher seats after the concerts were moved from 1300SMILES Stadium to the Townsville Entertainment and Convention Centre. Others said they turned up to the Saturday show only to be told their tickets had been transferred to the Friday concert.

But promoters said multiple attempts had been made to communicate with ticket-holders about the changes.

Skye Orsmond said she had no idea her ticket had been transferred to the Friday show until she received a text from Ticketek on Saturday afternoon inquiring about why she had not shown up. She said she was one of the lucky ones who was granted entry on Saturday but said plenty of others missed out after all the seats were filled.

'We had a text message saying the venue had changed but it didn't say anything about the day changing', she said. 'In the end we at least got to go but we spoke to a lot of people who completely missed out. There was a whole group of really angry people there. The show was fantastic and made up for all the negativity but it was just really poorly managed.'

A Ticketek spokeswoman said ticket-holders were updated on changes through email, phone and text and they were now dealing with any unresolved issues with individual customers directly. 'Ticketek made extensive efforts to contact all ticketholders impacted by the change … prior to the concerts to notify them of the new venue and, where necessary, new date of the show their tickets were valid for', she said.

The venue for this tour was changed due to the 'production requirements' of the show.

- Who is an authorised ticket seller?
- Who is an unauthorised ticket seller (reseller/scammer)?
- What do you think is a reasonable notice period for a change of venue?
- What rights does the consumer have when shows are relocated or cancelled?

For more information, see https://www.accc.gov.au/consumers/online-shopping/buying-tickets-online.

Source: Townsville Bulletin, 27 April 2015, Christie Anderson. Licensed through CAL. www.townsvillebulletin.com.au/news/ticketing-debacle-leaves-ricky-martin-fans-furious/news-story/9494b2585857b0e8c01d6e4ffcfabf8f

Check venue and registration set-up

On arrival at the venue, it is necessary to locate and check the registration set-up against the prearranged agreements and relevant safety and access requirements. Following this, carry out a site inspection in order to become completely familiar with the event venue (the first question you will be asked will be the location of the toilets). Finally, establish contact with the appropriate venue or site personnel and other operations staff to facilitate effective communication during the event.

Early delivery of materials ensures that the stand is ready when doors open

There are several safety considerations to bear in mind, including keeping an eye out for cables in public areas that present tripping hazards, and blocked emergency exits. Sun and weather protection is required for outdoor events. Where large numbers are expected at one time, barriers are required to manage queues.

SET UP REGISTRATION AREA

Event organisers need to arrive in good time to complete the set-up of the registration area. This is sometimes problematic, such as when the stands are still being built and the tradesmen are running over time. Here are some other problems that can occur:

- Vehicles are banked up in the loading area and materials have not been delivered.
- A ladder is needed for setting up and guests are due to arrive any minute.
- There are not enough pens for people to complete their registration forms.
- Traffic has been bad and lots of people have been delayed.
- Name badges are in order of first name and not surname.
- Some arrivals have not had name badges prepared for them.

- A speaker has lost her USB.
- Access to the registration area is blocked by people waiting to enter the conference room.
- People arriving in the lobby cannot see any clear directional signage.

In all of these cases, careful proactive planning can prevent problems arising. The set-up process can work more quickly and smoothly, for example, if trolleys are used to shift boxes from the loading dock, and software systems have been checked beforehand. The following sections give more advice about preparation.

Establish communication

On arrival at the venue, your first point of contact is the venue manager or the venue operations team. No doubt there have been many such events run at the venue and their experience and knowledge will be invaluable, particularly relating to electrical supply and technology.

Prepare materials

In some cases, organisers bring in boxes of promotional materials that need to be put in satchels on-site. This is one example of a task that should be done beforehand to save time. Name badges should be prepared in advance and spread out in alphabetical order by surname. Spare badges should be kept in readiness for attendees who arrive unexpectedly.

Check equipment

The most critical aspect of software-reliant event registration is the installation of materials and equipment to check their efficiency and working order prior to the commencement of registration.

PROCESS ON-SITE REGISTRATIONS

Once the equipment is set up for registrations, it is time to open the doors. While for some events people arrive at different times during the day, in most cases this is a very stressful period when everyone arrives at once but they are delayed by registration or ticket taking – unless, of course, they have pre-registered and can enter using their mobile phone apps.

Welcome attendees

Once people start arriving, it is necessary to process registrations efficiently but to also allow for friendly interaction with the customers. These are the steps to follow in processing registrations:

- Welcome attendees in a courteous and friendly manner and provide accurate and relevant information on the venue and event features.
- Check and accurately record registration details according to event procedures.
- Assist where possible with work overflow of other registration personnel.

- Identify, record and action any registration discrepancies with minimum disruption to the attendee. Registration discrepancies may include unexpected on-site registrations; incorrect details in name or payment information; or no-shows or incorrect pre-bookings for particular sessions, activities or inclusions.
- Accurately finalise documentation and pack or store registration resources according to event procedures.

These steps are summarised in Figure 3.3.

FIGURE 3.3 Steps in processing registrations

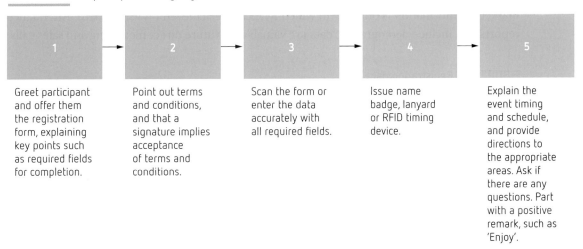

1	2	3	4	5
Greet participant and offer them the registration form, explaining key points such as required fields for completion.	Point out terms and conditions, and that a signature implies acceptance of terms and conditions.	Scan the form or enter the data accurately with all required fields.	Issue name badge, lanyard or RFID timing device.	Explain the event timing and schedule, and provide directions to the appropriate areas. Ask if there are any questions. Part with a positive remark, such as 'Enjoy'.

An important aspect of registration for sporting events is the signature on the indemnity form. The registration will include questions about physical fitness and the athlete must sign the form acknowledging any risks. Some inclusions in the **indemnity** could read as follows:

> Indemnity
> Exemption from liability for damages

I indemnify and will keep indemnified the Organiser and each Event Sponsor against all costs, losses or damages arising from or in relation to my attendance at or participation in the Event.

I declare that I am physically fit and have trained sufficiently to participate in and complete the Event.

The Organiser reserves the right to reject or cancel my entry at any time, including without limitation for safety or insurance reasons.

During events such as exhibitions and conferences, it is essential for staff and security guards to monitor registrations and accreditation. For events at which alcohol is served, there is the need to conduct age checks and, in some cases, issue wristbands. Entry and exit points to licensed areas need to be manned.

Lin and Lin (2013) conducted research in the exhibition industry, finding that exhibition marketing was the most important criterion to exhibitors, including Internet exposure and inviting specific overseas buyers. Service quality was another key factor highlighted in their research.

Check registration

Staff at the registration desk seldom understand the importance of the data provided by the visitor. In fact, the registration details of all exhibition visitors are an asset. This list allows all exhibitors access to names, job roles and other business details post-event for direct mailing purposes. The basic elements of a registration form are shown in Figure 3.4, and from this it becomes clear that answers to the questions posed enable exhibitors to judge the seniority and purchasing power of the exhibition visitors. With correct basic data, there is also the opportunity for follow-up after the exhibition.

Return on investment (ROI) is an important consideration for events, and targeted marketing information is one way in which ROI can be achieved (Wilson, 2013). Attendance reports that include demographic data are valuable for future direct marketing and sales calls.

FIGURE 3.4 Registration data

Basic information

Title _____

Name_____

Company_____

Address_____

Mobile_____

Email_____

Website_____

Job title (please select)

☐   Owner, manager or GM

☐   Branch or store manager

☐   Sales, marketing or purchasing manager

☐   Employee

☐   Media

☐   Other_____

Purpose of visit

☐   Visit current suppliers

☐   Research new suppliers

☐   Market-research new trends

☐   Evaluate products

☐   Look for partner and investment opportunities

☐   View products and order

☐   Other_____

Ushering

Once the attendees have arrived and registered, or have shown their tickets, they need to be shown to their seats. This is an important aspect of customer service. Tickets need to be checked for validity and seating location. Sometimes this is problematic; for example, when people arrive on the wrong day or at the wrong time. But in some cases this can be accommodated to the great relief of the customer. Most tickets are scanned electronically and this is a very useful deterrent to those who try to get in with fake tickets. Also be aware that many festivals have ushers at the gates who inadvertently let groups in when the last member of the group is showing the receipt stub and not a valid ticket.

Getting everyone seated before the conference or show begins is essential and this may mean hurrying the crowd in the foyer. It also means that entry may be refused if someone is late – they may be required to wait for a break in proceedings. Highly problematic is the person arriving late for their graduation ceremony, and contingency plans need to be put in place for this occurrence.

Once the audience is registered and seated, event service personnel are required to monitor safety issues, such as checking that no-one is sitting in an aisle or blocking an exit.

Finalise registration

The final stages of event registration involve processing final payments and reconciling financial information. This in turn leads to the preparation of final reports, which will include takings/income and attendance.

Finalise payments

In order to finalise cash payments, the float has to be checked and reconciled against summary records. Point-of-sale records for customer payments also need to be determined and balanced. Any discrepancies need to be investigated. It may also be necessary to transport and bank takings. For large events involving large cash amounts, it is preferable to employ a security company that will regularly collect, count and bank the takings.

Prepare reports

In addition to financial reports of event income from registrations or tickets, it is useful to generate reports identifying the number of tickets sold in different price categories, and the profiles of attendees. All of this is important marketing information for the next event.

Figure 3.5 shows the breakdown of revenues from a small exhibition.

FIGURE 3.5 Breakdown of an exhibition's revenues

VISITORS	TOTAL	PERCENTAGE	REVENUE
Registrations	120	90%	
Cancellations	10	7%	
No-shows	4	3%	
Type			
Attendee	100	83%	$2075
Exhibitor	20	17%	$5100
Payment method			
Credit card		19%	$654
Direct debit		81%	$6521
Total			$7175

Summary

In this chapter we have reviewed the stages of event registration. Hopefully, the key message of this chapter is understood to be 'attention to detail'. An athlete with the wrong timing device, a graduate without a certificate, a new citizen given the wrong information about a ceremony – all are examples of the things that can go wrong at important times for event attendees. People can also arrive late and be confused, needing direction and reassurance, as getting around some of the larger events is confounding. Thus, the role of anyone working at the point of registration is to provide a good first impression and give clear directions and instructions.

Registration software and devices, including RFID, are increasingly commonplace. This provides for seamless operation if managed correctly, or complete disaster if the system goes down without contingency plans for this possibility.

'Check, check and double-check' is the name of the game for weddings, conferences, expos, races and awards nights. Registration staff who check lanyards or monitor ticket gates also play an important role in managing the security of the event, ensuring that the organisers know exactly who is there.

Key terms

Accreditation	Process of issuing access to specific event zones or areas
Event program	The line-up of speakers or entertainers at an event
Indemnity	Exemption from liability for damages
RFID	Radio frequency identification chip or transponder
Trade show	A trade show is designed to sell products, mainly to retailers

REVIEW YOUR KNOWLEDGE

1   Explain the differences between registrations of visitors to the following event types, in each case using a specific event as an example:
    – conferences
    – exhibitions
    – sporting events
    – entertainment events.
2   Event registration software is useful for maintaining records of attendees, including payment information. Explain the features of an event registration software package you have identified and the reports or documentation that can be produced.
3   Conflict can occur during the registration process. Describe three problems that can arise and how these problems can be best managed.

APPLY YOUR KNOWLEDGE

1   Citizenship ceremonies are dignified occasions. Visit a range of citizenship websites, including the ones given below, to develop a diagrammatic plan for registration set-up, taking into account the following: space, registration area, seating, weather protection and safety. You can use any

venue for the event, including a school hall, council office or outdoor area. Your plan should show the location, parking, entry points, registration area, seating, exits and so on.
- www.australiaday.org.au/australia-day/australia-day-ceremonies/citizenship-ceremonies/citizenship-ceremonies-faq/ (Australia)
- http://wellington.govt.nz/services/community-and-culture/citizenship-ceremonies (New Zealand)
- There are many videos of ceremonies on YouTube.

2 Develop a run sheet for the day that illustrates the timing of set-up and the key components of the ceremony (what will happen when).
3 Describe the process of registration in a flow chart showing how recipients of the award will be processed and also their families and other visitors.
4 List the equipment and documents that are needed so that a checklist can be completed before the ceremony.

CASE STUDY

The Gold Coast Airport Marathon is held annually in one of the most popular holiday destinations in the world. It is Australia's premier road race and was the first marathon in the country to hold an International Association of Athletics Federations (IAAF) Road Race Gold Label.

The event is held on the first weekend of July and attracts more than 27 000 participants of all ages and abilities across a number of races including the Gold Coast Airport Marathon, Wheelchair Marathon, ASICS Half Marathon, Wheelchair 15 km, Southern Cross University 10 km Run, Suncorp Bank 5.7 km Challenge and Zespri Junior Dash 4 km and 2 km races.

Source: Gold Coast Airport Marathon (2017). About the Gold Coast Airport Marathon. https://raceatlas.com/event/gold-coast-airport-marathon

Assuming that you have been given a role as volunteer trainer at the marathon, prepare a portfolio of information for other volunteers that includes:
- the history and aims of the event
- the course layout
- the categories of entrants and details of different races
- race etiquette, weather policy and race policy
- registration and check in process.

Gold Coast Airport Marathon

Note that all of this information is on the marathon's website (http://goldcoastmarathon.com.au) and there is no need to contact the organisation directly.

Online resources

Visit **http://login.cengagebrain.com** and search for this book to access the study tools that come with your textbook.

References

China Import and Export Fair (2017). Statistics: 121st Canton Fair. **www.cantonfair.org.cn/html/cantonfair/en/about/2012-09/137.shtml**

Doshi, J. K., Furlan, A. D., Lopes, L. C., DeLisa, J., & Battistella, L. R. (2014). Conferences and convention centres' accessibility to people with disabilities. *Journal of Rehabilitation Medicine*, 46(7), 616–19.

Lin, C. T., & Lin, C. W. (2013). Exhibitor perspectives of exhibition service quality. *Journal of Convention & Event Tourism*, 14(4), 293–308.

Wilson, M. (2013). Making an exhibition. *Australasian Leisure Management*, 97, 40.

Websites

Accessible events – a guide for organisers, **www.meetingsevents.com.au** (search for 'accessible events')

etouches event registration software, **www.etouches.com/event-software/module/ereg/**

Exhibition & Event Association of Australasia, **www.eeaa.com.au**

Meetings & Events Australia, **www.meetingsevents.com.au**

Professional Conference Organisers Association, **www.pco.asn.au**

Ungerboeck Software International, **https://ungerboeck.com**

2

EVENT PLANNING

4 MANAGE PROJECTS

OVERVIEW

In this chapter, the key concepts of project management will be introduced and applied. These are used across many industries. In some, such as information technology and engineering, the role of project manager is a highly regarded professional job title. Event managers are project managers: the milestones and deadlines for execution of the plan are generally fixed due to live broadcast and other factors such as waiting wedding guests. This is one industry in which the project deadline is seldom extended. A number of stakeholders are also involved, creating a necessity for good project planning, communication, execution and evaluation.

LEARNING OBJECTIVES

On completion of this chapter, you will be able to:

1 define a project's scope by identifying the objectives, budget, scope of activities and deliverables

2 develop a project plan in consultation with stakeholders that includes project specifications

3 administer and monitor a project, implementing financial and quality control systems and meeting agreed timelines

4 evaluate a project's effectiveness and report outcomes to stakeholders.

INDUSTRY VIEWPOINT

Successful event management involves many people undertaking separate tasks in a coordinated manner. In Mosman, this involves staff from every section of Council, staff in several other state agencies, staff of companies and clubs, as well as volunteers. Events must be managed in accordance with not only Council's own policies, but also various state laws and regulations.

Only a small portion of this effort is visible to the general public. Even if the event runs smoothly there will be some negative feedback as some degree of inconvenience is inevitable. If the event is poorly managed, however, the impact can be profound, with damage to property and to the natural environment, with public safety threatened, and with widespread dissatisfaction by visitors and local residents alike.

Source: Mosman Council (2014). *Special Event Management Policy & Operations Manual*, p. 24.
http://mosman.nsw.gov.au/council/policies-forms/policies

INTRODUCTION

As this statement from a special event operations manual so clearly illustrates, planning and organisation are the key elements that determine the success of an event. For most event organisers, the first stop is the local council. The local council provides guidelines on the possible impact of events, such as the impact of noise. This may be a factor even if the event is not being held at a public venue. Another useful contact is the local tourism office. This office, with links to corporate offices in each State and Territory, plays an important part in the strategic management of events and, in many cases, provides support in a number of other ways, such as listing events on their website.

However, before making these contacts, it is necessary to develop the event concept and project plan. This involves defining the event's purpose and aims, as well as the specific objectives by which the success of the event will be measured. Funding for the event may come from grants or from sponsors, but all stakeholders have to be provided with a good understanding of the event concept and project plan before proceeding further. If the client is the one funding the event, the provision of a clearly developed concept, plan and evaluation strategy will generally avoid problems down the line, including legal ones.

The first stage of formal project management is referred to as **initiation**. This involves understanding the client's requirements so that expectations can be met. Setting off on a project without the target in sight is extremely dangerous. Too often, event planners get involved in micro-level planning before fully understanding the macro-level requirements.

> **Initiation**
> Project initiation is the first stage in the project management life cycle and involves defining objectives, scope, purpose and deliverables

DEFINE PROJECT SCOPE

In order to define the scope of a project, one has to understand the client brief well enough to agree on objectives, budget and activities. The next step is to agree on **deliverables**, these being the outcomes achieved along the project timeline, such as completion of safety training or design of the stage set. The

> **Deliverables**
> Project deliverables can be tangible, such as an operations manual, or intangible, such as completion of security briefings

importance of involving stakeholders in this process cannot be overstated. Any confusion will lead to dissatisfaction, conflict and costly changes, and these in turn will impact on the profit margin. The project life cycle is illustrated in Figure 4.1, definition of scope being part of the project initiation phase.

FIGURE 4.1 The project management life cycle

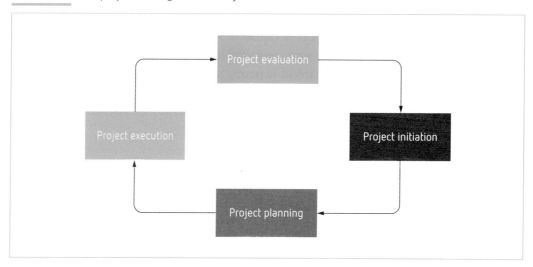

The overall project proposal should include the following:

* description of the project
* purpose of the project
* outcomes and deliverables
* scope statement (limits, boundaries)
* timeline
* cost.

The Project Management Body of Knowledge (PMBOK) was originally developed for construction and engineering and it has been through several revisions and updates. PMBOK is now applied across wide-ranging projects in all rapidly changing industries, particularly those impacted by new technologies. The Project Management Institute publishes the PMBOK guide, covering the processes that are common to most projects, including events (a link to the relevant website is listed at the end of the chapter).

There has been some discussion of whether or not events fit within the project management definition of a project. Although events are unique in having absolute deadlines, given their very nature, it is generally agreed that they are projects which function as such. The PMBOK and processes can be adapted for the event industry to serve its own specific needs.

Below, we discuss a number of concepts and terms that are used frequently in this system.

Feasibility

In the world of project management, feasibility is tackled more scientifically than creatively (and this is the criticism that some event directors have of a 'pure' project management approach to event planning). Feasibility under this approach is reviewed largely in terms of realistic dates for completion of tasks and subtasks. The financial viability of the project is evaluated and this includes developing a resource strategy for the project.

Stakeholder analysis

Stakeholder input is a consideration at every stage of project management, stakeholders being required to 'sign off' at critical points, which signals their agreement with the concept or plan. This is vitally important, and there are many examples of how this has paid off: a sponsor signing off on the use of their logo on the event poster may avoid a complete new print run if the colour is not 100 per cent correct. As an event manager, it is comforting to be able to say, 'This is what you signed off on. If you want anything else, it is going to cost you ...'

> **Stakeholders**
> May include internal and external customers, organising committees, funding bodies, regulatory authorities and other government authorities

Scope/work breakdown

Project managers recognise that any project is limited by time, scope and cost. *Time* is allocated according to the work breakdown structure (WBS). This is very similar to writing job descriptions in the traditional business environment, but in this case the tasks are more specific and clustered according to function. *Scope* refers to the extent of the project. Anyone who has planned a wedding will easily understand the concept of scope creep, particularly the person paying for the wedding who finds that the bride and her mother frequently have new and more expensive ideas as the date draws near. This will be discussed in more detail in Chapter 7 when we look at contract negotiation and, more importantly, contract variation.

Risk management

Risk management will be discussed in Chapters 9 and 18. It is mentioned here to stress that risk is not only safety risk, but rather any risk that can impact on completion of the plan by the due date. One of the most important risks relates to legal compliance. An event can be shut down or fined if it is in breach of liquor licensing legislation. Noise, safety and other issues can also present a high risk to the implementation of a plan. Collaboration with authorities and approvals are essential. If a popular event leads to traffic chaos, for example, this will not sit well with authorities or agencies on the ground if plans have not been discussed and approved. Effective communication with council, government agencies and emergency services can mitigate risks.

Deliverables

During the planning process, decisions are made about what is deliverable at each stage. These plans include ever-increasing detail; for example, equipment details for procurement (purchasing). A sample uniform is a more tangible example of a deliverable.

To differentiate between objectives and deliverables, the following examples are provided:

- *objective*: increase ticket sales by 15 per cent; *deliverable*: marketing campaign proposal approved by 16 June
- *objective*: meet food safety regulations and pass council inspections; *deliverable*: food safety plan approved and staff training completed by end August.

If you prepare a creative pitch and present to a sponsor, is this a deliverable? What are three of the deliverables you might identify in relation to sponsorship?

Milestones

Within the framework of project management, a milestone is an element that signifies the completion of a work package or phase. It is usually marked by a high-level event such as the signing of a deliverable. Typically, a milestone is associated with some sort of decision that outlines the future of a project.

Resources

An analysis of the resources required to complete a project is essential. Resources can include people, equipment, materials, money (funding) and facilities. These are all inputs and have to be considered in terms of cost and timing.

Control and creativity

Project management involves disciplined planning and control. Many of the tools suggested in this chapter, such as Gantt charts and PERT charts, are utilised in project management. It is important that careful attention be given to the critical path for completion as often timelines are interdependent. However, as mentioned above, some of the more creative people in the event business argue that this approach constrains creativity and is too limiting for the 'organic' environment of event management.

Reusch and Reusch (2013) suggest that event management has very specific characteristics for which the industry needs further developed methods and tools. The Event Management Body of Knowledge (EMBOK) is one such attempt at adaptation (a link to the relevant website is listed at the end of the chapter).

Finally, Serrador and Turner (2015) differentiate between project success (achieving outcomes) and efficiency (meeting time, scope, and budget goals). Their research indicates that efficiency is shown through analysis to be neither the only aspect of project success nor an aspect of project success that can be ignored. In a creative field such as event management, there can be no doubt that an efficient, well-run event that misses the mark for the audience would exemplify poor application of project management principles, possibly due to lack of emphasis on this early initiation phase.

Debate the following statement: 'The application of project management principles and processes destroys creativity. It is a ball and chain for the event producer'.

Analyse your own ability to undertake macro- and micro-level planning using examples from things you have done in the past. Should you do one or the other, or can you do both?

DEVELOP PROJECT PLAN

Following project initiation and general agreement, more detailed project planning can begin. This phase involves confirming the administrative structure for the project and developing an integrated project management plan using appropriate project management tools to communicate the plan to the relevant colleagues. The administrative structure could be a steering committee, advisory or reference group, or a consultative committee.

The level of detail required at this stage covers what (tasks), when (milestones and deadlines), who (staff, volunteers or contractors), and how (resources, risks). Maps and models, Gantt charts, PERT charts and run sheets are useful tools for presenting material and information to clients, members of staff and stakeholders. These are described in the following sections.

Maps and models

Maps are a useful way to represent an event, particularly to contractors who may be required to set up the site. It may be necessary to develop more than one map or plan using CAD (computer-assisted drawing) software, since different parties involved in the event will require this material for different purposes. These parties may include:

- builders and designers
- telecommunications and electrical contractors
- emergency response teams
- spectator services hosts
- artists, entertainers and exhibitors
- the event audience.

Models are also extremely useful, as most clients find it difficult to visualise three-dimensional concepts. A model can also assist in aspects of event management, such as crowd control. In this instance, bottlenecks and other potential problems can emerge from viewing a three-dimensional model. Most CAD software can present the information in this way, allowing the event management team to anticipate all design and implementation issues. Examples of models and maps are given in Figures 4.2 and 4.3.

FIGURE 4.2 CAD perspective views of an exhibition stand

Source: ExpoNet (2017). www.exponet.com.au

Work breakdown structure

The **work breakdown structure (WBS)** provides an overview of the work to be done in key areas. Note that at this stage it is not an organisation chart, with people assigned to specific roles. The WBS describes the tasks to be performed. It can take the form of diagram or table. A high-level WBS is shown in Table 4.1, indicating the key areas for planning. This can be enhanced by adding more detail later.

> **Work breakdown structure (WBS)**
> Involves organising key tasks into logical sections or clusters

FIGURE 4.3 Map of National Folk Festival

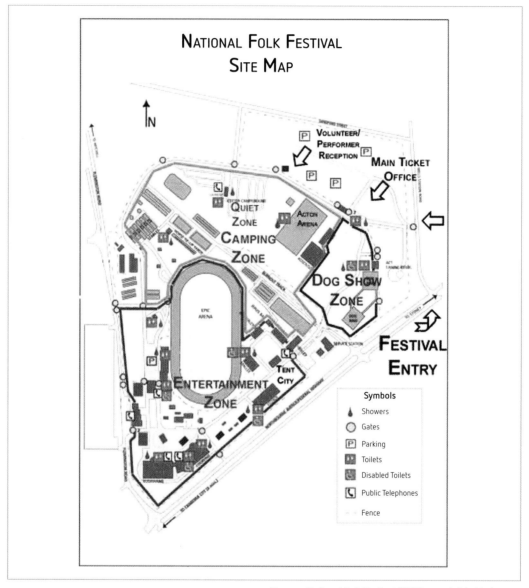

Source: National Folk Festival (2017). www.folkfestival.org.au

TABLE 4.1 A high-level work breakdown structure

Production (front of house, stage)	• plan line-up • select performers • negotiate contracts • plan staging • prepare budget • conduct rehearsals • manage rights

Operations (back of house)	• venue management • ticketing • safety, WHS, emergency planning • seating and ushering • catering and waste
Administration	• approvals • legal compliance • finance • fundraising • staffing • insurance
Marketing	• pricing • website • box office sales • promotion • sponsorship

The four key areas shown in the table cover artistic or entertainment type events. For sporting events, the production of the 'show' is replaced by the management of the sporting event, including teams, referees and so on.

The WBS illustrated here is quite simple. In practice, most events have many stakeholders managing different aspects of the event planning and execution. The venue management team at a stadium might work quite independently of the show or sport that is scheduled, although a great deal of collaboration is required. Catering might be provided by a number of concessions, and ticketing could be outsourced to a specialist ticketing agency such as Ticketek or Ticketmaster.

Business events also involve a number of key areas that require planning. Conference planning will be illustrated in Chapter 5, but one can see that the 'performance' aspect of any event can cover athletics, surf carnivals, conferences, street parades and the like. It is useful to think of this separation as looking after the performance/competition versus looking after the audience. At large, dedicated venues, the management team is highly effective in managing the audience. For unique events at outdoor sites, this becomes far more complex – all these services need to be planned, from parking to seating, from catering to waste, from safety to emergency. Chapter 24, the final chapter in this text, will deal with these complex aspects of organising event infrastructure from the ground up.

Gantt charts

A Gantt chart is generally used in the early planning days and in the lead-up to an event. The Gantt chart, developed by Charles Gantt in 1917, focuses on the sequence of tasks necessary for completion of a project. Each task on a Gantt chart is represented as a single horizontal bar on an X–Y chart. The horizontal axis (X axis) is the time scale over which the project will span. Therefore, the length of each task bar corresponds to the duration of the task, or the time necessary for completion. Arrows connecting interdependent tasks reflect the relationships between the tasks they connect. The relationship usually shows dependency, so that one task cannot begin until another is completed.

The benefit of this type of chart is that the interdependence of the tasks can be clearly seen. For example, once you have plotted the process of recruiting, inducting, training and rostering staff for an event, you may realise that the recruitment process needs to start earlier than expected to enable staff to be completely ready for the big day. The 2012 London Olympic Games faced just such a crisis with security staffing, and 3500 army, navy and air force staff were seconded to the event at the last minute.

Another aspect of planning is identifying the **critical path**: those elements of the plan that determine the minimum time needed to complete a project. Critical path analysis is beyond the scope of this text; however, the general principle of identifying planning elements on which all else is dependent can be done with a Gantt chart.

In the case of arrangements with sponsors, for example, these need to be finalised before the printing of promotional material can occur, as sponsors need to approve the use of their logos. If one sponsor pulls out of the arrangement, this will have an impact on print production which will, in turn, affect promotional activities and ticket sales.

Project planning software, including specialised event planning software, is available, while for smaller events a spreadsheet is probably sufficient. The trick is to identify the tasks that can be clustered together and to choose the ideal level of detail required in planning the event. At the extreme, the chart can be expanded to a point where even the smallest task is shown (but at this stage it will fill an entire wall and become unmanageable). As with maps, the Gantt chart must be a user-friendly planning tool in order to be effective.

Another point to take into account is that change is an integral part of event planning and it may be necessary to make significant changes that immediately make all your charts redundant. An experienced event manager is able to ascertain the level of planning required to ensure that everyone is clear about their roles and responsibilities, while remaining reasonably open to change.

A high-level planning chart for an event is illustrated in Figure 4.4. It provides a broad overview of the main event tasks and a general timeline. Each of these major tasks could also be used as the basis for a more detailed plan. This has been done in Figure 4.5, which shows

FIGURE 4.4 Sample Gantt chart for event planning

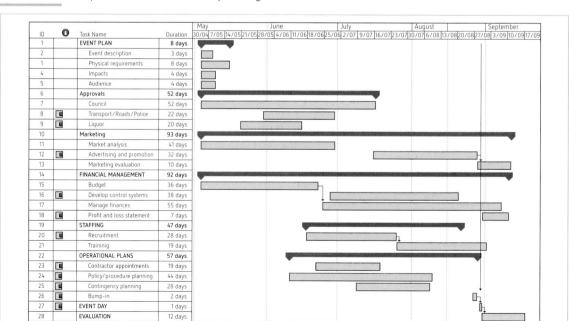

the planning process for recruiting and training staff for the above event. This Gantt chart is clearly an example of a fairly detailed level of planning although, even here, the training aspect is not covered fully as there would be many steps involved, including writing training materials and seeking approval of the content from the various functional area managers.

FIGURE 4.5 Sample Gantt chart for event staff planning

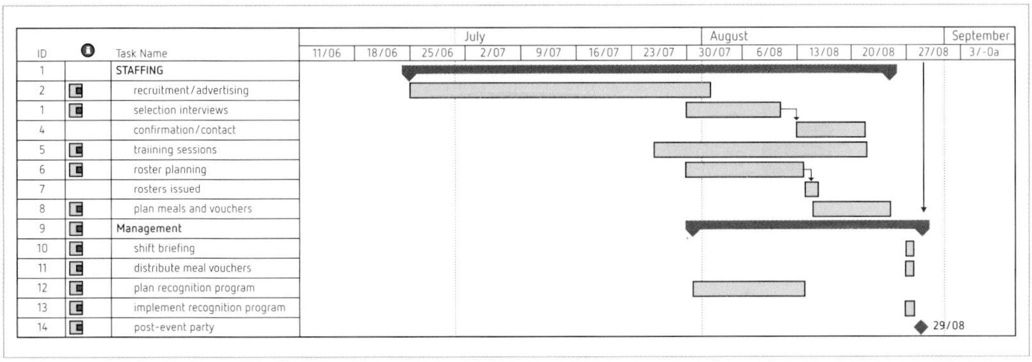

PERT charts

The program evaluation and review technique (PERT) chart depicts task, duration and dependency information and is very useful in defining the critical path. A PERT chart provides a graphical illustration of the project timeline with a particular focus on concurrent tasks. Simply put, a multitasker (or several members of a team) can achieve more in less time if some tasks are done concurrently. However, this is not always possible as there are often dependencies that lock in the critical path. Event managers need to multitask; if they can only follow through one process at a time, nothing will be ready on time.

The PERT chart in Figure 4.6 illustrates the development process for a festival website. The numbered nodes represent tasks completed, deliverables or milestones. Diverging arrows indicate that tasks can be completed concurrently. Thus, in this example, after the concept for the website has been developed (1), one person can source the text and graphics (2) while another works on the website structure/design and storyboards (3). Directional arrows represent dependent tasks that must be done sequentially. Thus, a direct arrow is drawn from uploading to website server (8) to the formal launch (9). Each of the arrows between the nodes shows how many days are needed for task completion. Since the critical path is the longest path, in this example the website cannot be launched in less than 45 days.

All graphical illustrations provide alternative ways in which to view processes. PERT charts, while not widely used, are particularly helpful in showing how a project's critical path can be shortened by developing as many parallel tasks as possible.

Run sheets

The run sheet (also called the production schedule) is an indispensable tool for most event managers. In the preliminary stages of planning, the run sheet is quite simple, with times allocated only to specific elements of the event (see the run sheet for a gala dinner in Figure 4.7). This overview of proceedings forms part of the event concept briefing.

FIGURE 4.6 PERT chart for development and launch of a festival website

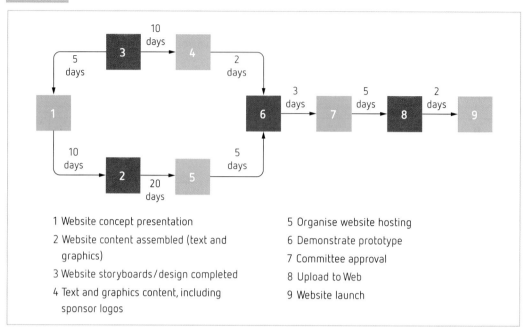

1 Website concept presentation
2 Website content assembled (text and graphics)
3 Website storyboards/design completed
4 Text and graphics content, including sponsor logos

5 Organise website hosting
6 Demonstrate prototype
7 Committee approval
8 Upload to Web
9 Website launch

FIGURE 4.7 Preliminary run sheet for a gala dinner — concept stage

1900	Guests arrive. Pre-dinner drinks in foyer.
1930	Doors to Royal open. Guests move to tables.
1935	MC welcome.
1940	Entrée served.
2000	First 'Championship' (demonstration dance routine).
2010	Main course served.
	Band starts playing.
2050	Band stops.
	Second 'Championship' (demo dance routine).
	Guests drawn onto dance floor at the end.
2115	Dessert served.
	Band plays.
2140	Band stops.
	ABTA Awards Presentation (1 award, with 2 finalists).
2225	Ms & Mr Sparkly awarded.
	Dancing for guests starts properly.
2355	MC announces final winners (all!) and last dance.
2400	Guests depart.

Source: Reproduced with permission of Events Unlimited

As planning progresses, however, the run sheet becomes even more detailed with, for example, timings for dancers, technicians and other staff. This is illustrated in Figure 4.8, in which bump-in and bump-out (set-up and breakdown, respectively) are also included. These processes will be discussed in greater detail in Chapter 12.

FIGURE 4.8 Complete run sheet for a gala dinner

0800	Lay dance floor and stage, and lower vertical drapes. Scissor lift ready. Audio subcontractor commences bump-in. Rear projection screen set.
0900	Dance floor and stage set. Stage designer bumps in for stage decoration.
1000	Production meeting.
1100	On-stage set-up commences (audio and video).
1230 (approx)	Band set-up.
1430	Technical set-up complete. Table set-up can commence.
1500	Technical run-through.
1730	All decorations complete.
1745	Rehearsal with MC and SM (probably walk through with music). Band sound check.
1830	All ready.
1845	External sign ON.
1900–1930	Guests arrive. Pre-dinner drinks in foyer.
1900	Dancers arrive. Walk-through and music check.
1915	Pre-set lighting ON.
1925	Walk-in music ON.
1930	Doors open. Guests move to tables. All dancers ready.
1935	MC welcome.
1940	Entrée served.
2000	First 'Championship' (Demonstration dance routine).
2010	Main course served. Band starts playing.
2050	Band stops. Second 'Championship' (Demo dance routine). Guests drawn onto dance floor at the end.
2115	Dessert enters and is served. Band plays.
2140	Band stops. Awards presentation (1 award, with 2 finalists).
2225	Ms & Mr Sparkly awarded. Dancing for guests starts properly.
2355	MC announces final winners (all!) and last dance.
2400	Guests depart. Bump-out commences.
Tue 0230	All clear.

Source: Reproduced with permission of Events Unlimited

From a project management point of view, correct sequencing, accurate timing and careful scheduling are the keys to good planning. Sequencing involves establishing the order of actions: what has to happen before another activity can start, and which activities can take place in parallel. For example, all mechanical handling equipment, particularly forklifts and scissor lifts, must be taken out of the site before seating can be laid out. Timing determines how long before the next action takes place. For example, how long is needed to clear the forklifts from the audience area to allow for seating layout to commence? Remember also that sometimes equipment such as chairs and tables will need to be delivered in several loads, and often the loading dock will be too busy for immediate offloading (in project management terms, this is a *limiting step*). Now, having planned the sequence and the timing, scheduling can take place. This involves listing the order and timings for bump-in on a run sheet or production schedule. In both cases, the responsibility for each action should be clearly indicated. Experienced contractors can often offer valuable assistance and advice on the sequence and timing of many tasks.

At this point, an even more detailed run sheet can be developed (at this stage called *the script*) to identify each person's role and cues. This is illustrated in Figure 4.9, where the timing of meal service and the cues for recommencement of the 'championships' after the main course are outlined in detail. Run sheets are an important tool for all stakeholders and participants, from the venue management team through to the subcontractors.

Suppliers waiting their turn to offload gear

FIGURE 4.9 Script for part of gala dinner

2010 As main nearly cleared	Main course served.	MC and dancers stand by. Dance 2 music ready.
When clear 2050	Band stops and exits.	MC mic ON. Band OFF. MC spot ON. House down.
	MC: Welcome to our next championship, The Self-Booking Samba. Amazingly the finalists are our previous winners. Please welcome them back. Dancers run on. (2nd dance routine 10 min).	Vision — Self-Booking Samba. Dance floor ON. MC spot OFF. Music 2 ON. MC mic OFF.
	Dancers pause at end. MC: And once again it's a tie, isn't that fantastic! Now I know that there are some aspiring champions out there who are probably thinking 'I could never do that!' Well our champions have graciously agreed to teach you some of their steps, so come on up and join in ... MC somehow coaxes people up. When enough on dance floor he cues music with: OK. Let's dance! (About 10 minutes dance coaching)	When music 2 finished cue music 3. MC spot ON. MC mic ON. House UP ½. Music 3 ON. MC mic OFF. Kitchen advised 10 min to dessert.
At end		Dance music 3 OFF. Cue march in — SB track 14. Kitchen 1 min to dessert.

Source: Reproduced with permission of Events Unlimited

ADMINISTER AND MONITOR PROJECT

Having initiated the project and completed the planning, it is time to move into execution. Naturally, this only occurs when all stakeholders have given their approval, particularly the major client and relevant government authorities. For example, when outdoor events utilise public spaces such as parks, very specific regulations apply. These can cover issues such as damage to grass and trees, dust control, access by vehicles and equipment, vibration and noise. The City of Port Phillip provides comprehensive guidelines that inform the development of detailed plans (the link is included at the end of the chapter). Of course, approvals for outdoor events involve numerous authorities above and beyond the local council. Traffic management, emergency services, and food authority bodies are examples. If any of these approvals are not forthcoming, then the project is delayed, which in turn will have serious ramifications. When moving into the execution phase, the structure of the project management team, including stakeholders, needs to be finalised for effective implementation and monitoring.

Committee or project management team

An event committee comprised of key stakeholders can be appointed to provide oversight for the whole project. Figure 4.10 shows a chart for an event committee. The committee has an important role to play in monitoring progress and approving any additional financial commitments. External stakeholders such as sponsors or local councils can be included on the committee or invited to meetings. In this way, the ongoing commitment of stakeholders is ensured during the evolutionary process of event project implementation. The committee plays an advisory function, making sure that the original scope and objectives are not lost along the way.

FIGURE 4.10 Event committee structure

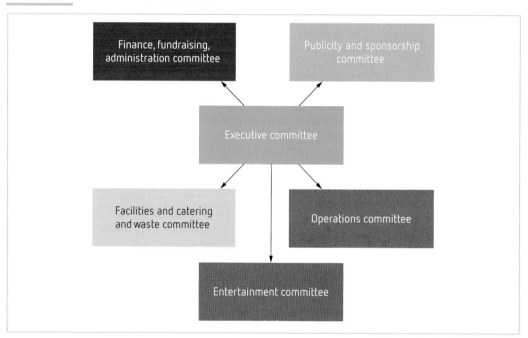

Regular meetings are necessary to ensure that objectives, deliverables, timelines, cost and quality control aspects of the project are managed effectively. At each of these meetings, planning documents such as revised Gantt charts and budgets will be reviewed. For these meetings to be successful, agendas need to be distributed beforehand listing the topics to be covered, and any associated reading material needs to be sent out with the agenda. The objective of the meeting should be clear, leading to actionable outcomes or decisions that are recorded in the minutes. Careful consideration of the people invited to meetings and sticking to the schedule are two elements of effective meetings.

The term 'organising committee' is generally associated with major events or those involving several external bodies, as you would find with a surfing competition. Here, governing bodies, administrators, venue managers and volunteers might all have a role to play.

For smaller and less formal events, the project management team would provide this level of oversight in the lead-up to the actual day of the event.

Organisation charts

An organisation chart is another important tool used in administering an event project. Once all tasks have been identified and grouped logically in the WBS during the planning phase, the staffing requirements for an event become much clearer and can be represented on an organisation chart. This chart may evolve as more project team members come on board closer to the implementation of the event, and this includes contractors as well as volunteers. There are thus several iterations of the organisation chart as the workforce grows; Chapters 10 and 11 will discuss and illustrate this in more detail. It is important that event organisation charts show the full workforce, including contractors (such as security) and services (first aid), with clear reporting relationships. It is also helpful to use colour coding to indicate paid staff versus contractors versus volunteers.

Financial and quality control systems

As previous chapters have illustrated, the event environment is a dynamic one involving many months and weeks of planning and administering a project, which is then executed in a very small timeframe. As the original plan evolves, any deviations from the plan need to be evaluated with care so that things don't spin out of control. The client is often the instigator of such changes, wanting more flowers, live music, a different menu, free parking, special lighting and so on. As these demands grow (outside the original scope), they need to be costed and approved by the client. A project variation document is one way to track these changes. Every event manager should keep a contract variation form on their clipboard at all times, so that every time there is an additional request it can be agreed to in writing. The alternative is that the additional requirements will eat into the small profit margin. In addition, very tight contract specifications make the issue of variation much less problematic.

A council recognises that circumstances may change after approval of a festival, and that this may result in, for example, changes in artistic personnel. Variations to the agreed project require prior approval by the festival committee.

List three other potential variations that have budget implications for a music festival.

EXTENSION ACTIVITY

Event planning software

Various different types of planning software for preparing plans, charts, run sheets and checklists are widely available. Microsoft Excel is the easiest and most commonly used software for small events. However, specialised software such as Microsoft Project is more sophisticated, assigning work and resources and creating a critical path. Gantt charts are the

Testing of wi-fi at the Singapore Convention and Exhibition Centre

foundation for project planning, whereby links between tasks can be created and modified easily. Many other event-specific software programs have been developed, with different levels of functionality and ease of use.

Most events also have their own website, which plays a vitally important role in marketing and ticketing. Specialist support is required for designing and hosting a website, particularly if tickets are sold online.

For many sporting events, technological solutions are needed for registration, timing, scoring and results processing. The media place heavy demands on information technology systems, including access to broadband Internet for transmitting video and image files. Higher-than-usual demands are placed on outdoor events, particularly if the site does not provide intranet and Internet connections such as those provided at every stand at an exhibition centre as part of the venue hire agreement. A conference or exhibition needs tailor-made software for registration and dealing with the specific requirements of speakers, exhibitors and visitors. Easily accessible wi-fi is a standard expectation.

In addition to these special requirements, standard office technology is required for administration. This includes software for word processing, spreadsheets and databases. Clearly, ongoing support and maintenance is essential, as is the routine backing up of data.

Communication

A communication plan ensures that everyone involved in an event project, from sponsors to volunteers, is informed of progress. Communications in various formats, such as meetings, focus groups, emails and broadcasts, all contribute to the motivation of the workforce and this in turn means that the event is likely to meet expectations. Poor communication leaves everyone scrambling, and this has a flow-on effect on the event audience.

Communication is conducted internally as well as externally, and can cover some of the following key messages for the workforce:
* key milestones
* fundraising
* safety initiatives
* risk management and contingency plans
* sustainability
* spectator services
* reporting requirements
* regulatory requirements and authorities (e.g. food safety, alcohol).

Overall, the fundamental thrust of the communication is achievement of the event's objectives. Communication should therefore include positive progress reports and messages of support from sponsors, athletes, host organisations and the like.

Effective communication is an essential feature of project management. Everyone involved needs to be aware of the goals and milestones and these have to be carefully monitored. In the stressful environment of event planning, trust and respect within the project team are essential. Ongoing consultation, in the form of meetings, telephone calls and emails, is one way to assess progress against project goals. Occasionally, additional resources will be required or the project timeline will need to be reviewed, but not the ultimate deadline – the event date – as that never changes! Actions must be agreed, with timelines and responsibility allocated. Everyone needs to be involved in ongoing communication – team members, colleagues and clients.

Checklists

At the most detailed level of planning, a checklist is indispensable. It is a control tool that ensures that the individual performing the tasks has not forgotten a single detail. For example, when checking fire-fighting equipment and emergency exits, it is imperative that a specific checklist be followed, and that it be signed and dated on completion. This is part of the record-keeping process, aimed not only at preventing potential problems, but also at reducing the risk of litigation if anything should go wrong. Detailed and correctly implemented plans reassure the client, allow the event team to work effectively, and build confidence in achieving the objectives of the event. A safety checklist is illustrated in Figure 4.11.

FIGURE 4.11 Daily safety checklist

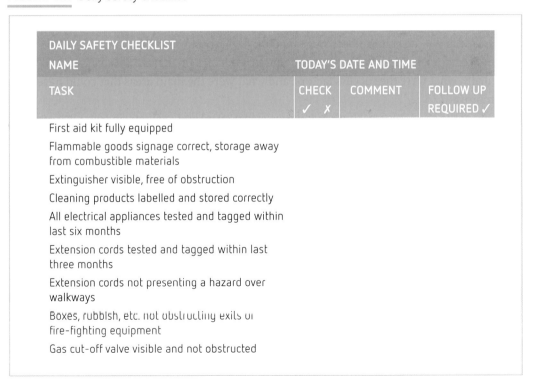

EVALUATE PROJECT

There are several ways to evaluate the success of an event, the most common approach being to survey the audience. But there are many other ways to review the project process, from planning through to implementation and closure. Focus groups are particularly useful, each having a specific group of attendees with key issues to discuss, such as traffic management, volunteer satisfaction or community responses. Focus groups provide qualitative feedback, and the resulting quotes and testimonials are very useful for inclusion in a final report.

EXTENSION ACTIVITY

If you were evaluating the success of a fashion show, which aspects would you analyse? How would you get this information?

Document analysis is also helpful. All the incident reports should be reviewed to identify common trends, and daily managers' logs should also be consulted. Key questions can include the following:

* Were there sufficient boundaries around the scope of the project or did the scope blow out along with the budget?
* How well did the timeline and task completion process work? Were there unexpected delays or limiting steps?
* Did the risk management plan anticipate the key risks or was something overlooked?
* Did any legal issues arise, or insurance claims, or applications for medical expenses due to accidents and injuries to the staff or audience?
* How well did the stakeholders work together? Did the communication plan (or lack of it) lead to complete chaos? (This is often due to a reliance on mobile phones; see p. 235.)
* Finally, what were the success factors, and what were the main areas that could have been improved?

One of the most informal but effective ways to control and evaluate an event is to observe it: to identify bottlenecks and queues or to investigate the reasons for delays or complaints. This can be done on the ground. Decisions that are taken, such as developing a multiskilled group of volunteers for deployment to different posts, should be noted. A final evaluation report is important for approving bodies and sponsors. It also allows for continuous improvement, documenting the lessons learned, and provides evidence of the success of the event. This is exceptionally valuable when tendering for the next project.

Budget
A financial plan or forecast; an estimate of income and expenditure

Financial report
Shows an organisation's financial status; may be done at the end of an accounting period

Budgets used for evaluation

Event budgets will be covered in detail in Chapter 8. For the time being, it is important to note that event **budgets** forecast income and expenditure. On completion of an event or at the end of the financial year, **financial reports** will show whether a specific event or the event business was profitable. Careful preparation and monitoring of budgets is fundamental to effective project management. Financial resources are always limited, and by adding tasks (such as labour), goods (decorative items) or services (security), the budget forecast may be compromised. From this, it is clear that project management is an iterative process involving ongoing monitoring. All the planning processes mentioned in this chapter need to be fully integrated. The work shown in the WBS should line up with the tasks in the Gantt chart, as well as the line items for expenses in the budget.

EXTENSION ACTIVITY

On the commencement of your event project, you understand the requirement to:
- keep records of project activities
- monitor project results
- keep proper accounting records for all project costs, including cash and in-kind contributions
- account in full for all expenditure on the activity.

Explain how you would go about ensuring that you can report on expenditure (both cash and in-kind).

Return on investment (ROI) is one way to measure the financial success of an event, or of multiple events. For a promoter, this is linked to investment and profit. Sometimes ROI is evaluated more widely by looking at economic flow-on effects. This is a key consideration for government agencies that support events, as was mentioned in the first chapter.

Evaluating other impacts

Events also have social and environmental impacts. These might be measured qualitatively as opposed to quantitatively, as above. Return on objectives (ROO) evaluates the achievement of objectives such as sponsorship recognition, brand image, social media engagement, publicity, and waste management education.

Event evaluation using the Encore event evaluation kit from CRC Tourism has been conducted for a diverse range of events. The website listed at the end of the chapter also includes an excellent example of a planning timeline.

Event evaluation using the Encore event evaluation kit from the Sustainable Tourism Cooperative Research Centre (STCRC) has been conducted for a diverse range of events such as the Elvis Festival in Parkes (Schlenker, Foley & Carroll-Dwyer, 2016) and the Formula 1 Australian Grand Prix (Fairley et al., 2011). The report on the review and redevelopment of the kit includes samples of questionnaires (Schlenker, 2010, p. 10). There has been a shift towards sustainability in more recent studies.

So with evaluation we return to where we started: having a clear purpose and objectives, and targeted plans to achieve them. The nature of the event business is that most of the allocated time is spent in planning, and very little is spent in the execution phase. In fact, it often comes as a shock when the event is over so quickly. Things can go bad in an instant in the event environment but good planning can prevent this happening. In the best cases, the plans have been so thoughtfully developed that the event manager's role is simply to ensure that procedures are correctly implemented, resulting in minimal incidents and satisfied clients. However, effective project management goes further than a celebration following a successful event. It includes evaluation reports to demonstrate why the event was successful and how it can be improved. Unless the event organisation sets out to measure the outcomes against the objectives, there will be no legacy from all those many months of planning and no criteria to prove a successful outcome.

Summary

In this chapter we have covered the important topic of project management and looked at various tools, such as maps, Gantt charts, checklists and run sheets, which are used to administer and monitor the progress of activities and timelines for events. Unlike most other projects, deadlines in event management cannot be postponed, since the date of the event and the place where it will be held must be advertised. The planning tools described and illustrated in this chapter will help you meet those deadlines, particularly as each aspect of an event is generally contingent on another. Effective planning ensures the provision of all necessary services and amenities at an event. Nevertheless, planning needs to remain flexible since this is a very dynamic industry in which change is inevitable.

Key terms

Budget	A financial plan or forecast; an estimate of income and expenditure
Critical path	Determines the minimum time needed to complete a project
Deliverables	Project deliverables can be tangible, such as an operations manual, or intangible, such as completion of security briefings
Financial report	Shows an organisation's financial status; may be done at the end of an accounting period
Initiation	Project initiation is the first stage in the project management life cycle and involves defining objectives, scope, purpose and deliverables
Stakeholders	May include internal and external customers, organising committees, funding bodies, regulatory authorities and other government authorities
Work breakdown structure (WBS)	Involves organising key tasks into logical sections or clusters

REVIEW YOUR KNOWLEDGE

1   What are the characteristics of an event that make it a project?
2   Explain the meaning of the following project management terms using event examples:
    – feasibility
    – stakeholder analysis
    – scope
    – deliverables
    – milestones.
3   Describe four tools that can be used for event project planning and control (for example, Gantt charts) and find an event-related example online that illustrates the use of each tool.
4   Discuss the pros and cons of establishing a unique project management model such as PMBOK for the events industry, as opposed to working with the standard principles outlined in the generic project management systems used by other industries.
5   The administrative structure for an event can vary enormously from project to project. Assume that a festival has the following structure: event chairperson, marketing committee, ticket sales

committee, finance committee, sponsorship committee, production committee, human resources committee and event operations committee. List the key responsibilities of each committee (no more than five each).

APPLY YOUR KNOWLEDGE

1   The concept 'chain of events' is very relevant to event planning. Review three different types of event (such as a product launch, fete and sporting competition) and identify potential weak links in the planning process that could jeopardise each event if they were not thoroughly considered. For example, the lack of a back-up system for electrical supplies at an outdoor venue could jeopardise an event.

2   Visit www.travelsmart.gov.au/events/eight.html and compare two case studies of transport planning in terms of their travel solutions.

3   Using the checklist at the above website, visit a public event and analyse its transport arrangements, making observations and recommendations for future project planning.

CASE STUDY

The last time One World College had a jobs expo, the number of exhibitors at the fair outnumbered the students who came along looking for jobs. Employers wasted a Saturday standing around and were unimpressed. This event was not a success for job providers or students.

A better result is expected this time. The student association of One World has been given permission to run a weekend event to help other students on campus to get motivated, plan careers and find jobs.

The college offers courses in event management, hospitality, child care, aged care, nursing and retail. Your brief is to plan an event with potential components such as a jobs expo, industry talks, entertainment and job-seeking skills workshops. The key idea is to provide something experiential that totally engages participants, leaving them with clear steps for achieving job outcomes. The college prides itself on innovation so your brief is to be creative.

TASKS

1   Your first step is to create an organising structure.

2   Next, develop an overview of the event (scope and objectives) to present to One World's director. This overview needs to include a Gantt chart illustrating the event planning timeline. The format of the event (talks, expo, entertainment and so on) also needs to be prepared.

3   You will need to raise funds to pay for catering, entertainment, speaker expenses and the like, so the budget needs to be prepared.

4   The event has to be 'sold' as appealing and interesting. Your promotional effort also requires planning.

5   The micro-planning phase needs to cover the event's production components with detailed run sheets and checklists. This should show your team's ability to keep an eye on the important details, such as food, fees, signage, identification and safety.

6   Finally, present your pitch to the college director, complete with a project plan, and showing how you will monitor success and evaluate outcomes.

Online resources

Visit **http://login.cengagebrain.com** and search for this book to access the study tools that come with your textbook.

References

Fairley, S., Tyler, B. D., Kellett, P., & D'Elia, K. (2011). Formula 1 Australian Grand Prix: Exploring the triple bottom line. *Sport Management Review*, 14(2), 141–52.

Reusch, P. J., & Reusch, P. (2013). Event management: A special kind of project management. *Intelligent Data Acquisition and Advanced Computing Systems (IDAACS), 2013 IEEE 7th International Conference* (vol. 2), 555–9.

Schlenker, K. (2010). *Encore Festival and Event Evaluation Kit: Review and Redevelopment*. Gold Coast: Sustainable Tourism Cooperative Research Centre.

Schlenker, K., Foley, C. T., & Carroll-Dwyer, E. (2016). The Parkes Elvis Festival: Attendee and host community perspectives. In *Focus on World Festivals: Contemporary Case Studies and Perspectives* (299–308). Oxford: Goodfellow.

Serrador, P., & Turner, R. (2015). The relationship between project success and project efficiency. *Project Management Journal*, 46(1), 30–9.

Websites

Business value of Meetings, Meeting Professionals International, **www.mpiweb.org/Portal/Business/BusinessValueofMeetings**

City of Port Phillip event guidelines, **www.portphillip.vic.gov.au/events-promotions.htm**

EMBOK (Event Management Body of Knowledge), **www.embok.org**

EPMS (Event Project Management Software), **http://epms.net**

Meander Valley Council event management planning guide, **www.meander.tas.gov.au/page.aspx?u=520**

PMBOK (Project Management Body of Knowledge), **www.pmi.org/PMBOK-Guide-and-Standards.aspx**

smart events evaluation service, **www.smartevents.com.au/public/evaluation.asp**

DEVELOP CONFERENCE PROGRAMS

5

OVERVIEW

Business events are a valuable component of the event industry, as delegates from around the world generally spend more than most other tourists. There are also intangible benefits associated with conference programs. They raise the profile of the city and country as well as contributing to knowledge capital. Conferences can be large or small, the larger ones attracting thousands of delegates who fill the hotels in the city. This is a highly competitive industry, with cities such as Hong Kong and Singapore bidding for the same conferences, often years before they are held. On the local scene, many industry associations move their conferences around the country, holding the annual event in a different city each time.

LEARNING OBJECTIVES

On completion of this chapter, you will be able to:

1. establish program requirements by analysing context, scope and objectives in consultation with stakeholders

2. design a conference program with objectives in mind, with attention to budget, venue and staging constraints

3. finalise program details, gain approvals and prepare final plans for implementation.

INDUSTRY VIEWPOINT

Matthew Hingerty, chairman of the Business Events Council of Australia (BECA), has been quoted as saying: 'Business events are an economic powerhouse of the Australian economy – they foster trade, export, investment, diplomacy, education and knowledge transfer. They also generate employment, tax revenue and stimulate the visitor economy, with their benefits spreading across both city and regional economies'.

The results of a 2015 BECA study indicate the following:

- 391 000 events attracted 26.5 million delegates
- majority were single or part-day events
- corporate events were the most common event type, followed by government and then association
- total direct expenditure was $23.2 billion in 2013–14
- contributed direct value-add of $11.3 billion
- generated over 147 000 jobs
- 3 per cent of meeting and convention delegates were from overseas, 20 per cent were from interstate and 77 per cent were from within the host State
- international delegates spent on average $440 per day (excluding flights); interstate delegates had a higher expenditure level per day at $586 (including flights).

Source: Adapted from *micenet* (2017). Business events a major economic driver. www.mice.net.au/article/business-events-a-major-economic-driver; Business Events Council of Australia (2015). *The Value of Business Events to Australia*, p. 2. www.businesseventscouncil.org.au/files/View_Report.pdf

The conference audience needs to be engaged

PCO
Professional
conference organiser

INTRODUCTION

As this extract regarding the Business Events Council of Australia (BECA) shows, the business events sector makes an important economic contribution. Visitors to conferences spend more than other tourism visitors.

This chapter will look at a number of different types of organisations that host conferences, the **PCOs** (professional conference organisers) who provide professional conference planning and advice, and suppliers such as hotels, conference centres and other exotic venues that provide the infrastructure, catering, audiovisual services and so on. This is illustrated in Figure 5.1.

FIGURE 5.1 Role of the PCO as intermediary

A PCO can act as an intermediary between the client and the **suppliers** in the same way as a wedding planner. The advantages of employing a professional in this role can include:

- keeping the event focused on the key strategy, goals and objectives
- advising on the best venues and suppliers
- keeping costs down by knowing where to look for discounts or concessions
- managing logistics of travel and accommodation
- assisting with the speaker program and selection of the appropriate **MC**
- providing creative ideas for social activities before and after the conference
- assisting with the huge administrative workload
- ensuring that all budget items are listed and there are minimal unforeseen costs
- advising on marketing and technology support for the event.

BECA is a peak body providing an umbrella structure for the business events associations operating in the business events sector. This provides an opportunity to liaise with the federal government and other agencies and to work together to support the sector as a whole. BECA members include the Association of Australian Convention Bureaux (AACB) and Meetings & Events Australia (MEA), among others. Collaboration at a high level ensures that Australia can compete when bidding for major events on the world stage. Similar bodies exist in other countries and key conference cities.

In Singapore, there are many government initiatives that support the business events sector, including qualification for the accreditation schemes ATF and AIF, the criteria for which include professional organisation of an international standard, being at the forefront of innovation, high-quality overseas visitors and buyers, the generation of substantial trade, and a proven track record.

Internationally, similar meanings are associated with the industry terminology for meetings of different sizes.

A **conference** involves information sharing between speakers and the audience, with limited participation in the form of audience questions and smaller workshops. Networking among delegates with common interests is a key component of conferences. Smaller meetings are often known as seminars. These are most commonly of a business or academic nature.

A **convention** is a larger-scale event, generally of a political nature, where people convene to share opinions, and sometimes to reach agreement on an issue; for example, the United Nations Convention on Climate Change.

A **congress** invites specific representatives, from different nations for example, with specific cultural, religious or political interests. These are formal meetings.

Supplier
Provides event goods (e.g. floral arrangements) and services (e.g. audiovisual set-up)

MC
Master of ceremonies

Conference
Gatherings focused on information-sharing and education, most commonly of a business or academic nature

Convention
Large-scale gathering with the intention of reaching agreement on an issue, generally of a political nature

Congress
Gathering that includes representatives from different groups; for example, the National Congress of Australia's First People

EXTENSION ACTIVITY

Visit the website for the World Congress on Family Law and Children Rights (http://wcflcr2017.com) and then answer the following questions:

* What are the aims of the congress?
* Why is this titled a congress rather than a conference?
* Is this a business or an academic congress?
* What are the key components of the conference program?
* How does the program (the line-up of speakers and other activities) link to the aims of the conference?

ESTABLISH PROGRAM REQUIREMENTS

As with most events, there is the buy side and the supply side. The buyer is the client paying for the event, and the supplier (in simple situations) is the hotel with meeting rooms. This is an oversimplification but it does help to clarify the roles.

Types of conference

Large conferences and events are organised (bought) with the following types of organisation in mind.

Association conference

An association is generally a formal body such as the Dietitians Association of Australia, the Organic Agriculture Association or the Institute of Public Accountants. These associations have members who share information and provide networks and educational activities.

LNG18 conference

Image courtesy of Staging Connections, an Encore Event Technologies Company

Corporate conference

Corporate events (business/conference-related) cover any number of areas, such as the LNG18 conference illustrated here. In relation to this gathering, Staging Connections was engaged by Arinex to propose an event solution for the world's largest global liquefied natural gas conference, attended by over 6000 industry personnel over the course of four days.

Government conference

Government organisations also host conferences, such as the Tasmanian Tourism Conference, the annual conference of the Local Government Association of Queensland, and the Australian and New Zealand Search and Rescue Conference. An international example is the United Nations Climate Change Conference.

Academic conference

Academic conferences cover all sorts of knowledge areas, highlighting current research in fields such as engineering, chemistry, medicine, physics and psychology. Academic papers are presented at the conference and are published afterwards. These papers are peer reviewed and are highly regarded academic research papers. The process involves a call for papers and a lengthy selection process, thus adding to the timeline for planning.

Other conferences

Of course, there are any number of smaller meetings and conferences held by sporting and community bodies on topics such as water safety, women in finance, health care and so on. As the next section shows, for a conference to be successful there are specific outcomes to be achieved, otherwise delegates might feel that the cost and time involved in attending has not been worth it. This may be because the client did not provide clarity from the start, perhaps running a conference without clear parameters. It is the conference organiser's skill that brings it all together successfully.

Conference scope and objectives

Every conference has objectives that need to be achieved, such as networking, education, knowledge creation, and dissemination of information. As with all events, the conference scope and objectives need to be agreed by key stakeholders at the start.

A Malaysian study has identified six critical success factors for successful MICE (meetings, incentives, conventions and exhibitions) event management. These factors are: clear objectives, location of venue, financial resources, code of conduct, marketing and promotion, and event sponsorship (Ismail, 2014). The project management principles discussed in the previous chapter are relevant here.

Design

Event design is the creative process that ensures that the objectives are achieved in ways that engage and stimulate the audience. Chapter 14 will elaborate on design elements, but suffice it say that a conference can be exceptionally dull if considerable thought is not given to the design elements. The name or title of the conference, venue, lighting, sound, props, seating and entertainment all contribute to the design. The most important aspect of a conference is the quality of the presentations. Everything should be done to select speakers who are credible, effective communicators with important and clear messages for the audience.

Date and duration

The date and duration of a conference need to be agreed upon. To do so, one has to look at the calendars of participants as well as the external activities occurring in the city of choice. These activities might be complementary to the conference or they might not be complementary, simply leading to premium prices for travel and accommodation.

Most conferences include a social event such as a cocktail party the evening before the conference for those people who have flown in during the afternoon. Many conferences also include a formal dinner. If this occurs in the middle of the event, then few people will be feeling energetic the morning after – pity the first speaker! Another period that is problematic is the final afternoon of the conference, when many of the audience leave early to catch flights. Speakers who are given these tricky times find it very hard to hold an audience. Finally, many events include a day or half-day of touring or sightseeing. If this is relevant to the achievement of event objectives, then this is valuable.

EXTENSION ACTIVITY

Welcome to the ABBA Conference: the premier annual event that brings ideas together in an entertaining way. Mix the highest-calibre speakers from around the globe together with the best local and international thought leaders and performers, and you have the perfect recipe for life-changing conversations, limitless innovation and energising personal motivation. Offering a mix of different formats including celebrity keynote speakers and specific, small breakout sessions, you too can join the conversation on emerging trends, leaving energised, informed and ready to improve the bottom line.

Imagine that this promotional paragraph is on a conference website. What do you think of it? Write a critique outlining your thoughts and what improvements, if any, you would make.

Innovation and point of difference

Innovation is another element that, added to the design aspects of the event, gives them a point of difference. A gaming app linked to key concepts in the presentations would be one such innovation. If networking is an objective of the event, then there are many software packages that make it possible for event attendees to interact with each other and provide real-time feedback to the speakers.

Rogers (2013), in his book *Conference and Conventions*, provides guidelines for winning conference business. For many countries, conference bidding is supported by agencies such as Tourism New Zealand. Tourism New Zealand works collaboratively with the business events sector, and undertakes business development and marketing activity to attract new conferences and incentives to New Zealand, as well as to grow delegate numbers and value. A key tool to achieve this is the Conference Assistance Programme that supports international conference bids. Rogers provides guidelines for conference organisers in far more detail than this chapter can do justice, particularly for the major conferences that attract international bids.

Stakeholders

This chapter has briefly mentioned the roles of the client or buyer, and suppliers such as hotels, travel agencies and conference centres. We have also referred to the role of the PCO. When a conference impacts on a whole city, then many different stakeholders are involved, ranging from hotels to fitness centres, restaurants, tourist attractions and the like.

Amway China sends 10 000 delegates at a time to leadership seminars around the world. Lasting for five days and four nights, these seminars support thousands of jobs in hotels, restaurants and shops, which contribute to the local economy both directly and indirectly.

Think about the logistics of managing such an event by estimating the number of hotels, hotel rooms and seminar sessions needed to cater for this group based on the maximum/size or capacity of your city for providing accommodation and event venues of this scale.

A large sales conference dinner

Delegate profiles

The profiles of delegates need to be considered in the planning process. Country and city of origin, languages spoken, demographics, languages, cultural etiquette, special needs and expectations all need to be taken into account. Here's a list to be considered for every conference:

- accessibility
- special dietary requirements
- religious observations
- rooming preferences (twin-share rooms or single occupancy)
- transportation
- language and translation
- interests (see iconic tourist attractions, or avoid clichés and do something active and exotic).

Budget

The conference budget forecasts the income expected from delegate registrations and sponsorship. The main expenses are for venue hire, catering, speakers, entertainment, staging, lighting and audiovisual support. Administrative costs should not be ignored either!

Generally, the accommodation rates in preferred hotels are advertised on the conference website but bookings are done independently, linking to the hotel site for payment and confirmation.

As later chapters on financial matters will illustrate, the deadline for registrations means that venue and catering costs can be predicted quite accurately, much more so than other types of events.

When negotiating with hotels, there are a number of areas in which concessions could be discussed:

- free wi-fi in rooms and meeting rooms
- access to a business centre for delegates not staying in the hotel
- complimentary or discounted rooms for organising staff
- complimentary or discounted hospitality suites
- late checkout
- discounted parking
- discount on published menus
- complimentary entry to health clubs
- computer workstations in the foyer
- reduced rates on audiovisual services.

Venue and staging requirements

Conference and exhibition centres are fully equipped to offer events of all sizes, and many set-ups can be changed very quickly as the conference moves from one model to another, say from theatre style to banquet. Figure 5.2 illustrates the capacity of different room configurations for different types of events. This information is generally provided on venue websites.

So dedicated venues seem the easiest option for the event buyer. On the other hand, a unique venue might be attractive as it is something different. A decision in favour of the latter should not be taken lightly, however, as there could be a multitude of problems, one of the most significant being power supply. The level of planning required for a unique venue is discussed in Chapter 15.

Another consideration is the location of the venue. Holding a conference on an island might be the most effective way to ensure that everyone is engaged with the content and can't escape! In a major city, boring presentations or dull topics can lead to delegates wandering off to the bar or the shopping mall.

External impacts

Political issues, weather, and competing or complementary events all need to be considered when finalising dates for a conference. The business calendar is also important, including the end of the tax year and summer holidays (northern and southern hemispheres), as well as semester breaks for academic conferences.

Risk assessment

Risk assessment will be covered in more detail in Chapter 18. At this stage, it's enough to say that an analysis of risk shows which things might go wrong and the consequences of

FIGURE 5.2 Perth Convention and Exhibition Centre, level 3, floor plan and capacities

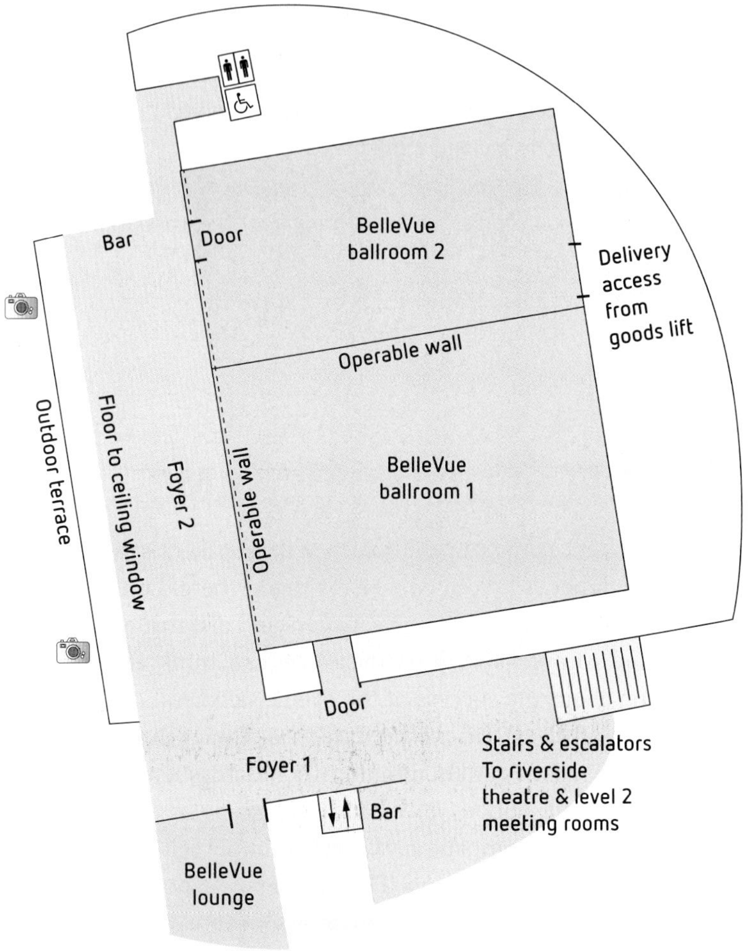

	BANQUET	COCKTAIL	THEATRE	CLASSROOM
BelleVue Ballroom 1	750	690	1000	680
BelleVue Ballroom 2	500	500	700	480
Ballrooms 1 & 2	1390	1195	1700	1150

Source: Perth Convention and Exhibition Centre (2017). Floor plans & capacities.
www.pcec.com.au/plan-an-event/floor-plans-capacities

this occurring. Technology failure is a common risk, and so too are delays in the arrival of key speakers on the program. Severe weather can delay the fights of arriving delegates, including cyclones and other disruptive events. Contingency plans help to prepare for potential risks.

The example that follows illustrates one of the most unexpected, heart-wrenching impacts on a conference. At least six delegates were killed on board flight MH17 on their way to a conference; however, organisers decided with a heavy heart to continue rather than cancel.

EXAMPLE

THE INTERNATIONAL AIDS SOCIETY (IAS) MOURNS THE LOSS OF FRIENDS AND COLLEAGUES ABOARD FLIGHT MH 17

The International AIDS Society (IAS) has today confirmed the devastating news that at least six delegates travelling to the 20th International AIDS Conference (AIDS 2014) in Melbourne, Australia, including former IAS President Joep Lange, were on board the Malaysian Airlines flight MH 17 that crashed over Ukraine, killing all 298 people on board.

'The extent of our loss is hard to comprehend or express', said President of the IAS, Françoise Barré-Sinoussi. 'We grieve alongside all of those throughout the world who have lost friends and family in this senseless tragedy.'

Source: International AIDS Society (2014). The International Aids Society (IAS) mourns the loss of friends and colleagues aboard flight MH 17. Press release, 19 July. http://www.iasociety.org/Web/WebContent/File/IAS_press-statement_190714_2.pdf

DESIGN CONFERENCE PROGRAMS

When designing a conference program, the quality of the speakers is the foremost consideration. One can talk about Herzberg's (1966) two-factor theory here. Lundberg, Gudmundson and Andersson (2009) applied the two factors – satisfiers and dissatisfiers – to the job satisfaction of employees. Applied to events such as these, we can think about the things that send delegates away talking about the success of the event (satisfiers) or talking about things that were disappointing (dissatisfiers). Dissatisfiers are those things that are largely tangible, things that one would expect to meet a certain minimum standard, such as air conditioning, lighting and wi-fi. If these are present, nobody goes back to work raving about them, but if they aren't up to standard there are many complaints. We could simply call these the basics: they have to be right; they are a minimum expectation. The satisfiers are intangible and motivational, and in this context an example is a speaker who inspires or motivates. Satisfiers can also include unique opportunities for increased knowledge or a wider business or academic network.

Other identifiable components of the program include:

* the welcome or opening, and the keynote speaker (discussed below)
* breakout sessions (small-group discussions or talks)
* plenary session (usually at the end of the conference and attended by all members; where key speakers wrap up the program in a semi-formal way, often answering questions from the audience).

Speakers, facilitators and talent

A number of people are involved in presenting a conference. The speaker line-up has to follow a certain order, with formal opening and closing speeches, often by VIPs or government authorities. The keynote speaker usually delivers the most high-profile presentation quite early in the program. Speakers can be quite choosy about when they speak as there are some times that are more challenging than others, say after lunch. The MC or facilitator manages the speakers, introducing them and making interesting and often lighthearted remarks the whole way through. There are agencies that offer people who are suitable for MC roles, as well as well-known motivational speakers who can add immeasurably to the program, athletes being a good example.

Talent is the collective term for anyone who performs, encompassing general entertainment, dancing and singing. A **stage manager** is someone appointed to oversee the production during the actual performance, ensuring that the right people come on and off stage at the right time; the stage manager 'calls the show'.

> **Talent**
> Speakers, actors, entertainers – anyone who is part of delivering the production
>
> **Stage manager**
> Organises the production

Technology requirements

Technology requirements can be very demanding, particularly when there is a live streamed talk from a senior executive based overseas. Specialist assistance can be required for most aspects of a conference. A TEDx event (a community-based version of the TED talks, discussed later in the chapter), for example, requires that a great deal of attention is paid to video production. Suggestions relating to webcasting and other aspects of these events are provided on the TEDx website in the *Organiser Guide*, which you can download (**www.ted.com/participate/organize-a-local-tedx-event/tedx-organizer-guide**).

The Perth Conference and Exhibition Centre app from AVPartners integrates social media tools, gamification, surveys and live polls with up-to-date event information to ensure PCEC events are accessible and relevant for attendees online, as well as offline.

Delegates can post updates, tag their location, like and comment on posts and send private messages, all from within the app. They can also access up-to-date event documentation, such as programs and flyers, speaker, attendee and exhibitor information. Using the PCEC app, event organisers can update event information and send targeted push notifications to attendees in real time. Designed for all smartphones, the app also facilitates reporting on active users and interactions within the app, thanks to a built-in analytics function.

Source: Perth Convention and Exhibition Centre (2017). Event services – events app from AVPartners. www.pcec.com.au / plan-an-event / event-services

EXTENSION ACTIVITY

What are the benefits of using this app versus commissioning an app specifically for your conference or exhibition?

Social activities

When a conference runs for more than a single day, and when delegates fly in from around the country (or from around the world), there is generally a social program that includes several options. The following components may be considered:

- a welcome reception the evening before the event so that people can meet and mingle
- a dinner which is often an awards night as well, combining speeches, awards, entertainment and dancing
- leadership breakfasts
- focus group meetings
- masterclasses
- other networking sessions.

Some conferences have quite formal opening and closing ceremonies. Partners are invited to all aspects of the social program and some conferences also include a kids' club.

More unusual offerings might include a cabaret street party, river cruise, BBQ in the park, visits by native animals, shopping tours, city walks, food tours or industry visits.

SOCIAL PROGRAM, INTERNATIONAL CONFERENCE OF IMMUNOLOGY

Opening ceremony and welcome reception

The official opening of ICI will include a special Australiana experience followed by an exciting Melbourne showcase. An invitation is extended to all delegates to attend the Opening Ceremony and Welcome Reception to be held at the Melbourne Convention and Exhibition Centre.

Come along to see and hear a sample of unique Australian culture with a traditional Welcome to Country, meet some of our native Australian animals, experience our local delicious foods and learn some of Melbourne and Australia's fun and quirky traditions. This function will be a great way to kick off your week in Melbourne at ICI 2016!

This is an 18 plus event.

www.arinex.com.au (all 6 images)

Congress dinner

The Congress Dinner will be a fun filled Australiana Outback experience at a waterfront venue on Melbourne's South Wharf. Enjoy a fun filled evening with a traditional bush band and then DJ whilst you mingle and enjoy delicious food stations, an array of canapés and admire stunning views of the Yarra River and Melbourne City Skyline at night. Places are limited so make sure you book early.

*The Congress Dinner is not included in any registration categories. Delegates may purchase tickets via the registration form as well as additional tickets for partners and guests. Places for the Congress Dinner are limited. This is an 18 plus event.

Source: International Congress of Immunology (2016). Social program. www.arinex.com.au

There may be parts of the conference that the delegate can claim as a business expense but other parts they cannot. This is why delegates often pay for these components separately. Many organisations and associations have a code of ethics on attendance at events, with careful separation of personal expenses. Many professional associations have guidelines prohibiting conferences that are thinly disguised free holidays. From a taxation viewpoint, delegates can claim the cost of attending seminars, conferences and education workshops that are connected to work activities. However, as stated, delegates need to separate personal expenses or costs associated with their partners attending social events, and may request separate invoices and payments for these.

Travel and accommodation

Many conferences involve travel, including flights and accommodation. In times past, before the Internet made competitive pricing and booking so simple for individuals, these tasks were undertaken by conference organisers, leading to useful commissions supporting the budget bottom line. However, the area is now so competitive that individuals (or their employers) generally make their own bookings for flights and accommodation. This avoids last-minute room cancellations when more competitive rates are available online.

In the design phase of conference planning, negotiations with hotels will result in a discounted 'conference rate', and a link on the conference website to the hotels in question will enable delegates to take advantage of these prices.

Hybrid events

TED talks are conferences with a difference. They are hybrid events with real audiences as well as virtual audiences: the talks are distributed free internationally, many of them attracting millions of viewers online and on YouTube. There are hundreds of videos, and these provide ideas for conferences that are creative, stimulating and interesting.

Watch the following example of a TED talk: www.ted.com/talks/ken_robinson_says_schools_kill_creativity

This is the type of talk that would normally be confined to a conference room and presented as a published paper to a small audience. This style of event, with both live and online audiences, is likely to experience a dramatic surge in popularity over the next decade.

Can you think of a conference topic that would draw a large online audience?

EXTENSION ACTIVITY

As mentioned earlier, the TEDx *Organiser Guide* for local events is exhaustive, providing practical ideas for conference planning, including choice of speakers, designs, experiences for the audience, and many other practical resources. These talks and guidelines will be very useful for the assessment tasks at the end of the chapter

FINALISE PROGRAM DETAILS

The last planning phase includes confirmation of all details and careful scheduling of the program. Costs need to be finalised based on bookings received prior to the deadline and this is linked to catering numbers and meeting-room bookings. Stakeholders involved in the process need to approve the program at this point (not for the first time, but hopefully the last).

A simplified timeline for the conference planning process is illustrated in Figure 5.3.

FIGURE 5.3 Small conference planning timeline

TIMING	KEY TASK	WORK BREAKDOWN
12 months prior to conference	Plan conference with stakeholders	• Appoint committee • Agree aims and objectives • Agree dates and duration • Arrange sponsorship
11 months prior	Select venue	• Develop venue specifications • Conduct site inspection • Formalise arrangements with hotel and suppliers
10 months prior	Event marketing and website	• Develop marketing and communications plan • Appoint website developer
10 months prior	Speaker program	• Call for papers • Select keynote speakers • Select other program speakers • Select MC
10 months prior	Plan social activities	• Dinners • Tours
9 months prior	Promote conference	• Direct mail campaign • Communications and promotional strategy • Offer early-bird discounts • Online registrations
9 months prior	Manage registrations	• Block hotel rooms • Make travel plans • Confirm meeting spaces • Confirm menus and numbers
1 month prior	Confirm hotel arrangements	• Confirm hotel rooms • Confirm AV requirements • Confirm room arrangements • Confirm run sheet
1 week prior	Technical rehearsal	• Assemble speaker presentations • Run-through with AV
2 weeks after	Post-conference	• Thank all stakeholders, speakers and participants • Publish proceedings • Finalise financials • Finalise final report

Final schedule and run sheet

The run sheet illustrated in the previous chapter (see Figure 4.7) is extremely detailed and includes more than the conference line-up of speakers. It shows minute by minute how the program will be realised, enabling lighting and sound technicians to take their cues and the MC to manage the speaker program, as well as allowing food and beverage staff to deliver service at the appropriate times. This is linked to the banquet event order (BEO), which is used by the hotel to deliver the contracted service.

A small sample of a BEO is illustrated in Figure 5.4.

FIGURE 5.4 Banquet event order (BEO)

TIME	ROOM	FUNCTION	SET-UP	GUARANTEED	EXPECTED
Sunday 4 July 6−8 p.m.	Foyer	Registration	Standard registration desk Flowers by Flora		
Sunday 4 July 6−8 p.m.	Rose Room	Welcome reception	Cocktail	90	105
Monday 9 a.m.−12 p.m.	Main Hall	Keynote presentations	Classroom	160	170

FOOD	SET-UP
Rose Room Serve 6−8 p.m. platters from kitchen; open bar	• Remove all tables and chairs • Set up 10 cocktail tables, 40 stools • Bar set left • Lectern and AV set-up for Welcome
• Mini quiche × 80 • Sushi roll × 80 • Chinese noodle box × 110 • Satay chicken stick × 220 • Mini-burger × 110 • Gluten-free vegetarian burger × 30 • Salad box × 30 • Mini-profiterole × 220	• Audiovisual • Music by Bob's Quartet on arrival 5.45−6.30 p.m. (own AV set-up) • Welcome speech with PowerPoint by MD 6.30 p.m., set up lectern and AV • Lighting design by Derek Day

Confirmations and registration

A cut-off date for registrations ensures that numbers and the budget can be finalised before the conference. This flows on to bookings for particular conference rooms, seating arrangements and catering. From an event planning viewpoint, it is always important that the group fits the room and there aren't acres of empty chairs because delegate numbers were not transmitted to the function staff doing the set-up. Naturally, the chef will need final numbers for planning catering well in advance so that food is ordered and prepared in the correct quantities. Ordering specific items for special diets is particularly important, as a vegan, gluten-free or lactose-free meal will require the right ingredients. It is estimated that up to 10 per cent of delegates order special dietary meals. Allergies to particular ingredients can be life-threatening and must be taken very seriously. This needs to be checked with the chef beforehand.

The trend for ordering gluten-free meals is growing, overtaking orders of vegetarian meals. In addition to **dietary preferences**, the chef also has to consider **religious requirements** such as kosher and halal meals. Finally, there is the important issue of **food allergies** such as peanut and fructose intolerance.

How can you best communicate delegate food requests to the chef? In the registration process, can you differentiate between general dislikes, healthy eating and life-threatening allergies?

Dietary preferences
Lifestyle-related food choices, such as a low-sugar or low-fat diet

Religious requirements
Halal and kosher food are prepared with religious requirements in mind, excluding prohibited ingredients or using specific preparation methods

Food allergies
Physical reactions to certain foods; in some cases, such as peanuts, these can be life-threatening

Publication

Post the event, there are a number of tasks to be undertaken. One is the need for conference presentations and papers to be published after editing. It is often surprising how disorganised presenters can be, leaving their materials in draft state until the night before! Chasing up final academic papers can also be time-consuming.

Evaluation and reporting

There are many people involved in running a conference and all need to be thanked, in particular the speakers and the master of ceremonies. Another task after the conference is the checking of registrations alongside payments and invoices paid, so that the conference finances can be reconciled. The final report should include not only financial information but feedback from stakeholders, presenters and conference delegates so that any suggested improvements can be applied to forthcoming events.

Summary

This chapter has looked at one type of event in considerable detail: the meeting or conference. As such, it has shown the full cycle of establishing program requirements, designing the conference program, and executing the event. As with other events, the chapter has illustrated the involvement of stakeholders and shown the importance of a program design based on the needs of the audience. From a delegate viewpoint, the things that are important are the schedule, speakers, and opportunities to network formally and informally as part of the social program. Room layouts, entertainment and catering all contribute to satisfaction levels. Academic conferences require particular attention to the process of calling for papers, peer reviews and publication.

Key terms

Conference	Gatherings focused on information-sharing and education, most commonly of a business or academic nature
Congress	Gathering that includes representatives from different groups; for example, the National Congress of Australia's First People
Convention	Large-scale gathering with the intention of reaching agreement on an issue, generally of a political nature

Dietary preferences	Lifestyle-related food choices, such as a low-sugar or low-fat diet
Food allergies	Physical reactions to certain foods; in some cases, such as peanuts, these can be life-threatening
MC	Master of ceremonies
PCO	Professional conference organiser
Religious requirements	Halal and kosher food are prepared with religious requirements in mind, excluding prohibited ingredients or using specific preparation methods
Stage manager	Organises the production
Supplier	Provides event goods (e.g. floral arrangements) and services (e.g. audiovisual set-up)
Talent	Speakers, actors, entertainers – anyone who is part of delivering the production

REVIEW YOUR KNOWLEDGE

1   Conference design is a key part of a successful production. Who are the potential stakeholders involved in putting on a business conference?

2   Explain why it is important to understand the scope and objectives of the stakeholders and audience. Provide an example of a conference design brief.

3   List the key steps involved in planning a conference in the lead-up period.

4   Once the conference is up and running, who are the potential stakeholders involved in the production of the event?

APPLY YOUR KNOWLEDGE

1   Visit two conference and exhibition centres to compare and justify your selection of appropriate meeting rooms for a three-day conference involving 300 physiotherapists. As well as general and plenary sessions, there will be several breakouts during the program for hands-on physiotherapy demonstration sessions, with a maximum of 20 delegates involved in each session.

2   For the above conference, choose a venue outside the conference centre for a banquet dinner on the final night where a sports theme will be the highlight.

3   For the above conference, plan a one-day post-conference tour of major sporting facilities in the area.

ALTERNATIVE

Using the TEDx guidelines, plan for a mini TEDx conference. You may do this as a simulated event or apply for a licence and go for full production. All planning documents must be submitted.

CASE STUDY

As a conference planner, you have been tasked with the job of choosing a keynote speaker for an adult education conference. The theme of the conference is educational innovation. The delegates are vocational and higher education teachers.

Below are three samples from potential speakers. You will not be using the specific speech but need to choose the speaker. Once you have done this, write a brief for the speaker explaining both the conference program and how you will be providing for their needs.

MAYSOON ZAYID: 'I GOT 99 PROBLEMS … PALSY IS JUST ONE'

https://youtu.be/buRLc2eWGPQ?list=PL0nKakcqb4tRMwpoDZOEVyt_p-QZrKlpC

'I have cerebral palsy. I shake all the time', Maysoon Zayid announces at the beginning of this exhilarating, hilarious talk. (Really, it's hilarious.) 'I'm like Shakira meets Muhammad Ali.' With grace and wit, the Arab-American comedian takes us on a whistle-stop tour of her adventures as an actress, stand-up comic, philanthropist and advocate for the disabled.

PRANAV MISTRY: THE THRILLING POTENTIAL OF SIXTHSENSE TECHNOLOGY

https://youtu.be/YrtANPtnhyg?list=PL68492A0FC99185C7

At TEDIndia, Pranav Mistry demos several tools that help the physical world interact with the world of data, including a deep look at his SixthSense device and a new, paradigm-shifting paper 'laptop'. In an onstage Q&A, Mistry says he'll open-source the software behind SixthSense, to open its possibilities to all.

HANS ROSLING: THE BEST STATS YOU'VE EVER SEEN

https://youtu.be/hVimVzgtD6w?list=PL68492A0FC99185C7

With the drama and urgency of a sportscaster, statistics guru Hans Rosling uses an amazing new presentation tool, Gapminder, to present data that debunks several myths about world development. Rosling is the professor of international health at Sweden's Karolinska Institute, and the founder of Gapminder, a non-profit that brings vital global data to life.

Online resources

Visit http://login.cengagebrain.com and search for this book to access the study tools that come with your textbook.

References

Herzberg, Frederick (1966). *Work and the Nature of Man*. Cleveland: World Publishing.

Ismail, F. (2014). The critical success factors of event management: A focus on meetings, incentives, conventions & exhibitions (MICE) in Malaysia. Doctoral dissertation, Universiti Tun Hussein Onn Malaysia.

Lundberg, C., Gudmundson, A., & Andersson, T. D. (2009). Herzberg's two-factor theory of work motivation tested empirically on seasonal workers in hospitality and tourism. *Tourism Management*, 30(6), 890–9.

Rogers, T. (2013). *Conferences and Conventions: A Global Industry* (3rd edn). London: Routledge.

Websites

Business Events Council of Australia, www.businesseventscouncil.org.au/

Business Events in Singapore (BEiS), www.stb.gov.sg/assistance-and-licensing/grants/pages/business-events-in-singapore-(beis).aspx

Business Events New Zealand, http://businessevents.newzealand.com/en

Exhibition & Event Association of Australasia, www.eeaa.com.au

Meetings & Events Australia, www.meetingsevents.com.au

NT Conventions, www.ntconventions.com.au

Perth Convention and Exhibition Centre Event Manual, www.pcec.com.au/plan-an-event/event-resources

Professional Conference Organisers Association, www.pco.asn.au

MANAGE EVENT STAGING COMPONENTS

6

OVERVIEW

Event staging can be considered in terms of the technical requirements for audiovisual, lighting, sound, sets, stage design and special effects. Event staging can also be considered more broadly to encompass other products and services such as catering, security, signage, entertainment, transportation and fencing, all of which are required to 'stage' an event. As this brief overview illustrates, many different suppliers or contractors are involved and it takes real talent to bring this all together to work seamlessly.

LEARNING OBJECTIVES

On completion of this chapter, you will be able to:

1. analyse event staging requirements, integrating regulatory, risk, safety and sustainability issues

2. source and negotiate with staging contractors using specifications and schedules, then evaluate quotations against quality criteria, select contractors and finalise agreements

3. monitor staging preparations by evaluating work against specifications and timelines, including the approval of changes, particularly those impacting on quality and budget

4. evaluate staging components by seeking feedback from stakeholders.

INDUSTRY VIEWPOINT

The biennial New Zealand Festival is presented by a charitable trust – The New Zealand International Festival of the Arts. Up to three hundred specialist arts administrators, communicators, production and technical staff are employed to help produce and present the Festival, but most are on short-term contracts, of between six weeks to eighteen months' duration. In the 'off' period between Festivals, a skeletal administration staff of only four is maintained.

The Festival operates on a financial knife-edge, with a mandate to break even at the end of each event, and the requirement to start from zero each time. It has 'core funding' by Wellington City Council, but relies heavily on public and private sector support for its existence; 62 per cent of income comes from ticket sales, and 31 per cent from sponsorship and grants. The Government, through its arts funding agency, Creative New Zealand, assists the development of new New Zealand work for presentation at the Festival.

Approximately 75 per cent of the Festival's operating budget is spent on buying, producing and presenting the events which make up the Festival, with the remainder split between administration and marketing costs.

Source: Adapted from New Zealand Festival (2017). www.festival.co.nz

INTRODUCTION

The New Zealand Festival, one of the top five festivals in Australasia, provides an introduction to the issues associated with staging. The staging of an event incorporates all aspects of the event that enable the performance to go ahead. Broadly speaking, by 'performance' we mean entertainment: the sport, the parade, the ceremony. The topics covered in this chapter, such as theme, venue, sound and lighting, as well as all the essential services, are relevant to every one of the free and ticketed events of the New Zealand Festival. For every event in that festival, the organisers would have had to look at issues such as capacity, seating arrangements, emergency access, stage requirements and staffing.

Staging is an ancient concept: the Roman gladiatorial events were staged in spectacular, albeit gruesome, fashion, but these events certainly had the enthusiastic atmosphere every modern event organiser aspires to – although the modern audience would be unlikely to enjoy the same level of bloodshed.

One of the largest outdoor music events held in Australia illustrates the complexity and logistics of staging. In 2005, Robbie Williams entered the *Guinness Book of World Records* for the fastest, and largest, number of concert tickets ever sold in one day – 1.6 million – when the European leg of his world tour went on sale. Williams sold out five London shows, each with a capacity of 75 000; his Leeds concert sold out in 90 minutes. In the Netherlands, four Amsterdam Arena gigs were sold out in a breathtaking 89 minutes. In Germany, a mass of 20 000 fans braved the cold to line the streets of Munich waiting for tickets to go on sale at midnight! Williams went on to tour Australia in November 2006, playing in five capital cities. According to promoter Michael Chugg, this was a rare occasion where Australia saw exactly

Robbie Williams concert, site set-up   Lighting effects transform the stage

the same concert as countries in the northern hemisphere. They brought two stage roofs and rigs from the UK, which ran in tandem and leap-frogged across the country. There were 57 semitrailers on the road, 30 steel containers, and 27 trucks to transport staging, production and the six 400-amp generators needed to power the pop-hunk's super-sized show.

> **Rigging**
> System of lines, blocks and counterweights that enable the crew to move stage equipment such as lights and special effects

This chapter looks in detail at the skills required to manage overall event staging from an organisational and contractor management perspective. It requires the application of advanced planning and organisation and communication skills, combined with a detailed knowledge of the event management process and a broad understanding of individual specialist services. It does not, however, require a specialist knowledge of these areas.

Event staging requirements may relate to:

* exhibition set-up
* audiovisual requirements
* display and decoration
* furniture
* temporary structures
* special effects
* entertainment
* sound and lighting
* stage design
* rigging
* catering, including set-up
* security
* disability and emergency access.

Pyrotechnics offer particular challenges for both the event organiser and the specialist contractor

Special effects, for example, may include pyrotechnics, which are used at many outdoor sporting and entertainment events. An event or venue manager would need to know that there are specific requirements for the use of pyrotechnics (fireworks) and would need to contract a licensed operator to provide these special effects. Close-proximity pyrotechnics are smokeless and have no fallout, making them suitable for parties, weddings and awards nights, where they contribute greatly to the WOW factor. This chapter aims to develop a broad understanding of specialist component services such as these.

ANALYSE STAGING REQUIREMENTS

There are many factors to consider when staging an event, the primary consideration being the suitability of the venue for the production and the audience. The production could be a performance, but it could also be a marathon, a meeting or an exhibition. In Chapter 5 we discussed the work breakdown structure. In this chapter we will return to this overview of the work to be done, and talk about the specialists who can provide these services, the outsourcing of some tasks, and the development of a detailed run sheet in order to facilitate the event build.

The staging environment

Selection of an event venue must take the needs of all stakeholders into account. Stakeholders include emergency services, catering staff, entertainers, participants and clients. Performers and their promoters are particularly fussy about the configuration of the venue, including the stage and the seating, as these can contribute to the success or failure of the performance. The sound qualities of the venue are equally important.

Frequently, the client has an unusual idea for a venue, but however imaginative this may be, selection of the site must be tempered with rational decision making. While a parking lot could be transformed into an interesting place to have a party, it would have no essential services, such as electricity, and would present expensive and time-consuming logistical problems. An existing event venue, such as a conference centre, could more easily lend itself to transformation using decoration and props.

Choosing a venue that is consistent with the event purpose and theme is essential. It can also lead to cost savings as there is far less expense in transforming it into what the client wants. The major considerations for selecting an event venue include:

* size of the event (including size of the audience)
* layout of the site and its suitability for the event
* stage, field of play or performance area
* essential services (water, electricity)
* transport and parking
* supply issues for goods and services providers, such as caterers
* technical support
* venue management support.

An inspection of the venue or site should reveal any limitations. The aspects to consider include:

* compatibility with the event theme
* audience comfort
* visibility for the audience (**line of sight**)
* sound quality

| Line of sight |
| Audience view of the stage |

- entrances and exits
- stage area (where relevant)
- storage areas
- available equipment
- cover in case of poor weather
- safety and security
- access for emergency vehicles
- evacuation routes.

In viewing a potential event site, there are three major stakeholders who need to be considered and whose perspectives could be quite different: the **performers**, the **audience** and the **organisers**. By performers we mean those in the limelight, whether this involves providing an educational talk, dancing in a parade, presenting an award or scoring over a tryline. Performers have specific needs that are fundamental to their success, such as the level of intimacy with the audience (often the result of the distance from the audience) or the volume of the sound. The audience also has needs, the primary one being to see what is going on! The level of lighting and sound, as well as access to and comfort of the seating, also contributes to audience satisfaction. Catering and facilities are generally secondary. Finally, from a management perspective, the venue must help to minimise risks, such as adverse weather, power failure, accidents and emergencies.

Performers
Includes dancers and singers, but in the broader sense refers to anyone in 'the show' – on stage (speakers) or on the field (athletes)

Audience
Anyone watching 'the show', including spectators and conference delegates

Organisers
Includes the event manager, event producer, management team and/or committee giving oversight to the event

Event staging requirements

Once the venue or site has been selected, it is necessary to analyse the staging requirements for the event based on a detailed review of all the proposed aspects of it. Safety and risk-management issues also need to be incorporated in planning for event staging. In order to plan an event involving a stage and set, it is necessary to know the types of props that will be required and the equipment needed to install them. If working outdoors, staging requirements may include stages, tents, scaffolding, fences, ground covering and seating. All of these are available from suppliers of staging products and services. An event manager needs to understand product and service terminology, features and options, as well as current technology in key areas of staging. This knowledge is essential for contractor briefing and development of specification documents for:

- catering
- venue or site services and set-ups
- technical services (e.g. audiovisual, lighting, sound, rigging, special effects)
- entertainers
- registration requirements and set-ups
- physical elements (e.g. display, furniture and temporary structures)
- security
- media coverage
- safety equipment.

As we have mentioned several times, the theme of an event must be supported in every aspect, including the décor, lighting, sound and special effects. The theme may be quite subtle;

for example, in the case of a high-tech theme for a conference, the audience would only be subliminally aware of some aspects of it, such as the colour scheme. In more dramatic cases, guests might be asked to support the theme by dressing appropriately or participating in entertainment that is consistent with the theme. Themes may be tried and tested, or unique.

A theme can be reinforced through such creative elements as:

- colour
- landscape and/or location
- film/theatre/art/dance
- humour
- fantasy.

As Silvers and Goldblatt (2012) point out, events in general are becoming increasingly sophisticated, experiential in their nature, and more elaborate. The format of events is constantly changing, thus highlighting the importance of creative flair together with technical knowledge.

Following are important aspects of the theme that need to be carefully considered by the event organiser. As you will see, there are many decisions to make! Detailed staging specifications may relate to price, performance standards, timelines, technical specifications for equipment, and regulatory requirements.

Entertainment

A wide range of acts can be used to enhance the theme of an event, and corporate events in particular often employ interesting performers such as snake charmers, hypnotists and belly dancers. Entertainment companies have a wealth of ideas, which you can explore on their websites. They need to be briefed in the early planning stages so that they become familiar with the event purpose and the event audience. They can then look at the event theme and come up with a range of concepts to suit the theme. If a band is recommended, the specific technical requirements should be discussed at this stage. (One event organiser illustrated the importance of briefing the entertainment provider by describing her own experience in organising an event for a 21st. When the parents of the young woman celebrating her birthday heard that one of the band members had made indecent gestures and remarks, they were furious with the organiser!)

Décor

Lena Malouf (2012) is one of Australia's foremost event designers and her work has earned her two major awards, the first for Best Event Produced for a Corporation or Association (overall budget US$200 000 to US$500 000) and the second for Best Theme Décor (décor budget over US$50 000). Her guests were submerged in a magical 'underwater' world reminiscent of the fantastical journey in the children's classic *Bedknobs and Broomsticks*. Malouf's events are characterised by extravagant displays, including imaginative moving art pieces that tie in perfectly with the chosen theme, her main aim being to surprise and transport the audience. She has served as the Worldwide International President of the International Special Events Society (ISES).

Décor encompasses many things, from the colour scheme to the drapes, from props to floral arrangements. The challenge is to bring them all together into a cohesive theme. Staging rental companies can be extremely helpful with this task.

Layout

The layout of the event venue is clearly integral to the success of the event. Anyone who has worked on conferences and formal dinners knows that table layout is something that needs to be negotiated with the client well in advance. With large dinner events in large venues, all too often the audience at the back of the room has very limited vision of the stage. Where this is compounded by poor sound and too much alcohol, it does not take long before the presenter is drowned out by the clink of glasses and the hum of conversation. This can be very embarrassing.

When planning an event at which guests will be seated around a table, it is essential to plan the layout according to scale. If the dimensions of the tables and chairs are not considered, as well as the space taken by seated guests, there may prove to be no room for waiters or guests to move around.

The timing associated with setting up a room needs to be taken into account when developing the run sheet. A large hotel might set up for small meeting sessions during the day and then turn the entire function space into a banquet by 7 p.m.

Watch the time-lapse video of a ballroom set-up at a Four Seasons hotel in the United States (https://youtu.be/rjlyK1Fz8o8). Now contrast it with the video showing the time and effort required to transform a non-traditional venue (a gym) (https://youtu.be/qQmzeCBk1rs).

Weigh up the pros and cons of using a fit-for-purpose venue and a non-traditional venue from the viewpoint of hiring equipment and labour cost.

EXTENSION ACTIVITY

Lighting and special effects

Lighting can be used to spectacular effect, and for this reason events held at night provide the opportunity for more dramatic results than those held during the day. Lighting can be used both to create the general ambience and to highlight particular features. It is often synchronised with sound for special effect at dances and fireworks displays, and can also be used to highlight sponsor advertising. As with sound, lighting is used to create a particular mood, although it is important to remember that this must be consistent with the event theme. Subtlety is required, for there has been a tendency recently to use some of the latest patterning techniques too often. Professional advice from a lighting designer is recommended as lighting is more often than not one of the main contributors to staging a successful event. Laser lightshows are becoming increasingly imaginative, including projections onto water screens and architectural lighting.

Lighting equipment can be rented or bought. However, designing a show is a specialist skill. With this in mind, discuss the following statement: Old-school event lighting (analogue tungsten and halogen lighting with gels) is completely out-of-date and has been supplanted by new technologies including a wide range of LED (light-emitting diode) options.

EXTENSION ACTIVITY

Lighting and special effects are increasingly driven by technology

Sound

Music is a powerful creator of mood. It can excite or calm an audience, while particular pieces can be highly emotive. The volume needs to be pitched at just the right level, and all members of the audience need to be able to hear clearly, particularly if the event is being staged in a large stadium. Professional sound engineers can be relied upon to give advice on equipment and the acoustic qualities of a venue. For example, a concrete venue with little or no carpeting or curtaining has a negative effect on sound, but this can be remedied by the incorporation of drapes in the design.

Vision

Vision incorporates all projected images, such as replays of sporting highlights on large screens or scoreboards. Data projectors can project images onto screens for dramatic effect, and this can be extended to live broadcasts with satellite links.

Digital styling

Digital styling takes audiovisual presentations to a new level, enabling organisers to select a range of themed projections, including sponsor logos, videos and photoloops. Digital styling creates visual works using images, video content and other media to create seamless and immersive displays. These can be projected onto non-traditional surfaces such as buildings, trees, water and so on. Long gone are the small screens and long delays involved in loading multiple presentations using different media.

Stage

The stage is used for many reasons, including performances, prize giving and presentations. Equipment rental companies can provide advice on the size and shape of the stage, as well as on screens and other devices on which to project images from the rear of the stage.

However, the needs of the audience are the prime consideration, particularly the line of sight, which must be considered when deciding on the size and shape of the stage and the placement of lecterns or screens.

Set

The **set** includes all objects on the stage: props, flats, lecterns, stairs, curtains and so on. Sometimes these are hired; at other times they must be built or made. The **cyclorama**, for example, is the curved white screen at the back of the stage used to create a sense of distance, with special lighting of the cyclorama providing different-coloured backgrounds. **Borders** are used to mask parts of the rigging system and to trim the sightlines so that only the set may be seen by the audience. A **traveller** is a type

---

Set
All objects on the stage

Cyclorama
Curved white screen at the back of the stage, used for light projections

Borders
Materials used to mask the upper portion of the stage area, such as fabric or canvas; also known as a valance curtain

Traveller
A curtain that moves along a track

of curtain that moves along a track. Often it is used as the main stage curtain, being configured so that one operating line moves curtains from both sides of the stage simultaneously. Other staging terms are described in Table 6.1.

TABLE 6.1 Technical terms used in event staging

PERFORMANCE	
Management and agent	Take care of performers' interests
Talent	Performers (although sometimes used as a demeaning term to refer to the people who are not the main performers)
Green room	Area where performers wait and watch monitors
Dressing room	Area where performers dress and are made up
Wings	Area used for assembling performers and props
Stage-in-the-round	Circular stage allowing the audience 360-degree views
Proscenium arch	Traditional theatre-style curtains at the side and above
Thrust	Stage projecting into the audience, such as at fashion parades
Tracks	Fixed tracks used to move props
Lectern	Stand for speaker
LIGHTING	
Mixing desk	Where the lighting engineer controls lighting effects, adjusting colours, brightness and special effects; also where the sound engineer controls sound, including volume and switchover between music and microphone
Rigging	Overhead truss
T-stand/tree	Upright stand for lights
Floodlight	Wide light
Spotlight	Narrow light
Fresnel	Circular soft-edged beam (can go from spot to medium flood)
Cyclorama	Curved white screen at the back of the stage for light projections
Parcan	Fixed beam with soft edge, cheaper than floodlights, usually above the front of the stage and used in groups of four
Lighting gels	Slip-over colours used to change the colour of spotlights and parcans
Wash light	General area cover
Key light	Used for highlighting an object
Back light	Rear lighting effect (should use for speakers)
House light	Lighting provided by venue

SOUND	
Sound spec sheet	Specifies the sound requirements for a particular group or performance
Sound amplifier	Used to project the sound (microphones are plugged into amplifiers which power up the sound and send it to the speakers)
Out-front speakers	Speakers which face the audience
Fold-back speakers	Positioned on stage, facing the performers, to help performers hear themselves
Microphones	Include battery, stage (dynamic voice), headset and lectern
EXHIBITIONS	
Floor plan	Two-dimensional layout of the venue
CAD drawing	Computer-generated, three-dimensional drawing of the design for a stand
Booth	Usually a 3 metre × 3 metre stand at an exhibition
Corinthian	Walling covered with fabric to which Velcro will adhere
Pit	Service duct located in the floor, providing power and data cables (for some indoor and outdoor events, water and compressed air and gas can also be provided in this way)
Tracker/reader	Device for scanning visitor cards to capture their data
GENERAL	
Pyrotechnics	Fireworks
Three-phase	Power for commercial use comes in three-phase (lighting, sound and vision equipment requires three-phase) and single-phase for domestic use

The stage specifications from the Adelaide Festival Centre shown in Figure 6.1 would be most useful in planning operations by the event organiser. Most larger centres provide this level of detail, as well as plans and drawings.

Tenting

Doug Matthews (2015) points out that a tent provides a blank canvas allowing for highly creative lighting and décor. Tents are also associated historically with circuses and entertainment, as well as providing an environment that many of the audience will not have experienced. In Australia, a tent is called a *marquee*, but in the United States this term refers to a canopy. There are many designs and colours of tents but the most commonly used is white. Movie-goers might remember the breach of protocol of Indian wedding planner Vijay Raaz in *Monsoon Wedding* when he erected a white tent rather than a red or orange one. In India, white is associated with mourning and death.

Field of play

Each sporting event has specific requirements. These may include gymnastic equipment, which must be properly set up to very clear specifications, or simply a good-quality pitch and wicket. In fact, there is nothing simple at all about a good-quality wicket, as cricket fans would know only too well! The quality of the grassed field is important for most sports. An Olympic Games soccer

FIGURE 6.1 Example of stage specifications

Stage specifications
Adelaide Festival Centre

STAGE FACILITIES

Stage
Timber, covered with 6 mm masonite.
Painted: Matt black.

Traps
The Space has an understage trap in a T formation across the centre of the floor area. The trap is covered by a series of steel framed and timber covered lids, each measuring approx. 1.2 m x 1.8 m. Please refer to the 'Space Plans and Drawings' for further details.
The space also has a shallow audience seating trap with two levels. Please refer to the 'Space Plans and Drawings' for further details.

Power Supply
In addition to the Stage Lighting Power (distributed from the Drama Centre Rack Room) the Space has one 32 amp 3 phase outlet located in the grid.

Control Rooms
The Space Sound Control Room is at balcony level with a fully opening window. The Space Lighting Control Room is also at balcony level with a fixed, double glazed window. Some stage managers choose to call the show from the Lighting Control Room, although there is limited space.

Music Stands and Sconces
Music stands, sconce lights and orchestral chairs can be supplied out of the Festival Theatre stock subject to availability.

Pianos
Concert and rehearsal pianos are available by arrangement with the Production
Co-ordinator. Moving and tuning charges apply.

Masking
The Space Theatre is stocked with the following masking items:

HARD MASKING
4 Flats	4500 mm high × 1600 mm wide	Wool covered ply
4 Flats	3000 mm high × 2000 mm wide	Wool covered ply
2 Flats	2300 mm high × 900 mm wide	Wool covered ply
2 Flats	3100 mm high × 600 mm wide	Wool covered ply
1 Flat	2700 mm high × 1500 mm wide	Wool covered ply
2 Flats	3400 mm high × 1400 mm wide	Wool covered ply (fit above balcony)
2 Flats	2800 mm high × 900 mm wide	Wool covered ply (fit below balcony)
1 Flat	2800 mm high × 1500 mm wide	Wool covered ply (fit below balcony)

SOFT MASKING
8 Curtains	5400 mm high × 3400 mm wide	Pleated velour (for hanging from bobbins on perimeter track)
6 Curtains	5400 mm high × 3100 mm wide	Flat velour (fair condition only)
7 Curtains	5400 mm high × 4000 mm wide	Flat velour (fair condition only)

Cyclorama
Cyclorama   approximately 36.57 m × 5.48 m drop (approx. 120 ft × 18 ft).
*Please note that one end of the cyc has visible water marks.

Source: The Adelaide Festival Centre

semi-final held in Canberra was threatened with cancellation due to the poor quality of the newly laid turf. Fortunately, the problem was solved in time for ticket-holders to enjoy the eagerly awaited match. Problems of this nature are not uncommon. For this reason, sporting fields are often covered when they are used for other events. However, while the cover protects the surface, it also blocks out the light so that damage can still be caused to the field. These days, professional grass specialists can replace an entire field within hours, but this is a very costly exercise.

The photos below illustrate the installation of protective flooring in parts of a stadium. This included two layers: the first, a mesh to protect the grass and limit flattening; the second, a series of boards which were laid by hand by a team of 20 workers over eight hours. This effort was repeated for each concert performance at the stadium as the flooring could not be left on the grass over a 24-hour period or the grass would not survive the heat and lack of light.

This mesh layer protects the grass and limits flattening

Laying protective flooring in a stadium

Successful flooring products need to sit on the ground but still allow air, light and water to permeate. They also need to have an acceptable load-bearing capacity. Terraplas, the first turf protection product, was developed in the United Kingdom and is used widely in stadia accommodating audiences of 80 000 or more people. An alternative product is PRO-FLOOR. Unlike Terraplas, which is rigid and flat, this Australian product follows the contours of the ground, rolls up for storage, and is easy to install and dismantle. This type of product allows light to permeate so it can be used for longer periods than the system illustrated in the photographs. It is commonly used for pathways at shows and festivals and in the queuing areas. When making a decision regarding turf protection, the labour required for installation and dismantling is a cost consideration.

Event services

The supply of essential services, a communications network, and transport and traffic management are essential to the staging of most events.

Essential services

Essential services include power, water and gas. While the provision of these may sound simple, various different electrical sources are often required, including three-phase power for some equipment and power back-up in case of emergency. Providing the venue kitchen with gas can also be a challenge. The choice of a complex site can add to the difficulties of providing these essential services to the event venue.

Communications

Many events have particular requirements for communications, which may even include the installation of a private communications network. Where there is a high level of demand on the communications network, the issue of bandwidth must be resolved, particularly if there is a significant amount of data being transmitted. High-speed wi-fi access to multiple concurrent users is essential for modern facilities.

In the staging of an event, power is an essential service

Transport and traffic management

Transport to the event, including air, rail, bus, train and taxi, needs to be considered. So, too, does the issue of parking and its impact on local traffic. In some cases, streets have to be closed, traffic diverted and special permission sought for this purpose, the event plan being an important part of the submission to the relevant authorities. Thought must also be given to access for people with disabilities, the marshalling of crowds, and the notifying of businesses affected by any disruptions. Most importantly, the stars of the show need to be able to find their way into the venue without any difficulty. Most large stadiums and convention centres have special entry at the rear or via an underground tunnel for the VIPs, players and/or performers.

SOURCE AND ORGANISE STAGING CONTRACTORS

From a legal and business perspective, it is essential to develop accurate and complete staging specifications detailing the precise requirements based on sound product and service knowledge for provision to contractors. (See Figure 6.2 for an idea of the types of technical specialists often required at events.) In turn, contractors should provide timely quotations for the provision of products and services, which should then be confirmed in writing, showing details of the products and services and their costs. The legal nature of these arrangements is discussed in Chapters 7 and 17.

The organiser's aim is to:

◆ identify and source appropriate contractors to provide services for the event
◆ provide accurate briefings or specifications on precise staging requirements to contractors
◆ obtain complete and timely quotations for the provision of services
◆ analyse quotations and select contractors in consultation with key stakeholders
◆ confirm agreements with contractors in writing, including details and costs of all services.

When monitoring contract implementation, the organiser needs to:

◆ monitor progress, including safety issues, at regular intervals through ongoing liaison with contractors and other stakeholders

FIGURE 6.2 Technical specialists

THE TECHNICAL TEAM

The production, or staging, of an event involves many specialists. As an example, members of the technical team supporting a performance would include:

- Artistic Director
- Production Manager
- Technical Director
- Stage Manager
- Choreographer
- Scriptwriter
- Lighting Designer
- Lighting Operator
- Sound Designer
- Sound Operator

- Vision Designer
- Vision Operator
- Front of House Manager
- Floor Manager.

The following staff would support the performance indirectly:

- Venue Manager
- Operations Manager
- Logistics Manager
- Catering Manager
- Cleaning and Waste Manager.

- identify the need for adjustments and organise appropriate changes, with confirmation in writing
- negotiate adjustments to maintain the integrity and quality of the event
- evaluate work completed against event requirements and time schedules, and take appropriate action to address delays.

The dynamic nature of the event environment generally brings about multiple additional requests or changes. For this reason, contract variations need to be negotiated and always documented in writing.

Safety is a major consideration in the staging area, and this work is generally done by licensed professionals. Staging contractors are able to interpret stage plans, and they have a detailed knowledge of:

Image courtesy of Staging Connections, an Encore Event Technologies Company

Technical know-how is an essential element of staging success

- the types of control desks which operate stage machinery
- techniques for working out the load capacity of stage machinery
- safe and efficient methods and procedures used in manoeuvring loads
- techniques for handling scenic elements (e.g. toggling flats and pin hinging)
- relevant legislative and/or organisational health and safety requirements (e.g. safe manual handling techniques, working at heights, moving loads safely)
- safety issues associated with using ladders

- signals to be employed when using stage machinery
- safety procedures to be followed in the event of lifting, revolving or trucking emergencies.

Tum, Norton and Wright (2006) point out that there are any number of potential causes for accidents, including *direct damage* to the venue or equipment, *consequential loss* due to the venue being unavailable, *legal liability* through failure to perform, and *personal loss*, including financial loss by the event organiser (p. 152).

Catering contractors

A catering contractor usually does the catering for an event, taking care of food orders, food production and service staff. These contractors (or the venue catering staff) should provide menus and costings relevant to the style of service required. Photographs of previous catering and food presentation styles can be helpful in making a decision.

There are many approaches to event catering, the most common being:

- a set menu, with table service
- a buffet
- finger food
- fast food.

The style of cooking and the type of service have the main impact on cost. Food that is prepared off-site and heated or deep-fried on site can be very cost-effective. If fully qualified chefs are to provide quality fresh food with superb presentation, and the guests are to be served by silver service-trained waiting staff, then clearly the costs will escalate enormously.

When discussing catering contracts, the event organiser needs to be very explicit about food quantities, the type of food required and speed of service. Despite expressions of interest in healthier food at sporting events, findings show that the old favourites, such as pies and chips, are still popular and that fruit salad and sandwiches do not sell well.

A food safety plan is another essential item when planning an event. Food safety involves protecting the customer from food poisoning by implementing a plan to prevent cross-contamination and other factors that cause bacterial growth. For example, food needs to be kept at the correct temperature all the way from the factory/market to the shop, into the kitchen and onto the buffet. Food safety plans look at every aspect of food handling and, if well implemented, ensure the measurement of temperatures at key points in the process in accordance with the guidelines of the plan. The best kitchens have refrigerated delivery areas and separate storage for vegetables, meat, seafood and other products at the correct temperatures. Planned food production processes, including plating food in a refrigerated area, can further reduce the risk of bacterial growth. Finally, it is essential for the food safety specialist to consider the length of time taken for the food to reach the customer (perhaps at the other side of the stadium) and the length of time before it is consumed. Health authorities in the various States and Territories monitor food safety.

Catering for an event is extremely demanding for those in the kitchen. Producing several hundred hot meals is not for the faint-hearted. The chef should be aware of the planned time for service of all courses and this should be confirmed at an early stage of the planning. Most floor managers will ask the chef how much notice is needed for service of the main course and they will monitor proceedings and advise the chef accordingly.

Beverages supplied at functions and banquets usually come in the form of beverage packages ('packs') which are available at a range of prices, depending mainly on the quality of the wine. A pack includes a specific range of wines, beers and soft drinks, and does not generally include spirits. The client may choose a selection of beverages, but this will clearly be more expensive, and may also specify a time limit for an open bar.

The logistics of catering from a site that has no kitchen are quite daunting. All equipment and ingredients have to be transported to the site and, as discussed above, perishable food must be maintained at the right temperature. This often involves hiring a coolroom. Workflow planning is particularly important; for example, certain ingredients must be pre-prepared, ready for use when needed.

Queue management is another consideration, as customers waiting or needing to use condiments can hold up the process if appropriate planning has not occurred.

Accommodation providers

For many conferences, exhibitions, shows and sporting events, accommodation is an essential part of the package. The packaging of air travel and accommodation demands that planning for such events occurs well in advance in order to acquire discounted airfares and attractive room rates. If such rate reductions are essential to favourable pricing of the event, it is preferable to hold the event in an off-peak season. However, as soon as an event such as the Formula 1 Australian Grand Prix in Melbourne reaches a significant size, discounted rates are out of the question as accommodation in the destination city will be fully booked.

The following extract illustrates the response of many accommodation providers as soon as they get wind of an event, although this approach to pricing is generally counterproductive. The negative image created by overpricing can have an impact on tourism in the long term.

> The normally sleepy town of Mongu (in Zambia) is about to come alive this weekend for the Kuomboka ceremony. The ceremony stretches back several centuries and is about moving Lozi people from the flooded Zambezi Plains to the plateau. Hotel owners in Mongu say they immediately hiked room rates as soon as the announcement of the event was made, by between 600 and even 1000 per cent in some cases. They are also quoting their room rates in United States dollars as they expect more than 5000 tourists to witness Zambia's foremost traditional event.
>
> The holding of the ceremony is dictated by the amount of rain that falls in a particular season. So much rain has fallen this year that staging the ceremony was never in doubt.
>
> Source: *Sunday Independent* (South Africa) (2001). 25 March.

This is a most unusual event – most event organisers dread the prospect of rain, while those organising this event require rain to ensure its success!

Waste management specialists

One of the legacies of recent mega events in Australia is an increased awareness of environmental issues. Biodegradable plates and cutlery are now commonplace at smaller events, replacing non-biodegradable foil pie plates and polystyrene containers.

Methods for reducing the environmental impact of noise, air and water pollution should be part of the planning process, and advice on these can be obtained from the Environmental Protection Authority which has offices in each State. With regard to air pollution, releasing helium balloons into the atmosphere has been shown to be environmentally unfriendly and this practice is slowly dying out around the world.

Waste management is another important consideration for event organisers and is often contracted out to specialists; this will be covered in detail in Chapter 16. Professional contractors can advise on the correct disposal of cooking oils and other toxic waste that could affect the water supply. As we know, clearly marked bins should be provided for the recycling of waste products. Waste management companies can provide the full range of equipment and services, including installation and removal of bins.

Biodegradable plates and cutlery

The number and type of toilets to be provided at an event, including the number allocated to men, women and people with disabilities, must also be decided. The composition of the event audience – the number of men and women attending – and the average time taken by each in the toilet also need to be considered! Theatre management has been working on this for years. Every woman has faced the problem of long queues at an interval and there is in fact a formula for working out how many toilets are required! Too many events provide substandard toilet facilities that cannot meet the demand, so it is essential to discuss the requirements for any event you are planning with a toilet facilities hire company, as they are the experts.

Cleaning contractors

Some cleaning contractors specialise in events, including Clean Event, the company

Temporary handwashing stand, including soap and towels

widely used for events in Australia. In most cases, cleaning is done before and after the event. Maintaining cleanliness during peak times is challenging, particularly if there is only a short changeover time between event sessions. This means that you have to get one audience out, the cleaning and replenishment of stocks done, and the next audience in on time. The timing is part of logistics planning, which we will cover in detail in Chapter 24. Cleaning staff are part of the event staff and should receive appropriate training so that they can answer questions from people attending the event.

Handwashing facilities are useful for guests and essential for staff preparing food. The temporary handwashing facility illustrated on page 115 is ideal for outdoor events. It provides soap and hygienic running water.

Other event services

Several traditional contractors have been identified above, ranging from catering to waste management. It is difficult for event organisers to focus on the operational aspects of planning for the event audience and simultaneously on the more artistic and abstract aspects of experience design. This involves establishing an environment focused on the audience or spectator experience; for example, providing street entertainment or laser lighting.

With some events, the staging process may even include managing the fans who queue for days before the event for places at it. At the Academy Awards, for example, the area designated for fans is occupied for up to two weeks before the big night, as one of the fans receives a free grandstand seat overlooking the red carpet.

Overall, many events can be conceptualised as theatrical events. According to Martin, Seffrin and Wissler (2004), this conceptualisation embraces characteristics of authorship, 'performativity', spatial and temporal dynamics, and performance–audience relationships (p. 91). Lissa Twomey's opening to the New Zealand International Arts Festival in Wellington certainly comprised all these characteristics. According to the reviews (Sorensen, 2010), thinking outside the box was not just a guiding principle but a leitmotif for Twomey's work as artistic director: 'Guided by her long experience with the Sydney Festival and her now shrewd understanding of the NZ audience, Twomey put together a triumphant program of calculated risk-taking'.

MONITOR STAGING PREPARATIONS

The event manager needs to monitor the pre-event progress of staging components at regular intervals through ongoing liaison with contractors and other stakeholders, and to evaluate work completed against event requirements and time schedules. Sometimes it is necessary to take appropriate action to address delays or other problems; these issues are more easily resolved if the specifications were clear in the first place. However, the event environment is a dynamic one and it is almost always necessary to make staging adjustments and changes. Staging adjustments may relate to changes in numbers, budgetary changes, demands by the performers, or unexpected difficulties with staging components. These, too, should be agreed in writing, however trivial they may seem at the time.

As will be shown in Chapter 7, it is essential to maintain good relationships with suppliers of event services and equipment as it is these contractors who may be needed to help with last-minute changes. If they are responsive, many crises can be averted.

Ferdinand and Kitchin (2012) remind us of the project management phases described in Chapter 4 and the importance of effective planning during the phases of event development.

Contract specifications

Contract specifications are the most important aspect of negotiations. A brief outline of the potential services required for audiovisual support are illustrated in the following extract from a tender specification (see Table 6.2). As mentioned earlier, other key terms of contracts, such as cancellation, will be covered in more detail in Chapter 7.

TABLE 6.2 Audiovisual services required

Pre-production: source, locations, video clips, graphics, rights and permissions

Renting, installation and maintenance of equipment

Provision of technical services in recording, editing, projecting multimedia and speaker content

Photographic services

Theming services, including lighting and displays

Post-production: editing with captions and graphics, music

Archiving: provision of archive material in the prescribed format, posted as online content

The specifications would accompany an agreed schedule for all of the activities illustrated in Table 6.2. Factors affecting staging specifications include:

- performance standards
- price
- technical specifications
- theme-related requirements
- timelines
- regulatory requirements.

Regulatory requirements include contractor licensing (for example, an electrician) and the quality of goods and services provided (consumer protection). There are many laws and regulations that should be considered and these will be covered in Chapter 17. Of these, workplace health and safety is arguably the most important (see Chapter 9), as the event organisation is the PCBU – 'persons conducting a business or undertaking'.

Stage equipment

Stage equipment can involve one or more of the following elements:

- framed scenery (e.g. flats, profiles, doors, windows)
- weight-bearing scenery (e.g. rostra, ramps, steps)
- non-weight-bearing scenery (e.g. columns, trees)
- soft scenery (e.g. canvas legs, borders, cloths, gauzes, cycloramas)
- furniture and other set props
- revolves
- trucks.

Working at heights, the equipment to be used could include the following (which must be used according to regulation limits and licensing requirements):

- tallescope
- maxi-lift or genie-type lifter
- cherry picker
- mobile scaffolding
- ladders and A-frames
- scissor lift.

Safety

A handbook developed by the Australian Government for independent contractors operating in Australia states:

> If you hire independent contractors, you are legally responsible for ensuring their health and safety at all times while in your workplace (to the extent that this is reasonably practicable). For example, you should ensure that your workplace, machinery, substances and facilities used are safe, and that all workers have adequate training, supervision and are properly licensed if required.

Source: Australian Government Department of Industry, Innovation and Science (2016). *Independent Contractors: The Essential Handbook.* p. 17.

Monitoring the safety of contractors is essential

Rehearsals

The importance of rehearsal cannot be underestimated. This is the opportunity for all involved to integrate their efforts – everyone from the stage manager (who calls the shots for the presentation) to the technical support staff (who follow the appropriate cues for lighting and sound). A technical run-through allows the staff involved to test the set-up and make sure that all elements work satisfactorily. Technical glitches at an event are unprofessional, to say the least, so a back-up plan for all aspects of the presentation is absolutely essential. This includes two copies of each video or sound clip, slide presentations in more than one format, and multiple microphones. Every potential problem should have a ready solution. The final aspect, over which the event manager has little control, is the quality of the presentation given by the speaker, particularly at business and academic conferences. Giving some basic advice and encouragement beforehand can assist a presenter enormously. If rehearsals have been conducted and everything is under control, speakers are far less nervous and far less likely to feel uncomfortable under the spotlight. A 'ready room' where the speaker can set up and test the presentation before going on stage is recommended.

EVALUATE STAGING COMPONENTS

As this chapter has illustrated, most events involve multiple contractors or suppliers. Integrating their activities is one of the most difficult challenges. All want access to the loading dock and venue at the same time and this might not be possible. Operational efficiency demands careful scheduling, with some contractors given priority over others; for example, those installing rigging need to be given first access. While the banquet manager might prefer to set the tables the night before (a time-consuming process), this is not possible until the staging equipment is installed.

If it takes four-and-a-half hours to put up a tent to be used as a bar, this clearly creates a scheduling issue as bar equipment and supplies cannot be installed until this is done, and of course the water and electrical supplies need to be considered. Post the event, it is important to review these schedules and obtain feedback from all parties involved in order to improve efficiency and customer service. A detailed understanding of staging requirements, supplier arrangements and scheduling, as well as careful monitoring, will ensure that things run smoothly. If stakeholder interests are not managed well, this will lead to serious operational problems and delays.

Briefing and debriefing

The most common approach to managing communication with suppliers and other stakeholders is the pre-event briefing and post-event debrief. For an event that runs over several days, this is a daily occurrence. Many of the issues of integrating operations can be resolved this way. Effective two-way communication via radio (rather than mobile phone) is another way to immediately resolve operational issues. If documented, this information is invaluable when next staging the same event.

Summary

In this chapter we have looked in detail at the staging of an event, including layout, décor, sound, lighting and vision. The staff and subcontractors have also been identified, and the services required at an event, including catering, cleaning, waste management and communications, have been discussed. Staging an event is probably the most creative aspect of event management, and there is enormous scope for making an event memorable by using the best combination of staging elements. Selection of the right site for an event is essential as this can have a big impact on the cost of staging the event and the level of creativity that can be employed in developing the theme. The integration of all staff and contractor roles is similarly essential, and the event schedule or run sheet is a valuable tool.

Key terms

Audience	Anyone watching 'the show', including spectators and conference delegates
Borders	Materials used to mask the upper portion of the stage area, such as fabric or canvas; also known as a valance curtain
Cyclorama	Curved white screen at the back of the stage, used for light projections
Line of sight	Audience view of the stage
Organisers	Includes the event manager, event producer, management team and / or committee giving oversight to the event

Performers	Includes dancers and singers, but in the broader sense refers to anyone in 'the show' – on stage (speakers) or on the field (athletes)
Rigging	System of lines, blocks and counterweights that enable the crew to move stage equipment such as lights and special effects
Set	All objects on the stage
Traveller	A curtain that moves along a track

REVIEW YOUR KNOWLEDGE

1   List and explain five staging challenges associated with the production of a concert.
2   List and explain five staging challenges associated with holding a marathon.
3   What are the issues associated with special effects and pyrotechnics?
4   Explain the following technical equipment and services:
   – audiovisual
   – lighting
   – sets
   – sound
   – stage design
   – rigging
   – special effects.
5   Why is the work breakdown structure and the subsequent run sheet important for integrating the work required?

APPLY YOUR KNOWLEDGE

1   Look at this explanation of the history of the Roman Colosseum – https://youtu.be/ 0OyID1KC6kc – paying particular attention to the staging components, such as using lifts to release the lions onto the stage and using water to stage sea battles. Discuss the statement, 'What it takes to run a stadium hasn't changed'.
2   Staging Connections is an audiovisual and event services company. Explore its website (www. stagingconnections.com/event-production-services) and summarise the work it does in the areas of styling, design, technical and digital services. For example, it is not adequate to simply say 'rigging'. You need to explain what this is. Note: do not contact Staging Connections or any other supplier for help with your assignments.

CASE STUDY

ANALYSING STAGING REQUIREMENTS – A STREET MARKET

You have been appointed to the role of event coordinator for a small country town. The council wants to host an annual food market and has asked you to make a preliminary analysis of the staging components.

· Watch the time-lapse video of Perth's Beaufort Street Festival (www.beaufortstreet.com.au/ festival-timelapse) to get you started.
· Speculate as to who are the stakeholders, staff and contractors working on this type of event.
· Develop a run sheet/schedule of tasks and timing for your proposed event similar to that illustrated in this chapter.

- List the various contractors who may be involved.
- Develop specifications for one of the contractors; i.e. requirements that they must meet that can be monitored, such as food safety and waste management.
- As entertainment has been proposed, are there special technical requirements for small bands to consider?

This does not have to be done in great detail at this stage but it should be sufficient to start the process of sourcing stallholders and contractors and negotiating their requirements.

Online resources

CENGAGE
brain.com

Visit http://login.cengagebrain.com and search for this book to access the study tools that come with your textbook.

References

Australian Government Department of Industry, Innovation and Science (2016). *Independent Contractors: The Essential Handbook*. Canberra: Australian Government.

Ferdinand, N., & Kitchin, P. (2012). *Events Management: An International Approach*. London: Sage.

Malouf, L. (2012). *Events Exposed: Managing and Designing Special Events*. Hoboken, NJ: John Wiley & Sons.

Martin, J., Seffrin, G., & Wissler, R. (2004). The festival is a theatrical event. In V. A. Cremona et al. (2004). *Theatrical Events: Borders, Dynamics, Frames*. Amsterdam / New York: Rodopi Publishers.

Matthews, D. (2015). *Special Event Production: The Resources* (2nd edn). London: Routledge.

Silvers, J. R., & Goldblatt, J. (2012). *Professional Event Coordination* (vol. 62). Hoboken, NJ: John Wiley & Sons.

Sorensen, R. (2010). NZ festival puttin' on the risk. *The Australian*, 4 March.

Tum, J., Norton, P., & Wright, J. (2006). *Management of Event Operations*. Oxford, UK: Butterworth-Heinemann.

Websites

Event staging and outdoor festival stages (Select Concepts), www.selectconcepts.com.au / event-staging. html

Audiovisual for events (ExpoNet), www.exponet.com.au / Events / Audio-Visual-And-Staging.aspx

Staging Connections, www.stagingconnections.com

Staging Rentals & Construction, www.stagingrentals.com.au

3

EVENT COORDINATION

ESTABLISH AND CONDUCT BUSINESS RELATIONSHIPS

MANAGE FINANCES WITHIN A BUDGET

7

ESTABLISH AND CONDUCT BUSINESS RELATIONSHIPS

OVERVIEW

This chapter illustrates the nature of the event business by highlighting the many negotiations conducted with stakeholders and the agreements reached. Constant monitoring of the implementation of such agreements is necessary, and in the process good working relationships are developed. There are many suppliers in the industry, including hotels, caterers, entertainers and decorators. If anything goes wrong during planning and event execution, these relationships are sorely tested. On the other hand, successful outcomes build loyalty and long-term business relationships that stand the test of time.

LEARNING OBJECTIVES

On completion of this chapter, you will be able to:

1 build business relationships using effective communication and negotiation skills

2 conduct negotiations by effectively communicating with colleagues and stakeholders

3 make formal business agreements, including approvals, evaluating the need for specialist legal advice as required

4 foster and maintain business relationships with key stakeholders such as sponsors and suppliers, monitoring agreements and performance indicators.

INDUSTRY VIEWPOINT

When you plan to use a venue, you should start your negotiations early, at least six to nine months before the event. If you schedule the event for a quiet period, such as during holidays or weekends (for a business hotel), or during the low season, you will save thousands of dollars. This gives you opportunities for leverage in your negotiations for the function room, hotel rooms and other venues. Your leverage is enhanced by the size (number of people attending) and duration of the event. You can also negotiate services, upgrades, complimentary hotel rooms (at least one for every 50 rooms) and other value additions if you are booking in a low season. It is essential that you shop around as hotels are highly competitive when it comes to group bookings. However, be cautious about food and beverage, as this is the most important aspect for most people attending meetings, as savings here may lead to many complaints. For example, sandwiches for lunch will not meet the expectations of most conference attendees. When negotiating food and beverage, compare the price charged with the cost of taking your group to a nearby restaurant. Whatever the nature of the event that you are running, indoors or outdoors, shop around for value – that can involve anything from an extra day to set up or provision of support services.

Anon

INTRODUCTION

The most talented event managers are highly effective communicators. This is the basis for ongoing relationships with a wide range of stakeholders with whom legal relationships in the form of agreements or **contracts** are developed. This can include sponsors who have high expectations of the value they will gain from the sponsorship arrangement. A similar situation exists regarding the media if the event is being broadcast, as these rights are worth significant amounts of money – a lot is at stake for all parties with a live broadcast. There are a multitude of smaller arrangements with food and beverage suppliers, security organisations, fencing contractors and so on. All contracts need to be negotiated and formalised. Clear expectations on both sides and a willingness to work through problems as they arise will ensure that these relationships are successful. See Chapter 17 for more information on the legal aspects of contract formulation.

> Contracts
> Legal agreement concerning an independent contractor's labour or skills whereby payment is made on the basis of hourly or daily rates; or relating to an independent contractor achieving a result where payment is made on the basis of a fixed fee

Following the Commonwealth Games held in India, it was reported that several Australian firms including Ric Birch's Spectak Productions, and world-renowned fireworks group Howard & Sons, still had substantial parts of their $1 million plus contracts unpaid three months after the closing ceremony. Delhi Games organisers claimed that services were not up to the mark.

EXTENSION ACTIVITY

Source: Tabakoff, N. (2011). Aussies owed millions from Delhi Commonwealth Games. *Daily Telegraph*, 20 January. www.dailytelegraph.com.au/sport/aussies-owed-millions-from-delhi-commonwealth-games/news-story/eeca5bca78a62c351764f201e73b553e

Review this story and debate the following issue: 'A contract is not negotiable after the fact. Changing conditions and perceptions cannot be considered'. You might like to think about this statement in the context of smaller, local events.

BUILD BUSINESS RELATIONSHIPS

In many sectors of the event industry, the consumer or client is a large corporation, association, government body or artist promoter. People working in event management can be on either side of this negotiation (as client or supplier) or they may sit in the middle. For example, a professional conference organiser (PCO) manages the planning of an event with the client on one side and the hotel or conference centre on the other. Of course, the ultimate customer is the person attending the event.

The following general guidelines are provided to aid event managers who often need to enter into detailed discussion and negotiation with a client about aspects of an event: the event concept, the parameters of the event, or its feasibility. As the extract at the start of the chapter illustrates, the event organiser can often negotiate favourable accommodation rates and venue prices for events to be held in the off-peak season, if these discussions are held a considerable time before the event.

In preparing for a business negotiation, it is necessary to understand the goals and positions of both parties, as these goals are often contradictory. Price is a good example. If price is being negotiated for a conference, the client will require the best outcomes for the lowest price, while the event organiser (or PCO) will want the highest possible profit margin, particularly if working on commission. Ultimately, it is necessary for both parties to identify their bottom line so that the process of negotiation can continue. Chapter 8 will deal with budgeting, which informs this aspect of the negotiation.

It is also important to ensure that the appropriate people are conducting the negotiation. Ideally, the event organiser should negotiate with the owner or manager of the company, or a person in the organisation with delegated authority. The event organiser should likewise have the authority to close the deal when the correct price and other conditions, such as conference specifications, have been agreed.

Taking the widest scope of definition, suppliers to the event client can include:

- host countries and host cities (competitive forces often result in considerable **value in kind** provided by government agencies)
- conference and exhibition centres
- venues (e.g. sporting, cultural, unique).

The more usual suppliers of services include:

- party, conference and wedding planners
- audiovisual experts
- sound and lighting technicians
- tradespeople
- caterers.

Suppliers of goods include those supplying:

- merchandise

> **Value in kind (VIK)**
> Also known as 'contra', occurs when a sponsor provides goods/services in exchange for sponsorship rights. In similar situations involving government or community groups, contribution is also given a monetary value and shown in the budget

- food and beverage
- signage
- equipment.

The most successful event managers are capable negotiators whose dealings are tough but friendly. During a career in events, you are likely to encounter the same venue managers and suppliers, so these relationships are vitally important. Of course, word of mouth will enhance your profile as a cool, calm and delightful person to work with even in the most stressful of situations!

As has been illustrated in previous chapters, the event business is complex. This chapter raises the question: Who is the client? For example, a council could be the client or simply a stakeholder. However, unless the event is fully funded by the bodies on the left-hand side of Figure 7.1, they are referred to as stakeholders.

Food stalls are generally run by independent suppliers

FIGURE 7.1 Identifying stakeholders and suppliers

STAKEHOLDERS	SUPPLIERS
• Arts council • Regional tourism body • State tourism body • Major sponsors • Local council	• Hire company • Staffing agency • Catering organisation • Security company • Bus company

Clarification of the hierarchy of organisations involved in the event is absolutely essential. All parties carry a certain level of risk and responsibility. For legal and business reasons, it is essential to know who, or which organisation, sits at the top of the hierarchy – and takes the most risk. In some cases this is unclear, while in others there is a fairly clear delineation; for example, between venue management and the event producer when staging a concert at a stadium.

As the first chapter illustrated, many event associations have a code of ethics. Sample code of ethics for event managers:

- Conduct business ethically giving consideration to sustainability principles including social responsibility, environmental and economic sustainability.
- Support the industry as a whole in all forms of business conduct when dealing with stakeholders.
- Ensure that clients and customers are satisfied, negotiating fair and transparent contracts and delivering on promises or exceeding expectations.

- Comply with all relevant laws and regulations and ensure that subcontractors do the same.
- Conduct risk assessments and provide optimal levels of safety for workers, guests and the public.
- Support and encourage staff in their work and professional careers, abiding with EEO laws and other legal requirements such as minimum pay rates.
- Demonstrate sound financial governance.

Range of relationships

As previously indicated, the range of relationships that exist in the event environment is enormous. In some cases cash does not change hands, as would be the case with a sponsorship arrangement whereby the sponsor agrees to provide goods and services in exchange for sponsorship exposure. VIK (contra) arrangements are commonplace, including for many smaller community events. A school fete can involve many cooperative partners in a variety of ways; indeed, there could be a whole network of relationships.

A relationship with a charity is another example of an important arrangement. The charity is likely to have a range of requirements that need to be met, and it will need to be involved

| PCBU |
| Persons conducting a business or undertaking |

in all negotiations if the event in question is a fundraiser. Workplace health and safety uses the acronym **PCBU**, which refers to 'persons conducting a business or undertaking', and this is a useful term for non-commercial, community or fundraising events. A chart identifying relationships between stakeholders is therefore essential.

For legal and financial reasons, it is also important to know who is the principal in the contractual relationship: the person or business that engages a contractor. In the event business, the term *hirer* is also used to refer to this person or entity.

The network of relationships might include subcontractors. For example, a major event organisation might contract a large and well-established security company. This company might not be able to meet the demands of a huge crowd on a peak weekend and might reach agreement with another security organisation to meet the requirements. The question then is whether this second security firm has a contractual relationship with the first as a subcontractor, or deals directly with the event organisation.

Regardless of the potential network of subcontracting relationships, the principal contractor oversees risk management and safety for all aspects of the work, and they should develop a WHS plan with this in mind. Each of the PCBUs – the principal contractor, any subcontractors and the client – must consult, coordinate and cooperate with each other to ensure that risks to health and safety are managed. This is a duty shared between the parties and must be carried out prior to and during the work.

For events held in public places, the most important relationship involves the local council (see Figure 7.2 for an example of a council's application process flow chart). Many councils provide extensive planning information; indeed, there are links to the best of these guides throughout this text. These clearly illustrate the wide range of stakeholders that need to be consulted before an event is approved.

FIGURE 7.2 Council application process flow chart

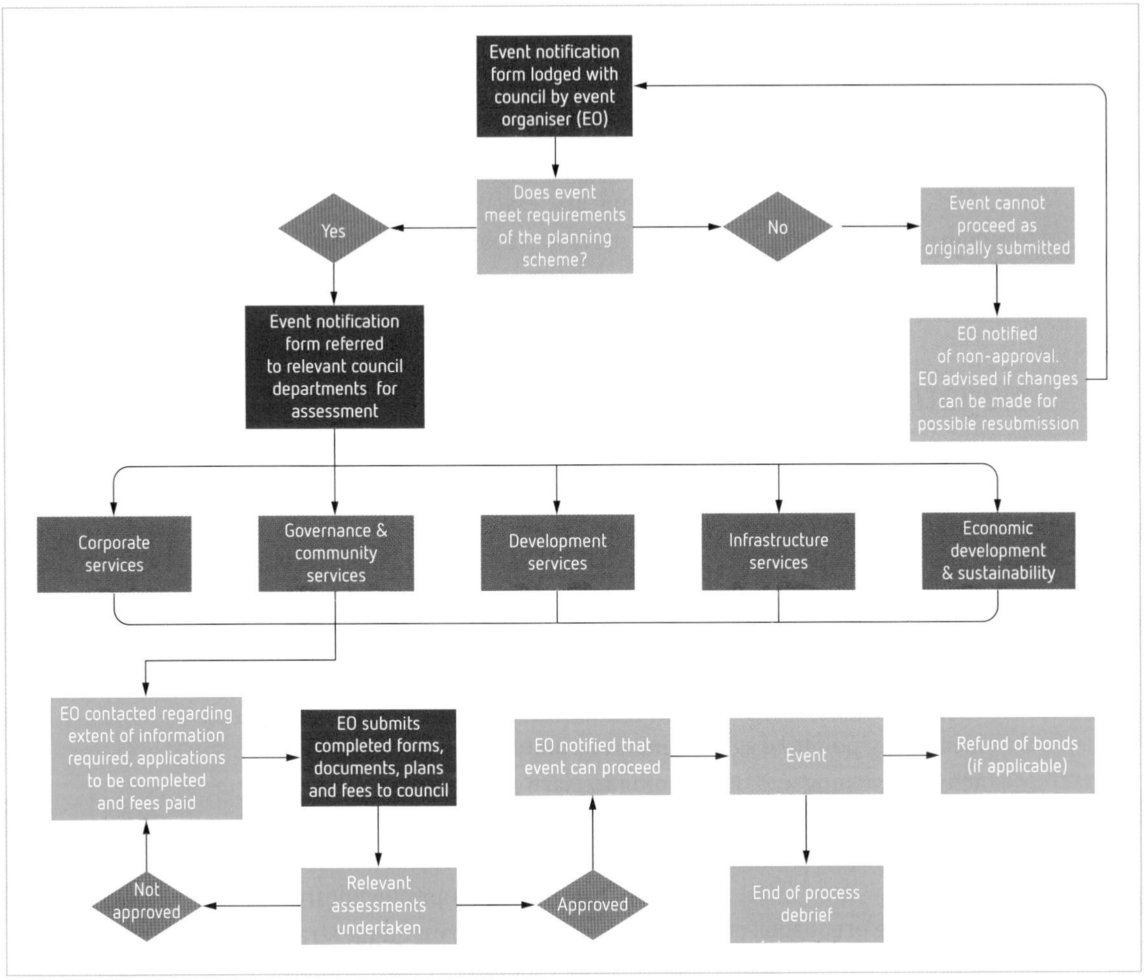

Source: Meander Valley Council (2011). Council application process flow chart.
www.meander.tas.gov.au / webdata / resources / files / Council_Application_Process_Flow_Chart_(Apr_2011).pdf

There are many opportunities to maintain business relationships informally. Regular contact with customers and suppliers can be maintained through:

* association membership
* cooperative promotions
* industry functions
* social occasions
* regular telephone contact
* social media.

In the next section, we will consider the skills, techniques and tactics of effective negotiation.

CONDUCT NEGOTIATIONS

There are professional and organisational protocols for negotiation, a key consideration being the level of authority held by the parties involved to close the deal. When in doubt, the input of your colleagues and careful reference to company policy is useful. You need to ask, 'What is the scope of my authority' and 'What is the scope of authority of the person I am dealing with?'

Active listening and questioning are essential negotiation skills, particularly when used in conjunction with one or more persuasive negotiation tactics. Active listening involves confirming and clarifying what a person has said by paraphrasing and checking assumptions.

Negotiation techniques

Before commencing the negotiation, it is useful to know the key issues and order the priorities. You need to know how far you can go before finalising the negotiation. Techniques for the negotiation itself may include:

- undertaking preparatory research of the facts of the business situation or parties to the agreement
- identifying the goals of the negotiation and limits to the discussion
- clarifying the needs of all parties, including third-party stakeholders such as suppliers and contractors
- identifying points of agreement and points of difference
- actively listening and questioning to clarify points of discussion
- using non-verbal communication techniques to reinforce messages
- using appropriate language, avoiding jargon, acronyms and colloquialisms
- using appropriate cultural behaviour
- adopting bargaining strategies, including attempts to achieve win-win outcomes
- developing options and alternatives using brainstorming
- confirming agreements verbally and in writing.

Where those involved in the negotiation exhibit a wide range of individual differences, particularly in language or culture, some strategies can help to develop effective communication. These include identifying the specific information needs of all participants in the negotiation, using plain English, developing subteams, using graphics, and providing all individuals with opportunities to participate.

Figure 7.3 outlines the five main steps in the negotiation process.

FIGURE 7.3 Stages in the negotiation process

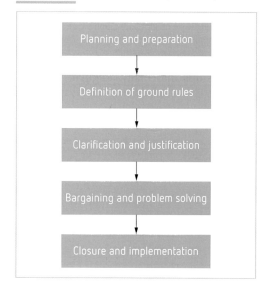

- Planning and preparation
- Definition of ground rules
- Clarification and justification
- Bargaining and problem solving
- Closure and implementation

Negotiation strategies

Many books have been written on the many different types of strategies that can be used, but here we will outline just a few of those strategies:

- *We will beat our competitors.* 'Name any price you have been given and we will beat it' is a common sales technique.
- *Try it out.* Once the customer or client has committed to trying a product (such as sampling the menu for a banquet), the deal is as good as done.
- *Take it or leave it.* Starting at a ridiculously high price, the aim is for the other party to feel that they have 'won' when the price is negotiated lower.
- *Pressed for time.* By creating pressure for a decision through an artificial deadline, 'by this date for this price', it is possible to force an early commitment.
- *Worn out.* Constant communication using different channels and reinforcing customer benefits can work in some situations.
- *Compromise.* The most common approach is to identify the extremes of, say, price and reach a mid-level compromise.

Each technique works in some negotiating situations and not in others. For the most part, a successful negotiation is one in which both parties strive for a win-win outcome (Kenworthy, 2010), with the aim of ensuring the long-term commitment of both parties to the business relationship.

Cultural sensitivity is also important. As mentioned earlier, different cultures approach bargaining and negotiation in different ways. In some cultures, the aim is to get straight to the point, while in others, relationship building is seen as more important than the specifics of the final agreement. Regardless, it is always best to negotiate face to face rather than over the telephone or via email.

Following agreement, the details should be confirmed in writing. Agreements then should be monitored over a period of time, since it is much more difficult to find new customers than it is to retain existing ones. Existing customers or clients with whom relationships have been developed should also be closely monitored to gauge their satisfaction level with the products or services supplied.

A study by Ogden and McCorriston (2007) of supplier management by conference venues in the UK highlights the benefits that can accrue from good supplier management within this sector:

> A survey of venue managers covering a cross-section of venue types was used. A significant proportion of venue managers report having long-term supplier relationships, placing considerable value on the non-financial benefits that can accrue from long-term supplier relations featuring mutual trust and good working relationships. These include consistency, responsiveness and flexibility in service delivery. Additionally, the familiarity of regular suppliers with the venue and its procedures can lead to seamless service delivery to the customer and free up venue managers' time.
>
> Source: Ogden, S., & McCorriston, E. (2007). How do supplier relationships contribute to success in conference and events management? *International Journal of Contemporary Hospitality Management*, 19(4), 319–27.

The results indicated that there were both financial and non-financial benefits to establishing and managing supplier relationships effectively.

MAKE FORMAL BUSINESS AGREEMENTS

While the scope of this text does not allow for a full explanation of contract law, the following summary may be useful. A **simple contract** is an agreement made between two or more parties, which is generally supported by a document expressing that agreement in writing but which can be made orally. A **formal contract** is a deed, or a contract under seal. Clearly, a dispute over an agreement that has been written up and signed is easier to resolve than a verbal contract. For a simple contract to be enforced, it must meet the following conditions:

> **Simple contract**
> Agreement made between two or more parties, generally supported by a document expressing that agreement in writing but which can be made orally
>
> **Formal contract**
> A deed, or a contract under seal
>
> **Consideration**
> For an agreement to be binding, something of value must change hands, usually money but could include goods or services

- The *offer* must be made with the intent to be binding; in other words, it must be a definite promise and not merely an inquiry. A court will not enforce an agreement if the material terms are vague or absent. In the case of hotel rate agreements, while it may not be possible to quote specific rates for the years to come, the offer should at least include a definite formula, or method, for setting rates for the future.
- There must be unqualified *acceptance* of the exact terms of the offer for an agreement to exist. Usually, this means both parties sign the agreement. There can be no additions or deletions unless these are agreed to and signed off by both parties.
- An *exchange of money* for goods and/or services is the normal transaction for a business agreement. **Consideration** is the payment for, or cost of, the performance promised in an offer. An example in the event industry would be a hotel's promise to deliver a function space, and a wedding organiser's promise to use that space and pay for its use.
- There must be an *intention to create a legal relationship*. In most business agreements this can be assumed. However, an agreement to buy drugs for distribution and sale at a nightclub would not be an intention to create a legal relationship in any sense!

At the higher levels of contract negotiation and exchange, such as for a major sponsorship agreement or a long-term lease on a venue, professional legal advice would be necessary for both parties. However, in most business negotiations carried out by an event manager, a letter of agreement is all that is necessary to formalise the terms of the negotiation.

A letter of agreement should stipulate the goods and/or services to be provided, the prices agreed, payment conditions, and in some instances delivery guarantees. Conditions regarding cancellation of bookings for rooms or food orders also need to be included in agreements with, for example, hotels and food suppliers, respectively. Note that all written agreements of this nature are contracts, even if they are referred to as 'letters of agreement' or 'confirmation letters'.

The agreement should contain certain information that is important for tax reasons because it establishes a business relationship (contract for service) as opposed to an employment relationship – particularly for service providers that work for the event company quite frequently, such as fitters, plumbers and electricians. This information includes:

- the names and ABNs (Australian Business Numbers) of both organisations
- a statement that it is a fee for service or a purchasing agreement

- the obligation by the service provider to use their own tools and equipment
- the obligation by the service provider to meet business legal requirements, including taxation, workers compensation insurance and public liability insurance
- payment for completed work (not hourly)
- control over work and delegation to staff where necessary (this may be implied).

As much as possible, the language of the letter of agreement should be simple, so that both parties are clear about their expectations. This allows the partners in the relationship to build trust and conduct their business in a professional manner. Variations to the contract should also be in writing.

Matthews (2015) suggests that the event details present in a contract should also include:

- venue details (time and location of event, specific room, times for bump-in and bump-out)
- specifics of the services and/or products to be provided (lighting, audio equipment, menus)
- specifics of additional services (change rooms, food and beverage for staff and suppliers)
- compliance with regulations and standards.

Where the standard or form contract is only one or two pages, it is too short to contain all the necessary information. But a rider or appendix that details all the services provided can be added as an attachment. For events, the phrase 'The devil is in the detail' is quite true – small things in plans, schemes and contracts that are overlooked can potentially cause serious problems later on.

The commercial negotiation of wedding catering is interesting in that there are expectations on the part of the whole wedding party, not just the client paying for the event. These expectations can change on a daily basis and, for this reason alone, both specifications and variations to the specifications need to be carefully documented. The provision of photographs of the floral arrangements, décor and menu items by the caterer can help to clarify the expectations of the wedding party and avoid conflict. Additionally, any exclusions need to be elaborated; in this case, the wedding planner might indicate that transportation arrangements are excluded.

Exclusions can be very important as they have the potential to blow out the scope of the arrangement and therefore the budget. Providing meals for sponsors or contractor employees is one example. Disclaimers and exclusion clauses are also used to limit liability. As you can see, professional legal advice may be necessary for effective contract negotiation.

Standard clauses of an event catering contract

As mentioned above, there are a number of clauses that are found in a typical contract or agreement. Those that typically appear in a catering contract are provided here as an example:

- *Parties to the contract.* These are the parties entering into the contract. Business names and ABNs should be specified. While the contract will list the parties involved, such as the two businesses, the caterer and the client, it may be useful to nominate who in these organisations has the authority to vary the terms of the contract.
- *Deadline and deposit (prepayment).* Each contract needs to include a start and completion date. Any deposit or prepayment should also be stipulated. A deposit or prepayment is generally required, as expenditure is usually incurred prior to provision of the service.

- *Specifications.* The inclusion of specifications and performance standards ensures that the parties have clear expectations of the service to be provided. In the case of a catering contract, a menu could be included as an appendix. The inclusion of food safety plans would illustrate the performance standard for food hygiene.
- *Attendance figure (number of guests).* In a catering contract, the number of guests must be specified and agreed to in advance to ensure that the appropriate amount of food and beverage supplies is ordered. In addition, a final date and time should be included for the finalisation of numbers. The customer will have to pay for that number regardless of attendance. This is vitally important, as business functions often experience a large number of last-minute cancellations or no-shows.
- *Beverage licence and arrangements.* The liquor licensing arrangements need to be clearly stated, as do the arrangements for meeting bar costs. Some customers meet bar costs until a certain time or amount is reached, after which guests pay for their beverages.
- *Other licences and permits.* It may be necessary to seek council approval for an outdoor event, and permits may be needed for some locations. The responsibility for lodging applications and payment must be made clear in the contract.
- *Services.* This section specifies the level of service to be provided, including the number of wait staff and bar staff.
- *Special requirements.* This clause covers special requirements such as disability access for guests.
- *Schedule of payments.* Payments are scheduled from the time of the deposit. In many cases, the full amount due for the catering is paid prior to the event.
- *Insurance.* The currency of public liability and workers compensation insurance needs to be specified.
- *Cancellation.* The terms of cancellation need to be specified.
- *Termination/non-performance.* The measures that need to be in place if the service provider cannot deliver on the contract as a result of illness, accident or other misadventure must be stipulated. This can prove particularly problematic if entertainment is part of the agreement, as the client may have to find another provider at a higher cost. Some contracts include penalties for non-performance.
- *Confidentiality.* The terms of a contract are generally confidential.
- *Arbitration.* Arrangements should be specified in the event that a dispute occurs.
- *Warranties.* Warranties are guarantees by the service provider (e.g. about the quality and suitability of equipment).
- *Signatories and date.*

A sample contract for venue hire is provided in Chapter 13. An Australian Government guide titled 'Contracts made simple' is also listed in the references at the end of the chapter.

> **Intellectual property**
> Intangible property such as copyright, designs, patents, trademarks and trade secrets

This includes more detailed information such as on ownership of intellectual property. For example, when employing a Web designer, are you careful not to provide images where others own the copyright (cutting and pasting from the Web), and do you have the code for the site in case this is needed in the future? If not, then you are bound to the designer for future changes to the site.

Benefits of written contracts

A written contract provides proof of what was agreed between the principal/hirer and the contractor, and helps to prevent misunderstandings from the outset. As a contractor, it is important for tax reasons to indicate your status as a contractor for services as opposed to taking on the role of an employee. For clarification of the differences between services contracts and employment contracts, visit any of the government websites listed at the end of the chapter, or that of the Australian Taxation Office.

Payments and timeframes, scope of work and deliverables need to be included in the contract, which should also specify how either party can end the contract before the work is completed if this is necessary, such as would be the case if the event was cancelled. Remember that when called to bid for an event, it may be advisable to provide an estimate as opposed to a quote in the early stages, when the scope of work is still unclear.

Inclusion of KPIs in contracts

Pearlman (2008) conducted research into key performance indicators (KPIs) for several international convention and visitor bureaus (CVBs). While it was difficult to find adequate comparative data, the study highlighted measures used within the industry, such as economic impacts, net square footage of convention space, occupancy of hotels and convention centres, and number of attendees. Clearly, these KPIs were relevant to those centres, while the KPIs given below apply to a specific contract between the exhibitors at an international IT exhibition to be held in Brisbane and a logistics company, and focus on how performance would be monitored and evaluated.

As the overseas exhibitors would need to send their state-of-the-art technology to the exhibition, along with cartons of marketing collateral (brochures, business cards, USBs and so on), this would need to be cleared by Customs (and in some cases quarantined), and it would have to be stored until the exhibition infrastructure was assembled and then delivered safely to the exhibition hall. In signing up with the logistics company to handle this part of the exhibition, the exhibitors (with your help) would need to develop KPIs, which would specify the service levels required for the following tasks:

- import documentation for exhibition equipment and displays
- international transportation
- loading and unloading
- Customs clearance
- local transportation
- warehousing
- delivery
- operation on-site.

Following the exhibition, the process would occur in reverse as the equipment would need to be packaged and sent back to the home country.

Contractors involved in an exhibition build

As the exhibition organiser, you would be the broker in the relationship between the company providing logistics support and the exhibitors, your clients. In negotiating performance standards with the logistics company, timelines would clearly feature at all stages. KPIs might specify:

- accuracy and reliability at all stages
- care in storage
- insurance for any damage incurred
- timelines for pick-up and delivery
- operational support during the exhibition
- troubleshooting.

KPIs are generally used in big business; for smaller events, the specifications are adequate. For example, wedding venues supply menus with photographs and in the best cases invite the bride and groom in for menu tasting. Clarity of expectations is the basis for good negotiations, whether they are for budget events or big corporate events.

Shutterstock.com / Antonio Truzzi

Photographs bring clarity to customer expectations

Provision for breach of contract

When negotiating contracts, it is essential to consider the possibility of cancellation of services at a critical time, and the financial and logistical ramifications of trying to find another contractor at short notice. A caterer not arriving on time to set up the kitchen and prepare the food would have disastrous consequences for an event. Such possibilities need to be covered by a clause for breach of contract, detailing the penalties for non-performance. Contingency planning for such a possibility should also form part of the risk analysis.

From a formal point of view, there are several ways to resolve a dispute, starting with negotiation, moving on to dispute resolution, and finally taking the matter to court. This can be costly and time consuming. Dispute resolution can involve a professional mediator to identify the issues in dispute, develop options, consider alternatives, and try to reach an agreement between the parties.

Conducting meetings

When planning meetings with clients and stakeholders, the style of meeting and the required level of formality will vary according to the meeting's purpose, the occasion, nature of the participants, and organisational procedures. In the author's experience, the best format is the *standing meeting*, which only lasts long enough for attendees' legs to get tired. This is a popular approach in the event business.

An agenda that reflects the purpose of the meeting should be prepared in advance, after asking participants for agenda items. This should be distributed well before the meeting in case the preparation of documents or other material is necessary prior to the meeting.

The chairperson should follow organisational procedures and meeting protocols. The primary task of the chairperson is to keep the meeting on track. Open and constructive communication should be encouraged. In order to avoid an aimless discussion, participants should be encouraged to present information and ideas clearly and concisely so that agreement can be reached on the meeting's goals and the required actions can be documented.

Minutes of meetings should be prepared, including unresolved issues and actions for which people should be assigned responsibility (see Figure 7.4).

FIGURE 7.4 Differences between positive and negative meetings

	SUBSTANCE OF THE MEETING	RELATIONSHIPS IN THE MEETING
NEGATIVE	• Lack of agenda • Lack of focus • Background information missing • Lack of action items • Lack of minutes	• Angry • Impatient • Distrustful • Time wasting
POSITIVE	• Clear agenda • Agreement on price, terms, conditions, etc. • Operational schedule agreement • Action outcomes • Minutes of meeting	• Listening • Finding common ground • Participation by all parties • Taking responsibility for outcomes

FOSTER AND MAINTAIN BUSINESS RELATIONSHIPS

Ethical behaviour is of supreme importance in maintaining business relationships. The code of conduct below is for a person whose primary role is that of procurer, but it could equally be used by anyone in the event industry:

- Conduct yourself at all times with objectivity, honesty and integrity.
- Act in accordance with laws and regulations.
- Perform your duties with care and diligence.
- Respond to stakeholders equitably, courteously and in a timely manner.
- Maintain confidentiality.
- Avoid conflicts of interest.
- Do not take advantage of your position in order to seek or obtain benefit (including gifts or other financial benefit) for yourself or for any other party.

Event planners should select suppliers on merit alone, and commissions or inducements from suppliers should be disclosed. Debate this point.

Ongoing communication with clients and customers is an informal way to gauge the success of these relationships. This can be done by telephone, email or face to face. More formal methods of monitoring client satisfaction and performance standards involve structured qualitative and quantitative research. Evaluation can be done only when the event concept has been clearly defined and its feasibility tested. Following this, more detailed plans can be developed involving negotiation with clients and stakeholders. Once KPIs have been agreed, these can be used as the basis for evaluating the services provided during the process of event planning and implementation. When the event is over, an evaluation report is written by the event organiser for the major clients, such as business partners or sponsors, thus fulfilling its role in closing the management cycle – beginning with planning and finishing with evaluation of both process and production regarding the event.

Communication is the key

Building industry relationships is essential for any event business. This not only applies to a single project but is an ongoing process that leads to a solid reputation in the industry. Conflicts stemming from poor business relationships can arise from such things as overdue payments on invoices, which will make a supplier less likely to come on board for the next event. Another issue for concessions such as food trucks and food stands is when the event organiser overestimates the size of the audience. This means that the supplier loses money.

Communication is the foundation for successful event implementation, starting with the project initiation phase and finishing long after the event. Effective early communication is needed to get approval to go ahead in the first place, and this should be based on sound project planning. During the execution phase, the successful implementation of the contracts negotiated with suppliers will depend on how clearly expectations were communicated. The media plays a role in determining the event's profile and success, and sound relationships built up with this sector will be rewarded.

A plethora of planning documents and contracts are the result of all this communication. These documents will be invaluable if something does go wrong. When it comes to investigations into accidents and fatalities occurring at events, hopefully, the relevant documents will show that 'duty of care' was exhibited, and that negotiations with business partners were conducted towards this end.

Summary

In this chapter we have covered the skills and knowledge required to establish, manage and maintain business relationships with customers and suppliers. In any business relationship there will always be issues that require negotiation, and guidelines for conducting successful negotiations have been provided. Considerable attention has also been given to the preparation of written contracts which formally document the outcomes of negotiations between client and supplier on such aspects as price, delivery and quality. Contracts are essential for ensuring that both parties are legally protected. Finally, we have discussed several key attributes of well-run, productive meetings, and have reiterated the importance of effective communication in business relationships.

Key terms

Consideration	For an agreement to be binding, something of value must change hands, usually money but could include goods or services
Contracts	Legal agreement concerning an independent contractor's labour or skills whereby payment is made on the basis of hourly or daily rates; or relating to an independent contractor achieving a result where payment is made on the basis of a fixed fee
Formal contract	A deed, or a contract under seal
Intellectual property	Intangible property such as copyright, designs, patents, trademarks and trade secrets
PCBU	Persons conducting a business or undertaking
Simple contract	Agreement made between two or more parties, generally supported by a document expressing that agreement in writing but which can be made orally
Value in kind (VIK)	Also known as 'contra', occurs when a sponsor provides goods/services in exchange for sponsorship rights. In similar situations involving government or community groups, contribution is also given a monetary value and shown in the budget

REVIEW YOUR KNOWLEDGE

1   Explain the term 'stakeholder' using an example.
2   Explain the term 'supplier' using an example.
3   What are the core elements of a contract? List and explain each of them.
4   Provide guidelines for effective negotiation.
5   In a meeting there are task elements (substance) and relationship elements. Explain how these work together for effective meetings.
6   Explain, using examples, why specifications or KPIs are useful in clarifying expectations in business relations.

APPLY YOUR KNOWLEDGE

A spate of 'no shows' by headline performers and personalities over the past few years serves as a harsh reminder for promoters that they must take active steps to try to reduce this risk.

The risk of a headline performer or personality being a 'no show' needs to be considered in the context of how performance contracts are drafted when engaging such artists. The payment terms in the contract are often rigid with the promoter commonly being required to pay a substantial up-front deposit to the performer. In fact it is not unusual for the full performance fee to have been paid by the promoter well before the performance dates.

Tip: Promoters should ensure that any up-front payments paid to the artist are instead paid to the artist's agent who should be required to hold the sum in an escrow account. The performance fee should only be able to be released to the artist pending the proper performance of the contract by the artist.

In circumstances where the promoter has paid a significant fee to a headline performer or personality who does not perform as required, the promoter will be left having to comply with all of its contractual obligations with regard to the event – including making payments due to third parties (such as venues) and in some cases having to refund to consumers the ticket price for the performance.

Source: TressCox Lawyers (2017). Promoters at risk of no shows by headline performers or personalities. www.tresscox.com.au/page/our-news/newsletter/promoters-at-risk-of-no-shows-by-headline-performers-or-personalities

Visit the website for TressCox Lawyers (**www.tresscox.com.au**) and investigate three live-performance contracts online in order to extend your list of 'top 10 tips' for event organisers employing bands and musicians. If you are more interested in event catering or weddings, you could investigate those areas instead.

CASE STUDY

As the newly appointed Film Festival coordinator, you will have the opportunity to screen 20 10-minute films developed by graduates of your State's high-profile Film and Television School. This event has attracted an enthusiastic audience in the past, achieved media attention, and launched some young artists into stellar careers.

TASK

Using a diagram, illustrate two different ways in which the event could be structured: one where the Film and Television School is the main client and the other where the major client is a sponsor. In addition, show on the diagram the other stakeholders involved and their relationships with one another.

Online resources

Visit **http://login.cengagebrain.com** and search for this book to access the study tools that come with your textbook.

References

Australian Government (2016). Independent contractors – contracts made simple. **www.business.gov.au/info/plan-and-start/start-your-business/independent-contractors**

Kenworthy, A. (2010). Service-learning and negotiation: An educational 'win-win'. *Journal of Management Education*, 34(1), 62–87.

Matthews, D. (2015). *Special Event Production: The Resources* (2nd edn). London: Routledge.

Ogden, S., & McCorriston, E. (2007). How do supplier relationships contribute to success in conference and events management? *International Journal of Contemporary Hospitality Management*, 19(4), 319–27.

Pearlman, D. (2008). Key performance indicators of the MICE industry and the top 25 United States and Canadian CVBs. *Journal of Convention and Event Tourism*, 9(2), 95–118.

Websites

Business planning (Australian Government), **www.business.gov.au/info/plan-and-start/templates-and-tools**

Independent contractors (Australian Government), **www.business.gov.au/info/plan-and-start/start-your-business/independent-contractors**

Government grant finder, **www.business.gov.au/assistance**

Managing suppliers (Victorian Government), **www.business.vic.gov.au/money-profit-and-accounting/managing-suppliers/how-to-negotiate-payment-terms-with-suppliers**

8 MANAGE FINANCES WITHIN A BUDGET

OVERVIEW

In this chapter, the emphasis is on understanding the existing budget, controlling expenditure and managing variations. This chapter therefore introduces budgetary management where others may have developed the budget — the preparation of completely new budgets is covered in Chapter 21. A budget is a plan or forecast, and for many managers the challenge is to stay within budget in order to realise the organisation's objectives. The preparation of financial and statistical reports is also a requirement at this level.

LEARNING OBJECTIVES

On completion of this chapter, you will be able to:

1 allocate resources (mainly financial) according to the budget and agreed priorities, maintaining accurate records of income and expenditure

2 monitor financial activities against the budget and report deviations from targets

3 identify and evaluate options for improved budget performance, including new approaches and new suppliers, and present recommendations to colleagues

4 complete financial and statistical reports to inform decision making.

INDUSTRY VIEWPOINT

The founder of Tropfest – the world's largest short film festival – has taken to crowdfunding to keep the Australian event alive. John Polson has launched a Pozible campaign, seeking to raise $100000 to prop up the festival moving into the future by finding a 'sustainable business model'.

The festival – which at its peak attracted almost 200000 to Sydney's Centennial Park – was cancelled one month out from its December event, due to what Mr Polson labelled a 'terrible mismanagement of funds'.

Source: Megan Mackander (2016). Tropfest turns to crowdfunding to keep world's largest short film festival alive. ABC News, 31 January. www.abc.net.au/news/2016-01-31/tropfest-turns-to-crowdfunding-to-keep-film-festival-alive/7127834

INTRODUCTION

Tropfest is a short film festival which began in Australia in 1993 as a screening for 200 people. It has since become the largest short film festival in the world, expanding to locations such as London, Bangkok and Abu Dhabi. The Sydney event was cancelled in 2015 due to financial difficulties following a dispute with the management company over a financial shortfall. However, a new sponsor was found and the festival went ahead a few months later. The festival is now being run by a non-profit company with a new board. Its founder, John Polson, believes the rebuilt festival will be run as a huge community event, with its new Parramatta venue expected to attract 70000 people (Maddox, 2016). This episode in the history of a demonstrably sustainable event shows the importance of effective financial management, including a realistic budget and careful monitoring of the cash flow situation.

WHAT IS BUDGETING?

A budget is a forecast, an estimate of income and expenditure, in monetary or quantitative terms. A budget translates management policies and goals into measurable outcomes. Strategic plans outline the long-term goals of an organisation and provide direction. Various other plans stem from the strategic plan, but it is the budget that breathes life into the strategic plan. Budgets give a sense of tangibility to a strategic direction. They allocate limited resources to achieve optimum results in quantifiable terms.

All plans cost money, either directly or indirectly, while the ultimate goal of a business is to make a profit. Even in not-for-profit organisations, costs need to be recovered in order to remain in operation. The process of planning, allocating resources and identifying measurable outcomes is called *budgeting*.

Event budgeting requires a good understanding of the events industry and the various sectors within it, as well as of external factors which impact upon the event business, such as economic conditions, future trends, competition and cost structures. Budgets allow for the monitoring of deviations, as mentioned above, and for management to initiate corrective action if necessary. This involves variance analysis of both actual results and forecasted figures and will be discussed in more detail later in this chapter.

Budgets provide organised estimates of revenue, expenditure, staffing levels and equipment needs. They can be used as a communication tool by management to express long- and short-term objectives, and to ensure responsibility and accountability. Budgets can also serve as a means of control.

Computerisation has also facilitated quick updates and communication with stakeholders, making budgets these days living documents. Budget revision may not be necessary if funds are allocated in accordance with the strategic plan and stakeholders are involved in the decision-making process. However, unforeseen circumstances, both internal and external, such as organisational restructuring, a change in management structure, the introduction of new legislation, a change in economic conditions, significant price movement for certain items or a shift in market trends, may cause management to have to review their budgets. In project work, budgets need to be revised if the scope of the project changes. In event budgeting, factors such as venue availability, last-minute changes to the event theme or cancellations by event speakers or performers can greatly affect the cost structure. Budgets will only work if controls are in place and formulated with careful consideration.

Information sources for budget preparation may include performance data from previous periods; financial proposals from key stakeholders; financial information from suppliers, particularly pricing; customer and supplier research; competitor research; industry trends; planned local events or issues which may have an impact on the budget; management policies and procedures; enterprise budget preparation guidelines; declared commitments in given areas of operation; and grant funding guidelines or limitations.

In summary, budgeting:

* allows for the evaluation of business decisions
* sets targets in quantifiable terms
* provides benchmarks
* is a good means of communication
* serves as a summary sheet for a large amount of information
* allows for controls and checks at various intervals
* ensures the accountability of managers and departments.

EXTENSION ACTIVITY

Discuss the following statement in terms of your knowledge of matters personal and business: 'A budget is a plan that reminds you that you can't afford to do what you would like to do'.

A simple budget for a party is shown in Figure 8.1. All of these items could be broken down into more detail, such as decoration, which could include flowers, lighting, chair covers and so on. This budget does not include furnishings, table settings, the stage, dance floor, cutlery or crockery. The assumption is that these are provided by the venue. Another assumption is that there is no need for an event planner, with this role undertaken free of charge by a family member. The only staff are agency food servers and a barperson. As the cost of the venue is so high, you could consider a venue that is not set up for an event, which would be much cheaper; however, then there are many things that would need to be obtained from a party hire company. The other alternative is a 'package cost', including venue and catering, from a dedicated event venue such as a club or hotel. This clearly demonstrates the importance of checking assumptions and alternatives.

FIGURE 8.1 Party budget

ITEM	COST	PERCENTAGE OF TOTAL COST
Venue	$2500	23%
Entertainment	$600	6%
Staffing	$800	8%
Catering and beverages	$5000	47%
Décor	$650	6%
Photography	$900	8%
Invitations	$210	2%
Total	**$10660**	**100%**

Budgeting techniques

Three budgeting techniques – zero-based budgeting, rolling budgets and activity-based budgeting – are discussed below. Each has positive and negative attributes. In terms of the nature of the event industry, some budgets are for one-off events, while others are for annual events. In other instances, an event company will run many events of different types during the financial year, and in this respect the organisation looks more like a traditional business that trades all year.

The various types of budgets include the following. The key ones will be discussed here in detail, with more information to follow in Chapter 21.

- cash budgets
- cash flow budgets
- departmental budgets
- event budgets
- project budgets
- purchasing budgets
- sales budgets
- wage budgets
- whole of organisation budgets.

Zero-based budgeting

As the name suggests, zero-based budgeting (ZBB) is a technique that sets all budgets to zero at the beginning of the year or period. Every function within an event organisation is analysed regarding its needs and costs, and money is allocated based on the merit of their requests. All functional areas (or departments, as they are described in a traditional business), such as marketing, human resources and security, compete for funds. So while it might be assumed that an event largely staffed by volunteers does not need a big budget, this is only partially true.

Volunteer programs still need to be funded for such things as uniforms, meals and recognition strategies. Brisbane City Council suggests that a value be put on volunteering, and it advocates the amount agreed on by Volunteering Australia and State volunteer centres: $28.99 per hour.

With respect to cost increases, zero-based budgets can help management rein in the entitlement mentality and make budget discussions more meaningful and realistic during review. In addition, ZBB focuses on a comprehensive analysis of objectives and needs, and therefore planning and budgeting are combined into a single process. This requires managers to evaluate the cost-effectiveness of their operations in detail.

The negative aspects of ZBB include increased costs in budget preparation due to the additional staff time required, which can lead to fewer resources being available for other aspects of event management that are equally or more important.

Rolling budgets

Annual budgets typically forecast income and expenditure for 12 months. They remain unchanged and serve as a static financial measure. Rolling budgets, by contrast, provide updated and adjusted figures. Quarterly or monthly updates are prepared according to current financials based on actual performance. Rolling budgets are often used to forecast one to two years in advance; an 18-month period is a typical timeframe for a rolling budget. The regular updating of budgets can be very time consuming but has the benefit of enabling a business to have current, up-to-date budgetary figures on hand and to take action more quickly to allow for changing economic conditions. This is advantageous for an event company that runs an ongoing operation such as annual exhibitions in several major cities. Long-term analysis and forecasting will help this business to make effective plans for its future. Bidding for events well into the future, up to five years ahead, requires a great deal of analysis and predictive ability.

Activity-based budgeting

Revenue
Sales revenues reflect income from sales of goods or services

As the name suggests, this is budgeting based on levels of activity rather than on cost elements. An activity-based budget incorporates a set of **revenue** and expense projections at various sales volumes. It shows how costs vary with different rates of output or at different levels of sales volume. With activity-based budgeting (ABB), the costs for each function of an organisation are established and relationships are defined between activities. This forms the basis for resource allocation. Information is then used to decide on the resources that should be allocated to each activity.

This approach is useful for major events such as the Melbourne Festival, which includes a number of paid and unpaid events across the program. Using an activity-based budget, the success of each of these events (dance, circus, music, theatre) can be monitored and evaluated. Ideally, an activity-based budget is reliant on historical data and ticket sales projections.

ALLOCATE BUDGET RESOURCES

In a large organisation, various functional areas/departments put in bids for budget resources. These bids are prioritised and resources are allocated by the senior executive team in the organisation based on its business and marketing plans. Each department will receive an allocation. Communication and consultation within the operational management team is vital at this stage. Changes in income and expenditure priorities since the initial discussions and planning stage need to be communicated to all sectional managers. The final approved allocation figures and the relevant account codes are important to the sectional managers as they need to draw against the relevant account codes for expenditure. Communication also increases the awareness of constraints on expenditure, which may have resulted in necessary controls. Indeed, detailed records of resource allocation according to the organisation's control systems are necessary for audit purposes and accountability. If the actual numbers delivered through the financial year turn out to be close to the budget, this will demonstrate that the company understands its business and has been successfully driving it in the planned direction. On the other hand, if the actuals vary greatly from the budget, this sends an 'out of control' signal. It highlights to management that the business is not moving towards the goals set out in the strategic plan and that investigation and possible corrective action is needed.

According to Kerrie Nash, who is arguably the most experienced HR professional in the world of mega events:

> Workforce is the biggest item of discretionary spend in any organizing committee, so clearly that's going to be a prime area of focus. Whenever we have to try and find money, which is all the time, HR never stops recalculating and re-versioning and rethinking the HR plan to make sure that across the business it's coming in within budget. We work very, very closely with finance to make that a reality and to get the right systems and processes and information in place to be able to do that. Recruitment needs to be handled very, very carefully.

> Source: Van der Wagen, L. (2015). *Human Resource Management for the Event Industry.*
> London: Routledge. p. 163.

This is true for all large-scale events. When the organising committee develops and implements grandiose plans that become unaffordable in the early stages, the event faces immense budget pressure at the worst possible time – just before the event goes live. This impacts on all areas.

Types of budgets

Budgets are financial management plans with two distinct features – they cover phases of operations and phases of time. They may be classified into different types based on their purpose or their time period.

In the event industry, the following budgets based on purpose are commonly found.

Capital budget

A capital budget relates to items requiring capital expenditure and often requires the allocation of substantial funds to projects. The measurable outcome is the timely installation of the asset or system within the budget. Staging and technology are two big-ticket capital budget items. Capital expenses such as these can be avoided by hiring equipment and outsourcing services, which is commonplace in the industry.

Operating budget

An operating budget relates to items of **income** and expenditure appearing on the operating statement. For an event company, the primary source of income would

> **Income**
> Generally in the form of sales but can also include sponsorships, donations and commissions

Expenses
Money spent or costs incurred in an organisation's efforts to generate revenue, representing the cost of doing business

be from corporate client fees. For festivals, income is most likely to include ticket sales. There may also be ancillary sources of income such as grants, sponsorship, donations, interest received, rent received and commission received. Items of expenditure as a result of ongoing activity represent the cost of goods sold, labour and overheads. The operating budget contains profit projections based on projected income and **expenses**.

Departmental budget

A functional area/departmental budget relates to the revenue and expenses for a given period of time, usually one year. It also projects departmental profit. The departmental budget of a banquet department, for example, would identify expenses such as cost of food, cost of beverages, food and beverage staff costs, cost of menus, beverage and wine lists, cleaning supplies, replacement crockery and laundry. The department head is responsible for the departmental budget, providing input into its preparation and working with the department team to achieve the targeted profit levels. Departmental budgets are prepared in larger-event establishments where there are several revenue-earning departments. Departmental budgets assist in responsibility accounting – a reporting structure whereby departmental heads are given feedback on the performance of their responsibility centres by the finance manager. For example, catering and banquet managers would be given regular updates on financial performance and this would be shared with the team during regular meetings.

For an event business running multiple events during a calendar year, it may be preferable to prepare a budget using event projects (activities) as the basis for the forecast. This makes it easier to adapt if events are changed (in terms of attendance numbers or pax) or cancelled. Figure 8.2 is a simple forecast based on events booked, including only income and expenses directly related to those events (and not general overheads).

FIGURE 8.2 Activity-based budget function packages

	WEDDING	GALA AWARDS DINNER	CONFERENCE
Attendees	300 pax	300 pax	120 pax
Income (sales)	$19 800	$24 000	$5400
Expense (direct)	$10 890	$15 600	$3638

Cash budget

A cash budget is a projection of cash flow in a business. Neither the income statement nor the balance sheet shows the flow of funds. The cash budget relates to the sources of funds and the application of funds on a monthly basis. The closing bank balance of one month is the opening balance of the next month. The opening bank balance plus all cash receipts indicates the cash available to the business at the end of each month. Payments are made from the cash available, and most businesses have a policy of maintaining a certain level of cash at the bank.

A cash budget is applicable to any business, small or large. Poor cash flow is, in fact, one of the main contributors to the high rate of failure of small businesses. Businesses may be profitable on paper, but without a healthy cash flow, they cannot operate efficiently. And it is not uncommon to find growing businesses with sound profits encountering liquidity problems.

Cash flow is necessary for timely payments and for putting plans into action, and cash budgets provide management with valuable information on the availability of cash. This enables them to make decisions on, for example, debt collection and credit terms with suppliers. Such budgets also enable management to identify alternative uses for surplus funds, to look for the cause of a cash deficit (such as slow ticket sales), to seek new ways of generating funds through different business activities, and to organise overdraft facilities to assist the business through deficit periods. Often, managers in the event industry focus on operations and overlook money management, which can be extremely detrimental to their businesses. Cash flow issues are a common form of event failure. A critical factor to the survival of any business is the ability to generate cash and to manage cash resources so as to meet the objectives of the business and service its debt.

A cash budget template is provided in Figure 8.3. As is clear from this, the cash budget is a working document. When compared with the actual figures, it provides objective data to management for decision making. It is similar to what happens on a personal level: we all watch our bank balance, looking at the money coming in and the money going out in the form of various payments, leaving us with a surplus or deficit!

FIGURE 8.3 Example of a cash budget template

PARTY CENTRAL EVENTS CASH BUDGET			
	JANUARY	FEBRUARY	MARCH
Opening bank balance			
Receipts			
Cash sales			
Cash receipts from accounts receivable			
Other			
Total receipts			
Cash available (opening bank balance plus total receipts)			
Payments			
Payments to creditors			
Salaries and wages			
Interest payments			
Operating expenses			
Loan repayments			
Total payments			
Surplus/deficit closing balance (cash available minus total payments)			

Master budget

The master budget is prepared for the entire organisation for a one-year period and relates to items which appear on the above four budgets. It is a comprehensive budget covering all activities of the organisation. It comprises a budgeted operating statement for the ensuing year and a budgeted balance sheet as at the end of the year. The master budget is prepared by the finance department of large event organisations. It involves collating information relating to the various departments of the operation and provides the general manager and the executive team with a holistic view of the entire operation, as well as with the tools for management decision making.

Budgets based on forecasted periods

Different event organisations have different approaches to monitoring financial activities; for example, in terms of the budgets they deem necessary. A freelance event coordinator is likely to have monthly and annual budgets, but they are unlikely to have a long-term strategic budget for a five-year period.

Budgets can be based on forecasted periods as follows:

- A *long-term budget* is a strategic plan. It ranges from three to five years. Because it contains long-term future projections, it needs to be revised and updated annually so that its projections remain realistic. It provides the business with a planning tool for the future. Budgeted income statements and balance sheets and capital budgets can be prepared for the long term, but usually they are set out in annual terms within the long term.
- An *annual budget* is an operational plan. It is a forecast for a one-year period. Any long-term budget can be prepared as an annual budget, but this term is predominantly used for budgeted operating statements. Each component of the budgeted operating statement, such as the sales forecast, payroll budget, administration budget, marketing budget, stationery budget, maintenance budget, or even a departmental budget, is known as a *mini-budget*.
- A *monthly budget* is a performance plan. Incentives for staff may be attached to this type of budget. Monthly budgets are commonly used for departmental sales, departmental profits, departmental payroll and departmental income statements. Because of its monthly timeframe, it provides short-term targets towards which staff can work, making corrective action or change possible with little delay.

Prepare budget information

Following marketing and pricing decisions, the budget can be developed and discussed to reach agreement on the planned targets.

The budgeting process is a cyclic process which involves:

1 assessing market and economic conditions and the strategic plan of the business
2 establishing attainable goals in light of market and economic conditions and the business plan
3 allocating resources to reflect enterprise policy
4 planning to achieve the established goals
5 setting standards, or benchmarks, in quantifiable terms and communicating these to all stakeholders
6 comparing actual performance with budgeted targets and investigating deviations

7   implementing corrective action, if necessary, and communicating this information to all stakeholders

8   revisiting the budgeting process for continuous improvement.

In a large business with several revenue-earning events, the formulation of an operating budget requires input from all departmental heads/functional area managers on forecasted revenue and related expenses. Sales projections need to take into account anticipated trends, competition, market conditions, economic activity, pricing policy, government policy and historical sales data. The sales budget is the preliminary budget, as the cost of goods and other operating costs are related to sales. After input from line managers, the master budget and the operating budget can be prepared by the accounting and finance division (or the accountant in a smaller establishment).

Preparation of the sales revenue forecast is the first step in formulating an operating budget, a departmental budget and a master budget. Costs are expressed as a percentage of sales in accordance with industry standards, or benchmarks. Projected costs deducted from forecasted sales revenue give profit projections. A departmental budget for banquets and catering is illustrated in Figure 8.4. At a later date, actual figures would be entered in order to monitor deviations.

FIGURE 8.4 Simplified budget showing income (sales) and expenses

BANQUET AND CATERING DEPARTMENTS BUDGET					
	FORECAST			PERCENTAGE	
Sales	$989 235			100%	
Department expenses					
Food and beverage	$105 911			20%	
Labour including on-costs	$286 213			53%	
Other overheads					
Cleaning	$16 523			3%	
Linen	$33 589			6%	
Laundry	$33 568			6%	
Uniforms	$18 589			3%	
Other	$44 590			8%	
Departmental profit	$450 252			46%	

Other factors which affect sales forecasts are seasonal demands and other fluctuations, the impact of promotions and advertising, the guest mix (for example, corporate functions, weddings, meetings – and what they spend), public holiday variance and local competition.

Operating budgets relate to the whole organisation and departmental budgets relate to individual departments, in this case the banquet and catering department. Budgets can be produced electronically using accounting software: the actuals are plotted against the forecasts and it is the variance analysis that gives true meaning to the budget.

Figure 8.5 illustrates the type and number of functions held by the banquet department, the largest source of revenue being corporate meetings.

FIGURE 8.5 Banquet department sales revenues

FUNCTIONS	FORECAST NUMBER	FORECAST REVENUE
Weddings	85	$2 975 000
Corporate meetings	360	$3 204 000
Awards nights	18	$504 000
Private parties	80	$768 000
Other	150	$235 350
Total	693	$7 686 350

Awards nights generate better revenues than most other events

MONITOR FINANCIAL ACTIVITIES AGAINST BUDGET

Financial record keeping is the key to monitoring financial activities. Financial records are necessary for the business so that cash flow can be managed, and in simple terms it is essential to know how the business is performing. Financial records are also required for legal reasons. Records should explain all transactions – be they electronic or in writing – and kept for five years.

The following records assist with the monitoring of financial activities:

- income and sales records (e.g. ticket sales, grants)
- expense and purchase records (e.g. venue hire, equipment)
- bank records (deposits, statements, summaries)
- tax records (business activity statements)
- end-of-year records (creditors who owe you money, debtors who you owe money to).

Every transaction should have a record, such as cash receipts and cash payment records.

For most department managers and small business managers, it is essential to keep on top of record keeping, reconciling and producing monthly reports. All of this can be done using simple accounting software. Often, a management committee is responsible for ensuring that accurate and complete financial records are kept. These can include a cash book, receipt book, bank statements, and asset register. This enables everyone in the organisation to understand its budget status in relation to targets.

Benchmarks are a valuable way in which to monitor finances for an event project. Qian and Simmons (2014) have undertaken a long-term study which reveals that most events have very small budgets. This shows, if anything, how important it is to carefully manage finances.

> More than 50 percent of the responding festivals had budgets below $24 999. Meanwhile, more than 20 percent had a budget of $50 000 or more. The most frequently reported festival/event income range was $50 000 or more, and the least frequently reported were $5000–$9999 and $25 000–$49 999. Income sources for the majority of festivals and events included sponsors (66 percent) and vendor fees (59 percent). Close to 30 percent of the responding festivals and events had 10 or fewer sponsors, while 10 percent had more than 30 sponsors. The most frequently identified sponsor type was private businesses (39 percent), followed by non-profit organizations (32 percent). Festivals and events were more likely to charge vendors of food, art, and alcoholic beverage a flat fee.

> Source: Qian, X., & Simmons, P. (2014). Minnesota festivals and events: Comparisons between 1989 and 2013, p. v. University of Minnesota Tourism Center. https://conservancy.umn.edu/handle/11299/167691

Unlike the hospitality industry where there are key ratios of income to expense and a limited range of income sources and major expense items, the event industry provides greater challenges given its diverse nature. It is most unusual to see long-term research such as the above, ranging across the years 1989 to 2013. Most importantly, the research showed that income sources for the majority of events included sponsors and vendor fees. Additionally, festivals and events were more likely to charge food and beverage vendors a flat fee rather than using a percentage of gross sales. The most frequently reported festival income was US$50 000 or more.

FIGURE 8.6 Festival and event total budget in 2013 ($n = 156$) compared with 1989 ($n = 84$)

TOTAL BUDGET (US$)	YEAR OF INQUIRY	
	1989	**2013**
Less than $1000	8%	13%
$1000–$9999	35%	27%
$10 000 – $49 999	33%	34%
$50 000 or more	5%	22%
Not sure	18%	3%

Source: Qian, X., & Simmons, P. (2014). Minnesota festivals and events: Comparisons between 1989 and 2013. University of Minnesota Tourism Center. p. 17. https://conservancy.umn.edu/handle/11299/167691

IDENTIFY AND EVALUATE OPTIONS FOR IMPROVED BUDGET PERFORMANCE

As we now know, a budget is a forecast, and the aim is to predict financial outcomes for an organisation. Actual performance is compared against budget forecasts and this needs to be monitored on an ongoing basis. Deviations in financial performance are analysed in detail, which is known as *variance analysis*. Variance is the difference between planned and actual performance.

Variance analysis can be used for both revenue and expenditure variance. Revenue variance may relate to price or volume, or both. Expenditure variance may relate to price, volume, efficiency, or a combination of volume and price. Variance analysis can best be explained by expanding on the earlier banquet department example. As shown in Figure 8.7, actual revenues for the period were lower than expected: a variance of 16 per cent below budget. The only event type that exceeded expectations was private parties, but these made up only a small proportion of sales. With a high average spend, a sales focus on weddings (average spend US$35 000) and awards nights (average spend US$28 000) would more likely produce better outcomes. Ten more weddings and five more awards nights would reduce the variance to 9 per cent, a much more acceptable figure.

FIGURE 8.7 Variance analysis revenues

FUNCTIONS	FORECAST NUMBER	FORECAST REVENUE	PERCEN-TAGE	ACTUAL REVENUE	PERCEN-TAGE	VARIANCE	PERCEN-TAGE
Weddings	85	$2 975 000	39%	$2 150 000	33%	−$825 000	−28%
Corporate meetings	360	$3 204 000	42%	$2 690 000	41%	−$514 000	−16%
Awards nights	18	$504 000	7%	$450 000	7%	−$54 000	−11%
Private parties	80	$768 000	10%	$989 000	15%	$221 000	29%
Other	150	$235 350	3%	$210 350	3%	−$25 000	−11%
Total	693	$7 686 350	100%	$6 489 350	100%	−$1 197 000	−16%

Involvement of staff at the planning stage will promote ownership of the budget and commitment to it by staff. In the previous example, the rationale for increased effort by the catering sales team targeting specific event types is illustrated. The second focus is on cost of sales. If expenses can be reduced, this too will improve the bottom line. Frontline staff can contribute to savings in many ways, such as making sure that cutlery doesn't end up in the bin, and that linen is not washed unnecessarily.

Budgets need to be realistic to make them work. Actual data should be measured against budgeted data as soon as possible to check for variance and to initiate timely corrective action. This corrective action may involve the introduction of time-saving methods and improved systems, the use of computerised systems, or staff training and development. Budget cuts and cost cuts should be made to enhance efficiency, rather than being done at the cost of customer service.

As a budget is a plan for allocating finite resources to obtain optimum results, funding should be allocated in accordance with a company's strategic business plan and business priorities, and this should be communicated to all relevant employees. Needless to say, the importance of budgetary control cannot be stressed enough. Appropriate records and systems should be in place to make budgets work. Though budgeting is a financial function, communication is the key to its success. All stakeholders should be involved in the planning process, and the financial goals and targets should be communicated to staff, as they are instrumental in making goals a reality

Comparisons with previous years and time periods are useful. Budget variance can be kept to a minimum except when external or other unavoidable factors cause change. For example, the threat of a terrorist attack would have a direct impact on the travel industry and, in turn, on event operations, resulting in a significant change to the projected figures. In such situations, management would need to review the forecasted budget and make it more realistic and achievable.

Rectifying budget variance

Below are a number of tips for rectifying budget variance. A drop in actual sales could be rectified by any one of the following actions or a combination of them. Areas to investigate would also depend on the nature and size of the business. Regarding an event business, the following are recommended:

- Check if the forecast was realistic in the first instance.
- Review sales and marketing.
- Revisit pricing strategies.
- Look at competition.
- Assess cashier controls.
- Audit record keeping.
- Introduce innovative ideas to boost sales.
- Review quality standards.
- Look out for adverse publicity.

In your household, how do you exceed your budget? Name five things that you could do to reduce expenses.

If you were running a birthday party and found that you had exceeded the budget by 10 per cent, how could you save money in the area of food and beverages?

EXTENSION ACTIVITY

If the actual cost of goods were more than the budget, the areas to investigate would be as follows:

- purchasing (specifications, alternative suppliers, tendering process)
- portion sizes and standard recipes
- receipt, storage and issuing of stock
- security of storeroom and stock
- wastage in preparation
- deterioration of food and storage conditions
- quality and condition of equipment
- need for further training.

If labour costs were too high when compared with the budget, it would be necessary to consider:

- a change in efficiency and productivity
- a mix of casual and full-time staff
- pay-rate fluctuations
- the rostering and optimum usage of staff

- the motivation levels of staff
- absenteeism and staff turnover
- the need for training
- the multiskilling of staff
- health and safety in the workplace.
    If there were a deficit in the cash budget, management would need to evaluate:
- the mix of cash and credit sales
- credit terms from suppliers
- the debt collection period
- strategies to increase cash sales
- the timeframe for servicing of debt
- overdraft arrangements with the company's financial institution
- inventory levels and stock tied up, especially wine and liquor
- capital expenditure timelines.

A financial spreadsheet

As seen above, budgets are a planning and diagnostic tool but they do not provide practical corrective action measures. It is the responsibility of the event manager to use this tool to manage the business effectively.

COMPLETE FINANCIAL AND STATISTICAL REPORTS

Besides standard budgets, event management needs to prepare other reports of a financial and statistical nature stemming from the budgets. Actual results can be reported against forecasts in the following reports:

- daily, weekly and monthly transactions and reports
- income and expenses breakdown by department/functional area
- sales performance
- yield management.

Yield management

Yield management is also known as revenue management, as it is a system designed to maximise revenue. Yield management originated in the travel industry, which adopted the system after airfares were deregulated in 1978, prior to which discounted fares were uncommon. The event industry has followed the travel industry's lead. Like seats on planes, stadium seats have a limited shelf life. As these products are perishable, it is prudent to sell unsold seats at a lower price rather than lose the revenue altogether. So in order to maximise profits, seating is priced at different levels depending on anticipated demand. If the game is a sellout, most tickets would sell at a higher price than would be the case for a local game where many seats are left empty. Differential ticket pricing is thus an approach aimed at maximising yield. The same concept applies to the functions department – quotes will vary depending on seasonal demand, March and November being the peak period for weddings.

Financial record keeping

Some small event businesses are extremely lax about record keeping; for example, paying for a food stall in cash, paying staff in cash, or not recording or banking cash received. A legitimate business is required to maintain all the appropriate financial records and to report activity (transactions) to the tax office. As a result, the following records need to be kept.

Income/sales records

This means all income, whether it's cash, EFTPOS or electronic banking. Records of cash sales could be cash register summaries/printouts or deposit slips. Income would be recorded in bank statements as credits.

Expense or purchase records

This refers to all business expenses, including outgoing cash expenditure. Receipts should be kept even for small items. Other amounts would be recorded in bank records as debits.

Bank records

Bank records apply to deposits, bank statements and credit card statements. All business transactions, debits and credits should be evident on bank records.

GST

If registered for the Goods and Services Tax (GST), all tax invoices from suppliers are necessary for preparing the Business Activity Statement (BAS).

Employee and contractor records

For employees, tax file numbers, the wages paid, tax withheld, superannuation paid, fringe benefits provided need to be recorded. For contractors, it is invoices and payments with an ABN, and contract details.

Records can be kept on paper or electronically. Accounting software is useful for this purpose, as it will automatically calculate amounts and produce reports such as the cash balance. In addition, it will produce invoices and summary reports for GST and tax purposes. These days, accounting records can be cloud-based, so that employees can work from any location or device. MYOB (Mind Your Own Business) is one of the software packages most used by small businesses.

Discuss the pros and cons of paper versus accounting software for an event stall holder. The following website is useful in completing this exercise: **www.bit.com.au/Review/344651,7-accounting-packages-for-australian-small-businesses-compared-including-myob-quickbooks-online-reckon-xero.aspx**

EXTENSION ACTIVITY

Budgetary tips for managers

Monitoring and control should be ongoing so that problems can be rectified without too much financial damage to the business. With small businesses, owners should have an understanding of finance as they do not have the luxury of a financial controller. It is of paramount importance that all event managers can interpret financial information and plan and monitor budgets.

The need for long-term planning and the heavy capital investment required in event businesses necessitates budgeting at both the operational and strategic levels. Budgets start managers thinking and get them more involved in the business operation. They can be a source of motivation and are certainly a good basis for communication. By setting goals or standards for revenue, costs and cash flow, which are directly linked to operations, budgets become instrumental in quality management.

Could the great philosopher Aristotle have been talking about budgets and control with the following words, even before budgeting had been formalised by accountants and finance managers?

1   First, have a definite, clear, practical ideal: a goal, an objective.
2   Second, have the necessary means to achieve your ends: wisdom, money, materials and methods.
3   Third, adjust all your means to that end.
    Finally, here are the golden rules of managing finances within a budget:
1   Monitor actual income and expenditure against budgets at regular intervals and communicate results to staff.
2   Follow process guidelines and include financial commitments in all documentation. This is required for monitoring and auditing, and will also assist in the accurate presentation of final results.
3   Identify and report deviations to senior management according to organisation policy and the significance of the deviation.
4   Conduct variance analysis on a regular basis as deemed necessary by the organisation.
5   Analyse the reasons for variance, take corrective action, and monitor its effectiveness.
6   Communicate budget status in terms of timeframes to the management team through financial and statistical reports.

EXTENSION ACTIVITY

When it comes to fundraising events, the costs for speakers, entertainment, the venue and catering can mean that very little is left over for the charity concerned. This is definitely the case for formal dinners. How would you go about raising money for a charity where the ratio of income to expense is higher and the charity receives a better donation?

Summary

In this chapter, the budgeting process and various types of budgets have been outlined, together with various factors involved in the preparation and monitoring of budgets, with special reference to the event industry. Examples have been used to explain some of the practical tools for managing finances within a budget, such as variance analysis. Overall, this chapter has looked at the functional use of budgets as a management tool in planning, monitoring and controlling the finances of a business.

Key terms

Expenses   Money spent or costs incurred in an organisation's efforts to generate revenue, representing the cost of doing business

Income   Generally in the form of sales but can also include sponsorships, donations and commissions

Revenue   Sales revenues reflect income from sales of goods or services

REVIEW YOUR KNOWLEDGE

1   What is a budget?
2   What are the different types of budgets?
3   Why are budgets important for a business?
4   What are some of the important factors you would consider before allocating budget resources?
5   Preparing a budget is as important as controlling a budget. Why?
6   How would you monitor and review financial activities against a budget in a medium-to-large event establishment?
7   Can you identify a minimum of three options for improved budget performance?
8   Is it possible to make a profit even if you have a deficit balance in your cash budget? Give reasons for your answer.

APPLY YOUR KNOWLEDGE

Using the following budget, and actual figures, calculate the variances for each item. Suggest ways in which profitability can be improved in relation to managing expenses.

BANQUET AND CATERING DEPARTMENT BUDGET					
	FORECAST	PERCENTAGE	ACTUAL	PERCENTAGE	VARIANCE
Sales income	$989 235	100%	$900 236		
DEPARTMENT EXPENSES					
Food and beverage	$105 911	21%	$99 562		
Labour, including on-costs	$286 213	53%	$303 000		

BANQUET AND CATERING DEPARTMENT BUDGET (CONTINUED)					
	FORECAST	PERCENTAGE	ACTUAL	PERCENTAGE	VARIANCE
OTHER OVERHEADS					
Cleaning	$16 523	3%	$15 000		
Linen	$33 589	6%	$26 300		
Laundry	$33 568	6%	$48 236		
Uniforms	$18 589	3%	$20 156		
Other	$44 590	8%	$41 302		
Departmental profit	$450 252		$346 680		

CASE STUDY

1   Given the following budget, decide on the best approach to managing festival income if sponsorship dropped by 30 per cent. You must explain your rationale.
2   Review the festival expenditure, adding any items that may be necessary for an outdoor event, including food and beverage stalls.
3   Review the whole budget and rationalise your changes.

FESTIVAL INCOME	DESCRIPTION	AMOUNT
Admission	16 000 people	$23 588.76
Merchandise	T-shirts	$300
Other (give details e.g. Raffles, donations etc.)	Raffles, bar, sideshow alley. Donation: Browns road butchers	$6 655
Other Contributions		
Sponsorships	Coca-Cola, Junior Leagues Club, Private individuals	$27 000
State government funding	Valuing diversity grant	$10 000
Recipient contribution (In-kind)	Wages, staffing & preparation costs at $35.00 per person	$1 400
Community contribution (In-kind)	Stall rent and QLD Times 1 page ad	$12 000
Brisbane City Council	**Grant/Sponsorship**	**$16 000**
Other Brisbane City Council Funding	Lord Mayor's Suburban Initiative Fund (Parkinson Ward)	$5 000
Other Commonwealth funds	Festivals Australia Grant	$10 000
Other income not specified above (give details)		–
Total income		$111 943.76

Source: Brisbane City Council (2017). Festival Funding program budget tips.

FESTIVAL EXPENDITURE	COSTS TO BE PAID FOR BY BCC GRANT	COSTS TO BE PAID FOR BY RECIPIENT
ARTIST COSTS		
Artist fees	$16 000	$11 235
Travel allowance (Local only) e.g. Taxis	–	$150
Accommodation	–	$750
Transport equipment (Local only) e.g. Road transport, fuel, insurance	–	$250
PRODUCTION COSTS		
Venue hire	–	$15 000
Event permits, road closures, security	–	$2 000
Costumes	–	$400
Light and sound, staging	–	$17 000
Other (e.g. catering)	–	$5 000
FESTIVAL ADMINISTRATION		
Project coordination	–	$8 000
Other (e.g. marquee & furniture, materials)	–	$10 500
MARKETING COSTS		
Brochures	–	$450
Posters	–	$300
Advertising/Marketing	–	$2 500
Total expenditure	**$16 000**	**$77 535**

Source: Brisbane City Council (2017). Festival Funding program budget tips.

Online resources

CENGAGE
brain.com

Visit http://login.cengagebrain.com and search for this book to access the study tools that come with your textbook.

References

Maddox, G. (2016). Tropfest's John Polson rebuilds the short film festival as it should have been. *Wingham Chronicle*, 6 November. www.winghamchronicle.com.au/story/4274138/tropfests-john-polson-rebuilds-the-short-film-festival-as-it-should-have-been/?cs_36

Qian, X., & Simmons, P. (2014). Minnesota festivals and events: Comparisons between 1989 and 2013. University of Minnesota Tourism Center. https://conservancy.umn.edu/handle/11299/167691

Van der Wagen, L. (2015). *Human Resource Management for the Event Industry*. London: Routledge.

Websites

Accounting and finance for event planners, https://youtu.be/J-XU75_IByY

Edinburgh Festival Fringe sample budget, www.edfringe.com/participants/planning-your-show/sample-budgets

Event planning guides:

https://publications.qld.gov.au/is/dataset/olgr-publications/resource/83339b0f-bd15-4d4a-847b-6784f15603fb

www.geelongaustralia.com.au/events/planning/eventplanning/article/item/8cdc2778104484a.aspx

www.melbourne.vic.gov.au/SiteCollectionDocuments/melbourne-event-planning-guide.pdf

https://parks.dpaw.wa.gov.au/sites/default/files/downloads/know/resource-for-events-in-wa-october-2012.pdf

PART 4

ON-SITE OPERATIONS

9

IDENTIFY HAZARDS, ASSESS AND CONTROL SAFETY RISKS

OVERVIEW

Health and safety are serious concerns, particularly for outdoor events and music festivals. Everyone working at an event venue needs to be watchful and concerned. While event organisers and stakeholders are responsible for formal risk assessments, these plans cannot be fully implemented unless everyone at every level communicates effectively. This chapter will stress the importance of identifying hazards, assessing safety risks, reporting incidents, and eliminating or controlling any risk. Frontline staff, including volunteers, need to know when to escalate a problem.

LEARNING OBJECTIVES

On completion of this chapter, you will be able to:

1 identify actual and foreseeable hazards that have the potential to harm the health and safety of workers or anyone else in the workplace

2 assess the safety risk associated with a hazard using systematic methods of risk assessment according to organisational procedures

3 eliminate or control the risks where possible, reporting or escalating the issue where necessary.

INDUSTRY VIEWPOINT

I think workplace health and safety is given too little consideration, especially for volunteers. Firstly, it is a new and unfamiliar environment and we are seldom told how to respond to accidents and emergencies. I am trained in first aid and I have worked as a life guard but I have no idea how to respond to a medical emergency such as a drug overdose.

Secondly I think there are situations when you act before thinking about safety. In the heat of the moment I have found myself doing things I would not normally do at the office, lifting stacked chairs for example. Finally, I have often worked at locations such as at race water stations, parking lots and entry gates without a radio and often without mobile reception. A particular concern of mine is leaving a shift in the early hours of the morning when it is dark, there is limited public transport and there are a few people wandering about who have had far too much to drink. Despite all this I love volunteering.

Event Volunteer

INTRODUCTION

In the management of music events, careful analysis of crowd behaviour and the procedures proposed for monitoring and managing emergencies needs to take place. This is often done with the assistance of specialists in this area of security, safety and first aid. *Crowd management* encompasses the steps taken to organise and manage crowds, while *crowd control* is the term used for dealing with crowds that are out of control. Security staff and security organisations play a major role in crowd control, particularly in the case of sporting events.

The likely behaviour of event visitors is a consideration in analysing the level of potential risk at a particular event. It should form part of the analysis that begins with the risk management policy and follow through to the contingency plans for safety and security (discussed in Chapter 18). The safety of the event audience, staff and subcontractors should be of paramount concern for every event manager, since all events carry safety risks which may result in anything from accidents to the evacuation of a venue.

Event worksites present numerous safety risks to workers

Another issue for consideration for most events is that of queuing. Queuing can be managed very well or very badly. The delays experienced while getting into events such as, for example, a football grand final are sometimes so long that the event manager has to direct staff to stop taking tickets and simply open the gates. Clearly this can lead to problems inside the venue if non-ticketed people manage to find their way in. On the other hand, if the grand final has commenced, and a goal is scored while the spectators remain outside, there is little else that can be done. However, this would not be a viable option if there was a large number of people without tickets outside the venue and a crowd crush was a possibility.

Investigate the following disasters at mass gatherings and identify the major cause of each:
· football match at Ellis Park, Johannesburg, South Africa on 11 April 2001
· football match at Hillsborough Stadium, Sheffield, UK on 15 April 1989
· Hajj pilgrimage at Mecca, Saudi Arabia on 25 September 2015
· Love Parade at Duisburg, Germany on 24 July 2010.

Orderly management of spectators leaving a venue is just as important, with clear directions and signage necessary to guide them to public transport. Sometimes revellers enjoy themselves so much at an event that they have to be marched out by security staff.

In this chapter we will deal with workplace health and safety; general security issues; hazard identification, assessment and control; and the effective communication of incidents.

WORKPLACE HEALTH AND SAFETY

Workplace health and safety (WHS) legislation aims to prevent accidents and injury in the work environment and is of particular relevance to the event organiser. The duties of employers, people in control of workplaces, and the suppliers of equipment and services are all described in the relevant State or Territory legislation. Since all follow the same model, in essence the laws are similar.

First, the person conducting a business or undertaking (PCBU) is the main duty holder under the relevant work health and safety act. They are usually the employer and may be a partnership, company, unincorporated body or association, a sole trader, a government department or statutory authority.

The WHS laws require organisations that employ any paid workers to ensure, so far as is reasonably practicable, the physical and mental health and safety of all of their workers, including volunteers. This means that volunteers are treated the same as all other workers.

Duty of care
Legal obligation of a person or organisation to avoid acts or omissions that could foreseeably harm others

Role of employers

Employers and business owners (PCBU) must, so far as is practicable, provide and maintain a working environment where their employees are not exposed to hazards. This means that they must show a **duty of care**, and this is covered in detail by WHS legislation.

General duties include the provision of:

- safe systems of work, such as the correct equipment for working at heights or transporting heavy items
- information, instruction, training and supervision
- consultation and cooperation
- personal protection such as high-visibility vests
- a safe plant and substances
- the reporting of fatalities, injuries and disease.

The basic aspects of WHS legislation focus on identification of hazards such as vehicles moving through crowds or stages collapsing in storms. This involves the assessment of risk and consultation with those involved. WHS committees play a formal role in the management of safety risk. An incident reporting system for hazards, accidents and injuries is needed and training is required to ensure that everyone on the work site is 'on-side' as far as health and safety is concerned. This will be elaborated on later in this chapter.

Role of employees and volunteers

The current WHS legislation has been expanded to cover volunteers, so a PCBU can be a voluntary organisation. Workers and volunteers are protected by the same laws and have the same responsibilities as employees.

The organisation must make sure that workers and volunteers understand their responsibilities, which Safe Work Australia summarises as follows. The organisation must:

- take reasonable care for their own health and safety
- take reasonable care to ensure they don't affect the health and safety of others
- carry out tasks in a safe way
- follow the reasonable work health and safety instructions given
- co-operate with the reasonable policies and procedures of the organisation that relate to work health and safety.

Essentially, what is reasonable care would be what a reasonable person would do in the circumstances considering things like their role, their knowledge, their skills, the resources available and the consequences to health and safety of a failure to act in the circumstances.

Ways of making sure that employees take reasonable care include:

- carrying out activities within the role they have been assigned
- not carrying out activities that they do not have the skills to undertake
- not doing anything that would seem to be unsafe.

Returning to the current legislation, it requires that all employers must take out workers' compensation insurance. This covers all staff for work-related accident or injury, including their medical expenses and payment for time off work and rehabilitation. The most important element of this legislation is the *responsibility placed on supervisors and managers* for ensuring that employees have a *safe place of work and safe systems of work*.

Policies and procedures in relation to safety are essential, and these procedures need to be part of all employee training. Standing on a wheeled trolley or on a box in high heels, as illustrated in the photos here, are unnecessary WHS risks. Small ladders would solve these problems, but staff are often in a hurry and cannot go searching for safer options. It is also better to go the long way round than to take short cuts on sites that provide limited access.

Provision of stepladders to these employees would have prevented this risky behaviour

Role of security companies

Laws exist in relation to security companies and security personnel. The industry is well regulated and an event company must ensure that the appropriate licences are secured. A master licence is held by the security company, and there are various classes of licence for officers, depending on training and experience. All security officers are required to undergo a criminal record check.

The roles of security officers include:

* acting as a bodyguard, bouncer or crowd controller
* patrolling or protecting premises
* installing and maintaining security equipment
* providing advice on security equipment and procedures
* training staff in security procedures.

Security companies must hold appropriate general liability insurance cover. General liability insurance cover is, in fact, a requirement of all contracts between event organisers and subcontractors. Subcontractors, including security companies, also need to cover their staff for work-related health and safety incidents.

Security is generally required for premises, equipment, cash and other valuables, but the predominant role of most event security staff is to ensure that the correct people have access to specific areas, and to act responsibly in case of accident or emergency. Accreditation badges allow security and other staff to monitor access effectively. Security staff are also responsible for removing people who are behaving inappropriately, sometimes in cooperation with the police.

There are several considerations in the organisation of security for an event. First, it is necessary to calculate the number of trained staff required for the security role. Second, if the venue covers a large area, vehicles and equipment will most likely be required. (Four-wheeled buggies are usually used to deploy security and other staff to outlying areas.) And third, the level of threat needs to be determined to ascertain whether firearms are needed, as would be the case when transporting money is involved.

In all cases, security staff should be appropriately licensed and the security company should carry the appropriate insurance.

Role of police

The police often provide some of the required support for event safety, generally at no cost to community events. However, with the growth of the event industry and the increased demands on police for spectator control, charges are now being levied by some police services for every officer attending a profit-making event. The role of the police is to uphold the law. Their role is thus different to that of security.

Mounted police are sometimes on duty at large street festivals and processions

IDENTIFY HAZARDS

Before looking at hazards in detail, it is important to have an overview of the risk management process.

The Australian and New Zealand standard for risk management (ISO 31000) simplifies the process of systems development and is a useful resource for supervisors and managers in the event industry – **risk management** is covered in detail on Chapter 18. Risk management plans for event safety can also be required from contract organisations working on-site.

> **Risk management** Involves forecasting and evaluating risks in order to minimise their impact

The risk assessment process

Risk management involves a five-step process:

1. Establish the context.
2. Identify the risk.
3. Analyse the risk.
4. Evaluate the risk.
5. Treat the risk.

Context for risk
Depending on the nature of the event, indoor or outdoor, a different context is presented, with specific risks; the weather, for example, can change the risk context very quickly

This process allows the manager or supervisor to establish and prioritise the risks, to take steps to prevent problems occurring, and to make contingency plans if problems do occur. The **context for risk** in this case involves WHS in the event environment. The focus of this chapter is on identifying hazards, as opposed to the more general business risks faced by an organisation, such as a cash flow problem, which will be covered in Chapter 18 in far more detail.

Crowd management is a specialised area illustrated by Figure 9.1, in which Aldo Raineri (2013) highlights the various factors that contribute to crowd safety risk for a mass gathering held in a rural area, using the Tamworth Music Festival

FIGURE 9.1 Assessment of crowd safety at outdoor music festivals

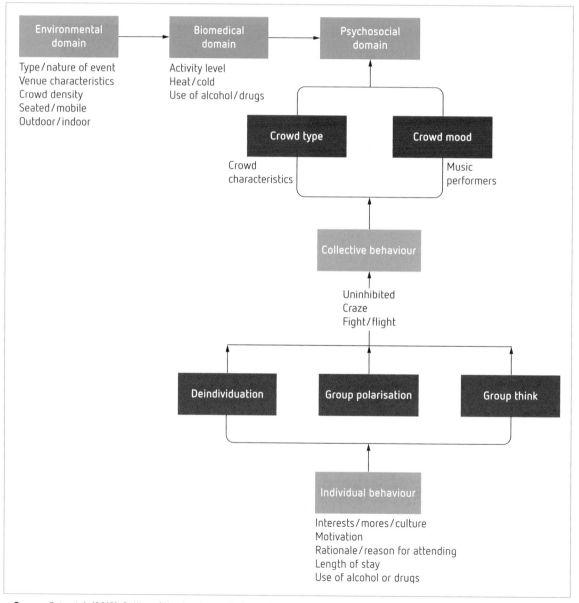

Source: Raineri, A. (2013). Outline of the development of a model to facilitate the assessment of crowd safety at outdoor music festivals. Presentation, Safety Institute of Australia Safety in Action, June. http://hdl.cqu.edu.au/10018/1044847

as an example. While this specialty is beyond the scope of this chapter, it clearly illustrates the context for risk, such as crowd type and mood, and some of the highest risks – one of them, in this situation, is drug and alcohol use.

Identifying a risk or **hazard** involves ascertaining when and how a problem might occur. Hazards representing potential risk include:

> **Hazard**
> Anything that has the potential to harm people

- fire hazards, such as an emergency exit blocked by staging equipment
- plant and equipment hazards, such as removal of safety guards
- hazardous substances, such as cleaning chemicals
- electrical equipment, such as exposed temporary wires or overloaded supply
- spills; e.g. oils on slippery kitchen floors causing falls
- stacking of unbalanced heavy items
- moving vehicles, such as buggies moving through a crowd
- hold-ups; e.g. when event takings are carried in a backpack
- threats to visitor/spectator safety caused, for example, by crowd crush
- threats to staff safety; e.g. departure in the early hours of the morning.

Brainstorming by the event management team helps to identify potential risks and hazards.

People often confuse hazards, risks and outcomes. When documenting hazards, risks and outcomes in a register, the facilitator should attempt to define the three separately. For example, a leaking gas cylinder is a hazard, the risk is potential explosion, and the outcomes could be burns or other injuries.

Temporary structures and ladders present a safety risk

Safety involves everyone

All employees, contractors and volunteers should be involved in WHS hazard identification. Generally, training is done by conducting site induction or briefing sessions with anyone working at the site, from managers to cleaners. WHS committee members play an important formal role, including inspections.

All of the following people may be involved in the assessment of risk:

- managers and supervisors
- WHS committee members
- WHS representatives
- peers and colleagues
- staff under supervision
- suppliers
- contractors
- volunteers.

There are many ways to identify hazards, both formal and informal. Observation and awareness are among the most important approaches of all, since the event environment is dynamic, evolving through processes of bump-in, show and bump-out. Hazards can emerge over a very short period compared with a conventional business. Checklists are an extremely useful tool, potentially expanded to a full audit of plans and reports. Consultation involving management, supervisors, employees and volunteers can be done via briefings, meetings, surveys or suggestion boxes. One of the most valuable approaches is to ensure that all incidents and accidents are reported, even in the case of a 'near miss', so that the hazard can be avoided in future. Therefore, ongoing observation and monitoring is the key to effective identification of workplace hazards and risks.

ASSESS THE SAFETY RISK ASSOCIATED WITH HAZARDS

Once potential hazards have been identified, the risks associated with them and the consequences of these risks need to be evaluated. This process allows the management team to prioritise the issues for attention. It is a good idea to set up a committee to manage risk, safety and security issues, and to establish operational guidelines for hazards that pose risk. The following questions need to be asked:

* What is the likelihood of this happening?
* What are the potential consequences?
* Who will be exposed to the risk/hazard?
* What impact has this risk/hazard had in similar circumstances?
* How will people react to this risk/hazard?

With hazards that might pose a risk to health and safety, the following three classifications are recommended:

* *Class A hazard* – This has the potential to cause death, serious injury, permanent disability or illness.
* *Class B hazard* – This has the potential to cause illness or time off work.
* *Class C hazard* – The resulting injury or illness will require first aid.

While this example refers mainly to incidents causing injury or illness, the potential consequences of fire, bomb threats, hold-ups, electrical failure and so on can be evaluated in the same way.

Likelihood

Assessing risk involves considering the likelihood of something happening – Table 9.1 illustrates the use of measures of likelihood. During a marathon, it is very likely that someone is going to experience heat exhaustion and therefore we use the rating of 'almost certain'. Clearly this is something we have to be prepared for. The next level is 'likely', followed by 'possible'. Other situations can be 'unlikely' and not expected, or 'rare', in which case it could happen but probably never will. This is not to say that we ignore any risks which are rare, such as lightning strike, since the consequences of this happening are potentially fatal. This is why we turn to the next scale, which rates consequence.

TABLE 9.1 Qualitative measures of likelihood of an incident occurring

LEVEL	DESCRIPTOR	EXAMPLE
A	Almost certain	Is expected to occur in most circumstances
B	Likely	Will probably occur in most circumstances
C	Possible	Might occur at some time
D	Unlikely	Could occur at some time
E	Rare	May occur, but only in exceptional circumstances

Source: Based on Standards Australia (2004). *Risk Management Guidelines: Companion to AS/NZS 4360:2004*. Table 6.4.

Consequence

Levels of consequence range from insignificant to catastrophic. It is highly likely that almost everyone running in a marathon will get blisters, but the consequence is 'insignificant' or 'minor' from a medical point of view. By contrast, if a runner has a heart attack, the consequences are 'major', requiring immediate treatment and hospitalisation. 'Catastrophic' is the descriptor used for potential fatalities and these have occurred at several events, resulting in coronial inquiries. The Kimberley Marathon fire that burned runners, including Turia Pitt, is one such example. This was a rare occurrence with near-fatal consequences. Overdoses and contaminated drugs can lead to multiple fatalities, and have done so several times recently. When a risk or hazard is assessed as minor, major or catastrophic, measures need to be taken to deal with the risk (reduction or treatment), no matter how unlikely it is to occur.

Table 9.2 illustrates the use of measures of consequence.

TABLE 9.2 Qualitative measures of consequence or impact of an incident

LEVEL	DESCRIPTOR	EXAMPLE
1	Insignificant	No injuries, low financial loss
2	Minor	First aid treatment, on-site release, immediately contained, medium financial loss
3	Moderate	Medical treatment required, on-site release, contained with outside assistance, high financial loss
4	Major	Extensive injuries, cancellation, major financial loss
5	Catastrophic	Death, coronial inquiry, reputation damage, potential bankruptcy

Source: Based on Standards Australia (2004). *Risk Management Guidelines: Companion to AS/NZS 4360:2004*. Table 6.3.

Risk register and ranking

Having analysed the safety risks, the headings shown in Figure 9.2 and Figure 9.3 can be used for the risk register and risk ranking in terms of 'extreme', 'high', 'medium' and 'low'.

FIGURE 9.2 Risk register

FIGURE 9.3 Risk analysis

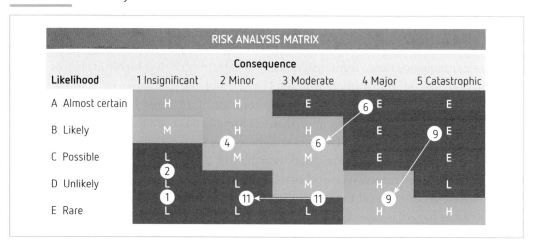

ELIMINATE OR CONTROL THE RISK

Risk treatment
Development of ways to modify or reduce risk

Contingency plan
Developed to respond to potential risk situations

Once the risks have been prioritised, the final step is to look at the most effective ways of managing them. This falls under the umbrella of **risk treatment**. Control measures include:

- elimination plans (e.g. removal of dangerous children's equipment)
- substitution plans (e.g. replacing slippery floor tiles in a wash-up area)
- isolation plans (e.g. isolating dangerous or noisy equipment)
- engineering controls (e.g. using fences to prevent access to waterways or busy roads)
- administrative controls (e.g. warning signs, trained staff and well-developed procedures all help to minimise risk)
- **contingency plans** (where risk cannot be completely avoided, contingency plans for, say, evacuation, need to be developed).

An example of a simple risk treatment plan is shown in Figure 9.4. This plan shows the analysis of risk associated with an armed hold-up, the potential impacts, and the management strategies (or controls) and contingency plans put in place to control them.

FIGURE 9.4 Risk treatment plan — armed hold-up

Nature of risk	Likelihood of event A (almost certain) – E (rare)	Consequences of event 1 (negligible) – 5 (severe)	Preventative measures NO SHORTCUTS, AVOID COMPLACENCY	Contingency measures MONEY AND PROPERTY NOT WORTH A LIFE, NO HEROICS
Hold-up	D (unlikely)	4 (major)	• Develop procedures relating to cash handling • Assign responsibilities • Conduct training • Distribute standard hold-up form • Develop posters — 'stay alert' • Report suspicious circumstances • Check doors and locks when opening • Lock rear entrances; monitor by CCTV • Monitor identification • Watch for bogus tradesmen • Remove excess cash and hold in strongroom • Check alarm systems weekly • Check CCTV monitors daily • Provide escorts for cash • Change routines and carriers • Alert employees to confidentiality requirements • Employ security when large amounts being handled	• Staff to stay calm • Staff to do as told by offender • Staff to stay out of danger • Observe bandits and vehicles • Avoid panic • Raise the alarm when safely possible • Phone police when safely possible • Provide name and address of premises to police • Provide offender's description to police • Provide vehicle description to police • Give travel directions to police • Close premises to public • Retain witnesses • Do not interfere with crime scene • Complete offender description form (all witnesses) • Avoid statements to media • Refer media to manager **Post hold-up** • Issue press release • Provide counselling for staff • Review procedures • Improve security for cash handling

Once controls have been proposed, you can revisit the risk matrix shown in Figure 9.3 and plot the intended changes to each risk based on the significance of the controls proposed, the reduction of their likelihood, and/or the reduction in consequence. For each of the combinations, there is an overall risk rating of low, moderate, high or extreme. As you can see from the matrix, two risks (6 and 9) have dropped from extreme to high as a result of improved control measures.

In the sections below, we will discuss the safe handling of items and the safe performance of certain activities that otherwise may be a threat to the health and safety of workers in the event environment.

Safe lifting techniques

Lifting techniques are generally part of training for anyone involved in lifting, carrying or moving heavy objects, such as sporting equipment or display stands. A useful training aid for this purpose is illustrated in Table 9.3.

TABLE 9.3 How to prevent injuries caused by lifting and moving heavy objects

AVOID	COMMON CAUSES OF INJURY	COMMON SOLUTIONS
Lifting and moving	Lifting boxes from the floor	Do not store items on the floor.
	Carrying boxes or equipment	Use proper lifting techniques. Get help or use a lifting aid. Use a cart. Avoid over-reaching, twisting or lifting over your head.
	Pushing carts	Maintain casters in clean, operating condition. Match the casters to the floor type.

The correct way to lift a heavy object is to squat close to the load, keeping your back straight. Do not stoop over the load to get a grip and pick it up. Test the weight of the object before attempting to lift it. Lift using your knees and legs (not your back) as leverage. Keep your back straight, not bent forwards or backwards. Do not twist or turn your body while carrying the object or putting it down.

Safe Work Australia's code of practice for hazardous manual tasks provides the following guidance advice for implementing control measures in relation to manual handling, which should include safe systems of work, work organisation and work practices.

> ### PUSHING AND PULLING LOADS
>
> Pushing loads is preferable to pulling because it involves less work by the muscles of the lower back, allows maximum use of body weight, less awkward postures and generally allows workers to adopt a forward facing posture, providing better vision in the direction of travel.
>
> Reduce the effort to keep the load moving by:
>
> * using motorised hand trucks and trolleys that are as lightly constructed as possible and have large wheels or castors that are sized correctly and roll freely

- using hand trucks or trolleys that have vertical handles, or handles at a height of approximately one metre
- ensuring that hand trucks and trolleys are well maintained
- treating surfaces to reduce resistance when sliding loads
- for pushing, ensuring handles allow the hands to be positioned above waist height and with elbows bent close to the body
- for pulling, ensuring handles allow the hands to be positioned below waist height allowing workers to adopt a standing position rather than being seated so the whole body can be used.

FIGURE 32 A trolley can eliminate many of the risks involved in manual handling, however, the load will still need to be manoeuvred onto the trolley and through the workplace.

Source: https://www.safeworkaustralia.gov.au/system/files/documents/1705/mcop-hazardous-manual-tasks-v2.pdf; pages 26 and 27.

A definitive absolute safe lifting weight is not possible to determine, and risk assessment needs to take into account factors such as load characteristics, the work environment and human characteristics.

Safe use of electrical equipment

Electrical equipment is a significant hazard in the event environment, particularly in wet weather. All safety steps must be taken to prevent accidents involving electrical equipment, including routine tagging, lockout and inspection of equipment. Many venues are extremely rigorous in their demands for documentation demonstrating correct licensing and inspection. Electrical safety should be a priority for all outdoor event sites.

What is an RCD?

An RCD is a residual current device. RCDs (or safety switches) provide added protection when using electrical equipment. They cut the power supply to the electrical appliance if a current leakage fault (a current imbalance between active and neutral) is recognised. They are designed to help prevent electrocution. RCDs should not be confused with lower-cost circuit breakers, which cut the power supply when the current draw exceeds a specified level (or in abnormal power conditions).

What types of RCDs are there?

There are hardwired RCDs such as those installed in homes. Householders also call them a 'trip switch' as they trip when safety is compromised. Portable RCDs, on the other hand, are plugged into power outlets, and appliances are then plugged into the RCDs. Where hardwired protection is not available, portable RCDs must be used with handheld appliances. They should also be used where electrical appliances are in close proximity to water. This can occur at outdoor events, particularly when it is raining. One can purchase portable power outlets with built-in residual current and overload protection.

What is the AS/NZS 3760:2010 'testing and tagging' standard?

This is a standard for the safety inspection and testing of electrical equipment. It applies also to cord extension sets, portable electrical outlet devices, portable RCDs and portable isolation transformers.

As you might recall from the discussion of risk management, if elimination of the hazard is not possible, other controls should be implemented to reduce potential risks. These controls may include the use of RCDs, which need regular monitoring and testing.

Provision of temporary electrical systems requires monitoring by licensed tradespeople

These cylinders contain a hazardous substance, requiring clear instructions for safe handling and storage

Safe use of machinery

Regulations for safeguarding machinery in the workplace are provided in the Australian Standard AS 4024.1-1996 Safeguarding of Machinery – General Principles.

This standard identifies the hazards and risks arising from the use of industrial machinery and describes methods for their elimination or minimisation, as well as for the safeguarding of machinery and the use of safe work practices. It also describes and illustrates a number of safety principles and provides guidelines by which it is possible to assess which measure or method it is practicable to adopt in particular circumstances.

This standard is intended for those who design, manufacture, supply, install, use, maintain or modify machinery, machinery guarding or safety devices, and identifies the existence of standards for a number of particular classes of machine. It is also designed to be used by those concerned with information, instruction and training in safe work practices.

Safe handling of hazardous substances

Because different chemicals have different safe use requirements, it is important for staff to know as much about hazardous substances used in the workplace as possible. Material safety data sheets should be used to provide the following advice on these substances to staff members:

* ingredients of a product
* health effects and first aid instructions
* precautions for use
* safe handling and storage information
* emergency procedures.

Safety signs

Safety signs are particularly important in the event workplace since staff are generally only at the venue for a very short period, which does not allow much time for reinforcement of safety issues. However, these should be stressed during briefing sessions. Posters and safety signs, such as those reproduced here, can be used to reinforce key messages, helping to prevent many accidents.

First aid and paramedic services

In most cases, first aid is provided by organisations such as St John Ambulance, although venue and event staff should also be trained in first aid procedures. Some of these procedures will be specific to the event in question. For example, at road races, common first aid emergencies that occur include exhaustion, collapse, dehydration, road burns, and bone and muscle injuries, and procedures should be in place for dealing with them. In addition, participants in races such as these sometimes do not wish to accept help and staff would need to be trained in the correct procedure for dealing with such an occurrence.

To deal with more-extreme circumstances, Tarlow (2002, p. 30) suggests the following four steps, known as APMC, as standard for a serious and life-threatening emergency:

1   Administer triage for/to the injured individuals.
2   Plan the next steps (rescue).
3   Manage the scene.
4   Control (avert additional injuries or loss of life).

When the level of risk is high, such as at music festivals where drug use is commonplace, then the services of an organisation such as EMS Event Medical should be considered. Organisations such as this provide on-site professional and experienced emergency care doctors, paramedics and emergency medical technicians (EMTs). This improves first response to medical emergencies and reduces the number of ambulance call-outs.

Health and safety training

Risk management is an ongoing process, involving constant evaluation of the impact of change and the risk factors associated with that change. Analysis and consultation are essential when change in the workplace occurs, as is health and safety training relevant to any change. Most major events will not allow work to commence before safety and evacuation training has been undertaken.

All induction and training programs should include a component on health, safety and security, with a particular emphasis on duty of care. The topics that should be covered in training sessions include:

•   review of the risks to health and safety
•   magnitude of actual and potential problems

- review of issues that could arise, such as public liability actions
- specific job and individual risk factors
- control strategies
- reasons for procedures, rules and regulations
- outline of the most prevalent areas of risk (e.g. slips and falls, manual handling)
- responsibilities of all parties.

Every staff meeting should have health and safety on the agenda so that employees are able to identify risks and consult on procedures and systems. Both awareness and action are necessary, and when serious risks are identified, they should be referred to the organisation's workplace health and safety committee. The role of this committee is to:

- help to resolve any health and safety issues
- carry out regular safety inspections
- develop a system to record accidents and incidents
- make recommendations to management about improving health and safety
- access any information about risks to health and safety from any equipment or substance or occupational disease.

All accidents and incidents need to be reported, even in cases where medical attention is not required.

Incident reporting

For any event, there are standard reporting relationships on all operational issues. On the whole, these reporting relationships concur with the organisation chart. However, there are many instances where communication is less formal and less structured, and this is the case in the event working environment where 'mayhem' or 'controlled chaos' may best describe it.

Despite some tolerance of rather haphazard communication just before and during the event, *any communication relating to an incident or emergency needs to be very clear.* (An example of an incident report card is illustrated in Figure 9.5.) The reporting of an incident must follow a short and specific chain of command. Workers need to know what constitutes an incident and what constitutes an emergency. The chain of command, or organisation chart, for an emergency is seldom the same as the organisation chart for the event as a whole. Emergency reporting tends to go through very few levels, and all staff must be trained in emergency reporting. Many stakeholders may be involved – general staff, security staff, first aid personnel, police, emergency services – but absolute clarity is needed as to who makes key decisions and how they are to be contacted. These lines of reporting and responsibility will be reviewed in the next chapter.

Communication methods

Most event teams use radios as they are the most effective tool for maintaining communication. Different channels are used for different purposes, and it is essential that the correct radio procedures be followed. In Figure 9.6, radio links to an Event Operations Centre are illustrated, with Control serving as the link to the decision makers. For example, in response to a request to remove a hazard, Control would ensure that the site team responded to the call. If a spill were reported, Control would report to Cleaning, requesting that the spill be cleaned up. The Operations Centre also has links to emergency services which can be called if required.

FIGURE 9.5 Sample incident report card

INCIDENT REPORT CARD

Date   Time

Your name   Your position   Functional area/department

Names of person/s involved in the incident

Contact details of person/s involved in the incident

Name and contact details of witness/es if any

INCIDENT DETAILS

Time of incident

Location of incident

Cause of incident

Consequences of incident

Can any action be taken to prevent reoccurrence?

Date and time received and logged

Outstanding actions

FIGURE 9.6 Channels of communication for radio incident reporting

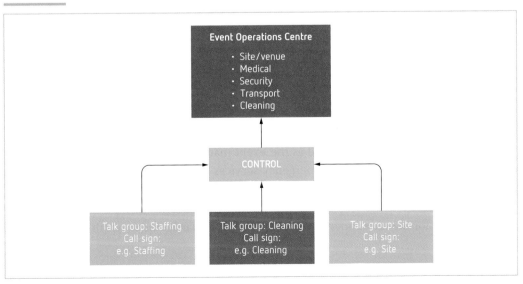

A railway security officer in radio contact with the operations centre

At some events, mobile phones are used, but the drawback of this method of communication is that the information transmitted can be overheard. Networks can also become overloaded if spectators are using their mobile phones, particularly during intermission and at the end of a match or concert.

Meetings between event staff, including security staff and emergency services, are necessary to plan and monitor security and safety, as difficulties can occur if the communications technology of the various services is not compatible. It is crucial that this issue be anticipated and that contingency plans be put in place to deal effectively with any communication problems.

Safety at outdoor events

The safety checklist for dance parties in Figure 9.7 can be modified for any event, large or small. When staging an event, organisers need to consider all of the points outlined in order to demonstrate their duty of care to employees, contractors and the spectators/audience, as well as additional considerations relevant to the particular event.

FIGURE 9.7 Checklist for planning and management of a dance party

- Communication with all stakeholders including emergency services
- Risk assessment and safety planning negotiated and agreed
- Pre-event venue or site assessment
- Access for emergency services
- Approvals and permits required
- Notification of emergency services and hospitals
- Briefing and debriefing of staff
- Security and crowd control; regular patrolling in areas of high risk
- Conditions of entry and a pass-out policy
- Communication systems, including emergency
- Event management centre and contacts
- Public liability insurance

A person also must be nominated as the 'event manager'. They must remain at the event and be contactable at all times by emergency services and all individuals and organisations providing a service or working at the event.

An area must be designated as the event management centre or operations centre and must be staffed for the duration of the event. The event management centre must be able to communicate with the event manager, emergency services and crowd control supervisors at all times during the course of the event.

EXTENSION ACTIVITY

Discuss the press release below by answering the following question from the viewpoint of the police, the event organiser and the individual concerned: Who has responsibility for managing the safety of drug users at festivals?

DRUG CHARGES AT MUSIC FESTIVAL FORTITUDE VALLEY

Police have charged more than 120 people during an outdoor music festival on December 6 and 7 in Fortitude Valley, Brisbane. A total of 123 people were arrested and charged with 127 offences including supplying a dangerous drug, possession of dangerous drugs and other associated drug and property related charges. The event attracted crowds of upward of 20 000 people on each day and was attended by officers from Brisbane City and Fortitude Valley, State Flying Squad, Public Safety Response Team (PSRT) and the Dog Squad.

The majority of those arrested are expected to appear before the Brisbane Magistrates Court over the coming weeks. A significant amount of illicit drugs were seized including MDMA (Ecstasy), Cocaine, Cannabis, Methylamphetamine, GHB and cash suspected from the sale of dangerous drugs.

Police would like to take this opportunity to remind the public of the health risks associated with the consumption of illicit drugs which can prove fatal.

Source: https://creativecommons.org/licenses/by/4.0/deed.en

There are many event and festival safety guidelines available online, including safety guidelines for live entertainment events with specific coverage of electrical safety, hazardous chemicals, event rigging, and working at heights. Some of these are listed at the end of the chapter.

Summary

The health, safety and security of staff and the event audience are very important concerns of the event management team. In this chapter we have focused on risk management relating to workplace safety, which involves identifying potential hazards, analysing and evaluating the risk of these hazards, eliminating or controlling the risk, and developing contingency plans for dealing with the risk. We have also discussed preventative measures such as the safe handling of heavy objects and hazardous substances, and the safe use of electrical equipment and machinery. Not only must people be protected but also assets, and security personnel and the police are there to assist the event manager in managing these risks. Most importantly, an effective system of communication for reporting incidents helps to prevent their escalation and assists staff in dealing promptly with emergencies.

Key terms

Context for risk	Depending on the nature of the event, indoor or outdoor, a different context is presented, with specific risks; the weather, for example, can change the risk context very quickly
Contingency plan	Developed to respond to potential risk situations
Duty of care	Legal obligation of a person or organisation to avoid acts or omissions that could foreseeably harm others
Hazard	Anything that has the potential to harm people
Risk management	Involves forecasting and evaluating risks in order to minimise their impact
Risk treatment	Development of ways to modify or reduce risk

REVIEW YOUR KNOWLEDGE

1 What are the essential duties of a PCBU in relation to WHS?
2 What are the essential duties of employees and volunteers in relation to WHS?
3 What are the key steps involved in risk management; i.e. the process?
4 The whole workforce should be involved in identifying hazards. Using one type of event as an example, explain who could be included in identifying hazards.
5 How can you identify hazards both informally (e.g. observation) and formally (committees)?
6 List five common methods applied to controlling risks.
7 Explain the difference between a hazard analysis form and an incident report form.

APPLY YOUR KNOWLEDGE

Strong winds develop at a community event at which there are several stall holders. One tent has already blown over. The other stallholders have adopted various measures for preventing this from happening:
- removing the canopy from the frame
- holding onto the frame for dear life
- tying the framework to nearby trees or council tables
- using sandbags to hold the tent down.

As the safety inspector, your role is to identify the hazards, assess the severity of the situation, and control or eliminate the risk. Explain the approach you would take as the wind grows stronger by the minute.

Hint: You may have had the foresight to anticipate this earlier.

CASE STUDY

WORKPLACE HEALTH AND SAFETY

The Gold Mining Company is a nightclub venue that is popular during the months of May, June and July for its Friday night dance events. The staff working at this venue are all casuals and turnover is high. During a conversation, two of the staff, Jason and Malik, find out that they have both been mugged on their way home from work in the early hours of the morning, but on different Friday nights. In both cases, the perpetrators waited in a nearby alley and threatened them with knives. Jason lost his wallet and $400 and Malik broke his ankle when trying to run away. Candice, another employee, has been harassed by patrons and was once burned deliberately with a cigarette by a particularly drunk and obnoxious customer. Management gave her some cash to get medical attention.

TASK

Discuss the WHS issues in relation to the staff concerned. What were the responsibilities of management in each of these cases? Did management fulfil its WHS duty of care in relation to Candice? Explain your answer.

Online resources

CENGAGE
brain.com

Visit http://login.cengagebrain.com and search for this book to access the study tools that come with your textbook.

References

Raineri, A. (2013). Outline of the development of a model to facilitate the assessment of crowd safety at outdoor music festivals. Presentation, Safety Institute of Australia Safety in Action, June. http://hdl.cqu.edu.au/10018/1044847

Tarlow, P. (2002), *Event Risk Management and Safety*. Milton, Qld: John Wiley & Sons.

Websites

Advice for managing major events safely (WorkSafe Australia), www.worksafe.vic.gov.au/__data/assets/pdf_file/0016/211345/ISBN-Advice-for-managing-major-events-safely-2006-04.pdf

ISO 31000 Risk Management, www.iso.org/iso/home/standards/iso31000.htm

Risk assessment – event safety checklist, www.casey.vic.gov.au/files/f9b9d987.../event-safety-checklist-outdoor-event.pdf

Safe Work Australia, www.safeworkaustralia.gov.au/sites/SWA

Safety guidelines for live entertainment events, http://liveperformance.com.au/safety_guidelines_live_entertainment_and_events_0

Safety Institute of Australia, https://sia.org.au/events

The event safety guide, www.qub.ac.uk/safety-reps/sr_webpages/safety_downloads/event_safety_guide.pdf#search=event%20safety%20guide

10

MONITOR WORK OPERATIONS

OVERVIEW

This chapter deals with day-to-day supervision. In order to monitor work operations effectively, managers and supervisors need to communicate policies and procedures to their workforce, plan and organise operational functions, and deal with the unexpected. Chapter 4 provided an overview of the project management process, the higher-level planning that is required to plan and deliver an event, often involving many suppliers of goods and services. This complicates matters, as suppliers and contractors have their own staff who do not take kindly to being instructed by anyone other than their direct manager. Detailed operational manuals, policies and procedures with clear responsibility for implementation are essential to avoid confusion. Given the stress and often unexpected nature of the many problems arising in the event environment, a cool head, good decision making and a charismatic personality go a long way.

LEARNING OBJECTIVES

On completion of this chapter, you will be able to:

1. monitor and improve workplace relations to support overall organisational goals and expected service levels

2. plan and organise workflow, scheduling of work, training and delegating to staff

3. monitor and support team members by working collaboratively, providing coaching and feedback

4. solve problems and make decisions, including on short-term solutions, looking also at the potential long-term impacts which should be discussed in consultation with colleagues.

INDUSTRY VIEWPOINT

In order to ensure that a volunteer is matched to the right role, the volunteer must have a clear understanding of what the role involves, what skills will be required to undertake the role and what standards are expected. The position description is a brief written summary of the duties and responsibilities of volunteers and ensures the aims and objectives of the program are being met. It is not a detailed record of every task and duty but a focus of expected outputs of the role and protects the rights of the volunteers. Role descriptions will be forwarded to volunteers once rosters have been set. Unlike paid workers, volunteers do not work under an award system and do not enter into an agreement based upon the provision of labour for a prescribed payment, which is protected by law. However, volunteers do enter into a contract with Council where they agree to perform certain tasks which are of benefit to the organisation and the community.

Source: Frankston Arts Centre (2014). Volunteer manual and application. http://artscentre.frankston. vic.gov.au/files/assets/arts_centre/arts_to_see_and_do/arts_access/fac_-_volunteer_ manual_-_2014-05-13_a1686066.pdf

INTRODUCTION

The importance of ensuring that both staff and volunteers have clear expectations of the duties that they will perform at an event cannot be emphasised enough. While the event environment is an exciting one for the audience, the workforce, including paid staff, contractors and volunteers, seldom has the opportunity to enjoy the event. For example, an event operations manager may sit behind CCTV monitors for the whole event, providing radio instructions to staff on the ground who may be dealing with spectator problems. The cornerstone of monitoring operations is careful recruitment, selection, induction and training, all of which contribute to a better understanding of the service levels expected.

In order to monitor work operations, policies and procedures need to be spelled out to the workforce – to paid staff and volunteers working for the event organisation, as well as to contractor or supplier employees. This requires a high level of organisation, integration and documentation. The three Ps of work operations are project planning (covered in Chapter 4), policy (statements of intentions) and procedures (the steps involved in achieving the policy.

A **policy** is a statement of intention which is implemented as a **procedure**. For example, there could be a policy on ticket transfers or refunds that would need to be elaborated as a series of procedural steps worked out in conjunction with a ticketing agency. There could be a policy that members of the audience do not use umbrellas. Volunteer ushers may be responsible for implementing the policy. If, however, a person refused to follow instructions, security would be called. In some situations, audience behaviour is so bad that the police are required to escort them out of the stadium. As you can see, the procedures developed would involve ushers, security and police, all of whom play a role in implementing them.

Policy
Statement of intention, such as to be environmentally sustainable

Procedure
Steps involved in implementing a policy, such as separating waste streams

At one festival, police arrested 23 people for drugs and other offences, which included suspicion of assault, handling stolen goods, and failing to comply with a direction to leave. The police also helped to evict 133 people.

Tasks

1   Visit two festival websites and read the terms and conditions relating to audience/spectator conduct. The intention is likely to evict anyone displaying inappropriate conduct. The procedures would be documented, including involvement of ushers, security, venue management and police, with the steps to be followed explained. At this stage, simply identify three aspects relating to conduct that interest you.

2   Discuss whether you think the terms and conditions are reasonable.

The social and environmental aspects of events mentioned in Chapter 1 form the basis for many aspects of the event design, and these flow through to operations. The permitted behaviours of a young audience may be quite different at an opera compared with those in a vineyard. Environmental sustainability might be high on the agenda of one event but not as high on another. These considerations, as well as economic impacts and thus budget considerations, underpin the implementation of the event objectives.

MONITOR AND IMPROVE WORK PLACE OPERATIONS

When allocating work in the early stages of event project planning, decisions have to be made regarding the operational implementation of various elements of the event plan. Workflow planning is essential to the allocation of work and resources. For example, loading materials at the rear of a convention centre is one aspect of event planning that needs to be carefully organised and monitored. If things do not run to schedule, trucks can wait for hours to offload staging equipment. Some items need to be installed before others, so rigging is unloaded long before catering supplies. Micro-level planning is crucial in the event environment. Anyone who has run an event on an island or at a similarly remote location will attest to it.

In addition to a focus on task performance, operations management is also the process of creating a work environment in which people are enabled to perform to the best of their abilities. It is a whole work system that begins when a job is defined as needed. The steps are as follows:

• Develop a clear work breakdown structure.
• Decide whether to outsource aspects of the work to contractors/suppliers.
• Develop job descriptions for paid and volunteer staff.
• Select appropriately skilled and experienced people or contractors.
• Negotiate requirements and accomplishment-based standards, milestones and deliverables linked to project planning.
• Provide effective orientation and training.
• Provide ongoing coaching and feedback.
• Design recognition systems that reward people for their contributions.

In the new world of 'experience-centric services', say authors Voss, Roth and Chase (2008), customer experience is the basis for the service operations strategy. They see the role of operations strategy as 'one of choreographing the service delivery system to create and deliver a realised total experience for the customer' (p. 33). This idea of service as performance goes back to the founding philosophy of Disneyland.

On-time arrival for staff at check-in is a key indicator

By contrast, many other event management experts focus on the tasks as opposed to the people that deliver the service experience, as it is all too easy to be consumed by issues such as logistics, traffic management and perimeter fencing.

Monitor efficiency

The use of key performance indicators and performance management systems to effectively monitor performance will be outlined below.

Certain tools are used by organisations for managing performance. One of the most useful and widely used tools today is the **key performance indicator (KPI)**, which helps to define and measure progress towards organisational goals. KPIs are quantifiable measurements, agreed to beforehand, that reflect the critical success factors, or key result areas, of the organisation. They differ depending on the organisation, departments (functional areas) within the organisation, or the specific project.

> **Key performance indicators (KPIs)**
> Indicators that help to define and measure progress towards organisational goals

KPIs are very useful when negotiating contracts with suppliers of goods and services. They form part of the 'specifications' described in Chapter 7. For example, when negotiating a catering contract, quality, quantity, cost, timeliness and compliance (food safety, workplace health and safety) could form the basis of KPIs.

Once KPIs reflecting the organisation's goals have been defined, they are used as a management tool. KPIs give everyone in the organisation a clear picture of what is important, of what they need to make happen. KPIs can also be used as an incentive. Letting employees know through various communication channels what the target is for each KPI and the progress that is being made towards that target is an excellent way of motivating people.

In long-life organisations, KPIs are usually long-term considerations. The definition of what they are and how they are measured does not change often. This is not always the case for events, with their short life and large component of contract and casual staff and volunteers.

One of the most important outcomes for the event industry is efficient and effective operations (zero complaints may be the KPI measure), so that the production (theatrical, sporting, concert) can go ahead on time as planned. A KPI for the artistic merit of a theatrical event may then be the number of positive reviews published in the media, while the organisers of a sporting event would be content with seamless operations regardless of whether the home team won. For all events, the most critical KPI is the show starting on time, though this is more easily said than done!

Banquet service levels can range from one waitperson for 16 guests to one waitperson for 10 guests

KPIs can cover the full range of business operations, including financial targets. Examples include:

- attendance, size of audience, ticket sales
- total labour hours
- total food cost
- total bar sales
- queue management (time taken to 'load' the venue)
- service numbers (people served during intermission)
- wait times (various event bottlenecks involving entry, the buffet, exit and car park)
- average spend (over and above ticket sales)
- employee and volunteer turnover (as a percentage)
- sponsor recognition.

Monitor service

Performance management is a process for managing organisational, functional, team and individual performances. In the event context it would be applied mainly to the performance of the workforce of the organising body – paid staff and volunteers. Logically, suppliers of goods and services are responsible for managing the performance of their own staff.

There are formal and informal methods of managing people performance, with informal approaches being more common in the chaotic environment of an event's 'hot action'. Sometimes supervisors resort to shouting instructions.

EXTENSION ACTIVITY

As the supervisor responsible for the checking of tickets at an entry point, what would you do if you saw a contract cleaner doing something unsafe, such as climbing onto the roof of a cart?

> **Performance appraisal**
> Formal process for providing performance feedback

Performance appraisal is a specific part of formal performance management. It is more likely to be used in relation to full-time event planning staff (the organising body) in the months and sometimes years leading up to an event. It is an evaluation of an individual's performance against standards, deadlines and deliverables associated with their job role. In the best of situations, this is an opportunity to acknowledge effort and commitment and congratulate the individual for achieving the objectives established. In the worst of situations, it involves a process of managing unsatisfactory performance, with the possibility of termination of employment. Figure 10.1 shows the generic items that are commonly found on a staff performance report.

FIGURE 10.1 Generic items on a staff performance report

- Review of current duties and scheduled tasks
- Quality and timeliness of project deliverables
- Areas of skills/strengths
- Communication and teamwork
- Areas of suggested improvement

- Training and development needs
- Long-term career development needs
- Level of satisfaction
- Action plan, including timeline

Non-performance or unsatisfactory performance in an employment context usually means that an employee (or volunteer) who has the capacity to perform their duties is not performing them or is performing them unsatisfactorily. Unsatisfactory workplace performance includes situations in which the employee is not meeting the required standards or is creating a safety risk to themselves and others, or where they are in breach of a code of conduct. If the latter is the case, it is important that in all but the most exceptional circumstances (such as intoxication, drug use or gross misconduct, which would result in summary dismissal), due process is followed, which means investigating the issue and providing the employee with opportunities for improvement.

A volunteer brings her children to an event and then leaves them outside the sponsor's marquee while she has a few drinks after her shift. One of the senior staff notices this and puts her and her kids into a taxi to go home.

How could this extraordinary situation have been prevented from arising in the first place? How would you deal with it? As the volunteer has finished her shift, is she considered to be 'off duty'?

EXTENSION ACTIVITY

To summarise, performance management is about developing a shared understanding of organisational objectives, including monitoring work on an informal basis. For larger organisations, this also involves conducting formal performance appraisals, generally on an annual basis. Thus, in order to monitor efficiency and service levels effectively against systems and procedures, quality measures need to be established beforehand. Managers and supervisors can then provide feedback that is meaningful to employees, as well as to organisations to whom work has been outsourced, such as contract caterers. In the best of circumstances, the event manager finds the quality and quantity of the food provided on the buffet to be of the highest standard, and the service flawless! Ongoing performance improvement is part of quality management and for this reason it is important to stay in touch with industry trends. As a simple example, if the delegates are being served espressos and scones with cream at your competitor's hotel, you might have to discuss your tired offerings with your functions manager.

PLAN AND ORGANISE WORKFLOW

Planning involves establishing systems and procedures and monitoring their implementation. An example of a simple procedure is making sure that there is sufficient change in the register before trading commences. If there is not, service will be delayed while someone runs to the bank for change – and regarding outdoor events, a bank might not be close by. Alternatively, customers may be asked to search for change, and this can turn into a collaborative exercise for a group of people in trying to work out the fastest way to assemble their combined funds. Customers do not walk away talking about an event in glowing terms when they are given prompt and correct change at the bar; however, they may never return if this simple procedural step has not been followed and the queues have been so long that they have missed part of the performance.

Systems and procedures

A system is a way of doing things and, as Figure 10.2 shows, food service systems at events often involve payment at the time of ordering, with a single cashier responsible for the float and till balance at the end of the period of trading. Monitoring and feedback are then clear to all concerned. In other circumstances, all waitpersons have access to the register. Both staff and customers need to understand the system for ordering and payment.

FIGURE 10.2 System and procedures, monitoring and feedback

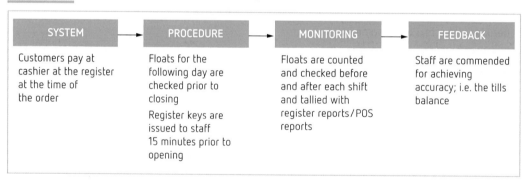

SYSTEM	PROCEDURE	MONITORING	FEEDBACK
Customers pay at cashier at the register at the time of the order	Floats for the following day are checked prior to closing Register keys are issued to staff 15 minutes prior to opening	Floats are counted and checked before and after each shift and tallied with register reports/POS reports	Staff are commended for achieving accuracy; i.e. the tills balance

Another example of a system with an associated workflow is the step-by-step process involved in preparing a self-service buffet. Within the scope of a system, such as preparing a buffet for service, there are numerous procedures for employees to follow; for example, setting up the display, preparing the food items, checking that there is sufficient food, and replacing items that are running low. In most situations, a team is involved in the preparation, service and clearing away. Detailed routine procedures are required for stocking and restocking the buffet, keeping bain-maries at the correct temperature, and discarding food that has been left out for too long. Fresh food should not be added to a dish that has been standing – this is why the whole tray is replaced. The food service should be planned so that guests can access the food from both sides of the table, thus speeding up the process (see Figure 10.3).

Workflow planning for a buffet involves arranging the room for the best flow, planning separate tables (stations) for dessert, tea and coffee, and setting plates at the start of the line and hot food at the end of the line.

A more abstract example (see Figure 10.4) shows the customer management process for a business function. Typically, the catering sales manager 'sells' the function and closes the deal, while the functions/banquet manager and chef deliver on the specifications on the day.

FIGURE 10.3 Customers accessing both sides of a buffet table will speed up the process

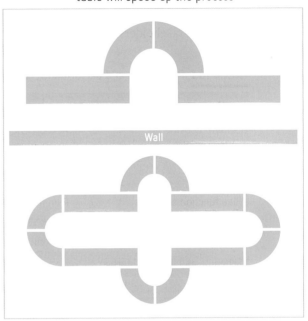

FIGURE 10.4 Organisation chart – catering sales and service

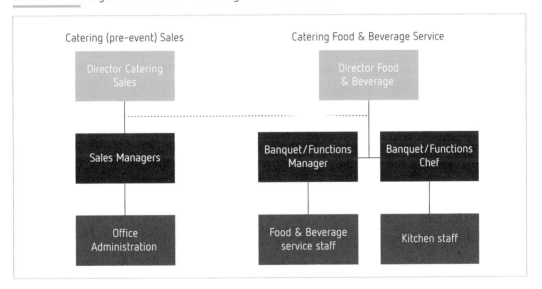

The example in Figure 10.4 is taken further in Table 10.1, where standard procedures are enhanced by adding performance measures. For example, if the customer expects a written quote within 24 hours, the staff involved must be aware of what they must do (procedure) and how they must do it (performance measure). One performance measure for the catering sales manager could be a nightly back-up of data. Client data is invaluable for any catering business and loss of a company's client list could be a costly error. For the current client, it would certainly signal incompetence if information had to be requested a second time. 'And what may I ask did we quote for your function?' would not inspire confidence! Similarly, it is essential that messages are taken correctly and transmitted in a timely way. Business clients expect immediate attention. Performance measures also establish timelines for negotiating with other stakeholders, such as the banquet chef in this instance.

TABLE 10.1 Procedures and performance for a functions manager

STANDARD PROCEDURE	PERFORMANCE MEASURE
Confirm bookings	• Acknowledge and confirm booking and reconfirm within 24 hours by responding to catering sales manager • Liaise with chef regarding function catering in week prior to function
Plan function set-up	• Plan function layout two weeks prior to event • Check stock levels (e.g. tablecloths, cutlery) • Develop function specifications such as table layouts
Schedule and manage staffing	• Plan staffing requirements • Roster staff • Contact staff one week prior to function • Confirm rosters 24 hours prior to function • Brief staff immediately prior to function set-up
Supervise function set-up	• Monitor function set-up in progress • Check all physical specifications have been met two hours prior to function (e.g. tables, stage set-up) • Schedule service of food and beverage and confirm with chef three hours prior to function (e.g. timing of main course and dessert)
Manage customer requests on the day or refer to catering sales manager	• Respond to customer needs with meeting requests, or refer to catering sales manager immediately
Clear and clean up after the function	• Supervise staff clearing and cleaning up • Monitor workplace health and safety • Evaluate function and record outstanding or emerging problems • Where necessary, supervise function set-up for following day

For the functions supervisor, the primary responsibilities are organising rosters, setting up the function and liaising with the client during the function. The functions supervisor's duties have a shorter timeline than those of the catering sales manager, but they are just as important to the client, since it is unlikely that the catering sales manager will do little more than call in to check that everything is going well once operational responsibility has been handed over from their department to the functions or banquet department.

As these examples illustrate, clear responsibilities and timelines can contribute to operational efficiency and avoid time-consuming and costly mistakes. A client who calls and asks for a different function room set-up and arrives on the day to find that the request has not been processed will be unhappy and demand a change to the seating plans. This could involve redeployment of staff and the time-consuming process of furniture removal, which in turn could lead to other responsibilities being neglected, timelines falling apart, and much panic and stress.

The management tasks of planning, organising, leading and controlling are well illustrated in the above examples.

MONITOR AND SUPPORT TEAM MEMBERS

Event employees are motivated by a wide range of factors, from hours compatible with study in unrelated fields to the potential for promotion and career development in the event industry. The first type of employee is probably looking for a position in which the tasks are simple, the work is routine and well paid, and the problems are few. The second is looking for a challenge: variable and complex work and new learning experiences. This diversity is matched by diversity in cultural expectations. Some employees are comfortable in a society in which individual effort is acknowledged, while others are more accustomed to a group-oriented environment in which social harmony is more important than competition.

With these challenges in mind, the event manager needs to monitor and support team members.

Workforce planning

Developing work rosters is one of the most difficult tasks for a manager because labour is so expensive. Overstaffing eats into profits very quickly and, for this reason, most managers allocate human resources with great care. Scheduling, or rostering, involves balancing the number of staff and the labour cost with the appropriate level of service required. The aim is for optimal efficiency and service quality. Volunteers can contribute to staffing levels, but as Chapter 23 will show, there are costs associated with volunteer management. Motivation is a key factor for the entire event workforce. As a temporary arrangement, there is often little incentive to last the distance, whether this applies to an employee, contractor or volunteer (this will be discussed in the next chapter). If an event is overstaffed with volunteers, their motivation levels will be low, particularly if they are not given meaningful work.

Coaching and training

Once the event workforce is on the ground, they need to be trained and then coached on an ongoing basis – many staff will be unfamiliar with the venue and the procedures. But before coaching begins, the objectives or outcomes need to be discussed with the participants. This creates a context for the coaching and enables everyone to understand the process. It is also essential to explain why a procedure is important and what can go wrong if it is not followed correctly. Sometimes the training approach has to be modified to meet the specific needs of training participants. People differ in terms of their language, literacy and numeracy needs; cultural and language backgrounds; physical ability; and level of confidence based on previous learning experiences in the workplace. Opportunities for practice and self-evaluation should be incorporated into every training program. In brief, 'show and tell' must be followed by 'do and review'.

Some event supervisors are superb demonstrators, but they are not there just to show off! The objective of training is that the participants should learn! A focus on learning is, in fact, the key factor in effective training.

There are a number of training methods that can be used, the most common being demonstration, as discussed above. Others include:

* informal coaching
* formal presentations, such as updates on legislative changes
* explanations, sometimes quite informal, to explain why things are important
* problem solving, including group discussion of problems experienced in the workplace
* mentoring by a supervisor, which is particularly useful for the development of service skills
* job rotation through different functional areas, which helps the employee to understand how service is integrated across teams and departments
* experiential learning, or ongoing learning through placement in a range of situations and scenarios.

Of course, a combination of any of the above methods can be used for both formal and informal training.

When coaching is complete, the supervisor should ask participants to evaluate their own performance and identify areas for improvement. If the training objectives were clearly stated at the beginning of training, this should not be difficult. Doing so also allows participants to take ownership of their learning and to identify areas in which additional training may be required.

There are many ways in which a supervisor can evaluate if learning has occurred. The worst trainers demonstrate and walk away; the best trainers assess learning progressively. The most common way of assessing if learning has taken place is through observation. Asking questions is another very productive method of checking knowledge and understanding. Open questions such as 'Why is this safety procedure important?' are more effective than closed questions, such as 'Do you understand?' Presenting problems, case studies and scenarios to participants are additional ways of assessing learning. Obtaining third-party opinions – from other supervisors, for example – also helps to establish the level of skill and knowledge gained by participants during training.

As mentioned previously, recording training and assessment of training according to enterprise and legislative requirements supports performance management. In many areas of risk management, such as fire safety training, staff are required to participate in regular fire drills to reinforce their knowledge and skills, and records of these must be kept, along with participants' responses to questions about the drills. Employees might never encounter a fire in the venue, but regular training ensures that, if they do, they are prepared.

For coaching to be successful, the supervisor must be able to say that the participant has:

* task skills (can follow the steps correctly)
* task management skills (can perform multiple tasks and prioritise correctly)
* contingency management skills (can identify when things go wrong and how to remedy the problem)
* job/role environment skills (can work in a team with customers from all walks of life)
* the ability to transfer and apply skills and knowledge to new contexts.

Once new employees have been through the processes of induction and training, they are ready to embark on their event roles. From this point, monitoring their performance and providing positive feedback to them are essential to the maintenance of their skills and enthusiasm.

In summary, when a supervisor, manager or trainer prepares for coaching, the following steps are recommended:

1   Explain the overall purpose of coaching to the employee.
2   Explain and demonstrate the specific skills to be coached.
3   Communicate clearly any underpinning knowledge required.
4   Provide the employee with the opportunity to practise the skill.
5   Ask the learner if there are any questions.
6   Ask open questions to check the learner's understanding.
7   Provide feedback in a constructive and supportive manner.
8   Ensure that the learner has enough opportunity to repeat the skill until confident.

This is far more easily done in conventional workplaces. With the temporary staff and volunteers working at most events, time allocated to training is typically very limited, which means that supervision needs to be 'tighter' and procedures made as clear as possible.

Collaboration

Prioritisation and delegation are two management techniques that can assist in monitoring work operations. In workplaces where there is a positive dynamic and the team works well together, service problems seldom emerge. Where there is a dysfunctional work unit and people are not willing to assist one another, the quality of service is usually compromised. This can easily occur if a team is not well trained, does not have the equipment and other resources it needs, or where there is limited positive performance feedback.

Team meetings, briefings and debriefings, in which systems and procedures are discussed, problems and service incidents (both positive and negative) are analysed and effective solutions are developed, are essential to meeting standards set by the event organisation.

The set-up team is soon to be replaced by the operational team

Conflict management techniques

Many factors, including cultural background, language differences and previous experience, can have an impact on communication between members of the event workforce and, indeed, between the workforce and the client or the customer. Conflict will occur – contractors will complain about delays; customers will complain about waiting, their seat allocation, the sound level, sometimes in an unpleasant way; and team members will come into conflict while working in this noisy, frantic and high-pressure environment. Diplomacy and empathy are essential requirements in managing all these types of situations.

Conflict management differs from country to country. Some cultures are more prone to complain, others to suffer in silence. Differences also exist in how problems are resolved. Some only want to air their grievances, while others want solutions. On the whole, clients don't want to hear excuses or to see blame being shifted.

The interactionist approach to conflict management proposes that there are two types of conflict: functional conflict, which is constructive; and dysfunctional conflict, which is destructive. Functional conflict occurs in a healthy, competitive environment where the goals of the organisation are being achieved and diverse management styles are represented.

When dealing with a conflict situation, managers can use a range of techniques: avoidance, accommodation, forcing, compromise and collaboration. These conflict management strategies are useful for the day-to-day management of operational issues.

Some conflict is trivial and may be best ignored, with intervention escalating the conflict rather than resolving it. For example, when work pressure causes a flare-up, it is likely to be resolved when everyone relaxes after the event. Accommodation involves giving way to the other party in the conflict, while calling upon formal authority means forcing a resolution. The latter is often appropriate in a crisis situation where there is no time for compromise or collaboration. Compromise occurs when everyone in the situation gives way to a degree to reach a mutually agreed solution, while collaboration involves brainstorming and negotiation to reach a solution which is advantageous to all involved.

While collaboration would seem to be the 'best' conflict resolution technique, this is not always the case. Situational factors, such as the time and risk involved, the gravity of the issue, the personalities and formal authority of those involved, all contribute to the decision as to which approach to take in resolving conflict.

In the event environment, where stress levels are generally high, conflict is almost inevitable. As a result, managing conflict and stress are key elements of managing people in this environment.

Provide feedback

Most feedback given in the event environment is informal, occurring during briefings and debriefings. Sometimes, feedback requires individuals to receive on-the-job coaching to improve their skills. It is important to document substandard operational procedures and the corrective measures being undertaken in accordance with organisational management systems.

Most importantly, it is essential to provide feedback on excellent performance, either formally or informally. Most events celebrate their successful conclusion with a staff party once the audience has left. More-novel ideas include having the workforce celebration before the event as a kind of bonding process, accelerating the 'mourning' phase. In other cases, success is celebrated a few days after everyone has caught up on lost sleep!

Manage follow-up

When individuals are not achieving the required outcomes, they need to be monitored and coached. The manager should agree the performance improvement required with the person, document this, and provide support services where necessary. If this proves ineffective, the manager needs to counsel the individual who is continuing to perform below expectations and implement a disciplinary process if no improvement occurs.

One of the most important principles in managing disciplinary measures is procedural fairness. In its fullest application, procedural fairness requires that the employee (or volunteer) is:

* provided with an opportunity to put their case, and to hear the case against them
* given clear reasons why the standard has not been met
* told what the expectations are for improved performance
* provided with a review date on which the situation will be re-evaluated.

In such circumstances, the action must be timely and consistent with the treatment of other employees. When serious misconduct occurs or ongoing poor performance continues, it may be necessary to terminate staff in accordance with legal and organisational requirements. This also applies to volunteers.

Retain staff

Management of people encompasses the all-important issue of staff retention. Retention of senior management personnel is vital. Hanlon and Jago's (2004) research into two major annual events shows that the period immediately following such events is typically flat in contrast to the adrenalin rush of the previous weeks. It is during this period that a number of retention strategies should be considered for permanent staff. In addition, organisations running annual events need to put some effort into maintaining contact with seasonal workers who often return annually to these events.

Table 10.2 shows the relevant retention strategies for full-time and seasonal workers before, during and after an event.

TABLE 10.2 A recommended guide for retaining full-time and seasonal personnel at the Australian Open Tennis Championships and the Formula 1 Australian Grand Prix

RETENTION STRATEGIES FOR PERSONNEL CATEGORIES		
EVENT CYCLE	FULL-TIME STAFF	SEASONAL WORKERS
Lead-up	Event's status	Event's status
	Recognition	Recognition
	Ownership	Ownership
During an event	Team debrief	Team debrief
	Team activities	Team activities

RETENTION STRATEGIES FOR PERSONNEL CATEGORIES (CONTINUED)		
EVENT CYCLE	**FULL-TIME STAFF**	**SEASONAL WORKERS**
After an event	Team debrief	Team debrief
	Thank you function	Thank you function
	Operations appraisal	
	Remuneration	
	Career management programs	
	Updated job descriptions	
	Re-establishing teams	
	Positive direction from management	
	Exit interviews	
	Loyalty payments	
During the year	Team meetings	Continuous contact (e.g. Christmas cards, birthday cards, organisation's newsletter, team meetings)
	Remuneration	Career opportunities
		Survey needs
		Employed for additional events

Source: Hanlon, C., & Jago, L. (2004). The challenge of retaining personnel in major sport event organizations. *Event Management*, 9, p. 47. © Cognizant Communication Corporation.

Lifelong friendships evolve from volunteers returning year after year to the same event

While there are few studies on retention in the short-life event workforce, there is anecdotal evidence of high absenteeism among volunteers on the second or third day of an event.

This chapter has illustrated the all-important differences between the event business environment and the event project environment from a human resource point of view. Managing people in these circumstances has special challenges during the often long lead-up to an event as well as during the event's execution.

SOLVE PROBLEMS AND MAKE DECISIONS

In monitoring work performance, the manager's role is to observe day-to-day operations, check reports and documents, obtain feedback from customers and suppliers, and discuss ongoing issues with the work team. When problems occur (for example, complaints about slow service), the manager should immediately identify the cause of the problem and adjust procedures. However, most problems can be avoided if there is good planning and preparation and diligent implementation of procedures.

The following workplace records may indicate a quality issue or a problem that needs resolving:

- media reports
- complaints (including noise)
- point of sale (POS)/cash register reports
- stocktake reports
- actions taken by food safety authorities
- calls from fair trading officials
- threats by suppliers over non-payment of accounts
- incident report forms
- supervisor's logbook, duty manager's report, mystery customer report
- checklists.

In the case of incident reporting, frequent reports of a similar type of incident would indicate that decisions need to be made and steps taken to prevent such occurrences. For example, burns reported by kitchen staff may require investigation and the development of new equipment or procedures.

In later chapters, there will be a focus on risk management as an approach used for decision-making. In the chaotic world of large audiences, complex productions and unanticipated operational dramas, this risk assessment approach is essential for problem solving and decision making. However, as this chapter has indicated, careful planning and monitoring can go a long way to preventing the unexpected.

Summary

In most circumstances, the event workforce is likely to evolve from a small planning team to a large and diverse workforce comprising paid staff, contractors and possibly volunteers just prior to and during the event. As we have seen in this chapter, managing operations in this difficult environment requires a great deal of planning as well as the development of effective systems and key indicators for measuring performance. The systematisation and simplification of procedures can go a long way to ensuring that tasks are completed correctly and on time. Extensive checklists are not only good planning tools, they also assist individuals on the frontline to understand what to do and how to do it. As with all other aspects of event management, the devil is in the detail. If all contingencies have been considered and plans made accordingly, the event will go without a hitch and everyone will be able to celebrate its success at the finish.

Key terms

Key performance indicators (KPIs)	Indicators that help to define and measure progress towards organisational goals
Performance appraisal	Formal process for providing performance feedback
Policy	Statement of intention, such as to be environmentally sustainable
Procedure	Steps involved in implementing a policy, such as separating waste streams

REVIEW YOUR KNOWLEDGE

1   The event workforce often includes contractor organisations to whom work is outsourced. Visit the website of an event security company to identify the operational aspects of an event that they can cover when planning the work breakdown.

2   The terms and conditions of entry to an event form the basis of several procedures. Give examples of two such procedures.

3   Explain the difficulties involved in monitoring work and delegation when the workforce is a diverse combination of paid staff, volunteers and contractors.

4   How can award conditions impact on your staff planning?

APPLY YOUR KNOWLEDGE

1   Project planning is about the lead-up to an event, the planning timeline. Following the macro-level planning, micro-level planning is necessary in the form of detailed procedures. Give an example of a system and corresponding procedures – for example, for food ordering, storage, preparation and service – to demonstrate that you can plan and monitor workflow.

2   Waste management is a key consideration for many events. Compare the initiatives undertaken by two events, focusing on practical application of the principles as well as the role the event has in educating the public. Explain how you can effectively evaluate the success of a waste management plan.

CASE STUDY

STAFF RETENTION

As the operations manager for a major event, your current concern is a rumour that one of the contractor organisations is trying to poach your staff. Having worked with your team for many months and enjoyed a mutual understanding of the operational problems posed by this major event, you are worried that the loss of one or more of your staff will lead to a setback of several weeks. For you, retention is a priority. In preparation for a discussion with the human resources manager about this rumour, prepare answers to the following questions.

QUESTIONS

1   How are employees' expectations of their roles developed?

2   What sort of targets or goals can be set to motivate people in senior event roles?

3   How can feedback, both formal and informal, help to retain key staff?

4   If career development is important to an individual working on a major event, how can these aspirations be met, given the limitations of short-life organisations?

5   How will you approach this interview?

Online resources

Visit **http://login.cengagebrain.com** and search for this book to access the study tools that come with your textbook.

References

Hanlon, C., & Jago, L. (2004). The challenge of retaining personnel in major sport event organizations. *Event Management*, 9, 39−49.

Voss, C., Roth, A. V., & Chase, R. B. (2008). Experience, service operations strategy, and services as destinations: Foundations and exploratory investigation. *Production and Operations Management*, 17(3), 247−66.

Websites

Event operational manual − example, **www.google.com.au/url?sa=t&rct=j&q=&esrc=s&source= web&cd=1&ved=0ahUKEwievbjT-e7VAhVJOFQKHQaXDrYQFggmMAA&url=https%3A%2F%2F www.lgtoolbox.qld.gov.au%2Fsystem%2Ffiles%2FEXAMPLE%2520-%2520Event%2520Guide. pdf&usg=AFQjCNG2Whw_hOraWqJgG8o1shfzuTvnHg**

Event operations manual − template (Leo Isaac), **www.leoisaac.com/evt/evt002.htm**

Event planning checklist (Resource Centre), **www.resourcecentre.org.uk/information/event-planning-checklist/**

Event waste minimisation guide, **www.zerowaste.sa.gov.au/upload/resource-centre/publications/ events/2010%20EVENTS%20GUIDE.pdf**

Meander Valley Council event management planning guide, **www.meander.tas.gov.au/page.aspx?u=520**

Plan a catered event menu, **www.thebalance.com/plan-a-catered-event-menu-that-will-impress-your-guests-1223525**

11

LEAD AND MANAGE PEOPLE

OVERVIEW

This chapter will view leadership through the lens of event projects, where the team is brought together for a single event, and event business operations, where the team works together across a number of events throughout the year. Regardless of which way you look at it, the event context is characterised by a long lead time for planning with a relatively small team (even for major events), followed by an explosion of volunteers and contractor employees. Leading and motivating teams in this environment requires careful planning as most jobs are temporary in nature.

LEARNING OBJECTIVES

On completion of this chapter, you will be able to:

1 model high standards of performance, interacting with the team in a positive and professional manner

2 develop team commitment and cooperation, communicating short-, medium- and long-term plans

3 manage team performance, providing coaching and mentoring, and recognition and rewards for team achievements.

INDUSTRY VIEWPOINT

The volunteer took one look at the uniform, refused to wear it and walked off the job. Of the 20 people I had in my team on the first day, only six remained by day five. Three of my best people were reassigned to another team on the second day. Some of those who remained beyond the second day found the work too hard; others found it too boring. People assume that when they work at a major event they will be directly involved in the action. We were long gone by the time the bike race began each morning, rushing ahead to set up the next night's camp. In reality, most event employees work behind the scenes, handling difficult situations such as spectators trying to gain access to secure areas. In our case, drunkenness, aggression and general horseplay by both riders and spectators were hard to handle. The work was physically hard too. Holding a team together is a real challenge, especially when there are many other opportunities for them, or nothing to hold them.

Cycling event manager

INTRODUCTION

This story illustrates the problems that confront many event managers. Staff are often hard to come by owing to the short-term or unpaid nature of the work. In the above scenario, the event manager is struggling to keep the event team together for the duration of a six-day, long-distance bike race. While her team may have been enthusiastic to support the charity involved in the race, as well as excited to be on the road with the cyclists, the harsh realities are often quite different from the team's expectations.

Although the event planning team may work together for months or even years, the bulk of the event team works together for an extremely short period, ranging from one day to about one month. Staff expectations are hard to manage under these conditions, and there is little time for building relationships and skills. Therefore, the focus of the event leader should be on giving clear guidelines, facilitating efficient work, energising people and celebrating successes. The event must be extremely well planned and the event leader must concentrate on developing tools for organising and controlling activities, as well as on innovative ways to inform, lead and motivate employees and volunteers who may need to reach job maturity within minutes or hours.

MODEL HIGH STANDARDS OF PERFORMANCE AND BEHAVIOUR

Much has been said about the challenges of the event environment. However, from a human resources point of view, it is also necessary to consider the long and stressful planning period leading up to an event. For a major event, this can be for a period of a year or more. Due to the number of uncertainties that need to be resolved and the diverse range of contractual and stakeholder relationships that need to be negotiated during this period, stress management is an important consideration. It is at this time, and during the event execution, that supervisory and management staff need to model high standards of performance and behaviour. In this of all industries, charismatic leadership goes a long way to maintaining motivation. Open and supportive communication is also extremely helpful. This includes:

* planned and informal exchanges of information
* open access to documents, including operational plans
* using technology to support effective communication (e.g. email groups)
* involving others in developing solutions
* being prepared to declare your own need for assistance
* providing constructive feedback.

Tyssen, Wald and Spieth (2013) confirmed that team cohesion is affected by charismatic leadership. They highlight the importance of transactional and transformational leadership in temporary teams.

In this chapter, we will look at the all-important topics of team development, motivation and leadership.

EXTENSION ACTIVITY

Colonel Sanders was 65 when he founded the fast-food chain Kentucky Fried Chicken. By that point, his famous secret chicken recipe had been rejected by potential partners over 1000 times.

Walt Disney said, 'Laughter is timeless, imagination has no age, dreams are forever'.

Both are examples of leaders who inspired. Investigate two leaders who inspire you and explain the reasons for their success.

FIGURE 11.1 Leadership model for temporary teams

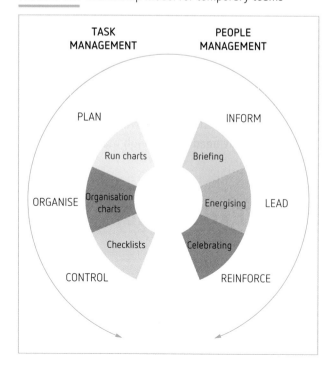

DEVELOP TEAM COMMITMENT AND COOPERATION

The leadership model on which this chapter is based is shown in Figure 11.1. The two main dimensions of this model are task management and people management, the basis for many other models used in organisational behaviour.

Task management

Task management involves the skills of planning, organising, coordinating and controlling work processes, using tools such as run charts, organisation charts and checklists.

Plan

Planning is probably the most important aspect of event management. It encompasses the development of policies and procedures to cover all situations, from disputes over ticketing/seating to the summary dismissal of alcohol-affected employees. Planning is necessary for the development of staff rosters and the provision of meals for paid and volunteer staff, as well as for restocking, the careful scheduling of stock being essential for multi-session events. When a venue is still under construction, architectural drawings are used in logistics planning to ensure, for example, that materials and equipment can be unloaded and set up easily.

There are a number of useful tools which can facilitate the planning process. A simplified version of a run chart is helpful for all team members, and charts and maps should be displayed and discussed during training. Sometimes, it is necessary to modify them so that they can be easily understood by all event staff. While the event management team needs to focus on the macro level of the event (the big picture), the micro level must not be ignored. It is essential that all members of the team are clear about the specific jobs that they are expected to do, otherwise they will become frustrated and their performance will deteriorate.

Organise

Organisation charts are covered in detail in Chapter 4. An organisation chart enhanced with task lists is a useful tool for providing everyone with a more accurate idea of roles and responsibilities at a glance. There should be no ambiguity as to who is responsible for what. In addition to the organisation chart, every person should have a job description listing their duties. This includes contractor employees.

Job rotation is an important organisational task, particularly where paid or volunteer staff are required to man remote locations. Change from one role to another during a shift can alleviate boredom and reduce feelings of inequity.

Control

Checklists are useful control mechanisms. They can be used to check cleanliness, monitor the temperature of food, check for safety or security risks, and to ensure that procedures are followed for setting up and shutting down. A completed checklist is also intrinsically satisfying for the person carrying out the tasks, especially if their job has no visible output. Most events are high-risk, making control measures absolutely essential for risk and hazard minimisation. Tours of the venue (both front and back of house) to check that everything is safe are invaluable. Frayed carpets, loose wiring and chairs stacked in fire exits can all be dealt with using simple control tools such as checklists.

People management

The three skills shown in Figure 11.1 that are required for good people management are informing, leading and reinforcing. Briefings, energising strategies and celebratory activities can achieve closure on short-term targets and are necessary for keeping staff interested and motivated.

People management is one of the most significant challenges for the event manager. Due to the short-term nature of events, the frontline staff do not have the commitment of employees embarking on careers with traditional organisations. A volunteer or casual employee who finds the work boring, the location unappealing, the weather unpleasant or the food unsatisfactory may simply not return the following day. Indeed, he or she may not return from a meal break! The ability to keep people informed, to inspire and motivate them through positive leadership, and to reinforce the attainment of specific results is the key to successful people management in this fast-paced environment.

Inform

Briefings before and after shifts provide the opportunity to advise staff on the order of proceedings and to clarify issues of concern. If a single important piece of information is left out, and several hundred spectators ask the same question about it, it is frustrating for everyone involved and a mistake most event managers make only once in their careers. If staff understand why they are performing what appear to be unnecessary tasks, such as checking accreditation or photocopying results, they are far more likely to understand how they fit into the big picture. Well-informed staff members, including all uniformed staff who are always the target for questions from customers, regardless of their role at an event, also respond well to positive feedback from guests and spectators.

Lead

Most event staff expect to have some fun at an event and most look forward to joining in the atmosphere. Positive actions on the part of management, including good verbal and non-verbal communication and the initiation of a range of activities to energise the team, can help to create positive staff morale. Event managers who are burnt out before an event begins are unlikely to provide inspired leadership or to solve problems with tact and diplomacy. Time and stress management are vital for everyone involved. As role models, event leaders demonstrate to their staff how to provide quality service to customers. Depending on the level of formality of the event, the service provided will vary in subtle ways. Staff look to management for these cues.

Finally, it is important that each staff member has accurate expectations of his or her role, especially the more mundane tasks. (Sometimes, jobs will be oversold and underdelivered, or undersold and overdelivered.) This provides the opportunity for the event manager to encourage the staff member to go beyond initial expectations by introducing motivational strategies such as job rotation, viewing the performance, meeting the stars and athletes, or assisting the public. Accurate expectations of the less exciting parts of the job, combined with a positive team spirit, are the outcomes of good leadership.

Reinforce

Positive reinforcement of key messages can enhance safety and service, two essential responsibilities of the whole event team. The range of ways in which core messages can be reinforced are outlined in Table 11.1. Event staff are well known for their capacity to celebrate success at every stage of a project, so recognition strategies for individuals and groups, including parties and prizes, are essential in this industry where people work under tremendous pressure to pull off an event.

TABLE 11.1 Communication strategies

VERBAL	VISUAL	WRITTEN	BEHAVIOURAL
• Briefings • Meetings • Radio conversations • One-to-one discussion • Instruction • Phone conversations • Training • Word-of-mouth messages	• Photographs • Displays • Models • Demonstrations • Printed slogans • Posters • Videos • Internet • Social media	• Training material • Memos • Letters • Email • Handbooks • Staff newsletters • Reports • Information bulletins • Checklists	• Videos • Working practices • Role modelling • Non-verbal communication

Summary

In summary, event leadership is about:

- planning for short-term assignments
- organising and simplifying work processes
- developing checklists and other control processes.
  It is also about:
- briefing and communicating with the team
- motivating and energising on an hourly or daily basis
- reinforcing key messages and targets
- celebrating success.

The work of the event leader may extend to some or all of the following challenging contexts, quite unlike those of the traditional business environment:

- one shift for one day
- single or multiple venues
- single or multiple session times
- a team separated by physical distance
- routine and dull jobs away from the action
- busy, pressured and high-stress roles in the midst of the action.
  And the team itself may include all or any of the following:
- contractors
- volunteers
- temporary workers
- students
- committee members
- police and other stakeholders.

TABLE 11.2 Differences between long-term and short-term teams

LONG-TERM TEAMS	SHORT-TERM (TEMPORARY) TEAMS
Commitment to the organisation's mission	Commitment to task
Decisions by consensus	Leader solves problems and makes decisions
Group cohesion over time	Limited relationship building
Career development within organisation	No career/organisation orientation
Intrinsic satisfaction	Tangible rewards
Empowerment	Limited responsibility
Lifelong learning	Limited learning
Positive performance management	Positive reference

MANAGE TEAM PERFORMANCE

The characteristics of short-term groups differ dramatically from those of long-term groups. Long-term groups are able to focus on quality improvement initiatives, with quality teams contributing to ongoing improvements over a period of time. This is seldom the case for short-term teams. The differences are summarised in Table 11.2.

Not only is the event team temporary, it is also, as a rule, extremely diverse. The general approach to managing a diverse workforce is to assimilate everyone into a strong organisational culture. When individuals share common codes of behaviour and communication, and solve problems in routine ways, the positive benefit is consistency and this can be achieved in the normal organisational life cycle. However, this is hard to achieve in the dynamic event environment where there tends to be more on-the-spot decision making and a wider acceptance of different standards of behaviour. With limited time, an event leader simply does not have the opportunity to assimilate the team into a strong organisational, or group, culture. Working with a diverse range of people with wide-ranging needs and interests is inevitable, but there are strategies that can be put in place to enhance team performance.

Let us now look at the main theories of group development and how these can be adapted by the team leader to enhance the performance of their team.

Group development

Studies by B. W. Tuckman as far back as 1965 and subsequently revised are still applicable today. They have shown that groups tend to go through five defined stages in their development:

1   *Forming.* This is the period during which members grow used to one another and tentatively formulate goals and behaviours that are acceptable.
2   *Storming.* In this stage there is generally some conflict over control and leadership, including informal leadership, known as sorting out 'the pecking order'.
3   *Norming.* Once the hierarchy and the roles of all group members have been defined, the group tends to adopt a common set of behavioural expectations.
4   *Performing.* During this productive stage, members focus on performance within the framework of the team.
5   *Adjourning.* Faced with disbandment, successful teams share a sense of loss. In this stage, feelings of achievement are tempered by sadness that the group will be disbanding.

One limitation of the model is that it makes team building appear linear and sequential. Although it's a useful analytical tool, we must remember that some teams may not follow this pattern, particularly where there is some form of disruption, such as new members joining the team. However, this analysis of group development is useful to those in the event industry because the process of group formation does require special attention in this environment. Sometimes, the early stages of group development can be accelerated so that the performing,

Briefing a security team, which is essential at most events

or productive, stage is reached quite quickly. This can be done effectively by using ice-breakers in team training sessions.

In a more recent study, Nixon, Harrington and Parker (2012) argue that leadership performance is significant to project success or failure. They conclude that no single leadership model is appropriate throughout the duration of the project. Performance, therefore, must be modified to align with the stages of the project duration.

Where group members exhibit a wide range of individual differences, particularly in language or culture, the following strategies can help to develop effective communication between them:

- Identify the specific information needs of group members.
- Use plain English.
- Allocate buddies or develop subteams.
- Use graphics to impart information.
- Rotate roles.
- Provide all members with opportunities to participate in the group.
- Develop group rituals and a group identity.

Geert Hofstede (1980), well known for his work in cross-cultural communication, has identified the following value dimensions in communication.

The first value dimension he termed **power distance**. This indicates the extent to which a society accepts differences in power and authority. In some cultures, employees show a great deal of respect for authority, so Hofstede suggested that these employees have a high power distance. They would find it difficult to bring problems out into the open and discuss them with senior staff. The low power distance prevalent in other cultures encourages closer relationships at all levels, and questions and criticism from employees are more readily accepted. As you can imagine, if employees in an event team were to come from both high power and low power distance backgrounds, the first would be aghast at the audacity of the second when they brazenly pointed out problems, and the low power distance employees would find it difficult to understand why the others did not speak up.

The second value dimension identified by Hofstede was **individualism/ collectivism**. Some societies have a strong sense of family, and behavioural practices are based on loyalty to others. Such societies display higher conformity

> **Power distance**
> First of Hofstede's value dimensions, indicating the extent to which a society accepts differences in power and authority

> **Individualism/ collectivism**
> Hofstede's second value dimension, highlighting the difference between individuality and conformity to group norms

to group norms, and it follows that employees of these cultural backgrounds would feel comfortable in a group. By contrast, employees from highly individualistic societies would defend their own interests and show individual (as opposed to group) initiative.

These are just two cultural dimensions. There are many other variations in people's responses to situations; for example, their different attitudes towards punctuality.

Hofstede suggests that the main cross-cultural skills involve the capacity to:

* communicate respect
* be non-judgemental
* accept the relativity of one's own knowledge and perceptions
* display empathy
* be flexible
* take turns (allow everyone to take turns in a discussion)
* tolerate ambiguity (accept different interpretations of what has been said).

Improving communication

While the topic of event briefings has been covered briefly above, here are some additional guidelines for improved communication in the event team.

Establish the level of priority

It is important to establish the level of priority immediately. Emergency situations are of course the highest risk for any event, and communication about an incident or potential incident should be given top priority.

Identify the receiver

By identifying the receiver, you will be able to match your message to the receiver's needs, thus demonstrating empathy. Your message will also reach the correct target.

Know your objective

Clarity in communication is often linked to the development of an action objective. If you know what you want to achieve, you will be able to express yourself more easily and clearly. Stating a problem and its ramifications is often only the first stage. By indicating what needs to be done, you can more easily achieve your objective and reach an agreed outcome.

Review the message in your head

In preparing to send a message, you should structure your communication effectively. It is also useful to review the receiver's likely response.

Communicate in the language of the other person

If you use examples and illustrations that the receiver will understand, your message will be more easily comprehended.

Clarify the message

If the receiver appears from their non-verbal behaviour not to understand your message, clarification is essential.

Do not react defensively to a critical response

Asking questions can help you to understand why your receiver has responded defensively and can diffuse the situation. By seeking feedback, you can ensure that you have reached a common understanding.

Think about what this event staffing manager has to say:

> In most event situations you are running on adrenalin from the start. There is never enough time. You have to deliberately stop yourself, focus on the person, look them in the eye and use their name. It is so easy to forget to do this when you have a hundred unsolved problems and the urge is to be short with them. Something as simple as using the person's name makes the difference between a good event leader and a mediocre one. The worst event leaders are so stressed they can't remember their own names!
>
> Source: Event staffing manager

Time management

As mentioned previously, the event environment is busy, noisy and often stressful. To work effectively with event teams, which may be together for a very short period of time, an event manager needs to:

- plan effectively
- build relationships quickly
- identify critical issues and tasks
- analyse and allocate tasks
- manage work priorities
- make quick, informed decisions
- provide timely information
- remove barriers
- simplify processes
- solve problems immediately
- manage stress for themselves and others
- develop creative, flexible solutions
- constantly monitor performance
- reward the achievement of outcomes.

From this list, it is clear that outstanding time management skills (on both a personal and a group level) are required in order to gain maximum benefit from the planning phases. An ability to develop an instant rapport with new people is also essential when time is limited.

Planning and managing meetings

Meetings are an important feature of the management of events, starting in the early planning phases and building to pre-event briefings and post-event evaluations. Meetings can be highly productive, or they can waste an incredible amount of time. In fact, a poorly focused, poorly managed meeting will simply confuse and frustrate everyone. Video conferencing is commonplace for stakeholder meetings, and these need to be structured well.

Timelines should be set and an agenda for discussion distributed beforehand with all relevant material so that everyone is prepared. During meetings, a chairperson should manage the pace and outcomes of the meeting and someone should be designated to keep notes for the record. The most important aspect of note taking is the recording of actions and deadlines for those attending. Documentation from the meeting should be distributed and actions identified, prioritised and included in the planning process.

Information from the wider environment which may affect the team and needs to be covered at meetings includes:

- overall organisational objectives
- rationale for management decisions
- changes in organisation policies
- marketing information and targets
- business performance information (including financials)
- technology updates
- plans for new equipment
- training developments.

In addition to focusing on tasks at event meetings, focusing on people should be a priority. Meetings can be an excellent venue for relieving stress, building team spirit and motivating all involved.

Motivational techniques

In common business operations, such as real estate and banks, most employees are permanent and motivational considerations are quite different from those in the dynamic and project-focused event environment. Here, the workforce is made up of contract, casual, temporary and volunteer labour and a small team of event staff who generally work much more flexible (and longer) hours than the norm. With this in mind, the modern event manager needs to evaluate contemporary theories of motivation to understand how best they can motivate their own work teams. A number of these theories are summarised below.

Getty Images / Andrew Milligan

Not all volunteers are highly motivated

Three needs theory

David McClelland (1961, 1975) suggests that there are three motivating needs: the need for achievement, the need for power, and the need for affiliation. Those motivated by achievement are goal oriented and focus on career development. Those who are motivated by a need for power prefer to influence others, either through formal or informal leadership. Where such influence occurs informally, it is essential that leadership skills are harnessed for the good of the organisation. If the informal leader is a troublemaker, then their goals will not be compatible with those of the organisation. Finally, those who are motivated by affiliation look for a friendly, group-oriented workplace where there is positive social interaction.

Equity theory

In the workplace, people make comparisons between the effort they make and the rewards they receive, and the effort and rewards of others. If there is a perception that other employees or volunteers are better rewarded or make less effort, this will result in a lack of motivation. To redress the issue, the person who feels that their treatment is inequitable is likely to become less productive or leave. Inequity can be perceived by teams as well, with employees at one venue comparing their rewards and effort with those of employees at another venue. 'Not fair' is the usual comment made in this situation and it is applicable to any number of rewards, including meal breaks, shift allocation, uniform design, and allocation of new equipment or incentives. The perceived imbalance between effort and reward is illustrated in Figure 11.2.

FIGURE 11.2 Perceived imbalance between equity and reward

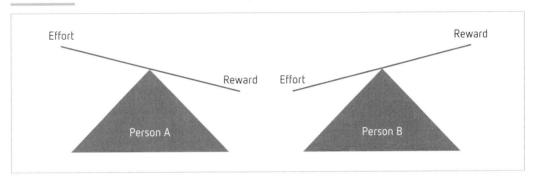

When evaluating the benefits and equity of rewards, another consideration is whether it is best to reward individuals or teams.

Opportunities for individual recognition, development and reward may include:

- internal training/professional development
- external training/professional development
- change in job responsibilities
- opportunity for greater autonomy or responsibility
- formal promotion
- contests and prizes
- rewards for loyalty
- incentives.

Goal setting

Edwin Locke et al. (1984) suggest that achievable goals are highly motivating. However, as well as being achievable, goals must be specific and relevant. Goal achievement is an **intrinsic (internal) motivator**, while prizes and other tangible rewards are **extrinsic (external) motivators**. Many events with social impacts attract volunteers who are intrinsically motivated, because their efforts are directed towards fundraising for charities and other social causes. If this is the case, these goals need to be well articulated, and communication of the milestones towards achieving these goals needs to be timely and encouraging.

> **Intrinsic (internal) motivator**
> Where behaviour is driven by internal rewards such as satisfaction or a sense of achievement
>
> **Extrinsic (external) motivator**
> Where behaviour is driven by an external tangible reward such as a bonus or public recognition

Reinforcement theory

The origin of the theory of reinforcement is the work of B. F. Skinner (1953). Reinforcement theory, more recently rebadged as incentive theory, is based on the premise that people's behaviour is determined by feedback. In the simplest sense, positive feedback is likely to enhance behaviour. So it follows that productivity will improve if the correct behaviours are identified, monitored, recognised and rewarded, often by praise, which is most effective when linked to specific behaviours and goals.

It is important to remember that unacceptable behaviour, too, can be reinforced by positive feedback or actions. For example, a lazy employee who arrives late to find that everyone else has set up the function room is being rewarded for laziness, and an employee taking credit for the work of others is being rewarded if management gives him or her a bonus. Managers need to be aware that they may be positively reinforcing the wrong behaviour. 'Let me do it' can encourage future demonstrations of incompetence!

Another outcome that can follow certain behaviours is punishment. In the event industry, this often involves criticism, and sometimes yelling. The effect is demotivating, even though the behaviour that provoked the outburst may be eliminated.

The use of rewards, including encouragement, can have wide-ranging benefits. A positive working environment can have a dramatic impact on motivation and, in turn, on customer satisfaction. Thus, there is a customer benefit associated with a positive environment. When an individual is rewarded for learning new skills or for working efficiently, this can have a direct, constructive effect on the reinforced behaviour. It can also have a spin-off benefit, by influencing other positive behaviours. Indeed, psychologists have shown that rewards do not have to be given every time the behaviour is exhibited. A variable ratio of reinforcement, given at random, can be even more effective. This principle is evident in the behaviour of gamblers. While gamblers may only win, say, once out of five times, that win is sufficient to encourage them to gamble again and again. This means that a manager can have a powerful influence over an employee's behaviour if the rewards follow the desired outcomes, even if these only occur from time to time. In addition, positively reinforced behaviours are stable, even in the absence of the reinforcer.

In contrast, when a manager has a punishing, critical style, employees may comply when he or she is present, but will take the opportunity to misbehave in his or her absence – 'While the cat's away the mice will play'. For many managers in busy event workplaces, the temptation is to notice errors and omissions. 'Your attitude towards customers is bad' is a negative, punishing reaction that will do little to improve performance. It takes a shift in thinking to provide constructive feedback and encouragement of good performance.

The challenge for the manager is to explain to the employee what a 'good attitude' looks like. 'Stop what you are doing, smile and acknowledge the customer, greet the customer and take time to listen' are some of the signs of a positive attitude towards the customer. Once these behaviours have been established, practised and understood, the employee can be encouraged for exhibiting a positive service ethic. The customer may also reward this orientation with an enthusiastic response. As mentioned, rewards can take many forms. However, in everyday life, simply noticing effort and complimenting it is often all that is needed to create an upbeat event environment which everyone on-site can enjoy.

Role modelling

Role modelling is often used in training in the service industries. At events where the ambience is created by senior staff, the tone is set for subsequent relationships with clients and colleagues. For this reason, behaviour by senior personnel should demonstrate best practice, and employees who model this type of behaviour and uphold the service vision of the organisation should be appropriately rewarded. This may sound very simple, but in practice far too many managers in event workplaces exhibit autocratic, egocentric styles of behaviour that are not conducive to a positive service ethic.

Expectancy theory

This theory, developed by Victor Vroom (1973), looks at the motivators of performance and the outcomes of performance. It also considers the important issue of perception and how the balance between effort and reward is perceived by the individual, thus combining elements of some of the preceding theories. If the expectation is high but the performance target is achievable, the individual or team will achieve the outcome, providing that the outcome has sufficient appeal.

Expectancy theory is one of the most comprehensive explanations of motivation and identifies three variables:
- expectancy (effort linked to performance)
- instrumentality (performance linked to reward)
- valence (attractiveness of rewards).

Expectancy theory stresses the importance of the individual's perception: their perception of effort leading to performance; their perception of the likelihood of rewards being delivered as promised; and their perception of the rewards promised.

Evaluating staff and volunteer satisfaction

Gina and Jeffrey Pauline (2009), in their study of volunteers at a professional tennis event, showed that volunteers were strongly motivated by material and purposive factors, and that volunteer satisfaction was higher when their motives were met. Gordon and Erkut (2004), in their study of volunteers at a music festival, showed that while people were enticed to volunteer by perks such as tickets, T-shirts and meals, their retention and willingness to return to the next event depended on intangible factors. One of these was a scheduling process that allowed for individual preferences.

In reality, the frenetic event environment does not provide the same context for performance management as a traditional

Volunteers ready to help with information

long-life organisation. For most event managers, retention of staff is a pressing issue. This is achieved by charismatic leadership, good project planning, achievement of milestones, and a sense of camaraderie, teamwork and commitment to the event purpose. For events such as the Olympic Games, volunteers are strongly motivated by pride in their country and culture.

Summary

In this chapter, we have discussed the time constraints in staging an event and the temporary nature of the event workforce, both of which have a major impact on event leadership. The event staff manager must be able to plan, organise and control tasks in such a way that all concerned are able to see their contribution to the aims and objectives of the event. In managing these temporary, and often diverse, teams, the event staff manager also needs to accelerate group development processes, communicate effectively, lead constructively, motivate team members, and develop recognition and reward programs.

Key terms

Extrinsic (external) motivator	Where behaviour is driven by an external tangible reward such as a bonus or public recognition
Individualism/collectivism	Hofstede's second value dimension, highlighting the difference between individuality and conformity to group norms
Intrinsic (internal) motivator	Where behaviour is driven by internal rewards such as satisfaction or a sense of achievement
Power distance	First of Hofstede's value dimensions, indicating the extent to which a society accepts differences in power and authority

REVIEW YOUR KNOWLEDGE

1   How does the event leadership environment differ from that of a conventional long-life organisation?
2   Make three suggestions for team development in the event environment.
3   Select one theory of leadership and apply it to the event context.
4   List 10 elements of an effective volunteer management program.

APPLY YOUR KNOWLEDGE

For this activity, you need to lead an event team showing evidence of planning and organising, making decisions, delegating, providing information and motivating through feedback. The team's performance should be effective and efficient.

There are many opportunities for you to bring together a team; for example, the Cancer Council gives you options such as Australia's Biggest Morning Tea, Pink Ribbon, Daffodil Day, Girls' Night In and Relay for Life.

For each of these events, a range of resources and the opportunity to raise money using a secure website are provided. The most inspiring aspect of fundraising is reaching a team target. The sites provide planning tips as well as ideas and inspiration. Resources and downloads include posters and promotional templates.

All that is left to do is to harness a team and achieve your fundraising target. Following the event, provide feedback to the team and evaluate the project's success.

CASE STUDY

VOLUNTEER MANAGEMENT

I knew what I had to do. I had to stand at an access gate all day on my own and check staff passes. I was prepared for the boredom but I didn't bring my thermos or a porta-loo! Can you believe it? I wasn't given a break for six hours! By then I was really looking forward to some relief. You would think that these managers would learn something about people's basic needs. In this situation I needed to keep warm and dry. A folding chair would have made all the difference. A drink and an opportunity to go to the toilet would have been welcome! In terms of the hierarchy of needs, I wasn't expecting self-actualisation, but I was hoping to have my physical needs met by being given scheduled breaks and possibly having my job rotated. In fact, by the time my shift was over for the day, my supervisor had long left the scene. It's good for some.

Event volunteer

QUESTIONS

1 How could this person's needs have been better catered for?
2 Are there any strategies for helping to motivate this volunteer?
3 What leadership approach would you take to manage an event team?
4 Is a different approach needed for managing paid staff as opposed to volunteer staff? Explain your thinking.
5 Explain one way in which you would energise your staff or celebrate success.

Online resources

Visit http://login.cengagebrain.com and search for this book to access the study tools that come with your textbook.

References

Gordon, L., & Erkut, E. (2004). Improving volunteer scheduling for the Edmonton folk festival. *Interfaces*, 34(5), 367–76.

Hofstede, G. (1980). *Culture's consequences: International Differences in Work Related Values*. Beverly Hills, CA: Sage.

Locke, E. A., Frederick, E., Lee, C., & Bobko, P. (1984). Effect of self-efficacy, goals, and task strategies on task performance. *Journal of Applied Psychology*, 69(2), 241.

McClelland, D. C. (1961). *The Achievement Society*. Princeton, NJ: Von Nostrand.

McClelland, D. C. (1975). *Power: The Inner Experience*. New York: Irvington.

Nixon, P., Harrington, M., & Parker, D. (2012). Leadership performance is significant to project success or failure: A critical analysis. *International Journal of Productivity and Performance Management*, 61(2), 204–16.

Pauline, G., & Pauline, J. (2009). Volunteer motivation and demographic influences at a professional tennis event. *Team Performance Management*, 15(3/4), 172.

Skinner, B. F. (1953). *Science and Human Behavior*. New York: Simon and Schuster.

Tyssen, A. K., Wald, A., & Spieth, P. (2013). Leadership in temporary organizations: A review of leadership theories and a research agenda. *Project Management Journal*, 44(6), 52–67.

Vroom, V. H. (1973). A new look at managerial decision making. *Organizational Dynamics*, 1(4), 66–80.

Websites

Motivating volunteers, www.volunteer.vic.gov.au/manage-your-volunteers/supporting-and-supervising/keeping-volunteers-motivated

Six leadership styles and when you should use them, www.fastcompany.com/1838481/6-leadership-styles-and-when-you-should-use-them

The best project management leadership styles, www.brighthubpm.com/monitoring-projects/64679-project-management-leadership-styles

MANAGE ON-SITE EVENT OPERATIONS

12

OVERVIEW

This chapter will provide an overview of event organisation from the standpoint of an event management company or event organiser. The next chapter will deal with the similar responsibilities of a venue-based or in-house event coordinator. The latter works for the venue, and the job is arguably easier as many systems and procedures are in place for the types of events run at a purpose-built commercial venue. In this chapter, the scope of organisation is wider, encompassing, for example, the provision of a complete overlay for several sporting competitions and including a wide range of stakeholders such as the media and sponsors.

LEARNING OBJECTIVES

On completion of this chapter, you will be able to:

1. oversee event set-up against prearranged service agreements, establishing contact with contractors such as set builders

2. monitor event operation through observation and communication, checking on compliance and liaising with the client

3. oversee event breakdown and sign invoices according to contractor arrangements

4. evaluate the operational success of the event through debriefings and review of documentation such as incident report forms.

INDUSTRY VIEWPOINT

It is a normal practice for any representative body, at any level, that has the responsibility to select which organisation will stage an event, to ask each and every rival organisation to supply a proposal detailing how they will organise and stage the event. This process of supplying a proposal is often referred to as the 'bid process'.

When organisations are required to enter into a formal bid process in order to win the right to stage an event, there are two tasks. The first task is to develop a bid proposal and to submit the document to the selecting authority by the required date. In addition, it is often advantageous to attend a meeting of the selecting authority and make a formal presentation that draws out the main points or highlights of their proposal and to answer any questions that may arise. This is the second task.

Source: Leo Isaac (2017). Bidding for events. www.leoisaac.com/evt/top074.htm

INTRODUCTION

When bidding for an event, a proposal needs to be submitted which covers several key areas, including the expertise of the event team, the venue and facilities selected, the event/sporting program, and of course the proposed budget. Multiple stakeholders can be involved, such as a national sports organisation, the government and sponsors.

This chapter will look at the organisational task of preparing event plans, planning for set-up, and managing event operations and the event breakdown. All major events also require a formal evaluation of the success of the event. Planning encompasses selecting the venue or venues required for the competition, and in some cases these are at different locations across a State or country.

Suncorp Stadium in Brisbane, for example, offers a wide range of services, making it an attractive option for event managers looking for a venue. This includes 75 per cent roof covering, 2196 dining spaces, corporate suites, 25 food and beverage outlets, merchandise outlets, ticketing facilities, ATMs, customer service help desks and video replay screens. The range of events held at Suncorp Stadium extends beyond sport to cover other types of events, and all of these have significant operational demands. First, there are the logistics of getting all equipment to the site and ready for set-up, as well as the athletes, participants or exhibitors. The bump-in period can fill several days before the event is open to the public. At the end of the event, everything has to be dismantled and stored, as most items are valuable assets, and the venue restored to its original state for the next operation. With all events, the cost of venue hire includes the period required for bump-in and bump-out, otherwise known as set-up and breakdown. Between bump-in and bump-out there is an event to run and the event audience expects a range of services such as those provided by this venue.

This chapter applies to all types of events, including the following:

- business and corporate

- entertainment and leisure
- exhibitions, expositions and fairs
- festivals
- fundraising
- government and civic
- marketing
- meetings and conventions
- sports.

For each of these events there is an event program which defines the activities that will engage the audience or participants. For example, the program of events for a fishing competition could be advertised as shown in Figure 12.1.

In addition to the program, there is the running order which describes the operational tasks and timing of event set-up and break-down. As described in previous chapters, this starts long before the visitors arrive. For example, in the case of this fishing competition, event staff would arrive long before 6 a.m. to check registrations and start to set up the kids' games, while another team would be working on the fireworks set-up. Bar and food

FIGURE 12.1 Event program for a fishing competition

facilities would likewise need to be prepared for service and products assembled. For an event like this fishing competition, there might be several stakeholders involved, including the harbour authority, the council overseeing the park, the fishing club, the surf club management team and a fireworks contractor. A hierarchy of reporting relationships is essential to ensure that the event manager can effectively coordinate operations.

FINALISE EVENT PREPARATIONS

Meeting the needs of the event participants or performers is part of the preparation process. These may be exhibitors, athletes, speakers, players or other talent. The **customers** may include the audience, spectators, visitors, ticket holders, delegates or media. When it comes to mega events, the importance of meeting the needs of the media crews reporting live results around the world cannot be understated. However, for most events, the aim is to meet the needs of the more tangible audience.

> **Customers**
> In relation to events, includes spectators, visitors, ticket holders, delegates and media

The event organiser needs to develop plans and procedures for on-site management based on an assessment of overall event requirements and to collate materials to facilitate effective on-site management. The event operations manual is the source document for the implementation phase of the event. Event briefings with operational staff and event contractors prior to the event are essential and must include clarification of roles and responsibilities. Naturally, the infrastructure needs to complement the services provided. For example, for security to be effective at a music concert, appropriate fencing and entrances need to be provided. Where the event is of the type where fans may jump or storm the fences to get in free, the fence needs to be a sturdy structure, otherwise it creates a safety hazard (your author was once nearly flattened in just such circumstances). The fence also needs to be covered with a material that prevents outsiders seeing the performance at no charge. Security personnel employed for this type of event have many specifications for managing their roles, including the set-up of the entry points, pass-out systems and lighting. Thus, infrastructure providers and service providers work closely together. During the briefing session, some of these requirements may be revised or improved; for example, initiating additional crowd management measures.

Crowd management requires effective planning

Plans and procedures for on-site management can be extensive. Depending on the nature of the event, they may include any of the following elements, all of which impact on the talent (the performers) or the players.

Travel and accommodation arrangements

Speakers, athletes and entertainers sometimes come from distant locations and their travel arrangements need to be organised, allowing for sufficient time for delays or missed connections. It would be most embarrassing for the event manager if the star of the show was still at the airport when the audience was seated! Accommodation bookings during a peak festival period are hard to come by and the performers need the best of these offerings, as close to the event venue as possible. Most major performers and players travel with a lot of equipment, some of which is potentially unsuitable for use with local electrical and other services, thus presenting further logistical challenges.

Technical requirements

Meeting technical specifications for technological and other equipment is another aspect of services management. The event manager generally has the role of organising all technical elements, including design, scheduling, staging, sound, lighting, audiovisual, entertainment and décor for the production aspect of the event. The stage is replaced by the field of play for a sporting competition and there are quite different specifications for the preparation of football fields and racetracks. In most cases, sporting venues are specialists in this area. The bigger challenges occur when a sporting stadium is used for a music event or other untested event.

Accreditation

Accreditation is the process whereby every person working on-site (other than a ticket holder) is easily identified and enabled to access one or more specific areas or zones; the more senior members of the workforce have access to all zones. Usually, this involves a pass or lanyard which is used for:

- access (to parts of the venue such as the field of play or a VIP area)
- identification (of performers or athletes, or volunteers)
- security (ensuring that everyone is accounted for in specific areas and limiting access to some).

Control areas are installed for a music event

The zones that are likely to be used are for media; athletes and officials on the field (or performers on stage); VIPs; sponsors; as well as operational staff areas around the venue and its surroundings. For major events, some areas are highly secure, with limited access only by accredited personnel with police clearance.

In the context of exhibitions, the visitor accreditation pass can be scanned on entry and when visiting particular stands. Increasingly, radio frequency identification (RFID) devices are used, as they can be read over short distances without swiping a card. RFID devices are used for timing in races, too, usually embedded in ankle bands.

Bump-in and rehearsal

The bump-in and rehearsal processes for performers (singers, speakers) or participants (athletes, cheerleaders) need to be as smooth as possible, so that these people can do their best. This is all scheduled and run by the production/competition team. All participants need to be briefed on their rehearsal schedules and the event program. The event is usually 'called' by the event producer and the stage manager executes these instructions, making sure people appear on stage at the correct time. All production elements need to be run on cue, including lighting, sound and visuals. A green room or change room should be provided for the performers.

Security

Security staff play a role in both of the main areas of the event – behind the stage area and front of house (FOH). Protecting talent, sponsors, VIPs and dignitaries is essential and once again accreditation processes come into play. Security also acts at the interface between the stage or field and the audience, watching for crowd-related problems. A security plan which links with an emergency plan is developed by venue/site management, security management and local authorities such as the police, fire brigade and ambulance services. A separate security plan may be needed for VIPs, performers or players.

Booking and ticketing

Most tickets to larger events are sold online or through ticketing agencies, bringing a whole range of efficiencies to booking and allocating tickets. A streamlined booking process is absolutely essential for all events, both commercial and not-for-profit.

FRINGE WAS WARNED OF BOX OFFICE DEBACLE MONTHS IN ADVANCE

A damning report into the failure of the Edinburgh Festival Fringe's box office has revealed how warnings of potential chaos were being made behind the scenes months in advance. Consultants have blamed a series of 'flawed' decisions by Fringe officials and board members for the ticketing debacle, which brought the world's biggest arts festival to the brink of financial ruin.

The review of last year's box office failure, published today, reveals how a new computer system was still not ready to be tested with a month to go before sales opened ... The consultants have condemned a lack of proper planning, poor project management, inadequate risk assessments and a breakdown in communications both within and without the Festival Fringe Society.

Source: Ferguson, B. (2009). Fringe was warned of box office debacle months in advance. *The Scotsman*, 3 February. www.scotsman.com/news/fringe-was-warned-of-box-office-debacle-months-in-advance-1-827689

A facility for lost tickets or badges needs to be in place if there is no ticket office on-site. Mobile phone technologies have led to many changes to the booking and ticketing process as customers become even easier to reach and registering using their phones is now possible. For many exhibitions, visitors register online.

As mentioned earlier in the book, the anticipation of attending an event is part of the event experience and this is enhanced by an event's website or app featuring the line-up of artists or the current competition results.

Registration/entry

With the advent of remote scanning devices, runners can now wear microchips that have their identity code and finishing time recorded as they pass the start and finish line. The identity of the runner is stored in a barcode-like format which can be scanned over a short distance, the principle being the same as when a person uses a data card to swipe in or out of a building. Microchips that can be scanned remotely will no doubt replace the lanyard worn at exhibitions in future, and each exhibitor will have a report showing how long each visitor spent looking at their stand. Technology, both hardware (microchips) and software (databases), has solved many problems with registration of event participants.

For events such as exhibitions where visitors either register or pay, this process must be carefully planned to avoid delays and frustration. Where visitors register, the data to be collected must be agreed with the client. As with ticketing, registration is often performed online. Registration can be a complex action and consideration should be given to using a specialist company.

Ushering

Security staff, volunteers and ushers all have the role of greeting visitors to an event, and they play an important role in customer service. By briefing contractors, such as security and cleaning staff, the level of customer service can be improved at all stages of the event. Then, as the guests stream out and thank the security staff for a great show, they too can feel that they have contributed to the event experience. Pass-outs or wristbands are an important consideration for facilitating on-site service.

All staff need to provide customer service

Other customer service requirements at an event include information services, lost and found, cloakrooms/lockers and merchandising. First aid and ATMs are essential if pass-outs are not permitted.

Functional areas

While the division of responsibilities into different functional areas has been discussed in previous chapters, it is useful to review the roles of these areas, known in most other businesses as 'departments'. Each of these functional areas develops its own policies, procedures and performance standards.

Procurement and stores

This area is responsible for purchasing, storing and distributing the products required for the event. Such items may include radios, computers, sound equipment and drapes, and these are often hired from specialist suppliers.

If catering, for example, were contracted out to a subcontractor, the subcontractor would be responsible for food purchasing and storage, and the same would apply to other subcontractors. They, too, would be responsible for their product or equipment procurement and storage.

One of the main roles of this functional area during an event is the supply of event merchandise to the sales outlets.

Marketing

In the lead-up to an event, this functional area is responsible for the overall strategy for product, pricing and promotion. As the event draws near, image, sponsor liaison and sales promotion become priorities.

Ticketing

The ticketing area looks after ticketing in the lead-up to an event and during the event. For most profit-making events, the ticketing function is managed wholly by a major ticketing organisation which may also be represented on-site.

Registration

Most sporting events and exhibitions, particularly those with large numbers of participants or visitors, need a functional area to manage the registration of participants in the race or other event. This involves completion and processing of relevant forms by participants, as well as acknowledgement that participation is at their own risk.

Merchandising

The merchandising area is responsible for the sale of merchandise, ranging from caps and posters to T-shirts. The range is frequently extensive and is sometimes advertised online. Merchandising is usually subcontracted to one or more companies.

Finance

As the event draws near, the main concern of this functional area is to maintain control processes, minimise expenditure and manage cash during the event.

Legal

In most cases, legal advice is sought before the event and it is only with very large events that a specific functional area is established to cover this role.

Technology

Networks linking different reporting systems can be developed to include those for sales of tickets and merchandise, registration of attendees and athletes, and recording of results, as well as managing rosters and payroll.

Media

This functional area deals directly with the media, and during an event it needs to be constantly informed of progress. If a negative incident should occur, it is the media unit that writes the press releases and briefs the press. It also manages media interviews with the stars or athletes.

Community relations

Generally speaking, this functional area is only represented when there is a significant community involvement; for example, at non-profit events or those with a social or environmental impact.

Staffing

As the event approaches, the staffing area looks after training, uniforms, rosters and other schedules, and staff meal vouchers. Recognition of their efforts is needed to ensure that all personnel are retained to the end of the event, particularly if the event runs over several days and fatigue is a factor.

Services and information

The provision of guest services and information to the event audience is obviously at its peak during the event, requiring staff to be extremely knowledgeable and resourceful. Most large event venues and sites can be confusing to the audience, so clear traffic flow for ingress and egress, as well as routes, areas and facilities, should be planned with clear signposting.

Cleaning and waste management

Very often this function rests with venue staff who undertake cleaning as a routine operation before, during and after an event. For larger events, such as street festivals, the local council may ask current contractors to expand their role for the period of the festival. For other events, contract cleaners are often called in to manage this functional area. An important consideration today is to make the

Cleaning services are vitally important

event as green or environmentally friendly as possible. Waste management is covered in more detail in Chapter 16.

Catering

In most cases, venue catering is outsourced to a catering company and there is generally a longstanding contract in place with that company. Sometimes, however, a decision needs to be made as to whether to employ one caterer to take on this role or several caterers, each offering different types of cuisine or beverages. Most event organisers leave this area to catering professionals. A food and beverage manager is often employed to oversee this aspect for complex events.

Venue operations

The management of the venue, in particular the operation of facilities and equipment, maintenance and the like, is the responsibility of the venue team. Health, safety and emergencies are the key areas of concern of this functional area. If the event is held at an exotic or unusual location, the appointment of a site manager is recommended to ensure that the obtaining of permits and such things as perimeter fencing, plumbing, cabling, gas and power are under control.

Security

Security services are essential for monitoring and managing crowds. The crowd management plan covers readily available information, such as the dimensions of the venue or site, but it also goes further to encompass the probable number of spectators at particular times of the event and their flow through the site. Clearly, the peaks are the most problematic from a crowd management perspective, and the plan needs to address this and other challenges by carrying out the following tasks:

- Estimate the level of attendance for specific days and times.
- Estimate the number of people using public corridors, specific entrances, specific aisles and seating at particular times.
- Estimate the number of ushers and service and security personnel needed for spectator management.
- Establish the requirements for crowd control measures, such as barriers.

- Identify the areas that need to remain restricted.
- Develop accreditation plans for restricted access by specific staff.
- Identify particular hazards (e.g. scaffolding, temporary structures).
- Identify routes by which emergency services personnel will enter and leave the site.
- Establish the means of communication for all staff working on the site.
- Establish a chain of command for incident reporting.
- Check safety equipment (e.g. the number of fire extinguishers, and also that inspections have been carried out according to legal requirements).
- Identify the safety needs of specific groups of people, such as people with disabilities, children and players/performers.
- Identify first aid requirements and provision.
- Develop an emergency response plan.
- Develop an evacuation plan and initiate training and drills for the staff concerned.

As we know, there are many different types of event venue, each having specific features and some being safer than others. They range from outdoor environments, such as streets and parks, to aquatic centres, indoor facilities and purpose-built venues. The last of these is generally the safest since crowd management and evacuation would generally have been considered at the time these structures were built, and would have been rehearsed again and again by the venue team. However, a crowd management and evacuation plan would still need to be developed for each event held at the venue, as factors such as spectator numbers and movement would generally be different.

Production

Matthews (2015) points out that the term 'event producer' can be used interchangeably with 'event manager'. However, 'producer' generally refers to the role of coordinating and executing the technical side of the event: the production. The production team usually comprises several specialist staging contractors.

Technical equipment and services can include the following:
- audiovisual
- lighting
- rigging
- sets
- sound
- special effects
- stage design.

Sports operations

All aspects of a sporting competition, including results management and award ceremonies, are managed by sports operations.

Medical

The medical functional area provides first aid and other medical services to both attendees/ spectators and performers/athletes. In some cases, this area is responsible for athlete

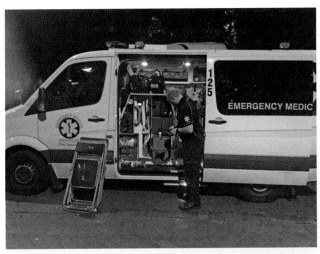

EMS Event Medical is a mass gathering medical specialist

drug testing at major sporting events. Mass gatherings present any number of medical emergencies and this can be outsourced to specialist organisations such as EMS Event Medical, an organisation providing trained paramedics using GPS tracking for fast response, and supported by on-site pre-hospital emergency care.

Summary

These functional areas, and their roles and responsibilities, should be spelled out in the operations manual, which should also contain emergency contact details for all event contractors. Run sheets, production schedules or running orders should be available to everyone who has responsibility for an action or actions included on these schedules. Some people will need only summaries, while others, such as the lighting engineers, will need minute-by-minute cues. Maps and layouts of the event overlay are also essential for event personnel. Exceptional personal skills in communication and people management assist in reducing the anxiety level of all concerned. Contractor communication mechanisms and protocols need to be put in place, including the appointment of a main liaison person for each contracted supplier. Two-way radios or walkie-talkies are recommended, as mobile phones are unsatisfactory tools for communication in the event environment. The benefit of two-way radio is that several listeners can be on the channel at one time.

OVERSEE EVENT SET-UP

As mentioned previously, attention to detail is essential, which is why it can take years to plan an Olympic Games or Commonwealth Games. During this phase, attention needs to be paid to planning in all the areas mentioned, with a specific focus on the following safety features of planning:

- safety risk identification assessment and control
- communications and consultation

Loading the venue requires detailed scheduling

* security
* event operations
* crowd management
* construction
* contractor management
* traffic management.

Figure 12.2 provides a checklist of tasks that need to be done in preparation for sporting events. Leo Isaac also offers an event operations manual on his site that provides the basis for comprehensive planning.

FIGURE 12.2 Checklists for indoor and outdoor venues

CHECKLIST FOR INDOOR VENUES	CHECKLIST FOR OUTDOOR VENUES
• Moving competition equipment into place	• Mowing and marking grass
• Erecting sponsor signage	• Putting up crowd-control ropes
• Erecting flags, banners and bunting	• Erecting tents and marquees
• Fixing direction signs	• Erecting sponsor signage
• Setting up microphones, amplifiers and speakers for public address	• Fixing direction signs
• Positioning podiums for speeches and medal ceremonies	• Setting up microphones, amplifiers and speakers for public address
• Positioning scoreboards	• Positioning podiums for speeches and medal ceremonies
• Setting out tables and chairs	• Checking playing surfaces for hazards
• Painting, fixing and/or cleaning equipment, furniture and premises	• Erecting flags, banners and bunting
• Checking security of windows and doors	• Erecting portable toilets
• Working out lighting and air-conditioning controls	• Positioning of first aid equipment
• Positioning of first aid equipment	

Source: Leo Isaac (2017). Venue set-up. www.leoisaac.com/evt/top096.htm

EXTENSION ACTIVITY

Watch the following time-lapse video of an event set-up – **https://youtu.be/nTxx1GAWK5w** – pausing from time to time in order to complete a run sheet for the build.

Hint: The project set-up took two days from about 7 a.m. on the first day through to the opening of the event at 7 p.m. on the second day.

The key environmental and social impacts of event delivery, and the minimum-impact procedures needed to reduce them, must be considered during this phase, including:

- reducing impact on the lifestyle of neighbouring residents
- maintaining natural and cultural integrity
- recycling and disposing of waste, especially hazardous substances
- planning for safety for crowds and the movement of large numbers of attendees
- managing traffic and parking
- monitoring use of energy, water and other resources during event set-up, operation and breakdown.

Service agreements with event contractors should be reconfirmed and checked during event set-up. Problems with power supply, noise, waste and ticketing cannot be solved during the event execution phase and need to be checked and double-checked during set-up and rehearsal. The gates will open on time and the event set-up has to be completed successfully beforehand.

MONITOR EVENT OPERATION

Murphy's Law says that if something can go wrong, it will! Here are some things that can go wrong, and have gone wrong, in the event business:

- All volunteer contact details and rosters are accidentally deleted two days before the event.
- The sprinklers come on during an outdoor cocktail party.
- The speaker is so short she cannot be seen behind the lectern.
- There is no accessible toilet for someone in a wheelchair.
- Fans find their way into the VIP area.
- The beer runs out.
- Children vomit in public.
- The ATM is stolen.
- The seat numbers are so faint they can't be read.
- The prawns are left out overnight.
- The toilets get blocked.

The event manager's role is to monitor event operations through observation and appropriate communication and control mechanisms and to identify and analyse operational problems, such as the need for additional services, as they arise and take prompt action to address them. As this chapter so clearly illustrates, careful contingency planning is absolutely essential. If all reasonable 'what if' questions have been answered, then there will be fewer problems to deal with.

Common deficiencies and discrepancies for business events may include:

- incorrect room set-ups
- incorrect staging
- faulty or unavailable technical equipment
- lack of equipment to manage displays and signage
- shortage of food and beverage
- insufficient or dirty toilets
- inappropriate space in registration areas.

Of these, the importance of sufficient food and beverage promptly served cannot be overstated. Nothing upsets a business client more than a long queue that leads to an almost empty banquet table.

Detailed run sheets are used for the timing of the actual event, irrespective of the type of event (sporting, concert, dinner and so on). The actual implementation of these schedules is normally vested in one person, the producer/director/stage manager (depending on the type of event), who 'calls' the show using instructions to staff to ensure that all aspects are on cue. Under their direction may be performers, lighting, sound and vision. It is a very skilled and highly responsible role.

Crowd management

Crowd management is one aspect of event monitoring that needs careful attention at all times. Preventative measures (such as barriers) can be put in place, but close supervision is also required. To reduce congestion at turnstiles, staff should be deployed to assist spectators and to monitor the area. However, impatient crowds might simply jump over the turnstile or knock it down, so there would need to be a contingency plan in place for dealing with this situation. Property damage by spectators would also need to be covered and procedures put in place for ejecting the offenders. At worst, the police may charge them. (Streakers who disrupt play during sports matches spring to mind.) The more serious risk, however, is that non-ticketed spectators will gain illegal entry.

First aid

A number of services exist to cater for different levels of coverage for first aid services. As part of the risk management process, you need to consider which type of service will meet your needs. For example, two volunteer first aid personnel would be nowhere near sufficient to cover a professional motor sports event. Equally, a team of six paid doctors and paramedics would definitely be overkill for a school sports carnival (and would probably never fit in such an event's budget).

The level of service available at an event is influenced by the number of first aid personnel on-site and their qualifications. Whether they are paid or volunteers will also have an impact on service, as generally the more highly trained specialists are those working in a paid capacity.

Emergency response plan

In order to effectively implement emergency procedures, the following steps should be taken:
- Review implementation issues and integrate them with all other event operational plans.
- Ensure broad awareness of the procedures through wide dissemination of information and consultation with all concerned.
- Use signage and well-designed communication materials in a simple format to provide information.
- Train all staff.
- Test the procedures by conducting evacuation exercises.
- Review procedures to check effectiveness.

Unfortunately, there are many examples of events at which people have lost their lives through fire or riot, and there are many more examples of near misses. For this reason, it is necessary to prepare both a crowd management plan and a risk management plan for every event, as well as emergency response plans (ERPs) for crowd control and evacuation in case of fire or other major risks. As indicated, these plans must comply with the relevant legislation and standards and be properly implemented. All possible preventative measures and contingency plans need to be put in place prior to an event, and appropriate staff training is essential.

Communication

Workforce communication during the event period when everyone is 'slammed' is vitally important. Mobile phones that are so busy that all they do is go to voicemail each time are not the answer. Two-way radios with associated protocols for emergency reporting are an essential component of managing on-site event operations. Channels need to be coordinated with any outsourced services such as security, first aid and cleaning.

What do you imagine the administrators of a surfing event require to set up the event?

EXTENSION ACTIVITY

imagetalk / Bjorn Svensson

OVERSEE EVENT BREAKDOWN

When the event is over, the event manager has to ensure that event breakdown (bump-out) is completed according to contractual arrangements. This may involve supervising the packing and removal of items (but not before the audience leaves, please) and liaising with venue and site personnel to check the site before leaving, in particular making sure that everything has been turned off, lost property logged and a full inspection of any damage conducted. It may be necessary to debrief operational staff and contractors, with a view to future operational and service improvements. Finally, after a good night's sleep, accounts need to be checked against contractor agreements and any matters requiring post-event action assessed. Any legal issues are likely to emerge post-event, so careful analysis of duty logs and incident reports is recommended. For major events, the legal team is the last to leave the building as they have to deal with outstanding issues such as claims for compensation.

During this phase, consideration is given to:

- documentation and records
- security
- contractor management
- incident investigation
- monitoring and assessment
- system audits and management review
- audience satisfaction
- stakeholder debriefing.

EVALUATE OPERATIONAL SUCCESS OF THE EVENT

An event evaluation report is an important document, particularly if the organisation plans to bid for future events. This should report on financial reporting, attendance and ticket sales, client satisfaction, media reports, safety and incident management, sponsor feedback and other matters. Proof of success is not given enough attention in the event industry, possibly because there are so many stakeholders involved.

Summary

This chapter has looked at operational management during the performance itself, when a wide range of on-site services need to be provided to both the performers/players and the audience. This requires exceptionally careful planning and implementation, using checklists developed for previous similar events. Acute observation skills, quick thinking and problem solving are essential skills required of the management team. Anxiety in the management team will transmit quickly through the whole production, damaging the ambience and inhibiting the enjoyment of the audience. Thus, a cool head and gallons of charm are necessary when something goes wrong, as inevitably it will. However, careful planning for contingencies will ensure that most problems are likely to be minor. An upbeat management style contributes in a positive way to the event experience for all concerned.

Key term

Customers   In relation to events, includes spectators, visitors, ticket holders, delegates and media

REVIEW YOUR KNOWLEDGE

1   Who do we refer to in this chapter when we talk about the needs of the performers / players?
2   Who do we refer to in this chapter when we talk about the needs of the audience?
3   Who are other potential customers?
4   Explain the following requirements of the performers using specific examples:
    - travel and accommodation
    - technical
    - catering
    - security.
5   Explain the following requirements of the event audience using specific examples:
    - booking
    - registration
    - ushering
    - problem solving
    - exiting the event.
6   What is a functional area? Give two specific examples.

APPLY YOUR KNOWLEDGE

Conduct your own survey titled 'The things I hate most about events' with 20 colleagues to see which aspects of customer service are most important. Contrast these results with a survey about the things customers like most.

SurveyMonkey is widely used for online surveys. Use this tool if you have access to it.

CASE STUDY

ON-SITE SERVICES FOR AN AWARDS NIGHT

You are running a graduation and awards night for a school, which 300 people will attend. Using the concepts explained in this chapter, describe how you would provide event services for:

- the graduates
- the award winners
- the parents and visitors
- the school's staff.

You will need a layout diagram for the venue and a run sheet that includes tasks, timelines and responsibilities. The names and certificates will need to be checked against RSVPs more than once and a contingency plan put in place for a missing certificate.

This should not be just like any other awards ceremony, so think about lighting, sound and other effects that could create the right atmosphere.

You need to submit the following documentation:

- budget
- venue or site selection
- organisational chart of stakeholders involved
- communication plans
- registration plans

- operational documents including the event program and the schedule for set-up and breakdown
- event service agreements (e.g. entertainment)
- risk assessment
- other documents such as maps and rosters.

    Given an opportunity to run a live or simulated event, you also need to write a final report.

Online resources

Visit http://login.cengagebrain.com and search for this book to access the study tools that come with your textbook.

Reference

Matthews, D. (2015). *Special Event Production: The Resources* (2nd edn). London: Routledge.

Websites

Event operations manual – template (Leo Isaac), www.leoisaac.com/evt/evt002.htm

Event planning guide (Wodonga), www.wodonga.vic.gov.au/leisure-arts-visitors/events/images/
    Event_management_planning_guide.pdf

One-week banquet set-up and breakdown, https://youtu.be/KfUt2jv9VOE

PLAN IN-HOUSE EVENTS OR FUNCTIONS

13

OVERVIEW

This chapter looks at the role of the in-house venue coordinator in a facility such as a conference centre, hotel or stadium. Up until now, the focus in this text has been on the wider role of the event planner (or coordinator) who has been putting a project together for a client, with the venue as one element of the package. Here, the important role of venue coordinator or venue manager is discussed in detail. Key responsibilities for someone in this position are negotiating bookings for the venue and finding out about client specifications, such as layout, access, timing, food and beverage service, and special requirements. The main duty of the venue manager is to ensure that the event space is clean and set up correctly, and that services are provided as per client specifications. Regarding any building or facility, it is also assumed that security and emergency planning are in place.

LEARNING OBJECTIVES

On completion of this chapter, you will be able to:

1. liaise with event customer or clients to satisfy service expectations, determining operational needs, preferences and budget

2. prepare and confirm event proposals and negotiate and agree on final event details

3. coordinate event services, including internal areas and external suppliers, preparing and distributing operational documentation

4. finalise an event and evaluate operational success, including finalising payment.

INDUSTRY VIEWPOINT

A venue coordinator works for the venue, not directly for you. They'll act as a liaison between you and the venue's operations team, which means they'll show you the venue, help coordinate any services offered on-site (from in-house catering to valet parking), and process the final invoice.

They'll typically deal with the logistics of a wedding on the day of, like giving vendors access to the site for set-up and breakdown, setting up tables and chairs, ensuring the power and plumbing works, cleaning the space before and after the event, keeping things safe (cleaning up that glass your drunken uncle dropped on the dance floor), and more …

If the venue you're considering does not offer an on-site coordinator, you may want to hire an event coordinator. This person is separate from the venue and will be hired directly by you, which means you'll need to factor this expense into your budget …

Your event coordinator's goal is to make sure you are able to enjoy every moment of your wedding without worrying if the right people are in the right place at the right time or about whether or not you're sticking to the schedule. Consider them your big day BFF, there to guide you and your partner through the whole process as smoothly as possible. After all, they'll be by your side from the moment you start planning until you make your grand exit.

Source: Loverly (2015). What's the difference between a venue coordinator & an event coordinator, anyway? https://lover.ly/planning/wedding-101/wedding-need-to-know-venue-coordinator-vs-event-coordinator

INTRODUCTION

The distinction between an in-house/venue coordinator and an event coordinator becomes clear when reporting and payment are analysed. A **venue coordinator** is employed by the venue to manage the client (see Figure 13.1), which takes in all of the logistics of the event from booking through to payment. The client pays the venue for the services delivered by it, generally including food and beverages. If other external services are required, such as a DJ or limo, the client will pay for this directly.

> **Venue coordinator**
> Works for the venue to manage the event from booking through to payment
>
> **Event coordinator**
> Organises all aspects of an event for a client

By contrast, an **event coordinator** works for the client and is paid by them to undertake all planning for an event; for example, RSVPs, as well as travel and accommodation arrangements for attendees. There are several ways in which event coordinators (including wedding planners) are paid. It can be by the hour, as a percentage of expenses, or as a flat project fee. Event coordinators may also earn commissions from suppliers such as hotels or photographers. In these

FIGURE 13.1 Role of in-house or venue coordinator

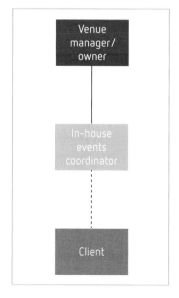

circumstances, the client would pay the suppliers directly. This is shown in Figure 13.2, where the dotted lines illustrate the relationship of the parties in terms of planning, through to payment.

Remember that a **commercial venue** can take the form of a convention centre, hotel, restaurant, entertainment complex, nightclub, club or stadium. People who supply services such as DJs, entertainers and celebrity speakers, are generally referred to as *suppliers*, while businesses that provide goods (such as coffee carts) are often called **vendors**. For example, at a stadium you would refer to an ice-cream vendor – the vendor typically sells directly to the client. Technically there are differences between the two, but in this industry the terms are used more or less interchangeably. The key point is who pays the supplier or vendor? If an event coordinator were to pay the suppliers, this would create completely new legal and financial arrangements, and this is why most wedding and party planners prefer to work on the basis of hourly or project rates, working more or less as consultants and thus carrying fewer financial and legal risks.

Lastly, it is important to note that the role of venue coordinator is similar in most respects to that of a banquet manager. The banquet manager supervises venue staff in the set-up process, liaises with the chef in the kitchen, coordinates food and beverage service, and monitors guest satisfaction in the hotel environment. (A job description for a venue manager is shown in the following section.)

Terminology is tricky as there are a variety of roles that fall within the scope of in-house event coordination, such as a facilities event coordinator or catering sales assistant. The catering manager, while mainly responsible for the kitchen side of the business, might also be in charge of service if the venue is small.

FIGURE 13.2 Role of event coordinator or wedding planner

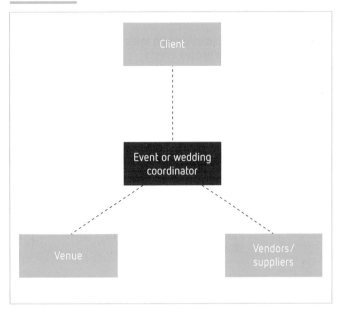

Commercial venue
Venue that charges for hire or offers event packages, usually designed for the purpose of staging events

Vendor
Generally supplies direct to the customer, such as a hot dog vendor or concession

LIAISE WITH EVENT CUSTOMER TO SATISFY SERVICE EXPECTATIONS

In the sections that follow, we will discuss the responsibilities of the venue manager (see Figure 13.3) and venue coordinator and compare these with those of the banquet manager, who has more of a **front-of-house** role in service delivery,

Front of house
In the event context, the area where customers are served

FIGURE 13.3 Job description – venue manager (at a sporting venue)

- In conjunction with sales and marketing, maximise bookings to ensure the viability of planned and proposed events
- Prepare quotes for hire and organise all aspects of this
- Ensure all services are operational at scheduled times, and standards are maintained for service delivery
- Ensure that the venue is run in a safe manner and in accordance with all legislative requirements, including workplace health and safety, security and emergency planning
- Manage cleanliness and waste management
- Liaise with suppliers/vendors
- Deliver key performance indicators in providing food and beverage
- Manage venue staffing
- Monitor sales, margins, budgets and cash control
- Proactively plan and implement operational plans so that best-practice operational and service standards are achieved

> **Back of house**
> In the event context, the operations area, which includes kitchens, stores and so on

as opposed to a **back-of-house** role. Using the term 'venue manager' rather than 'in-house event coordinator' will help us to avoid confusing these roles with those of event planners or conference organisers, who are not venue-based.

The venue manager needs to develop plans and procedures for on-site management based on an assessment of overall event requirements, and to collate materials to facilitate effective on-site management. The operations manual is the source document for the planning phase of the event.

A venue operations manual will include the following:

- facilities and services
- event layout plans
- fees and charges
- menus for food and beverages
- cleaning and waste
- technology, including audiovisual
- emergency plans
- crowd management.

The Perth Convention and Exhibition Centre, for example, has an event manual which it provides to clients for planning purposes, as do all large venues of this type. These manuals form the basis for ensuring that all booked events deliver on the clients' selection of goods and services and final specifications. This negotiation process will lead to a proposal for the client that also includes booking conditions, a confirmation letter and contract documentation.

Once the negotiations for venue use are finalised, the operational phase begins. As many venues run a wide range of events such as meetings, trade shows, banquets, awards nights, entertainment events, ceremonies and competitions, the venue manager has a lot of work to do in planning the configuration of the venue and providing the staff required to deliver the event. Numerous external suppliers are needed to provide lighting and sound, décor, floral arrangements, stages and so on. Internal event services generally include catering, cleaning and waste, security and technical services.

Event briefings with operational staff and event production contractors prior to the event are essential and must include clarification of roles and responsibilities.

Different types of events run at the Perth Convention and Exhibition Centre

PREPARE AND CONFIRM EVENT PROPOSAL

When negotiating the event booking, there are several things that need to be discussed, including the issues discussed in the following sections.

Event specifications and running order

The essential items are the date and times of the event, a brief idea of the running order, the space(s) required, food and beverages required, technical equipment, total budget, and estimated number of attendees (to be finalised by a cut-off date).

Rooms required

Rooms and spaces can include breakout rooms, conference rooms, and evening banquet room. Hotel rooms may be needed for speakers and other key guests. Styles of room set-ups (see Figure 13.4) include the following:

- banquet
- classroom
- conference
- theatre
- U-shape.

Food and beverages

Menus and food and beverage packages are generally offered to clients, but they may have special requests for menus to match the theme of an event. In a survey done by Special Events (Hurley, 2012), caterers report that the percentage of special meal requests at events has risen from 5 per cent to 20 per cent over the past 10 years. The difficulty faced by the chef here is differentiating between serious allergies and food preferences. Table 13.1 illustrates some of these options.

FIGURE 13.4 Styles of room set-up

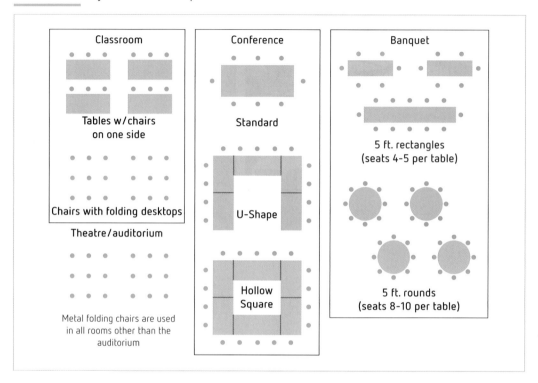

TABLE 13.1 Special food requests

RELIGIOUS	VEGETARIAN	DIETARY	ALLERGY
• Kosher/Jewish • Halal/Islam • Lactovegetarian/Hindu, Buddhism	• Raw food • Indian style • Chinese style • Vegan	• Diabetic • Fat free • Low salt • Low calorie • Non-carbohydrate	• Nut and other allergies, such as shellfish • Lactose intolerant • Gluten intolerant

Food is an integral part of any event, so the preparation of a catering concept is essential at an early stage of event planning. This is necessary to ensure that the catering concept complements and enhances the overall event or function concept.

Any experienced event manager knows that complaints about food are serious indeed and extremely difficult to remedy during or after an event. Conversely, where client expectations are surpassed, food quality can contribute to high satisfaction ratings for the entire event. Since, generally speaking, the cost of food in relation to all other costs is relatively low, food should always be served in reasonable portion sizes and reasonable quantities. Careful planning is essential, and advice must be given to the client on menu selection and service style to ensure that they meet the needs of the audience or spectators at the event.

The costing process

Menu costing is usually the domain of the executive chef in a large establishment. However, someone running a small catering business needs to give careful consideration to costing. Figure 13.5 shows an example of the costing sheet for one menu item. Figure 13.6 illustrates the preparation time and labour cost involved in one banquet order.

FIGURE 13.5 Labour costing

ITEM	FRIDAY	HOURS	SATURDAY	HOURS
Puff pastry smoked salmon bites	Slice salmon	10	Assembly	11
	Make crème fraiche	5	Baking	6
	Prepare garnishes	2	Plating	3
	Set-up and clean-up	5	Set-up and clean-up	5

Once the preparation time has been calculated for all menu items, the spreadsheet would show the total kitchen labour cost and food cost for the banquet menu – total labour cost is shown in Figure 13.6. A similar costing would need to be done for the food and beverage service aspects of the event, including the cost of setting up the function area. Using spreadsheets provided by industry software is the best way to manage costing and quotations, as the number of attendees can be easily modified.

FIGURE 13.6 Labour costing

EMPLOYEE	HOURS FRIDAY	LABOUR COST	HOURS SATURDAY	LABOUR COST
Chef	10	$250	11	$275
Apprentice	8	$144	10	$455
Total labour cost		**$394**		**$730**

Styles of service

There are several styles of service, ranging from plated meals to self-service buffets, from which a client may choose.

Buffet

A buffet style set-up offering a wide variety of foods will usually guarantee customer satisfaction. However, a major mistake often made with buffets is not providing sufficient vegetarian dishes. As these appeal to non-vegetarians too, it is common to find that such dishes have run out before the vegetarians get to the front of the queue. Buffet queues are another matter of concern – if a queue forms, it can take some time for the last person to help themselves, by which time some dishes, such as seafood, may have run out. But with careful planning and layout, they can be avoided.

Buffet food

Plated meals

For many functions and conventions, the food is pre-plated and everyone gets the same meal unless a special dietary request has been made. Sometimes, there is a 50/50 drop, with different meals served to alternate guests. Guests at the table are then free to swap meals if they please. Again, demand for vegetarian meals is often higher than expected, even though guests are asked about special meal requests at the time of booking. One of the many menus offered by Suntec Singapore Convention & Exhibition Centre is illustrated in Figure 13.7. This convention centre can organise events ranging from small cocktail parties for 10 people to weddings, corporate dinners, banquets, functions and other special events for 10 000 people. The centre's world-class chefs provide a gourmet selection of Asian, Western and halal menus. In the competitive field of convention bidding, catering plays a big part in the decision-making processes of organisers.

FIGURE 13.7 Example of a gourmet menu offered by a convention centre

GOLDEN PEONY MENU

Sashimi on Ice
taro, deoduck clam, salmon and lobster

Buddha Jumps over the Wall
top broth with abalone, sea cucumber,
shark's fin, scallops and fish maw

Stuffed Spiny Sea Cucumber
served with crab roe

Braised Abalone
served with Hong Kong kai lan

Pepper Beef Tenderloin
served with Oriental apple sauce

Imperial Pearl Rice
with crabmeat, dried scallops and prawns

Double-boiled Bird's Nest
with hasma, ginseng, red dates in young coconut shell

Suntec Singapore International Convention & Exhibition Centre

Source: Suntec Singapore Convention & Exhibition Centre. www.suntecsingapore.com

Grazing stations

A contemporary approach to function food is a grazing station – a small table with light snacks such as cheese and fruit. Healthier items are becoming increasingly popular, with fruit often served for morning and afternoon tea. A large basket of red apples is a welcome change from a platter of processed biscuits.

Food stalls

Food stalls are commonplace at many events, and here it is essential that food quality and food safety are carefully monitored. The caterers should be evaluated before the event, menu and food specifications agreed, and food safety plans reviewed.

Beverage service

Prices for alcohol at functions such as weddings should be negotiated beforehand. This can be done on the basis of an open bar where the host pays for all individual drinks, or a cash bar where guests pay for all their own alcohol. A compromise is an agreement by the host to pay for all beer, wine and soft drinks but not spirits. In other cases, the host might set a limit on the budget, and once this is reached guests must pay for their own drinks. Or a full package deal might be negotiated where the establishment charges a flat rate based on average drinking at a similar type of function. This, of course, includes a margin for profit. In rare cases, the client may wish to provide the wine, in which case corkage rates need to be discussed before the event.

A survey of weddings in the UK showed that almost one in five people has problems with at least one aspect of their wedding – one in 10 reported problems with the photographer or DJ, and one in 20 reported issues with catering.

Search online for favourite 'wedding fails' moments and look for some of things that can go wrong, such as 'Drone knocks out groom'. List 10 complaints that fall within the responsibility of the reception venue, in order of importance.

EXTENSION ACTIVITY

Technical requirements

Technical requirements for indoor venues can be met in-house, or if they are complex, by an external specialist. Considerations include:

* the stage and props
* audiovisual services, projectors and screens
* hanging points and rigging
* load capacity, room access and loading dock
* laptops and clickers
* power availability and capacity.

Support is essential for an event with sophisticated technical requirements, but even for small weddings where the father of the bride wants to show a PowerPoint display and can't manage without a mouse.

Invoicing and payment

The terms and conditions of the contract are very important. As mentioned previously, a guaranteed number of guests and deadline for confirmation are essential. The chef will base all menu planning on the basis of the guaranteed and set numbers. Food orders need to be taken into account when agreement is reached on deposit and payment schedules. The payment schedule can vary considerably – some highly sought-after wedding venues require full payment one month before the wedding, with no refund for a cancellation.

Public liability insurance

Many venue-hire contracts include the following requirement for insurance:

> The hirer shall, at all times during the term of this agreement, be the holder of a current public liability policy of insurance, which covers it in respect of the activities that are the subject of the use of the facility and be for an amount of at least $10 million.

In some cases, councils offer limited liability insurance for casual hirers. Regardless, the venue manager or event coordinator is obliged to monitor the currency of insurance arrangements and certification. This is generally not a requirement for conventional, purpose-built commercial facilities such as hotel venues and function centres.

If your event is in your home and the general public does not have access, you still need to check the terms and conditions of your home and contents insurance, which often includes a public liability component. (Needless to say, this is equally important at any other venue.) Your insurance may be void if illegal activity is taking place, including the sale of alcohol to minors or the sale of illicit drugs.

Visit **http://theothertalk.org.au/hosting-a-teenage-party** and answer the following: What happens if the event is advertised on Facebook and hundreds of gatecrashers turn up? Who takes responsibility: the venue or the host?

Special requests

Banquet event order (BEO)
Specifies the client's specifications and the event booking details

The final stage of preparation for a venue-based event is the event order form, also known as the **banquet event order (BEO)** (see Figure 13.8). Note the important difference between 'guarantee' and 'set'. The guarantee is the minimum number of guests the client has agreed to in the contract. However, one generally sets for more, just in case. If additional guests turn up, the client will pay for them. If less than the guaranteed number of guests turn up, the client still pays for the guaranteed number.

COORDINATE EVENT SERVICES

The set-up of a venue for an event is best understood by watching time-lapse videos such as those included in the weblinks at the end of the chapter. The most useful ones tell you the full duration, such as the Amway Center 72-hour overlay. There are numerous examples of

FIGURE 13.8 Banquet event order (BEO)

DAY Friday	DATE 17 May	TIME 6 p.m. start 11 p.m. end	VENUE Grand Ballroom	GUARANTEE 185	SET 200
Event client			Billing instructions		
Event planner			Authorised signer(s)		
Email address			Advance deposit amount		
Contact details					
Billing address					
MENU Guarantee guest count and deadline			BEVERAGE DÉCOR		
STAFFING AND SET-UP			AUDIOVISUAL REQUIREMENTS		
			BILLING		
			Food		
			Beverage		
			Room rental		
			AV		
SPECIAL REQUESTS			Total		
			Deposit		
			Amount due by		
Prepared by			Terms and conditions		
Issue date					
Signature					

banquet set-ups in this format, which illustrate the huge effort, equipment, expertise and timing required.

Consideration needs to be given to four phases:

1 The *build phase* is needed for the installation of ceiling fixtures and stages, for example.

2 The *set-up phase* is needed for moving banquet furniture and setting tables.

3 The *service phase* presents the biggest challenge, particularly in working out how long it will take to serve each course. For example, 20 tables of 10 people could require five servers and two runners, and it would take approximately 20–30 minutes to serve the main course. Staffing needs to be scheduled accordingly.

4 The *breakdown phase* involves clearing and packing everything away. In many venues, the room is set up for the next day's event before staff leave in the early hours.

From these examples, one can see that costing and scheduling are key skills required in this role. Looking at the job description for a banquet manager shown here (Figure 13.9), one can now understand the complexities of 'supervise service', particularly if you have also watched a time-lapse video of function service.

FIGURE 13.9 Job description – banquet manager

- Plan event service with meticulous attention to detail included in banquet order
- Manage daily staff roster
- Oversee room set-up according to specifications
- Coordinate with staff and relevant departments to arrange for the delivery of requested services
- Coordinate with kitchen regarding food production and service planning
- Inspect tables for place settings: linen, china, glass and silverware
- Supervise service and ensure customer satisfaction
- Manage special requests such as seating and food preferences
- Conduct regular meetings with catering managers and catering director to ensure the needs of the clients are being met

A banquet manager has a thousand details to supervise

Per-person calculators are available online for all types of event set-up. Event planning software provides for easy calculations and tailor-made diagrams for clients showing the spaces and capacity for different set-ups (see the example in Table 13.2). Remember that space is required between tables for seating and service aisles, with wider aisles and less seating per table if wheelchairs are to be accommodated.

TABLE 13.2 Sample event set-up calculation

TABLE TYPE	NUMBER OF TABLES	NUMBER OF PEOPLE	METRES (SQ)
Round (1.8 metres)	20	200	242

It is evident from all of the above that the venue manager and event coordinator need to work with internal personnel and external suppliers in the process of effective event planning and implementation. A detailed schedule including all components and timings is the most critical element of planning, and then it is essential to be proactive, flexible and calm during the service phase. Requests for special meals not booked beforehand can put a spanner in the works, while late guests and more people than expected attending are other potential problems.

Trade shows and exhibitions

Trade shows and exhibitions place different demands on the venue manager. Most exhibition spaces are a blank canvas and the first step is planning the layout of stands and pricing them accordingly. For example, the largest exhibition space closest to the entrance can be charged out at the highest rate. This is likely to be a custom-built stand. At the back of the exhibition, it is likely that the stands will be standard builds and attract correspondingly lower fees.

The design of custom builds can vary greatly. Look at exhibition websites such as **www. exhibitoronline.com** to see illustrations of some of these designs, one of which is the 'Plaza' (see Figure 13.10).

FIGURE 13.10 The 'Plaza' exhibition structure

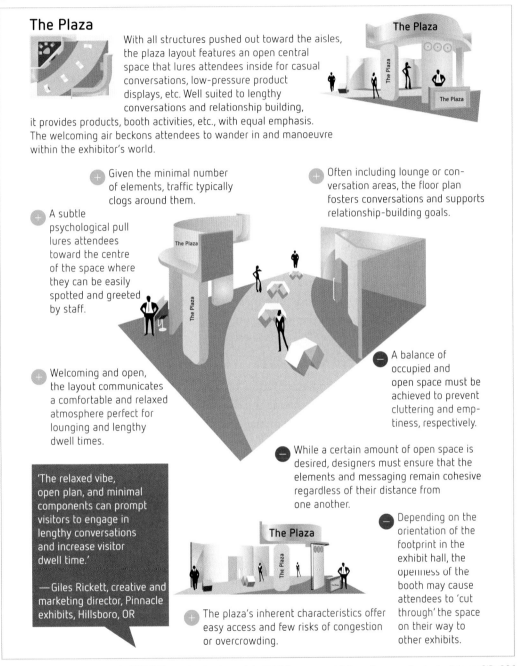

The Plaza

With all structures pushed out toward the aisles, the plaza layout features an open central space that lures attendees inside for casual conversations, low-pressure product displays, etc. Well suited to lengthy conversations and relationship building, it provides products, booth activities, etc., with equal emphasis. The welcoming air beckons attendees to wander in and manoeuvre within the exhibitor's world.

Given the minimal number of elements, traffic typically clogs around them.

A subtle psychological pull lures attendees toward the centre of the space where they can be easily spotted and greeted by staff.

Often including lounge or conversation areas, the floor plan fosters conversations and supports relationship-building goals.

Welcoming and open, the layout communicates a comfortable and relaxed atmosphere perfect for lounging and lengthy dwell times.

A balance of occupied and open space must be achieved to prevent cluttering and emptiness, respectively.

'The relaxed vibe, open plan, and minimal components can prompt visitors to engage in lengthy conversations and increase visitor dwell time.'

—Giles Rickett, creative and marketing director, Pinnacle exhibits, Hillsboro, OR

While a certain amount of open space is desired, designers must ensure that the elements and messaging remain cohesive regardless of their distance from one another.

Depending on the orientation of the footprint in the exhibit hall, the openness of the booth may cause attendees to 'cut through' the space on their way to other exhibits.

The plaza's inherent characteristics offer easy access and few risks of congestion or overcrowding.

Source: Armstrong, L. (2017). Floor plan fundamentals. Exhibitor. www.exhibitoronline.com/topics/article.asp?ID=906

The venue manager has to schedule the build process very carefully, installing rigging and flooring, then overseeing the building of stands, potentially by different contractors. Exhibitors will require power and some will need a water supply. Lighting is another consideration, with the requirement to select the right type and amount of light.

Exhibitors can only enter the exhibition space after the build is completed in order to finalise the set-up of their stands with their displays. Typically, bump-in for exhibitors is on the afternoon before the event, although if the stands are simple, preset standard arrangements, then this can be permitted only a few hours beforehand – if exhibitors do not meet their deadlines for ordering services, sending freight and bumping-in on time, then late fees can be levied. Throughout the event, though, they will have wide-ranging demands, complaining, for example, about noise from adjacent stands or lack of visitor numbers.

The logistics of exhibition management require advanced project management skills, planning, negotiating with exhibitors, working with exhibition stand contractors, managing loading and freight, and so on. In summary, the job of an exhibition manager involves:

- planning exhibition layouts and associated programs such as seminars or demonstrations
- negotiating prices with exhibitors and confirming requirements
- organising visitor registrations
- checking on insurance, WHS and other legislative considerations
- arranging catering and other services
- arranging lighting
- organising loading, parking and security
- managing budgets and administration
- supervising bump-in and bump-out.

There are, of course, special requests that make life more interesting. Exhibitions involving animals (particularly snakes), guns, jewellery and new model sports cars provide additional challenges.

Environmental considerations

In all aspects of planning and implementation of the event, attention should be paid to minimising impacts. These include reducing the disruption to neighbouring residents, using resources efficiently, using effective waste management reduction initiatives, ensuring crowd safety, and managing security, particularly in licensed venues.

FINALISE EVENT AND EVALUATE OPERATIONAL SUCCESS

Chefs play an important role in customer satisfaction

The last phase in finalising arrangements is the issue of invoices and payment of suppliers. One also needs to obtain feedback from the client regarding the success of the function, this being the most satisfying part of the event or venue manager's job. Finally, a staff debrief is essential to iron out any remaining issues, and regular meetings with the catering sales team, the chef and the banquet staff will enhance all future event planning activities.

Summary

This chapter has looked at the delivery of events and functions in commercial venues. For most hotels and function centres, as well as sporting venues offering event packages, preparation of the proposal for a client is the starting point. Often, menus and layouts are already prepared but these just provide the basis of the negotiation. Clarity of expectations is essential, and the event order is a commonly used approach (software being available for this purpose) to ensure that the booking captures all requirements and special requests. Agreement on payment terms, confirmation of numbers and cancellation are key aspects of this.

Service delivery is clearly a major challenge for large events such as a sit-down meal for 600. Systematic planning and on-the-ground improvisation are required when problems occur. But when the event is over, the customer's enjoyment is the highlight for anyone working in this type of role.

Key terms

Back of house	In the event context, the operations area, which includes kitchens, stores and so on
Banquet event order (BEO)	Specifies the client's specifications and the event booking details
Commercial venue	Venue that charges for hire or offers event packages, usually designed for the purpose of staging events
Event coordinator	Organises all aspects of an event for a client
Front of house	In the event context, the area where customers are served
Vendor	Generally supplies direct to the customer, such as a hot dog vendor or concession
Venue coordinator	Works for the venue to manage the event from booking through to payment

REVIEW YOUR KNOWLEDGE

1. This chapter is about work as an in-house event coordinator in a commercial venue. Give some examples of commercial event venues.
2. Give five examples of in-house events and functions mentioned in this chapter.
3. Explain the purpose of the banquet event order.
4. What are the ways in which negative impacts of events can be minimised, such as noise?

APPLY YOUR KNOWLEDGE

Compare and contrast several venue booking arrangements, paying attention to the terms for cancellation and payment. Draw a table showing at least four of these, and analyse the differences.

CASE STUDY

The Melbourne Convention and Exhibition Centre has floor plans and capacity for a wide range of events, as do all major convention centres. Select one of these spaces and develop an event proposal for two different clients who have different specifications. For this task, you will need to work with two colleagues to simulate the role of an event venue coordinator.

TASKS

- Analyse and document the event staging requirements.
- Develop ideas for concept theme and format.
- Prepare a proposal for products and services.
- Estimate costs based on packages generally available on the Internet.
- Negotiate and agree on the final details with your 'clients'.

Do not contact a venue for a quote. A wide variety of standard industry operational material is available online. See the websites listed at the end of this chapter for examples of convention centres that offer event planning resources/tools, but note that there are many others.

Online resources

Visit http://login.cengagebrain.com and search for this book to access the study tools that come with your textbook.

Reference

Hurley, L. (2012). Caterers respond to growing tide of special diet demands. Special Events, 3 October. http://specialevents.com/catering/caterers-respond-growing-tide-special-diet-demands

Websites

Hilton event planning checklists, www.hilton.com/en/hi/groups/checklist_meeting.jhtml
How to read a banquet event order, http://planningitall.com/2014/03/27/how-to-read-a-banquet-event-order-beo/
Marriott event planning checklists, www.marriott.com/meeting-event-hotels/event-planning-checklist.mi
Melbourne Convention and Exhibition Centre (event planning tools), http://mcec.com.au/plan-an-event/event-planning-tools
Perth Convention and Exhibition Centre (plan an event – go to resources), www.pcec.com.au/plan-an-event/event-resources
Room capacity calculator, www.confpeople.co.uk/free-venue-finding/room-capacity-calculator
Set-up and capacity guidelines for banquets, www.banquettablespro.com/banquet-table-setup-diagrams
Time-lapse event set-up (Amway Center), https://youtu.be/VF-NJrKUvnc
Time-lapse event set-up (sports centre), https://youtu.be/o7r8UYWT1Zo
Wedding, start to finish, https://vimeo.com/131009717

EVENT CONCEPTS AND BIDS

14

DEVELOP EVENT CONCEPTS

OVERVIEW

Event concept development is not to be confused with theming or décor. Concepts are generally much broader ideas, and often more innovative. Sculpture by the Sea is an example of an innovative idea brought to fruition. Sometimes the concept is developed as part of a bidding process where several organisations are hoping to host a high-profile international event; for example, different cities bid for the Commonwealth Games. Extensive consultation is necessary to ensure that the client brief is fully understood and met. Other stakeholders, including sponsors and government bodies, are also involved when testing the operational feasibility of the ideas. Concept development is thus a highly collaborative process.

LEARNING OBJECTIVES

On completion of this chapter, you will be able to:

1. evaluate and explore needs and opportunities for events, researching a diverse range of ideas and innovations, and consulting with stakeholders to meet the client brief
2. develop a range of creative approaches to event concepts in a collaborative process, experimenting with new ideas
3. refine event concepts based on feasibility, including budget and risk
4. progress the event concept to the operational stage after verifying operational practicality.

INDUSTRY VIEWPOINT

Why an Elvis Festival in Parkes? Parkes has a bunch of passionate Elvis fans – one local Elvis fan has even changed his name to Elvis by deed poll and another local couple operated Gracelands Restaurant for many years. The Festival concept was conceived by these and other passionate community members, who saw potential for a fun event. January was identified as the perfect time to stage the event, being a slow time in local tourism and also coinciding with Elvis Presley's birthday (8th January). The first Festival was held in Parkes in January 1993. The Festival has sparked a boom in awareness of Parkes as a tourist destination. Since the Australian movie *The Dish* hit the big screen, Parkes has been best known as the home of Parkes Radio Telescope, but now the town has become widely recognised as the 'Elvis Capital of Australia'!

Source: Parkes Elvis Festival (2017). Festival history. http://parkeselvis.wpengine.com/about/festival-history

INTRODUCTION

The Elvis Festival in Parkes highlighted above has grown over the years, expanding from a few hundred people attending 10 years ago to the current level of 10 000 attendees. Many festivals and events grow in this way, often surprising their founding bodies. In other cases, the concept is carefully researched and linked to market trends, consumer behaviour and emerging fashions. Perhaps this is indicative of the art–science balance of the event business: it takes real flair to develop innovative, creative ideas, and a lot of hard work and attention to detail to pull it off. Some events develop organically over time, while others are carefully planned and plotted, developing in a linear manner. As this chapter shows, the team that runs an event needs to attend to the creative core concept as well as the logistics of its implementation.

EVALUATE AND EXPLORE NEEDS AND OPPORTUNITIES FOR EVENTS

Event concepts are developed for any number of clients, including private clients (parties and weddings), corporate clients (product launches, conferences) and government bodies (regional events and major festivals). In the case of corporate and government organisations, a good starting point for event concept development is understanding the organisational vision. In the case of Tourism Victoria, grants are available for regional tourism development. The Visit Victoria Regional Events Fund aims to 'support the attraction, development, marketing and growth of events in regional Victoria in order to increase economic benefits by driving visitation from outside of the region and the State, extending the length of stay and yield' (Visit Victoria, 2017). Any event concept would need to achieve the vision of showcasing, for example, the Goulburn Valley, while other objectives include increasing tourism visitation and spend. If we look back to Parkes as the Elvis Capital of Australia, and the level of visitation that town achieves, you can see that an equally innovative concept could achieve the desired outcomes. The Goulburn Valley is branded 'the heart of Victoria', and any proposal would emerge from detailed research on the region and its tourism potential.

Information sources that could shape event concept development include:

- the organisational vision
- market research, including tourism statistics
- the client's creative brief or grant parameters
- the event objectives.

Once these are reviewed, then creative ideas can be generated and tested by exploring new and interesting concepts, challenging assumptions, making connections, and researching current social trends.

External and internal factors

External and internal factors affecting event concept development are summarised below, bearing in mind that some client briefs are purely commercial and not tourism related. In each case, however, understanding the market, the competition, operational considerations and resource availability are fundamental aspects of a feasibility study. The aim is to develop a proposal 'with legs', a concept that is on trend and sustainable. Not every event needs to be a completely new innovation or something that has never been done before. Things can be done better and they can be done differently.

- Market factors:
  - competitive environment
  - potential levels of participation and interest
  - media interest
- Operational considerations:
  - access
  - climate
  - regulatory requirements
  - risk
- Resource availability, constraints and potential:
  - human
  - physical
  - financial
- Sustainability.

Other external factors relevant to event planners are demographic and social trends, and every event planner needs to be fashion-forward by having a detailed understanding of emerging cultural practices.

Stakeholder management

Before clarifying and agreeing on the purpose and key objectives of an event, it is necessary to take into account the different perspectives of the event stakeholders. It is most important to understand the concept of 'a stakeholder' in relation to event management. This is because there are generally multiple stakeholders who contribute to the development of the event concept and its implementation. There are various definitions of this term, ranging from the broad idea that a stakeholder is a person who can affect or will be affected by the event, to the more specific idea that a stakeholder is a person of influence but not directly involved in the work. Clearly, this definition could also include an organisation, such as a government authority.

Getz (2007) states that 'stakeholders are those people and groups with a stake in the event and its outcomes, including all groups participating in the event production, sponsors and grant-givers, community representatives, and anyone impacted by the event' (p. 15). Alternatively, the model developed by Allen et al. (2012) includes six major event stakeholder groups: the host organisation, host community, co-workers, event sponsors, media, and participants/spectators.

To clarify the concept of stakeholder, the best example is that of a wedding, where everyone has an opinion about how things should be done, including the mother-in-law. In the tradition of most weddings, the father is the client as he is paying for the wedding, and the bride and groom are the participants. Presumably the father would veto ideas that were too expensive and the mother-in-law anything that was too outlandish. There are also contractors, such as the celebrant, florist and caterer, who have a stake in the planning as they too have limitations, not least of which is the budget. In all event environments there are many stakeholders, sometimes with conflicting opinions, ideas and objectives. There are also constraints that limit the scope of the event project, including the aforementioned budget, size of the venue, accessibility, availability and so on.

Thus, in developing an event plan, analysing event information and consulting with stakeholders to determine the broad scope of the event is the first step. As mentioned, these stakeholders may include the following (see also Figure 14.1):

- event principal (key person in host organisation, or client)
- organising committee
- sponsors, donors

FIGURE 14.1 Event stakeholders

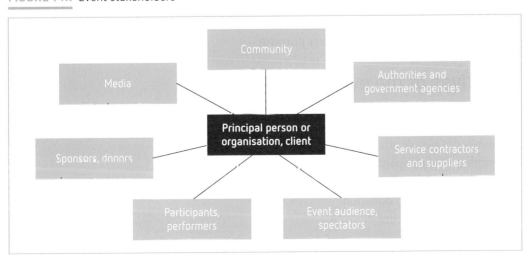

- local community
- local authorities (e.g. council, emergency services, environmental authority)
- service contractors (e.g. staging, cleaning, catering, security)
- suppliers
- performers, entertainers, participants
- spectators, audience
- media.

Purpose of the event

Numerous factors need to be considered in developing the event concept. The most important of these is the purpose of the event, although the purpose is also strongly linked to both the theme and the venue. In some instances, defining the purpose may be difficult. For example, a discussion with 10 people about the purpose of a wedding is likely to lead to many different ideas, such as 'to formalise a relationship', 'to make a commitment', 'to show off to relatives' and 'to have a big party', and these ideas do not even include a religious element. However, they will need to work out the purpose – the one thing that summarises the primary aim of the wedding – to ensure its success.

The purpose of the event should drive all planning and assist in sorting out differences of opinion and managing conflict. For example, if you were running a conference for financial planners, there could be two quite different purposes:

1   To facilitate an exchange of information, bringing participants up-to-date with the latest changes in financial planning software products.
2   To achieve a memorable out-of-body experience for financial planners in order to develop a positive association with a new software product.

Achieving the first purpose would be quite straightforward, as this would require a fairly standard meeting or convention. Fulfilling the second purpose, however, would be more difficult. For this unforgettable experience, you would need a unique venue and carefully planned activities that the participants would enjoy. At the same time, the product would need to be reinforced constantly so that attendees would leave with an inescapable association with it. To have the fun without the positive association would defeat the purpose. The focus of the first of these purposes is *information*, while that of the second is *entertainment*.

Also consider that while for many events the main purpose is making a *profit*, for many it is not. The mission statement of the Maleny Scarecrow Carnival in Figure 14.2 is an excellent example of an event with a *community* purpose.

Objectives of the event

Planning for an event should also involve defining specific, measurable objectives. These might include targets for the following:

- number of people attending
- number of participants
- contributions of sponsors
- value of grants and donations
- break-even or amount of profit

FIGURE 14.2 Example of an event with a community purpose

Maleny Scarecrow Carnival

Mission Statement (purpose)

To make this unique event an annual celebration of Maleny's rich cultural and social diversity. To present an opportunity for the community to unite and share creative energy, spirit and pride.

Background

The aim of the celebration is to enrich the social and cultural fabric of our community. Since ancient times, scarecrows have been used by almost every culture in a rural context; in most instances, in the belief that their presence would increase fertility and enrich the harvest.

The Maleny Scarecrow Carnival began in 1998 with the concept of a cultural event that would enhance Maleny's distinctive rural qualities and offer a unique opportunity for the local and wider communities to express their creativity. It is difficult to imagine a more perfect setting for hundreds of artistic and whimsical scarecrows than the rolling emerald green hills of Maleny. The event is based on the creation and display of scarecrows throughout the Sunshine Coast hinterland. It is comprised of four major facets:

- Scarecrow Masquerade
- Scarecrow Discovery Trail
- Scarecrow Contest
- Scarecrow Fiesta.

The Carnival coincides with the September school holidays to maximise the opportunity for families, the local community and visitors to participate in a wide range of activities.

The Maleny Scarecrow Carnival provides broad-based regional economic benefits consistent with community values and encourages involvement from all sectors of the community. In doing so, it heightens community awareness of various local groups and services as well as providing the opportunity for entertainers and artisans to showcase their creative skills. Most importantly, the Carnival is based on whole family participation, from toddlers right through to grandparents. Following on from the overwhelming success of the inaugural event in 1998, the organisers are building on the framework already in place. Interactive skill development workshops will add a new dimension and greater opportunities for members of the community to participate.

People involved include community and support groups, hospitals, libraries, Chambers of Commerce, schools, preschools and kindergartens, tour groups, garden clubs, retirement villages, businesses, sporting clubs, service groups and, of course, individuals. It is most interesting to note that 14 towns outside Maleny participated in the Scarecrow Contest; many well beyond the Sunshine Coast hinterland. We even received international involvement, including 30 miniature scarecrows sent by the children of the Australian International School in Singapore.

We have initiated relationships with other scarecrow festivals throughout the world, including Japan, Canada, USA and Europe, and our aim in the future is to seek international participation, with a view to expanding the cross-cultural elements available to the community.

- goals for charitable contributions
- level of media exposure
- number of repeat visitors
- value of merchandise sold
- value of food and beverage sold
- number of exhibitors, stall holders.

Establishing objectives helps keep the organisers or the event manager focused on what they wish to achieve. Measuring the outcomes against the objectives assists in the planning of future events.

Scope of the event

Related to the purpose and objectives of the event is its scope. This encompasses the date, time and duration of the event and its size. The scope of the event is dependent on the available resources. Resources that may be required include human resources (for example, the number of volunteers), physical resources (equipment or infrastructure) and financial resources (sponsorship) – there's nothing like a tight budget to get the committee focused!

Timing is another critical factor here. It is essential to ensure that the event does not clash with similar events during a peak season. In almost every country, spring is the time when most festivals and sporting events are held. This creates a competitive environment as the general public has lots of options for the first week in September (or April in the northern hemisphere) and few for weekends in mid-winter. Clearly, a night-time outdoor event in mid-winter would not be a sensible option.

Let's now look at some of the factors that may have a bearing on the development of the event concept.

DEVELOP A RANGE OF CREATIVE APPROACHES TO EVENT CONCEPTS

All of the above factors – the purpose, the objectives and scope of the event, available and potential resources, timing – will impose restrictions on concept development. The extent of the lead time may also impose limits on the concept. For example, a short lead time may mean that the performers or venues that the organisers were considering may not be available. Support by the management of potential host organisations, such as sporting associations or councils, may be withdrawn. But the most constraining factor, generally, is the extent of financial resources and/or voluntary commitment to the event.

Of course, there are events where money is no object. Many celebrity weddings immediately come to mind, as do elaborate corporate events. But with a little imagination, it is still possible to come up with an event concept that is innovative and appealing and does not break the bank. This may involve adapting existing ideas, developing new ideas, or incorporating or experimenting with new technologies.

Once the concept is clear, a suitable location needs to be found, bearing in mind that many event-specific environments provide ready-made décor and tried-and-tested services. However, the concept may be designed for a more exotic location or venue, requiring more complex planning, particularly if the event is to be held outdoors.

Risk management is an important consideration in both concept development and event planning. Risk management involves analysis of the likelihood and consequence of potential risks, such as threats to health and safety of staff and attendees, volunteers not contributing as much time as expected, or a sponsor deciding to withdraw at the last minute. (Risk management is covered in depth in Chapter 18.)

A wide range of implementation factors also needs to be considered, beginning with the theme and venue, which are closely tied to the event concept.

Theme

The theme of the event should be linked to the purpose. It should be completely compatible with guest/audience needs and consistent in all respects. Most events adopt a colour scheme that is repeated on all items produced for the event, such as tickets, programs, uniforms, décor, posters and merchandise. This helps attendees to identify with the theme.

Potential themes are endless, limited only by your imagination and the customer's pocket. Examples include:

- historical
- geographical
- cultural
- sporting
- musical
- entertainment
- artistic
- food and wine
- objects (e.g. CDs, boats).

When coming up with ideas for a theme, it is most important to consider the range of suitable venues available, keeping in mind the constraints of budget and other considerations.

The event concept can be pitched to the client as a presentation, and in some cases event planners use storyboards in the same way that they are used in interior design and movies. A **storyboard** is a collection of items that can include illustrations, images, colour palettes, sketches and 3D dioramas, now much easier to produce using CAD design and 3D printing. This gives the client a good visual idea of the 'look and feel' of the event.

Middle Eastern theme

Props used for styling

As Goldblatt (2010) points out, the theme should ideally appeal to all senses: touch, smell, taste, sight and hearing. If the aim of the event is to transport the audience, appealing to all the senses will contribute positively to the outcome. Keep in mind, once again, the needs of the audience when planning; for example, what music will be played. As we all know, taste in music and the desirable sound level vary enormously from one audience to another.

> **Storyboard**
> A collection of graphical items used to illustrate creative designs

Venue

The event manager needs to carefully consider the planning implications of choosing an unusual venue in preference to a standard venue requiring decoration only to match the theme. Lighting, sound and catering also provide challenges in unusual settings.

The following are examples of unusual venues:

- demolition site
- parking lot
- tunnel
- museum
- research facility
- amusement park
- orchard
- vineyard
- aquarium.

The remaking of the Australian Open Tennis Championships is an example of a fully integrated event venue and theme. The Australian Open is the only sporting event in the world boasting two retractable roofs at its venue. When not in use for tennis, retractable seating moves away to reveal a velodrome, which is used for cycling events.

Many venues provide enormous flexibility and can be readily transformed to meet the requirements of the theme. The range is extremely wide, from hotel banquet rooms, conference centres and theatres to sporting venues.

When considering the choice of venue, the event organiser needs to look at a number of factors, including:

- potential to fulfil the purpose of the event
- ambience
- location
- access by public transport
- parking
- seating capacity
- built features (such as stages)
- cost of decoration, sound and lighting
- cost of labour
- logistics of setting up
- food and beverage facilities
- safety.

There are many, many other factors that need to be taken into account in selecting an event venue, but the overall strategy should be to aim for the best possible fit with the client's and the audience's needs at the lowest possible cost. If all stages, props, carpets, seating, portable kitchens, refrigerators and so on have to be hired, the cost will be very hard to justify – even if the venue seems perfect in other ways.

Event audience

When organising an event, the needs of all participants must be considered before finalising the concept. When one of Australia's best-known athletes was invited to give a presentation at an event attended by approximately 200 people, the rental agency said that they were unable to provide a ramp to the stage for her wheelchair and wanted to compromise by asking members of the audience to lift her chair onto the stage. This was clearly unacceptable. In this situation, the response from the event coordinator is 'Find one!'

In the example of an entertainment-based event held for financial planners (conservative stereotype!), an organiser would be wise to challenge normal behaviour and encourage participation in unusual activities. However, great care would need to be taken to ensure that such an audience was not pushed beyond its conservative limits. At a similar event, an event coordinator found that persuading the audience to wear unusual hats was all that it took to break them out of their normal patterns of interaction. Of course, every audience is different, and the event manager needs to go with the flow and direct the event to meet audience response. This can involve sudden changes in plan.

Visit the Red Bull events site (**www.redbull.com/au/en/events**) to see how Red Bull runs a wide range of events all around the world. Read up on some of their more innovative events.

How do these events fit with the slogan 'Give wings to people and ideas'?

EXTENSION ACTIVITY

Resource requirements

The topic of financial management will be covered in detail in Chapter 21. However, it is an important consideration at this early stage of event concept and design. Initial financial estimates can get out of control very easily, and the choice of event concept can certainly contribute to this. Otherwise, good ideas should be knocked on the head at an early stage if they do not appear financially viable, as it is possible to come up with concepts that are startling in their simplicity and also cost-effective. This is where the creative and rational aspects of the event manager's abilities can come into conflict. Very often, the creative aspect wins – sometimes at the expense of the company's profit on the event.

Financial resources are not the only resources that may be required. One also needs to think about physical resources (event venues and infrastructure will be covered in detail in Chapter 15) and human resources (covered in Chapters 22 and 23). The skills of the event team and, just as importantly, the contractors, such as lighting technicians and catering staff, are an important consideration in terms of concept development. Staff working at most events have very limited opportunity for training, making job breakdowns and task sheets essential aspects of planning. In addition, stakeholders such as the waterways police, the Environmental Protection Authority and transport authorities have all sorts of requirements that could challenge the feasibility of an event, and these must be investigated.

The following list is not exhaustive but provides an idea of the many people involved in staging an event:

- talent/performer/team and manager
- cast and crew
- contractors (service providers)
- suppliers

- employees
- volunteers
- emergency services.

Timing of the event

The timing of an event is often linked to the season or weather. For example, depending on the location, a food and wine festival would be better programmed for early autumn than for mid-summer when the heat would be intolerable for both the audience and the stall holders. And mid-winter is certainly not the time to hold a flower show. While this might seem obvious, it is surprising how often events are programmed to occur at very unsuitable times. The timing of sporting events is, of course, limited by the sporting season and their traditional competitions. Broadcast to international audiences is another consideration. Television schedules for local and international events are tightly managed, and live television broadcasts need to be carefully planned. Not every sporting enthusiast is keen to stay up all night for a delayed broadcast and this is always a consideration for major sporting competitions held in one time zone and broadcast in another.

The evaluation of an event concept must take into account the following four time-related factors:

1 season
2 day of the week
3 time of day
4 duration.

Generally, mid-winter events are poorly attended, while event audiences are faced with an oversupply of events in spring.

Closely linked to this concept of timing (in the sense of scheduling on the event calendar) is the topic of lead time. This is the time available for planning and implementation. Last-minute requests are very difficult to manage. For the event manager, a long lead time is preferable, allowing adequate time to develop the event specifications and commence contract negotiation with suppliers and other contractors.

The duration of the event is another consideration, with multiple-day events providing the biggest challenges, as the venue has to be cleared, cleaned and restocked between sessions.

REFINE EVENT CONCEPTS

The following elements are covered only briefly here since they are revisited in a number of other chapters. The aim of discussing them here is to raise awareness of the problems and pitfalls that can occur if they are not considered at this early stage of concept development. In addition, if not dealt with, they can have a negative impact on the event planner's creativity.

Competition

Prior to involvement in any event, it is essential to conduct an analysis of your competition. This involves looking at the timing and duration of other events, even if they are unrelated. People have limited disposable income and festivals and events tend to be non-essential items in most family and tourist budgets. A wider study would include an analysis of the political, environmental, social and technological impacts, known as environmental scanning. This would place the event in a broader context.

Regulations

A wide range of laws and regulations have an impact on the staging of events and these can severely limit creativity. As a simple example, releasing balloons into the atmosphere is considered environmentally unfriendly. Parking, traffic and neighbourhood impact, especially in terms of timing and noise, are all aspects that require the event manager's liaison with local or State/Territory government.

Marketing

How to sell an event is a very important part of the initial planning, the timing of your marketing efforts being crucial. Do you advertise months beforehand or the day or week before? Will the audience turn up on the day? How can you encourage them to do so? Should you sell tickets in advance? (Many events actually have no advance ticket sales.) All these questions require the decision-making skills of the event manager or the event management team.

Community impact

The impact of an event on the local or wider community and others is a major consideration of the planning stage. Local traders and other lobby groups can raise hell for the unprepared event organiser, so it is absolutely essential that community benefits are explained and other impacts considered as part of the event proposal.

Risk

The weather is the greatest risk to attendance, enjoyment and success for most events. (You will be reminded of this at several points throughout this book.) Drought-breaking storms forced the evacuation of 400 campers at the 2004 Tamworth Country Music Festival, and created a muddy mess reminiscent of Woodstock at Brisbane's Big Day Out. However, participants were excited to see the rain at these events, which were both scheduled at times when heavy rain was least expected. Measures to counteract the impact of the weather are essential aspects of event feasibility planning. You must also be aware that insurance premiums will be linked to the perceived risk to the safety of participants.

There are many risks associated with events and Chapter 18 covers this topic in detail. Risks may include, among many others:

- cancellation by a key performer
- non-arrival of equipment
- technical failure
- transportation crisis
- accidents.

Revenue and expenditure

Losing money is the fastest way to get out of the event business. For this reason, the event concept (and the investment in event design) needs very careful analysis. So too does the topic of cash flow. In almost every case, contractors for catering, security and other services require deposits and payment in full prior to the event, which can cause cash flow problems if there are no advance ticket sales.

Matthews' (2015) book on special event production can assist with costing all the resources required for a large-scale event, including lighting, entertainment, décor, audio systems, visual technology, special effects staging and set design. An event concept needs to be costed, and to do this effectively one has to contact suppliers to assist with quotes. Many suppliers, such as Staging Connections, can cover most of the technical requirements. Venues, on the other hand, are one of the main considerations, ranging from dedicated event venues and sites (the easy option) to non-traditional venues (such as museums and tunnels) and finally to greenfield sites that have to be built from the ground up.

For the event manager, careful attention to budgeting will provide a reasonably accurate idea of the costs involved in running the event, which is essential in making a decision as to what to charge for tickets. This judgement is also informed by knowledge of the particular consumer market and likely perceptions regarding value for money.

> **Break-even point**
> The point at which there is enough income from an event to meet expenses

The **break-even point** is the point at which there is enough income to meet expenses. After reaching the break-even point, the event organiser will make a profit. Even for a community event that is not aiming to make a profit, break-even is the target.

The two models illustrated in Figure 14.3 and Figure 14.4 show how variable costs impact on event planning. Variable costs change according to the number of customers. For the conference in Figure 14.3, daily delegate costs are $79 (including conference room and meals) and accommodation is $150 per night. One night's accommodation and two days' delegate fees are used to calculate the variable costs based on the number of delegates. Delegates are charged at a rate of $550 for the conference.

FIGURE 14.3 Modelling a conference with high variable costs

	Number of delegates		
	150	250	300
INCOME (delegates charged $550)	$82 500	$ 137 500	$165 000
Variable costs			
Delegate fees paid to venue per head	$23 700	$ 39 500	$ 47 400
Hotel accommodation per night	$22 500	$ 37 500	$ 45 000
	$46 200	$77 000	$ 92 400
Fixed costs			
Office and related costs	$15 000	$ 15 000	$ 15 000
Commissions	$ 4 500	$ 4 500	$ 4 500
Speaker accommodation and fees	$15 000	$ 15 000	$ 15 000
	$34 500	$ 34 500	$ 34 500
TOTAL COSTS	$80 700	$ 111 500	$126 900
PROFIT OR LOSS	$ 1 800	$ 26 000	$ 38 100

As this example shows, the organisers cannot break even unless they have just under 150 delegates. Once they have over 300 delegates, the conference is extremely viable. As bookings for the conference come in by telephone, email and online, the organisers are in a good position to estimate the number of hotel rooms and the size of the conference room needed. Therefore, they may be able to negotiate a lower delegate fee with the conference centre and lower room rates with the hotels based on volume, thus contributing to better bottom-line performance. This level of financial flexibility is envied by other sectors of the industry.

In contrast, for a music festival, nearly all costs are fixed and there are few, if any, variable costs. This makes it much more difficult to assess financial viability, particularly if tickets are sold just before or on the day of the event. In the simplified model shown in Figure 14.4, all costs are fixed, including the fees paid to the artists. Unless audience numbers reach 2000, the production will run at a loss.

FIGURE 14.4 Modelling a music festival with high fixed costs

	Number of tickets sold		
	1500	2000	3000
INCOME (tickets charged at $65)	$ 97 500	$130 000	$195 000
FIXED COSTS			
Artists	$ 70 000	$ 70 000	$ 70 000
Travel and related	$ 15 000	$ 15 000	$ 15 000
Office and related	$ 15 000	$ 15 000	$ 15 000
Marketing	$ 12 000	$ 12 000	$ 12 000
Equipment and rental	$ 15 000	$ 15 000	$ 15 000
TOTAL COSTS	$127 000	$127 000	$127 000
PROFIT OR LOSS	−$ 29 500	$ 3 000	$ 68 000

The total costs are almost the same for the final model in both figures, but the music festival is more profitable. On the other hand, the level of risk is much higher. Anyone looking at the two events in terms of financial feasibility would conclude that the possibility of losing money would appear greater with the music festival (with a potential loss of $29 000 if ticket sales were not high enough), while the profit would be higher if a large audience was attracted.

As these models demonstrate, feasibility analysis – looking at the best- and worst-case financial scenarios – is extremely useful. The timing of the event audience's decision making will impact on cash flow and cause significant anxiety for the event organiser if these decisions are made at the last minute. Picture the sleepless nights of the music festival planner if only 1500 tickets had been sold a week before the event! The conference organiser's task seems less financially stressful in this example as there is a heavy reliance on variable costs. These costs can be closely monitored and linked to deadlines for delegate registration. While to some extent these models are oversimplified, they do demonstrate the importance of making assumptions and using these to look at the break-even point and various feasibility scenarios.

Unlike retail stores that can discount merchandise that is slow to sell, event organisations must sell before the event and as far ahead as possible. Tickets cannot go on sale the day after an event is over, nor can the merchandise produced for the event. If T-shirts, caps and other merchandise are not sold, this too will mean lost revenue. Even the concession outlets that sell food and beverages do not get a second chance at sales. For these reasons, the decision on price point is extremely important in ensuring that the event audience reaches a viable level.

However, not all events are ticketed. An exhibition, for example, involves renting stands to exhibitors, and the price charged for exhibiting is based on the cost of staging the exhibition and the likely number of exhibitors. For non-profit events, financial decisions involve keeping within the budget, which may be established by another body (for example, the local council). Where a client is paying for the staging of an event, the event management company will develop a budget for the event based on very clear expectations from the client as to the benefits expected from the event. Often, the event management company earns a fee and the client is ultimately responsible for the cost of the budgeted items and any variations.

Compare concepts

Once an event concept's feasibility is agreed, it is then possible to create a number of operational and financial models. In the example in Figure 14.5, there are two models, one in which the main source of income is ticket sales and the other in which ticket sales projections drop from 66 per cent of income to 42 per cent of income. In Model B, there is a much stronger push for sponsorship and fundraising is abandoned. However, as a result, the festival is in a loss situation. Given the difficulty associated with raising sponsorship, the first model would appear to be the better one. These models are simplified and do not take merchandise or fixed and variable costs into account. However, for this purpose, they illustrate the value of modelling techniques.

FIGURE 14.5   Financial modelling

Income	Model A	% of Income	Model B	% of Income
Ticket sales	$ 175 758	66%	$ 102 301	42%
Memberships	$ 12 036	4%	$ 25 123	10%
Sponsorship	$ 10 230	3½%	$ 52 146	22%
Grants	$ 32 156	12%	$ 32 513	14%
Donations	$ 12 351	5%	$ 12 351	5%
Fundraising events	$ 9 856	3½%	$ –	–
Stall rentals	$ 15 623	6%	$ 15 623	7%
Total Income	**$268 010**		**$240 057**	
Expenses		**% of Expenses**		**% of Expenses**
Artist performance contracts	$ 68 952	28%	$ 68 952	28%
Festival production	$ 35 612	15%	$ 35 612	15%
Marketing and fundraising	$ 22 613	9%	$ 22 613	9%
Salaries and wages	$ 62 133	26%	$ 62 133	26%
Office and related costs	$ 22 613	9%	$ 22 613	9%
Postage	$ 5 021	2%	$ 5 021	2%
Other	$ 27 591	11%	$ 27 591	11%
Total Expenses	**$244 535**		**$244 535**	
Net Income	**$ 23 475**		**–$ 4 478**	

Another form of modelling, based on historical data, is very useful for annual events or events that are reasonably predictable in terms of demand. Differential ticket pricing is based on a concept of revenue management initially popular in the airline industry and now used widely in many other service industries.

Using information systems, it is possible to allocate different prices for different shows, seats, sessions and market segments. It is also possible to monitor advance sales and offer special deals. For example, if it is anticipated that an event is going to be a sellout, then more tickets can be sold at Model A prices than for a match that is unlikely to fill the stadium.

In the case of mega events, many tickets are allocated to overseas bodies or sold as part of tour packages. Consequently, these tickets may return unsold at the very last minute, causing much consternation when some of the best seats come onto the market very close to the event. To manage differential pricing well, historical data is required to predict demand. Yield management is a variable pricing strategy based on historical data and consumer trends in order to maximise revenue.

> **Yield management**
> Variable pricing strategy based on historical data and consumer trends in order to maximise revenue

Layout

This creative element is so often given far too little consideration. Consider events that you have attended in which you have felt socially uncomfortable. Your discomfort was generally the result of too much open space, too much light, or a limited opportunity for people to mix. The worst scenario is being seated at a long, wide table where you are too far away to talk to those opposite and are stuck with people you have little in common with on your left and right. And to add insult to injury, the venue is ablaze with light. Worse still is the cocktail party in a huge ballroom where a small circle develops in the centre – not small enough, though, for everyone to talk. The audience needs to comfortably fill the venue to create a positive ambience.

Event with an Australian theme

Styling

Fabrics, decorative items, stage props, drapes and table settings can all be hired, and it is generally worthwhile investigating these options before settling on the event theme as hiring items can reduce costs enormously. Floral arrangements need to be ordered from florists experienced in larger events. Australian native plants, some of them up to 2 metres high, can produce a stunning effect. In many ballrooms the floral arrangements are elevated above the table, on tall stands, so that guests can talk to each other more easily. The effect is quite dramatic, with the floral arrangements dominating the décor. There are specialist event stylists who can provide advice, and many event hire companies offer this service too.

Suppliers

Good relationships with suppliers of all commodities will ensure that only quality products will be received, including the freshest flowers and the best produce the markets can supply. During most large events, suppliers are pressed for the best quality from all their customers at a time when volumes are much larger than usual. This is when a good longstanding relationship with a supplier is invaluable. It was reported that at Atlanta during the 1996 Olympic Games you could not buy tissues or towels anywhere. The success of the Olympic Games in Sydney was due to early planning (especially of menus), allowing farmers and other suppliers to sign contracts well in advance. Consider for a moment that some of the flowers had to be planted years before the event! So, too, some of the fruit and vegetables, which were in good supply despite it being the off-season.

Technical requirements

Few people would have attended an event or meeting where there wasn't a single technical glitch. Speakers put their notes on the laptop and the screen starts changing at a phenomenal rate. Screensavers come on when the speaker goes on for too long, the presentation is halted, and file names appear on the screen. While none of these problems are caused by technical support, there are ways in which they can be reduced. Technical glitches by the contracted company are unacceptable. Microphones must have back-ups, the power supply must be assured, and stages and video screens must be visible to all in the audience. There is no substitute for wide-ranging experience, and this is a key attribute that should be sought when choosing technical contractors. New technology, especially anything used to demonstrate new products, needs to be tested thoroughly through many rehearsals. A back-up system is essential.

There are times when an event concept should remain just that because it is technically impossible.

Staging

Many events require professional staging and there are companies which specialise in this. Staging Rentals, for example, has completed a wide range of projects over 20 years of operation, including product launches, road shows, fashion shows, exhibition stands, conferences, award presentations, media launches, concerts, gala dinners and fabulous parties, to name a few. Staging Rentals has a wide range of specialist skills resident in the company, including logistics and installation. However, technical effects, such as firework displays, may require other specific specialist skills.

Entertainment

For some events, entertainment is central; for others, it is peripheral. The most important thing is that the entertainment suits the purpose of the event, not detracts from it. The needs of the event audience must be carefully considered when making this decision.

A clown creating balloon art is something one would consider for a children's party. However, the same idea (with different designs) could also work extremely well at a wedding reception while guests are waiting for the photography session to finish.

Talent

Closely allied to the previous point, talent may come in the form of musical performers, dancers, athletes, golfers, conference speakers and so on. When the talent is the focal point for an event, management of the talent is exceptionally important. This includes meeting their essential needs as well as their many personal preferences for hotel rooms and unique foods! Most performers and top sports men and women have very clear requirements that must be obtained well in advance, particularly if there are staging needs for which equipment is specialised and perhaps not readily available.

Catering

Nothing makes participants at an event more frustrated than delays in service and poor-quality food – except for, perhaps, a lack of toilet facilities! While guests may have patience with other delays, they will become very agitated if hours are spent in queues, especially if these are away from the action. Food quality and selection are notoriously bad, and outrageously expensive, at many events and planning must take this into account. These days, an espresso coffee cart can be found every few metres at most events, reflecting changes in the expectations of the audience and event managers' response to this. Creative event planning frequently requires unique or unusual food and beverage products and these can take time to find. They may even need to be imported. Time means money, as does importing, and both can contribute to an escalation in cost.

Service

Finally, the service elements of the event need to be considered. As Matheson (2009) suggests, the intangible aspects of the event are vitally important. These include the atmosphere or ambience and the factors that contribute to the uniqueness of the visitors' experience. This is provided largely by staff and/or volunteers. Outsourcing to service contractors is a consideration, but these employees need to make their contribution to the event ambience. First impressions count, and being greeted by a surly security officer certainly won't enhance the atmosphere. The outfits worn by the event workforce also contribute to the atmosphere, as does their enthusiasm and energy. In some cases, actors are employed to ramp up the drama of the event experience still further.

Having given consideration to the above factors, the operational practicality of the concept, theme and format needs to be considered. For a banquet on a beach, for example, catering provided the biggest challenges, the bluebottles being a secondary inconvenience. For this event, lifesavers were seconded to provide service despite their lack of training in this area. They were, however, able to respond knowledgeably to questions and no doubt contributed far more to the event experience than agency waiters.

Fine dining with a beach theme

Berridge (2007), the author of *Events Design and Experience*, stresses the importance of design having a focus and considering the use of space and flow of movement (p. 97). He gives the example of an exhibition in which the zones provided different experiences for the visitors. This is illustrated locally in the royal (agricultural) shows held in Australia and New Zealand. Clearly, there is more to design than just the visual impact of the event. Berridge's text is recommended for the creative aspects of event design.

PROGRESS THE CONCEPT TO OPERATIONAL STAGE

The next stage involves developing a summary of key logistical requirements based on the overall concept, theme and format. Accurate and complete information should then be provided to all relevant stakeholders, including councils and other authorities, so that any necessary formal approvals can be received before planning is too far advanced.

The following logistical elements must be taken into account when considering an event concept:

* access to the site (Can vehicles come close enough for off-loading or parking?)
* physical limitations (Will the size or shape of the stairs make it impossible to move heavy equipment?)
* dimensions of the site (Is it too high, too low, too narrow?)
* refrigerated storage (Is it sufficient?)
* physical space for food preparation (Is it too small?)
* toilet facilities (Are they fixed or portable?)
* cleaning (Is it contracted?)
* catering (Will there be any physical problems with transporting, storing and serving food?)
* safety (Are patrols, exits, fire procedures, first aid etc. all in place?)
* potential damage to the site (Is there a danger of flowerbeds being trampled?)
* provision of basic services (Are water and electricity laid on?).

This chapter illustrates the careful balance required between the creative and rational aspects of decision making when considering an event concept. Brainstorming by the planning team will generate ideas but these then need to be considered as to their feasibility in terms of the issues raised in this and subsequent chapters.

While a full-scale operational manual is not required at the concept development stage, the client needs to be convinced that the idea is viable. The proposal should also include legal compliance and insurance considerations. Finally, the credentials of the event organisation making the submission or bid need to be included, ideally with hard evidence of past success. This is why the evaluation phase of all event planning is emphasised throughout this text. Most clients are looking for a return on investment (ROI) or return on objectives (ROO) and need to be persuaded that you can deliver this.

Summary

It is essential that the event concept is workable, creative but not fanciful. In this chapter, we have shown that determining the purpose/objectives of the event in conjunction with all stakeholders is critical in ensuring that the event concept will work. Early in the process, it is also necessary to identify the potential audience as well as the financial and other resources required to support the event. The event concept can then be further developed to include the theme and the décor, and a suitable venue can be selected. Any logistical requirements of the event must also be identified early in the planning process. The purpose, theme, audience and venue need to be compatible elements for the event concept to be successful.

Key terms

Break-even point	The point at which there is enough income from an event to meet expenses
Storyboard	A collection of graphical items used to illustrate creative designs
Yield management	Variable pricing strategy based on historical data and consumer trends in order to maximise revenue

REVIEW YOUR KNOWLEDGE

1 Explain the external and internal factors that need to be considered when planning an event concept.
2 From a financial point of view, many event concepts are influenced by the arrangements for financial underwriting of the event. Give three specific examples of existing event concepts that match the following financial outcomes: not-for-profit, for profit and fully subsidised.
3 Use figures in a table similar to Figure 14.3 to illustrate how variable ticket pricing can be used to maximise revenues for an event.
4 What does Goldblatt (2010) say about the appeal to the senses of an event concept? Use an event that you have experienced to illustrate the importance of engaging all the senses.
5 List the pros and cons of using an existing, fully functioning venue versus a unique but untested building for an unusual event where the aim is to create a WOW factor.
6 Think of a highly creative and innovative event concept and then briefly summarise the technical and operational opportunities or limitations of this concept.

APPLY YOUR KNOWLEDGE

Your client is a well-known retailer who runs department stores in all the major cities. Their vision is to engage customers in the stores by improving on their customer experience. Their new slogan is 'Beyond service, customers want an immersive experience'. Department heads and supervisors will all attend the event, which will roadshow around the capital cities.

Come up with two concepts and develop a storyboard for two different events that will enable you to pitch these ideas to the client. The emphasis is on creativity rather than operational detail for this task.

CASE STUDY

IT'S A WRAP!

In many ways Mercedes-Benz Fashion Festival really is a circus. A gorgeous celebration of colour and movement, of the innovative and the unpredictable, that always generates excitement and wonder when it comes to town.

Our models who, like the acrobats under the Big Top, have wowed us all week with their grace, their beauty and their poses. They performed at the Cloudland Wrap Party for free, which proves their beauty is much more than skin-deep!

To our designers who manage, each year, to conjure the remarkable and the mysterious, just like the travelling magicians of old. They have taught us to expect the unexpected — but even then, they still manage to surprise us.

To our retailers, the tightrope walkers who walk the highwire every day, seeking to strike a balance between the cold hard world of business and the ethereal and airy stratosphere of style.

To our sponsors who really are the strong men of an event like Fashion Festival, supporting our efforts, lifting our spirits and catapulting our dreams into reality, even when times are tough. A particular thanks to the strongest of them all, Mercedes-Benz, our naming rights sponsor and enduring supporter.

And, of course, to Brisbane City Hall, for this year providing a truly stunning Big Top for our circus.

To the Queensland Government Department of Employment, Economic Development and Innovation. This year they were the lion tamers, taking on the fiercest of economic conditions, staring down those who'd like to take a swipe at the value of a Fashion Festival, and generally taming the most conservative budget beasts.

To our fabulous volunteers. Because when any circus comes to town, there is always an army of people working away from the spotlight to get the Big Top up in time, to welcome visitors and answer questions, and generally to make sure the show runs smoothly. And our little army did it for free!

And to our team at MBFF. You are truly talented jugglers, keeping all the balls in the air, spinning the plates and dodging the flying knives, to put on a terrific show.

And finally, to you. Our fabulous MBFFashionistas, those who bought tickets, got involved, participated in events and proved how beautiful Brisbane really is.

Thank you for your support and we look forward to sharing plans for next year in the coming months.

MBFF will further enhance Brisbane's positioning as a city of creativity and style and its reputation to stage a dynamic, consumer-driven event that will:

- boost retail sales and the city's economy by supporting another home-grown industry
- increase awareness for our local industry
- increase visitation to the city, and
- positively reinforce the city's ability to stage international standard events.

Source: Lindsay Bennett Marketing Pty Ltd.

QUESTIONS

1   What was the theme of the event?
2   How does the theme fit with the idea of a fashion festival?
3   Who were the stakeholders who were thanked for their contributions? Draw a diagram to summarise these relationships.

4   What are three operational or logistical challenges associated with running a fashion show?

5   If you were to develop some measurable objectives for this event, which elements could be chosen to develop these targets?

6   Choose or develop a single statement that summarises the purpose of this event.

7   Develop a proposal for a fashion festival, surf carnival or other event of your choosing, including two completely different concepts for the client. This proposal must include:
   - client overview (naming rights sponsor), including company strategic direction and target markets
   - client/sponsor creative aspirations and event brief
   - two innovative concept specifications of your design
   - an overview of operational planning considerations
   - resourcing, including people, equipment and budget
   - risk benefit analysis
   - staging requirements overview, including technical feasibility.

Do not contact industry suppliers for quotes or proposals. Online research will provide sufficient information.

Online resources

Visit **http://login.cengagebrain.com** and search for this book to access the study tools that come with your textbook.

References

Allen, J., O'Toole, W., Harris, R., & McDonnell, I. (2012). *Festival and Special Event Management*, Google eBook. Milton, Qld: John Wiley & Sons.

Berridge, G. (2007). *Events Design and Experience*. Oxford, UK: Butterworth-Heinemann.

Getz, D. (2007), *Event Studies: Theory, Research and Policy for Planned Events*. Oxford, UK: Elsevier.

Goldblatt, J. J. (2010). *Special Events: A New Generation and the Next Frontier* (vol. 13). Hoboken, NJ: John Wiley & Sons.

Matheson, V. (2009). Economic multipliers and mega-event analysis. *International Journal of Sport Finance*, 4(1), 63–70.

Matthews, D. (2015). *Special Event Production: The Resources* (2nd edn). London: Routledge.

Visit Victoria (2017). Regional Events Fund. **www.visitvictoria.com/Regional-Events-Fund**

Websites

Business Events delegate research, **www.tourism.australia.com/statistics/business-events.aspx**

Consumer events (Tourism Australia), **www.tourism.australia.com/events/consumer-events.aspx**

Event styling (Decorative Events & Exhibitions), **www.decorativeevents.com.au**

Fvent suppliers and venues (Australasian Special Events), **http://specialevents.com.au/find-suppliers-venues**

Goulburn River Valley tourism-related grants, **www.goulburnrivervalley.com.au/grants**

15 SELECT EVENT VENUES AND SITES

OVERVIEW

In this chapter, we will look at the selection of suitable venues and sites for events. Each event has specific site requirements, such as perimeter fencing if a temporary liquor licence is needed, and of course there are creative elements too. The most exotic places for festivals and events generally have limited infrastructure and so pose the most problems. Therefore, a careful balance is needed between creativity, risk and budget. For those with the biggest budgets, there are exciting spaces that can be transformed with imaginative styling.

LEARNING OBJECTIVES

On completion of this chapter, you will be able to:

1. determine venue or site requirements by developing site specifications in consultation with stakeholders, primarily the client

2. source the event venue or site by researching and inspecting venues or their websites while being mindful of risk and regulatory issues

3. confirm venue or site bookings, finalising contracts within appropriate timeframes.

INDUSTRY VIEWPOINT

The *Disability Discrimination Act* (1992) requires that people with disabilities are able to access and use places open to the public and to access any services and facilities provided in those buildings. People with disabilities can face barriers to attending and participating in public functions in a variety of ways. They may experience difficulty hearing what is said, seeing small print on an invitation, climbing steps to the venue, understanding signage or using a rest room in the building. Public events need to be planned to ensure they are accessible to all members of the community. Consideration of aspects such as the venue, a continuous accessible path to the venue, invitations, and hearing augmentation are important.

Source: Government of Western Australia, Department of Communities, Disability Services (2017).
www.disability.wa.gov.au

INTRODUCTION

The terms 'venue' and 'site' are used almost interchangeably by event managers, with **venue** used mainly for built structures and **site** for outdoor spaces. 'Site' also has more general use for a range of locations, which in turn can be transformed into event venues. Events are also held at convention centres, hotels, clubs, restaurants and many other places. The term **facility** is also used extensively, particularly in North America in the context of a 'sports facility' or 'convention facility'. An event **precinct** usually incorporates a number of venues.

In this chapter, the various attributes of event sites will be considered, particularly for outdoor events where all infrastructure has to be brought in and erected on-site. This chapter will also look at disability access, since best practice in this area is likely to meet the needs of all visitors, particularly in the areas of signage, lighting, pathways and emergency exits.

> **Venue**
> Generally refers to a built structure where an event takes place
>
> **Site**
> Generally an oudoor space with limited infrastructure
>
> **Facility**
> Alternative term used for an event location, particularly in North America
>
> **Precinct**
> Covers a large area that includes several venues (e.g. Commonwealth Games precinct)

DETERMINE VENUE OR SITE REQUIREMENTS

When evaluating the suitability of a venue or site, there are two main considerations: the functionality of the venue and the suitability of the site for the event's creative purpose. Natural features of some sites lend themselves well to creating an extraordinary event experience. Concerts held in caves and natural amphitheatres are good examples. In such situations, however, the event manager needs to be mindful of the costs of using unusual, untested sites and the functional problems inherent in using them, as well as their legal obligations for access to public places.

When planning an outdoor event, the onus is on the management team to ensure that the infrastructure meets the needs of everyone in the event audience.

For the event manager considering an established venue, a site inspection would determine whether the venue was suitable for the planned event, particularly from a functional perspective. Building codes ensure that most modern buildings comply with other aspects such as disability needs; for example, that doorways are wide enough for wheelchair access.

The size and scope are considerations when looking for appropriate cities and venues for staging major events. When a major event such as the FIFA World Cup, Olympic Games

or Commonwealth Games is planned, various cities bid for the event. During this process, the city presents the infrastructure available for the event – not only specific competition venues but also descriptions of transportation, accommodation and so on. The city must demonstrate that it has the full range of physical and human resources to support the bid, as well as the financial resources for the event to succeed. In bids for such international events, the infrastructure is promised but sometimes not delivered. For example, the steel and glass roof for the Athens Olympic Games swimming centre could not be finished in time for the games. Bids also need to address the issue of accessibility for both athletes and audience. This topic is covered briefly in this chapter. The challenge of providing accessible public spaces is fairly easily met when the venues and transport networks are new; however, it is much more difficult when the event is held in an ancient city like Athens.

When bidding for a large conference of, say, medical professionals, the bid would again cover the city, its accommodation, entertainment options and attractions. Indeed, conference centres in Singapore and Melbourne would differ little in what they could provide regarding

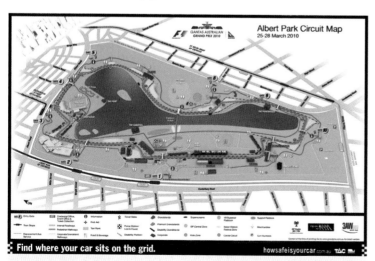

Aerial photograph and customer circuit map of the Formula 1 Australian Grand Prix site, Albert Park, Melbourne

the conference venue and meeting rooms. Delegates arriving at the conference are more interested in the city that hosts the event and the attractions it has to offer.

Prior to selecting a venue or site, it is essential to analyse the overall venue or site requirements based on a detailed review of all aspects of the proposed event. Developing accurate venue or site specifications will facilitate the research process. Of course, this links to the event purpose and objectives discussed in the previous chapter.

The client specifications could include, for example:

* contemporary wedding for 200 guests
* industrial look, girders, polished concrete floor
* tables of industrial scale joined together in a square shape so that when dinner is cleared, the bride and groom can dance around the room on the tables-turned-catwalk
* kitchen as centrepiece – food preparation as entertainment
* rigging suitable for enormous hanging flower arrangements
* professional lighting design.

This would continue to cover more mundane matters such as parking and security. All stakeholders need to be consulted in this process, as illustrated in the previous chapter and on many reality wedding shows; the bride and groom, for instance, might not agree on the creative brief and specifications.

The role of the event manager as a walking, talking checklist will become evident in this chapter. Key to the search for requirements is attendee capacity and the size of the area, including the type of layout and staging considerations (working at heights). Safety and security are other issues, particularly if there are special effects or a temporary liquor licence.

Research can take many forms, with multiple venues and suppliers listed online. However, one can also use industry associations and networks to find new ideas and recommendations. Most government bodies will put large-scale events up for tender so that any interested party can bid. Once the specifications are agreed, the research and selection process begins. A site inspection checklist is essential for this purpose.

SOURCE EVENT VENUE OR SITE

In the previous chapter we discussed the importance of analysing the feasibility of the event concept. Now we will consider the aspects of an event that must be taken into account when developing venue or site specifications. These include:

* creative theme or image required
* estimated number of attendees
* audience composition
* facilities and services to be provided
* staging/competition requirements
* budget parameters
* location
* capacity of site or venue
* timing (including availability and access for set-up and breakdown)
* accessibility.

The requirements of all stakeholders also need to be considered. Stakeholders may include:

* attendees/delegates/guests/spectators (including those with a disability)
* host organisation
* sponsors
* contractors
* emergency services
* regulatory authorities.

Imagine, for example, that a client has requested a small event, the purpose of which is to introduce newly appointed executive staff (and their partners) following a merger of two banks. The client wants to 'break the ice' and for this reason wants something a bit different from a conventional dinner, with more of a team focus. However, it cannot be a tacky team-building theme or an outdoor activity. Pretending to be spiders in a web, walking over logs, or something similar is absolutely out of the question.

This elegant solution could well meet the needs of this client:

> A chef's table dinner in a five-star commercial kitchen where guests, guided by the executive chef, 'prepare' the food. A chef's table is usually located inside a commercial kitchen, providing a unique venue, surrounded by glimmering stainless steel and professional cooking equipment. Usually the chef invites selected people to dine at the chef's table and this is a privilege few enjoy. The food is generally unsurpassed in quality and creativity. This concept is unique in that guests at an event would never normally get their hands dirty. Guests would arrive expecting a conventional dinner, be surprised by the location, and further surprised when given a large apron and asked to assist. Since all ingredients would already be prepared, as on a television cooking show, none of the guests would find the situation daunting. Each guest would be involved, with movement around the kitchen and the table, observation, questions, congratulations and so on. No time for embarrassing conversational lapses when discussing the jobs people have lost in the merger process! Rather, an unforgettable dining experience that would really 'break the ice'!

The number of guests would be the major consideration when sourcing the venue. Only five-star commercial kitchens would be suitable and the size of the chef's table would be limited by the space available in the kitchen. The dining area would also need to be a safe distance away from the heat and flames! One solution would be a banquet table in a function room outside the kitchen but this would destroy the energy and creativity of the concept. For the concept to work, a dining table in the kitchen would be essential. Such a space could well be available in a convention centre on a Saturday night, but would be hard to find in a busy five-star hotel conducting normal peak business.

As this example illustrates, décor, availability, capacity, safety and access issues are all relevant when selecting an appropriate venue. Schwarz (2012) provides a case study of the Love Parade in Duisburg as an example of site failings, leading to the death of 21 people from suffocation.

EXTENSION ACTIVITY

Watch the Love Parade disaster unfold on You Tube (**https://youtu.be/8y73-7IFBNE**). Explain the issues surrounding site access for the event audience that contributed to the disaster. For this exercise, ignore the actions of police.

Following this, look at other examples of crowd-crush disasters involving ramps and tunnels, such as the Falls Festival where 80 people were injured, the tragic death of 700 people at the Hajj in Mecca, and the Cambodian Water Festival stampede in 2010 (Hsu and Burkle, 2012).

For one of these events, briefly outline how the venue (or surrounding area) was unsuitable for the crowd, contributing to the crowd-crush disaster.

Venue information sources

When looking for a venue, there are various sources that can be utilised:

- local/regional/State/Territory tourism organisations
- convention and visitor bureaus
- venue publications and directories
- destination brochures
- trade journals
- Internet searches.

In conducting such a search, it is useful to compare services and specifications. Some venues have interactive websites that allow you to configure function rooms, depending on whether the event is a cocktail party, meeting or dinner function. These CAD designs are most useful in showing the space available (not forgetting any space needed for a stage and possibly wheelchair access). Clear communication of requirements is essential, particularly if the event is so large that it will be sent out to tender.

Site inspection – conference

Figure 15.1 provides a checklist of the technical requirements for a small conference, as this is the most important consideration for an event of this nature. A more detailed analysis of the site for the conference would cover other fundamentals such as parking, public transport, accessibility and smoking areas, as well as registration, seating and catering.

FIGURE 15.1 Conference technical requirements

Registration desks	Flipcharts
Display screens	Lecterns
Staging	Speakers
Data projector	Audio equipment
DVD player	Laptop with presentation software
Remote controls	Sufficient power supply
Overhead projector	Accessible power outlets
Extra lenses and bulbs	Extension cords
Laser pointers	Lighting effects (including dimmer)
Projection screens	Microphones and stands
Projector trolleys	Radio microphones (hand-held and lapel)
Whiteboards	Technician on site

All elements of an event need to be itemised to ensure that even the smallest detail is given attention. For an outdoor music concert, for example, the site inspection checklist would run to many pages, including site elements such as perimeter fencing, lighting, signage, pathways, parking and so on.

Site inspection – accessibility

The Western Australian Disability Services Commission provides a checklist for creating accessible events, which is reproduced in Figure 15.2. This covers invitations and promotional materials, external access, internal access, communication and function space requirements. A more detailed planning approach to a major event might cover these elements and more:

- way-finding
- signage
- transport
- parking
- footpaths
- ramps
- stairways

- lifts
- surfaces and finishes
- entries and exits
- doorways and doors
- toilet facilities
- emergency provisions (must comply with Australian standards).

FIGURE 15.2 Checklist for creating accessible events

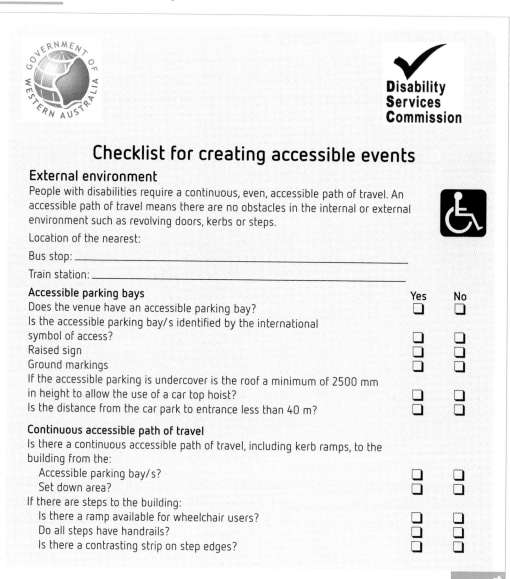

Checklist for creating accessible events

External environment

People with disabilities require a continuous, even, accessible path of travel. An accessible path of travel means there are no obstacles in the internal or external environment such as revolving doors, kerbs or steps.

Location of the nearest:

Bus stop: _____

Train station: _____

	Yes	No
Accessible parking bays		
Does the venue have an accessible parking bay?	☐	☐
Is the accessible parking bay/s identified by the international symbol of access?	☐	☐
Raised sign	☐	☐
Ground markings	☐	☐
If the accessible parking is undercover is the roof a minimum of 2500 mm in height to allow the use of a car top hoist?	☐	☐
Is the distance from the car park to entrance less than 40 m?	☐	☐
Continuous accessible path of travel		
Is there a continuous accessible path of travel, including kerb ramps, to the building from the:		
Accessible parking bay/s?	☐	☐
Set down area?	☐	☐
If there are steps to the building:		
Is there a ramp available for wheelchair users?	☐	☐
Do all steps have handrails?	☐	☐
Is there a contrasting strip on step edges?	☐	☐

If there is a ramp to the building:
  Is the gradient no steeper than 1:14? ❑ ❑
  Does the ramp lead to the main entrance? ❑ ❑

The building

Entrance

Is the entrance threshold level? ❑ ❑
If there is a step/s at the entrance of the doorway:
  Is there a ramp of not more than 450 mm in length and with a gradient
  of 1 in 8? ❑ ❑
  Is the entrance door easy to open? ❑ ❑
  Is the clear door space 800 mm (preferred)? ❑ ❑

Internal environment

Is the inquiry or reception counter low enough for a wheelchair user? ❑ ❑
Does the venue have an accessible path of travel from the front entrance
to all areas guests will use? ❑ ❑
If there are internal steps:
  Do all steps have handrails? ❑ ❑
  Is there a contrasting strip on step edges? ❑ ❑
If there are ramps:
  Are they no steeper than 1:14? ❑ ❑
  Do they have handrails? ❑ ❑
Do all doors have a clear space 760 mm (essential) or 800 mm (preferred)? ❑ ❑
If there is only a side approach to the door, is there 1200 mm clear space in
front of the door? ❑ ❑
Does the venue have a non-slip floor surface or carpets with a firm low pile
of 6 mm or less? ❑ ❑

Visibility

Are facilities in the venue clearly signed? ❑ ❑
Is the venue well lit? ❑ ❑
Are there any areas of high reflection or glare? ❑ ❑

Toilets

Does the venue have a unisex accessible toilet? ❑ ❑
Is the toilet situated on the same floor as the function? ❑ ❑
Does the door have a clear space of 800 mm (preferred)? ❑ ❑
If there is only a side approach to the door, is there 1200 mm clear space in
front of the door? ❑ ❑
If the door of the toilet opens inwards, is the space large enough for the
person in a wheelchair to shut the door once inside? ❑ ❑
Is there 950 mm space at one side of the toilet pan? ❑ ❑
Is there a grab rail next to the toilet at 800 mm – 810 mm high, preferably
in an 'L' shape? ❑ ❑

Signage

Does the venue have clear, directional signage to:
  The function room? ❑ ❑
  The toilets? ❑ ❑

Please note that disabled facilities in older buildings will only have a clear space of 760 mm. The
standard has now been revised to a clear space of 800 mm.

Source: Government of Western Australia, Disability Services Commission (2017).
State government access guidelines for information, services and facilities. pp. vii – ix.

Site inspection – outdoor events

For an outdoor event, significant considerations include:

- access for emergency services
- public access
- service access and loading docks
- parking
- public transport
- power supply
- potable water (cold)
- sanitation.

For a sporting competition, considerations include:

- competition area cleanliness, maintenance and safety
- competition area clearly marked
- adequate lighting for competition area
- spectator area cleanliness, maintenance and safety
- marked out-of-bounds area
- perimeter fencing
- buffer between spectators and competitors
- competitor change rooms
- sports equipment of appropriate standard
- all areas clear of non-essential equipment
- exits and entrances clearly marked and unobstructed
- electrical systems in good condition
- waste containers provided
- walkways clean and well maintained
- stairs non-slip
- wheelchair access to all areas
- compliance with fire safety regulations in all aspects.

Viewing platforms can be provided for people in wheelchairs

The checklists could be endless, including also loading docks, storage areas, access and refrigeration space. In particular, the special requirements of large items such as stages and athletics equipment need to be considered to ensure that they can be brought into the event area, otherwise known as loading restrictions. The logistics of boat shows and car shows are complex and have to be linked to both space and scheduling, making sure that items arrive in an orderly and timely way.

Fit with audience profile

An overriding consideration in the choice of an event venue is the fit with audience needs. It is easy for an event manager to lose sight of this when inspired by a concept and unusual location or bogged down with checklists. Will the event audience travel to the venue? Will the venue provide too little or too much space for the number of people? This psychological factor contributes a great deal to the event experience. What is the event purpose? Being constantly mindful of the event purpose and the needs of the event audience is necessary throughout the venue selection process. Being able to think three-dimensionally in terms of height and décor is another beneficial attribute for an event manager.

Set-up for a half-marathon start

Fun runs are popular, but it can be difficult to balance the needs of the most fun-loving runners with limited fitness, and those of the most professional and experienced runners. How would you select a site or course that meets the needs of both groups?

Venue safety

The subject of venue safety has been mentioned several times and will be covered in more detail in Chapter 18. Safety is a crucial issue and the event manager cannot be too careful. Unfortunately, there are several examples of structural failure at large events that have led to fatalities.

Staging an event at a modern, state-of-the-art stadium, using professional contractors, is a low-risk option from a safety point of view, as is running a conference in a purpose-built conference centre. Outdoor events using hire equipment present a much higher level of risk. Checking engineering and other certification, as well as contractor references, can reduce this risk. There are no short cuts or savings in the area of venue safety – old buildings may not meet fire safety standards, for example – and attention to detail is essential.

Figure 15.3 outlines the type of detail provided to contractors to ensure the safe delivery of goods at the loading dock. Figure 15.4 outlines the process for venue and site selection.

FIGURE 15.3 Detailed instructions for access and delivery

**The Adelaide Festival Centre
Access Details**

Vehicle access
Passenger vehicle access is via Festival Drive (off King William Street).
Height clearance is 2.1 metres.
Heavy vehicle access to dock is from North Terrace down ramp (in front of Casino).
Height clearance is 4.5 metres.

Loading dock

A 'Cab Over' prime mover is essential when manoeuvring a semi-trailer flush against the dock.

The Space, Dunstan Playhouse and STC Workshop, share a common dock. The dock is an 'end loading' facility service, one vehicle only at any time.

There is a 1500 kg capacity hydraulic lift platform from ground level to dock floor immediately in front of the dock. This lift platform is 2.75 metres wide × 1.5 metres deep.

The dock door is 3.15 metres high × 2.75 metres wide.

Scenery and equipment must be moved from the dock to the Space stage via a 4355 kg capacity hydraulic lift 7.3 metres long × 2.4 metres wide × 2.75 metres high. Scenery must then travel through the STC Workshop and onto the Space stage. The door from the STC Workshop into the Space is 3 metres wide × 5.5 metres high with full acoustic isolation.

Source: The Adelaide Festival Centre (2008).

FIGURE 15.4 Venue and site selection process

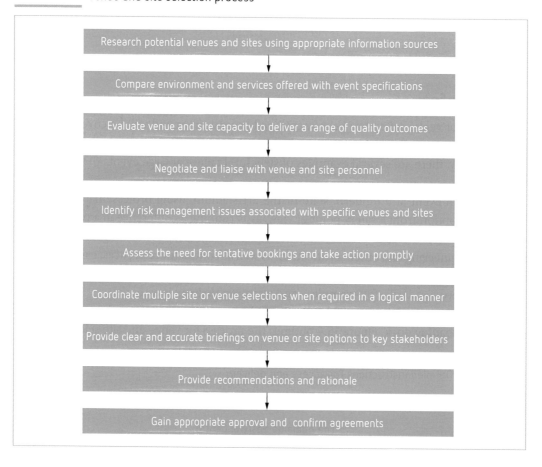

Research potential venues and sites using appropriate information sources

Compare environment and services offered with event specifications

Evaluate venue and site capacity to deliver a range of quality outcomes

Negotiate and liaise with venue and site personnel

Identify risk management issues associated with specific venues and sites

Assess the need for tentative bookings and take action promptly

Coordinate multiple site or venue selections when required in a logical manner

Provide clear and accurate briefings on venue or site options to key stakeholders

Provide recommendations and rationale

Gain appropriate approval and confirm agreements

CONFIRM VENUE OR SITE BOOKINGS

On completion of the investigative and evaluation phase, and with approval from stakeholders for a site or venue, arrangements must be confirmed in writing with the venue provider. The contract may include estimated numbers, facilities and services to be provided, audience or delegate profile and location, event theme and image, and of course the budget (see Figure 15.5). Other important considerations include access and timing for set-up and breakdown, size of the area and equipment, technical capacity or potential, and staffing.

FIGURE 15.5 Sample venue contract

CONDITIONS OF HIRE AGREEMENT

Between the VENUE MANAGEMENT and the hirer.

BOOKING PROCEDURE: Every person applying to hire the VENUE must provide a permanent address and contact details. This booking is unconfirmed until such time as a signed copy of the Conditions of Hire Agreement has been returned to us together with payment of the required deposit and other actions as specified within this and supporting document(s). Our return of this countersigned agreement with deposit receipt will provide formal acceptance of your confirmed Hire Contract.

CANCELLATION: Any cancellation after confirmation of this agreement, or part thereof, will result in forfeiture of the total deposit value, plus any other costs incurred.

SET-UP AND BREAKDOWN: Set-up and Breakdown (bump-in and bump-out) shall be agreed and stated within the Conditions of Hire Agreement. In the event of any performance or use continuing beyond these times, the Tenant shall pay to VENUE MANAGEMENT such further sum or sums as is specified in the Venue Rental Schedule. The keys of the Building shall be kept by the Caretaker or nominated deputy. Labour costs for access outside normal operating hours shall be payable by the Tenant.

SUBLETTING: The Tenant may not sublet the venue or any part thereof.

DEPOSIT: On the signing of this Conditions of Hire Agreement and receipt of the deposit invoice, the sum shall be payable to secure confirmation of this document.

The balance of the account as invoiced by VENUE MANAGEMENT shall be payable within seven days of the event date.

CATERING: VENUE MANAGEMENT, through their in-house caterers, retain sole and exclusive right to supply to persons attending the premises with food and beverages. A separate catering deposit may be required should there be any pre/post-performance catering required by the Tenant. Numbers and menu confirmation must be made not less than 72 hours (3 days) prior to the function date.

SMOKING: Smoking shall not be permitted in any part of the building. The Tenant shall be liable for any damages or costs should any person smoke within the venue.

FURNITURE AND EQUIPMENT: The Tenant shall be accountable for the replacement of all furniture and equipment to where it came from at the conclusion of the event unless set-up and dismantling fees are being paid as detailed in this agreement. The Tenant shall be accountable for damages or breakages. At the conclusion of the event, the Tenant shall be responsible for removing any furniture, equipment items or decorations introduced to the venue at that time, unless alternative arrangements have been made with VENUE MANAGEMENT.

LABOUR: VENUE MANAGEMENT can provide labour for the set-up and dismantling of your event. This is charged out at a $30.00 per hour per person (normal working hours) and $35.00 per hour per person (after hours). This does not include technical staff.

CLEANING: The Tenant is expected to leave the facilities in the condition they were found. If this is not so, additional cleaning charges will be incurred and charged on the final invoice. The final decision will be made by VENUE MANAGEMENT.

NOISE LEVELS: These shall be restricted to a maximum of 100 decibels within the venue, or less if determined by VENUE MANAGEMENT.

FIRE ALARMS: The Promoter / Tenant shall be liable for any charges incurred due to the activation of the fire alarm by 'false alarm' during the hire period.

EVACUATION PROCEDURE: As a requirement of the Fire Safety Regulations, the Tenant and their staff should familiarise themselves with the Venue Evacuation Procedure, copies of which are on display in all areas of the venue. If the Tenant and their staff are unsure of any part of the procedure please contact the Caretaker.

THE TENANT covenants with VENUE MANAGEMENT as follows:

(a)   Not to infringe or breach, or permit to be infringed or breached, any copyright, performing right or other protected right by or in the conduct of any performance.

(b)   Shall make no alteration to the structure, fittings, decorations or furnishings of the buildings without previous written permission of the Caretaker and shall after each performance or use leave the building in as good a condition as they were in before any permitted alteration to the satisfaction of the Caretaker. Any damages or costs associated with alterations, or other activities, shall be made right, with the full cost met by the Tenant.

(c)   Shall not introduce, display, attach or suspend any equipment, fittings or furniture without previous written permission from VENUE MANAGEMENT.

(d)   Shall meet all Australian standards in the use of electrical equipment.

(e)   Shall pay the cost of any special electrical equipment installation or fittings which may be required for the purpose of the Tenant's event, and shall obtain written permission prior to any such work from VENUE MANAGEMENT.

(f)   Shall permit the VENUE MANAGEMENT (or Caretaker) to visit at any time all parts of the premises.

(g)   Shall ensure that they operate with current policies as required under the Workplace Health & Safety Act, Australian Standards for building evacuation and any other Acts or local by-laws as may be relevant. The Tenant will accept total liability, as the lessee of the facilities, for adhering to these laws.

(h)   Shall provide certificate of currency for Public Liability Insurance Policy and Workers Compensation Insurance. Shall do likewise if subcontractors are employed.

VENUE MANAGEMENT agrees as follows:

(a)   Shall provide such staff, equipment and services as are specified at the full cost to the Tenant, or as included within Venue Rental as determined within the Venue Rental Schedule.

(b)   The Fire Safety Officer is a separate charge to the Tenant, to be present in the venue one hour before the doors are due to open, through until the building is vacated at the conclusion of the performance or use.

(c)   Shall reserve the right to revise fees and charges from time to time as may be found necessary.

(d)   Shall reserve the right of entry to any of our venues for our staff members or management at no charge.

(e)   Shall have complete supervision and control over admission of the public, the Tenant or subcontractors.

(f)   VENUE MANAGEMENT shall not be responsible for the loss or damage to any article of any kind brought to or left in the building.

Matthews (2008, p. 152) says that:

> The first point to bear in mind is that when in any venue or on any outdoor site, the event producer is a guest and not an employee or even a contractor for that venue. Certainly the event producer is usually a contractor of the client who is also a client of that venue or site, but that does not automatically allow the producer to demand whatever he or she wants of the venue.

Source: Matthews, D. (2008). *Special Event Production: The Process.* Oxford, UK: Butterworth-Heinemann. p. 152

He goes on to highlight the importance of maintaining good relations and understanding internal management hierarchies in hotels, convention centres and other venues.

In some cases, such as for touring events, multiple sites or venues are involved. In other cases, such as for a major festival, related events are held in multiple locations. Both require careful integration in the planning phase.

On finalisation of the contract, it is necessary to draft the physical dimensions of the event in order to develop more detailed equipment specifications. A scale map, plan or CAD drawing of the event and two- or even three-dimensional models help to clarify expectations to all stakeholders. Many events are set up at the last minute and the most difficult thing for all concerned is visualising the event and the work environment. Check all measurements, or you may not hire enough carpet! An example of the Formula 1 Australian Grand Prix circuit map was shown at the start of the chapter.

On completion of the event, a report should be prepared, providing an assessment of the venue or site, the level of cooperation shown by venue personnel, and their willingness to negotiate on products, services and costs. The initial risk assessment should be reviewed for the post-event report as well.

Risk and regulatory issues

Responsibility for risk assessment is generally shared between the venue operator and the event organiser. Generally speaking, when hiring premises for an event, the building owner is responsible for the safety of the space, including, for example, fire exits and kitchen equipment. The person booking and running the event is responsible for other aspects of the event; for example, the potential for gatecrashers to turn up. Therefore, although the venue operator has a standard building risk assessment process, it is absolutely necessary to prepare a risk assessment that highlights issues for the particular event and which identifies who is responsible.

For example, if you were running a stage performance in a shopping centre involving child performers, the various stakeholders would need to identify who is responsible for stage set-up and safety, who does the roll call and deals with toileting emergencies, who announces a lost child, and how the search process and police notification would occur. These responsibilities would fall to the centre management, staging contractor, event organiser, teachers and parents.

Other risk and regulatory issues associated with venues could occur in the areas of:

- liquor licensing
- security and safety
- crowd control
- noise.

The social and environmental sustainability issues associated with an event can occur in the areas of:

- water and energy use
- waste management
- relationships with the local community and business operators
- antisocial or illegal behaviour
- damage to the natural environment.

From this, it is fairly apparent that using a tried-and-tested venue with formalised policies and processes, such as you would find at a hotel, convention centre or club, means that half the job is done. If the site is built for the event from the ground up, a great deal more planning is needed. This will be discussed in more detail in the final chapter.

Summary

The creativity of an event concept is often tempered by the suitability and availability of a venue or site to stage the event. Of course, many venues and sites can be totally transformed if there are unlimited funds available to the event manager! As this is not the case in most instances, choosing the right venue for an event is crucial to its success. In this chapter, we have covered what you need to know to develop accurate site specifications for different types of events and how to source suitable venues or sites. For the event manager, there are many aspects to consider when preparing site specifications, not least of which is safety. We have also stressed the importance of confirming venue arrangements in writing, and reviewing and signing a venue contract for which an example has been provided.

Key terms

Facility   Alternative term used for an event location, particularly in North America
Precinct   Covers a large area that includes several venues (e.g. Commonwealth Games precinct)
Site   Generally an oudoor space with limited infrastructure
Venue   Generally refers to a built structure where an event takes place

REVIEW YOUR KNOWLEDGE

1   When an overseas group is visiting for a conference, what are some of the considerations for the choice of venue?
2   List five key areas that need to be considered concerning accessibility to a venue or site.
3   How can the event manager ensure everyone's understanding of the proposed layout of the site or venue (two-dimensional) and the concept (three-dimensional)?
4   What do we mean when we talk about technical equipment and production services?
5   What are the risk and regulatory issues associated with venues in the areas of:
    - liquor licensing
    - security and safety issues

- crowd control
- noise?

6   What are the social and environmental sustainability issues associated with outdoor music festival sites in the areas of:
  - water and energy use
  - waste management
  - the natural environment
  - relationships with the local community and business operators
  - antisocial behaviour
  - damage to the natural environment.

APPLY YOUR KNOWLEDGE

Visit a large convention centre in your State or Territory to look at the facilities available and their event planning tools. You can also use the event planning manual provided by the Perth Convention and Exhibition Centre (PCEC) in the online resources that accompany this textbook (the link is also provided here: http://www.pcec.com.au/plan-an-event). Review scale diagrams of meeting and function rooms and check the suitability of the convention centre for a two-day conference for 200 Chinese delegates, including a gala dinner.

Develop your own site specifications and inspection checklist based on your research into the needs of this inbound market. You can select another market profile if you wish (see www.tourism.australia.com/statistics/market-profiles.aspx).

In undertaking this task, you need to identify the staging products and services required, including but not limited to:

- accommodation
- catering
- technical equipment and services
- staffing
- security
- storage facilities.

Do not contact industry suppliers for quotes or proposals. Online research will provide sufficient information.

CASE STUDY

Your local council has plans for an organic food market and community entertainment event. You are an event organiser and you are tendering for this.

While you are not running a mobile food stall yourself you will have oversight of all operations and need to select a suitable site for this event. You need to show how the site offers or can offer the following minimum requirements:

- The area is big enough for vehicle access.
- There is adequate space for equipment.
- The area can be kept clean.

A mobile food stall

- There is clean water available for equipment and hand washing.
- Garbage and waste can be collected and cleared regularly.
- There is sufficient lighting and ventilation.
- Temporary storage facilities are provided, including refrigeration.
- Toilets are available.

It is recommended that you access the Shoalhaven City Council guidelines for mobile food stalls (**www.shoalhaven.nsw.gov.au/For-Business/Public-Health/Food-stalls**) or a similar document, of which there are many online.

Your overall task is to demonstrate to the council that you can select a suitable site and plan for the temporary infrastructure required for the stall holders and the public. Food safety, WHS and public safety are key compliance issues that need to be addressed. Alcohol will not be sold or served.

Online resources

Visit **http://login.cengagebrain.com** and search for this book to access the study tools that come with your textbook.

References

Hsu, E. B., & Burkle, F. M. (2012). Cambodian Bon Om Touk stampede highlights preventable tragedy. *Prehospital and Disaster Medicine*, 27(05), 481–2.

Matthews, D. (2008). *Special Event Production: The Process*. Oxford, UK: Butterworth-Heinemann.

Schwarz, A. (2012). How publics use social media to respond to blame games in crisis communication: The Love Parade tragedy in Duisburg 2010. *Public Relations Review*, 38(3), 430–7.

Websites

Academy for Venue Safety and Security, **www.iavm.org/avss/avss-home**

Creative Spaces, **www.creativespaces.net.au/find-a-space#!**

Crowd control at venues and events, **www.worksafe.vic.gov.au/forms-and-publications/forms-and-publications/crowd-control-at-venues-and-events**

Unique spaces in Brisbane, **www.hiddencitysecrets.com.au/unique-spaces-brisbane**

Venue Safety and Security Magazine, **www.ifea.com/p/resources/iemagazine/venuesafetyandsecuritymagazine**

IMPLEMENT AND MONITOR ENVIRONMENTALLY SUSTAINABLE WORK PRACTICES

16

OVERVIEW

The event industry is a leader in environmentally sustainable practices. There are many festivals and events that champion the environmental message, educating the public while implementing careful management of resources. This chapter will highlight many of these practices, and will show how monitoring environmental impacts can lead to continuous improvement. Working with stakeholders is part of the process, as an integrated approach involving all contractors is essential. Ideally, environmental targets are discussed during contract negotiation and key performance indicators (KPIs) are set for monitoring purposes.

LEARNING OBJECTIVES

On completion of this chapter, you will be able to:

1. investigate current practices in relation to resource usage, analysing relations and industry practices
2. set targets for improvements and evaluate alternative solutions
3. implement performance-improvement strategies, working with stakeholders
4. monitor performance using evaluation tools and technologies.

INDUSTRY VIEWPOINT

The Queensland Folk Federation (QFF) is committed to environmental sustainability. We recognise that sustainable resolutions to environmental issues can be brought about through a cultural agenda. This provides us not only with opportunities to engage and advocate in this area, but a responsibility to do so.

In staging the Woodford Folk Festival (WFF) and the Dreaming, our first responsibility is to create a safe and healthy site for the Festival friends. As land managers we believe we have an obligation to conserve and enhance the natural environment

Source: Woodford Folk Festival (2017). The festival – environmental statement. https://woodfordfolkfestival. com/the-festival/environmental-statement.html

INTRODUCTION

The Woodford Folk Festival aims to become 'a leader amongst cultural organisations in environmental matters', and the aims are to enhance the environment through planting, weed control and other landscaping initiatives. Additionally, the event provides the opportunity for education in environmental sustainability. There are many components to their strategies to enhance the environment, including waste management, recycling, sewerage and wastewater management, and chemical use.

Woodford Folk Festival

Environmental issues are important considerations for all mega and major events, including the Olympic Games and Commonwealth Games. These issues are also considered in competitive bids for major sporting events such as the FIFA World Cup and Rugby World Cup. Bid documents need to clearly spell out details of the intended plans for managing solid waste, sewage treatment and energy, and state how the organisers see this influencing the city and region in the future. Planning for even the smallest event must also consider the environment. Local councils are responsible for waste management and will look for a waste management plan. They will demand assurances that the environmental impact will be minimal and that the area will be left in pristine condition. Environmentally friendly waste disposal is a major consideration of event organisers.

Greenshoot Pacific, founded by Meegan Jones, provides a guide to understanding the international standard for Sustainable Events Management Systems (SEMS) (visit **www. greenshootpacific.com/iso-20121-short-guide-download**). The organisation's website provides case studies, guides and checklists for this specialised area. ISO 20121 is an international standard developed to manage sustainability issues, including social, environmental and economic impacts. It was put to use at the London Olympics soon after it was finalised. This standard covers all types of events, cultural as well as sporting. Numerous resources are available, including an event waste checklist, event energy checklist, supply chain analysis, and legal procedures. These can be purchased at minimal cost from the site.

EXTENSION ACTIVITY

Watch this guide to event sustainability management systems (SEMS): https://youtu.be/izsLhtOqOl8?list=FL6vUa3a6_qGynWrBbZiKtdg

Now watch the two more controversial clips 'Sustainable Olympics, fact or fiction?' and 'What Rio doesn't want the world to see':

https://youtu.be/l4hiDuBuoIg

https://youtu.be/1W_zM7koJy8

Do you think that London and Rio achieved their environmental sustainability promises? These short clips will provide lots of ideas for both sides of the argument:

https://youtu.be/wmOmS-vHdzo

https://youtu.be/mIlMODRwGxU

This chapter will review current practices at festivals and events, show how setting targets can assist with monitoring improvements in this area, and demonstrate how festivals and events can also play a role in environmental education.

INVESTIGATE CURRENT PRACTICES IN RELATION TO RESOURCE USAGE

In general terms, the goal of any event organisation is the minimisation of environmental risks and the maximisation of opportunities to improve business environmental performance. This may include minimisation of waste through implementation of the waste management hierarchy, which will be described in detail in this chapter. An additional role for all event staff is to model environmentally efficient work practices such as switching off lights and appliances when they are not being used or monitoring waste management streams to avoid contamination. Efficient water use is another area in which everyone working on-site can assist. Seeking alternative sources of energy is, however, the role of organising bodies.

In order to comply with environmental regulations, the following practices are usually necessary:

- Analyse the use of resources, such as individually packaged tomato sauce and overuse of packaging materials in general.
- Discuss with suppliers how to minimise other packaging waste and use of items such as polystyrene boxes.
- Examine invoices from suppliers and conduct resource audits to see if there are better alternatives.
- Take measurements under different conditions (the measurement of waste streams is discussed later in the chapter).
- Monitor the use of equipment.

Laws and regulations

In addition to the recommended (and voluntary) international ISO standard as the basis for an international event industry code of practice, the event organisation must comply with Australian laws. The overriding national environment law is the *Environment Protection and Biodiversity Conservation Act 1999* (*EPBC Act*), the most relevant section for event organisers concerning heritage properties, protected species and ecological communities.

State and Territory governments also have local environmental protection authorities (EPAs) that provide guidelines and procedures applying to sea, land, water, air and people. In addition, Australian event industry codes of conduct, such as the Waste Wise principles outlined later in this chapter, provide specific policies, procedures and templates for festival and event organisers, and there are also industry accreditation schemes such as the Restaurant & Catering Australia's Green Table initiative (visit **http://rca.asn.au/rca/what-we-do/products-programs/environmental-sustainability-green-table**).

Most event venues describe their environmental credentials on their websites, as this is an important consideration for organisations making bookings. One example is the Melbourne Convention and Exhibition Centre which has been recognised for its environmental attributes, having at one time been named the winner of the Urban Development Institute of Australia's Environmental Excellence Award.

EXTENSION ACTIVITY

You will be flying from Brisbane to Townsville for a festival, staying in a modest hotel for five days and spending money on various things like food, beverages and merchandise. Using a carbon emissions calculator, work out the impact of your visit. Now think of three ways in which you can reduce the footprint size of your visit to the festival.

You can also complete a fun, interactive baseline quiz to calculate how many planets it would take to support your lifestyle: www.wwf.org.au/get-involved/change-the-way-you-live/ecological-footprint-calculator

Health and safety at public events

It is also important to consider all aspects of health and safety when planning a public event, particularly a large outdoor event such as a concert. The Department of Health in South Australia produces useful guidelines for the management of all important aspects of health and safety at public events, ranging from waste disposal to sewerage and wastewater management for an event site which is not served by sewerage facilities.

EXAMPLE

WASTE DISPOSAL

Public events generate a considerable amount of waste including rubbish, wastewater and sewerage. A system for dealing with this waste needs to be adequately addressed by event organisers and must include clean-up after the event. Event organisers need to allocate enough resources to ensure that all waste is managed during and after the event to prevent insanitary conditions and environmental harm.

Event organisers should consult with the following authorities to determine who has legislative responsibilities and requirements for the management of solid and liquid wastes:

- the local council
- the Environment Protection Authority
- the Department of Health.

An accumulation of waste must not give rise to insanitary conditions, which are prohibited under the *Public and Environmental Health Act*. Premises are in an insanitary condition if:

- the condition of the premises gives rise to a risk to health
- the premises are so filthy or neglected that there is a risk of infestation by rodents or other pests
- the condition of the premises is such as to cause justified offence to the owner of any land in the vicinity
- offensive material or odours are emitted from the premises
- the premises are for some other reason justifiably declared by the relevant health authority to be in an insanitary condition.

Solid waste such as refuse and food waste are the biggest risk for nuisance and offensive conditions as well as infestation by vermin if not adequately controlled. Event organisers must provide an adequate number of refuse bins with lids with regular emptying as often as needed to prevent infestation and overflow.

Food businesses must implement a pest control program to ensure that:

- all practicable measures have been taken to prevent pests and vermin from contaminating food and/or entering food premises and
- all practicable measures have been taken to eradicate and prevent the harbourage of pests and vermin on the premises and vehicles that are used to transport food.

All temporary refuse, sewage and wastewater disposal sites constructed for the event must not create nuisance or offensive conditions. Disposal of refuse or liquid wastes must not result in the contamination of ground, surface or stream waters or provide breeding sites for rodents, vermin or insects. Special arrangements must be in place for the collection and disposal of decomposable and hazardous waste including food waste, clinical waste and waste from first aid and sharps.

Solid waste disposal

Public events must have suitable and adequate facilities for the storage, collection and disposal of solid waste that:

- contain the waste
- prevent animal, pest or vermin access

Bins are overflowing and there is no option for recycling

- are easily identifiable and accessed by patrons, food vendors and waste collectors
- are able to be easily and effectively cleaned
- ensure that materials such as glass, cardboard, plastic, etc. are recycled through provision of clearly designated and labelled containers.

Note: All putrescible or offensive waste should be in lidded containers.

As the availability of appropriately licensed waste disposal depots is often limited in remote outback areas, it may be necessary to consider alternative options. The Environment Protection Authority should be contacted in this eventuality.

Needle and syringe disposal

Illegal and prescription drug use at events must be considered and planned for. The presence of injecting equipment may pose a safety hazard for patrons and staff. Sharps containers should be provided at the event. Generally these are located within toilets, however other locations may be considered appropriate.

Cleaning and security staff must be briefed on the dangers associated with used injecting equipment and instructed on safe handling methods.

Dust control

A common problem at outdoor events is dust control. Large amounts of dust may develop as a result of the event itself. Dust caused by large crowds or vehicle movement can contaminate food, create a nuisance, and cause problems for performers and patrons, especially asthma and allergy sufferers. Consideration must be given in the planning stages to the need for lawn or grass mowing, light watering, and ground covering (artificial or otherwise) – when it is to be carried out, how and by whom. For dust caused by frequent or heavy vehicle movement, event organisers should consider laying a gravel road, compacted rubble, and/or frequent wetting down.

Water supply

An adequate supply of water must be provided at public events the quantity and quality appropriate to the intended use. All water for drinking and use within food premises must be of potable quality; that is, it must be suitable for human consumption. The quantity of water supplied will depend on a range of factors, including:

- the nature of the event and crowd activities
- event duration
- location of event and the time of the year
- environmental conditions such as temperature, wind, rain etc.
- number of people (patrons, performers and other staff) attending the event
- proportion of persons camping on the site
- flush toilets and other ablutions
- food handling arrangements
- dust control.

Event organisers should refer to the NHMRC/ARMCANZ Australian Drinking Water Guidelines for information in relation to microbiological and chemical standards for drinking water.

The Emergency Management Australia Manual, Safe and Healthy Mass Gatherings, recommends 20 litres of potable water per person per day, of which 4 litres is the drinking water component. Event duration, location and expected ambient temperatures should be considered in determining the quantity of drinking water required.

Non-potable water supplies may be used for toilet flushing, fire fighting or dust suppression. Where camping is permitted, water for showers needs to be bacteriologically safe although not necessarily of potable quality. Non-potable supplies, including piped outlets, are to be clearly identified as not suitable for drinking.

Water supply must be constant and at a sufficient pressure to withstand peak demands at all outlets. Water should be readily accessible at all food premises, toilets, ablutions, laundry facilities, designated standpipes for patron use, fire fighting and first aid posts.

Toilets and ablution facilities

Depending on the nature and duration of the event, event organisers need to ensure that adequate toilet facilities are provided for patrons, entertainers and support staff. These facilities should include water closet pans, urinals and hand basins. Showers are required where camping is proposed in conjunction with the event. Facilities should be adequate in number, conveniently located and suitable for the event. The toilet facilities must have the necessary provisions for the collection, treatment and disposal of sewage and wastewater. The facilities must be operated and maintained in a clean and tidy manner so that insanitary conditions do not occur.

Unless otherwise permitted by the relevant health authority, all toilets will be water flush and have hand basins provided, connected to a cold water supply. Portable water flush toilets must be provided when existing toilet facilities are inadequate. When planning for public toilets, the following should be taken into consideration:

- type of event
- duration of the event
- crowd type and activities
- number of patrons
- alcohol and food consumption.
  Toilet and ablution facilities should be:
- clearly designated for each sex, with unisex toilets for disabled persons
- separate from food service preparation and storage areas
- cleaned and maintained for the duration of the event
- well lit and clearly identified
- situated and screened to ensure privacy
- preferably having separate approach for each sex
- provided with handwashing basins with cold running water, soap (bar or liquid), disposable towels or air dryers and waste containers
- provided with toilet paper
- provided with provisions for disposal and removal of sanitary napkins, nappies and incontinence pads, condoms, needles and syringes and other refuse
- provided to enable feeding and or changing of infants.

Where showers are provided, suitable provisions for holding of clothing during shower use are needed.

In hot areas, shade should be provided in conjunction with the facilities.

Event organisers should ensure that all support staff are briefed on the proper procedure for handling needles and syringes, on the risks of needlestick injuries and the correct procedures should a needlestick injury occur.

To maintain facilities in a sanitary condition, they must be cleaned at least daily or more frequently where necessary to prevent nuisance or offensive conditions and infestation/harbourage by nuisance insects or pests. A cleaning schedule should be established for toilet facilities and ablutions to cover frequency of cleaning, monitoring, equipment and chemicals to be used. There must be adequate maintenance personnel available to repair any blockages, and sufficient supplies need to be available for use by the cleaning staff, including soap, toilet paper, buckets, mops, brooms, protective clothing etc.

At least one unisex toilet for patrons with a disability should be provided at each group of toilet facilities. Refer to the Building Code of Australia as a guide for further information.

As a means of alleviating long line-ups, particularly at female toilets, event organisers should consider the provision of additional unisex toilets.

Portable toilets must be situated so that they can be pumped out during the event. Vehicles pumping out portable toilets must not block access for emergency services.

Signs directing patrons to toilet facilities should be prominently placed at locations where patrons can see them. Toilet and ablution facilities should also be sited to allow easy access and minimum queuing. Toilet locations could be included on site maps that are provided with tickets to the event and at information centres.

If an event is to be held within a building, for example in a building that is specifically built for the purpose of entertaining or holding an event, then the number of toilets must comply with the requirements for South Australia as set out in the Building Code of Australia.

Toilet and ablution facilities must not give rise to insanitary conditions. The *Public and Environmental Health Act* prohibits insanitary conditions which includes conditions posing a risk to health, conditions where offensive material or odours are emitted, and conditions that could cause justified offence. The Act also prohibits the unlawful or inappropriate discharge of wastes into a public or private place.

Sewerage and wastewater

When the event site is not served by a sewerage system, or the sewerage system is inadequate, the relevant health authority or agency must be contacted to determine the requirements for all types of sewage and wastewater disposal. This includes sewage, wastewater from handwashing, food stalls, ablution blocks and from any crowd comfort measures such as spray tents and foam parties.

Sewage and wastewater collection, treatment and disposal systems must be constructed and operated to prevent contamination of the food or water supply or other water bodies, or insanitary conditions. In areas administered by local government, contact the local council.

The Minister for Health through the Environmental Health Service of the Department of Health is the relevant health authority in all other areas of the State (see also Section 11.3).

Source: South Australia Department of Health (2006). Guidelines for the management of public health & safety at public events. www.sahealth. sa.gov.au/wps/wcm/connect/ b650500045c7337a9262fbac725693cd/ publicevents-phcc-100531.pdf? MOD=AJPERES&CACHEID= b650500045c7337a9262fbac725693cd

People making the most of event facilities

Notes: The guidelines for the Management of Public Health and Safety at Public Events were prepared in 2003 and last revised in 2006. Please note that some parts of the guidelines are now out-of-date and contain references to various regulations, standards and programs that have since been superseded. When using or referencing information provided in the Guidelines, care should be taken to ensure that up-to-date advice is sought from relevant agencies.

These and many other guidelines are available online; a few weblinks are provided at the end of the chapter for more information.

Cleaning

The cleaning function for most events is handled by the venue staff or by a contract cleaning company. The staff involved must be trained in all areas of waste management, including policies and procedures developed specifically for such things as cleaning routines and inspections. The responsibility for specific areas needs to be clearly defined. For example, while public areas and toilet facilities are generally the responsibility of the cleaning contractor, the catering contractor may be responsible for cleaning in the kitchen, particularly during service. The staff involved in cleaning need to be very knowledgeable about the event itself as they are frequently the targets of questions, the most common one being 'Where are the toilets?'.

Cleaning services for outdoor events are most likely to be outsourced to companies such as Clean Event, well known around the world for event and venue presentation and waste management consultancy services. This company can even provide, through a subsidiary, executive washrooms stocked with toiletries, perfumes and flowers – and every washroom comes with its own attendant!

Professional waste consultants can provide assistance in:

- identifying the event venue's total potential waste stream
- tailoring the waste stream to maximise the use of recycled materials
- identifying biodegradable, cost-effective food and drink packaging
- providing recycling collection, storage and transportation equipment
- providing environmental audits post-event.

If waste management is not outsourced, it is the responsibility of the event organiser or local council to decide on the method of dealing with waste streams.

Standard colour codes and bin labels are recommended to simplify waste disposal for the organiser and to educate the public. Other types of bins and recycling equipment, such as recycling cages, are also recommended where needed.

Medical and contaminated waste needs special care, as these items must be collected, stored and disposed of in accordance with legal guidelines. This is particularly relevant where there is doping control at an event and blood tests are carried out. Oil used in catering also requires special treatment (in a restaurant a waste trap is used) and should not be disposed of in the sewerage system.

Purchasing

Current resource usage can be measured for many conventional business operations, but for most events this is not possible unless comparisons can be made from year to year. One of the most effective approaches, then, is to ask venues, suppliers and contractors about their environmental credentials. The Darwin Convention Centre, for example, strives for ongoing improvement and participates in numerous sustainability initiatives. The Gold Coast Convention and Exhibition Centre, meanwhile, has achieved EarthCheck Gold status. Some of the Gold Coast centre's achievements include the following:

* 75 per cent of waste recycled or reused
* 100 per cent of the cleaning and pesticide products used on-site are biodegradable
* light sensors installed throughout all toilets and storerooms
* 500 power-saving LED lights installed throughout the foyers, replacing less-efficient lighting
* use of recycled (non-potable) water for the landscape irrigation systems
* centre has worked with local suppliers to change the way goods are packaged and delivered; for example, most suppliers are now using cardboard boxes that are then recycled on-site
* menus consist of 85 per cent locally grown and sourced ingredients
* excess, freshly made and packaged foods are donated to OzHarvest (Gold Coast Convention and Exhibition Centre, 2017).

These statistics demonstrate the current figures. As the organisation is committed to continuous improvement it can set targets to improve performance based on these benchmarks.

Planning sanitary facilities

Planning the correct number of toilet facilities for an event is a very scientific matter. In fact, council guidelines can sometimes be very specific in respect of the number of toilet facilities to be provided for events. This is illustrated in Table 16.1, Table 16.2 and Table 16.3. As you can see from these tables, there are a number of considerations for the event planner, including the duration of the event, the number of males and females attending the event, and service of alcohol. Provision of toilets for people in wheelchairs and for baby change rooms also needs to be considered. Facilities provided can range from the most basic to the luxury complex. (There is no question as to which one the consumer would prefer.) If not enough facilities are provided, the resulting crowd behaviour is something one prefers not to imagine. This can also occur where camping areas are not adequately supplied with facilities.

TABLE 16.1 Toilet facilities for events where alcohol is not served

PATRONS	MALES			FEMALES	
	WCs	URINALS	HANDBASINS	WCs	HANDBASINS
<500	1	2	2	6	2
<1000	2	4	4	9	4
<2000	4	8	6	12	6
<3000	6	15	10	18	10
<5000	8	25	17	30	17

Source: Blue Mountains City Council (2014). Application: festivals and events. www.bmcc.nsw.gov.au/files/misc005_
festivalseventsapplicationformupdated2july2014.pdf

TABLE 16.2 Toilet facilities for events where alcohol is served

PATRONS	MALES			FEMALES	
	WCs	URINALS	HANDBASINS	WCs	HANDBASINS
<500	3	8	2	13	2
<1000	5	10	4	16	4
<2000	9	15	7	18	7
<3000	10	20	14	22	14
<5000	12	30	20	40	20

Source: Blue Mountains City Council (2014). Application: festivals and events. www.bmcc.nsw.gov.au/files/misc005_
festivalseventsapplicationformupdated2july2014.pdf

TABLE 16.3 Reductions for duration of event

DURATION OF EVENT	QUANTITY REQUIRED
8 hours plus	100%
6–8 hours	80%
4–6 hours	75%
less than 4 hours	70%

Source: Blue Mountains City Council (2014). Application: festivals and events. www.bmcc.nsw.gov.au/files/misc005_
festivalseventsapplicationformupdated2july2014.pdf

Note that in Table 16.1, Table 16.2 and Table 16.3, figures are a guide only. Each event needs to be assessed on a case-by-case basis.

No doubt this type of analysis can be refined even more, with more variables such as the number of intermission periods and type of seating being taken into account. What is clear is that careful consideration must be given to this issue, particularly for events held out of doors or at temporary venues. Anyone who has spent some time in a long toilet queue at an event will agree that this important element of customer service is sometimes poorly planned. At one event, organisers forgot to turn on water supplies to the toilet facilities, causing dismay on the part of the event audience and incredulity on the part of the emergency plumber who was called in after most toilets had blocked up. The importance of using pre-event checklists is well illustrated by this story.

SET TARGETS FOR IMPROVEMENT

One of the most common measures of environmental impact is the 'carbon footprint', which is the amount of greenhouse gases produced by human activities, usually expressed in the equivalent tons of carbon dioxide. CO_2e is the abbreviation of 'carbon dioxide equivalent'.

Other measures (or key performance indicators) include:

* energy consumption
* percentage or volume of recycled materials
* water consumption
* percentage or volume of water recycled or reused
* total weight of waste by type
* weight of waste to landfill
* proportion of spending on local suppliers.

For example, the Gold Coast Convention and Exhibition Centre achieved waste reductions equivalent to filling 17 shipping containers in 2014. A key aspect of the centre's approach involves communication with suppliers and stakeholders.

A Waste Wise Event is one where the event organisers integrate simple and cost-effective waste, recycling and litter management systems in their events. The NSW Government Department of Environment, Climate Change and Water provides outstanding guidelines for planning such an event. Guidelines for planning prior to the event are given below.

> Communicate and gain support for your intentions to host a Waste Wise Event with your relevant stakeholders by focusing on the benefits of being involved. Your key stakeholders will most likely be:
>
> * **Councils.** Most events in NSW are held on council-managed public land. Your local council can help achieve Waste Wise aims for an event through policy initiatives, waste management and resource recovery experience. By doing this the council will be more able to fulfil community expectations and give positive reinforcement to their residents by mirroring the at home recycling behaviour when away from home.
>
> * **Event site owners.** The benefits to them of a Waste Wise Event can easily be explained, such as reduced costs for waste management, a positive environmental image and public acceptance of recycling strategies. The site owners may need to establish the costs and benefits of running their site differently – from social, economic and environmental perspectives. Once gained, the commitment from the site owner can be formalised by putting some Waste Wise clauses in your contract/agreement with them.
>
> * **Sponsors** can gain promotional benefit, and are attracted to events that send a sound environmental message. They need to be made aware of exactly how their brands will be enhanced by being involved with or

endorsing a Waste Wise Event. It's wise to check whether the landowner has a policy about sponsors or branding. Be careful of sponsors whose products may not be consistent with Waste Wise aims.

• **Stallholders and vendors'** commitment can be gained by inserting a short standard clause in their agreement, permit or contract that commits them to using certain materials for packaging and to following Waste Wise procedures. They need to be informed early of the goal to minimise waste and packaging, and their expected compliance with the Waste Wise aims. The businesses could even develop their own Waste Wise Plan for their operations throughout the event. Using less costs less.

• **Waste services contractors** will usually be private contractors, but may be council's own staff. They are critical to the success of your Waste Wise Event. The best way to gain commitment to Waste Wise aims is to insert a short standard clause in their contract/agreement. Included in this should be a commitment to providing accurate data of quantities taken to both landfill and recycling facilities, probably in the form of a weighbridge receipt. (Check what data is available at no extra charge.)

• **Other service contractors,** including businesses supplying fencing, portable toilets, power supply, sound systems or marquees, need to fully understand the Waste Wise aims of the event. It is advisable to negotiate a mutually agreeable clause in the agreement or contract for waste avoidance well in advance.

• **The public** will respond positively to a well organised Waste Wise Event. Mention the benefits of being Waste Wise in all promotional material through clear communications and signage during the event. Messages of encouragement and support will have a positive impact by reinforcing their at home Waste Wise behaviour. It may also be worth conducting a survey during the event to gauge their commitment to being Waste Wise.

Source: The content relating to the Waste Wise events guide has been reproduced with permission of the NSW Environment Protection Authority.

Figure 16.1 shows a useful waste management flowchart for before, during and after an event.

The website of the NSW EPA also provides many templates, including clauses that could be included in legal contracts with suppliers and other stakeholders. Similar guidelines are available for other States and Territories, such as South Australia's *Waste Minimisation Guide: Events and Venues.* The South Australian publication has particularly useful guidelines for exploring better catering options to increase the amount

FIGURE 16.1 Waste Wise flowchart

of environmentally friendly, compostable waste and reduce the waste that ends up as landfill. Goldblatt's (2011) *The Complete Guide to Greener Meetings and Events* is also recommended.

Drink Bottles, Cans and Cartons

Compostables

Handy labels for a Waste Wise event

Source: Green Industries SA. http://www.greenindustries.sa.gov.au/publications-events

Logistics of waste management

Suppliers of waste bins and recyclable products are available through an Internet search. Event organisers need to plan the location of bins and the best time to have them installed. Clearing bins and storing waste is a major consideration for event organisers. In many cases, clearing is done by the cleaning contractor and waste is removed by a recycling/waste contractor, and it is essential that these companies work in partnership. In other situations, councils may provide waste management solutions. At the time of tendering and contracting waste management services, the following should form part of the clauses:

* commitment to the event waste management plan and targets
* methods to achieve the targets
* separation of waste streams
* waste measurement (recyclable, compostable and so on)
* bins and placement and signage.

   All of the above will assist with a post-event analysis of the waste management plan.

IMPLEMENT PERFORMANCE IMPROVEMENT STRATEGIES

The most important element of any waste management program is effective communication with stakeholders to enlist their support in the implementation of green initiatives. Stakeholders include staff, contractors, volunteers and, of course, the event audience.

One of the biggest problems with recycling is contamination of the waste stream. This occurs, for example, when a load destined for composting is contaminated by plastic, foil or other non-biodegradable items having been placed in the wrong bin, necessitating its disposal as landfill.

The concept of a composting stream is new to most people attending events. As mentioned previously, only food scraps and biodegradable foodware (plates, cutlery and cups made from cornstarch and sugarcane) should be placed in the bin provided for this purpose. The important message is 'right rubbish, right bin'. When procedures work well, the amount of landfill resulting from an event can be reduced dramatically.

The following principles form the basis of the waste management plan and need to be communicated to both internal and external customers.

Reduction

Waste reduction can be achieved through purchasing strategies aimed at reducing the amount of material brought into a venue; for example, by ordering supplies in large boxed quantities rather than small plastic packages. However, there is sometimes a conflict between waste management and food hygiene; for example, where food safety authorities recommend provision of individual portions of sauces, butter and jam to customers. If individual portions are dispensed with in favour of jars, bottles or other larger containers in the interest of waste management, the caterer must be confident that the condiments can be dispensed in a hygienic way, in accordance with food safety legislation. The pumps illustrated on the Heinz stand shown here meet this requirement. Using this system avoids small plastic sauce packages being included in the compost waste stream. The idea is that all food-related items are binned together in this one stream – a simple message for inattentive event fans.

Reuse

Waste reduction can also occur if items are reused. A good example is the polystyrene boxes in which some vegetables are delivered. These should not be allowed to remain on the site and should be removed for reuse if this can be done hygienically.

Dispensing units for ketchup are more environmentally friendly than individual sauce packages

Recycling

Most members of an event audience will be familiar with recycling messages in relation to glass bottles, plastic bottles, paper and cardboard.

MONITOR PERFORMANCE

Monitoring performance and communicating results is essential to motivate everyone involved. Environmental performance can be measured using the KPIs listed earlier, and these in turn can be reviewed also in terms of financial and social benefits.

The questions to be asked include the following:

- Have we considered the widest possible scope for improvement on environmental performance (not only recycling but a wide range of measures)?
- Which areas provide the most positive impacts and should therefore be prioritised?
- Are there problems and pitfalls in some areas that can be overcome?
- Have we considered the supply chain – how far consumables are travelling?
- Are all stakeholders on board?
- Do contracts with suppliers include environmental guidelines and targets?
- Do we have a communications plan?

Once baseline measures have been developed, the data can be compared and monitored. Discrepancies need to be investigated.

To recap, event operations planning needs to ensure that there are suitable policies (such as procurement/purchasing), minimal impact, education, and continual improvement. For each policy, procedures and responsibility need to be assigned, and an **action plan** developed.

> **Action plan**
> Indicates the specific tasks to be undertaken, by whom and when; ongoing improvement is also part of action planning

Public education is a common aim and this too needs to be planned, implemented and evaluated. Mair and Lang (2013) have investigated this in terms of visitor behaviour change. This is another measure that goes beyond awareness to lifestyle changes in the direction of pro-environmental behaviour.

Progress reports need to be circulated, and following the event an evaluation report provides essential evidence for future events and bids for other events.

Summary

This chapter has focused on how the event manager can comply with environmental laws, regulations and codes of conduct. To this end, an environmentally friendly approach to waste management at every event is recommended and, in many cases, a waste management plan is a requirement of local councils. Waste management is an important element of operational planning and one likely to cause dissatisfaction on the part of the customer if anything goes wrong. An increasing level of sophistication is evident at most large events in the provision of facilities, cleaning procedures and waste management, with customers having increasingly higher expectations. Effective communication with all stakeholders, including the audience, is imperative for the successful implementation of all environmental initiatives.

Key term

Action plan   Indicates the specific tasks to be undertaken, by whom and when; ongoing improvement is also part of action planning

REVIEW YOUR KNOWLEDGE

1   What does 'environmental sustainability' mean?
2   List three events which have environmental sustainability as a theme or message.
3   Explain the compliance issues associated with environmental impacts, including laws, codes of conduct and accreditation schemes.
4   Resource efficiency can be practised by event organisers. Explain this term and give three examples of how targets can be set and monitored.
5   When registering for a conference, it is possible to purchase carbon credits. Explain this concept.

APPLY YOUR KNOWLEDGE

The Department of Sport and Recreation in Western Australia provides guidelines for environmental sustainability in sport. Using the framework illustrated, develop a proposal for an adventure race *focusing only on environmental considerations* in order to get the go-ahead from the local authorities to continue to the next level in bidding for the event. You need to demonstrate that you can analyse information from a range of sources to identify current procedures, practices and compliance requirements in relation to environmental and resource sustainability.

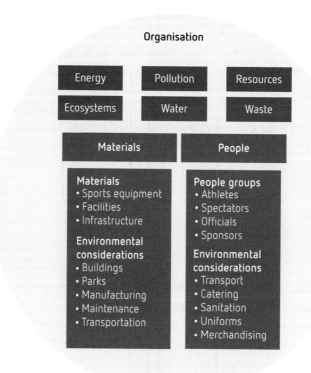

Source: Western Australia Department of Sport and Recreation (2012). Environmental sustainability pack for sport and recreation organisations in Western Australia. p. 2. www.dsr.wa.gov.au/docs/default-source/file-support-and-advice/file-facilitiy-management/sustainability-pack.pdf?sfvrsn=0

CASE STUDY

ADVENTURE RACE – IMPLEMENTATION AND EVALUATION

Having won the bid to host the adventure race, the final stage involves developing an action plan for environmental sustainability.

Part A of this plan shows the steps that will be taken to minimise impacts on the environment. You will outline organisational systems and procedures that relate to environmental and resource sustainability improvements, showing that you can:

- evaluate and implement strategies to improve resource usage
- plan, implement and integrate improvements into operations
- meet environmental requirements.

Part B of this plan shows how you will communicate with suppliers, stakeholders and the workforce, as well as the audience, to ensure that everyone is aware of these initiatives.

Part C of this plan shows how you will monitor and report on environmental performance.

A link to the *Environmental Sustainability Pack for Sport and Recreation Organisations in Western Australia* is provided below along with other online resources for this text.

Online resources

Visit http://login.cengagebrain.com and search for this book to access the study tools that come with your textbook.

References

Gold Coast Convention and Exhibition Centre (2017). Sustainability initiatives. www.gccec.com.au/sustainability-initiatives.html

Goldblatt, S. (2011). *The Complete Guide to Greener Meetings and Events*. Hoboken, NJ: John Wiley & Sons.

Mair, J., & Laing, J. H. (2013). Encouraging pro-environmental behaviour: The role of sustainability-focused events. *Journal of Sustainable Tourism*, 21(8), 1113–28.

Websites

Darwin Convention Centre sustainability, www.darwinconvention.com.au/sustainability-initiatives.html

Environmental Sustainability Pack, www.dsr.wa.gov.au/docs/default-source/file-support-and-advice/file-facilitiy-management/sustainability-pack.pdf?sfvrsn=0

Gold Coast Convention and Exhibition Centre, www.gccec.com.au/sustainability-initiatives.html

ISO20121, www.iso.org/iso-20121-sustainable-events.html

Sustainable Event Solutions, www.sustainablebrands.com/solutionproviders/sems-sustainable-event-solutions

Using the SEMS tool to enhance event sustainability performance, www.greenshootpacific.com/sems-green-event-download

17

RESEARCH AND COMPLY WITH REGULATORY REQUIREMENTS

OVERVIEW

The exhaustive number of laws and regulations and their attendant exhaustive detail can be quite daunting for the business owner or event planner. The aim of this chapter is to provide an overview of the most important and relevant regulatory requirements. Its focus is on the ongoing research needed to determine the scope of compliance required and the continuous review of policies and practices in response to any changes. If you are submitting an event proposal to a council, their guidelines will take you a long way to understanding what is required, as this is usually spelled out in some detail.

LEARNING OBJECTIVES

On completion of this chapter, you will be able to:

1 research the information required for legal compliance, evaluating the scope of compliance requirements for an event business or specific event

2 develop and communicate policies and procedures for legal compliance to relevant personnel and stakeholders, ensuring that all understand their roles and responsibilities for compliance

3 ensure compliance with legal requirements, including checking on contractor compliance and occupational licences to avoid risk of non-compliance

4 maintain personal and organisational knowledge of regulatory requirements, continuously reviewing, updating and distributing plans, policies and procedures for compliance with current laws and licensing requirements.

INDUSTRY VIEWPOINT

Unruly and disruptive patron behaviour is often an indication of intoxication which may result in penalties for licensees under the Act. A number of licensees have been successfully sued for failing to demonstrate the necessary duty of care towards their patrons. An event manager may also be liable for an incident resulting from a poorly organised event or irresponsible serving of alcohol. There is increasing government and community awareness of the legal responsibilities of event managers, specifically in relation to duty of care, negligence and workplace health and safety issues. Event managers need to be aware of these responsibilities and, as much as possible, ensure that event management plans account for the health, safety and comfort of event patrons and staff, and minimise the disruption and harm caused to the community.

Source: Queensland Department of Employment, Economic Development and Innovation (2010). Event management planning guide. p. 4. https://publications.qld.gov.au/storage/f/ 2014-06-24T23%3A47%3A44.633Z/event-management-planning-guide.pdf

INTRODUCTION

This extract illustrates the overlap between compliance considerations, in this case between alcohol service and public safety. It is unnecessary, and indeed almost impossible, for event managers to fully understand all laws pertinent to their industry and all their ramifications. For professional legal advice, most managers would contact their professional association or their organisation's own solicitors. The key issue for managers in the event industry is knowing when to seek professional legal advice.

In order to be able to make such a judgement, the event manager must remain abreast of general changes to legislation that could have an impact on daily operations. For example, public liability issues have brought about many legislative changes in the Australian States and Territories, so anyone operating an event business would need to carefully research the implications of those changes. They would also need to seek advice from their insurance company, as well as from their solicitor, regarding appropriate indemnity forms that their customers may need to sign. Indemnity forms can reduce or remove liability in certain circumstances (but not all), but they must be carefully prepared by a competent legal person. Sudden increases in insurance premiums may be the stimulus needed to research this issue further.

The aims of this chapter are therefore to provide a general understanding of the legislation that could have an impact on event operations, and to underline the importance of updating knowledge on any changes to this legislation.

RESEARCH INFORMATION REQUIRED FOR BUSINESS COMPLIANCE

Creating the right environment to minimise litigation is every manager's and every supervisor's role. Indeed, every staff member has a part to play in this regard. Reporting safety issues, for example, can help prevent accidents, often the cause of customer complaint and, at times, legal action. One major change to the law has been in the WHS legislation that introduced the need to report incidents as well as accidents. Dealing with incident reports and fixing them will usually result in reduced accidents. It is therefore the responsibility of management to create awareness of legislative compliance requirements, to develop appropriate policies and procedures, to undertake induction and training of employees, and to provide leadership that motivates employees to meet the highest professional standards.

Up-to-date information can be obtained from:

* print and news media
* reference books
* the Internet
* industry associations
* industry journals and magazines
* clients and suppliers
* legal experts.

Most event industry associations run seminars to update their members on any changes or trends and these are recommended to anyone working in the event business. Examples of these associations are listed at the end of the chapter.

Sources of law

In Australia, the law consists of:

* *Acts* passed by the *federal parliament* within the scope of its powers under the Australian Constitution (statute law) and *Acts* passed by *State parliaments* and the *legislative assemblies* of the Northern Territory, the Australian Capital Territory and Norfolk Island (statute law).
* Australian *common law*, which developed from English common law and is interpreted and modified by the *courts*. This results in decisions of courts that interpret the law, which are called precedent cases. These precedent cases usually alter the interpretation of the law or legislation and a number of important precedent cases are generally decided every year. Lawyers are required to stay up-to-date on all these relevant cases.

The Australian Constitution does not allow the Commonwealth parliament the power to make laws on all subjects. Instead, it lists the subjects about which the Commonwealth parliament can make laws. These include taxation, defence, external affairs, interstate and international trade, foreign affairs, trading and financial corporations, marriage and divorce, immigration, bankruptcy, and interstate industrial arbitration. Economic considerations have resulted in all the States agreeing that income tax be imposed solely by the Commonwealth.

Although the State parliaments can pass laws on a wider range of subjects than the Commonwealth parliament, the Commonwealth is generally regarded as the more powerful partner in the federation. If a Commonwealth law is clearly within the powers of Section 51 of the Constitution and is inconsistent with a law of a State parliament, the Commonwealth law operates and the State law is invalid to the extent of the inconsistency.

The *Racial Discrimination Act 1975* is an example of a Commonwealth Act, and is an important Act for event managers to take into consideration. The *RDA* makes racial discrimination in certain contexts unlawful in Australia, and overrides State and Territory legislation to the extent of any inconsistency. This is the principal Act, and there have been numerous amendments. Section 9 of the Act states that:

> This Act is not intended, and shall be deemed never to have been intended, to exclude or limit the operation of a law of a State or Territory that furthers the objects of the Convention and is capable of operating concurrently with this Act.

It states further that:

> It is unlawful for a person to do any act involving a distinction, exclusion, restriction or preference based on race, colour, descent or national or ethnic origin which has the purpose or effect of nullifying or impairing the recognition, enjoyment or exercise, on an equal footing, of any human right or fundamental freedom in the political, economic, social, cultural or any other field of public life.

Related Acts have been passed in the States and Territories which cover a range of issues in more detail. Under the *Anti-Discrimination Act 1991* (Qld), for instance, it is discriminatory to refuse to allow a guide dog onto premises.

As we learned in previous chapters, local governments and various government agencies (such as the transport authority) are responsible for implementing Acts and regulations under their jurisdiction. Examples of such regulations are building codes, signage limitations, lighting, street closures and noise restrictions, all of which are important considerations for the event coordinator. Local council offices generally give advice on their requirements but they are not permitted to give advice on legal compliance, and they will request the event organiser not only to comply with council requirements but also to contact the police or the Environment Protection Authority, for example, if applicable. Some councils have event planning templates which cover all relevant council regulations, as well as higher-level legal compliance requirements. When councils provide consent for an event to take place, they place great emphasis on the positive and negative impacts of the proposed event. In approving an event to proceed, the council is making a decision on behalf of the community. This is why they have extensive planning guidelines that must be satisfied, these guidelines being based on the Acts and regulations pertinent to event management.

The three levels of government discussed above are illustrated in Figure 17.1.

It must be made clear that local government powers are all delegated from the State and do not rank in the same level of law as State or Commonwealth legislation. However, from the viewpoint of an event organiser, the requirements of the local council are usually the most important parts of the law that need to be dealt with.

Common law

The second source of law in Australia, as mentioned above, is common law. Common law was introduced in Chapter 15 with the illustration of the venue hire agreement/contract. For a contract to be valid, there must be an offer and acceptance, an intention by the parties to be legally bound, and a consideration (an exchange, usually money, for goods and services

FIGURE 17.1 Levels of government

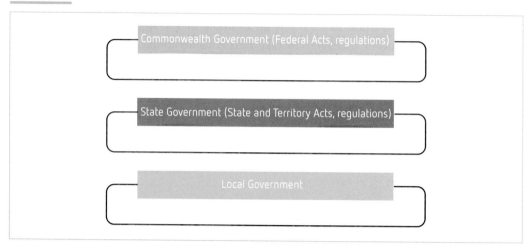

rendered). Where there is a dispute about a contract it is taken to court. In this circumstance, a judge needs to make a decision, largely based on precedent. Precedent cases vary and interpret the common law, so it is critical that event organisers are aware of all relevant precedent cases that may affect them. Contracts will be covered in detail in the second half of this chapter.

One of the most fundamental areas of common law for event organisations is *duty of care*. Where lack of *reasonable* care can be shown in court, the resulting claim for *negligence* can lead to an award for damages being made by the judge. Accidents occurring at events are usually brought to court with the plaintiff arguing negligence. This argument could be made against the event organiser, the venue management, the security company, or the ride operator. In fact, the claim might be made against all four, and it would be up to the courts to judge whether the defendants had shown the appropriate duty of care. Risk management strategies and contingency plans demonstrate that all reasonable steps have been taken to prevent an accident. A theme recurring through this book is therefore concern for the safety and welfare of everyone on the event site, with policies and procedures to reduce or eliminate risks where they are foreseen.

A situation such as the one described here demonstrates the legal concepts of duty of care, safety and negligence.

EXAMPLE

In 2003 Fox Studios was ordered to improve its public safety after coronal findings regarding the preventable death of a nine-year-old child.

In 2001 the child, who had wandered away to use the bathroom, was killed at Fox Studios after being crushed by an unsecured fence panel during a storm. A large-scale search was undertaken but the child's body was not found for 13 hours.

The coroner, while stating there was no criminal negligence, found Fox studios responsible for several factors contributing to the child's death: the failure of an inexperienced site supervisor to remove and securely store fencing panels; poor missing child protocols; and inadequate lighting which led to the body not being discovered until the following day.

As a result of the enquiry, Fox Studios was directed to improve its public safety through revision of its missing child protocols, by appointing an overseer for safety issues, ensuring fence panels are stored in a designated storage area away from public areas and having adequate lighting available for emergencies.

The coroner made the following recommendations.

Recommendations to:

The Minister for Fair Trading:

That all service providers for temporary fencing provide all users with appropriate information regarding safe use and storage of their product. That the Department of Fair Trading consider reviewing the standards applicable to shade cloth and other materials attached to temporary fencing with regard to wind resistance and fence stability.

The Minister for Police:

That all operational police be personally issued with torches as part of their official appointments.

The State Management Board:

That the board consider the possibility of the search coordinating role at high risk incident searches be undertaken by Police Rescue Squad in the Sydney Metropolitan Area or by the State Emergency Services and volunteer rescue associations in regional areas.

Fox Studios Australia:

- *That the protocols for dealing with 'lost children' be immediately revised to ensure all contingencies are catered for. The current protocol is based on the assumption that the majority of 'Lost Children' are found within a very short time frame. Within the protocol, there needs to be an emergency plan catering for children that may have been forcibly dealt with.*
- *That a compound be established to store equipment such as bollards, fence panels and other removable items used within the public areas of the complex.*
- *Advise each event production manager that only experienced personnel are to erect and dismantle temporary structures.*
- *That Fox Studios Australia ensure all licensed events submit a 'Risk Assessment and Management Plan' prior to approval being granted. It is suggested that a pro-forma be developed by Fox to ensure consistency of approach, particularly when temporary structures are being used.*
- *That Fox Studios Australia provide flood lighting for all Public Areas for use in emergency situations.*

Organisations have a duty to take reasonable care not to cause foreseeable harm to other people or their property. This is also known as the law of negligence. A large number of civil law cases involve what are called 'torts', which are legal wrongdoings. The term 'tort' is derived from the Latin word *tortus*, meaning 'a wrong'. Tort law exists to protect an individual's bodily safety and security, to protect tangible property and intellectual property, and to protect an individual's reputation. If any of these things are compromised or damaged by another person or organisation, a remedy can be sought by an action for negligence that will result in an order to pay damages and *compensation*, which usually takes the form of monetary damages. Civil law, for example, covers accidents, contract disputes, or the dividing up of a will. In general, civil law deals with private disputes between private people or organisations. The standard of proof required to succeed in negligence is one of *balance of probabilities*, as opposed to criminal law, which is *beyond reasonable doubt*. The level of compensation decided in a court case in which a plaintiff is seeking compensation is decided by a judge, or in major claims by a jury, the findings and compensation being based on precedent. By contrast, a breach of a statute, such as the WHS Act, can lead to fines and these are clearly stipulated. WorkCover inspectors are given inspection powers for the purpose of the Act, including the taking of samples, and the carrying out of a range of tests. There are very clear sentencing guidelines, and specific fines for breaches of the Act, thus illustrating the difference between legislation enacted by parliaments and common law negligence, which is judged in the courts and based on precedent. Table 17.1 lists a number of legal terms with their corresponding explanations.

TABLE 17.1 Legal terms

Agreement (legally called a contract)	Parties reach an agreement in contract law when an offer is accepted that creates rights and obligations enforceable by law.
Breach of contract	Failure by one of the parties to a contract to satisfactorily perform the service or action agreed to in the contract.
Common law	This is a collection of rules based on the decisions of judges in the most important courts. It is also called precedent law.
Compliance	Following the Acts and regulations of government bodies.
Consideration	Usually money (price), something of value that is exchanged in contracts.
Copyright	The rights belonging to the owner or licensee of literary, artistic and dramatic works, films and sound recordings, to reproduce, perform or otherwise deal with these works.
Duty of care	The obligation of a person to exercise reasonable care in the conduct of an activity. Breach of a duty of care which causes damage or loss to another may give rise to an action in tort.
Implied terms	Terms set out in legislation that are automatically part of a contract, without having to be stated in the contract document.
Indemnity	Compensation for a wrong done, or an expense or loss suffered as a result of the act or default of another. Verb: indemnify.
Jurisdiction	The laws of a particular State/Territory; the power to define unlawful conduct, enforce laws and adjudicate disputes.
Legislation	Laws made by parliament, referred to singly as an Act.

Mandatory	Having to be strictly complied with. Mandatory reporting: obligation to report cases of child abuse, for example, to authorities. Mandatory sentencing: automatic jail term for certain offences.
Negligence	A tort involving the breach of a duty of care resulting in loss or damage to another person.
Regulations	Laws which are not made by parliament but by other bodies to whom the power to make law is delegated in legislation.
Sue	To take legal action.
Tort	A civil wrong; an act which causes harm, intentionally or otherwise, for which the remedy is an action for damages.

Non-compliance

The previous section discussed the issue of negligence in the context of common law (court-made) decisions. Non-compliance occurs when an organisation breaches a specific Act, such as relates to liquor licensing, food safety or WHS. In these circumstances, inspectors can impose fines or cancel the event. For example, breaches under the *Liquor Control Reform Act 1998* (Victoria) include a maximum fine for permitting an underaged person on licensed premises (other than as permitted) of $19 028. There are many such non-compliance possibilities, such as permitting unauthorised consumption of liquor on a party bus – maximum penalty $7929 (Victorian Commission for Gambling and Liquor Regulation, 2017).

The Victorian Commission for Gambling and Liquor Regulation (VCGLR) has guidelines for running raffles, as do the regulatory bodies in other States and Territories – some require permits, while others do not. An organisation can hold a raffle without a minor gaming permit as long as the prize value is $5000 or less.

Find out from the VCGLR website (**www.vcglr.vic.gov.au**), or a similar site in your State or Territory, how to answer the following questions relating to a fundraising event:

- Are raffles classified as gaming?
- Can you run a raffle on behalf of a community or charitable organisation?
- Is there a ratio of value of tickets for sale, to the value of the prizes?
- How long should records be kept?

EXTENSION ACTIVITY

DEVELOP AND COMMUNICATE POLICIES AND PROCEDURES FOR LEGAL COMPLIANCE

As the previous discussion illustrates, events are a legal minefield! This is why industry professionals are highly sought after for their understanding of compliance issues and, more importantly, their understanding of the implications of the legislation for undertaking risk analysis and developing policies and procedures. In summary, compliance with legislation can be improved by:

- developing policies and procedures
- recruiting knowledgeable staff

- inducting and training new staff
- reinforcing legal responsibilities in meetings and in written communications
- conducting ongoing risk assessments in relation to non-compliance
- developing a culture of commitment by employees, volunteers, supervisors and managers.

A stakeholder communication plan is essential for all events. A communication plan ensures that you achieve your communication objectives – one highlighted here is that everyone understands their specific roles and responsibilities in relation to legal compliance. A stakeholder communications plan is not a marketing plan.

Objectives

The primary objective of a stakeholder communication plan is to ensure that a diverse range of stakeholders, including, for example, sponsors and emergency services, and in particular all contractors, are involved in planning, delivery and execution of the event. One of the objectives would be to identify areas of legal compliance, while another would be to identify risks.

Key messages

Legal compliance and risk management are aimed at achieving the highest possible levels of public safety. This message is generally communicated to stakeholders, including the workforce (staff, contractors, volunteers) but also security, traffic and emergency services personnel.

Audience

For each element of the communications plan, the audience needs to be identified. So, for example, sponsors would need to be told about any issues that might arise with naming rights or potential copyright infringement.

Tools

There are many ways in which communications can be managed. For example, one-way informational communication using a website, versus two-way engagement via meetings and action plans. In any emergency, effective channels of communication need to be chosen.

Timetable

Lastly, the timetable for communications needs to align with operational considerations.

Development of the event operations manual in collaboration with all parties concerned is the capstone of event planning. It is a powerful and effective document that is available to internal staff and the wider workforce, detailing policies and procedures that have been agreed upon following careful planning with legal compliance and risk management in mind.

The event operations manual should be very clear when nominating roles and responsibilities for legal compliance. Clear and specific procedures will avoid having things fall through the cracks. Sometimes these omissions can be the very things that have serious and even fatal consequences.

ENSURE COMPLIANCE WITH LEGAL REQUIREMENTS

The principles of the major Acts and regulations relevant to event management are covered below, in general terms.

Local government regulations

As mentioned previously, councils play an important role in approving a public event. Some councils have detailed guidelines, while others have less formal requirements. The size of the event largely determines the detail required in the submission since smaller events tend to have a lower impact on the community.

If an event has already been held in one council area, with approval, it is still usually necessary to obtain approval for a second similar event in another location. Likewise, if the event covers more than one jurisdiction, additional proposals may need to be submitted.

If the event requires the building of permanent structures, a development application would most likely be required, and this would link to the local environment plan (LEP), which is the community's vision for the future of the area. Application for the use of the premises and property for entertainment may also be necessary. Plans would need to be developed for the erection of temporary structures and approval would need to be sought for them.

Approvals are required by most councils for:

- using loudspeakers or amplifiers in public spaces
- installing amusement devices
- singing or providing entertainment in public places (fees would also apply)
- using a building or structure for entertainment (change of approval classification)
- building a temporary structure.

Councils are also very concerned about cleaning programs during and after an event, noise and disturbance of local residents, and traffic management.

Street fairs such as the one pictured here require local councils to undertake extensive planning and consultation with stakeholders, including traders in the affected areas Tourist buses are more likely to stop off during a festival period, which can have a significant impact on provision of services and facilities.

Street fairs must be approved by the council and local authorities

Business registration

Every business must be registered with an Australian Business Number (ABN) for taxation and goods and services tax (GST) purposes. The name of the business must also be registered. A business can take the form of a sole trader, a partnership or a company.

A *sole trader* is an individual who is trading on their own. That person controls and manages the business. The income of the business is treated as the person's individual income, and they are solely responsible for any tax payable by the business.

A *partnership* is a legal relationship between two or more people to carry on a business with the intention of making a profit. There are many problems associated with partnerships and they must be carefully documented by a partnership agreement that covers profit sharing, work practices, death and divorce and so on. This should be prepared by a legal person.

A *company* is a legal entity separate from its shareholders. It is a separate legal body created under the *Corporations Act* but does not include a partnership. Companies are regulated by the Australian Securities and Investments Commission (ASIC). New companies must be registered with ASIC. The first step in the registration process is to ensure that the proposed name is available for registration as a company. The ASIC National Names Index can be used to check if a proposed company name is identical to another name already registered.

There are also *associations*, which are similar to companies but are non-profit, and there are also *cooperatives*, which are also similar to companies but are registered under State/ Territory law. To decide which legal entity is best suited to your needs, you need to consult a lawyer and an accountant.

Taxation

For anyone running a commercial business (fee for service), compliance with taxation rules is essential. All businesses must be registered and this can be done by contacting the Australian Taxation Office (ATO). Advice will be provided on all types of taxation applicable, including deductions of PAYG (pay-as-you-go) tax for paid employees. Deductions for superannuation must also be made. All commercial businesses must pay GST, although charitable bodies and some educational institutions are exempt from GST.

Industrial relations

Employers and employees have certain obligations or duties to each other under common law and legislation. These obligations or duties are regarded as legal standards of behaviour in the employment relationship.

Some rights and obligations of employers as interpreted and applied by the courts are to:

- pay wages
- reimburse employees for work-related expenses
- ensure a safe working environment suitable for the performance of the employee's duties
- not act in a way that may seriously damage an employee's reputation or cause mental distress or humiliation
- not act in a way that will damage the trust and confidence necessary for an employment relationship
- not provide a false or misleading reference (should one be provided)
- forward tax instalments to the ATO.

The employee's main obligations are to:

- obey the lawful and reasonable commands of the employer
- exercise due care in the performance of the work and do it competently
- account to the employer for all moneys and property received while employed
- make available to the employer any process or product invented by the employee in the course of employment
- disclose to the employer information received by the employee relevant to the employer's business
- be faithful to the employer's interests; for example, by not passing on to a competitor information about the employer's business or denigrating the employer's products.

The employment relationship between employers and employees is also covered by legislation at the Commonwealth and State/Territory level. The legislation deals mainly with the framework for negotiating working conditions, including wages, holidays and other leave. In particular, employees may be paid under industrial awards (which tend to cover an industry or occupation, such as the catering industry) or workplace agreements (which cover a particular place of work). For more information regarding awards or agreements relevant to the event industry, the Fair Work website (**www.fairwork.gov.au/awards-and-agreements**) is a good starting point. Departments of industrial relations in the States and Territories will also provide information relating to employment.

Entertainment industry legislation

Licences for the entertainment industry apply to agents, managers and venue consultants. The disbursement of fees and trust accounts for performers are covered by this type of legislation. There is also a code of ethics. Entertainment industry legislation allows for complaints to be heard and resolved regarding payments to performers, agents, managers and venue consultants.

Copyright

The right to use music in a business or commercial operation requires a licence from the Australian Performing Rights Association (APRA) for the copyright in the song, composition or lyrics. A licence is also required from the Phonographic Performance Company of Australia (PPCA), the association representing music publishers and record companies. Therefore, if a sound recording were to be played at an event, the event company would need to apply for licences from both APRA and PPCA. The fees, while nominal, recognise the copyright and commercial value of the music. They vary according to the use of the music (from background music, live performance, music played or sung at sporting venues or function centres, to karaoke).

To clarify, there are two copyrights in each recording: first, the copyright in the sound recording of the recorded performance and, second, the copyright in the song, composition or lyrics. There are usually at least three copyright issues in a music video clip; namely, copyright in the cinematographic film that embodies the recorded performance, copyright in the recorded performance itself, and copyright in the song (composition or lyrics).

A liquor licence is required to serve alcohol

Copyright on text is generally held by the writer, artist or publisher, and permission is required from the copyright holder of any text or image that you wish to reproduce. In the same way, you hold the copyright in your own work. Logos and trademarks must be registered separately.

Liquor licensing

In general, this legislation covers the age of drinkers, the venues and the situations (for example, with meals) in which alcoholic drinks can be served, as well as the legal hours of alcohol service. Liquor must be correctly labelled and sold in legal measures. A sign must be displayed to say that it is an offence to sell or supply liquor to, or obtain liquor on behalf of, a person under the age of 18 years. The licensee must be able to show that reasonable steps (including requests for identification) have been taken to ensure that minors have not been served alcohol. Every person serving alcohol must hold a current Responsible Service of Alcohol (RSA) certificate. It is the obligation of event organisers to ensure that this is verified. Complaints about noise or indecorous behaviour can be made to the Licensing Board.

Consumer law

Consumer law aims to ensure that advertised goods and services are provided in accordance with the advertising. For example, at one concert featuring an overseas performer, the stage design was so poor that many members of the audience could neither see nor hear the performance. As a result, the event management company was forced to refund the money paid for the tickets to those who had been affected. The staging problem was resolved to everyone's satisfaction before the next performance.

The *Competition and Consumer Act 2010 (Cth)* and the various State and Territory Acts protect the consumer against misleading advertising and deceptive conduct. This means that conduct that is liable to mislead the public as to the nature, characteristics, suitability for the purpose or quality of any services must not occur. This is particularly relevant to event organisers if the event is cancelled or changed at the last minute (for example, a change in the headline act or venue). In this situation, the consumer is entitled to a refund. Recently, a New Year's Eve event was cancelled at the last minute and the organiser tried to postpone the event for a week. You can imagine the outrage in the media and the resulting pressure to comply with the requirement to make refunds!

Privacy

Information kept on a database provided by a client, exhibitor or spectator can only be used for the purpose for which it was given; that is, registration or ticketing. This data cannot be used for any other purpose, or used or sold to another business for direct marketing. The event business works closely with celebrity performers and athletes and a breach of confidentiality should never occur. Thus, all employees should know that personal information should not be given to the media.

Anti-discrimination legislation

The Australian Human Rights Commission investigates discrimination on the grounds of race, colour or ethnic origin, racial vilification, gender, sexual harassment, marital status, pregnancy and disability. A case can be made for unlawful discrimination if management or staff refuse entry to a premises on the basis of any of the above factors. Equal employment opportunity legislation is a subset of anti-discrimination legislation referring specifically to workplace discrimination. It is unlawful to discriminate when advertising for new staff, when selecting new staff, when offering training opportunities, and when selecting staff for promotion and other career development opportunities.

Environmental protection legislation

This legislation aims to prevent pollution, including air and waterways pollution. Discharge of sewage, oil and other waste into water systems is illegal and our waterways are protected by a number of State and Territory Acts, all relating to protection of the environment. Noise is covered in this category. Noise is a troublesome problem for festivals and events since by their very nature they attract crowds, entertainment events being particularly problematic. It is therefore essential to check noise limitations in terms of allowable decibels and the times during which loud music is permitted.

Food safety

Food Acts provide guidelines for safe food handling. Every contract caterer is required to develop a food safety plan covering food safety at all stages of delivery, preparation and service. This is necessary to guard against bacteria which may develop if food is

Safe plating of food – these trolleys are designed to be stored in refrigerators

left standing after delivery, or during preparation and service, and not kept at an appropriate temperature. Buffets where food is left unrefrigerated are notorious for high bacteria levels. Generally, food needs to be kept cool or heated to a hot temperature. The mid-temperature range is the most dangerous. A qualified caterer should know all about food hygiene and should follow correct procedures to avoid contamination. A food safety plan should be part of any catering contract, which should also include menus and prices. It is also important that all menus clearly indicate if there are any products included in them that may cause allergic reactions (for example, nuts).

Charitable fundraising legislation

The aims of this legislation are to:

* promote proper management of fundraising appeals for charitable purposes
* ensure proper record keeping and auditing
* prevent deception of members of the public who desire to support worthy causes.

A person who participates in a fundraising appeal that is conducted unlawfully is guilty of an offence. Authority is required to conduct a fundraising appeal; this is obtained by applying to the relevant body in your State or Territory.

Security legislation

This legislation provides for the licensing and regulation of persons in the security industry, such as crowd controllers, bouncers, guards and operators of security equipment. In general, there are different levels of licences requiring different levels of training.

Summary offences

Summary offences legislation covers issues such as the desecration of public and protected places, shrines, monuments, statues and war memorials. One very common offence is urinating on or in these protected places.

Workplace health and safety

This legislation is designed to prevent workplace accidents and injuries. The legislation has specific requirements for employers to provide safe workplaces and safe work practices. This topic is covered in detail in Chapter 9.

Workers compensation insurance

Workers compensation insurance, which is obligatory, covers the treatment and rehabilitation of injured workers. There are penalties for businesses that do not insure their employees for work-related accidents and injuries. Through workers compensation schemes, claims may be made for medical expenses and time off work. It is also important to ensure that the various categories of workers are correctly designated in the insurance proposal. If you say a worker is merely taking tickets when in fact they are a bouncer, the insurance company can cause major problems when there is a claim by the worker because they can say that the risk of injury to the worker had not been correctly assessed.

Where rehabilitation is necessary, redeployment to another role may occur until the person is fit to return to their original position. Employers have a responsibility to:

* register with WorkCover
* pay insurance levies by the due date
* send end-of-year reconciliation statements to WorkCover
* submit all claims for compensation on the prescribed forms
* assist with the rehabilitation of injured workers.

When an event is organised, all contracting organisations on-site (employers) should carry this type of insurance for their workers, and a certificate of currency is generally required when negotiating such contracts with service suppliers of security, maintenance, staging, catering and so on.

Volunteers and spectators are covered, in most cases, by *public liability insurance* since they are *not paid workers*. In some cases, event organisations take out specific insurance for volunteers to cover accidents and injuries. In the absence of this type of cover, volunteers fall under the umbrella of public liability (see below).

Business insurance

The various different types of insurance are summarised below, some being obligatory, others voluntary.

Public liability insurance

The most important insurance required by an event management company is public liability insurance. This covers a business owner's legal liability to compensate any person who is not an employee or a family member (a third party) for injury, damage to property or death as a result of the business operations should the owner and/or employees/volunteers be shown to be negligent.

Claims against this insurance can be reduced by careful risk analysis and prevention strategies. One council requires a $10 million level of insurance for minor events and a $20 million level of insurance for major events. As with most local government requirements, these may change from one council or municipality to another. Assets and motor vehicles also need to be insured.

Event organisers sometimes require participants to sign a disclaimer to reduce their liability. Essentially, the person who signs a disclaimer is taking responsibility for his or her actions. However, from a legal point of view, there is nothing to stop the contestant from making a case for negligence against the event organiser. Clearly, it would have to be shown that this negligence led directly to the injury, and the extent and impact of the negligence would then be investigated. In other words, an event organiser cannot avoid liability for negligence by having participants sign an indemnification agreement. The person has the right to sue in any circumstances and the case would be judged on its merits.

In addition to the public liability insurance which must be taken out by the event management organisation, all contracts signed with subcontractors, such as a company that erects scaffolding, should also include a clause requiring the subcontractor to hold a current policy covering them against liability for incidents that may occur. As you can see, there are a number of different stakeholders who are potentially liable, and the event organiser needs to limit their own liability by managing risk and ensuring that subcontractors are also insured. It is also essential that the event organiser actually sees a current insurance policy covering the required areas and preferably takes a copy of the policy to put in their file.

In the following article, the honorary vice-president of Clowns International advised 70 members to take out insurance against potential claims for custard pie injuries!

> Clowns gathered at a special Big Top conference last week – to discuss the legal risks of chucking pies. They got serious as they discussed whether circus audiences sitting in the front row were wilfully placing themselves in the line of fire. Clowns fear they could be liable for compensation if a member of the public got it in the face.
>
> Source: *International Express*, 10 April 2001.

Sports injury

This type of insurance provides injury protection during sanctioned practices, games and related travel that is approved and under the supervision of a proper authority. The policy can cover all participants: managers, coaches, trainers or officials, volunteers, auxiliary workers and employees.

Professional indemnity

Another policy which should be considered is professional indemnity insurance. This indemnifies the insured against any claim for breach of professional duty through any act, error or omission by them, their company or their employees. It is essential cover for lawyers and accountants who may be sued for their 'unprofessional' advice, as well as for anyone providing consultancy advice in the area of event safety, security and fire risk.

Product liability

Product liability is another type of insurance, essential if selling tangible products such as food or beverages and event merchandise, particularly toys, but not generally required as the event experience is intangible. With product liability insurance, damages arise out of product failure. However, should the scaffolding collapse, the event company would expect that the hire company and manufacturer of the scaffolding carry this insurance. As with all other insurance, make sure the policy is current and adequate.

Superannuation

It is now compulsory to provide for employee superannuation.

Fire insurance

Fire insurance covers the building, contents and stock of the business against fire, lightning, storms, impact, malicious damage and explosion. It is critical that all insurance cover is current market value. If you are underinsured, you will be paid only a percentage of your claim. So if your cover is for $1 million and the insurance company decides the true value is $2 million, you will only be paid half of any claim you make!

General insurance

General insurance covers property, including equipment, fixtures, fittings and miscellaneous property.

Business interruption or loss of profits insurance

This insurance provides cover if a business is interrupted through damage to property by fire or other insured perils. It ensures that a business' net profit projection is maintained and pays employee wages and additional working costs if alternative facilities have to be used.

Burglary insurance

Theft of property and damage caused by burglars breaking into property are covered by this type of insurance. It does not cover theft by shoplifters or staff.

Fidelity guarantee

Fidelity guarantee insurance covers losses resulting from misappropriation of goods or cash (that is, embezzling or stealing).

Money in transit

This covers loss of money on the business premises or when being taken to and from the bank. It can be extended to cover money taken home overnight or deposited in a bank night safe. Responsibility for money in transit should be made very clear when negotiating with stall holders, concessions or merchandise outlets. Security organisations can provide cash management services, including delivering change, receiving takings, transportation, counting and banking. The event organiser should make it clear to contractors that they should take out their own insurance for money in transit.

Machinery breakdown

Designed to cover breakdown of all mechanical and electrical plant and machinery at a work site, this type of policy can be extended to cover spoilage of foodstuffs consequent of such breakdown.

Cancellation or non-appearance (contingency insurance)

Where the cause is beyond control, such as the non-appearance of the main performer or abandonment by financial supporters of the event, this insurance would cover the costs incurred through cancellation of the event.

Weather

While insurance can be obtained for event cancellation due to weather conditions, this type of cover is extremely costly and claims are hard to fully substantiate.

Stakeholders and official bodies

While mention has been made of industry bodies, tourism authorities and professional associations, the number of government authorities that may need to be involved in the planning of a major event can be quite daunting. A number of these are outlined below.

Traffic and transport authorities

Any potential impact on traffic by an event must be discussed with the relevant traffic authority. If a road closure is necessary, this would involve preparation of a detailed plan and a lengthy period of consultation. Transport authorities may also need to plan for additional or alternative public transport. Most councils require that, where possible, you ensure that all parking is off the street and either on the venue property or some adjoining parking venue.

Emergency services

Emergency services need to be alerted to the risks associated with an event. At a minimum, lines of communication and incident reporting procedures would have to be submitted, as well as plans for dealing with potential emergencies and crowd control (see Chapter 18).

Police

It may be necessary for additional police to attend an event and often a charge is incurred by the event organisers for these services.

Preparing for the Monaco Grand Prix – an event of this size would need to comply with the regulations of many official bodies

Authorities for parks and public places

Depending on the venue or site selected, it may be necessary to find out about the rules and regulations governing use of the site. A submission to the authority is generally necessary, together with a set or negotiated fee. This is true even for the smallest wedding at most city beaches.

Government authorities may include:

* sport and recreation
* facility managers (e.g. stadium, city hall)
* licensing (including alcohol, transport, storage and handling of food)
* waste management
* utilities (use of additional or temporary supplies of electricity, gas or water)
* information services (such as tourism information centres).

The level of involvement of these authorities is determined by the scope of the event, the nature and complexity of the event, the requirements of regulatory bodies, the level of safety risk, and the potential impact on the physical environment (including noise). Essentially, the more complex the event, the wider the range of stakeholders that needs to be consulted.

Contracts

This topic is the most important in this chapter and could become a book in its own right. A contract is an agreement between two or more parties which is enforceable at law. There are three sources of contract law: common law (case law), statute, and the specific agreement between the parties. Statutes such as the *Trade Practices Act* apply to contracts. The effectiveness of the contracts between the parties involved in an event is crucial. Specifications need to be incredibly detailed in order to avoid disputes. Clarity and agreement between all parties is essential. The contract provides the basis for variation in price every time the customer has new demands. For this reason, time invested in the writing of the contract will reap rewards and often resolve legal disputes. Professional legal advice is essential for a new event management business.

The bulk of contracts used by event organisers are legally referred to as simple contracts. Figure 17.2 gives an outline of the inclusions in a simple contract. These should be in writing but legally do not need to be written to be enforceable. Formal contracts are written documents referred to as 'a contract under seal'. For a contract to be valid, there has to be an offer, intention to be legally bound, acceptance and consideration (usually money).

FIGURE 17.2 Content of contract/agreement

- Parties to contract
- Deadline and deposit
- Specifications (e.g. space booked, timing, food and beverage, accommodation)
- Services to be provided
- Special requirements
- Schedule of payments
- Insurance
- Cancellation
- Termination/non-performance
- Contingency
- Consumption
- Confidentiality
- Arbitration
- Warranties
- Signatories
- Date

Many events involve a range of contractors for services such as catering, cleaning, sound, lighting and security. While it is tempting for an event organiser to take on all roles, the benefits of employing contractors are many. Specialist organisations generally have more expertise and better equipment, they generally carry their own insurance, and they have a lot of experience in their particular field. By dealing with a range of contractors and using professionally prepared, well-negotiated contracts, the event organiser can dramatically reduce risk and liability. On the day, the main role of the event organiser is to monitor the implementation of the agreed contracts.

Many different types of contract are entered into by event organisers, including the implied conditions of a ticket held by the participant. Contracts are made between the event organiser and:

- participants (any member of the event audience, ticketed or registered)
- funding bodies (any donor, sponsor, contributor, bank or financing institution)
- the owner or controller of the site/venue
- employees (the employment relationship is a form of contract, with many elements determined in law, but not usually in writing)
- providers of goods and services (plumbers, scaffolding and staging suppliers, caterers, security companies, including preferred providers).

Contracts also cover:

- licences (music, liquor, rides, fireworks)

- trademarks/branding (logos, trademarks, images)
- transfers of contracts or rights (such as rights to a musical performance)
- franchises (operational guidelines, branding and marketing agreements).

Where there are chains of contracting parties, it is essential to identify who is acting as principal and as agents down the chain. The event organiser is potentially liable all the way down the chain and this is why insurance certification is advisable.

A standard contract for a live performance by a musician is provided on the companion website to this text. Specifications particular to this type of contract might include the following clarification.

Set Up and Load Out: The Hirer will provide the Artist and personnel with reasonable access to the venue before the performance to load in, set up, do sound checks and load out after the performance. The Hirer will provide secure on-site parking for the Artist and personnel.

Staging: The Hirer will provide safe working conditions and ensure all equipment and facilities are in good working order. The Hirer will be in compliance with all statutory requirements (including adequate staging with protection from sun and bad weather) and will obtain all permits, consents and licences necessary for the performance.

Power Supply: The Hirer will provide safe and adequate power supplies operated by competent persons in accordance with all statutory requirements. If any of the Artist's or the personnel's instruments or equipment is damaged by malfunction or improper operation of the power supply, the Hirer will reimburse any cost incurred to repair or replace the instruments or equipment.

Source: © Media, Entertainment and Arts Alliance (WA branch).

Most contracts include generic terms and conditions such as cancellation or insurance. However, the specifications are an essential component, clearly delineating responsibilities to help prevent operational problems.

MAINTAIN PERSONAL AND ORGANISATIONAL KNOWLEDGE OF REGULATORY REQUIREMENTS

Maintaining up-to-date legal knowledge is essential, and it is also necessary to be aware that in many instances specialist advice is required from a legal professional or an insurance company. Government agencies, such as the ATO, can also provide assistance. Record keeping is equally important as there are many documents that must be kept for legal and insurance purposes. Any claims or disputes are likely to occur after the event, so documents such as certificates of currency for insurance for all contractors must be kept on file. So, too, with risk assessments, action plans and incident reports. All approvals, permits and licences should be filed logically. With so many stakeholders involved – committee members, sponsors, suppliers, contractors – attention to detail is essential. A fully documented event operations manual and associated documentation (meeting minutes, registers, certification and so on) will all show that an event manager has been prepared and organised before the event and this could assist in any lawsuit brought against the event manager or organising committee. There are also obvious benefits for future planning in keeping a record.

Finally, the potential impact of a terrorist act, though unlikely to impact on most event managers, always needs to be considered, however remote the possibility. For Hu and Goldblatt (2005), the goal is to develop online solutions for facilitating knowledge management in both individual and organisational learning in the context of safety and security of planning festivals and events. This would mean that knowledge is maintained at individual, corporate and global levels, hopefully achieving higher levels of event safety.

Summary

In this chapter, we have outlined the legislation and related issues, such as licensing and approvals, that must be considered during the planning of an event. Legal compliance is one of the major risk issues for organisers of an event and research into the relevant legislation is essential. Tight contractual arrangements with the client and subcontractors are equally important as these can ensure the financial viability of an event or completely derail it. Insurances of various types are also required, including workers compensation and public liability, while workplace health and safety should always be a major consideration of the event organiser. Finally, the importance of staying abreast of changes in legislation and filing all relevant legal and other documentation has been noted in this chapter.

REVIEW YOUR KNOWLEDGE

1   Explain the meanings of the following terms:
    − compliance
    − duty of care
    − indemnity
    − negligence.
2   Explain the two sources of law in Australia.
3   List five different types of insurance and explain which of these is compulsory.
4   Briefly explain the intention of the following legislation, including objectives and primary components:
    − anti-discrimination
    − workplace health and safety (WHS)
    − food safety
    − privacy
    − Australian consumer law (ACL)
    − environmental protection
    − liquor law.
5   Explain five ways in which you can maintain and update your knowledge of regulatory requirements

APPLY YOUR KNOWLEDGE

Investigate two venues offering weddings and compare their advertised services / products, contracts and checklists from the point of view of the customer and the owner of the business. In addition, compare the contracts of the two venues in terms of the potential for misunderstandings to develop and legal disputes to follow.

CASE STUDY

In 2015, Camp Gallipoli hosted 40 000 people, mainly children, for an Anzac Centenary commemoration. Each person paid $70 – $120 to camp under the stars. The event was supported by the Department of Veterans' Affairs with a grant of $2.5 million and the organisers were given rare permission to use the word 'Anzac' in their promotions. Other sponsors contributed more than $5 million. Excess funds were promised to veterans and their families.

However, the organising body, Camp Gallipoli Foundation Incorporated, subsequently had its charitable status revoked by the regulator for reasons of governance.

Read more at www.adelaidenow.com.au / news / south-australia / camp-gallipoli-charity-held-on-to-58000-surplus-for-own-operations / news-story / f127ce694c1ef42949f34f1da17fc42b

QUESTIONS

1   Explain the roles of the charity, the federal government and the Australian Charities and Not-for-Profits Commission (ACNC).
2   Explain the difference between a charity and a 'for profit' event organisation.
3   Find out the key steps for registering a charity with the ACNC.
4   Summarise the governance standards for a charity.
5   Visit the Fundraising Institute of Australia and summarise their code of ethics.
6   List six different areas of legal compliance for this event, identifying the primary components of the legislation.
7   As this event involved children, develop policies and procedures necessary for events involving children.

Online resources

CENGAGE
brain.com

Visit http://login.cengagebrain.com and search for this book to access the study tools that come with your textbook.

References

Hu, C., & Goldblatt, J. J. (2005). Tourism, terrorism and the new world for event leaders. e-Review of Tourism Research (eRTR), 3(6), 139 – 44.

Victorian Commission for Gambling and Liquor Regulation (2017). Liquor licensing fact sheet: Breaches under the *Liquor Control Reform Act 1998*. www.vcglr.vic.gov.au / sites / default / files / Breaches_under_the_LCRA_1998_July_2017.pdf

Websites

Association of Australian Convention Bureaux (AACB), http://aacb.org.au

Australian Charities and Not-for-Profits Commission, www.acnc.gov.au/ACNC/Home/ACNC/Default. aspx?hkey=3e39ac62-4f04-44fe-b569-143ca445c6bf

Exhibition & Event Association of Australasia (EEAA), www.eeaa.com.au

Family welcomes finding after festival overdose, www.abc.net.au/news/2013-03-08/family-welcomes-coroners-finding-after-festival-drug-overdose/4561286

Guidelines for concerts, events and organised gatherings (WA Department of Health), ww2.health.wa.gov. au/~/media/Files/Corporate/general%20documents/Environmental%20health/Concerts%20 and%20Mass%20Gathering%20Guidelines.ashx

18 MANAGE RISK

OVERVIEW

In an earlier chapter, the assessment of risk was discussed in relation to workplace hazards. This chapter looks more broadly at the topic of risk, covering many types including financial risk and technology risk. For an event to be financially viable and sustainable in the long term, strategic planning is necessary. This involves a careful analysis of trends, anticipation of things that could go wrong (risks), and long-term plans for monitoring responses to the event by all stakeholders, including the audience and the client.

LEARNING OBJECTIVES

On completion of this chapter, you will be able to:

1. establish the risk context involving all stakeholders, identifying critical success factors and risk management processes

2. identify risks as they apply to the scope of the project and use tools and techniques to generate a list of risks in consultation with the relevant parties

3. analyse risks in terms of likelihood and consequence in order to evaluate and prioritise for treatment

4. select and implement risk treatments, following through with action plans after agreement with all involved parties.

INDUSTRY VIEWPOINT

This year, more than 2500 of Australia's toughest modified cars descended on Exhibition Park in Canberra. Coming from around the country and the world, this diverse tribe gathers to show off their love of the street machine to an enthusiastic crowd of over 100 000 people.

The Summernats delivers four days of high octane extreme auto action including Australia's top street machine judging competition, the world's biggest and best burnout battle, two nights of massive concerts, horsepower heroics, and more. It's all set against a backdrop of burnt rubber, rock and roll, and one of Australia's biggest motor retail trade shows, as we search for the Street Machine Summernats Grand Champion.

So much more than a motor show, the Street Machine Summernats is a celebration of the street machine lifestyle and the people who live it. Whether you know nothing about cars, or you can talk about them from the moment you wake up till the moment you got to sleep, the Summernats is Australia's best place to party in January.

Source: Summernats (2017). What is the Summernats? www.summernats.com.au/pages/? ParentPageID=2&PageID=62

INTRODUCTION

While not everyone's choice of event, the Summernats car festival is extremely popular, attracting a crowd of enthusiastic rev heads to the world's only purpose-built burn-out facility. This crowd has been described as high spirited, so the organisers insist on the following rules in an effort to minimise risk: no alcohol to be brought in, no glass bottles, no pets, no fireworks, no weapons, and no illegal drugs.

However, as this chapter will show, risk is about much more than safety. In the case of the Summernats, no doubt one of the risks that the organisers would have initially needed to consider would have been the response from the local community. The selection of Exhibition Park (outside Canberra's CBD) as a venue would have assisted in mitigating risk to the organisers caused by a disgruntled community calling for the closing of the event. The 'Save Albert Park' movement, for example, has lobbied against holding the Formula 1 Australian Grand Prix in Albert Park, Melbourne, arguing that it is an inappropriate and very costly venue and suggesting that the race should be held at a permanent purpose-built track well away from residential areas.

In chapters 4 and 14 we stressed the importance of establishing a clear event purpose and specific, measurable objectives. The focus of risk management should be the attainment of the event's objectives through identifying any foreseeable risk that might prevent these from being achieved. The following list, while not exhaustive, covers the key objectives for most events and event organisations:

The Summernats car festival

- meeting budget (e.g. when an event is managed for a client or charity)
- minimising losses (e.g. due to cancellation by a key player or artist)
- making a business profit or contribution to a charitable cause
- meeting project deadlines (extremely important when the event will be broadcast live)
- achieving a positive environmental impact (e.g. reducing landfill).

This chapter provides guidelines for identifying and assessing risks to business operations, controlling these risks, and monitoring and evaluating risk management practices.

RISK MANAGEMENT

> **Risk**
> Effect of foreseeable uncertainties on objectives – simply, things going wrong

This chapter will use this risk management approach to look beyond safety to the wider scope of risk, including financial and other risks. **Risk** is defined in terms of the effect of uncertainties on objectives. The process of managing risk involves:

- establishing the risk context by defining the environment in which the organisation's processes take place, describing external and internal influences and identifying risks
- undertaking a risk assessment, which involves risk identification, analysis and evaluation
- treating the risk, either by avoidance (by discontinuing a specific activity), taking on or increasing the risk in order to pursue an opportunity, removing the risk source, changing either the likelihood or consequence, sharing or transferring the risk (either partly or fully outsourcing the activity), or retaining the risk by informed decision
- monitoring and reviewing risk treatment plans.

The emphasis in the international risk management standard is on continual improvement through a systematic and structured approach, which is used in all aspects of management. The benefits of such an approach include:

- improved legal and regulatory compliance
- improved corporate governance (financial management)
- improved stakeholder relations
- improved organisational learning.

This framework and process, which was introduced in Chapter 9 in relation to safety and security, will now be discussed more broadly here. The framework is illustrated in Figure 18.1, highlighting the importance of continual monitoring.

As this diagram shows, the event risk management *framework* guides the risk management *process* from which procedures can be developed.

Before looking at policy and procedures, let's look at several generic sources of risk.

FIGURE 18.1 Framework for risk management

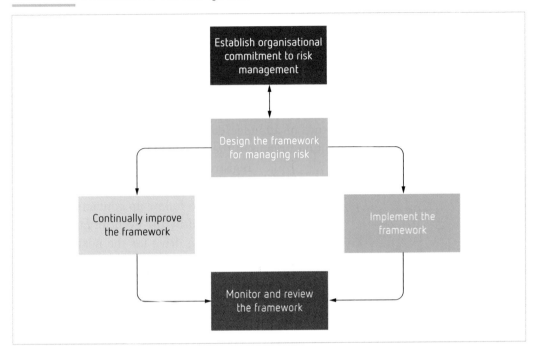

Natural disasters

Heavy rain is a disaster for an outdoor event, as too are hail, snow and extreme heat. Flooding can affect event venues, particularly temporary ones, and it can also cause damage to electrical wiring – potentially a very serious risk. Of course, fire is one of the risks venue managers fear, and must plan for, since evacuation of large crowds is extremely difficult. High winds are commonplace, illustrating the importance of daily risk assessment based on weather forecasts. High winds caused the collapse of the stage at the Indiana State Fair in 2011 – five people were killed and many injured. Brown and Hutton (2013) provide insights into audience behaviour in this specialist area.

Financial risk

Financial risk may involve unforeseen costs, lower than expected revenue, high exchange rates, a general decline in economic circumstances and disposable income, fraud, fines and cash flow problems.

Legal risk

Legal risks include disputes over contracts between the event organiser and the client and/ or between the event organiser and a subcontractor. These can occur if expectations are unrealistic or if a gap develops between the expectations of the client and the product the event organiser can produce for the price negotiated. Disputes can also occur if the venue hired does not meet the required standards in terms of such things as reliable electricity supply and suitable access for delivery vehicles. Breach of legal requirements is another form of legal risk, an example being a venue losing its liquor licence for a violation of the liquor laws.

Technology-related risk

Technological failure is an increasing risk for high-profile events, particularly those delivering live streaming. For example, a problem with guest registration at a trade exhibition would prevent the successful capture of attendee data, which is essential information for all stall holders. For the exhibition organiser, the attendance list (generated during registration) is their most valuable asset. It is made available to current exhibitors wanting to follow up contacts, as well as being used by the event organiser in the advertising drive for the next event of a similar nature.

Technology drives pyrotechnic displays

New Year's Eve fireworks displays are probably one of the events that are most reliant on highly sophisticated technology. Pyrotechnics planners for major fireworks displays need many back-up systems. If an event is simulcast live around the world, the preparation and planning have to be flawless. Every possible contingency has to be anticipated, such as a delay to the telecast or even cancellation of the event.

Mismanagement

A successful event requires good management, detailed planning and sound interpersonal relationships at all levels. Mismanagement can prevent an event reaching its objectives, and so too can people-related problems, such as disputes at the top level of management, leading to the dismissal of key personnel. Both are potentially serious risks.

Safety and security risk

Accidents, riots, terrorism and sabotage are all safety and security risks. These were discussed in detail in Chapter 9. The complex nature of event organisations (involving many stakeholders and a diverse workforce) contributes to the level of risk. Important tasks can 'slip through the cracks', and when things go horribly wrong, all stakeholders are in the spotlight. Coroners' reports and government inquiries, such as that conducted following the 2011 Kimberley Ultramarathon, when several runners were seriously burned in a bushfire, illustrate that multiple stakeholders are often found to have contributed to the outcome. There have been several reports into festival deaths and there is ongoing community concern that better preventative measures have not been taken.

View the following news report on the Kimberley Ultramarathon fire ordeal and list the potential stakeholders who could be implicated: www.abc.net.au/7.30/content/2012/s3439275.htm

Risk at sporting events

While the risks associated with most community, commercial and entertainment events are largely financial, with sporting events there is the additional risk of danger to the sportspeople involved and, in some cases, to the audience. For example, most bike and car races carry the risk of injury to both drivers and spectators, whether on the track or off-road. Bike races, and even fun runs, generally experience a number of medical emergencies and the occasional fatal heart attack.

Bike races carry risk for the competitors – one mistake can cause a pile-up

The challenge for organisers of such events is to reduce risk to an acceptable level through careful planning and by introducing new procedures and technologies where available, as safety standards change over time. Working out the safety standards for a particular sporting event at a particular time involves looking at a number of factors:

- perceived level of acceptable risk for participants and audience
- current legislation and legal precedents
- availability of risk management solutions
- development and implementation of plans, procedures and control mechanisms.

Well-designed sporting venues such as this one help to improve safety

The last of these is extremely important for event organisers, for if they can show that their procedures for managing risk were well considered and well implemented, this will stand them in good stead if a charge of negligence is laid.

Another important risk issue for sporting event organisers concerns temporary fencing and seating. Recently, a theatre company was fined $40 000 for two breaches of the *Occupational Health and Safety Act* because a temporary seating stand collapsed at a play, resulting in four people being hospitalised. According to *WorkCover News* (Issue 16), the judge determined that the theatre company had not obtained a report from a structural engineer and had not taken steps to ensure that correct safety standards had been met.

From the discussion of the types of risk the event organiser could face, it is clear that a first-rate risk management strategy is essential.

ESTABLISH RISK CONTEXT

Strategic risk management is not only about dealing with threats. It is also about dealing with opportunities. There are many situations in which an event business may be poorly placed to capitalise on opportunities – for example, when an unexpectedly high number of people turn up for an event, or when an annual show is expecting approximately a million visitors over five days, and rainy weather for the first three days sees attendance at a record low, followed by a huge surge on the fourth day when the sun comes out. While it may have been feasible to manage this number if the event audience was fairly evenly spread over this period, it would be almost impossible to do so under the above conditions unless planning and procedures were in place to deal with such an occurrence. In these situations, venues could be stretched beyond capacity, leading to dissatisfaction on the part of those attending, long queues, delays and, in the worst case, risks to safety. Spectators arriving at soccer matches that have been oversold have been known to storm the stadium, leading to fatal crowd crush. Human stampedes at religious festivals have occurred on several occasions (Illiyas et al., 2013).

> **Risk-management process**
> Has five main steps: establish context, identify risks, analyse and evaluate them, then treat the risks; review and consultation are also part of the process

The **risk-management process** is shown in Figure 18.2. Risk management is fundamental to the event manager's role. Indeed, the capacity to think strategically and to plan at the micro level is a valuable attribute for an event manager.

Risk management strategies must be put in place during the following developmental phases of an event:

- concept and marketing strategy development (identify strategic risk)
- logistics planning; e.g. development of registration or ticketing policies (identify operational risk at macro level)
- equipment safety and food safety planning (identify operational risk at micro level).

Having identified the potential risks to the event or the event business, the next step is to assess these risks in the relevant context.

The process of establishing the context for the risk management process provides guidance for decision makers, as well as establishing the scope for the development of risk management policies and plans.

Strategic context

The focus of the strategic context is on the external environment. For the event manager, this means looking at the global economy, the local economy, tourism trends, political

FIGURE 18.2 Risk management process

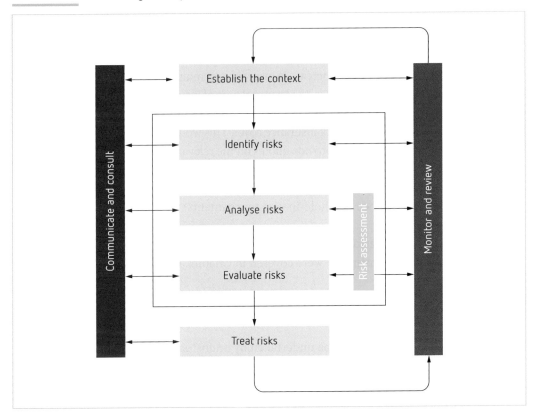

initiatives, competitive forces and social trends. As the world becomes globally oriented, consideration must be given to scheduled competitive major events (particularly sport and entertainment events).

Organisational context

The size of the event or the event business and its dependence on market segments creates the organisational context. All factors involving markets, products and timing are part of this context. For example, an event business that specialises in conference organisation for the accounting profession (with associated tours, entertainment and so on) may find that new probity guidelines will limit the scope of all future events and, in turn, have a major impact on profit margins. Reliance on any one market, including a particular source country for overseas tourists, is another aspect of organisational context that might need to be reviewed with a view to diversification. Extreme sports events clearly carry a higher risk than many others, as do some music concerts. However, these may be niche markets for a particular event company and they may need to accept (to some degree) the level of risk involved. Effort would be made to treat these risks, rather than avoid them, by planning different types of events.

Safety and security context

Specific security threats, such as terrorism, would be a significant factor in the risk context. Close liaison with the relevant authorities and task forces would provide more-specific information about the level of threat for different types of public event.

As a further example, a dramatic increase in insurance premiums may necessitate a review of all organisational and operational activities, the level and type of insurance coverage the organisation holds, and the level of risk the organisation is prepared to bear. The issue for the organisation would be to decide on the appropriate level of insurance cover. This would mean looking at replacement costs and policy limits. Insurers can provide quotes on the relevant insurance, such as:

- public liability (for corporate and community events)
- volunteer personal accident and weather cover
- prize indemnity insurance (for hole-in-one tournaments, sporting events and corporate promotions)
- equipment cover (for performers and artists, event organisers and promoters).

The different types of insurance were covered in Chapter 17.

IDENTIFY RISKS

The process of identifying risk can be undertaken by brainstorming the following questions:

- What are the worst things that could happen?
- Where are we exposed?
- What are the best things that could happen?
- How would we cope?

There are a number of sources of risk. Table 18.1 includes a framework for looking at the generic sources, together with specific examples from the event industry.

When considering generic sources of risk, an event organiser needs to look at a range of potential risk events which could conceivably impact on their specific operation. For example,

TABLE 18.1 Strategic sources of risk

SOURCE OF STRATEGIC RISK		EXAMPLES OF EVENT RISK
HUMAN BEHAVIOUR		• Celebrity endorses an event unexpectedly, resulting in wide positive media exposure and crowd crush. • Security staff member critically injures a fan. • Senior management disguises significant losses.
TECHNOLOGY AND TECHNICAL ISSUES		• Videoconferencing facility at conference centre fails during high-profile session with global audience. • IT specialist leaves company. • Lighting and sound systems are incompatible with local conditions.
WORKPLACE HEALTH AND SAFETY		• Excessive noise and hearing damage claims impact on insurance premiums. • Negative media exposure resulting from an accident causes damage to reputation. • Rides declared unsafe by authorities.

ECONOMIC
- Decrease in family disposable income due to rapid increase in interest rates leads to lower patronage.
- Budget tightening results in cancellation or downsizing of all corporate Christmas functions.

LEGAL
- Public liability costs lead to cancellation of a community festival. Contractual arrangements, such as naming rights, result in disputes between the organisers and competing sponsors.

POLITICAL
- Emphasis and support for regional events in overseas advertising on Australian tourism has negative impact on capital city events.
- Funding sources for festivals and events dry up.

FINANCIAL/ MARKET
- Economic recession in overseas source country impacts on a major inbound tourism market, in turn impacting on ticket sales. Financial institution refuses to cover cash flow crisis.

PROPERTY AND EQUIPMENT
- Gas supply fails over a sustained period, rendering cooking equipment inoperable.
- Rented equipment does not meet safety standards.

ENVIRONMENTAL
- Fans damage the environment at the Botanic Gardens.
- The local community protests about the approved decibel level of a music concert.

NATURAL EVENTS
- Constant rain during event leads to cancellation of performances/games.
- Cyclone devastates marquees and temporary buildings.
- Heat exhaustion causes problems for tennis players and spectators.

a major breakdown of lighting equipment at an event could be nothing short of catastrophic. If preventative measures and contingency plans were in place, this risk could be minimised (as will be discussed later in the chapter).

When identifying risks, it is essential to consult with and involve key people to achieve broad input into the risk assessment process, to use a systematic hierarchical process to conduct the risk assessment, and finally, to document this ongoing process.

ANALYSE RISKS

Risks need to be assessed from various viewpoints. First, what is the *consequence* or impact of the risk event likely to be? Second, what is the *likelihood* of the risk event occurring? Fires tend to have a major or even severe impact, but they are extremely rare. A long, rainy holiday season could have a moderate financial impact, and in the life of certain event businesses the likelihood of this is almost certain.

Once the consequence and likelihood have been evaluated, it is then necessary to look at the *level of risk* and decide which risks need treatment. Clearly, a potentially catastrophic risk, such as fire, while having a low probability, would still be rated as a high-level risk. The level of risk is calculated by finding the intersection between the likelihood and the consequences (see Table 18.2).

TABLE 18.2 Level of risk determined by likelihood and consequence

LIKELIHOOD	EFFECT (CONSEQUENCE)				
	INSIGNIFICANT 1	MINOR 2	MODERATE 3	MAJOR 4	CATASTROPHIC 5
5 (Almost certain)	M	H	E	E	E
	5	10	15	20	25
4 (Likely)	L	M	H	E	E
	4	8	12	16	20
3 (Possible)	L	M	M	H	E
	3	6	9	12	15
2 (Unlikely)	L	L	M	M	H
	2	4	6	8	10
1 (Rare)	L	L	L	L	M
	1	2	3	4	5

Key

Extreme (E) An extreme risk requires immediate action as the potential could be devastating to the organisation.

High (H) A high level of risk requires action, as it has the potential to be damaging to the organisation.

Medium (M) Allocate specific responsibility to a medium risk and implement monitoring or response procedures.

Low (L) Treat a low level of risk with routine procedures.

The final rating can be calculated as the product of the two numbers for likelihood and effect, ranging from 1 (low) through to 25 (extreme); see the example in Figure 18.3. For each of the combinations, there is an overall risk rating of Low (L), Moderate (M), High (H) or Extreme (E), as shown in the matrix.

SELECT AND IMPLEMENT RISK TREATMENTS

The next steps are to assess the organisation's capability to eliminate or control the risk, to determine specific elimination or control measures, to develop and document contingency plans, and to communicate these to the key people involved in operational activity. Of course, it is preferable to eliminate the risk, but if this is impossible then control measures must be put in place to minimise the risk. The event management team needs to continually monitor specific risks and controls to ensure the effectiveness of the approach taken.

Risks can also be transferred by outsourcing the risk to professional organisations. The most obvious example is transferring the safety risk of a high-profile VIP to a security company. Financial risks can likewise be shared by, for example, increasing the number of investors in a production. Insurance is another way to transfer risk.

The possibility of failure also has to be countenanced, as it needs to be when a performer cancels. Contingency plans are designed to deal with risks like this that cannot be avoided or controlled.

A risk analysis form similar to that illustrated in Figure 18.3 might be used, although for most events they are larger and more complex. The columns in this form that are most important are 'Treatment' and 'Contingency'. From this form it is evident that a number of risks can be expressed in generic terms.

FIGURE 18.3 Risk analysis for an event management company

IDENTIFIED RISK	LIKELIHOOD	CONSEQUENCE	LEVEL OF RISK	TREATMENT	CONTINGENCY
Main sponsor withdraws support	Possible	Major	High	• Sign long-term contracts with blue-chip business partners • Maintain ongoing business intelligence activities • Maintain ongoing communication to develop business relationship with sponsor	• Approach other sponsors • Approach government bodies for assistance • Take out a short-term loan • Extend other sponsorship involvement • Cancel the event
Cash flow crisis	Possible	Major	High	• Careful budgeting • Short-term contracts • Monitoring and control of expenses • Review pricing • Review promotional activities	• Increase borrowings • Search for new markets • Extend promotion • Discount tickets • Find more sponsorship or funding
Major fatal accident	Unlikely	Catastrophic	High	• Safety policies and procedures • Staff training • Insurance coverage • PR crisis plan	• Implement crisis management plan • Provide accurate information to the media
Maintenance systems failure	Rare	Major	Low	• High-calibre staging/ engineering staff • Systems and procedures for preventative maintenance • Insurance	• Contingency plans for breakdown of major plant or equipment

An organisation can take steps to prevent a risk event. Such steps may be based on legal obligations; for example, the installation of a fire detection system.

Contingency planning is necessary in case the risk event occurs. Fire-fighting systems would be put in place for such a contingency, as would evacuation procedures. Contingency plans need to be developed for all of the following emergency situations:

- prohibited access to a facility or venue
- loss of electric power
- communication lines down
- ruptured gas mains
- water damage
- smoke damage
- structural damage

- air or water contamination
- explosion
- chemical release
- trapped persons.
  Security risks could include:
- cash stolen in transit
- hold-up at ticket booth
- goods stolen from site
- illegal entry (e.g. climbing fences)
- illegal entry to performance or VIP areas
- vandalism to facilities and equipment
- insufficient number of security personnel on duty to control crowds
- untrained and unqualified security staff
- use of excessive force by security staff.

It must be stressed, however, that not all risks are physical or tangible. For each event, risks need to be categorised and evaluated. Figure 18.4 provides a risk analysis for human resource management, illustrating again that this approach can be used with all generic sources of risk and not just safety.

FIGURE 18.4 Risk analysis for human resource management

IDENTIFIED RISK	LIKELIHOOD	CONSEQUENCE	LEVEL OF RISK	TREATMENT	CONTINGENCY
Unable to recruit critical staff with specific technical experience	Possible	Moderate	Medium	• Workforce planning • International recruitment • Database of applicants	• Use agencies, network of contacts, head hunt • Meet relocation expenses • Provide incentives
Key staff member resigns or becomes ill shortly before the event	Likely	Major	Extreme	• Document policy and procedure • Maintain records • Work in teams • Appoint assistants • Provide incentives for staying until close-down	• Restructure • Recover lost ground • Reshape plans • Reassign responsibility
Volunteer and staff attrition during the event	Likely	Moderate	High	• Provide a reason to be there • Reward attendance • Acknowledge support	• Ensure rosters allow for attrition (inevitable) • Have a redeployment team

→

IDENTIFIED RISK	LIKELIHOOD	CONSEQUENCE	LEVEL OF RISK	TREATMENT	CONTINGENCY
Contractor defaults on service immediately prior to or during the event	Possible	Major	High	• Appoint contractors based on selection criteria, including past performance • Contracts to have penalty clauses • Work breakdown extremely detailed • Monitor activities	• Invoke penalties • Hire another contractor • Undertake work using own staff
Misconduct by staff member causes bad press	Rare	Major	Low	• Code of conduct • Disciplinary policy • Counselling and dismissal processes	• Dismissal • Press release
Fatal safety incident resulting from inadequate staff selection and training	Unlikely	Catastrophic	High	• Job analysis • Safety risk analysis • Selection based on experience and, in some cases, specific licences • Training in safety procedures • Documented procedures and signed checklists • Supervision	• Incident reporting system • First aid services • Communication system • Crisis management team • Press release
Non-compliance with industrial legislation	Unlikely	Minor	Low	• Assign responsibility for HR compliance • Monitor compliance, including of contractors	• Resolve with authorities

Source: Van Der Wagen, L. (2007). *Human Resource Management for Events*. Oxford, UK: Elsevier. p. 32.

Risk treatment involves identifying the range of options for treating the risk, assessing those options, and preparing risk treatment plans. There are a number of options for most risk events:

- Avoid the risk by abandoning the activity (e.g. abandoning children's rides).
- Reduce the likelihood of the occurrence (e.g. by implementing prevention programs such as a maintenance program).
- Reduce the severity of the consequences (e.g. contingency planning for first aid training).

Risk treatments are linked to the management functions of planning and control. Planning for prevention includes many of the processes described in this book, such as the development of sound contractual arrangements, inspection processes, training, supervision, technical controls and compliance programs.

It is important to note that waivers do not release an organisation from its duty of care to the person who signs the waiver. They do not protect organisations which act negligently or fail to act when they should. Disclaimers (statements that responsibility is not accepted for certain incidents) also do not exempt organisations from their duty of care.

Action plans

Once the most appropriate options for treating risk are selected, action plans can be developed. In summary, risk treatment generally identifies the following:

Source of risk	How could the risk arise?
Risk event	What could happen?
Priority	What priority does this risk have in relation to others?
Likelihood	Almost certain, likely, possible, unlikely, rare?
Consequences	Insignificant, minor, moderate, major, catastrophic?
Level of risk	Extreme, high, moderate, low?
Risk treatment	What will be done to eliminate the risk, control the risk, transfer the risk or retain the risk?
Responsibility	What is the name of the person who will implement the risk treatment option?
Resources required	What physical and human resources are needed to implement the risk treatment?
Performance measure	How will it be known that the risk treatment is working?
Timetable	When will the treatment option be implemented?

The outcome of a risk analysis is a prioritised list of risks for further action. The cost of managing the risk needs to be commensurate with the benefits obtained. Often, large benefits can be obtained for a reasonable cost, but to continue to strive for reduction incurs an escalating cost disproportionate to the result. This is called the law of diminishing returns, illustrated in Figure 18.5.

FIGURE 18.5 Cost of reducing risk can become uneconomic

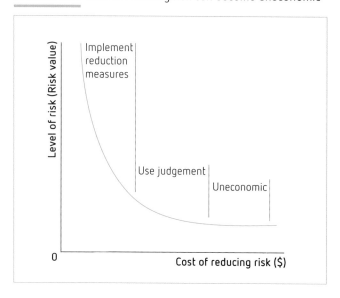

The event or organisation's capability to eliminate or control risk requires access to accurate information, expertise within the organisation to determine and implement appropriate control measures, analysis of legal liability, and consideration of the financial or other resource constraints on implementing sufficient control measures.

Action plans are used to develop risk treatments in detail. An action plan lists the steps that must be taken in order to achieve a specific goal, in this case treating the risk. The purpose of an action plan is to clarify what resources are required to reach the goal, formulate a timeline for when specific tasks need to be completed, and determine what resources are required. For each step, an action plan also identifies who is responsible. This is particularly useful for event planning when multiple stakeholders are involved, assigning one part to the organiser, another to the client and yet another to the security company. An action plan provides clarity and is an invaluable aspect of consultation and agreement with stakeholders. For example, at an event involving schoolchildren and their teachers at a shopping centre, one would need to develop an action plan for dealing with missing children. Who is responsible for taking a roll call? How is a child reported missing? Who makes the announcement on the PA system? How is a search instigated? And so on.

Evaluate risk management practices

A surf carnival involves many stakeholders and faces multiple risks

Finally, it is essential to continually monitor operational activities for a changing risk profile (for example, checking the weather, sometimes hourly) and to identify, assess and control risks on an ongoing basis. The importance of consulting with key people and stakeholders to elicit feedback on the effectiveness of all risk management practices cannot be stressed enough.

Clear documentation of identified risks and the outcome of assessment of these risks may include:

- checklists
- completed risk identification and assessment reports
- comprehensive file notes
- correspondence with customers, suppliers or specialist advisers
- reports
- meeting notes or minutes
- action plans.

Several event planning guides are listed at the end of the chapter, and there are many more examples of forms and templates on the Internet. The most useful are those provided by government agencies.

Four years following the death of teenager Gemma Thoms from a drug overdose at Perth's Big Day Out in February 2009, the coroner who worked on the case visited the festival to see the improvements that had been implemented in response to the tragic situation. He said the following:

In my opinion, the medical services at the 2013 Big Day Out were of a high standard. They reflected a capacity well beyond that which could reasonably be expected from volunteer

EXTENSION ACTIVITY

first-aiders alone. The medical services were well beyond the standards mandated by the 2009 Guidelines, which did not call for tertiary qualified medical staff or require the presence of an ambulance.

The total cost to the organiser of the St John Ambulance Service's involvement at the Big Day Out was about $18 000, which in my opinion is a modest impost considering the size of the crowd and the significant safety advantage provided by the presence of the ambulance and tertiary qualified professional staff.

Thoms' family welcomed the findings. 'The fact that the Coroner said it was inadequate in 2009 when Gem was there and the massive improvements that have been made since with St Johns and also the Big Day out having the 2013 one, they made such a big difference. I'm really, really happy about it', said Thoms' mother, Peta Davies (ABC News, 2013).

In response to the investigation, the *Guidelines for Concerts, Events and Mass Gatherings* (2009) were developed. These were far more detailed than the earlier guidelines, and more extensive than most. The document, as well as full reports from other inquests and inquiries, are included with the online materials provided with this text. They illustrate the complexity of each situation, both legal and ethical, and the responses of experts in an attempt to improve event operations.

By way of illustration, at Perth's Big Day Out in 2009, the investigation found there had been:

- 569 people seeking medical attention
- 23 major medical incidents
- 450 minor medical incidents
- 37 injuries
- 49 wounds
- eight emotional / behavioural incidents
- two incidents of multiple injury (combination of above).

There were five first-aid posts manned by a total of 74 volunteers who worked two shifts. Additionally, there was a six-person communications team (three per shift) and four people in the retrieval team (two per shift).

The coroner made the following finding:

In my view the medical precautions taken during the Big Day Out on 1 February 2009, to identify and treat those suffering the ill-effects of illicit drug use, were not adequate. It would have been prudent to have tertiary qualified practitioners (paramedics, nurses, doctors) employed at the Big Day Out …

I should emphasise that my comment should not be read as suggesting that either the promoter of the Big Day Out or the St John Ambulance Services did not comply with any standard imposed by law or legislation as to the manner in which a large event should be run.

Source: Mulligan, D. H. (2013). Coroner's report: Inquest into the death of Gemma Geraldine Thoms. Western Australian Government, 8 March. pp. 28, 29 & 39. www.coronerscourt.wa.gov.au/_files/Thoms_finding.pdf

Debate the issues by taking a position on the following argument, having done some research into the roles of all stakeholders and their responsibilities: 'Event organisers have no responsibility in relation to drug use.'

Develop a risk management policy

One final consideration for event managers is that of policy development. This goes beyond the steps of process and procedure to ensure that risk management forms a core element of policy in event planning. Policy development ensures that all stakeholders work together to mitigate risks.

The following steps are recommended for developing a risk management policy:

- Obtain the support of senior management for ongoing risk analysis, evaluation and treatment.
- Decide who is responsible for managing risks.
- Develop the required documentation.
- Develop a timeline for implementation and ongoing review of the policy.
- Integrate risk management with strategic and operational planning.
- Communicate with staff on an ongoing basis.
- Manage the program at each relevant level and integrate with all other management responsibilities.
- Monitor and review the policy, procedures and outcomes.

In the following situation, a policy was developed to stop participants over the age of 50 from participating in an event. In light of the feedback obtained with regard to this policy, no doubt it will be reviewed.

EXAMPLE

Peter Biscoe reckoned he was in good shape for yesterday's Rough Water swim at Bondi Beach. But the former champion swimmer, lifesaver and water polo player didn't get his chance. He was among about 90 swimmers aged over 49 who were excluded from the 1-kilometre swim because of rough surf.

Organisers said they had made the decision based on the greater health risks – particularly of heart attacks – among older swimmers. It didn't sit well with Mr Biscoe. '[Age] is an extremely arbitrary and irrational basis on which to exclude people', he said. 'Any of my children could go in the race, even though I am a much stronger swimmer than any of them.'

Last night, the head of the Anti-Discrimination Board, Chris Puplick, said such a decision based on age, not fitness, might breach the state's discrimination laws.

Source: Jacobsen, G. (2003). Fit and in his 50s, but swimmer sidelined because of surf. *Sydney Morning Herald*, 13 January. www.smh.com.au/articles/2003/01/12/1041990181655.html

Risk management is an iterative, ongoing process. It occurs during the event planning phase but must also become part of the minute-by-minute management of an event. Activities must be monitored on an ongoing basis using an incident report form (illustrated in Chapter 9). These incidents must be analysed and 'near miss' incidents given special attention. Likewise, any incidents that indicate a risk to health, safety or security should be given special attention and action taken immediately to reduce or eliminate the risk.

Summary

The event industry has experienced many economic downturns that have had a serious impact on business. Many music festivals have come and gone. Extreme weather has also resulted in the cancellation of events. Internal forces such as lengthy contract disputes or serious accidents can also impact negatively on a business in this industry. For these reasons, this and other chapters in this book stress the value of risk management planning during all stages of event planning, from concept through to execution. This chapter has also outlined the steps in identifying, assessing, evaluating, controlling and monitoring risk, with emphasis on the ongoing nature of this process. Strategic and operational risk management can prevent damage to a company's financial status and/or reputation, enhance opportunities and improve relationships with stakeholders.

Key terms

Risk	Effect of foreseeable uncertainties on objectives – simply, things going wrong
Risk-management process	Has five main steps: establish context, identify risks, analyse and evaluate them, then treat the risks; review and consultation are also part of the process

REVIEW YOUR KNOWLEDGE

1 Outline the purpose and key elements of current risk management standards.
2 Explain the risk management process using a diagram.
3 Explain the concept of risk treatment.
4 Explain, with examples, five sources of strategic risk for an event organisation.
5 Identify one event that has not properly evaluated the level of risk, with serious consequences.

APPLY YOUR KNOWLEDGE

Consider some of the social and legal issues relating to the use and abuse of alcohol and drugs at events.
1 Outline the legislative context in relation to the use of alcohol and drugs as well as the social context.
2 Identify policies and procedures relevant to this risk; e.g. searches.
3 Ensure that you discuss the roles of various stakeholders and their viewpoints.
4 Identify some of the factors that increase the level of this risk for the event organiser, and ways in which this risk can be managed by the event organiser.
    There are several references and weblinks at the end of the chapter that will help you answer these questions.

CASE STUDY

Conduct a risk management analysis using a table format and appropriate headings (see Figure 18.3 as an example) for at least two of the following events:

- outdoor launch of a soft-drink product, with entertainment, for a target audience of children aged nine to 14
- surf carnival (run, swim, paddle) for all age groups, with a handicapping system based on heat times
- school swimming competition for high school students of the Asia-Pacific region, with finals in a major city
- global warming conference and concert involving politicians, scientists, activists and the media.

Online resources

Visit **http://login.cengagebrain.com** and search for this book to access the study tools that come with your textbook.

References

ABC News (2013). Family welcomes finding after festival overdose. 8 March. www.abc.net.au/news/2013-03-08/family-welcomes-coroners-finding-after-festival-drug-overdose/4561286

Brown, S., & Hutton, A. (2013). Developments in the real-time evaluation of audience behaviour at planned events. *International Journal of Event and Festival Management*, 4(1), 43–55.

Illiyas, F. T., Mani, S. K., Pradeepkumar, A. P., & Mohan, K. (2013). Human stampedes during religious festivals: A comparative review of mass gathering emergencies in India. *International Journal of Disaster Risk Reduction*, 5, 10–18.

Websites

Advice for managing major events safely, **www.worksafe.vic.gov.au/__data/assets/pdf_file/0016/211345/ISBN-Advice-for-managing-major-events-safely-2006-04.pdf**

Event risk management and planning (City of Greater Geelong), **www.geelongaustralia.com.au/events/planning/eventplanning/article/item/8cdc2778104484a.aspx**

Risk management for public events (Launceston City Council), **www.launceston.tas.gov.au/files/assets/public/events/10-rfx-052-risk-management-of-public-events.pdf**

19

COORDINATE MARKETING ACTIVITIES

OVERVIEW

In this chapter we develop an understanding of the important topic of marketing, which is so closely linked to event management. To do this, we review marketing opportunities and select strategies to meet those opportunities, often using new and innovative technologies. Public relations involves working with promotional networks, including print and other media, but this is only one part of the strategy. Social media campaigns and other forms of promotion are also considered, with the end result being evaluated for success (for example, ticket sales, attendance and product sales) in order to inform the organisation when next planning an event marketing activity.

LEARNING OBJECTIVES

On completion of this chapter, you will be able to:

1 plan and organise marketing activities seeking innovative opportunities, including the use of new technologies and media

2 undertake a general public relations role in developing media releases and other media support material

3 review and report on promotional activities to inform sales and marketing planning.

INDUSTRY VIEWPOINT

Promotions work is not as glamorous as some might imagine – there is a lot less VIP entertainment and champagne involved! The daily role involves hard work and perseverance but is often rewarding. Ultimately, my role for our charitable fundraising event is to help bring our organisation and event to the attention of our target audience to increase donations.

In order to achieve this, extensive planning and research is required to identify the audience, key messages, communication channels and media opportunities to generate interest. The role involves extensive writing and requires strong communication skills.

Public relations activities are just one part of the broader marketing mix, which includes other communications disciplines and promotional activities. For example, direct marketing involves distribution of promotional materials directly to the customer. Personal selling involves meeting the customer face to face, or at the very least speaking on the telephone. It is all about strategic positioning of the organisation or event and communication of the right messages to reach and engage the target audience.

My role in assisting with the promotion of our fundraising event has involved begging family and friends to play rent-a-crowd for photo shoots. I have also helped prepare our spokespeople for media interviews, and speak with journalists to line up interviews in advance of the event, during the key promotional period. Lining up photo shoots and coordinating interviews are just some of the many tasks I perform to support the overall marketing plan. And then of course, I look after all social media …

Event marketing and promotions assistant

INTRODUCTION

Promotion and public relations are a crucial part of the marketing of any event, as we have mentioned in previous chapters, and these responsibilities will be discussed below in some detail.

The types of promotional activities commonly used in the service industries include trade and consumer shows, in-house promotions, advertising, public relations, familiarisations, signage and display, as well as social media activities.

As part of the marketing strategy, event promotion involves communicating the image and content of the event program to the potential audience. Broadly, the aim of a promotional strategy is to ensure that the consumer makes a decision to purchase and follows up with the action of actually making the purchase. It is essential to turn intention into action, and this is often the biggest obstacle facing a promotional campaign.

The digital landscape has changed dramatically in recent times and continues to do so. At World Expo 2010 in Shanghai, China Mobile, a global partner of the event, customised many applications for that event. Visitors were able to choose between 100 shows daily – over the six months of the expo there were 2000 performances over 35 venues. After booking online, entry was by mobile phone. The audience could also make purchases of food, beverage and merchandise using their mobile phone. And radio frequency identification (RFID) card visitors were able to go to certain terminals on the expo site to find their location and check which pavilions they had already visited. They could also see in advance if pavilions they planned to visit were crowded. Organisers were even able to control LCD advertising with their devices.

These innovations are likely to change the face of event marketing in the future, with customers having better information just in time, potentially delaying their decision making. It is therefore clear that staying abreast of current and new trends in marketing and consumer behaviour is essential for the event manager.

What is marketing?

The UK Chartered Institute of Marketing defines marketing as:

> The management process responsible for identifying, anticipating and satisfying customer requirements profitably.

The American Marketing Association provides the following definition:

> Marketing is the process of planning and executing the conception, pricing, promotion, and distribution of ideas, goods, and services to create exchanges that satisfy individual and organizational goals.

Another definition involves satisfying customer wants and needs through an exchange process. In this definition, the concept of profit is not included, suiting many non-profit community events. Most people think that marketing is only about the advertising and/or personal selling of goods and services. Advertising and selling, however, are just two of the many marketing activities. Marketing activities are all those associated with identifying the particular wants and needs of a target market of customers, and then going about satisfying those customers better than your competitors. This involves doing market research in relation to customers, analysing their needs, and then making strategic decisions about product design, pricing, promotion and distribution.

THE MARKETING MIX

Marketing action plans can be considered in terms of the marketing mix (see Figure 19.1). In other words, how will the event be positioned well, priced well, promoted effectively and distributed through different channels efficiently. All these factors must work together if success is to be the outcome.

The considerations of product, price, promotion and place (the four 'P's) need to be finalised at an operational level, ready for implementation.

FIGURE 19.1 The marketing mix

Product

Each event offers a range of potential benefits to the event audience. These may include one or more of the following:

- a novel experience
- entertainment
- a learning experience
- an exciting result
- the opportunity to meet others
- the chance to purchase items
- dining and drinking
- an inexpensive way to get out of the house
- the chance to see something unique.

Many marketing experts are unable to see past the main motivating factor for the event, which may be the opportunity to watch an international cricket match. There may, however, be some members of the audience who have little interest in cricket, but are motivated by some of the other features of the product such as the opportunity to see and be seen. Generally, people attending an event see the product as a package of benefits. Convenience and good weather, for example, could be benefits associated with an event product. Most products also carry negative features. Like a pair of jeans that is just the right fit but not the perfect colour, the event may have features that are not desirable, such as crowding, heat and long waiting times.

When marketing an event, therefore, alignment between the product benefits and the needs of the audience is necessary to guide the design of the event and the promotional effort. Pre-match and mid-match entertainment are good examples of adding value to the main benefit offered by a sporting event product.

The ambience, food, lighting and many other features also form part of the product. For a conference, the program of events or speakers is the main product. The members of the audience, and their behaviour, contribute to the audience perception of the product, albeit peripherally.

Transportation, seating, shelter against the elements and nearby tourism attractions are other potential features of the product. All these detailed elements need to be finalised so that the audience is provided with the information required to make an informed decision.

Think of the last big event you visited and identify your motivations for attending. Explain whether your expectations were met. Contrast your experience with that of someone else who attended the event in question.

Price

Pricing for an entertainment event is very tricky. It depends on the size of the potential audience and the selected venue. If the ticket price is too high, and the featured artist not as popular as expected, then the half-empty venue will result in a dismal financial outcome. The pricing of food and beverage items is also an important consideration because customers become annoyed if mark-ups are excessive. For events involving travel, the price often includes the cost of transportation and accommodation. Decisions must therefore be made in a timely manner regarding 'early bird' purchases, last-minute discounting and special prices for groups.

Promotion

Promotional activities need to be chosen carefully and timed effectively. There are many forms of promotion, including personal selling, brochures, posters, banners, websites, social media, news, radio and television advertising, and press releases. Balloons and crowd pleasers (people balloons with moving arms) are examples of eye-catching promotional strategies that can be incorporated into the marketing plan. Promotion is a costly exercise, radio and television advertising being two of the most expensive. Overall, the most cost-effective methods of promotion for many events are feature articles in local newspapers and banners. Events are also promoted by tourism bodies and tourism information offices at minimal cost.

Place/distribution

Tickets can be distributed as part of package tours, through ticket sellers (who take commission) or at the venue. In many cases, the event product is produced, distributed and consumed at the venue. This contrasts, for example, with goods that are imported for sale and ultimately consumed by the customer at home. The effectiveness of the channels through which an event is promoted and sold is a crucial aspect of its success.

The event venue is the location at which the product is enjoyed, playing an important part in meeting the needs of the consumer. Easy parking, good seating, excellent visibility, cleanliness and the provision of suitable facilities are often determined by the physical location of the event.

Illustration of the four Ps

The example of a motor show below illustrates the four Ps for an exhibition of the latest wheels on the road:

Product

* featured motor vehicles (high-tech concept cars)
* number and variety of exhibitors/brands
* dates and hours of exhibition
* associated events (such as seminars)
* prizes (door prizes, competitions)
* entertainment
* décor, lighting, special effects
* staffing
* parking
* transportation.

Price

* price of admission
* free tickets for sponsors and exhibitors.

Promotion

* website
* motor magazines
* print news (e.g. motoring supplements)
* direct mail.

Place/distribution

* city location (capital city, distance to travel)
* type of venue (and proximity)
* accommodation options (and proximity)
* tourist attractions (and proximity)
* ticket purchase (online, at venue, from dealers).

PLAN AND ORGANISE MARKETING ACTIVITIES

Marketing activities include far more than advertising. Indeed, most community events rely on free editorial publicity in the local media. Other forms of promotional activity include direct marketing, sales promotion and personal selling. **Digital marketing** refers to advertising delivered through digital channels such as search engines, websites, social media, email and mobile apps. All of these approaches will be discussed in detail later in this chapter.

> **Digital marketing**
> Marketing using digital channels, including social media and apps

Event promotion involves planning and scheduling marketing and promotional activities according to the overall marketing plan and marketing objectives. It is vital to identify relevant market information and use it to inform your short-term promotional planning. The market analysis may be based on marketing reports, sales reports, financial statistics, marketplace trends and competitive activity. A carefully crafted, integrated approach to communication with the client or customer is also needed to ensure that the marketing objectives are achieved in the established timeframes (see Figure 19.2).

FIGURE 19.2 Marketing communications mix

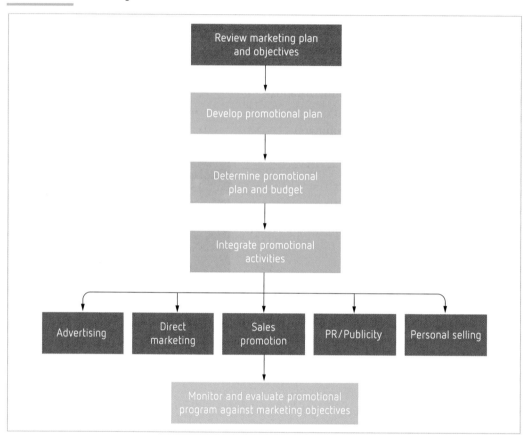

Having undertaken the market research, the marketing department is in a better position to decide how to promote a particular product or how to launch a new product. A number of activities are used for the marketing and promotion of event products and services, but not all will be applicable to every situation. Indeed, one key skill is the ability to determine which promotional activities are most appropriate, based on the current marketing focus and other relevant information.

Image and branding

The first step for most events is the development of a name, logo and image for the event. This includes the colour scheme and graphics that will appear on all event material ranging from registration forms to tickets to merchandise. Image and logo are closely linked and need to be agreed on well in advance. Together they are referred to as 'branding'. Where sponsors are involved, it is essential to obtain their approval of the branding, otherwise there could be conflict over the use of colour or the positioning and size of logos. The design must meet the needs of all stakeholders, as well as appealing to the event audience, particularly if the design forms the basis for merchandise such as T-shirts and caps. A slogan is sometimes developed as part of the image for an event and incorporated wherever possible. The result should be a consistent theme and colour scheme for all promotional material. In most cases, the colour scheme is also carried through to the décor, including signs, fencing, flags, table settings, banners and posters.

Identify target groups

Target groups for marketing and public relations activities may include event organisers, media representatives (for example, journalists, editors, producers and directors), patrons, sponsors, funding bodies, promoters, staff, volunteers, suppliers, vendors, related businesses, visitors and, of course, audiences.

Each of these different target groups is likely to have different communications needs or expectations. It is important to bear them all in mind when considering a marketing strategy, as well as to consider specific communications activities to ensure each important group is addressed. Later, when planning the communication methods or channels to reach these audiences, it is important to remember that some groups have particular communication needs or restrictions (for example, non-English-language speakers), or no access to the digital platform, or some other limitation. For this reason, as well as identifying target audiences, it is worth spending some time understanding them also.

You are planning to run an under-18 music event and you are developing a communications strategy. Summarise your key message/s for anxious parents sending their under-18s to the event. (What do they want to hear?) Then summarise your key promotional messages to the prospective participants/audience. (How will you generate interest?)

EXTENSION ACTIVITY

Identify customers

Planning is a cyclical process in which target market segments (customers) are identified, events are developed to suit their needs, and the event is competitively positioned. The aim is to develop a perception on the part of the customer that the event is desirable – indeed, more desirable than the products and services of competing organisations. Fun runs and craft fairs, for example, attract completely different target markets.

Market segmentation is the process of analysing customers in groups. Some groups may enjoy a particular type of country and western music. Others may enjoy line dancing. Yet others may visit a music festival just for the excitement and the atmosphere. It is absolutely essential to analyse the different motivations of the event audience and to develop a profile for each of these groups.

Tamworth is well known for a number of festivals, the most notable being the Tamworth Country Music Festival.

> The Tamworth region has a rich and diverse cultural heritage, which is reflected by the festivals and events, both small and large, that are held across the region. Nundle's gold mining history is celebrated during the annual Go for Gold Chinese Easter Festival while the region's rich agricultural history and the part played in it by the 'Little Grey' (Massey) Ferguson tractor is commemorated by the Grey Fergie Muster in Bendemeer every three years.
>
> It is not just history that is celebrated. The Tamworth Country Music Festival, the largest music festival in the southern hemisphere, combines street theatre, free public concerts and ticketed events to air the talents of country music artists,

Motor sports and music concerts are pitched at different audiences

from those just starting out as buskers, those participating in music colleges and quests, through to those receiving the prestigious Golden Guitar Awards.

Source: Tamworth Regional Council (2017). Festivals and events. www.tamworth. nsw.gov.au/Community/Festivals-and-Events/Festivals---Events

Attendee profiles form the basis for all marketing plans and activities. Báez and Devesa (2014) studied the profiles of attendees at a film festival and found, perhaps unsurprisingly, that while many were film lovers, others were there for other reasons, described as discovery and entertainment. Different marketing approaches would be required for each of these market segments.

Set goals and objectives

Setting goals and objectives at the outset, based on information gathered on organisational and/or marketing objectives, is key in any promotional plan. It will not only provide the context for developing the strategy but will also provide the ability to measure the success of the plan at its conclusion.

Goal setting is an effective way of ensuring that all internal parties have a clear understanding of the 'big picture' and desired outcome for the organisation, division or event. Any new idea or opportunity should be considered against the set goals.

A helpful rule to apply when setting the marketing plan's objectives is to consider the well-known management tool SMART objectives, developed by management authors Doran (1981) and Miller and Cunningham (1981).

The SMART method specifies that all goals or objectives must be:

- specific
- measurable
- attainable
- realistic
- time-bound.

For example, a goal may be to increase the number of unique visitors to the event website during the two-month period prior to the event by 20 per cent compared with the same period last year.

This goal would be helpful in driving the promotional strategy and assisting with measurement, as it is specific (focused on driving people to the event website), measurable (website hits are recorded by web hosts), attainable (a 20 per cent increase could be viewed as attainable depending on the previous year's results and the upcoming planned level of activity), realistic (since successful public relations efforts, which would raise awareness of the event, should help lift website hit rates) and time-bound (as the period to be measured is specified as the two months prior to the event – the key time to help drive visitor numbers or ticket sales for the event).

A simplified marketing plan is illustrated in Figure 19.3 to show the importance of SMART objectives and the rationale for the marketing activities that follow.

FIGURE 19.3 Simplified marketing plan for launch of an alcoholic beverage

Event Launch: Alcoholic Beverage

Target Audience

Direct target audience: 'A list' celebrities and key television media.

Indirect target audience: 20 – 30 year olds, mainly female, responding to associated promotion and publicity.

Marketing Objectives
- Achieve 80% attendance by invitation-only guests, VIPs and celebrities.
- Attract two of three key television channels for publicity purposes.
- Achieve $3000 publicity value in print media write-up.
- Achieve 15% increase in retail and wholesale beverage sales within the first three months.
- Establish the brand as first choice for 5% of target market segment.
- Achieve 45% brand sampling or recognition by target audience.

Action Plan
- Conduct market research in February (pre-event).
- Plan launch and obtain budget approval by 31 March.
- Prepare promotional brief and objectives by 4 April.
- Employ PR company to achieve publicity objectives by 12 April.
- Finalise promotional campaign plans by 29 April.
- Approve promotional material, including advertising, invitations and guest list by 30 April.
- Issue invitations and press releases by 10 May.
- Implement promotional campaign as per schedule.
- Launch advertising campaign on 15 May.
- Follow-up RSVPs by personal calls by 25 May.
- Stage launch 31 May.
- Conduct market research (post-event) in June.
- Media coverage final report due 3 July.

Event Marketing Budget
- Public relations campaign $95 000.
- Advertising campaign $250 000.
- Invitations – design, printing and postage $8000.
- Marketing staff and administration $60 000.

Monitoring and Evaluation
- Media monitoring done by PR company.
- Market research conducted pre- and post-launch.
- Value of retail and wholesale liquor sales monitored.
- Follow-up telephone survey of invited guests.

Having developed specific marketing objectives, action plans and corresponding budgets, the event manager can be more confident that the event will attract a good audience and meet customer expectations. Success must be monitored to identify whether the marketing plan is working, and modifications made to the plan if necessary. Ongoing inputs into the planning process should encompass competitive activity, marketing reports, marketplace trends and sales reports. For events that attract tourists, government tourism bodies provide considerable market research on their corporate sites. The tourism forecasts released by Tourism Research Australia provide trend analysis in inbound and outbound tourism. For example, destination weddings continue to grow at a fast pace, with as many as 25 per cent of couples opting to get married away from their home town.

Legal and ethical issues

Legal and ethical considerations must always be incorporated into the planning process. A public relations program or activity that is illegal or unethical risks major reputation damage to the event organisation and possibly its sponsors, and leaves the organisation open to litigation or charges from authorities.

Legal issues that need to be considered include consumer protection, copyright, child protection and privacy laws and guidelines. These were covered in Chapter 17.

Ethical considerations for marketing activities cover the appropriate use of images and text, and the sensitivities or cultural concerns of particular groups in the community. Event marketing and promotional activities provide an ideal opportunity to embed sustainability considerations, using sustainability as a marketing tool and highlighting positive social and environmental impacts.

FIGURE 19.4 Stages in buyer behaviour

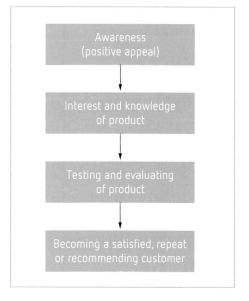

Advertising

Advertising is paid communication, using one or more types of media to reach potential buyers. It can be extremely expensive, particularly radio and television advertising, and for this reason it is essential to accurately identify the market and target the advertising as cost-effectively as possible.

Advertising is one of the most effective ways of raising awareness of an event or event business. However, from a marketing point of view, the aim is to achieve more than awareness. Awareness and interest need to be converted into sales and loyalty. The four steps to becoming a loyal customer are illustrated in Figure 19.4.

Whereas advertising might attract a potential customer to a convention centre as the possible venue for a wedding reception, a tour of the establishment and a display of photographs from previous receptions would create interest and allow the client to evaluate the product. An invitation to sample various menus, in consultation with the chef, would more than likely clinch the deal – provided the food was of an appropriate standard. The buyer has expressed interest, developed knowledge of the product and tested some elements of the product. For such an important decision, these steps are critical. Signing the contract is almost guaranteed and so, too, are the couple's expectation of the event's success and the possibility of recommendation to others.

In the event industry, expectation and anticipation are part of the product. Anything that can be done to enhance this is adding to the product benefit. A well-designed website can help to develop loyalty, while a website for an agricultural show is an essential source of information for visitors wanting to see specific exhibitions. Full multipage colour brochures and programs are used less frequently as more visitors access the required information online.

Various popular types of advertising are described in detail below.

Digital

Website and mobile app design and adequate listings with search engines – incorporating SEO (search engine optimisation) efforts to improve page rankings – are critical factors in the success of marketing and advertising. Security for online transactions and privacy of information given by customers are other very important considerations. The potential of this method of advertising is well recognised, with exponential growth expected in the coming years, many events being leaders in the field.

Digital advertising can assist with decision making on all types of bookings by providing detailed knowledge of the facilities, such as accessibility for displaying large items such as cars and boats. Some convention centres have interactive planning available, so that when the customer chooses a type of function (banquet, conference) and identifies the number of guests, various room configurations are shown on-screen using CAD software. Most websites also offer email links to facilitate questions and answers.

Digital platforms provide more than advertising – they can translate interest into purchase with bookings made, paid and confirmed online.

Print

Newspapers and magazines are the print media commonly used for advertising. Cost is related to the medium chosen and to the size and positioning of the advertisement. The front and back covers and inside front and back covers are usually the most expensive spaces to purchase, followed by the top part of right-hand pages. Choosing the appropriate newspaper or magazine is essential, as wide coverage or untargeted advertising tends to produce a very limited response. The circulation statistics for the publication need to be analysed, including the demographic profile of readers, and matched to event target markets.

As part of the marketing plan, it is necessary to identify the market to be reached and then to establish where these people live and which of the print media would be most likely to reach them. When selecting the most appropriate media, cost is generally the biggest issue. Then you need to decide when to advertise – a month before, a week before or the day before? Faced with budget limits and potentially expensive advertising, these are all crucial decisions.

When preparing an advertising budget, you should be aware that different time slots on radio and television cost vastly different amounts, as do different positions on the pages of print media, as mentioned above. Local newspapers and local radio stations are always more cost effective than national ones and are generally a most effective way to reach a local audience. Larger events may aim to attract international audiences and, if this is the case, you will need to clearly identify the potential overseas audience and perhaps develop a tourist package to include accommodation and other attractions. Partnership arrangements can often be reached with travel companies and the assistance of State/Territory and national tourism bodies obtained to support and promote the event.

The content of advertisements must be informative but, most importantly, it must inspire decision making and action to attend or purchase. Let's look at the following advertisement by an event company for their wedding hire products and services:

> We provide six-arm gold candelabra in the Victorian style, silk flowers, tea lights,
> fairy lights, table overlays (in organza, Jacquard and cotton), chair covers with
> sashes and ceiling drapes. We set up for you.

In this advertisement there is a lot of information but absolutely no inspiration. A number of descriptive adjectives would certainly have enhanced the text, as well as the possibility of customers buying their services!

By contrast, the advertisement for the unusual event in Figure 19.5 is much more creative.

FIGURE 19.5 A creative advertisement designed to attract an 'audience' to an unusual event

---

YOUR BLOOD!

Greendale Clinic Big Bleed Week

May 10–15 with the grand finale (don't miss this) on May 15

Greendale Clinic's last Big Bleed was a huge success. This year our target is 3000 units of blood. Sponsors have donated 10 major prizes as well as minor prizes for all other donors. The biggest prize, a trip to Cannes, will be presented at the grand finale. We will have free health advice, coffee shop and food stalls, a craft fair, children's entertainment, celebrities, races, a jazz band in the late afternoon and fireworks at the close each evening. Attendance is free and all donors receive a sponsor prize, plus go into the draw for the major prizes. Parking is available in Macleay Street. We start at 10 and finish at 9 pm.

It would be very difficult to attract an event audience if only the facts of a blood donation were presented, and the promotional team has realised this by turning this event into something not to be missed.

The advertising message needs to meet the motivational needs of the audience, at the same time assisting the decision-making process by supplying the necessary facts.

Radio

Radio advertising is effective if the message is clear. However, it is not possible to show images or provide very specific information and is thus used infrequently by all but the biggest event operators.

Television

While the impact of television advertising is greater than for most other media, it is extremely expensive. Specific marketing objectives would need to be developed and an advertising agency fully briefed on the proposed campaign. The timing of the advertising campaign should be linked to consumer decision making, which is generally possible only when market research has been conducted on similar previous events. Celebrity endorsement does not come free unless the event supports a charity. It costs around $2000 to $3000 for a minor celebrity and between $100000 and $250000 for a high-profile celebrity.

Direct mail

A substantial client list is a valuable resource for direct mail advertising and selling. A client list can be developed rapidly if an organisation is promoted at trade exhibitions where the list of attendees is made available to exhibitors. If the market can be clearly identified, then direct mail is a most effective form of advertising, and one that is cost-effective too. Where customers are transient, the expense of direct mail is unwarranted. Of course, an invitation is a form of direct mail advertising.

Displays and signage

Signs are one of the most effective ways by which small event businesses advertise, even though most councils place limitations on the size of signs. Lighting, too, is an important element of outdoor signage, and one that is often neglected. Sky writing is expensive: one display of up to 12 characters costs $2600. For a second display on the same day, the cost comes down to about $1800.

Signage — one form of advertising

Brochures and fliers

Brochures and fliers are essential advertising items for many types of small events, and they need to be descriptive, informative and colourful. The quality of any photographs or artwork used in them is most important too.

Advertising collateral

This interesting term covers a range of advertising media, from tent cards to billboards. Posters and billboards are often displayed in public places and tourist information centres.

Personal selling

Personal selling involves face-to-face contact between seller and buyer. This enables the salesperson to talk directly to the buyer, and to persuade the buyer through negotiation to purchase the product. This type of promotion is most common for booking conferences, exhibitions, parties and incentive travel events. This is because the event details need to be planned and a quote provided.

For all personal selling, it is essential to prepare in advance by finding out as much as possible about the potential customer. Following are the steps and stages involved in meeting a potential client or making a sales call:

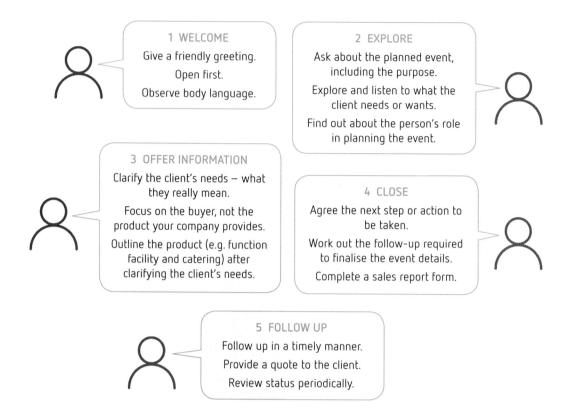

Completion of sales call reports is essential since face-to-face meetings are costly and business development managers need to show a return on the time invested. An example of a sales call report is illustrated in Figure 19.6.

Sales promotions

Sales promotions are intended to persuade a buyer to purchase immediately, so they often include incentives or discounts. Sales promotions may follow the introduction of a new product or may be implemented during a slow period. Examples of sales promotions include discounted event tickets, discounted off-season function facilities, incentive meeting packages, and newspaper or magazine competitions to win prizes such as tickets to a premiere. Giveaways would also fit into this category.

The Australasian Promotional Marketing Association provides a code of conduct for promotional activities, as well as advice to member organisations. For example, if a discount is available to only a limited number of customers, this should be clearly stated on all promotional material. In both Australia and New Zealand, gaming and trade practices Acts outline specific rules for promotions offering prizes.

FIGURE 19.6 Example of a sales call report form for meeting room/function bookings

SALES CALL REPORT

Event venue details

Name of representative _____

Date and time of sales call/client meeting _____

Client details

Name of client, department and address _____

_____

Contact person's name and position/role _____

Person responsible for bookings and their department (if not as above) _____

Sales and promotions information

Purpose and type of event _____

Types of rooms/facilities required _____

Other services_____

Number of guests/attendees _____

Specific entitlements or limitations (e.g. budget) _____

Other facilities currently used (competitors) _____

Opportunities for preferred supplier status (tendering) _____

Other needs (e.g. sales meetings, training sessions, conferences) _____

Outcomes of meeting _____

Action required _____

Promotional events and trade shows

Hotel groups, casinos, resorts and convention centres frequently exhibit at promotional events where they distribute information to potential buyers, particularly in the area of incentive travel. So, too, do suppliers to the event business, such as staging and rental companies, event software companies and event planners.

Issues to be considered when assessing whether to participate in promotional events or trade shows may include:

- consistency of the activity with the overall marketing direction of the organisation
- level of exposure to be achieved by attendance at an event, or sponsorship of an event
- matching of attendees to an organisation's target markets
- available financial resources
- human resource requirements
- timing of the activity or event
- social media.

UNDERTAKE A GENERAL PUBLIC RELATIONS ROLE

Public relations is stimulation of demand for a product or service by providing commercially significant news about the product or service in a published medium, or obtaining favourable editorial review in a medium, such as a newspaper, free of charge. The most commonly used form for public relations is the press release. Most major events have a press release page on their websites, although such releases would be sent primarily to specific contacts in the media. Editorial publicity in the form of an article or a story is highly sought after and valued. Of course, this is not completely free as there is a significant time cost involved in preparing and issuing press releases, following up journalists and producers by telephone, planning launches and so on. Thus, while there is no cost associated with the space allocated to the story, a public relations budget (in the form of human resource requirements or outsourced supplier fees) must be factored into the marketing budget.

Publicity for an event can be secured by running a careful publicity campaign with the media. Sometimes, photo opportunities and interviews with a spokesperson or celebrity will also be necessary to develop the feature.

There are different types of media materials:

1   backgrounder – providing general information about the event, history, previous success, etc.
2   press release – story, newsworthy information
3   media alert – invitation-style alert to the fact that the event is imminent.

There are several points of contact. In the print media, these include the editor, the feature writers, and the editors responsible for individual sections of the newspaper or magazine. In the broadcast media, the people to contact include the station manager, producer or news director who in turn provide the story to the news announcers and radio personalities. In each case, the first question asked will be 'What makes this event newsworthy?' and the answer to this must be clear.

The aim of a press release is to stimulate media interest in the event and thus achieve positive and cost-effective publicity. Many large event organisers post their press releases on their websites. For mega and hallmark events, a launch is usually held prior to the event to which the media and the stars of the show are invited. These occasions are used to distribute the press release. It is essential that a launch be well attended and that the media report the event in a positive way, otherwise it will be counterproductive. The launch must be staged for photo opportunities and interviews. In the case of smaller events, sending a press release to a local paper is generally the best option. Since the staff working on these smaller publications are extremely busy, it is advisable to provide them with a ready-to-go article, including quotes as well as photos and logos where possible. The example in Figure 19.7 is the sort of press release/article that would draw the attention of a local newspaper.

The following guidelines for preparing a press release will help to ensure that the reader sits up and takes notice:

* There must be something newsworthy to appeal to the reader in the first two sentences: he or she must be motivated to read the whole press release.
* All the facts must be covered: what, when, why and how. This is particularly the case for negative incidents. The reader wants to know what happened, when it happened, why it

FIGURE 19.7 Press release for a local newspaper

Media Release

WE HOST THE COUNTRY'S LARGEST CYCLE RACE

Thousands Pedal the Peninsula

This year's 54 km race will see 15 000 riders tackle the most scenic mountain and beachside race in the country. The race is the largest sporting event in the state and the largest bicycle race in the country. This indicates a trend towards competitive physical competition for all age groups and cycling is a popular choice. Contestants will be visiting from overseas countries including Japan, Korea, India and Holland. Some riders are fiercely competitive, while others ride as family groups. All age groups are represented, and last year's race was completed by an 84-year-old and his 7-year-old grandson. The race will raise funds for a community parkland project and will be run by 5 local clubs. An additional $3 million is the target for other deserving causes. To register for the event, contact Richard on 9879 6543 or register on-line at www.pedal.com.au.

happened and how things will be resolved. When something goes wrong, the facts are important because unsubstantiated opinion is dangerous. If the press release is promoting an event, all information such as the venue, date, time and so on should be included.

- The press release should be short and to the point.
- Layout should be professional.
- Contact details should be provided.
- Photographs should be captioned.
- Quotes from senior staff and stakeholders (including sponsors) must be included.
- If the press release is promoting an event, it should describe all potential benefits for the audience.
- An action ending for booking or registering should include all necessary information.
- The style of writing should be appropriate for the targeted publication.
- There should be no errors in grammar or spelling.

Apart from media attention, it is also possible to obtain exposure through a number of official tourism organisations. They provide tourist information to visitors through offices or websites at the State/Territory or national level. Brochures distributed to such offices or listings on their event calendars can provide valuable information to the potential (and sometimes very hard to reach) event audience. Every effort should be made to ensure that the event is listed as widely as possible.

The role of public relations is to manage the organisation's and the event's image in the mind of the audience and the public. This is mainly done through press releases as described above. These up-to-date information sources, together with photographs, provide the media with the background information they need to develop stories about the event. Media briefings can also be conducted before and during the event, particularly if high-profile people such as celebrities, entertainers and athletes can enhance the publicity.

One of the most critical public relations roles is to inform the media if there is a negative incident of any description. For this reason, an incident reporting system needs to be in place so that senior members of the event management team are fully informed, including the public relations manager, if this is a separate role. It may be necessary to write a press release or appear in an interview if such an incident occurs. In some situations it is essential to obtain legal advice regarding the wording used in the press release. The public relations role can be a highly sensitive one, and in some situations words need to be chosen carefully. A simple expression of regret, for example, would be more tactful than suggesting the cause of an accident before a thorough investigation or inquiry.

Another more positive public relations role is the entertainment of guests and VIPs attending the event, in some cases from other countries. In this public relations role you need to be:

- attentive to the needs and expectations of your guests
- mindful of their cultural expectations
- flexible in your response to their behaviour
- informative and helpful as a host
- proactive in designing hosting situations to meet the required protocol
- able to make easy conversation.

Particularly with overseas guests or guests of event sponsors, you need to know in advance who they are (official titles, correct names and correct pronunciation) and where they come from. Most importantly, you need to know the reason why your company is acting as a host to these guests, as often business objectives, such as sponsor product awareness or negotiations, are involved. Research is therefore essential to determine how to meet the needs of the guests and the expectations of, for example, the sponsors.

The effective multicultural host is able to:

- be respectful
- tolerate ambiguity
- relate well to people
- be non-judgemental
- personalise their observations (not make global assertions about people or places)
- show empathy
- be patient and persistent.

As you can see from the above, there are a number of roles for the public relations manager, or indeed for any member of the event team. The opportunity to sell an event occurs every time the telephone is answered or an inquiry is made by a potential customer. Customer relations becomes the role of everyone involved in an event and for this reason training in this area is recommended. This training should focus in particular on the event information likely to be requested by the customer, which is more difficult than it sounds since plans are often not finalised until very close to the event. Training ties in closely with the planning process, and the distribution of information to all concerned right up to the last minute is very important.

There are a number of situations in which an event manager might become involved in public relations, including:

- making travel arrangements by telephone or email
- meeting and greeting at the airport
- providing transport
- running meetings
- entertaining at meals

- entertaining at events
- providing tours and commentary.

If you had to lead a small group around a venue or an event, there are a number of additional recommendations:

- Plan the tour so that enough time is allocated to see everything.
- Advise your guests of your plan, however informal the group.
- Make sure that there is time for a break and refreshments.
- Provide maps so that people can get their bearings.
- Pause frequently so that the guests can ask questions.
- Be gracious – questions are never trivial or stupid.
- Make sure that everyone can see and hear.
- Treat everyone equally.
- Speak slowly and at an appropriate volume.
- Be patient and speak positively.
- Be flexible and change plans if necessary.
- Be attentive to fatigue or boredom and accelerate the tour if necessary.

In promoting an event, it is essential to analyse and understand the needs of the target market or markets. If, for example, one of the target markets was children aged eight to 12, it would be necessary to understand the motivations of this group and to match the product to these motivational needs. It would also be necessary to keep in mind that the person purchasing the product might not be the consumer – in this case it could be the parent, and promotional efforts would need to assist with decision-making processes within the family. Likewise, a sponsor might be making a substantial investment in the event, and might have general, as well as specific, expectations of the event, which might or might not be consistent with those of the event audience.

To summarise, the task of promoting an event to the optimal audience at the most beneficial time is the first challenge. The second is to meet the needs of all stakeholders and to maximise public relations benefits to the satisfaction of customers at all levels.

Create promotional action plans

Once the marketing and promotions strategy has been agreed, the following issues need to be considered when creating detailed plans for the various promotional activities outlined above:

- objectives and nature of the activity
- budget availability
- public relations implications
- staffing requirements and briefings
- availability of brochures and other promotional materials
- equipment requirements
- contracting of other services (e.g. app developer)
- strategies to ensure maximum benefits
- possible cooperative approaches (proactive or reactive)
- available technology
- potential e-commerce opportunities.

The promotional budget allocates funds to the various components of the promotional mix. This is illustrated for an event company in Figure 19.8.

FIGURE 19.8 Budget allocation to event company promotions

TYPE OF PROMOTION	TIMING	COST (INCLUDING PRODUCTION, MEDIA AND HR) $
Advertising		
Website management and search optimisation	Ongoing	2 700
Social media	Ongoing	2 200
Direct marketing		
Mailing list	Ongoing	450
Publicity/PR	Linked to key events (est. 4)	8 000
Trade exhibition	June	950
Sales promotion	August	810
Personal selling	Ongoing	21 000
Contingency		550
TOTAL		36 660

The promotional effort is often closely linked to ticket sales. Box office software enables the capture of information on peak booking periods, the profile of the audience, ticket yield, ticket sales in the various price ranges and group bookings, as well as providing addresses for direct marketing, allowing further promotions to be directed towards the areas of lowest sales.

For mega events, the postcodes of ticket holders are used to anticipate demand for public transport. Ticket sales can form the basis for domestic and international travel packages, including hotel accommodation and transportation. In some cases, large numbers of tickets are reserved for organising bodies and returned for sale if not utilised. The primary benefit associated with ticketing programs is the opportunity to manage cash flow. For events where tickets are sold only at the gate, it is impossible to monitor promotional efforts and extremely difficult to anticipate audience numbers, particularly if the event can be affected by inclement weather.

For an annual event, ticketing data – part of customer relationship management (CRM) – is a valuable source of information for planning subsequent years' events. The popularity of ticket grades, profiles of customers and timing of decision making are a few of the trends that can be monitored through ticket sale data.

Action plans at their most detailed look like Table 19.1, with specific social media platforms selected, the core message agreed and the posts planned and approved by the marketing team, together with any links. All that remains is for the plan to be put in place as scheduled.

TABLE 19.1 Outline for the social media plan

TUESDAY 24 MAY				
PLATFORM	TIME	MESSAGE	POST	LINK
Twitter	1 p.m.	Artist profile	Millie Marvel has joined our line-up	Photo Link to MM account
Instagram	3 p.m.	Change to line-up	New stage to expand local artist line-up	Photo

Crisis management

Crisis management is an important part of public relations planning for any event or organisation. Plans need to be prepared as a contingency measure to minimise the impact of any unfavourable press or respond to unforeseen operational issues (for example, shortages), major incidents, accidents and other crises.

Many things can go wrong and the media are ready and willing to report on interesting, dramatic, tragic and controversial stories. For mega events, the media may actually actively search for negative stories that would reflect poorly on the event organisers, sponsors and, in particular, the government bodies involved. These can range from stories about the mismanagement of the event (particularly about wasting public money) to stories about crowd misbehaviour. While most organisations cannot predict the exact nature of a crisis, it is useful to develop a communications strategy to match the most likely scenarios.

REVIEW AND REPORT ON MARKETING ACTIVITIES

All activities included in the promotional action plan must be able to be reviewed against agreed evaluation methods set during the planning stages. It is important to take 'learnings' from this review process to be incorporated into future planning to ensure that the most successful activities are used again, where appropriate, and activities that did not live up to expectations are either improved or avoided altogether in future planning.

Reports should be prepared according to organisation policy and within required timeframes so that those within the organisation are informed in a timely manner. They should assess activities against the marketing and promotional goals set at the planning stage.

Measures that can be used to evaluate the success of promotional activity may include:

- lift in customer inquiry levels
- lift in event ticket sales
- quality and quantity of media coverage
- level and quality of exposure to target market (percentage of target market present at promotional/sponsored event)
- consistency with the overall marketing direction of the organisation
- ability to meet set financial resources
- ability to meet set human resource requirements

- activity executed in the timeframe originally set
- results of event feedback forms or anecdotal feedback from key contacts/customers/ clients or organisational representatives.

Blythe (2010) suggests that trade shows often waste promotional effort due to their sales-led approaches. He suggests that exhibitors need to rethink their management of trade fairs in terms of communication models and focus on creating dialogue rather than using one-way communication processes.

As previously discussed in this chapter, market intelligence gathered as the basis of planning the marketing and promotions plan is a key step in the early preparation stages, and it is important that all market intelligence gathered is reported in a clear and concise way to those responsible for planning sales and marketing. Providing informal reports and updates to relevant colleagues also helps to maximise the likelihood that team targets will be met.

Summary

In this chapter we have dealt with event promotion in some detail, and have seen that branding or image is linked to the event purpose and theme, and that all of these aspects must be consistent and compatible in order to create the greatest impact on the consumer or event audience. There are many media options for advertising and these are often determined by the promotional budget available. Advertising and publicity need to be carefully planned to ensure the highest possible level of attendance at the event. We have also discussed the public relations role, communication with the media and other stakeholders being important during the planning phases and equally important when there are problems or incidents that threaten the success or reputation of the event. A more positive public relations role is the entertainment of guests and VIPs for which certain attributes are essential, including tolerance, patience, persistence, respectfulness, and an ability to relate well to people of all cultures.

Key term

Digital marketing   Marketing using digital channels, including social media and apps

REVIEW YOUR KNOWLEDGE

1   Explain the four Ps of marketing using event examples.
2   What is the difference between public relations and advertising?
3   What are the legal and ethical issues involved in marketing?
4   Explain, using examples, three forms of advertising.
5   Give guidelines for personal selling when providing a quote to a conference customer.
6   List five key elements of a good media release.
7   What is included in a promotional action plan?

APPLY YOUR KNOWLEDGE

Event brand congruence (fit) is essential, and several companies have taken this a step further by running events rather than sponsoring them. The case of Red Bull and its brand messaging is a case in point.

There are several academic papers listed at the end of the chapter and in Chapter 20 discussing the Red Bull case study. After reading these and accessing other online resources, explore the trend towards active participation of target groups in events. The trend is towards planned events for experiential marketing.

Harley-Davidson has approached you to write a report for them on this trend. They want to achieve the best possible outcomes and want your recommendations on whether they should sponsor events to run them as experiential marketing. List the pros and cons and provide a recommendation. Be sure to talk about ROI (return on investment).

CASE STUDY

PERTH FESTIVAL

We exist to enrich life through art.

Perth Festival has been disrupting and celebrating Perth and Western Australia for 65 years.

The Festival was born out of the University of Western Australia's annual summer school entertainment nights as a "festival for the people" on January 3, 1953.

Since then, Perth Festival has seeded and cultivated decades of cultural growth as the oldest arts festival in the Southern Hemisphere. It is Australia's premier curated multi-arts festival and one of the greatest in the world, known for commissioning major new works, celebrating the unique qualities of Perth and engaging diverse audiences.

At Festival time in Perth, there is no other place like this on Earth. For a few weeks every glorious summer, the best artists from Western Australia and the world stand shoulder to shoulder in creative unity with the community.

The Festival and its city share the most dynamic region in the world, the Indian Ocean Rim and East Asian time zone where more than 60% of the world's population lives.

Source: Perth Festival (2018). About Perth Festival.
https://www.perthfestival.com.au/about-us/aboutperth-festival

TASKS

1   Use the above information, and any other details you can find on the event website, to prepare the following materials:
    — content for a travel brochure that includes this festival
    — a backgrounder to explain the history of Perth Festival
    — a media release designed for a feature story
    — a list of media that could be used for promotion of this festival.
2   Develop two marketing activities for this festival that meet with the following criteria:
    — consistency with overall marketing direction
    — exposure that will be achieved, and target reach

- matching activities to target market
- cost-effectiveness of financial and human resources required to implement the activities
- timeframe for implementation.

Note: It is not necessary to contact the organisers to complete these tasks. There is sufficient information on the festival website.

Online resources

Visit **http://login.cengagebrain.com** and search for this book to access the study tools that come with your textbook.

References

Báez, A., & Devesa, M. (2014). Segmenting and profiling attendees of a film festival. *International Journal of Event and Festival Management*, 5(2), 96–115.

Blythe, J. (2010). Trade fairs as communication: a new model. *The Journal of Business & Industrial Marketing*, 25(1), 57–62.

Doran, G. T. (1981). There's a S.M.A.R.T. way to write management's goals and objectives. *Management Review*, 70, 35–6.

Drengner, J., Jahn, S., & Zanger, C. (2011). Measuring event–brand congruence. *Event Management*, 15(1), 25–36.

Gorse, S., Chadwick, S., & Burton, N. (2010). Entrepreneurship through sports marketing: A case analysis of Red Bull in sport. *Journal of Sponsorship*, 3(4), 348–57.

Miller, A. F., & Cunningham, J. A. (1981) How to avoid costly job mismatches. *Management Review*, 70(11), 29.

Websites

Australasian Promotional Products Association, **www.appa.com.au**

Destination Weddings, **www.destinationweddings.com/media/trendreport2016**

Event marketing strategy, **www.eventbrite.co.uk/blog/event-marketing-strategy-ds00**

How to use a marketing campaign to easily promote your next event, **www.shortstack.com/how-to-use-a-marketing-campaign-to-easily-promote-your-next-event**

How top music festivals use social media, **https://blog.hubspot.com/marketing/music-festivals-event-social-media**

OBTAIN AND MANAGE SPONSORSHIP

20

OVERVIEW

Sponsorship is often an essential requirement for an event to be financially viable. In this unit, we look at determining sponsorship requirements, sourcing and negotiating with potential sponsors, and then managing sponsorship arrangements during event execution. The fit between the sponsor and the event concept is a primary consideration, as the first question a potential sponsor asks is whether they will get a return on their investment. The level of negotiation and cooperation necessary to manage multiple sponsors (who sometimes have conflicting interests) is often underestimated.

LEARNING OBJECTIVES

On completion of this chapter, you will be able to:

1. determine sponsorship requirements and opportunities in consultation with colleagues and clients

2. source sponsorship, providing full costs and benefits, and negotiating/finalising contracts or agreements

3. service sponsors by monitoring and evaluating activities and maintaining effective communication with the sponsor.

INDUSTRY VIEWPOINT

It's been seven years since ANZ signed on to sponsor the Australian Open, and in that time the bank has gone from a logo to the tennis being one of its biggest marketing investments. The growth in the program has seen ANZ extend its offering beyond Australia and the Australian Open to China and the Shanghai Rolex Masters, with the tennis now being almost a year-round event for the bank.

ANZ has several different campaign aspects associated with the tennis, from a partnership with Novak Djokovic to its Hot Shots campaign for young up and coming tennis stars. The bank's general manager of marketing, Louise Eyres, wouldn't be led on the cost of ANZ's investment in the tennis, but she did say it was the bank's most significant investment to date, highlighting that it well and truly delivers in terms of ROI.

'Across Asia we're looking at a broadcast reach of 250 million through the tennis as a cumulative audience number. It's a significant reach for our brand; on that basis the investment is certainly warranted', Eyres says.

This year the brand has also launched a social campaign with Djokovic called #HeadbandForGood, which sees the bank donate $2 for every social post featuring a person wearing a tennis sweat band to World Vision. The bank has pledged to donate a maximum of $100000 for the campaign, with Eyres saying that ANZ will not struggle to hit that target.

Source: Homewood, S. (2016). ANZ embarks on 'most significant' investment in tennis ever. AdNews, 18 January. www.adnews.com.au/news/anz-embarks-on-most-significant-investment-in-tennis-ever

INTRODUCTION

As this extract illustrates, most large organisations have long-term strategic plans for sponsorship that are closely linked with their marketing plans. The concept of return on investment (ROI) is raised in this quote, as is the idea of corporate social responsibility (CSR), demonstrated by the program supporting World Vision. These will be discussed in more detail later in this chapter.

The 'fit' between a sponsor and an event is critical, which is discussed in the literature in terms of 'congruence' (Drengner, Jahn and Zanger, 2011). A sponsor seldom commits to an event on purely altruistic grounds. There is generally a motive, such as developing brand awareness in association with a particular product. For example, the sponsor will choose a sport that attracts an event audience that has the appropriate characteristics. This is why a beer company will select a sporting code (such as football) with a corresponding audience demographic, and a car manufacturer will choose another sporting code (such as rugby union) with a different demographic. The Red Bull approach involving the full integration of advertising into entertainment or sport is an innovative approach (Kunz, Elsässer and Santomier, 2016).

Inexperienced event organisers often assume that big companies will be generous with sponsorship for small events, and often the first step suggested by the committee is to contact corporations. Unfortunately, this seldom works because companies of this size already have well-established plans, with specific objectives to be achieved as part of their sponsorship deals. In fact, in most cases the outcome is a joint marketing effort by the sponsor and the event organiser. Most large organisations also have policies with regard to sponsorship and for this reason will reject a request from a fringe arts festival; for example, if this is not consistent with their marketing plan and policy to support a sporting code.

Many organisations have corporate charity partnerships as a means of achieving CSR goals, one example being the sponsorship of Merry Makers Australia, a dance troupe with intellectual or physical disabilities, ranging in age from six to 56. Festivals and events offer the opportunity for organisations to meet their CSR goals by establishing links with the local community. One legacy of the London Olympic Games was the outcome of volunteer training – transferable customer service skills. Similar legacies are expected to result from the Gold Coast 2018 Commonwealth Games.

If a straightforward donation, or patronage, is made to an event, without strings attached (no logo, publicity and so on), this is known as *philanthropy*. When seeking assistance for an event, it is important to identify whether the request is for a donation or a sponsorship arrangement. Sponsorship is defined as follows:

> A 'partnership' between an organisation and another organisation or event in which the sponsor publicly endorses an activity and ties its reputation with that of the organisation or event being sponsored.

> Source: Murdoch University

Sponsorship is a business relationship between a provider of funds, resources or services and an individual, event or organisation which offers in return some rights and association that may be used for commercial advantage.

> The key distinction between sponsorship and patronage is that no commercial advantage is sought or expected in return for the support of a patron.

> Source: BDS Sponsorship

With these definitions in mind, it is clear that any hint of poor media exposure (for example, drugs in sport, crowd safety issues) is likely to make the sponsor very edgy!

Potential sponsors may include:

- individuals
- private companies
- corporations
- government agencies
- industry associations
- educational institutions
- community organisations.

Sponsorship may cover:

- naming rights for events or event venues (e.g. Suncorp Stadium)
- media coverage (e.g. a particular channel always broadcasting a particular series or event creating viewer loyalty)

- staging or performances costs
- telecommunications expenses (e.g. providing communications equipment and service for the event)
- IT support (e.g. scoring, results processing)
- overall sponsorship of the event (e.g. agricultural conference sponsorship)
- physical items (e.g. satchels, prizes)
- food and beverage (e.g. morning and afternoon teas)
- travel for performers, artists or athletes
- entertainment (e.g. new talent)
- speaker sessions (e.g. supporting topical research such as salinity)
- ongoing organisational activities (e.g. annual publications)
- one-off promotional activities or projects.

However, planning a sponsorship program is not a haphazard process; it requires a targeted approach with specific outcomes for both the sponsor and the event organisation. Sponsorship arrangements can, in fact, make or break an event. The longevity of these arrangements is essential for success for both the event organiser and sponsor. Frequent changes, particularly with respect to event and stadium naming rights, simply confuse consumers.

Prior to the development of a sponsorship proposal it is useful to discuss the plan with the relevant industry sector. For example, consultation with the music or dance community could produce ideas and leads. Many associations have funding partnerships that support the sector.

EXTENSION ACTIVITY

Ausdance Queensland has a number of program partners listed on its website (http://ausdanceqld.org.au/funding-partners). If you were running an event involving contemporary dance, which of these partners would you select as the top five prospects for a sponsorship proposal?

The keys to successful sponsorship arrangements are communication and consultation. This occurs in three phases: prior to the event when the agreement is negotiated and confirmed; during the event when sponsors have high expectations of brand exposure; and post event when sponsors anticipate an evaluation of the program's success.

Potential sponsors and activities

Having targeted the appropriate organisations as potential sponsors, the package or 'sponsorship prospectus' needs to be finalised. A summary of the inclusions in one such package is shown in Figure 20.1 and illustrated in more detail later in the chapter, in the example titled 'Principal sponsorships'.

FIGURE 20.1 Sponsorship program

SPONSORSHIP BENEFITS	GOLD	SILVER	BRONZE
Naming rights	√		
Category exclusive rights	√		
Sponsor logo and link on home page	√		
Presentation opportunity	√		
Sponsor logo and link on sponsorship page of website	√	√	
Printed conference program and company profile	√	√	√
Logo on-screen during general session	√	√	√
Display table in foyer	√	√	

The opportunities provided to sponsors need to be mutually beneficial and expressed explicitly so that expectations can be realised. From the event organisation's perspective, the financial feasibility of the event is at risk if sponsorship is a major source of income. If this is the case, the sponsorship program is a high priority.

The first step in determining sponsorship requirements is to establish the amount of financial or other support needed. The second step is to identify items, activities or projects that may have sponsor appeal. Only then is it possible to identify potential sponsors for a particular activity and the fit with the sponsor organisation's profile.

DETERMINE SPONSORSHIP REQUIREMENTS AND OPPORTUNITIES

When approaching a potential sponsor, it is essential to address the motivational factor(s) that will spark the potential sponsor's interest. (This is particularly important when making an approach in writing.) Motives for sponsoring events fall into five major categories, as outlined below. Once the sponsor's motives have been clarified, it is then a matter of developing (where possible) measurable objectives, so that when the event is over the benefits of the sponsorship arrangement can be demonstrated.

Broad corporate and social objectives

Broad corporate and social objectives for a sponsor organisation include community involvement, promoting the organisation's image, and linking the company's image to success. Any change in audience attitude to corporate and social objectives of sponsors is, however, hard to measure. Public perception of an organisation shifts very slowly and it is difficult to evaluate this shift over a short time span. Qantas, for example, promotes its corporate image by linking advertising to sporting achievement and national pride, thus cementing its image as the national carrier. Other organisations prefer to support local rather than national events.

Product/brand-related objectives

Many sponsors use events to promote a product. Examples of products include airline travel, beer, wine and communications products. Examples of sponsoring organisations include Qantas, Heineken, Lion Nathan, Lindeman's and Telstra. They in turn may have a number of brands. For example, Lion Nathan has several brands in Australia: Toohey's New, Toohey's Extra Dry, XXXX Gold, Hahn Premium Light, Heineken, James Squire Golden Ale and Beck's. The organisation may choose a specific event to promote just one of its products. In many cases, the brand can be sampled at the event (especially beer at sporting matches), hopefully leading to higher brand awareness and strengthening brand preference.

Sponsors can achieve immediate online sales — 'see now, buy now'

Product sales objectives

Product sales objectives are far more specific, having to do with direct increases in sales of merchandise following the event (or, indeed, during the event). For example, many fashion shows offer the opportunity to buy online off the runway, the trend being 'see now, buy now'.

Business-to-business relationships can result from networking between a number of sponsors for a particular event, in turn leading to long-term benefits to all sponsor organisations in the alliance. Events such as the Olympic Games offer exclusive rights and all sponsors must work inclusively with other sponsors, using only their products and services.

Data capture is of significant benefit to sponsors of trade exhibitions and conferences because the contact information of all attendees is available to be used at a future date for direct mail purposes.

Media coverage

Gaining media exposure is one of the most obvious objectives of sponsors. Who has not seen the winning team's captain put on a cap featuring the sponsor logo before being congratulated on prime-time television and thanking the sponsor in front of hundreds of thousands of television viewers? There are many ways in which the sponsor organisation can gain media coverage before, during and after the event. Outdoor advertising, publicity activities, branded clothing items and extensive signage are all part of this package. Events also provide exceptional content for sponsor digital media channels.

Shutterstock.com / K2 Images

Corporate hospitality

Hospitality (in the form of corporate boxes) is often a key element of a sponsorship package. The guests are generally current or prospective clients who are entertained during the event. In some cases, the hospitality is also provided to key staff as an incentive for good performance.

SOURCE SPONSORSHIP

According to Philanthropy Australia (2017), businesses may give money, goods and services – usually 66 per cent, 17 per cent and 18 per cent, respectively. In 2015–16, businesses gave $17.5 billion, comprising $7.7 billion in community partnerships, $6.2 billion in donations and $3.6 billion in non-commercial sponsorships. In the commercial sponsorship arena, figures are hard to come by, but *Marketing magazine* (2014) puts the value of Australian sports sponsorship at $774 million and New Zealand's at NZ$182 million.

A sponsorship proposal should outline the benefits to the sponsor and associated costs. Once a sponsor indicates interest in the proposal, a period of negotiation generally ensues. It is important to note that the timelines for sponsorship negotiation are generally significant. Three to five years should be allowed for locking in a major sponsor and, during this time, frequent contact should be made with the potential sponsor to maintain their interest in the proposal. Agreement to the sponsorship concludes with the signing of a written contract, including full details of the commitment made by both parties.

Finalisation of the sponsorship agreement has to occur before any of the following can be planned and implemented:

- printing brochures and posters
- developing a website
- ticketing
- merchandising
- signage.

Sponsorship may include sponsorship packages, value-in-kind sponsorship and/or naming rights. These are outlined below.

Sponsorship packages

The following example illustrates the ways in which sponsorship packages can be developed to meet the needs of different types of sponsor, with several levels of sponsorship. For small events, there is often only one type of sponsorship or one sponsor.

PRINCIPAL SPONSORSHIPS

Diamond & Government Agency Sponsor

The Diamond & Government Agency sponsor is the highest level of sponsorship and will receive an outstanding level of exposure through the event. The Diamond Package includes sponsorship of:

National conference dinner – This event provides an ideal networking opportunity and provides a high level of exposure. Conference dinner tickets are much sought after by both delegates and non-delegates alike. The conference dinner will be held on the evening of Wednesday 25 July at Frasers State Reception Centre in Kings Park, Perth overlooking the Swan River and CBD. Delegates will attend the dinner and partners are welcome. The evening will also include after-dinner entertainment.

Major Sponsorships

These sponsorships provide opportunities for exposure in the lead-up to the conference through recognition in the monthly newsletter and website, and during the conference. In addition the Major Sponsorship packages provide complimentary or discounted trade-booths and conference registrations.

Gold Sponsor

The Gold Sponsor is the key private sector or local government sponsor for the Conference and will receive a very high level of exposure throughout the event. The Gold Package includes sponsorship of:

Welcome cocktail reception – The cocktail party represents one of the premier events of the conference. As the opening event, it has traditionally attracted eminent local dignitaries and political leaders to senior officials of State and Local Government. The Welcome Cocktail Reception will be held on Tuesday 24 July commencing at 5:30 pm and running through until 8 pm.

Conference handbook – Each delegate will be provided with a Conference Handbook outlining the program of speakers, paper/presentation abstracts and a page for delegate notes. The Conference Handbook sponsorship is an excellent opportunity to have your company logo and/or key message prominently displayed on every notes page within the handbook.

Silver Sponsor

The Silver Sponsor packages provide value for money with high levels of exposure. The Silver Sponsor is provided with a number of opportunities to attract potential clients and demonstrate skills and experience. The Silver Package includes sponsorship of:

Conference luncheon – The stand-up luncheon will be held on Wednesday 25 July and will be attended by all delegates.

Source: Australian Institute of Traffic Planning and Management (2018). AITPM National Traffic and Transport Conference 2018: Sponsorship and exhibition prospectus. p. 5. https://www.aitpm.com.au/national-conference-2018/

Value-in-kind sponsorship

In the examples illustrated so far, sponsors were asked to make a cash contribution. In many cases, however, sponsorship is provided as 'value in kind'. This means that the sponsor provides its goods and services free as part of the sponsorship arrangement. For example, air travel could be sponsored by Virgin Blue, vehicles provided by Holden and advertising could be underwritten by Fairfax Publications. A value is placed on this contribution and this value must be reflected in the event budget even though there is no cash contribution.

Naming rights

The primary sponsor of an event is often able to obtain naming rights; for example, Mercedes-Benz Fashion Week Australia, Billabong Pipe Masters, and Gatorade Triathlon Series.

In some cases, sponsors negotiate naming rights for event venues or facilities, such as Etihad Stadium in Melbourne, ANZ Stadium in Sydney, and the Pepsi Center in Denver. These are generally long-term strategic agreements with associated sponsor benefits such as tickets, hospitality, parking and so on. The exposure of the sponsor's name in all media communications in relation to the facility is a key element of this negotiation.

Contractual arrangements

Event sponsorship contracts and agreements have inclusions similar to those mentioned in Chapter 17. In summary, there are several elements:

- *parties* – these are the event organisation (or venue) and the sponsoring organisation
- *term* – this is the duration of the contract, ideally a lengthy fixed term
- *termination* – what happens if the contract is breached by either party
- *fees* – whether fees are paid upfront, in instalments, or linked to incentives such as attendance figures
- *obligations* – clarification of responsibilities on both sides
- *force majeure* – unforeseen event beyond control
- *insurance* – appropriate insurance, including public and product liability if relevant.

As mentioned previously, the contract can include specifications as appendices such as the sponsorship prospectus.

SERVICE SPONSORS

Sponsorship often plays a crucial part in an event and therefore sponsors need to be 'massaged' by event management throughout the entire process leading to the performance – and beyond. Issues that sometimes arise include ambush marketing, incompatibility between sponsors, or a sense of inequity in the profile achieved by other sponsors. In this last situation, one sponsor may feel that its company profile has been eclipsed by another because it has achieved more air time or its signage was of superior quality. Sponsors can become quite competitive, insisting that one or other has been given higher exposure, a more prominent logo, a taller flag and so on. Logos must also be handled with care by the event coordinator with regard to correct reproduction in terms of colour and style, as there have been many occasions when a whole production run of T-shirts, banners and posters has had to be written off due to sponsor complaints. When sponsor logos are used in any public arena, a sign-off by the sponsor is an essential procedure.

Sponsors are always concerned about ambush marketing, which can occur when competitors muscle in on the media attention gained by the event. This may happen if T-shirts with a competitor's logos are distributed free or body paint is used to achieve similar exposure. Picture if you can the blue and red colours of cola products and the potential for ambush marketing.

Incompatibility between sponsors is another issue, although it is fairly obvious that an approach would never be made to more than one organisation in a particular product category: never two beer companies, two soft-drink companies or two breakfast cereal brands. Since some of these organisations are major conglomerates with many products and many brands, this can be a minefield only avoided if the organisation and its products are carefully researched prior to negotiation. 'Who are the other sponsors?' is one of the first questions asked of the event manager. Sponsors want to be associated with appropriate partners, and this includes the event company as well as other sponsors. Athletes, models, actors and performers also have their own sponsors and they may not be compatible with the sponsors of the event. Rules about exhibiting logos and promoting competing sponsors must be very clear. For example, a competitor logo cannot appear in the event precinct, particularly if worn by a high-profile celebrity.

Monitor arrangements

Ongoing evaluation of the sponsorship arrangements is essential. For most large events there is a dedicated sponsorship manager to look after these sometimes temperamental partners. They can be demanding, and often the minor sponsors expect outcomes beyond their original brief. This delicate balancing act can be managed well if sponsorship documentation is maintained throughout. This includes:

* agreed contract with detailed specifications
* activity reports and schedules
* financial records
* minutes of meetings
* records of correspondence and agreements.

Finally, sponsors want to be associated with success. Any hint of failure in the press causes major consternation. This can result from the cancellation of acts, ticketing problems, accidents on-site and other unforeseen problems that can crop up. For this reason, a risk management plan in relation to sponsorship is essential, with contingencies in place for every eventuality.

Evaluate sponsorship

Evaluation is an essential component of the sponsorship arrangement. For a contract to be renewed, there must be demonstrable gains made by the sponsorship organisation. These are measured in terms of the sponsorship objectives discussed earlier. Figure 20.2 shows the process for sponsorship planning and evaluation. Unless evaluation in its various forms is carried out, it is impossible to demonstrate the success or otherwise of the sponsorship arrangement after the event. A warm glow is not enough to convince future sponsors that the event can produce tangible marketing benefits.

There are numerous measures of sponsorship evaluation, including:

- value of 'free' editorial media exposure (measured as hits or minutes × advertising rates)
- column centimetres in the press (publicity)
- geographic scope of media reach (number and location of media exposures, such as five country radio stations)
- social media likes and other digital metrics
- consumption of sponsor's products at the event
- purchase of sponsor merchandise such as caps and T-shirts
- spectator figures
- spectator demographics
- sponsor name recall surveys
- product awareness surveys
- alliance with other sponsors (value of business generated)
- increased product sales post-event
- success of hospitality provided
- analysis of corporate image (need pre- and post-event surveys).

Sales of merchandise can be a most effective form of measurement, providing that good estimates of sales are made beforehand. Merchandise is becoming increasingly popular with event spectators and audiences – the event audience wants a tangible reminder of their event experience. Big shows sell bags, cups, soft toys, caps, pens, posters and any number of other products. At sports events people buy hats, T-shirts, pins and stickers. However, these are generally beyond the scope of smaller events. For many events in the small to mid-sized range, sponsorship is one of the largest risk factors regarding the financial outcome of the event, even if the target is break-even.

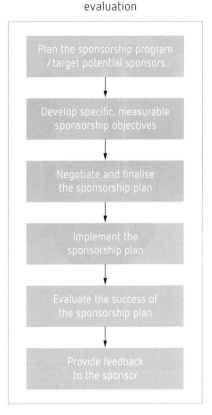

FIGURE 20.2 Process of sponsorship planning and evaluation

Plan the sponsorship program /target potential sponsors

Develop specific, measurable sponsorship objectives

Negotiate and finalise the sponsorship plan

Implement the sponsorship plan

Evaluate the success of the sponsorship plan

Provide feedback to the sponsor

Sports merchandise

Brand recall or awareness are other measures used in evaluating sponsorship; however, some studies have looked at 'congruence' between the brand and the individual's profile or event personality (Close, Krishen & Latour, 2009; Lee & Cho, 2009). The Lee and Cho study showed that the personality congruence between the sponsoring brand and the sporting event was the most significant attitude predictor towards the sponsoring brand. In other words, those individuals whose 'personality' matched the brand image were most likely to have a positive attitude towards the brand. However, for marketing purposes, more than a positive attitude towards a product or brand is needed: the positive attitude has to be converted to a purchase action. The impact of event sponsorship on brand use is hard to predict as there are so many variables involved in the purchase decision. The consumer process can be summarised in this way: sponsor awareness → sponsor attitudinal response → decision to purchase → purchase action.

Research is generally undertaken by a professional market research organisation in order to produce reliable and valid statistical information for reporting. Research consultants Sweeney Sports conduct regular surveys to provide information to sports sponsors.

Event organisations must ask:

* Are we giving sponsors what they want?
* Are they getting value for their investment?
* Are we managing the relationship well?

Sponsors can withdraw funding if they do not perceive value for their investment or if they are not managed well. Ongoing attention must be paid to this important aspect of event management, with a proactive approach being taken to managing these important stakeholder relationships. Maestas (2009) highlights the importance of these measurements: **return on investment (ROI)** and **return on objectives (ROO)**. The first measures the direct relationship between sponsorship and product sales or company profits. The second measures performance against objectives, such as sponsor recall or Internet search hits. In both cases, plans need to be made and implemented to obtain the data necessary to make these evaluations.

Return on investment (ROI)
Return on an investment in financial terms

Return on objectives (ROO)
Return on objectives such as brand recognition

Grohs and Reisinger's (2014) research suggests that image improvement is the most important company objective. They hypothesise that this is more complex than one would expect and suggest that sponsor image has several drivers, as illustrated in Figure 20.3.

One thing is certain. In past decades, sponsors were satisfied with measures of brand recognition. These days they demand a return on investment, with a trend towards event-based experiential marketing. For a critical review of this field, see Schmitt and Zarantonello (2013). **Experiential marketing**, engagement marketing and participation marketing all refer to marketing initiatives that actively engage participants. An example would be a track day event for potential buyers to experience driving a new-model sports car. The other major trend is engagement via digital media. Messaging prior to and after the event can lead to longer-term engagement with the audience and thus sponsor product consumers, leading to more 'followers' for the brand.

| Experiential marketing |
| Active participation in a marketing initiative |

FIGURE 20.3 Sponsor image formation

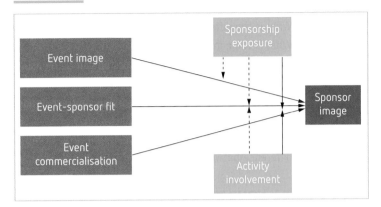

Event image – consumer perceptions of the event and its associations

Event sponsor fit – attributes of product overlap with attributes of event, such as motor racing, or product is sold at the event

Event commercialisation – some event audiences respond negatively to perceived overcommercialisation

Sponsorship exposure – amount of time the audience is exposed to sponsor message, especially in the media

Activity involvement – consumer involvement is active (activity-based) as opposed to passive

Source: Grohs, R., & Reisinger, H. (2014). Sponsorship effects on brand image: The role of exposure and activity involvement. *Journal of Business Research*, 67(5). p. 1019.

Summary

Sponsorship is a partnership arrangement between the event organiser and the sponsor organisation, usually formalised in a legal contract. Developing marketing and publicity objectives as part of the sponsorship plan provides the opportunity to evaluate the success of the event from the sponsor's perspective. This is essential for maintaining ongoing relationships with primary and secondary sponsors from one event to the next. As we have seen in this chapter, all parties have expectations of these relationships and they need to be clarified before operational planning begins. Staff need to be briefed about sponsorship arrangements, and activities (for example, hospitality, signage, merchandising) must be organised in accordance with sponsorship agreements. Every opportunity to enhance the value to the sponsor/s should be taken and every effort must be made to keep sponsors involved and up-to-date with ongoing plans.

Key terms

Experiential marketing	Active participation in a marketing initiative
Return on investment (ROI)	Return on an investment in financial terms
Return on objectives (ROO)	Return on objectives such as brand recognition

REVIEW YOUR KNOWLEDGE

1 What is the difference between sponsorship and philanthropy?
2 What is value in kind (VIK)?
3 Explain how the impact of sponsorship can be measured.
4 What is ambush marketing?
5 What are the features of a sponsorship contract or agreement?
6 How do you manage sponsor expectations?
7 Sponsors look for a return on investment (ROI) or return on objectives (ROO). What is the difference between the two?

APPLY YOUR KNOWLEDGE

1 Visit the websites of two major organisations to find out about their sponsorship arrangements. Then explain how the sponsorship arrangements meet their corporate objectives.
2 Review the sponsorship agreement provided online with the text or any other online resource and explain the following contractual terms:
   - in-kind support
   - intellectual property
   - insurance
   - hospitality, in the context of sports sponsorship.

CASE STUDY

SEEKING SPONSORSHIP

You have just been appointed sponsorship manager of a four-wheel-drive motor show. In addition to exhibitors, there is a range of other organisations that may wish to be associated with the show, such as camping, clothing and wine companies.

TASKS

1 Develop a sponsorship package for various types of sponsor.
2 Identify 10 potential sponsors as targets.
3 For one potential sponsor, explain why they may be motivated to enter into this arrangement.
   - Write a letter of introduction to send with your sponsorship proposal.
   - Clearly explain the costs and benefits.
   - Identify which areas are open to negotiation in the agreement.
   - Develop a sponsorship pitch, including a presentation and print material.

Online resources

CENGAGE

Visit **http://login.cengagebrain.com** and search for this book to access the study tools that come with your textbook.

References

Close, A., Krishen, A., & Latour, M. (2009). This event is me! How consumer event self-congruity leverages sponsorship. *Journal of Advertising Research*, 49(3), 271–84.

Drengner, J., Jahn, S., & Zanger, C. (2011). Measuring event–brand congruence. *Event Management*, 15(1), 25–36.

Grohs, R., & Reisinger, H. (2014). Sponsorship effects on brand image: The role of exposure and activity involvement. *Journal of Business Research*, 67(5), 1018–25.

Kunz, R., Elsässer, F., & Santomier, J. (2016). Sport-related branded entertainment: The Red Bull phenomenon. *Sport, Business and Management: An International Journal*, 6(5), 520–41.

Lee, H., & Cho, C. (2009). The matching effect of brand and sporting event personality: Sponsorship implications. *Journal of Sport Management*, 23(1), 41–64.

Maestas, A. (2009). Guide to sponsorship return on investment. *Journal of Sponsorship*, 3(1), 98–102.

Marketing (2014). Good sports sponsorships: industry trends, best practice and risk management. 28 July. www.marketingmag.com.au/news-c/good-sports-sponsorships-industry-trends-best-practice-and-risk-management

Philanthropy Australia (2017). Fast facts and statistics on giving in Australia. www.philanthropy.org.au/tools-resources/fast-facts-and-stats

Schmitt, B., & Zarantonello, L. (2013). Consumer experience and experiential marketing: A critical review. *Review of Marketing Research*, 10, 25–61.

Websites

How to get event sponsors, www.activenetwork.com.au/event-management-resources/articles/how-to-get-sponsors-for-an-event.htm

McDonald's Australia – sponsorship, https://mcdonalds.com.au/learn/responsibility/maccas-community/get-sponsored

Sports sponsorship report, www.imrpublications.com/newsdetails.aspx?nid=44

The new rules of event sponsorship, www.eventbrite.com.au/blog/free-download-new-rules-event-sponsorship-dsOd

Write a letter requesting sponsorship, www.wikihow.com/Write-a-Letter-Requesting-Sponsorship

EVENT BUDGETS AND FINANCE

21

PREPARE AND MONITOR BUDGETS

OVERVIEW

This chapter covers the key managerial skills of analysing financial information to inform budget development, then drafting a budget and monitoring budget performance over time. As the event business or event project needs to be financially viable, this involves detailed research with respect to expenses such as venue hire and staffing, and of course income. Event income can come from a variety of sources, including ticket sales and sponsorship. Cash flow is often a concern, which needs to be addressed in the planning stage. Whether break-even or profit is the objective, good financial management will ensure that the event is sustainable over time. Events that fail often do so for financial reasons.

LEARNING OBJECTIVES

On completion of this chapter, you will be able to:

1. prepare budget information, analysing internal and external factors that impact on budget
2. prepare a budget based on estimates of income and expenditure using valid, reliable and relevant information
3. finalise a budget following the negotiation and confirmation of supply contracts
4. monitor and review a budget to assess actual performance against estimates and prepare accurate financial reports.

INDUSTRY VIEWPOINT

Funding for WA's biggest regional literary event

The Liberal National Government has signed a three-year deal to sponsor Western Australia's biggest regional literature event – the Margaret River Readers and Writers Festival. Premier and Tourism Minister Colin Barnett said the three-day event would attract poets, authors, playwrights, journalists, comedians, illustrators, magazine editors, screen writers and radio hosts.

'The event will not only promote literature but also the extraordinary Margaret River region, helping to raise its profile as a destination for the arts', Mr Barnett said. 'Since its inception in 2009, the event has grown from 600 attendees to now attracting about 5000 people. The funding will help the festival secure high profile internationally renowned authors and increase its marketing to attract an even greater attendance over the next three years.'

Source: Western Australian Government (2016). Funding for WA's biggest regional literary event. Press release, 29 November. https://news.wa.gov.au/funding-for-was-biggest-regional-literary-event/

https://www.mediastatements.wa.gov.au/Pages/Barnett/2016/11/Funding-for-WAs-biggest-regional-literary-event.aspx

INTRODUCTION

Many events are dependent on funding from government bodies as one source of income. A total contribution of $80 million to the Margaret River Readers and Writers Festival from Royalties for Regions, through the Regional Events Program, is expected to bring significant economic, social and cultural benefits, potentially engendering higher levels of tourism visitation in the area, which in turn creates positive direct and indirect economic impacts in the region. According to Litvin (2013), 'festivals and special events should consider growing their events such that they attract new monies to the community, putting heads in beds and generating revenue for tourism providers and other merchants across the local economy' (p. 184). Government funding for cultural and sporting events also has a positive social impact. For example, the Significant Sporting Events Program, a Victorian Government initiative, is designed to assist in attracting international sporting events to the State.

As explained in previous chapters, event organisations fit into two key categories: for-profit and not-for-profit. A for-profit event is planned with a margin in mind in order to achieve a return on investment. However, a not-for-profit organisation has to budget just as carefully as a for-profit business, as it is essential that it covers all or most of its costs. Suppliers also expect a mark-up, except for charitable and other not-for-profit events, for which they might provide goods and services at cost.

Event budgets differ in other significant ways. Some event budgets, such as those illustrated in Figure 21.8 and Figure 21.9 at the end of the chapter, are for a single event. The budget template provided at the end of this chapter and on the website for this text is also for a single event, something we call a short-life or project organisation. Budgets are also developed by long-life event organisations, such as event suppliers of goods (stage rentals) and services (audiovisual support) and conference and exhibition centres, which run events almost on a daily basis. Long-life event organisations need to develop more-traditional budgets such as sales budgets, departmental budgets and cash flow forecasts. Reviews are then conducted on a weekly or monthly basis to check performance against the annual budget.

A conference and exhibition centre is a venue and charges for space and services. It manages the budget for the operation of the venue. A professional conference organiser (PCO) or exhibition organiser manages the event budget for a conference or exhibition held at the venue, and the client manages the budget for its organisation. This is illustrated in Figure 21.1. The interrelationship between these stakeholders on financial matters highlights the importance of ongoing communication between the parties.

FIGURE 21.1 Three interrelated budgets

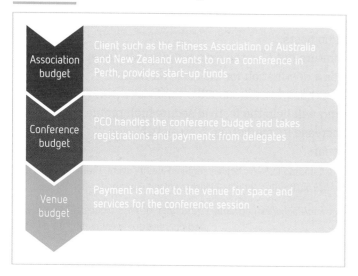

Not all events have profit or break-even in mind; they can have other non-financial objectives. For example, a promotion for a new product, such as a brand of perfume, would be part of a marketing initiative, with the expectation being a long-term return through product sales. Similarly, a company awards ceremony or incentive event might be paid for by the organisation with the expectation that this would lead to increased employee motivation. In some cases, the company expects a return on objectives (ROO) rather than a return on investment (ROI). These objectives are often marketing objectives where the event's purpose is to communicate several messages to the audience. In all cases, it is essential that the contracted event company has a clear idea of the financial and other objectives of the client, which may be a business, a government agency, or an individual.

According to Goldblatt (2010), there are three categories of event budgets:

1   profit-oriented events where revenue exceeds expenses (e.g. ticketed events)
2   break-even events where revenue is equal to expenses (e.g. community events)
3   hosted events where the client meets the cost of the event (e.g. product launch, 21st birthday party).

Financial objectives

The first step in the financial management of an event is to ask the following questions.

Is the aim to make a profit?

As explained above, many events have a range of objectives that do not include making a profit. For example, street parades or music festivals may be offered to the public free of charge, the expenses being met by government agencies and/or sponsors. Or goods and services are provided by businesses and individuals to assist in the running of an event, thus making it difficult to accurately estimate the actual costs. However, it is still essential that all other expenses are properly approved and documented.

Where the objective of an event is raising money for charity, a target needs to be set and, once again, both the expenses and the funds raised need to be accounted for correctly.

How much will the event cost?

In the example of the fundraising event above, as indeed for any non-profit event, it is important to estimate how much the event will cost as well as to keep track of the actual expenses incurred. With every event, money changing hands must be properly documented and, in most cases, the financial records should be audited. Expenses, or costs, include fees, hire costs, advertising, insurance and so on.

What are the revenue sources?

Generally, revenue is raised by selling tickets or charging admission or registration fees. Merchandise sales also contribute to revenue. Merchandising items, such as T-shirts and caps, may be sold by the event organiser or under arrangement with retailers whereby the event organiser earns a percentage of any sales. The same arrangement may occur with food and beverage sales.

How many tickets must be sold to break even?

This is a critical question. In essence, it relates to whether you decide on a large venue, large audience and low price, or a small venue, small audience and high price. This will be discussed in more detail later in this chapter.

What is the cash flow situation?

Events are fairly unique in that, for many, revenue comes in only on the day of the event. This means that all costs, such as salaries, office expenses and fees, have to be met up-front from existing funds. When ticket sales occur long before an event is staged, as they do with major concerts, this puts the company in the enviable position of being able to pay for its expenses from revenue while also earning interest on this money until the remaining bills become due. Very few events fit this category. Cash flow planning is an essential part of the event planning process for the above-mentioned reasons.

What control systems are needed to avoid fraud?

All businesses are accountable and systems need to be put in place to ensure that moneys are accounted for. Systems and procedures are needed

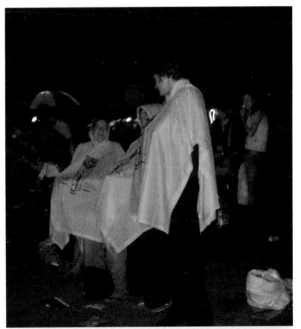

Ten thousand emergency ponchos may be required for an outdoor event and should be included in the budget unless the supplier will take returns; if sold, the margins could be high

Equipment rental – a common expense item for events

so that every transaction is recorded and all expenditure approved, including payment of invoices, cash payments, tax and so on. Cash management systems for the day of the event are often lacking and it is not uncommon for registers to be left open, for staff to take handfuls of change without substituting notes, and for bags of cash to be left lying around. This is clearly unsatisfactory.

How will legal and taxation obligations be met?

Employing the services of a properly qualified accountant will ensure that your organisation maintains accurate records and meets its legal obligations.

Budget terminology and formats

Almost everyone understands the three concepts of income, expense and budget because most people use them in their daily lives. Simply, income is money that comes in, expense is money that goes out, and a budget is a plan to ensure that expenses aren't higher than income. Cash flow management is ensuring that you always have enough money to pay the big bills like car insurance when they come in.

Running a financially viable event business with the ever-increasing challenges of the current business environment is not easy. These challenges include competition, economic uncertainty, increased government regulation and continuous change. In this context, it is imperative that today's event managers have an understanding of finance and management accounting. Effective operational management, marketing management and human resource management generally ensure excellent service, quality and the other attributes of a successful business. However, sound financial management is necessary to ensure financial viability, which is the key to the success and longevity of a business. A manager who has an understanding of accounting and finance is better equipped to make management decisions based on objective data. Accounting and finance are important to every business, regardless of its nature.

The first chapter in this text highlighted some of the key differences between events, event organisations and more-traditional long-life businesses. Understanding these differences is important as some events are one-off or annual activities and therefore from an accounting point of view are treated more as *projects* than ongoing business concerns. However, for other event operations, such as staging rental companies, wedding planners and conference organisers, the business is an *ongoing concern*, with multiple events and activities occurring on a daily and annual basis. This type of event business looks much like any other business in any other sector.

Usually, non-accountants struggle to understand what figures mean. But, as mentioned earlier, to run any event or event business, an understanding of the key accounting concepts is essential, as is an ability to interpret this financial information. First, we will discuss the types of budget, and then the main concepts you need to understand to be able to read an income statement.

Types of budget

Different types of budget were mentioned in Chapter 8, including:

- sales budgets
- departmental budgets
- event/project budgets
- purchasing budgets
- wage budgets
- cash flow budgets
- whole-of-organisation budgets.

In the rest of the chapter, we will focus mainly on event/project budgets and cash flow. Any event business that runs multiple events such as a function centre would work in a similar way to most conventional businesses.

Income statement

An income statement (previously known as a profit and loss statement) is a summary of an organisation's revenue, expenditure, gross profit and net profit (or net loss) for a specific period.

Profit

Profit is the positive gain from a business operation after subtracting all expenses from the income. Profit is what most businesses are trying to achieve. However, in the event industry there are two types of organisation: for-profit and not-for-profit. The first of these expects income to exceed expenses, thus making a profit, to be regarded as successful, while the second aims to break even, or simply meet expenses.

The event manager also needs to be aware of a rather unique concept relevant to the industry. This is value in kind (VIK), also known as 'assistance in kind'. This relates to contributions made by individuals and organisations to support an event. These contributions are not cash and are not purchased by the event organiser; they are goods or services provided free of charge as value in kind. At charity auctions, for example, many of the items are contributed by celebrities, businesses and other supporters of the event.

KEY TERMS

Accounting	The systematic recording, reporting and analysis of financial transactions of a business
Cash flow	Cash received minus cash payments over a given period of time
Expense	Any cost of doing business
Finance	Put simply finance deals with matters related to money; financial management has the aim of managing money well
Income	Also called revenue; basically, money earned
Profit	The positive gain from a business operation (or specific event) after subtracting all expenses from the income; the opposite of loss
Sales	Income received for the accounting period

EXAMPLE

From an accounting perspective, the event organiser needs to place a value on such contributions so that the financial records give an accurate portrayal of the success or otherwise of the event.

Income accounts

Income is revenue earned by the organisation, but also includes grants, donations and so on as discussed above. For most events, income comes from the client (for example, the parents of the bride) or from ticket sales. Sponsorship comes either in the form of cash or as VIK.

Typical income accounts for a small event organisation might include:

- sales revenue (from ticket sales and so on)
- grants
- donations
- rentals
- value in kind.

Adding them together yields *gross revenue.*

Expense accounts

Most companies have a separate account for each type of expense they incur. Typical expense accounts include:

- salaries and wages
- advertising
- telephone
- interest paid
- electricity and gas utilities
- rent paid
- equipment hire paid.

So profit is the difference between the income of the business and all its costs/expenses. It is normally measured over a period of time.

Profit = Income − Expenses

For events that run as a one-off affair, this is adequate for the income statement. In a perfect world, the income statement would match the budget. The budget is the plan, and if everything went to plan this would be reflected in the income statement.

In the event industry, the budget is generally prepared before the event and the income statement afterwards, while in most ongoing business operations, budgets and income statements are done regularly and routinely.

Turning to conventional layouts for reporting revenue and expenses, particularly for events businesses that are ongoing concerns, we need to look at some additional concepts, those of gross revenue (all sources of income), gross profit and net profit.

On the income statement, the most important source of revenue, such as sales of tickets, appears as the first item. If the event is paid for by a single client, this will be the first item as it is the predominant source of revenue. Gross revenue is the total revenue before any costs have been deducted. This is a similar concept to gross (not unpleasant) wages – the amount you would receive if there weren't all sorts of deductions such as tax before it reached your pocket.

If you deduct the direct costs (also known as cost of goods sold) from the gross revenue, you get the gross profit. If the gross revenue from an event were $750 000 and direct costs of $520 000 were deducted, this would result in a gross profit of $230 000. Cost of goods sold covers those costs which relate directly to the revenue earned. They might include cost of venue hire, labour and equipment rental. After calculating the gross profit, you would then deduct your overheads, such as administration costs and rent costs, of, say, $165 000, and you would be left with an operating profit of $65 000. Finally, your net profit is your profit after all other costs (such as interest paid) and tax would be deducted, giving you your net profit, in this case $41 000. This is illustrated in Figure 21.2.

FIGURE 21.2 Income statement

Income Statement as at 30 June 20XX		
Gross revenue	$750 000	
Less cost of goods sold	$520 000	
Gross profit		$230 000
Less adminstrative and other overhead costs	$165 000	
Operating profit		$65 000
Less other income expenses (such as interest)	$6 000	
Profit before tax		$59 000
Less tax	$18 000	
Net profit for the year/event		$41 000

To summarise, gross profit takes into account the direct costs of sales, while net profit is the bottom line.

Gross profit

As we have seen, gross profit is the difference between *sales income* and the *direct costs* of the product. (In the event business, the product is the 'show' or other event such as a surf carnival.) Gross profit is used as a performance indicator to help the business make decisions on its pricing policies. For example, sales income would be ticket sales, and direct costs would be the cost of performers, staging and venue. Thus, the most likely costs to appear as direct costs would be:

- venue rental or site costs
- performance costs (e.g. staging)
- event operational costs (e.g. food and beverage)
- talent costs (e.g. speaker, band, players).

Food and beverage costs relate directly to the numbers attending an event

Net profit

Net profit represents gross profit less all expenses associated with the normal running of the business. Net profit shows how well the business performs under its normal trading circumstances. Normal *running costs* for an event business generally include administration and office expenses, as well as advertising, as the key expenses.

Therefore, when producing an income statement, the headings would be:

> *Sales income*
> *Less cost of sales*
> *GROSS PROFIT*
> *Less administrative and other overhead costs*
> *NET PROFIT*

Figure 21.3 shows these terms for a normal business on the left and an event 'translation' on the right.

FIGURE 21.3 Illustration of net profit

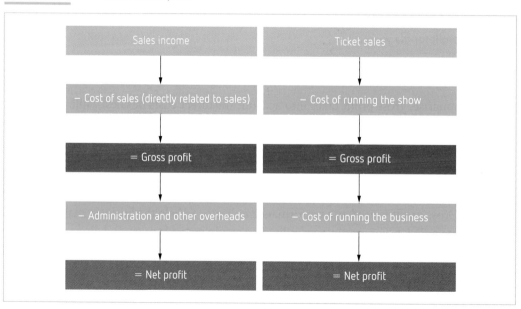

Having dealt with the idea of 'in', 'out' and what is left over, 'profit', let us move on to another way to look at the financial status of a business. Here we take into account assets (things of value) and liabilities (usually bank loans or other debts).

EXAMPLE

KEY TERMS

Physical assets   Items of value, such as property and equipment

**Intangible
assets**   Something of value that cannot be physically touched, such as an event
concept, brand, franchise or reputation (opposite of tangible assets). When a
business is sold, this is sometimes known as 'good will'

Debts   Money owed

Liabilities   Amounts owed by a business to its creditors; the debts of the business

Owner's equity   The net worth of the company; also called owner's capital. Equity comes from
investment in the business by the owners, plus accumulated net profits of the
business that have not been paid out to the owners

Balance sheet

If only life were so easy – now there are assets and liabilities to consider. An event company
might own a vehicle and a store full of staging equipment. These items are assets as they have
a value. On the other hand, the company might also have liabilities. These are amounts owed
by the company (such as bank loans).

While the income statement (or statement of financial performance) captures results for
a given period, such as a financial year, the balance sheet (or statement of financial position)
gives you an idea of what a business is worth at a certain point in time. Where the owners of
the business have acquired assets (for example, sound and lighting equipment), this becomes
very relevant; likewise if there are outstanding bills to be paid. The balance sheet shows what
the result would be if all bills were paid and everything were sold (assets minus liabilities).
This result is the owner's equity in the business:

$Assets - Liabilities = Owner's\ equity$

The problem for many event management businesses is that many of their assets, such as
their reputation, are intangible and difficult to value!

Figure 21.4 illustrates the concept of owner's equity for a normal business on the left, with
another event 'translation' on the right. Generally, of course, the assets and liabilities are listed
in detail. However, as mentioned previously,
an event business is quite different from most
others as it is service oriented and doesn't
carry stock as does, for example, a fashion
boutique. Consequently, reporting is simpler
as the owner generally has little equity. Assets
and liabilities are often minimal for event
businesses run by professional conference
organisers or party planners, for example.

Equipped with a good understanding
of these important financial concepts,
the research and negotiation involved in
preparing budgets can begin.

FIGURE 21.4 Illustration of owner's equity

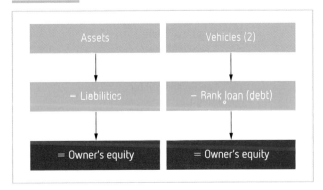

PREPARE BUDGET INFORMATION

Preparing a budget is part of the initial planning stage for any event. A budget includes projected revenue and expenditure from which an estimate of the net profit (or sometimes net loss) for the proposed event can be ascertained. It is a plan based on accurate quotes from all contractors and suppliers and careful research to ensure that no expenses have been overlooked. It provides guidelines for approving expenditure and ensuring that the financial aspects of the event remain on track. The budget is part of the event proposal or the basis of the quote by the event management company to the client.

An example of an event budget is provided in Figure 21.5. This budget illustrates the difference between fixed costs (administration and overheads) and variable costs (those

FIGURE 21.5 Budget items for a music event

Fixed Costs

Venue hire
Artists
   Speaker
   Actor/scriptwriter
   Singer/composer
   Choreographer
   Technical director
   Set designer
   Make-up designer
   Props designer
Production Team
   Stage manager
   Asst stage manager
   Asst technical
Costumes
   T-shirts @ $ (+10% extreme sizes)
Sound
   Copyright
   Hire
Lights
Vision (for presentation and speaker)
   Based on powerpoint presentation and video
   Preparation of visuals
Staging
   Preparation of production detail
   Set backdrop, paints etc.
   Props materials
   Expendables
   Posters for theatre × 6
   Props
   Laptop and printer
Printing
   Individual group labels
   Invitations
   Programs—shell plus insert
   Reviews
Onsite staff (catering)
Other hire (catering)
Gifts
Photography (digital camera)

Video recording
   Video camera hire
   Tapes
Set-up/dismantle
Freight
Airfares
   SYD−AKL return × 1
   SYD−AKL return × 1 (bus.class)
   SYD−MEL return × 5 @ $
Transfers
   Airport
   Coach—Hotel−theatre−hotel
   Coach—Office−theatre−office
   Coach—Airport−theatre−hotel
Accommodation and meals
   AKL 2 × 2 days
   MEL 4 × 2 days, 1 × 1 day
Miscellaneous
   Phone, fax, courier estimate
Contingency
Management fee

Total Fixed Costs

Variable Costs

Catering
   Coffee on arrival   @ $
   Morning tea with muffins   @ $
   Lunch—working type   @ $
   Afternoon tea   @ $
   Pre-show canapé and buffet dinner   @ $
   Beverage   @ $
   Total $ per head
   Breakfast for interstate arrivals 15   @ $

Total Variable Costs

Total Each Location

GRAND TOTAL

Source: Reproduced with permission of Events Unlimited

directly related to the number of customers; for example, catering costs), which vary in relation to the size of the audience.

The following factors also need to be taken into account when preparing budgets.

Internal and external factors

During initial budget discussions, these internal and external factors need to be considered and clarified:

- organisational and management restructures
- organisational objectives
- new legislation or regulations
- growth or decline in economic conditions
- supplier availability
- significant price movement for certain goods or services
- shift in market trends
- scope of the project
- venue availability and cost
- human resource requirements.

Consider the organisational objectives and human resource requirements for the Surry Hills Festival, which is staged annually in inner-city Sydney. With 60 000 attendees each year, the organisation of an event of this scale is a complex process which needs to start at least a year in advance. Particularly since the non-profit festival aims to raise funds for local community programs, its success relies heavily on volunteers and with only a handful of employees to act as Festival Directors. Several hundred community volunteers are enlisted for all aspects of the event, including fundraising, art and décor installation, running public workshops and tours, and talented live performers. The implications from a budget perspective are immediately obvious: the budget for this event would be largely built from VIK contributions and donations.

By contrast, it appears that nothing comes free in the wedding business. A few years ago, *Choice* magazine reported that soon-to-be married couples were paying a premium for their venue and services; in one case, the venue charged double for a wedding!

HERE COMES THE BRIDE: AND UP GOES THE PRICE

Mention the word 'wedding' and events can cost you more. A CHOICE undercover shadow shop has revealed that if you mention the word 'wedding' when booking an event more than half of the venues and suppliers will charge more than for an identical birthday event. CHOICE sought quotes from 60 reception venues, cake makers, hire car businesses, entertainments, florists and photographers in Sydney and Melbourne. One shopper asked for prices for her wedding and another for her 40th birthday. Both events had the same number of guests and identical

EXAMPLE

requirements in terms of cars, cakes, flowers, photographers, entertainment and venue. All the venues, bar two, wanted extra for the nuptials with one Melbourne business wanting to charge almost double.

Photographers were told shots were only needed at the reception centre. Of the ten approached five charged a higher rate for the wedding. One asked for $2200 extra. Seven of the ten hire car businesses quoted more for the wedding. Two Sydney operators upped the ante by 54%. Six of the ten DJs did likewise with one quoting 87% extra for the wedding.

Suppliers said that the demanding nature of weddings and 'sky-high' expectations meant higher costs and justified the more expensive quotes. The average cost of a wedding in 2008 was $33 349, with Australian couples expected to spend a collective $3.7 billion on their big days in 2009.

Source: Choice (2009). Here comes the bride: And up goes the price. Press release, 11 December.

Management fees

In many cases, an event organiser charges a management fee to oversee an event. As a ballpark figure for planning purposes, this is generally in the region of 10–15 per cent of total costs. While an event might have a low budget, it might still require considerable time and effort in its organisation and the lower end of the range, 10 per cent, would simply not cover management costs. In this case, or in the case of smaller projects, clients can be billed on a per-hour fee basis. In a fiercely competitive environment, there may be situations in which the event planner may look at business as a short-term opportunity with long-term gain.

Prior to contracts being signed, the event organiser should work out the tasks involved in the event, allocate staff to the various roles and determine their pay rates – plus on-costs such as superannuation, workers compensation insurance, payroll tax, and sick leave and annual leave (for permanent employees) – in order to come up with a more accurate estimate of management costs and therefore the management fee to be charged. In some situations, the event organiser might wish to involve themselves in a collaborative entrepreneurial arrangement with the client whereby the management fee is based on income earned or sponsorship raised.

If a management fee is charged, the client is usually responsible for all pre-event payments to venues and subcontractors. The fee is for the management and coordination of the event by the event organisers, and for their expertise, from concept through to execution. By charging a management fee only (and not assuming financial risk), the event organiser is to some degree at arm's length. This in turn is linked to other risks, such as public liability risk. Since many events are structured with cascading responsibility through many layers of client, contractor and subcontractor, it is essential that all these contractual relationships are clear, including financial and legal responsibilities at each level.

Contingencies

Most event budgets include a contingency for unexpected expenses. This ranges from 5 per cent of the costs (if the event organiser is confident that the costs are controllable) to 10 per cent (if there are a number of unknown variables or the costs are uncertain).

PREPARE THE BUDGET

The budgeting process is as follows:

1   Draft the budget, based on analysis of all available information, ensuring that income and expenditure estimates are clearly identified and supported by valid, reliable and relevant information.
2   Analyse the internal and external environments for potential impacts on the budget.
3   Assess and present alternative approaches to the budget.
4   Ensure that the draft budget accurately reflects event/business objectives.
5   Circulate the draft budget to colleagues for comment and discussion.
6   Negotiate the budget with all relevant stakeholders, including the client where relevant.
7   Agree and incorporate modifications to the budget.
8   Complete the final budget in the required format within the designated time.
9   Inform colleagues of final budget decisions and ramifications in a timely manner.
10 Review budget regularly to assess performance against estimates.
11 Analyse and investigate deviations (variances).
12 Collect information for future budget preparation.

Break-even point

To work out the break-even point, the event organiser has to estimate the number of tickets that need to be sold in order to meet expenses (see Figure 21.6). These expenses include both fixed costs and variable costs. Fixed costs, such as licensing fees, insurance, administrative costs, rental of office space, advertising costs and fees paid to artists, generally do not vary if the size of the event audience increases and are often called overheads. Variable costs increase as the size of the audience increases. If food and beverage were part of, say, a conference package, clearly these costs would escalate if the numbers attending the conference increased. Once the total revenue is the same as the total expenditure (fixed and variable), then the break-even point has been reached. Beyond it, the event is profitable.

FIGURE 21.6 Break-even point

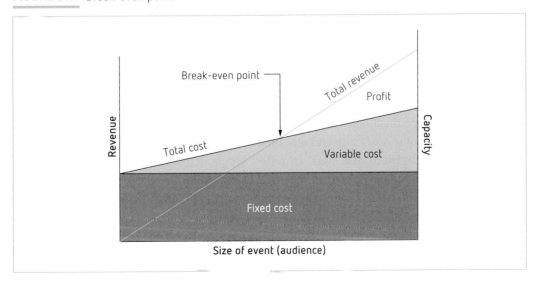

In the case of an exhibition, the organiser would be using the budget to establish how many exhibitors were needed to break even. The price charged for exhibiting could clearly be quite low if there were a lot of exhibitors; the price charged would have to be high if there were few exhibitors and if the aim were to meet the budget (particularly for fixed costs). However, this is not an altogether feasible way of setting prices or fees since there is a maximum price the market will bear and a minimum level at which the event becomes viable. This iterative process of analysing ticket prices or fees charged and the break-even point is part of the financial decision-making process.

Income strategy

Income strategy is a most complex issue for both large and small events. Even the smallest school fete committee wonders whether to charge an entry fee at the gate, and how much, to meet all the costs of running the event, and whether to allow stall holders and ride operators to charge individually and then to take a commission from these operators.

Event income can come from the following sources:
- entry tickets
- rental for stalls, stands and exhibitors
- merchandise sales (hats, t-shirts and so on)
- licensing
- sale of programs
- sale of food and beverage
- sponsorship or grants
- parking fees.

Licensing the sale of products can be a major source of income. When, for example, there is significant demand for merchandise associated with a major event (such as the FIFA World Cup, Le Tour de France or *The Lion King*), an agreement may be reached with another organisation to manufacture and sell products such as toys, clothing, pins and souvenirs. This licensing arrangement will include a royalty for use of logos, names and images of the event on specific products, and the products will often be sold in retail outlets outside the event precinct, such as Kmart, as well as at the event. Each item sold will attract a royalty payment for the event organising body.

Food and beverage items are often sold by concessionaires who pay a retainer to the event organiser or client to operate on the event premises and sell at the event. This arrangement is also common for bars and coffee stalls.

Ticket pricing

All sources of income must be factored in when making a decision on ticket prices. Clearly, the higher the level of sponsorship and other income, the lower the ticket price.

Ticket pricing decisions also need to reflect the anticipated size of the audience, the potential for different pricing levels (for example, seating allocations), the price the audience will bear, the opportunity for last-minute discounting, and many other factors. The logistics of ticketing include printing, distribution, collection and reconciliation, which all have implications for cash flow. A ticketing agency charges a commission on sales and distribution; however, pre-event ticketing does provide a source of cash when it is most needed.

Ticket sales and distribution on the day of an event can be problematic in terms of service and safety if not managed well – crowds forming at an entrance and long queues are to be avoided at all costs.

In addition to the numbering of tickets and development of an interval pass system, the event organiser needs to consider the logistics of delivering cash for change and banking large amounts of money (often necessary when banks are shut) at the close of the event.

FINALISE THE BUDGET

Once the budget has been negotiated and approved, it needs to be monitored on an ongoing basis to see whether forecasts were accurate. Modifications may be necessary and these should be carefully documented, particularly if the client is paying the bills.

Management accounting refers to the establishment of the budget, while cost accounting (part of management accounting) refers to establishing the actual cost of operations. Management accounting also involves analysis of variance: that is, areas in which there is a variance between the budget and the actual cost. In the organic event environment (in which every hour brings a new idea – more lights, better sound, bigger stage), it is difficult to manage the budget. Every change requested needs new agreement and this should be done in writing. The formal processes (approvals) involved here depend on the nature of the event and the financial arrangements. As with the management structure, the financial structure of a large event can be very complex, involving, for example, promoter, venue, sponsors and suppliers.

Software solutions

There are numerous event software packages available (see the websites listed at the end of the chapter). While Excel is suitable for small events, these software packages offer a number of advantages, the most useful being the integration of all event planning from registration through to execution and evaluation of the event. Figure 21.7 shows the features of event management software.

FIGURE 21.7 Features of event management software

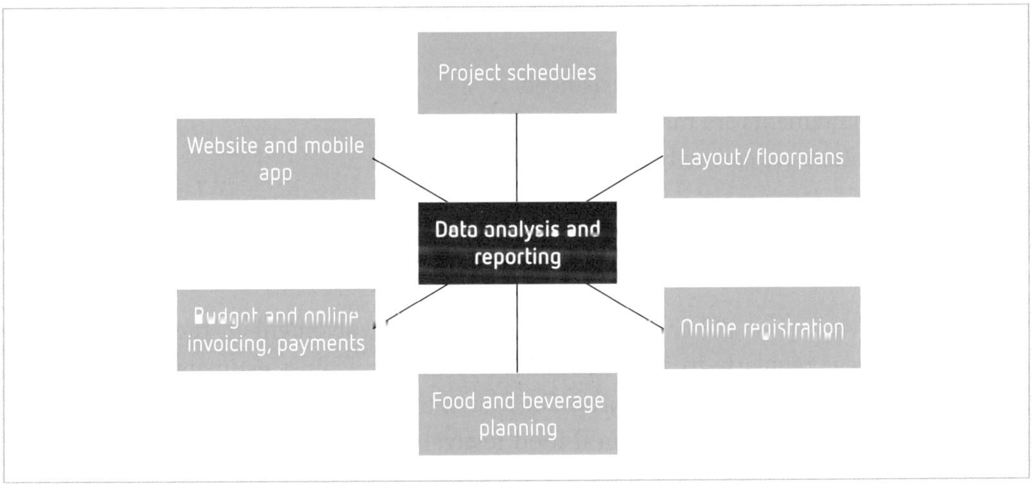

What are the software features that you would be looking for if corporate events were your core business? Visit this website for some ideas: www.cvent.com/au/event-management-software

Panic payments

This unusual accounting term is not exclusive to the event industry, but this industry is one in which inflated panic prices are often paid. In an ideal world, the event manager has all the quotes sewn up and the budget locked in long before the event. There should be few unforeseen contingencies – but don't forget this line in your budgets!

In reality, Murphy's law dictates that something will always go wrong. And the closer it is to the event, the more difficult it is to negotiate a reasonable price for what you require to put it right. In fact, if it is a last-minute crisis, it could easily lead to a high premium price – a panic payment. Essentially, the supplier has the event manager over a barrel. Careful planning, budgeting and detailed contracts negotiated well in advance can prevent this situation occurring.

Financial control systems

All purchases must be approved and usually a requisition form is used for this purpose. This means that the manager has the opportunity to approve costs incurred by employees. Once goods are ordered, or services provided, checks must be made that they meet specifications before the bills are paid. Fraud could occur if an employee had authority to make purchases, record and physically handle the goods, and pay the bills. This is why these roles are usually carried out by different people. In any case, the system should have checks and balances to make sure that:

- purchases or other expenses are approved
- goods and services meet specifications
- payment is approved
- accounts are paid
- incoming revenue is checked and banked
- revenue totals are recorded correctly
- debts are met
- all transactions are recorded and balanced
- taxation requirements are met
- financial matters are correctly reported to stakeholders.

MONITOR AND REVIEW THE BUDGET

As mentioned earlier, all stakeholders with a financial involvement in the event need to review the budget regularly to assess actual performance against estimated performance and to prepare accurate financial reports. The first of these steps is illustrated in the budgets for a family fun day and a multicultural food festival in Figures 21.8 and 21.9. In both of these, the difference between budget and actual expenditure is shown. As you can see from

Figure 21.8, an essential item for NAIDOC week, a flag, was not included in the original budget and for some reason catering costs were not considered in the planning stages either. Fortunately, savings were achieved in some other areas.

FIGURE 21.8 Budget items for a family fun day

NAIDOC Week Family Fun Day

EXPENDITURE		BUDGET $	ACTUAL $
Promotion			
	Promotion	2 500.00	103.50
	Flyer Print (9000)	1 000.00	928.00
	Roadside Signage—Design and Print	400.00	90.00
	Flags (Indigenous)	–	159.00
	Flyer Delivery	390.00	375.00
		4 290.00	1 655.50
Catering			
	Biodegradable Cups	–	473.00
	Luncheon and Consumables	–	883.00
			1 356.00
Infrastructure			
	Cool Room	250.00	–
	Stage/Stage Cover	4 600.00	4 273.00
	Chairs/Tables/Marquees	250.00	6 718.00
	Flag Poles	275.00	364.00
	Generators/DBs/Cables	350.00	1 567.50
	Mini Skip	243.00	182.00
	Rubbish Pickup	–	126.50
	Chemical Toilets	900.00	1 038.00
	Barrier Tape/Gloves	–	91.70
		6 868.00	14 360.70
Entertainment			
	Face Painting	–	800.00
	Performers (DJ, NSA, Bassonovas)	2 392.00	1 254.55
		2 392.00	2 054.55
Day Labour			
	Security Staff (× 2)	500.00	1 660.00
	First Aid	200.00	540.00
	Council Labour (P&G)	600.00	233.25
	Event Assistance	750.00	600.00
	Parking Coordination	500.00	–
	Cleaning (Toilets)	200.00	80.00
	Cleaning—Grounds	200.00	120.00
	Contingency	1 000.00	180.00
	Photographer	500.00	200.00
		4 450.00	3 613.25
TOTAL EXPENSES		18 000.00	23 040.00
INCOME		BUDGET	ACTUAL
Council Contribution			
	Budget Allocation	15 170.00	19 202.00
Grants and Sponsorship			
	Lotterywest		805.00
	Healthway	2 000.00	2 000.00
Other Income			
	Stallholder Fees	830.00	1 033.00
TOTAL INCOME		18 000.00	23 040.00

Source: © Town of Bassendean

FIGURE 21.9 Budget items for a multicultural food festival

MULTICULTURAL FOOD FESTIVAL 2009

EXPENDITURE		BUDGET $	ACTUAL $
Promotion	PR Activities	2 000.00	2 140.00
	Brochure	1 000.00	928.00
	Brochure—Distribution	400.00	285.00
	Signage—Roadside	400.00	451.00
	Fireworks Notification	60.00	
		3 860.00	3 804.00
Infrastructure	Tables/Chairs/Marquees	2 800.00	4 500.00
	Generators/DBs/Cables	1 500.00	1 788.00
	Lighting Towers	1 000.00	840.00
	Cool Rooms	300.00	240.00
	Chemical Toilets	2 000.00	920.00
	Sound/Stage/Stage Cover/Op	8 500.00	7 600.00
	Bulk Bin	360.00	265.00
	Dance Floor		1 295.00
	Wheelie Bins	300.00	182.50
	Two-way Radio Hire		256.00
		16 760.00	17 886.50
Entertainment	Performers' Fees	5 000.00	4 910.00
	Community Art Project	2 000.00	3 500.00
	Activities	–	–
	MC	300.00	400.00
	A Kickett—Welcome to Country	0.00	300.00
		7 300.00	9 110.00
Day Labour	SES—Excl. Zone and torches	–	–
	Cleaning—Toilets	250.00	250.00
	Cleaning—Grounds	300.00	300.00
	First Aid	400.00	325.00
	Security	3 000.00	1 599.50
	Parking Coordination— Jnr Footy	700.00	700.00
	Council (P&G/Leisure)	750.00	500.00
		5 400.00	3 596.00
Other	Food Vouchers	200.00	200.00
	Contingency	655.00	0.00
	APRA Licence	125.00	125.00
	Photography	200.00	200.00
		1 180.00	525.00
TOTAL EXPENSES		34 500.00	34 796.50

INCOME		BUDGET	ACTUAL
Council Contribution			
	Budget Allocation	27 950.00	29 167.00
Grants and Sponsorship			
	Lotterywest	5 000.00	5 000.00
Other Income			
	Site Fees	1 200.00	465.00
	Parking Income	350.00	164.00
TOTAL INCOME		34 500.00	34 796.00

Financial reports may include periodic reports showing budget versus year-to-date, actuals and financial commitments, periodic sales reports, taxation commitments, and funding acquittals in relation to grants received. Fundraising and charitable events are required to maintain accurate records of their financial affairs and in some cases these records are audited. Post-event, a report needs to be prepared showing actual income and expenditure against the budget.

Most accounting concepts, such as income, expense and profit, are easy to understand. But in business money does not generally change hands immediately as accounts operate on a 30-, 60- or even 90-day credit cycle. So at any one time a business owes money for goods and services that have been purchased, and is also owed money for goods and services it has sold. Unless creditors are carefully monitored, cash flow problems will inevitably occur. And unless a close watch is kept on income and expenses, the result could be a loss to the business.

Summary

This chapter has covered the important subject of preparing and monitoring budgets. We have learnt that the budget developed prior to an event must anticipate all revenue and expenditure and that steps should be taken to finalise contracts as early as possible to ensure that expenses do not exceed budget forecasts. The event manager also needs to take into account the cash flow situation in the lead-up to an event since most expenses occur early in the planning process, while the bulk of the revenue is generally collected close to, or during, the event. In this chapter we have also emphasised the importance of financial control systems for managing expenditure. Reporting systems need to be in place so that complete and accurate records are available for the final post-event report.

REVIEW YOUR KNOWLEDGE

1 Describe the three categories of event budgets using event examples:
    − profit-oriented
    − break-even (not-for-profil)
    − invitation, client-sponsored event.
2 Explain these internal and external factors that impact on budget development:
    − economic conditions
    − human resources requirements
    − legislation or regulation
    − price movement or seasonality
    − borrowing conditions.

3   In order to prepare a budget, you need to do your research. Explain the following sources of research information:
    −   competitors
    −   suppliers
    −   stakeholders
    −   historical data
    −   grants, VIK support,

4   List and explain three possible revenue sources for a festival.

5   What is a management fee?

6   What is a budget contingency?

7   Describe the budgeting process.

8   Use a diagram to illustrate and explain the concepts of:
    −   variable costs
    −   fixed costs
    −   break-even point.

9   Your business has been retained to stage the end-of-season celebration for the local softball association. It is to be held on grand final night, to celebrate the participation of players in the sport. It has been decided to hire the ballroom at the Sea Rider Hotel, which is in the heartland of the association's catchment area, at a cost of $1000. The association has requested a theme of 'Denim and Diamonds' to celebrate the tough game and environment, and the primarily female participation. It is expected that the decoration of the ballroom will cost approximately $2500 and that the entertainment will be a Mobidisk hooked into the ballroom's sound system at a cost of $1250. The event should break even if sufficient funding is raised via entrance fees to cover the hire of the room, the decoration, entertainment and a reasonable food/wine package at a cost of $25 per head. It is expected that approximately 300 players, officials and partners will attend the event.

    Establish (a) the break-even selling price; and (b) the selling price if the following event wanted to make a profit of $5000 to fund the purchase of new equipment for the association.

APPLY YOUR KNOWLEDGE

Prepare a budget for a sporting event using the following template (also available as an Excel file on the text website or online), which is used when applying for grants up to $15 000. You can add or delete items as required, depending on your event concept. Once completed, write a report explaining the concept and budget to the event committee.

Budget summary grants up to $15 000

EVENT NAME:	
EVENT DATE:	

Please Attach to Application Form
All figures are to be GST Exclusive
Do not include proposed Major and Regional Event sponsorship in this budget

INCOME

Item	Description	Cash ($)	In-Kind ($)
I-1	Federal Government Sponsorship Funding or Underwriting		
I-2	State Government Sponsorship Funding or Underwriting		
I-3	Local Government Sponsorship Funding or Underwriting (excluding Sunshine Coast)		
I-4	Sponsorships		
I-5	Ticket Sales		
I-6	Merchandising		
I-7	Other Income		
I	**TOTAL INCOME (Items I-1 to I-7)**	$0	$0

EXPENDITURE

Administration

Item	Description	Cash ($)	In-Kind ($)
A-1	General Administration		
A-2	Insurances — General & Event		
A-3	Travel & Accommodation		
A-4	Salaries & Fees		
A-5	Other Administration Expenses		
A	**TOTAL ADMIN EXPENDITURE (Items A-1 to A-5)**	$0	$0

Event Expenses

Item	Description	Cash ($)	In-Kind ($)
E-1	Event Evaluation/Bid Costs		
E-2	Sanction Fees		
E-3	Facility/Venue		
E-4	Ceremonies		
E-5	Entertainment		
E-6	Other Production Costs		
E-7	Merchandising		
E-8	Travel, Accommodation & Services		
E-9	Communication		
E-10	Ticketing Production		
E-11	Other Event Expenses		
E	**TOTAL EVENT EXPENDITURE (Items E1-E11)**	$0	$0

Marketing & Promotion Expenses

Item	Description	Cash ($)	In-Kind ($)
M-1	Marketing/Advertising		
M-2	Promotions		
M-3	Other Marketing & Promotional Expenses		
M	**TOTAL MARKETING EXPENDITURE (Items M1-M3)**	$0	$0

W	**TOTAL EXPENDITURE (ITEMS A + E + M)**	$0	$0
X	ADD CONTINGENCY (5% OF TOTAL EXPENDITURE)	$0	NA
Y	TOTAL EXPENDITURE + CONTINGENCY (ITEM W + ITEM X)	$0	NA
Z	OPERATING SURPLUS / (DEFICIT) (ITEM I - ITEM Y)	$0	NA

Source: Sunshine Coast Council (2017). Major and regional events sponsorship program: Budget summary – section B up to $15 000. https://d1j8a4bqwzee3.cloudfront.net/~/media/Corporate/Documents/Business/Major%20Events%20Sponsorship/section_b_budget_up_to_15k_2017.xls?la=en

CASE STUDY

EVENT PROPOSALS

Your event business, Rave Reviews, has the opportunity to quote for two major parties. Having experienced some financial difficulties in your first year of operation, you want to ensure that you choose the most feasible of these for which to prepare a proposal and produce the winning quote.

The first party is for a top celebrity and will be held at her waterside mansion. The party will be outdoors and the brief is to transform the garden through the use of a spectacular theme. The party will be attended by 350 guests and a lavish dinner is expected.

The second party is much larger – 500–600 people will be invited. A company is giving the party to celebrate its 50th year of tractor and farming equipment operations. The party will be held in a large airport hangar in the country. The food will be pretty basic and alcohol will be plentiful. Décor is not important, but entertainment is.

TASK

Discuss which of these two events you would choose in terms of its ease of financial management and its potential profitability, supporting your discussion with a detailed analysis of the internal and external factors taken into account, and developing a high-level draft budget for each. In your analysis, consider the financial risks associated with each event.

Online resources

Visit http://login.cengagebrain.com and search for this book to access the study tools that come with your textbook.

References

Goldblatt, J. J. (2010). *Special Events: A New Generation and the Next Frontier* (vol. 13). Hoboken, NJ: John Wiley & Sons.

Litvin, S. W. (2013). Festivals and special events: Making the investment. *International Journal of Culture, Tourism and Hospitality Research*, 7(2), 184–7.

Websites

Cvent event budget software, www.cvent.com/en/event-management-software/event-budget-management.shtml

etouches event software, www.etouches.com/event-software/module/eBudget

How to create a winning event plan, www.eventbrite.co.uk/blog/event-plan-and-template-ds00

How to get your event budget planning right, www.eventbrite.co.uk/blog/event-budget-planning

Special event budget worksheet, www.specialolympics.bc.ca/sites/default/files/Event_Budget_Worksheet.xlsx

Sunshine Coast Council, major and regional events sponsorship program, including budget templates, www.sunshinecoast.qld.gov.au/Business/Major-Regional-Sponsorship-Program

EVENT WORKFORCE

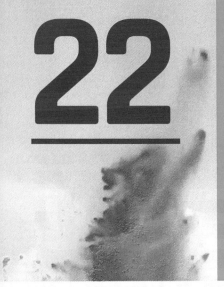

22

RECRUIT, SELECT AND INDUCT STAFF

OVERVIEW

This chapter describes the skills and knowledge required to recruit, select and induct staff and volunteers within the framework of existing human or staffing resource plans or policies. It requires the application of significant planning and organisational skills combined with sound knowledge of current recruitment, selection and induction practices. The chapter also applies to the process of volunteer management, including confirming need, establishing the recruitment program and monitoring implementation. With the complex nature of the event workforce in mind, this phase of managing people is challenging and critical to the success of the event program.

LEARNING OBJECTIVES

On completion of this chapter, you will be able to:

1 identify recruitment needs based on service and efficiency levels required by the organisation in line with goals and objectives

2 administer recruitment by placing advertisements or planning other methods to attract applicants to apply

3 select staff and volunteers based on clear selection criteria and an equitable selection process

4 plan and organise induction programs covering all organisational requirements, including WHS.

INDUSTRY VIEWPOINT

Two key questions guided our analysis of the planning and organization of a mega event – the Olympic Games in London 2012 – as a large-scale project. First we were interested in how the huge temporary organizations set up exclusively for these Games manage to mobilize the resources – particularly the knowledge and capabilities – necessary for the task.

The answer to this question, on a general level, is quite straightforward. Mobilization for a large-scale temporary venture mainly happened through recruitment of qualified professionals into single-project organizations. However, this recruitment occurred mainly through particular channels, namely predecessor projects, personal networks and permanent organizations in order to both increase speed and reduce uncertainty.

Source: Grabher, G., & Thiel, J. (2015). Projects, people, professions: Trajectories of learning through a mega-event (the London 2012 case). *Geoforum*, 65, p. 8. www.researchgate.net/profile/Gernot_Grabher/ publication/272889590_Projects_people_professions_Trajectories_of_learning_through_a_mega-event_the_London_2012_case/links/55881b8808ae1dfa49d22f26/Projects-people-professions-Trajectories-of-learning-through-a-mega-event-the-London-2012-case.pdf

INTRODUCTION

Traditional recruitment practices have evolved to include seeking and interacting with candidates using digital media. LinkedIn and Facebook, for example, are good places to find prospective employees. The value of staff word-of mouth (SWOM) has been demonstrated in the retail sector (Keeling, McGoldrick and Sadhu, 2013), and personal networks are widely used for recruitment in the event industry. Data analysis is also enabling recruiters to search thousands of résumés. The recruitment phase involves attracting just the right number of prospects: not too many and not too few. For the 2016 Rio Olympic Games, for example, there were 240 000 applications for 70 000 volunteer jobs.

The next phase of selection is quite difficult for the event industry as the criteria are quite broad. There are many skills and attributes one can bring to the job in event management. Employers who were interviewed as part of People 1st's (2010) research found that the following skills were in demand: understanding the client's industry/needs, managing suppliers, customer service, crowd management, and understanding legislation/ standards such as those relating to health and safety and sustainability. Applicants with these attributes can come from a wide range of occupations. Selecting volunteers on the basis of the 'ability to think on your feet' and 'provide proactive customer service' is more demanding as these attributes are not concrete or easy to assess. Equal employment guidelines apply to the recruitment and selection of everyone, from senior management to frontline volunteers.

IDENTIFY RECRUITMENT NEEDS

When planning for optimal staffing, the first consideration is the number of full-time, fully trained and competent employees the business can afford. These are the mainstay of the event enterprise – the core members of the team – who will establish and maintain the ambience and efficiency of the business. Therefore, it is sometimes advisable to offer special incentives to key personnel, such as senior managers, based on the success of the event business or project. Recognising employees' critical role in the success of an event encourages long-term retention of those employees. Even in the smallest event business, there is generally at least one person who carries a valuable knowledge resource with them, such as the names of regular clients, detailed knowledge of an ancient and tricky software package, or contacts for suppliers of staging equipment. For all of these reasons, and many more, employers are increasingly recognising the importance of investment in selecting, training and retaining their permanent and even temporary staff, who may be inclined to leave at a critical time just before an event deadline. For most event projects, many of the workers are contractors, and outsourcing is another consideration at the recruitment stage. This has the advantage of involving experts in a particular field in a specific event project. On the other hand, loyalty does not generally develop in a short time. It can only be established if there is a preferred provider relationship with these contractors; this was discussed at length in Chapter 11. Finally, the event management team has to decide whether the involvement of volunteers is appropriate. This, too, will be discussed in this chapter. In summary, the composition of the event workforce needs to be decided at an early stage of the planning process. Possibilities include:

* full-time paid staff, permanent or temporary
* temporary paid staff
* agency personnel
* contractor organisation staff (as a result of outsourcing elements such as catering)
* volunteers.

For most large public events, the workforce also comprises the many stakeholder personnel who are involved, such as emergency services or employees of sponsors. These members of the workforce, while not recruited specifically for the event project, need to be taken through the induction process. Most events of this nature require workplace health and safety (WHS) induction prior to entry to the site as well as a general overview of the planned proceedings.

Let's now turn to another issue that will have a big impact on recruitment – the federal government employment standards.

The industrial context

In many industries, such as hospitality, the pay and award conditions are highly structured. In the rather organic event environment, however, arrangements are often more ad hoc, providing that minimum guidelines are met. It is essential to know what these are before embarking on recruitment drives.

The National Employment Standards (NES) are the minimum entitlements for employees in Australia. In addition to the NES, an employee's terms and conditions of employment may come from an award, employment contract, enterprise agreement or other registered agreement. This cannot provide for conditions that are less than the national minimum wage or the NES.

The NES entitlements are set out in the *Fair Work Act 2009* and comprise 10 minimum standards of employment. In summary, the NES covers the following minimum entitlements:

1 *Maximum weekly hours of work* – 38 hours per week, plus reasonable additional hours.
2 *Requests for flexible working arrangements* – allow parents or carers of a child under school age or a child under 18 with a disability to request a change in working arrangements to assist with the child's care.
3 *Parental leave and related entitlements* – up to 12 months unpaid leave for every employee, plus a right to request an additional 12 months unpaid leave, plus other forms of maternity, paternity and adoption-related leave.
4 *Annual leave* – four weeks paid leave per year, plus an additional week for certain shiftworkers. Part-time employees will accumulate leave at a pro-rata rate.
5 *Personal/carer's leave and compassionate leave* – carer's leave is time to take care of immediate family but comes out of the employee's personal leave balance.
6 *Community service leave* – unpaid leave for voluntary emergency activities.
7 *Long service leave (LSL)* – most employees' entitlements come from laws in each State or Territory.
8 *Public holidays* – a paid day off on a public holiday, except where reasonably requested to work.
9 *Notice of termination and redundancy pay* – an employer has to give minimum notice when dismissing an employee, depending on the period of continuous service; e.g. one year or less, one week's notice.
10 *Provision of a Fair Work Information Statement* – must be provided by employers to all new employees; contains information about the NES, modern awards, agreement making, the right to freedom of association, termination of employment, individual flexibility arrangements, union rights of entry, transfer of business, and the respective roles of the Fair Work Commission and the Fair Work Ombudsman.

The information statement, which is available from the Fair Work Ombudsman website, elaborates on the following additional arrangements:

Modern awards

In addition to the NES, you may be covered by a modern award. These awards cover an industry or occupation and provide additional enforceable minimum employment standards. There is also a Miscellaneous Award that may cover employees who are not covered by any other modern award.

Modern awards may contain terms about minimum wages, penalty rates, types of employment, flexible working arrangements, hours of work, rest breaks, classifications, allowances, leave and leave loading, superannuation, and procedures for consultation, representation, and dispute settlement. They may also contain terms about industry specific redundancy entitlements.

If you are a manager or a high income employee, the modern award that covers your industry or occupation may not apply to you. For example, where your employer guarantees in writing that you will earn more than the high income threshold, currently set at $138 900 per annum and indexed annually, a modern award will not apply, but the NES will.

Agreement making

You may be involved in an enterprise bargaining process where your employer, you or your representative (such as a union or other bargaining representative) negotiate for an enterprise agreement. Once approved by the Fair Work Commission, an enterprise agreement is enforceable and provides for changes in the terms and conditions of employment that apply at your workplace.

Source: Fair Work Information Statement. © Fair Work Ombudsman
www.fairwork.gov.au. https://creativecommons.org/licenses/by/3.0/au/legalcode

From this limited information regarding employment entitlements, one can see how much work is required in the area of workforce planning. In the event environment, the temptation to outsource most elements of human resource management and development is almost overwhelming. However, engaging staff employed by a disparate range of supplier/ contractor organisations works against the aim of a committed, dedicated service team. For the most part, workforce planning needs to take into account the nature of the event; that is, whether it is a one-off event, a periodic event, or an ongoing event business running multiple events. Also taken into account should be the type of event, the ratio of volunteers, and the level of management expertise required.

EXAMPLE

SERIOUS MISCONDUCT

When an employee is terminated on the grounds of serious misconduct, the employer does not have to provide any notice of termination. However, the employer does have to pay the employee all outstanding entitlements such as payment for time worked or annual leave.

Serious misconduct includes when an employee:

- causes serious and imminent risk to the health and safety of another person or to the reputation or profits of their employer's business; or
- deliberately behaves in a way that is inconsistent with continuing their employment.

Examples of serious misconduct include theft, fraud, assault or refusing to carry out a lawful and reasonable instruction that is part of the job.

Contractor organisations and their employees

Turning now to the other significant component of the event workforce, the contractor organisations and their employees, there are a number of considerations for human resource planning that need to be taken into account.

Independent contractors can provide more flexibility and can bring specific expertise to an event. From a legal perspective they:

- decide how to carry out the work and what expertise is needed to do so
- bear the risk for making a profit or loss on each job
- pay their own superannuation and tax, including GST
- should have their own insurance (workers compensation and public liability)
- are contracted to work for a set period of time (e.g. two months), or to do a set task
- decide what hours to work to complete the job
- generally submit an invoice for work completed or are paid at the end of the contract or project
- do not receive paid leave.

It is essential that these matters are given due consideration and are clarified in contractual arrangements in order to prevent later claims for missing pay or injuries.

Deciding on the optimal mix of paid staff (permanent, temporary, full-time or part-time), contractors and volunteers is an important process. The principal (usually the event organiser) is also potentially responsible for remuneration, workers compensation and payroll tax for any defaulting subcontractor. For this reason it is essential to obtain an undertaking from all contractors and subcontractors that these obligations have been honoured. Completion of a form known as a Subcontractor's Statement (available from Revenue NSW and similar organisations in other States/Territories) is recommended. This form states in part:

- In completing the Subcontractor's Statement, a subcontractor declares that workers compensation insurance premiums payable up to and including the date(s) on the Statement have been paid, and all premiums owing during the term of the contract will be paid.
- In completing the Subcontractor's Statement, a subcontractor declares that all remuneration payable to relevant employees for work under the contract has been paid.
- In completing the Subcontractor's Statement, a subcontractor declares that all payroll tax payable relating to the work undertaken has been paid.

Source: Revenue NSW (2013). Subcontractor's statement. www.revenue. nsw.gov.au/sites/default/files/file_manager/opt011.pdf

From the above discussion, it is evident that human resource management for events is far more complex than for most long-life organisations.

Organisation charts

When planning for staffing needs, it is helpful to draw up separate organisation charts for each different stage or task.

Pre-event charts

Prior to the event, the focus is on planning and, as we know, this lead time can be quite long. The charts required during this period show:

- all those responsible for the primary functions during the planning stage, such as finance, marketing, entertainment, catering and human resource management; for example, the core event team for the Melbourne Comedy Festival includes the festival director, general manager, marketing manager, development manager, marketing executive, marketing coordinator, ticketing manager, office manager, production and technical manager, artist coordinator, senior producer and producer's assistant
- small cross-functional teams which manage specific issues such as safety and customer service
- the stakeholders committee (including external contractors, suppliers and public bodies).
  The graph in Figure 22.1 shows the cumulative recruitment of full-time staff for the 2002 Commonwealth Games in Manchester. In this case, the organisation chart would change every month as more and more people were employed. However, for the purposes of most small events, a pre-event organisation chart showing the planning structure in the early days

is adequate. Figure 22.1 also illustrates the steady increase in the number of people being taken on as the Commonwealth Games approached. Most business organisations have a much more stable and long-serving workforce.

FIGURE 22.1 Cumulative monthly recruitment of full-time employees, Manchester Commonwealth Games

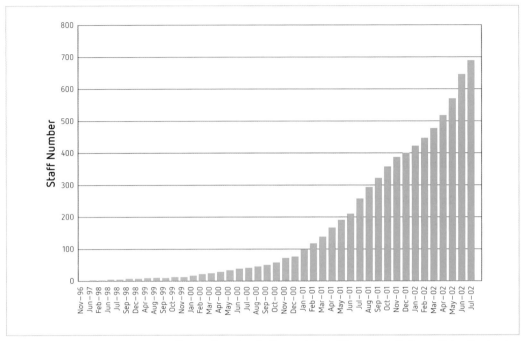

Source: Reproduced with permission of Commonwealth Games Federation, London

Charts during the event

When staffing levels for an event expand to the requirements of a full-scale operation, the size of the organisation generally increases dramatically. In some cases, there may be more than one venue involved, so each of the functional areas, such as the catering manager for each event venue, needs to be indicated on the chart. Charts should show the:

- full staff complement, together with reporting relationships for the overall event operations
- emergency reporting relationships (simplified and streamlined for immediate response).

Post-event chart

After the event, the team frequently disperses, leaving only a few individuals and a chart showing the key personnel involved with evaluation, financial reporting and outstanding issues.

Other chart elements

An organisation chart can also include a brief list of tasks performed by individuals or the people performing each role. This clarifies roles and improves communication. An organisation chart for a team involved in a product launch is illustrated in Figure 22.2 and an organisation chart for a fun run is illustrated in Figure 22.3.

Figure 22.4 shows the organisation chart for Clean Up Australia. More than 300 000 volunteers turned up for the first Clean Up Australia Day and this number continues to rise each year.

FIGURE 22.2 Organisation chart for a product launch

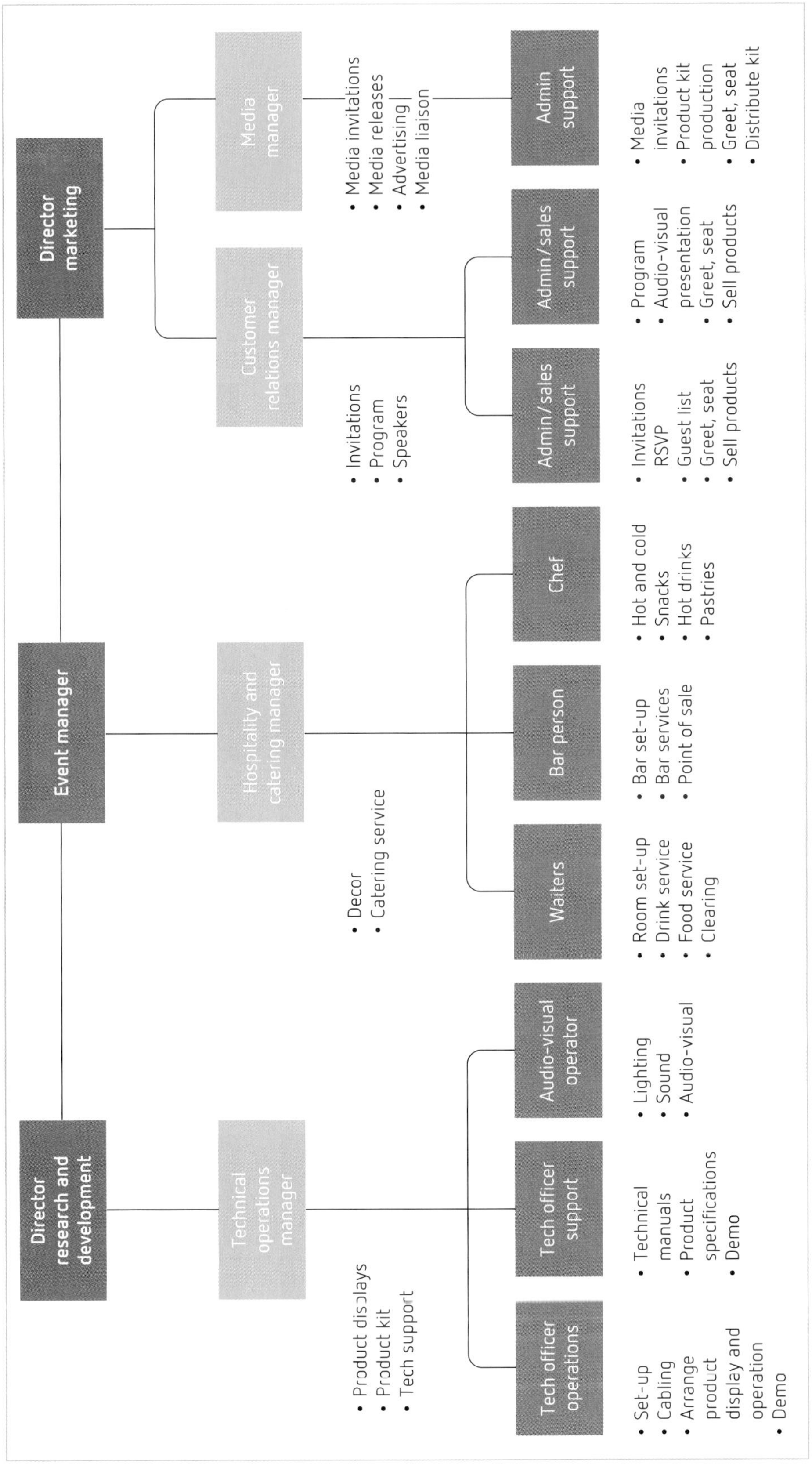

FIGURE 22.3 Organisation chart – day of fun run

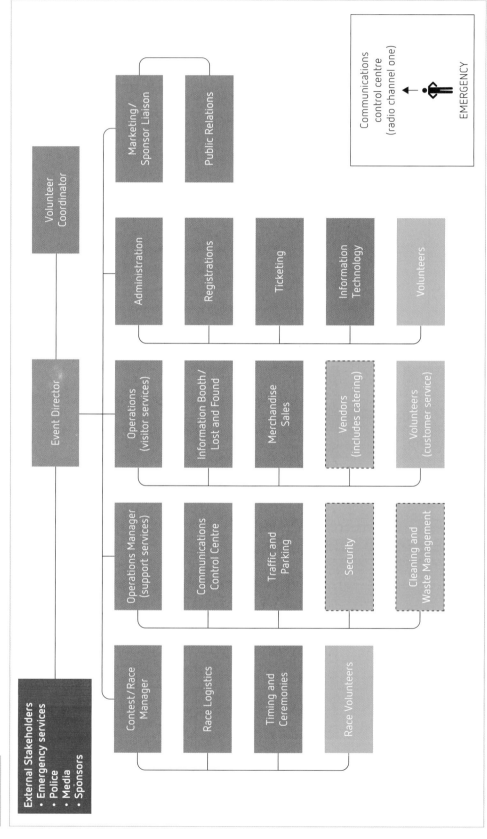

Source: Van der Wagen, L. (2015). *Human Resource Management for the Event Industry.* London: Routledge. p. 223.

FIGURE 22.4 Organisation chart for Clean Up Australia

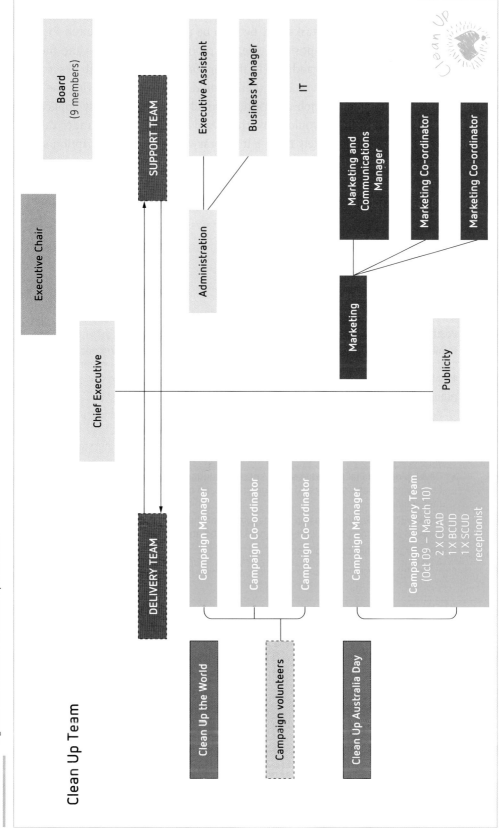

Preparing job descriptions

A job description, outlining the tasks that need to be performed, is required for each role. This document should show the position title, the reporting relationships and the duties. A position summary is optional. In addition to the sections shown in the job description for a catering services manager in Figure 22.5, there should be a section showing the terms and conditions of employment. This job description would indicate the salary applicable, while those for many other positions would show the award and the pay rate under the award or agreement. As this position is likely to be a temporary one, the job description should also show the start and finish dates.

FIGURE 22.5 Sample job description

Job Description

Position title: Catering Services Manager
Reports to: Venue Services Manager
Responsible for: Subcontracts with caterers/concessionaires

Position summary:
To meet the food and beverage needs of all customer groups through the selection and management of appropriate subcontractors and concessionaires. To ensure compliance with the negotiated agreements regarding menus, pricing, quality and service.

Duties
- Develop tender documents for provision of food and beverage, including bars, fast food, coffee stalls, snack bars, VIP and staff catering.
- Select subcontractors and confirm agreements regarding menus, pricing, staffing and service levels.
- Develop operational procedures with special attention to integration of services, food hygiene plans, supply and storage of food and beverage, staffing and waste management.
- Work with venue operations on the installation of the required facilities and essential services (including power, water and gas) for food and beverage outlets.
- Monitor performance of contractors.
- Deal with daily operational and customer complaint issues.

As you can see from the job description, this person would not have a direct role in catering. Instead, he or she would be managing catering subcontractors. This means that experience in selecting organisations to tender for the catering contracts and managing supply of the products promised in the contracts would be essential.

Once the job description is complete, a person specification is developed, as shown in Figure 22.6. This identifies the skills, knowledge and experience required for the role. This is used to inform the selection process. In this case, experience in a similar role, particularly in relation to tendering and contract management, would be required. In addition, knowledge of menu planning and costing would be essential, as would knowledge of food hygiene planning.

FIGURE 22.6 Sample person specification

Person Specification

Position title: Catering Services Manager
Reports to: Venue Services Manager
Responsible for: Subcontracts with caterers/concessionaires

Position summary:

To meet the food and beverage needs of all customer groups through the selection and management of appropriate subcontractors and concessionaires. To ensure compliance with the negotiated agreements regarding menus, pricing, quality and service.

Knowledge:
- Legal contracts (with professional advice where necessary)
- HACCP (food hygiene plans)
- RSA (responsible service of alcohol)
- Catering for large numbers
- Installation and management of bar and kitchen facilities

Skills:
- High level negotiation skills
- Verbal and non-verbal communication skills
- Preparing budgets and planning
- Development of operational procedures
- Problem solving

Experience:
- Managing large-scale catering subcontracts, multiple subcontractors, concessionaires
- Menu planning and catering control systems for large-scale catering
- Operational planning for new installations

Desirable:
- Experience in an event environment

As you can see from the requirements for the position, experience in an event environment is desirable. However, experience in managing multiple contracts, such as in a resort, hotel or catering organisation, may be relevant in the absence of event experience.

The actual position description for a volunteer for a music festival in Figure 23.2 in the next chapter is an excellent example.

ADMINISTER RECRUITMENT

Once the job description and person specification have been completed, they can be used to develop advertisements and interview questions.

The most common approach to recruitment is to advertise the position in local or major newspapers, on the event's website or event-related sites, or on employment sites such as SEEK. Employment agencies can also provide event staff – for a placement fee. This is an attractive method of recruitment as it cuts down your work by providing you with a shortlist of suitable applicants, as well as managing the administrative side of employment, such as taxes and insurance.

The best places to look for volunteers are volunteer organisations, schools, colleges and universities.

Advertising the position

While the event website is the most common channel for advertising positions, other social media sites and informal networks can also be considered. By creating an advertisement that is positively worded, the event business is likely to achieve a good response. However, if the positive features of the job are not balanced with realistic requirements, such as the necessity for qualifications or a requirement to work on weekends, an overwhelming response from poorly advised applicants can waste a lot of time.

An employment advertisement must create strong appeal for a number of readers, but deter applicants who do not meet the minimum requirements. In some cases it is necessary to actually limit the response. By stating the selection criteria developed in the person specification, only those with the appropriate qualifications, knowledge and skills who are interested in the position will apply.

In general, an advertisement should include the:
- job title
- necessary qualifications
- required skills and experience
- essential attributes, such as the ability to do shiftwork
- location
- wage/salary and any other benefits.

SELECT STAFF

The selection process involves reviewing applications, shortlisting applicants, checking their references (the job description and person specification can act as a guide for asking relevant questions) and interviewing shortlisted candidates.

Selecting the best applicant

Interviewing is carried out with reference to the selection criteria and to equal employment opportunity (EEO) guidelines, which indicate that selection and promotion should be based on merit.

During interviews, there are a number of questions that should not be asked of the applicant as they are discriminatory:
- Where were you born?
- Have you changed your name?
- Do you have any children?
- What language do you speak at home?

The following questions should not be asked of the applicant because they are irrelevant to the job:

- What do you do in your spare time?
- What sports do you play?
- What does your spouse do?

As a general rule, questions should be directly related to the position requirements and to applicants' behaviour and reactions in previous positions, and should allow the candidate to demonstrate their previous experience and its relevance to the position. Consider, for example, the following questions:

- Can you tell me how you would handle a customer complaint?
- Can you give me an example of a situation in which a customer experienced a problem or wanted to make a complaint and explain what happened?

The first of these questions is hypothetical and most people would find it easy to answer. The second question, which asks about previous experience, is much more difficult to answer but would provide more information about how the applicant has dealt with complaints in the past.

Once the interview questions have been developed, the same questions should be asked of all candidates in order to maintain equity. Using behavioural questions allows the interviewer to rate the performance of applicants against specific and relevant selection criteria. This greatly assists the process and formalises the documentation of the selection process. Many interviewers start off with good intentions, but by the time they have interviewed the fifth candidate they cannot remember the first. Careful record keeping is therefore essential. If the questions have been prepared well, there is little risk of a claim of discrimination. Essentially, selection is a process of careful discrimination. A manager must be able to show that the process of selection was based on relevant criteria, not irrelevant criteria, such as hobbies, or discriminatory criteria, such as sex or marital status.

Skills tests are an effective way to make selection decisions, particularly in the area of hospitality service. Volunteers and interns who have talent and promise are also good candidates, as long as they have provided good evidence of skilled performance.

Making an offer to the successful candidate

Once the candidate has been decided, it's time to make an offer in writing in accordance with enterprise policy and industrial/legislative requirements. The employment offer is a contract like any other and should include the following details:

- position offered
- compensation/pay
- benefits
- trial period
- start and finish date (if project or temporary)
- reference to the attached job description for duties and responsibilities
- reference to the attached employee handbook for policies and rules
- signatures of both parties.

A signed copy of the acceptance letter, as well as clear and complete details of the selection process, should be kept on record.

All unsuccessful applicants should be contacted promptly and appropriate colleagues should be informed of the decision. If necessary, recommendations for improvements in the recruitment process should also be communicated to appropriate colleagues.

Validating candidate information

In the process of assessing the individual's suitability for the position, a number of checks may need to be carried out:

* visa and other requirements for official employability status
* licences and permits (e.g. to drive a forklift)
* educational and other qualifications (e.g. responsible service of alcohol certificate, food safety training and first aid certificate need to be checked for currency)
* police check (mainly for major events)
* training and register of offenders (for positions involving work with children)
* references from past employers.

Record keeping

The recruitment and selection process needs to be documented. Decisions need to be made on the basis of specific criteria and EEO guidelines and this needs to be proven if necessary. These documents include administrative documents, interview schedules, interview records, criteria and score sheets, comments by interviewers or a panel, and recommendations.

PLAN AND ORGANISE INDUCTION PROGRAMS

Orientation
A new employee's introduction to the organisation

Induction
The embedding of individuals in the workplace with the aim of allowing them to 'settle in'

According to many human resources experts, **orientation** is an introduction to the organisation you are going to work for (or volunteer for), and it includes a company overview, important company policies, organisational values and various codes of conduct. In traditional organisations, a formal session is generally run by the human resources staff and provides the opportunity to understand key senior managers and their departments.

Although the term **induction** is often used synonymously with orientation, it is different in that it describes the embedding of individuals in the workplace, giving them an understanding of their colleagues and customers, policies and procedures and specific job role context with the aim of 'settling in'. The term *socialisation* (discussed later in the chapter) is also used to describe this broader, longer process; regarding long-life organisations, this could cover the first months of employment. Clearly, there is less time for settling in when you hit the ground running as an event worker or volunteer.

EXTENSION ACTIVITY

View the YouTube animation on induction, orientation and socialisation (**https://youtu.be/ isR8rXPzPVg**). Apply these concepts to your experience as a worker or volunteer and make three recommendations for the event environment.

Event staff must be trained in three basic areas:

1   *General outline.* Staff should be presented with a general outline of the event, including its objectives and organisational structure, and they need to be motivated to provide reliable information and outstanding service to every member of the event audience.

2   *Venue information.* A tour of the venue enables staff to become familiar with the location of all facilities, functional areas and departments, and the spectator services provided. This is the ideal time to cover all emergency procedures.

3   *Specific job information.* Event staff need to know their duties and how to perform them. Maps and checklists can be extremely useful for this purpose, while rehearsals and role-plays help to familiarise staff with their roles before the onslaught of the event audience. Most trainees would rather move from the specific, which is more personally relevant, to the general. However, in some cases, access to the venue is only permitted at the very last minute and training has to focus on the more general aspects first.

Training days provide an ideal opportunity for team building. Team-building activities, such as quizzes, games and competitions, should be included in all training so that comfortable relationships develop. Such activities should be relevant to particular tasks. Event leaders need to accelerate all processes as much as possible in order to hold the attention of the trainee group and develop team spirit.

Reinforcement is essential and, at the end of training, the event manager should be confident that all staff have achieved the training objectives for knowledge, attitudes and skills. Too often, these sessions are a one-way process, trainees becoming bogged down with an overload of information. Training materials need to be prepared in a user-friendly, jargon-free format for participants to access online. A hotline staffed by volunteers who can answer staff questions about everything (for example, rosters, roles, transport) is also a good idea.

The following checklist covers the type of information that might be included in online training manuals and in training sessions:

1   **Shift routine and specific tasks**
    - location of check-in area and check-in procedure
    - reporting for shift and briefing
    - uniforms and equipment
    - incident reporting system
    - supervision
    - specific roles
    - breaks and meals
    - debriefing and check-out.

2   **Venue operations**
    - venue organisation and support operations
    - staffing policies/rules
    - emergency procedures
    - radio procedures
    - other relevant procedures.

3   **General event information**
    - event outline and objectives
    - event audience expectations

- transport
- related local services information
- contingency planning.

Customer service training is a key component of all event training. As the general principles of quality service are well known, the focus should be on the specific information required by staff in order to properly assist customers, rather than on general skills. Most event staff rate training on specific event information for the event audience as being the most relevant to their training needs and to providing quality customer service. Staff, however well intentioned, find themselves helpless and frustrated when asked questions that they cannot answer. Figure 22.7 shows the attributes of staff that event customers value.

FIGURE 22.7 Key aspects of professional customer service

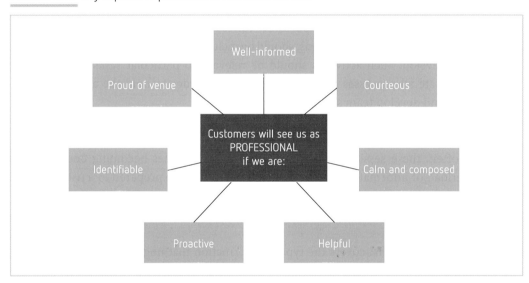

Briefing volunteers

Briefing staff prior to every shift is essential. It is an extension of the training sessions and allows the venue or event manager to impart important, relevant information to staff before they commence work. Some information may be new, such as changes to spectator transport arrangements, while other elements may be a reinforcement of key information, such as incident reporting or emergency procedures.

Socialisation

Socialisation, also referred to as induction, is the process whereby people adapt to a working community and become fully integrated into the workforce. In doing so, they adopt the norms and values of the organisation. Socialisation is a broader concept which goes beyond the early formal process, which in the event environment often occurs days or even weeks before the event begins. If we are interested in assimilation into the event team and workforce motivation, we need to look at the aspects of socialisation that are important to staff and volunteers.

Aisbett and Hoye (2015) researched two specific elements of human resource management in the sporting events context, looking at perceived organisational support and perceived supervisor support:

> The findings indicate that volunteers' satisfaction can be attributed more to the informal support (or lack thereof) provided by their supervisor (PSS) than the formal procedures implemented by the organization (POS). Volunteers' AC however, can be attributed more to POS than PSS. These results suggest that for some volunteers the supervisor may embody the organization; the support provided by the supervisor on the day of an event can become more important than support provided by the organization prior to the event. A poor supervisor's performance in providing the requisite support may therefore impact more on a volunteer's satisfaction than any failings (or otherwise) of the overall HRM system.

> Source: Aisbett, L., & Hoye, R. (2015). Human resource management practices to support sport event volunteers. *Asia Pacific Journal of Human Resources*, 53(3). p. 351.

These findings illustrate the importance of leadership and teamwork in the specific context of the job role. This is a challenge for events, as formal orientation often occurs some time before the event and describes the event organisational context. Meanwhile, the event workforce (staff and volunteers) are more interested in the place where they will work (often not yet determined), the people they will work with (also not yet confirmed) and the role they will undertake, which at this stage is often described in the briefest of terms. Thus, for the event manager, the aim is to familiarise everyone with the broader event context, also being mindful that job role clarity is a priority for most members of the workforce. Staff and volunteers will arrive on the job, possibly only hours before the audience, and this will present significant challenges. The quality of training and supervision provided will have a big impact on motivation and retention.

The event employment website called Sitecrew can assist festival and event organisations in the following ways:

- job and position listings
- recruitment of specialist site crew
- online induction
- training
- payroll.

What are the pros and cons of using an organisation such as Sitecrew, or a similar service like I Need Helpers, to meet event staffing needs?

EXTENSION ACTIVITY

Summary

Staffing is a very important part of event management and is crucial to the smooth running of an event. To cover this adequately, we have discussed many topics in this chapter, from identifying recruitment needs to planning and organising induction programs. Recruitment and selection help to bring staff on line, while induction and training prepare them for their event roles. We have also looked at the types of events that lend themselves to recruiting volunteers, how to maximise volunteer retention, and strategies for recognising their involvement. The event manager needs to be able to prepare human resource policies, job descriptions and person specifications, prepare organisation charts to enable employees to understand their reporting relationships, and manage workforce and WHS issues.

Key terms

Induction   The embedding of individuals in the workplace with the aim of allowing them to 'settle in'

Orientation   A new employee's introduction to the organisation

REVIEW YOUR KNOWLEDGE

1   Discuss the pros and cons of outsourcing services such as catering and security.
2   What are the minimum entitlements of workers under the National Employment Standards?
3   What are the WHS responsibilities of the primary or principal contracting agency (the event organiser) in relation to staff working for subsidiary contractors (subcontractors)?
4   How does induction and training for the event environment differ from induction and training in traditional long-life organisations?
5   Explain EEO and its application to recruitment and selection.

APPLY YOUR KNOWLEDGE

1   You are the staffing and volunteer coordinator employed by the local council working towards staging an annual food, wine and music festival. The two-day weekend festival will include 20 food stalls, 15 beverage stalls and two stages. Approximately 10 000 people are expected to visit over the two-day period. Over 100 volunteers will be required in the areas of vendor liaison, parking, ticket selling, information, merchandising, promotions, bump-in and bump-out, music, safety and waste management / recycling. Other roles will be full-time and part-time temporary; that is, paid roles.
2   Your task is to develop a recruitment, selection and induction program for all of the following jobs: casual, contract or temporary; full-time or part-time permanent; volunteer.
3   Conduct and record an interview for a volunteer with the assistance of a colleague.

CASE STUDY

You have been asked to run a tourism destination promotional forum. The aims are to raise the profile of your region as a tourist destination, provide a platform for the public and private sectors of the local tourism industry, discuss and address regional tourism issues, and help expand marketing networks and opportunities to promote local tourism destinations and events.

The Buyers and Sellers Business Session of the forum will enable delegates to network and conduct business with high-level government officials, and national, State/Territory and local tourism organisation representatives, as well as entrepreneurs, hoteliers, travel agents, tourism operators and media. Open breakout sessions will aim to generate ideas and solutions. Issues such as standards, product ranges, joint promotional efforts, and marketing opportunities and strategies will also be discussed.

TASKS

1   Develop an organisational chart similar to the one illustrated in Figure 22.2 in this chapter.
2   Develop your own job description as tourism forum event manager.
3   Develop a recruitment, selection and induction plan for this role.
4   Conduct and record two interviews for this role with the assistance of a colleague and make a selection decision.

Online resources

CENGAGE
brain.com

Visit http://login.cengagebrain.com and search for this book to access the study tools that come with your textbook.

References

Aisbett, L., & Hoye, R. (2015). Human resource management practices to support sport event volunteers. *Asia Pacific Journal of Human Resources*, 53(3), 351–69.

Keeling, K. A., McGoldrick, P. J., & Sadhu, H. (2013). Staff word-of-mouth (SWOM) and retail employee recruitment. *Journal of Retailing*, 89(1), 88–104.

People 1st (2010). Labour market review of the event industry. http://webarchive.nationalarchives.gov.uk/20100515084435/http://people1st.co.uk/research/reports

Van der Wagen, L. (2015). *Human Resource Management for the Event Industry*. London: Routledge.

Websites

Fair Work Ombudsman – National Employment Standards, www.fairwork.gov.au/employee-entitlements/national-employment-standards

I Need Helpers, http://ineedhelpers.com

Sitecrew, www.sitecrew.com.au

Volunteering Australia, www.volunteeringaustralia.org

23 MANAGE VOLUNTEERS

OVERVIEW

Managing an event workforce comprised mainly of volunteers is not easy. For some events, everyone wants to volunteer; for others, no-one is interested. For most festivals and events, volunteers have high expectations regarding the interesting roles they will play, imagining that they will overlook the stage or field of play. Well, as they say, 'If you want to enjoy the event, buy a ticket'. Thus, the volunteer program needs to ensure that volunteer motivations are understood and that the experience will be sufficiently rewarding that everyone lasts the distance. Most importantly, volunteer and intern programs should not exploit people, particularly if the role is better identified as a paid position.

LEARNING OBJECTIVES

On completion of this chapter, you will be able to:

1 research, determine and define needs for volunteer involvement, assessing benefits, costs and risks

2 undertake volunteer recruitment, developing job descriptions, selection program and communications strategy

3 maximise volunteer retention by developing a climate of recognition, planning and delivering training and supervision.

INDUSTRY VIEWPOINT

There were two training sessions for volunteers. The first was very general and did not answer any of my questions. In fact, I was so confused I almost didn't return for the second session. All I really wanted was a realistic idea of where I would be and what I would do. Instead we were told about reporting relationships, incident reporting and emergency evacuation. When they started to talk about the VERP and the chain of command I was totally lost. The final straw came when the manager talked about the contractors 'attempting to claw back service in response to price gouging'. I had absolutely no idea what he was saying. All I really wanted was a map and my job description.

Event usher

INTRODUCTION

This comment, made by a volunteer usher, illustrates the importance of effective communication and understanding the listener's needs and expectations. In this chapter, we will look at the volunteer programs for festivals and events, being mindful of the social benefits associated with volunteering.

According to the results of a survy conducted for Volunteering Australia by PricewaterhouseCoopers (2016), the most common reason for volunteering is 'to give something back to the community'. The methods of getting involved in volunteering varied across the age groups in the survey, with 26 per cent of those under 24 more likely to use the websites GoVolunteer or Seek, or the organisation's own website. In the higher age brackets, a personal approach was most common after word of mouth. The results therefore indicate that online sources are critical to engaging younger volunteers. The report on the survey says a key question is whether there is alignment between the types of roles volunteers want to undertake, the volunteer's individual skills and experience, and the needs of the organisation.

Volunteers, such as the event usher quoted at the start of this chapter, sometimes have a difficult time and as a result do not feel that the experience was worth it. As a student of event management and a volunteer at a festival, what are three of the best and three of the worst things that could happen to you?

EXTENSION ACTIVITY

The profiles of volunteers and their needs and expectations also need to fit in well with the event organisation's profile. The Red Frog program for assisting with schoolies week safety is a good example, and Volunteering Australia offers several guidelines on policy and best practice.

There are many reasons why a volunteer program is a good idea, over and above the rationale that it will save money. Volunteers can play a vital role as hosts of the event,

CLEAN UP AUSTRALIA DAY

The first Clean Up Sydney Harbour Day in 1989 achieved an enormous public response, with over 40 000 Sydneysiders donating their time and energy in an attempt to clean up their harbour. The next year, Clean Up Australia Day was born, after Ian Kiernan, AO, and his committee thought that if a city could be mobilised into action, then so could the whole nation. Over 300 000 volunteers turned out on the first Clean Up Australia Day and the numbers have risen ever since.

The subsequent challenge was to take the concept of Clean Up Australia Day to the rest of the world. After gaining the support of the United Nations Environment Programme (UNEP), Clean Up the World was launched in 1993. The success of Clean Up the World (an estimated 35 million people take part in over 120 countries annually) has shown that environmental effort in Australia has been noticed and the environment is a concern to all people globally.

Every official clean-up site needs to have at least one supervisor on Clean Up Australia Day. Site supervisors must be over 18, and should be responsible people who are happy to commit their services for the entirety of the clean-up activity. Site supervisors are volunteers who report to the national coordinator of the event.

- Site supervisors are responsible for:
- Ensuring they have read the Clean Up Australia Day Site Guide
- Selecting and surveying a site
- Registering the site with Clean Up Australia
- Correct registering of volunteers
- Volunteer briefing and ensuring volunteers are aware of safety requirements
- Distributing Clean Up bags and gloves
- Reporting back to Clean Up Australia.

It is easy to organise a Clean Up Australia Day site in your local area. Once you register your interest in joining the national campaign, Clean Up Australia will provide you with a step-by-step guide explaining exactly what you need to do to get involved! Simply register online at www.cleanup.org.au or contact Clean Up Australia by telephoning us today on CUADAY 1800 282 329.

Source: Clean Up Australia Limited. Permission for reference to Clean up Australia Day is granted by Clean Up Australia Limited.

The contribution of volunteers needs to be recognised: not only customer relations volunteers but also volunteers working for other organisations, such as the first aid provider.

Generally speaking, the personal benefits, as perceived by volunteers, are:

- personal satisfaction
- social contact
- helping others in the community
- doing something worthwhile
- personal or family involvement
- learning new skills
- using skills and experience
- being active.

There are many academic studies on the topic of volunteer motivation (for example, Güntert, Neufeind & Wehner, 2015; Rogalsky, Doherty & Paradis, 2016). The findings of such studies are useful in understanding the contribution and motivation of volunteers, and the importance of developing recognition strategies to meet their needs. In the job description for volunteers shown later in this chapter (see Figure 23.2), a number of benefits are listed that would meet the stated needs of volunteers for social contact and being active. These volunteers also received rewards in the form of merchandise and meeting musicians. After the 2000 Sydney Olympics, IOC president Juan Antonio Samaranch described Australia's volunteers as the 'most dedicated and wonderful volunteers ever'. This was a richly deserved accolade for a country in which volunteering is part of the social fabric. Furthermore, Kemp's (2002) evaluation of volunteer satisfaction with the Sydney Olympics and also the Winter Olympics in 1994 showed that all volunteers in Sydney and Lillehammer were very positive about their participation as a volunteer. The mean satisfaction score for Lillehammer was 7.7 and for Sydney it was 9.2 (on a Likert scale of 1 to 10).

However, during the Sydney Olympic Games, it was not only volunteers who embraced the Olympic spirit. An experiment by one of the radio stations showed that a person posing as an American tourist with a map and a puzzled look was offered immediate assistance by those who witnessed his dilemma. The average response time to offer help was 66 seconds (Column 8, 2000). This illustrates the positive attitude of most Australian citizens towards tourism and the importance of the role of events in increasing tourist numbers.

Better access for people with disabilities, targeted volunteer opportunities for young people and more respect for other cultures are some of the legacies of the 2006 Commonwealth Games held in Melbourne, with all Victorians 'equal first' in their involvement in the games. The Office of Commonwealth Games Co-ordination (OCGC) was established within the Victorian public service with a staff of around 600 at its peak. At the time of the games, 13 150 volunteers assisted. Research outcomes from the 2018 Commonwealth Games on the Gold Coast are now eagerly anticipated – approximately 15 000 volunteers will form the cornerstone of the event workforce.

WHS and insurance

Work health and safety (WHS) laws apply to all workers, including volunteers.

> Under WHS law a volunteer is a person who works for an organisation without payment or financial reward (but they may receive out of pocket expenses). The

law also recognises volunt
must provide the same pro
As a worker, a volunteer ha

If the WHS laws app
is reasonably practicabl
including volunteers. Th
same protections to its
The protection covers th
including volunteers ...

The WHS Act requir
volunteers, so far as reason
that affect them. Talking to
ensure they contribute to
control of any risks they face when they carry out their work.

WHS Act

Covers paid Workers just as Volunteers.

In summary, volunteers are regarded as workers under WHS legislation, and event organisations need to extend the same rights and responsibilities to volunteers as they do to the paid workforce with respect to workplace safety. In the 'hot' environment of feverish activity during bump-in and bump-out, volunteers often undertake work beyond their level of capability and without the appropriate safety resources and procedures. Working at heights is a common occurrence. Risk management with respect to volunteer programs should follow the format described in Chapter 18. Regular safety briefings are recommended and close supervision is necessary.

As volunteers are usually not covered by workers compensation insurance, event organisations should take out public liability insurance as well as volunteer personal accident insurance. The Volunteering Australia website provides information about the most common types of insurance that cover volunteers.

The skills and confidence developed by volunteers can provide pathways to employment.

Benefits, costs and risks

When planning a volunteer program, one has to think about the benefits, costs and risks. The main benefits go to the community, first through engagement and second through training and development. The skills and confidence developed by volunteers can provide pathways to employment. Certainly, events enhance community spirit.

In terms of risks, a significant concern given the number of for-profit event organisations taking on volunteers is exploitation. In parallel, this has an impact on the paid workforce: if lots of people are keen to take on the work for no pay, then this will reduce local employment. This concern is raised below regarding the 2016 Melbourne Fashion Festival, which echoes concerns raised at a similar event in London recently.

Finally, it is a mistake to think that the volunteer program is 'free'. There are many costs associated with running a volunteer program: planning and implementing recruitment and selection, planning and delivering training and recognition, and of course, an ongoing communication strategy to keep everyone motivated. Generally, a small team of paid staff is required to manage the volunteer program. Other costs include uniforms and meals. A budget template is provided in Figure 23.1.

FIGURE 23.1 Template for volunteer program budget

PROJECT BUDGET – VOLUNTEERS	COST
Volunteer coordinator/s: recruitment and selection	
Volunteer website development; communications strategy	
Orientation and on-the-job training	
Uniforms	
Meals	
Recognition strategy; social event	
Total	

After working 13-hour shifts in stifling conditions, some of the volunteers at the Melbourne Fashion Festival in March were on the verge of collapse. Tough conditions for volunteers at Melbourne's marquee fashion event are laid bare in dozens of leaked feedback reports obtained by Fairfax Media. Some of the volunteers say they went without food and water.

The documents point to the ugly underbelly of Australian fashion — the working reality beyond the glamour of the runway. They highlight a growing problem of exploitation of unpaid interns and volunteers, people trying to get a break in competitive industries such as fashion and the media.

Source: Schneiders, B., & Millar, R. (2016). Fashion's real victims: Melbourne Fashion Festival volunteers tell of mistreatment. *The Age*, 18 October. www.theage.com.au/national/investigations/fashions-real-victims-melbourne-fashion-festival-volunteers-tell-of-mistreatment-20161018-gs4vjg.html

EXTENSION ACTIVITY

Many event students return from 'work experience' feeling that they have been exploited, or even worse, left to stand idle. What are five key guidelines/requirements that a college or university should establish before sending students to volunteer at festivals and events?

UNDERTAKE VOLUNTEER RECRUITMENT

[handwritten: Volunteer rewards]

...sideration must be given to the volunteer's ...nteer rewards need to be incorporated into ...rget areas from which volunteers might be

Plan for recruitment

EvenTeamworK is an organisation specialising in volunteer management, offering consultancy services in all the areas discussed in this chapter; some similar organisations were discussed in the previous chapter. What this indicates is that running a volunteer program requires expertise and dedication. It also needs a budget! According to the founders of this business, 'the lack of resources allocated and expertise available for volunteer

Cleaning seats is not rewarding or enjoyable

[handwritten: EvenTeamwork]

management often leads to a high staff turnover, a dissatisfaction of volunteers and ultimately to organisations and events not achieving the anticipated outcomes'.

The planning activities discussed in the last chapter were recruitment, selection, induction and on-the-job training. The foundation for planning is the analysis of job roles/work breakdown structure and the development of job descriptions. This process enables the event management team to decide how many volunteers are needed – exactly enough to be busy, not hammered, and not idle. This can vary across the days of the event and peak periods. An example of a very comprehensive job description is shown in Figure 23.2.

Conduct recruitment

Recruitment is the process of attracting applicants by appealing to motivational factors. There are many options for advertising, some internal and others external. As mentioned previously, there are volunteer specialist agencies that will undertake this whole process. Another approach is to develop a strong relationship with a college or university in order to offer experience for students studying in a related field. There are also many specialist community organisations such as St John Ambulance and the Australian Red Cross. Others involve active seniors such as Rotary and Lions Club, and there are many associations for ethnic groups such as the Australian Chinese Community Association.

The festival or event website is the most common avenue for volunteer applications. For the most popular events, volunteers return year after year.

FIGURE 23.2 Excellent example of a position description

VOLUNTEER JOB DESCRIPTION

RESPONSIBLE TO:	• Event Coordinator
	• Volunteer Coordinator
LOCATION:	Central Park, Wendell Street entrance; meet at the volunteer tent.
DATE & TIME:	Friday 25th (12.00–17.00) AND
	Saturday 26th (9.00–14.00 or 13.00–18.00 or 15.00–20.00 depending on shift allocation OR
	Sunday 27th (9.00–14.00 or 13.00–18.00 or 15.00–20.00).
POSITION OBJECTIVE:	To assist in a community event set-up, and provide customer assistance on the day to enhance audience enjoyment.
ACTIVITIES AND TASKS:	**During bump-in/set-up**

During bump-in/set-up
- set out barriers
- set up backdrops
- set up chairs and tables
- put up sponsors' signs
- set up equipment for sound
- assist stallholders
- set up traffic, parking barriers signage
- place signs around festival—directional, parking
- place no-smoking signs around site

During the event
- check tickets at the entrance
- ensure patrons have valid tickets
- meet and greet patrons with enthusiasm
- supervise the queue
- conduct general minor security (e.g. ensuring patrons are not going through artists entry, etc.)
- assist with tidiness and cleanliness of the event site
- look out for lost children
- assist disabled and elderly patrons into the venue
- in the event of fire or emergency, assist with safe evacuation of patrons
- hand out and collect patron surveys

In general
- assist the Event Coordinator and Volunteer Coordinator as directed to deliver the festival
- follow directions as given to effectively carry out tasks
- present a positive image of the festival
- respect other volunteers and performers
- provide assistance to performers
- provide assistance to the public
- identify safety hazards
- report all incidents (including 'near miss')
- assist with customer complaints
- escalate issues to your supervisor if in any doubt

ATTRIBUTES:	· Excellent time management skills
	· Good service ethic
	· Self-motivated
	· Able to relate well to others and follow directions
	· Prepared to promote the festival
	· Willingness to support the Coordinator and other team members
	· Trustworthy and a reliable team member
	· Show understanding of safe work practices
	· Desire to meet people of all ages and backgrounds
	· Ability to assist with physical but not arduous tasks
	· Previous event experience is desirable but not essential
SELECTION CRITERIA:	The applicant should:
	· have a genuine interest in the festival values
	· be available for a minimum of 5 hours on each day
	· be flexible and comfortable taking on role(s) as required, especially minor lifting and carrying
	· demonstrate verbal and non-verbal communication skills for assisting customers of all ages and backgrounds
	· be trustworthy and reliable
	· show ability to work unsupervised and as part of a team
	· demonstrate absence of a criminal record
	· show agreement to undergo a police check
	· demonstrate ability to apply WHS and safety procedures
	· have the ability to stand and walk for long periods (up to 6 hours)
ORIENTATION AND TRAINING:	An orientation session will be held one week beforehand to familiarise volunteers with their roles
REWARDS:	THESE POSITIONS ARE VOLUNTARY AND SUCCESSFUL APPLICANTS WILL NOT BE PAID A WAGE.
	They will however enjoy the following benefits:
	· festival T-shirt and festival cap
	· other event merchandise including music CD
	· pass to the event during leisure time, and non-work day
	· one hot meal break and one short tea break
	· opportunity to meet with performers
	· increased knowledge of festivals and music
	· meeting people from different walks of life
	· future work experience
	· a reference will be provided for each volunteer
	· a get-together will be held to celebrate the success of the event
THE WORKING ENVIRONMENT:	· work independently and as part of a team
	· work in a busy, noisy and sometimes hot environment
	· wear comfortable shoes, neat casual attire and sun protection
	· demonstrate safe work practices
	· show concern for the safety of others

Select volunteers

The initial selection process is generally a desk job, an analysis of all online applications. This is usually done by human resources, the volunteer coordinator and the functional area manager. The number of applications should be monitored carefully and a cut-off applied once it is deemed that there are sufficient numbers. As it is an equal employment opportunity (EEO) requirement that all applicants are considered against selection criteria, it is important to ensure that applicant numbers are not excessive. Where an interview is not possible, teleconferencing or Skype offer options, particularly for the more senior volunteers.

Getting dirty is part of this job

Once checks have been done – for some events, police checks and child safety, and for others reference checks – the volunteer position can be offered and confirmed.

Induction

Induction was covered in detail in the last chapter, so suffice to say that this process establishes an important relationship with the volunteers, creating those lasting first impressions. Whether done online or during face-to-face training sessions, the information delivered needs to be inspiring and informative. It needs to address all the volunteer FAQs and ensure that everyone has realistic expectations. For the volunteers, three important areas are the benefits (for example, a free ticket), responsibilities (safety) and rights (a non-discriminatory environment).

As a collective overview of the event, induction and training should cover the goals and objectives of the event, the character of the event audience, and details of the show, performance or competition.

Develop communications plan

Staffing policies should be developed as part of any human resource planning strategy and should cover such aspects as health and safety, misconduct, poor performance, sexual harassment and contravention of safety procedures. These policies, such as those below, should be simplified and summarised as a code of conduct for all paid and volunteer staff, and then clarified at induction:

1   Work in a safe manner.
2   Do not endanger the health and safety of others.
3   Report all accidents and incidents.
4   Protect the confidentiality of the event organisation and sponsors.
5   Do not say anything derogatory about any aspect of, or person involved in, the event.
6   Refer media questions to the correct person.

7   Look after equipment, uniforms and other assets.

8   Act in a polite and courteous way when dealing with spectators and team members.

9   Use and abuse of alcohol or drugs while on duty is prohibited.

10   Act in a financially responsible manner.

11   Follow reasonable instructions of supervisors and senior event staff.

The policies can be discussed during induction and issued to all members of the event workforce. It is useful to assess the understanding of these matters, especially WHS, through the use of a questionnaire. This provides evidence that the induction process has been thorough. For an example of online WHS induction, see the Playbill Venues safety induction on the website listed at the end of the chapter.

A volunteer communications plan would likely include the following elements to address implementation:

- objectives
- target audience
- strategy
- key messages and Q&As
- tactics (including material to be used and medium of delivery, such as a website or social media)
- timeline
- responsibilities
- budget and anticipated costs.

Each element of a volunteer communications plan should be thoroughly thought through and describe the process by which it will be executed. For this reason, plans should be detailed, specifying exact dates, all the parties involved, and all the tools and resources required.

Colleagues and other important internal stakeholders should be provided with timely opportunities to contribute to the volunteer program. As mentioned previously, a volunteer communications strategy is not created or implemented independently of other management processes. In particular, senior executives or founders of the event should be consulted to contribute to the volunteer program goals, overarching strategy, resourcing, budget and evaluation plans.

Draw up rosters

Volunteer planning also includes the development of work rosters. This can be quite difficult, particularly if multiple sessions and multiple days are involved and interrelated tasks have to be considered, as sufficient time needs to be factored in for each task. For example, if the site crew has not completed the installation of essential equipment for a particular session, work cannot begin on related tasks. Volunteers scheduled to be on duty will stand idle and become frustrated, knowing that deadlines are slipping. Having got out of bed at 3 a.m. to arrive as scheduled at 4.30 a.m. to set up for the day will contribute further to their frustration. In the event environment, there is often limited time for a transition from one session or show to the next, and there are usually many interrelated jobs to be done, requiring extremely detailed planning and scheduling. A staffing crisis in the hours preceding an event can also contribute to the risk of accidents and poor service, again emphasising the importance of effective planning.

Gordon and Erkut (2004) looked at volunteer scheduling for the Edmonton Folk Festival, which is run almost entirely by 1800 volunteers. The authors' study supports the idea that accessible online scheduling software enables volunteers to manage their schedules based on personal preferences and limitations.

MAXIMISE VOLUNTEER RETENTION

Recognition of the work of both paid and volunteer staff can have a significant impact on motivation and retention. One of the most effective strategies is the development of realistic goals for staff, as this allows individuals to see that their work has contributed to the success of the event.

Intangible rewards include:

- goal achievement through individual and team targets and competitions
- job rotation
- job enrichment
- meeting athletes, stars, musicians and artists
- working with people from overseas
- providing service and information and performing other meaningful tasks
- praise and verbal recognition
- training and skill development
- opportunities for building relationships and friendships
- media recognition.

Tangible rewards include:

- merchandise
- tickets
- post-event parties
- recognition certificates
- statement of duties performed
- meals and uniforms of a high standard
- badges and memorabilia.

A volunteer at work at a community event

Linking performance to individual or team goals should be considered carefully by those in charge of motivating staff. When recognition is given to individuals, it needs to be done with caution, otherwise it can lead to accusations of inequity. Team targets are more likely to improve team performance and to develop camaraderie.

Cuskelly et al. (2006) caution against a one-size-fits-all approach to retention. Their study found that 'HRM practices and their association with volunteer retention problems vary within and across different categories of volunteer positions' (p. 158). Volunteers can fill any number of positions, from chairperson to ticket taker, and they work across a wide variety of event types, some of which align with their interests and others which do not.

Volunteers are thanked for their efforts

FIGURE 23.3 The volunteer journey

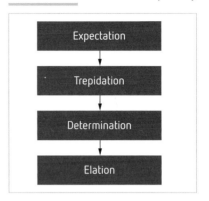

The volunteer journey is quite often an emotional as well as a physically draining one. From an emotional point of view, volunteers go through four stages, as illustrated in Figure 23.3. Initially they have quite high expectations, particularly if the event is well publicised or supports an important cause that they can relate to. As the event draws near, trepidation sets in because there is so much that is unfamiliar: the venue, the team, the role and so on. Having survived the first day, most volunteers then settle down emotionally but start to get very tired. Completing all the shifts requires determination, which is rewarded at the end of a successful event with feelings of elation.

Summary

Volunteer management is crucial to the smooth running of many events. Initially, one has to identify roles suitable for volunteers and then plan recruitment, selection and induction programs. Recruitment and selection help to bring volunteers on line, while induction and training prepare them for their event roles. We have looked at the types of events that lend themselves to recruiting volunteers, how to maximise volunteer retention, and strategies for recognising their involvement. A communications plan is necessary to ensure that volunteers are engaged from the start of the process to the end of the event. Leadership training for supervisors is equally important, as volunteer motivation is a key element of retention.

REVIEW YOUR KNOWLEDGE

1   List five reasons why people volunteer for events.
2   What are the benefits, costs and risks of a volunteer program for an event organisation?
3   Explain the key elements of the following legislation with respect to volunteers:
    −   EEO
    −   WHS.
4   What are the 10 most important elements of a volunteer program as outlined by Volunteering Australia's *National Standards for Volunteer Involvement*? (See the list of websites at the end of the chapter.)

5   What are the unique features of the event industry that make the processes of recruitment, selection and induction of volunteers somewhat different to these HR processes in a traditional business?

APPLY YOUR KNOWLEDGE

A PCBU is a 'person conducting a business or undertaking', and this includes an organisation that involves volunteers as part of the event workforce. Investigate the WHS legislation in your State or Territory with respect to volunteer management. In the process of this investigation, answer the following questions:

1   Do volunteers have to comply with the WHS Act?
2   Can volunteers be prosecuted under the WHS Act?
3   Is a volunteer entitled to workers compensation?
4   Explain the following insurances and their relevance to volunteer management:
    – volunteer workers personal accident insurance
    – public liability insurance.

To check your answers, visit: www.safeworkaustralia.gov.au/system/files/documents/1703/volunteers_guide.pdf

CASE STUDY

MUSIC FESTIVAL

A music festival usually runs over a three-day long weekend. Over 200 volunteers are needed in a wide variety of roles. You have just been appointed the new volunteer program manager.

Last year the dropout rate (attrition rate) for volunteers was 25 per cent. Those who stayed complained about a number of factors, and in a post-event survey only 10 per cent said that they would volunteer again.

The festival's organisers want to provide effective management of volunteers and to abide by best practice in line with the *National Standards for Volunteer Involvement*. They want you to develop a volunteer management plan to cover the following:

*   workforce planning – volunteer roles
*   recruitment strategy
*   selection strategy
*   induction and training plan
*   retention strategy
*   communications plan / online support
*   pre- and post-event evaluation of volunteer expectations and level of satisfaction.

Online resources

Visit http://login.cengagebrain.com and search for this book to access the study tools that come with your textbook.

References

Column 8 (2000). *Sydney Morning Herald*, 18 September.

Cuskelly, G., Taylor, T., Hoye, R., & Darcy, S. (2006). Volunteer management practices and volunteer retention: A human resource management approach. *Sport Management Review*, 9(2), 141–63.

Gordon, L., & Erkut, E. (2004). Improving volunteer scheduling for the Edmonton Folk Festival. *Interfaces*, 34(5), 367–76.

Güntert, S. T., Neufeind, M., & Wehner, T. (2015). Motives for event volunteering: Extending the functional approach. *Nonprofit and Voluntary Sector Quarterly*, 44(4), 686–707.

Kemp, S. (2002). The hidden workforce: Volunteers' learning in the Olympics. *Journal of European Industrial Training*, 26(2–4), 109–16.

PricewaterhouseCoopers Australia (PwC). (2016). State of volunteering in Australia: Help create happiness. April. Volunteering Australia.

Rogalsky, K., Doherty, A., & Paradis, K. F. (2016). Understanding the sport event volunteer experience: An investigation of role ambiguity and its correlates. *Journal of Sport Management*, 30(4), 453–69.

Van der Wagen, L. (2015). *Human Resource Management for the Event Industry*. London: Routledge.

Websites

EvenTeamworK, http://eventeamwork.com.au/about-us

National Folk Festival volunteer program, http://folkfestival.org.au/volunteers

Playbill Venues safety induction, http://venues.playbillvenues.com.au/safety_induction/wizard/step1

Volunteering Australia – National Standards for Volunteer Involvement, www.volunteeringaustralia.org/wp-content/uploads/National-Standards-Document-FINAL-3004.pdf

10

EVENT IMPLEMENTATION

24 ORGANISE EVENT INFRASTRUCTURE

OVERVIEW

This chapter covers the coordination of infrastructure and facilities for a complex event comprising multiple components, where these do not already exist at a venue or site. Many events take place at outdoor venues or at locations where infrastructure and facilities are minimal. Significant event operations knowledge combined with organisational and management skills are required to establish that infrastructure and make it operational. Consultation with suppliers, colleagues and broader event stakeholders is integral to planning for this type of event.

LEARNING OBJECTIVES

On completion of this chapter, you will be able to:

1. identify event infrastructure requirements based on a detailed review of the proposed event and venue and undertake planning activities, including risk management

2. establish and organise event infrastructure by preparing specifications and evaluating suppliers of goods and services, confirming arrangements in writing

3. monitor event infrastructure, evaluating work against schedules and specifications

4. evaluate the success of event infrastructure operations, noting improvements for future event planning.

INDUSTRY VIEWPOINT

The convergence of two separate student research projects occurred when a comment made by one respondent linked the two themes. The research projects investigated, firstly, satisfaction with provision of toilet amenities at music events and, secondly, drug use associated with different music genres. The female respondent stated that the queues at events were so long that she did not drink anything so that she would not miss acts or lose her place. This has potentially serious ramifications, including death from dehydration due to ecstasy use, exacerbated by lack of adequate toilet facilities. While this risk may be overstated, the findings from the research showed high levels of dissatisfaction with toilet amenities at festivals and events among female respondents. On a satisfaction scale, this aspect of the event was rated as important as food/beverage and parking/transport and clearly deserves greater attention from event organisers.

Source: Van Der Wagen, M. (2009). Ecstasy, dehydration and inadequate provision of toilet amenities for female music fans. ACEM 5th International Event Management Research Conference, Gold Coast, 6–7 July

INTRODUCTION

In terms of waiting time to use toilet facilities, most respondents to this survey waited for 5–10 minutes. However, over 30 per cent waited for 10–20 minutes, 8 per cent waited for 20–30 minutes and 4 per cent waited for up to 60 minutes. One respondent reported going home early as she could not face the waiting required. Just over 50 per cent of respondents missed part of the show as a result of this wait and 24 per cent said that this would impact on their decision to attend a future event.

The provision of toilet facilities is just one aspect of event infrastructure that needs to be considered and, judging from this research, it needs to be considered more carefully than it has been in the past. As well as toilet facilities, event infrastructure requirements include fencing, stages, catering facilities, provision of drinking water, data cabling and electrical cabling. All need to be considered at the concept stage and installed just before the event opens. An event that is staged in a park, for example, requires more detailed site planning as many of the services need to be established (for example, the cloak room, first aid tent, information kiosk, ticketing booth, backstage area and site office). All of these involve the erection of temporary facilities.

The focus of this chapter is managing the set-up, operation and pack-up of the event infrastructure, which is the culmination of many months, at least, of careful planning.

ANALYSE EVENT INFRASTRUCTURE REQUIREMENTS

The first stage of event operational planning involves establishing the event infrastructure requirements. These requirements could be for an indoor venue, such as a sports centre, community hall or an exhibition centre. They could also be for an outdoor site. Where the venue or site has been used frequently for events, this can be helpful, as the venue or site management team will have many more answers to the numerous questions organisers may ask. The planning challenges will be greater if the site or venue has never been used for the type of event you are planning.

Effective planning ensures the provision of all necessary infrastructure and amenities at an event

The first step is to liaise with the relevant authorities at the commencement of the event management cycle to ensure regulatory requirements are integrated into the planning process. The second step is to identify and analyse infrastructure and facility requirements based on a detailed review of all aspects of the proposed event and venue.

These requirements could include:

- staging
- power supply
- water supply
- heating or air-conditioning
- public toilets
- erection of temporary structures (in addition to staging)
- scaffolding
- emergency services
- car and coach parking
- transport systems
- contractor access
- camping sites or other temporary accommodation
- signage
- technology requirements (data cabling, Internet access)
- disabled access
- waste management
- security
- any ecological, environmental or heritage requirements.

From this list, it is immediately evident that many of these requirements can be met by existing, dedicated event facilities, providing a powerful incentive to use such a venue. However, there are also occasions where an untested site (such as a city precinct or a commercial building) is the most appropriate for the planned event. Consideration should also be given to utilities: air-conditioning, power, water and waste disposal.

Once a detailed list of the infrastructure requirements has been developed, it needs to be discussed with the approving authority or venue management. Relevant authorities may include local government, a State or Territory government, the police, ambulance and fire services. At all stages it is necessary to incorporate safety, security and risk management issues into all planning documentation and processes, as safety aspects are the most likely to lead to a rejection of event plans.

> **Utilities**
> Utilities include supplies of water and electricity

A map or diagram of the event overlay (site plan) is part of the planning process and needs to involve all stakeholders before it can be finalised and approved. For example, emergency services need to approve the location of first aid tents and other services for ease of access. There may be road closures in the surrounding area as part of the traffic management plan. Crowd flow planning is considered carefully – at a festival near the Victorian coastal town of Lorne in December 2016, more than 60 music fans were injured in a crowd crush while trying to leave the performance.

The site plan will assist with the planning submission made to the council and communication with stakeholders, including emergency services and contractors. Closer to the event, it will provide the audience with graphic information about the event. Figure 24.1 shows an example of a site plan.

FIGURE 24.1 Audience-friendly event map (site plan)

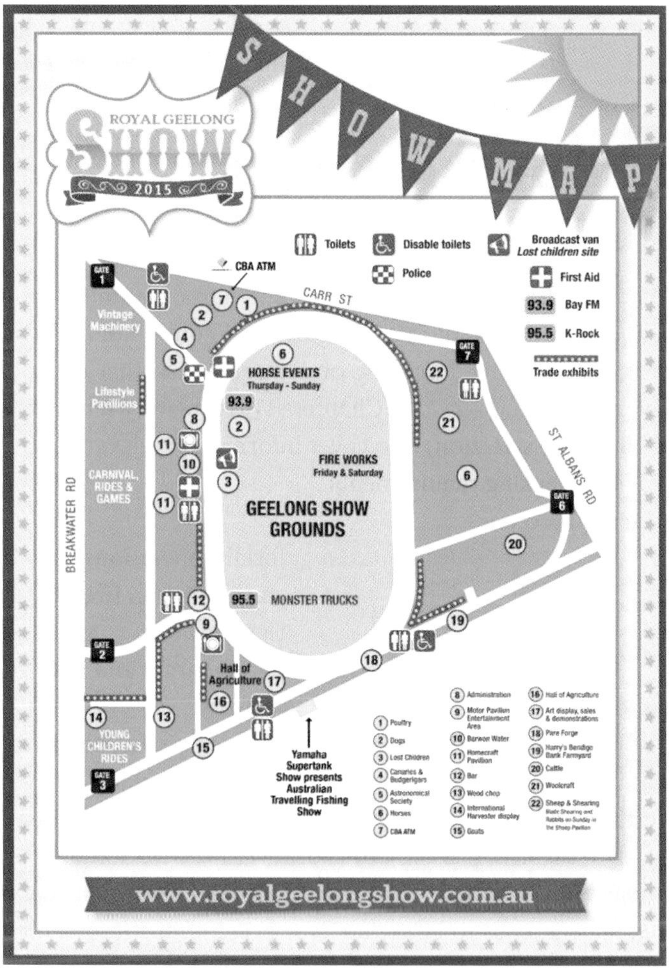

Source: https://www.weekendnotes.com/im/002/02/geelong-showground-map-show-rides-showbags-aimals-1.jpg

The site plan checklist provided in the appendix of this book shows the level of detail that is required for a council submission.

Regulatory considerations

An event overlay on a park or similar site requires careful planning, as the council or landowner will be concerned about environmental impacts. Fortunately, there are many methods of turf protection, including temporary access paths. There are many other considerations, such as waste, run-off, and potential damage to plant life, and an environmental strategy is needed to plan for all of these. Barriers and hazard tape are useful tools for treating the risks of environmental damage.

Built infrastructure and facilities will involve the services of builders, plumbers and electricians, all of whom are required to be licensed and insured. The build schedule ensures that these contractors arrive in the right sequence.

The many laws and regulations that might apply were covered in Chapter 17. In brief, they relate to issues such as:

- environmental protection
- food safety planning
- noise regulations
- WHS

- waste management
- building regulations
- traffic management
- liquor licensing.

SOURCE AND ORGANISE EVENT INFRASTRUCTURE REQUIREMENTS

Following approval from the relevant authorities and site or venue manager, steps can be taken to establish and organise event infrastructure and contractors. This requires accurate requests for tenders or the detailed briefing of contractors so that quotes can be obtained from suppliers of equipment and services. Chapters 17 (regulatory requirements), 7 (business relationships) and 15 (venue selection) also cover information relevant to this aspect of event management, including licensing requirements.

Licences may be required for:

- building work
- electrical work
- plumbing work
- gas fitting
- handling hazardous materials

- forklift operations
- stage sets (e.g. fire retardant certification)
- rigging
- pyrotechnics and special effects
- security.

The logistics of event management planning involves getting things organised, getting things (and people) in the right place at the right time, and pulling everything down. Rock concerts and entertainment events featuring international artists present many logistical problems, particularly if the group is on a tour of several cities. Sometimes a complex array of musical equipment, some of which might have been airlifted into the country only days, or even hours, before the event, has to be set up. However, in most cases, the team supporting the artists would have identified specific requirements, at times down to the last detail, to be met locally. (These might even include requests for exotic foods, special dietary items and dressing room layouts.)

The most amusing example of a logistical dilemma was that reported by the organisers of an equestrian cross-country event. A decision had to be made as to how to manage 'comfort breaks' for volunteers deployed over an enormous open venue. Should a buggie pick up the staff member and take them to the facilities? No, it was decided that a roving portaloo on the back of a small truck was the answer. Take the toilet to the staff member, not the staff member to the toilet! This avoided the redeployment of replacement staff. Naturally, also, the event organisers did not want to impact on the 'look' of the event on television by having temporary portaloos littered all over the cross-country course.

The level of difficulty associated with running an outdoor event at a temporary site cannot be underestimated. Each element of the proposed infrastructure must be discussed with key stakeholders and suppliers. Careful coordination and monitoring is essential, particularly during the bump-in phase when several contractors will be working simultaneously. As the expression goes, 'Time is money', and contractors who waste time during bump-in are not going to be responsive to later requests from event managers who have not planned the logistics of bump-in carefully enough to ensure an efficient process.

Bump-in (or set-up)

Once final arrangements have been checked and staff and contractors have been briefed, the process of setting up all structures and facilities required for the event begins. Setting up can be a time-consuming process and a run-through must be built into the planning. This is absolutely essential as it is imperative that all facilities and equipment work. For some tasks, such as installing sound and lighting equipment, the services of specialist engineers are needed.

For outdoor sites, an all-terrain vehicle may be needed to avoid damage to grass. This is illustrated in the accompanying photograph, in which first aid tents and ATM facilities can be seen in the background. Where an ATM is available on-site, delivery of cash to the tent is a logistical issue: ideally, there will be access from the rear for the armoured vehicle and also security guards. Perimeter fencing is another requirement for most outdoor events. Computer networks are tested to ensure that the network is up and running.

The collage of images from a food and wine festival shows the many facets of bumping in such an event. Most infrastructure is installed on the day before the event (and there are safety issues with this if members of the public, including children, have access to the site). Food and wine vendors bump in early in the morning (so neighbours need to be notified) so they can be ready to commence sales mid-morning. Vehicles should be prohibited at this stage. While this should be obvious, vans driving through crowds is a common sight at many outdoor events.

All-terrain vehicles are useful for various purposes at outdoor events and are designed to avoid damaging the grass

Figure 24.2 illustrates the level of checking that needs to be done to ensure that the set-up of an event will run smoothly.

FIGURE 24.2 Overseeing event set-up

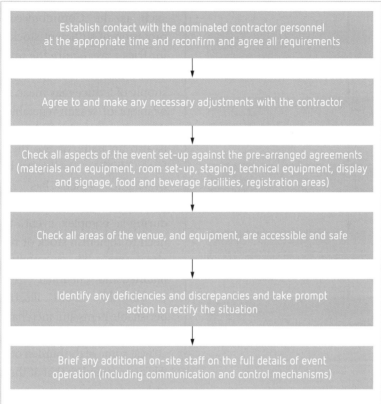

Establish contact with the nominated contractor personnel at the appropriate time and reconfirm and agree all requirements

Agree to and make any necessary adjustments with the contractor

Check all aspects of the event set-up against the pre-arranged agreements (materials and equipment, room set-up, staging, technical equipment, display and signage, food and beverage facilities, registration areas)

Check all areas of the venue, and equipment, are accessible and safe

Identify any deficiencies and discrepancies and take prompt action to rectify the situation

Brief any additional on-site staff on the full details of event operation (including communication and control mechanisms)

Bump-out (or breakdown)

Essentially, the bump-out sequence is the reverse of the bump-in. The timing, though, is usually a lot quicker. Again, a detailed schedule needs to be developed and agreed with contractors. This may include restrictions and/or scheduling of vehicle access to the site. All temporary structures and equipment need to be dismantled. If this has to happen immediately after the audience has left, sufficient staff will be required because at this stage everyone is generally exhausted, which itself presents a safety risk. If bump-out does not occur immediately, security staff will be needed to monitor the site until all equipment and materials have been removed. Some items are very expensive, and if they are lost, stolen or damaged this can have a dramatic effect on the bottom line of an otherwise successful event.

Figure 24.3 shows what is involved in efficiently managing the breakdown of an event.

In most other industries, logistics involves managing the processes of manufacture, supply and distribution (including storage and transport) of the product to the ultimate consumer. The same general principles apply in event management, where an organised and structured alignment of key logistics functions is required. Procurement, transportation, storage, inventory management, customer service and database management are all examples of logistical aspects of such event activities as merchandise sales. In the same way, the supply of

FIGURE 24.3 Overseeing event breakdown

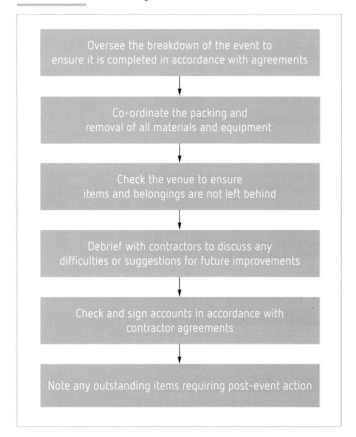

food and beverage to the event audience starts right back with the producer of the food and beverage products. For most events, food supply is unproblematic. However, in the case of a very large event, such as the Commonwealth Games, provision of sufficient stock of potatoes for fries may require the importation of frozen fries, while ensuring an adequate supply of lettuce may mean the sourcing of an out-of-season vegetable. For events that run over multiple days, food storage is also an issue, as are the logistics of fresh supplies needing to be delivered overnight, which has ramifications for staffing rosters and security. Often during a complex event, there is the need to replenish stock or refurbish and clean areas. These activities must be planned and scheduled.

As the above illustrates, most perishable items and merchandise should be sold during the event, thus alleviating at least some of the burden of moving out. Always remember that at the completion of bump-out the venue or site must be handed back to the owner or operator and any damages checked. This will be stipulated in the contract, and this final check and handover should be carefully documented, no matter how tired the event team.

MONITOR EVENT INFRASTRUCTURE

During the bump-in process, the event organiser needs to monitor progress with the infrastructure build. Specific times are allocated to this process in the exhibition industry and, for safety reasons, exhibitors are not allowed access to their stands until the build is complete. Ongoing liaison with contractors is necessary so that any need for adjustments to infrastructure can be identified and appropriate changes organised and confirmed in writing. This process is facilitated by well-prepared bump-in schedules, or run sheets, and a detailed operations manual. Sharing information with stakeholders, contractors and other staff is essential. One manager who did not follow this advice was seen on a children's scooter riding haphazardly from one part of an exhibition hall to another, leading to total meltdown when he could not cope with the hundreds of questions asked by stall holders. Keeping all the plans in your head is not advisable.

Monitoring progress, by itself, may not be enough. A good event manager anticipates possible changes that might be required and develops positive action plans to keep progress on time and on budget. A delay in one area can cause a significant flow-on effect in many other areas. This proactive approach is called 'active monitoring'.

Policies, procedures and performance standards

Every event requires policies. These describe the general principles, or 'what is to be done'. For example, policies may be drawn up to prevent accidents, avoid theft, or prioritise access to the site by emergency services crews. Having prepared the policies, the procedures for implementing them are then developed. The policy equates to 'what is to be done' and the procedure equates to 'how it is to be done'.

A procedure can take the form of a list of tasks or a checklist. Once procedures have been developed and integrated across the event functions, all the pieces begin to fit together. Sometimes, the timing of a procedure needs to be modified to meet the needs of another functional area. For example, if the grass surrounding the greens of a golf course was scheduled to be mowed the day before a golfing competition, it would not be possible to erect the crowd control fencing until this had been done.

A procedure for checking the safety of a kitchen could be outlined in a checklist, as shown in Figure 24.4. This procedure could also be shown as a flowchart or it could be based on a logical tour of the kitchen, with items rearranged to match the kitchen set-up.

FIGURE 24.4 Checklist for kitchen safety procedure

Kitchen Safety Checklist

1 Food contact surfaces are clean and clear. ☐
2 Chopping boards for meat, chicken, vegetables are colour coded. ☐
3 Non-food surfaces clean and clear. ☐
4 Floors are clean and not slippery. ☐
5 Equipment is correctly cleaned and stored. ☐
6 Wiping cloths and cleaning equipment for different purposes correctly colour coded. ☐
7 Plumbing is functional. ☐
8 Refrigerator and freezer temperatures meet standards. ☐
9 Hand-washing facilities meet standards. ☐
10 Garbage disposal containers are labelled and covered. ☐
11 Storage areas are clean and clear. ☐
12 No evidence of insects or rodents. ☐
13 Lighting and ventilation is adequate. ☐
14 Gas supply is checked. ☐
15 All cooking equipment is functional. ☐
16 First aid box is fully equipped. ☐

By establishing performance standards and inspection schedules, the operational success of an event can be more confidently assured. For example, in the case of a contract with a cleaning company, with clear expectations on both sides the result should be excellent customer service. In the case of the cleaning contractor, specific details about the level of service required would be outlined for the following:

- pre-event day cleaning
- in-session cleaning
- turnover cleaning (between sessions)
- post-event cleaning
- removal of waste materials.

The criteria for performance standards may include efficiency for example, speed of set-up and breakdown – see Figure 24.5), accuracy (checklist 100 per cent), revenue (dollar sales per outlet) or courtesy (customer feedback).

FIGURE 24.5 Effective planning ensures efficient set-up and breakdown

The Black Ice World Tour was a 2008–10 concert tour in support of AC/DC's 15th studio album, *Black Ice*. In total, the tour played to 4.9 million people, making it one of the highest-grossing concert tours in history.

Most rock tours are measured by the number of semitrailers it takes to cart the show. At the time of the Black Ice tour, U2 and the Rolling Stones used 40 rigs – AC/DC needed 80. It took the 200-strong production crew five days to set up the show. AC/DC brought everything to the party, including speakers, lights, amplifiers, scaffolding and their own power generators. At Sydney's ANZ Stadium, 10 000 square metres of terraplas were laid to protect the turf. However, after the show was over, it took only 24 hours to pack up and leave.

The operations manual

An extract from the contents page of the Perth Convention and Exhibition Centre's *Event Operations Manual* is shown in Figure 24.6. This is indicative of the level of detail required for a venue operator. (The full details of this manual can be found on the companion website or PCEC website.) While this would form the basis for further operational planning for an exhibition, this is not the full picture. The event organiser – in this case the exhibition planner – is responsible for running the event. This requires negotiation with the tradespeople needed to build the exhibition stands and the development of run sheets for unloading and installing the equipment. Signage and other visual items hanging from the ceiling would almost certainly require the use of a cherry picker or scissor lift.

So, in this case, there are several bump-in phases: build for large infrastructure, build for exhibition stands, bump-in for exhibitors, and finally the opening. Thus, in addition to the plan for the layout of the exhibition, a run sheet for the build phase of the event would be required. The sequence would be as follows:

- Equipment and contractor bookings confirmed.
- Stakeholders fully briefed: staff, venue, suppliers, exhibitors.

FIGURE 24.6 Extract from table of contents, event operations manual

CONTENTS

Emergency Plan

1. Introduction
1.1 The Purpose of the PCEC Event Manual
1.2 Layout of Contents
1.3 Glossary of Terms
1.4 Manual Updates
1.5 For Further Information
1.6 Welcome to the Venue Overview
1.6.1 Preferred Suppliers
1.7 Working with the PCEC
1.8 Fees and Charges
1.9 Payment Procedures
1.10 Exhibitor Accounts
1.11 Advertising and Promotions
1.12 Public Access and Facilities
2.1 Air Conditioning
2.2 Audio Visual Services
2.3 Business Centre and Reception
2.4 Car Park
2.5 Cleaning Services
2.6 Communication & Information Technology Solutions
2.7 Compressed Air
2.8 Concierge and Cloakrooms
2.9 Disabled Facilities
2.10 Exhibition Services Desk
2.11 Food and Beverage — Event Catering
2.12 Loading Dock Access and Management
2.13 Power Connections and Consumption
2.14 Registration
2.15 Rigging
2.16 Room Set-ups for Meetings and Seminars
2.17 Security
2.18 Signage
2.19 Special Events in the Pavilions
2.20 Stages and Dance Floors
2.21 Storage on Site
2.22 Ticketing Services
2.23 Ticketing, Ushers, and Cloakroom Services
2.24 Water and Drainage

3 General Policies and Procedures

3.1 Animals
3.2 Amusement and Other Entertainment Devices
3.3 Balloons and Other Inflatable Devices
3.4 Building or Construction Work
3.5 Candles
3.6 Children
3.7 Contractors and Production Companies
3.8 Contractors' Passes
3.9 Dangerous and Noxious Substances
3.10 Deliveries to the PCEC
3.11 Damage to the PCEC
3.12 Dynamic Exhibitions
3.13 Electrical Equipment
3.14 Emergency Evacuations
3.15 Exhibitor Manual
3.16 Exits, Egress, Aisles and No Build Zones
3.17 Fire Safety Regulations
3.18 First Aid
3.19 Floor Plan Approval
3.20 Floor Load Weight Limits
3.21 Foyer Areas
3.22 Gas Storage/Appliances
3.23 Guard Rails for Stages, Risers and Platforms
3.24 Hanging Objects
3.27 Housekeeping
3.28 Insurance
3.29 Material Handling Equipment
3.30 Move In/Move Out
3.32 Occupational Safety and Health
3.33 Plant and Equipment
3.34 Prizes and Lotteries
3.35 Pyrotechnics — Requirements for Use
3.36 Risk Assessment
3.37 Seating in Exhibition Pavilions
3.38 Security
3.39 Smoking Policy
3.40 Special Requirements/Services
3.41 Sponsorship

Source: Reproduced with kind permission of the Perth Convention and Exhibition Centre

- Documentation checked and distributed.
- Venue security briefed.
- Venue clear and clean.
- Production management team on-site.
- WHS officer on-site.
- Implement WHS induction and monitoring process.
- Load in and install rigging (requires lift equipment).

- Load in and install rigged lighting, audio and projection.
- Load in and install aerially rigged signage.
- Install and distribute power and Telstra cable.
- Exhibition floor all clear.
- Mark up floor.
- Allocate subfloor services and install.
- Load in and install flooring: carpet, floating.
- Load in and install shell scheme and customised stands (including stand lighting and audiovisual).
- Load in and distribute graphics and signage.
- Load in and distribute furniture and fittings.
- Load in and install exhibitor materials.
- Load in and set up food and beverage outlets.
- All clear for doors to open for public entry.
- Exhibition commences.
- Exhibition concludes.
- Bump-out commences (in reverse sequence).

Several event planning guidelines are included on the companion website to this text; in particular, Events Geelong provides exhaustive guides to planning, including risk management. Guides are also provided with other resources accompanying the text. These give all the information needed to plan different types of events, indoor and outdoor, at dedicated venues and untested sites. It is a good idea for manuals to include copies of contractors' quotes and agreements, as it is likely that the person who conducted the negotiation with the contractors will not be present at the time of bump-in. By keeping these quotes and specifications handy, problems can be more easily resolved and conflict avoided.

EVALUATE SUCCESS OF EVENT INFRASTRUCTURE OPERATIONS

In the scramble to break down event infrastructure and leave the site, opportunities to review and evaluate are often lost. This is important knowledge as it informs future event planning and operations. There are many arrangements that can fall down in terms of service quality and operational efficiency, such as the following:

- People don't turn up on the night and the organiser has paid $120 per head for catering.
- There is no audience for the event despite widespread advertising.
- A beach event is planned without reference to tides and the weather.
- The power supplied is not enough to drive all the AV equipment.
- Long queues mean that people miss part of the event.
- People unexpectedly turn up to a graduation event and there are no certificates for them.
- The performers don't arrive because they have missed a connecting flight that was planned with too little leeway and the audience is left waiting for over an hour.
- The bar is dry or the buffet empty.

- People jump over the barriers or knock them down.
- Ticket takers abandon their places at the gates and the event is overcrowded and dangerous.

As this and previous chapters have indicated, there are many suppliers and stakeholders involved in event planning, which can introduce problems with RSVPs, fencing, technology and all manner of other planning details. There are, however, several potential sources of information that can be tapped in order to improve future operations:

- analysis of incident report forms
- visitor surveys
- stakeholder debriefings
- management focus groups
- review of event documentation
- photographic and observational evidence (CCTV).

All of this information, some of it very positive, can be harnessed in order to analyse performance in light of feedback against predetermined performance criteria.

Summary

This chapter has looked in more detail at logistics, including the often problematic bump-in and bump-out phases of an event. The task of identifying the resources and equipment needed, bringing them on-site and setting up in the required time takes careful planning. The emphasis in this chapter has therefore been on organisation and coordination to ensure that all functional areas work together smoothly and cooperatively through all phases of the event. The development of policies and procedures can assist in the fulfilment of this goal by outlining the interrelationship between functional areas, and they will also help ensure that the event performance standards and objectives are successfully achieved. The operations manual, including all plans, layouts and schedules, is invaluable in this regard.

Key term

Utilities   Utilities include supplies of water and electricity

REVIEW YOUR KNOWLEDGE

1   What do we mean by the terms 'infrastructure' and 'utilities'?
2   List and explain 10 differences between a dedicated event venue and an untested site from an infrastructure point of view.
3   What are the safety issues for an event that is being built in an open space and how can these be managed?
4   Explain how policies and procedures can be used to streamline bump-in.
5   Coordinating contractors is an essential part of planning. How would you reduce the risks associated with failure to integrate supplier services?

APPLY YOUR KNOWLEDGE

MUSIC EVENT

The event shown in the image provides for on-site camping.

1   Identify the temporary structures and utilities that would be required for this event.

2   What are the regulatory considerations for this music event?

RACE FINISH

You are organising a race for 20 000 runners. The biggest logistical problem you face will arise at the end of the race. At this time, runners crossing the finish line are exhausted and don't want to run or walk another step. Media wanting to take photographs and interview front runners compounds this problem. Enthusiastic supporters wishing to congratulate those who finish only adds to it. All runners need to get across the line without hold-ups, otherwise their times will be affected.

You need to make plans to ensure that all runners cross the line, that they are advised of their times, and that they receive free sponsor products, retrieve their belongings and attend the prize-giving ceremony. Some participants and spectators will not wait for the final ceremony and will wish to take the transport provided back to the race starting point and go home.

Develop detailed operational plans for the end of the race, using estimates of finish times and crowd flow patterns for participants and spectators.

CASE STUDY

EVENT PROPOSAL FOR A STREET FESTIVAL OR SIMILAR EVENT

Using the tools and templates provided by Events Geelong (or similar), develop an event plan. The event can be any type of outdoor event on public land. For this proposal, you need to cover the following components:

- event overview
- event program
- event budget
- event site plan
- event build schedule
- staff roles
- risk management.

    Do not contact Events Geelong, local councils or suppliers for assistance with this proposal.

Online resources

CENGAGE
brain.com

Visit **http://login.cengagebrain.com** and search for this book to access the study tools that come with your textbook.

Websites

City of Sydney event guidelines, www.cityofsydney.nsw.gov.au/__data/assets/pdf_file/0003/235830/Event-Guidelines-V2.3.pdf

Event management planning guide (Queensland Government), https://publications.qld.gov.au/he/dataset/olgr-publications/resource/83339b0f-bd15-4d4a-847b-6784f15603fb

Events Geelong event planning guide, www.geelongaustralia.com.au/events/planning/eventplanning/article/item/8cdc2778104484a.aspx

Perth Convention and Exhibition Centre event manual, www.pcec.com.au/plan-an-event/event-resources

Planning and running sporting events, www.ipswich.qld.gov.au/__data/assets/pdf_file/0017/8045/event_management_workbook.pdf

Writing an event proposal, www.leoisaac.com/evt/top075.htm

APPENDIX

EVENT MANAGEMENT PLAN

Summative assessment

The following task relates to the final chapter 'Organise event infrastructure' (SITEEVT009) in which you are required to analyse event infrastructure requirements; source and organise event infrastructure requirements; and monitor the build of event infrastructure. Finally, you are required to evaluate the success of event infrastructure operations. In doing so you need to develop comprehensive plans, showing that you can work with local authorities and other stakeholders. The appendix that follows offers the groundwork for this live event or simulation. You will also be able to apply the knowledge of project planning, staging, budgets, risk management and workplace health and safety you gained from earlier chapters.

Section 2 of the *Geelong Event Planning Guide*, 'Developing an event plan', has been reproduced here as an appendix with permission. There are many guides available from government organisations, but this is one of the most comprehensive. Overall, there are five sections as well as tools and templates available online:

- Section 1: How to apply for an event
- Section 2: Developing an event plan
- Section 3: Event risk management and planning
- Section 4: Event emergency management and planning
- Section 5: Other useful event planning information

You need to work in a team to develop a comprehensive plan for an outdoor event requiring council approval. You can plan the event for your local area and can also access other event planning guides and templates. These guidelines suggest the following:

Contents of a basic event plan:

- event overview
- event program
- event site plan
- event build schedule
- staff roles and contacts list
- risk management/planning.

Depending on the nature of your event, additional event planning documents may also be required. Additional plans may include a:

- traffic and transport plan
- power management plan
- lighting plan
- water management plan
- waste management plan
- recycling plan
- noise management plan
- food management plan

- liquor management plan
- asset protection plan
- accessibility plan.

Finally, to meet the requirements of this competency unit, you also need to show how the event can be evaluated to enhance future planning.

You are reminded that it is not appropriate to contact a council such as this one (or any other industry suppliers) for help with assessments or quotes unless it is a real proposal. Sufficient information is provided online for you to do assessments.

WHY DOES THE EVENT NEED A PLAN?

Every event regardless of its size and nature needs an event plan. The plan is a collection of all of the decisions and arrangements that the event organiser has made to ensure that the event is set up according to the site plan, to ensure that all the contractors know what their responsibilities are and so the public have a safe and enjoyable experience.

You will be required to submit your event plan to the Event Services Unit. Final approval will be contingent on you applying for the relevant permits and ensuring your event plan meets the requirements of the City of Greater Geelong and the relevant agencies.

HOW TO MAKE A BASIC EVENT PLAN

This section of the Guide will help you develop a basic event plan. Additional event planning documents that may be required in the event plan are listed in *Section 2, The Event Plan, Part B, Additional Event Plans* of this Guide. Your Events Officer will advise you if any of these extra plans are required.

The contents of a basic event plan as follows:

- event overview
- event program
- event site plan
- event build schedule
- staff roles and contacts list
- risk management/planning – go to *Section 3* of this guide.

Once the event plan is developed and finalised you should distribute copies to:

- City of Greater Geelong – Event Services Unit
- asset managers and agencies that have issued permits and approvals
- your safety officer and chief wardens
- your event staff
- your contractors
- the emergency services
- your volunteers
- your participants (vendors, traders, performers etc.)
- your event committee and key stakeholders.

Note: If the event is required to apply for a Division 2 Occupancy Permit (POPE) the event plan will also need to include planning information requested in the POPE Permit application.

EVENT OVERVIEW

An event overview includes:

- name of the event
- organisers of the event (businesses or group)
- place/location of the event
- time of the event
- reason for the event: e.g. 'national under-23 qualifiers for the junior triathlon championships' or 'annual Christmas carols'
- expected number of participants
- expected number of spectators.

EVENT PROGRAM

How to develop an event program

Include the draft activities planned for your event and show when and where these activities will happen.

Two basic event program examples have been provided below; one program is arts focused and the other sports focused. Changes to the event program can be updated at any time during the planning phase.

EXAMPLE 1 Arts/entertainment event

ACTIVITY	LOCATION	SATURDAY 12 SEPTEMBER
Event starts – public arrives		10.00 a.m.
Food vendors open	See location on site plans	10.00 a.m.
Mechanical rides start	See location on site plans	10.00 a.m.
Stage program commences	On main stage marked on site plan	11.00 a.m. – 9.00 p.m.
Bar opens	Licensed marquee marked on site plan	12 noon
VIP function starts	Licensed marquee marked on site plan	1.00 p.m.
Community race ends	At finish line marked on site plan	5.00 p.m.
Presentations and speeches	At main stage	5.30 p.m.
Fireworks display	On barges located on site plan	9.00 p.m. – 9.30 p.m.
Event finishes		9.30 p.m.

EXAMPLE 2 Sporting event

ACTIVITY	LOCATION	SATURDAY 12 SEPTEMBER
Participant registration	Registration tent	6.00 a.m.
Participant briefing	Transition area	6.30 a.m.
Food vendors open	See location on site plan	7.00 a.m.
Commentary starts	Stage area	7.00 a.m.
RACE start – women amateurs	Swim ramp	7.00 a.m.
RACE start – men amateurs	Swim ramp	7.30 a.m.
RACE start – elites	Swim ramp	8.00 a.m.
VIP function starts	Licensed marquee marked on site plan	10.00 a.m.
Stage program commences	On main stage marked on site plan	9.00 a.m. – 4.00 p.m.
RACE fin – women amateurs	Finish line – Transvaal Square	3.00 p.m.
RACE fin – men amateurs	Finish line – Transvaal Square	3.30 p.m.
RACE fin – elites	Finish line – Transvaal Square	4.00 p.m.
Presentations and speeches	At main stage	4.00 p.m.
Stage program finishes	At main stage	5.00 p.m.
Event finishes		9.30 p.m.

EVENT SITE PLAN

What is a site plan?

A site plan is a map that shows the area on which the event is being staged or held within.

Throughout the site planning section in the Event Application Form you are asked to show information such as placement of equipment, existing services etc. This is so you can manage the site safely and determine in the planning stages how many people can attend the event site at any one time and the best location for the event's services and equipment.

Why is a site plan required?

A good site plan will assist you in applying for permits, positioning equipment and communicating with contractors, suppliers, vendors, performers, participants and spectators. A user-friendly version of the site plan could also be used in promotional information and made available at the event site. The site plan will also be used to communicate with emergency services providers during planning phases as well as during the event.

How to make a good site plan

Start with a good map

This map will become the basis for the site map. Find a map on Google Earth or ask your Events Officer for assistance. The map should show the immediate area surrounding the event site and include the names of the main roads or streets. It should also include all of the area's pathways, roadways, buildings and fences. Ideally this plan is to scale, and includes measurements of the area and its structures.

The site plan should include every single bit of infrastructure that you plan to put on or use at the site. You should show the dimensions (width and length) of all temporary infrastructure and equipment. Consider using a legend in your site plan so the site is clear of boxes and arrows and easier to interpret.

Use a program or engage a professional

Start adding the event infrastructure/equipment to the map to build a site plan. Programs such as PowerPoint or Microsoft Word can be useful in building a site plan. Depending on the scale of the event, event contractors may be able to assist in developing the site plan. This can be a good idea, especially if the event is of a larger scale and complex.

Maintain access

Many events are held in an area where the road is closed and it is assumed that the whole area including the roadway and the footpath is available for the placement of infrastructure and equipment. This is not the case. The event organiser is required to keep the following areas clear and free of infrastructure:

* *On a footpath:* an access path 1.8 metres out from the building line. This is to ensure that vision-impaired people are able to use the building line as a guide to access the area safely.
* *On a roadway:* a 4-metre-wide access path from the start of the road closure to the end is required to be maintained and be free of infrastructure and equipment for the purpose of emergency vehicle access.

Other requirements

If your event requires a Division 2 Occupancy Permit (POPE) or Siting Approval for the prescribed structures, then your site plan will need to be detailed and meet the requirements as set out in *Part C & D* of this Section. You will need to know though how many patrons you can fit into your site once you have added the infrastructure and back of house areas. An easy way to calculate how many people can fit into the site is as follows.

Square metreage of site boundary *minus* the square metreage of all infrastructure and back of house areas = the space that is left for the public attending the event. If 1500 square metres was left and each person generally needs 1 square metre of space, then 1500 people could fit in this event space.

Note: The dimensions of structures (temporary and permanent), the distance between immovable objects and the square metreage of the overall site must be shown on all maps.

Site plan checklist

EXISTING ELEMENTS	TEMPORARY ELEMENTS
Direction of north	
Significant trees Sensitive fauna or flora sites, bodies of water	
Adjacent property owners; i.e. railway land, shopping centres	
Public telephone/s	
Existing fences, gates, barriers, bollards SHOW DIMENSIONS	Temporary fencing (mesh and picket) SHOW DIMENSIONS
Existing entry and exit points SHOW DIMENSIONS	Temporary entry/exit points SHOW WIDTH DIMENSIONS OF EACH POINT
Existing buildings and structures SHOW DIMENSIONS	**Large** temporary structures: SHOW DIMENSIONS • tents & marquees (over 100 m^2) • stages (over 10 m $\times$ 15 m) • prefabricated building • (over 100 m^2) • aerial rigs • cordoned-off areas **Small** temporary structures: SHOW DIMENSIONS • tents & marquees (under 100 m^2) • portable structures (site huts, toilets) • stages (under 150 m^2)
Permanent grandstands SHOW DIMENSIONS	Temporary viewing areas – grandstands that accommodate more than 20 patrons SHOW DIMENSIONS Location of POPE/siting approval permit
Permanent seating areas	Temporary seating areas – show chairs, rows and aisles, and show distance between each row and aisle and seating area for wheelchairs SHOW DIMENSIONS
Existing pedestrian paths and walkways	Temporary pedestrian paths and walkways, including disabled paths
Existing steps and ramps	Temporary steps and ramps (including stages)
	Start/finish gantries and lines
	Route and direction of race (land, road and water)
	Pyrotechnics firing area and public exclusion zone

EXISTING ELEMENTS	TEMPORARY ELEMENTS
Existing amusement rides	Air castles and mechanical rides
	Animal nursery
Existing picnic and seating areas	Temporary picnic, quiet and seating areas
Restaurants, canteens	Temporary food vendors
	Licensed areas (show how area is cordoned off from public – type of fencing used, position, height)
	Ticket Offices / Registration areas Site Offices Operation or communication centres Media areas Public information areas Lost children / property area
Existing lighting towers / or lights	Temporary lighting towers / or lights
• Existing power sources • Power cables from power source to equipment • Show if leads are on the ground or strung overhead	• Temporary power sources, generators and distribution boxes • Show where area is cordoned off • Power cables from power source to equipment • Show if leads are on the ground or strung overhead
Existing sewerage outlets	
Existing toilets: • show male • show female • show disabled	Location of temporary toilets: • show male • show female • show disabled
Existing showers	Locations of temporary showers
Existing gas points	Gas bottle locations and size
Existing water fountains	Temporary water sources like taps, fountains and water trailers
Existing garbage bins	Temporary garbage bins Temporary skips
Pedestrian paths (1.5 m in width minimum) and cross-over points	Pedestrian barriers and temporary cross-over points
Existing car parks, including access car parks Existing bus stops / train stations Existing traffic lights and pedestrian crossings Existing disabled car parks	Temporary parking areas for: • public • temporary access parking (disabled) • contractor entry/exit and drop off pick up areas • bus stops • taxi ranks • emergency vehicles
Existing fire extinguishers and type, hoses and or water points (taps)	Fire fighting equipment (tankers, blankets, extinguishers and type of)

EXISTING ELEMENTS	TEMPORARY ELEMENTS
Emergency access/egress routes Show direction of travel SHOW DIMENSIONS	Access path (min 4 m wide) for all emergency services to all key locations within the venue Show direction of travel SHOW DIMENSIONS
Emergency assembly areas	Emergency assembly areas Align with exit gates (evacuation routes) SHOW DIMENSIONS
Evacuation route	Show evacuation routes: showing public flow routes, security point locations, exit gates and widths and evacuation areas
Existing location and size of first aid facility	Location and size of first aid facility Position of security guards
Existing unsafe areas	Restricted or unsafe areas (fireworks discharge areas, fuel storage, generators, back of house for performers etc.) Signage positions, showing position of key information signs to inform the public of amenities and services

Extra plans

Some areas shown on the site plan may also need to have separate detailed plans. For example, a catering marquee may need to show how the equipment is positioned within the marquee. A stage may need to show the wings, ramps, speaker stacks, canopies etc. A seating area may need to show how the rows or seating are to be positioned and the distance between each, the aisle widths shown, measured and marked. The clearance between rows of fixed seats should not be less than:

* 300 mm if the distance to an aisle is less than 3.5 m; or
* 500 mm if the distance to an aisle is more than 3.5 m.

EVENT BUILD SCHEDULE AND SUPERVISOR ROLES

You are responsible for the site, your contractors and for the safety of the public.

As the event organiser you are responsible for providing a safe environment for the public in and around your event's site, and this includes ensuring that your contractors are entering and exiting the site safely, that you have cordoned off the site so the public cannot access unsafe areas. It is your responsibility to manage any persons or contractors who are erecting, depositing or building equipment on the site. This applies during the set-up, staging, delivery and pack-up phases of the event.

Some event sites or structures on an event site may be deemed 'constructions' or 'structures' and therefore they must meet the Victorian Construction Regulations and comply with the *Occupational Health and Safety Act 2004.* Some contractors may need to provide you with Job Safety Analysis or Safe Work Method statements to show you how they are going to construct their equipment safely.

Section 3, Risk Management/Planning of this Guide provides advice on complying with these regulations.

Most sites are deemed to be places of work and therefore they must comply with the 2004 *OH&S Act.* Serious fines can be issued by WorkSafe, as well as Provisional Improvement Notices (PIN) which can cease your build and may result in the cancellation of your event. As the event organiser you must nominate appropriate staff or volunteers to manage the site build at all times that there are contractors on-site. You should equip your site supervisors with safety vests, a build schedule and contractor contact list; they should also have copies of the relevant Job Safety Analysis and Safe Work Method statements.

This is what you will need as a minimum when you are setting up and packing up a site:

- supervisors in high visibility vests or jackets who are scheduled to be on-site BEFORE the first contractor and until the LAST contractor or piece of equipment has been removed
- supervisors with the final site plan
- supervisors with the final build schedule
- supervisors with contact names and phone numbers of contractors
- spotters at the entry and exit areas to walk vehicles onto the site
- enough hazard tape and orange plastic bollards to safely cordon off the work zones
- rubber or grass matting to fix trip hazards
- pedestrian barriers to fence off unsafe areas
- cable ties and red gaffer tape.

Note: Once the set-up or build of the event has been completed, the bollards and pedestrian barriers can then be used to cordon off back of house and unsafe areas.

Once you have your event program and site plan, you need to develop an event build schedule.

A detailed event build schedule is invaluable to control the build of the site and communicate with everyone involved – whether on- or off-site. You can use the schedule when ordering equipment, advising contractors as to when they should arrive, and on-site during the event so that key staff know what is happening and when.

EXAMPLE Event build schedule

DATE	ACTIVITY	CONTRACTOR	EVENT REP.	TIME
Friday 11 Sept	Site hand over with local council	N/A	David Hands	8.00 a.m.
Friday 11 Sept	Site services marked	Council	David Hands	8.30 a.m.
Friday 11 Sept	**Site supervisor arrives on-site**		David Hands	8.10 a.m.
Friday 11 Sept	Site cordoned off, advisory signage	N/A	David Hands	9.00 a.m.
Friday 11 Sept	Shipping container arrives	Ships Australia	Simon Walk	9.30 a.m.

→

DATE	ACTIVITY	CONTRACTOR	EVENT REP.	TIME
Friday 11 Sept	Fencing erected	AFF – Sarah Wire	Simon Walk	10.00 a.m.
Friday 11 Sept	Portable toilets arrive	Toilet Hire – Karen Tipp	Simon Walk	10.30 a.m.
Friday 11 Sept	Marquees, trestles, chairs	Marquees 4 Hire – Eric Hair	Steve Fast	10.30 a.m.
Friday 11 Sept	Bins and skips arrive	Event Clean – Chelsea Cans	Simon Walk	11.00 a.m.
Friday 11 Sept	Generators arrive	General Gens – Peter Power	Simon Walk	11.00 a.m.
Friday 11 Sept	Fire extinguishers arrive	No Fire – Heath Mades	Simon Walk	11.00 a.m.
Friday 11 Sept	Gas bottles arrive	Go Gas – David Das	Simon Walk	11.00 a.m.
Friday 11 Sept	Electrician on-site	Event Electrics – Jamie Pleg	Simon Walk	11.00 a.m.
Friday 11 Sept	Speakers installed	Speak away – Jess Tell	Simon Walk	11.30 p.m.
Friday 11 Sept	Barwon Water trailer arrives	BW – Plumber	Steve Fast	12.00 noon
Friday 11 Sept	Sound check	Speak away – Jess Tell	Simon Walk	12.00 noon
Friday 11 Sept	Stall holders set up	Various	Steve Fast	1.00 p.m.
Friday 11 Sept	Mechanical rides set up	KT Rides – Fred Spin	Steve Fast	2.00 p.m.
Friday 11 Sept	Contractors/vendors off-site	Various	Steve Fast	5.30 p.m.
Friday 11 Sept	Security arrives	SSE – Mike Seccy	Simon Walk	6.00 p.m. Sat 7.00 a.m. Sun
Saturday 12 Sept	Roads closed	Stop Traffic – Fred Sign	Steve Fast	6.00 a.m.
Saturday 12 Sept	Site safety check	Safety Officer	David Hands	8.30 a.m.
Saturday 12 Sept	Volunteers briefing at site office		David Hands	9.15 a.m.
Saturday 12 Sept	Staff and security briefing at site office		Simon Walk	9.30 a.m.
Saturday 12 Sept	Vendors arrive	Various	Steve Fast	10.00 a.m. 9.30 p.m.
Saturday 12 Sept	St John arrive	St John – Mike First	Simon Walk	10.00 a.m. 10.00 p.m.
Saturday 12 Sept	Cleaning staff arrive/start	Clean Site – Sara Spring	Simon Walk	10.00 a.m. 11.00 p.m.
Saturday 12 Sept	Event opens		David Hands	10.00 a.m. 9.30 p.m.
Saturday 12 Sept	**Event closes/safety check of site**		David Hands	9.30 pm
Saturday 12 Sept	Roads opened	Stop Traffic – Fred Sign	Steve Fast	9.30 p.m.
Saturday 12 Sept	Security arrives	SSE – Mike Seccy	Steve Fast	9.30 p.m.

EXAMPLE Event pack-up schedule

DATE	ACTIVITY	CONTRACTOR	EVENT REP.	TIME
Sunday 13 Sept	**Site supervisor arrives & checks the site**		David Hands	6.40 a.m.
Sunday 13 Sept	Site cordoned off, bollards opened	N/A	David Hands	7.00 a.m.
Sunday 13 Sept	Contractors/vendors pack up	Various	Steve Fast	8.00 a.m.
Sunday 13 Sept	Marquees, trestles, chairs pack up	Marquees 4 Hire – Eric Hair	Steve Fast	10.00 a.m.
Sunday 13 Sept	Portable toilets leave	Toilet Hire – Karen Tipp	Simon Walk	10.00 a.m.
Sunday 13 Sept	Mechanical rides pack up	KT Rides – Fred Spin	Steve Fast	10.00 a.m.
Sunday 13 Sept	Electrician on-site	Event Electrics – Jamie Pleg	Simon Walk	10.00 a.m.
Sunday 13 Sept	Fire extinguishers collected	No Fire – Heath Mades	Simon Walk	10.00 a.m.
Sunday 13 Sept	Gas bottles collected	Go Gas – David Das	Simon Walk	10.00 a.m.
Sunday 13 Sept	Speakers dismantled	Speak away – Jess Tell	Simon Walk	10.00 a.m.
Sunday 13 Sept	Generators collected	General Gens – Peter Power	Simon Walk	10.00 a.m.
Sunday 13 Sept	Barwon Water trailer leaves	BW – Plumber	Steve Fast	10.00 a.m.
Sunday 13 Sept	Fencing dismantled	AFF – Sarah Wire	Simon Walk	11.00 a.m.
Sunday 13 Sept	Shipping container leaves	Ships Australia	Simon Walk	12.00 noon
Sunday 13 Sept	Cleaning arrive final site clean	Event Clean – Chelsea Cans	Simon Walk	12.00 noon
Sunday 13 Sept	Bins and skips leave	Event Clean – Chelsea Cans	Simon Walk	2.00 p.m.
Sunday 13 Sept	**Site supervisor checks & leaves the site**		David Hands	2.15 p.m.
Monday 14 Sept	Site hand back with local council		David Hands	9.00 a.m.

STAFF ROLES AND CONTACT LIST

During the event planning period, you will have allocated people to be responsible for different aspects of the planning and running of the event. Distribute this list of people's roles and contacts so they can communicate with each other and understand who is responsible for which element.

EXAMPLE Staff roles and contact list

EVENT STAFF		
RESPONSIBILITY	**EVENT REP**	**PHONE NO.**
Site manager/supervisor	David Hands	0411 xxx xxx
Site management support	Simon Walk	0415 xxx xxx
Liquor licence	Joan Beard	0412 xxx xxx
Food vendors	Josie Noone	0417 xxx xxx
Stall holders	Josie Noone	0417 xxx xxx
Safety officer	Liz Laylor	0478 xxx xxx
Chief warden	David Hands	0411 xxx xxx
Volunteer coordinator	Sarah Tiff	0415 xxx xxx
VIP host	Meg Tiff	0452 xxx xxx
Media management	Meg Tiff	0425 xxx xxx
Stage production	Josh Gross	0418 xxx xxx
Race director	Lara Lane	0415 xxx xxx

CONTRACTORS AND SUPPLIERS			
SERVICE	**COMPANY NAME**	**STAFF**	**PHONE NO.**
Traffic management	Stop Traffic	Fred Sign	0415 xxx xxx
Fencing	AFF	Sarah Wire	0425 xxx xxx
Portable toilets	Dunniroos	Sam Flush	0485 xxx xxx
Marquee hire	Tents Australia	Fred Pole	0485 xxx xxx
Cleaners	Clean Site	Sara Spring	0415 xxx xxx
Waste hire	Go Aways	Dave Dert	0425 xxx xxx
Electrician	Sparky Time	Eric Tass	0417 xxx xxx
Staging	On Stage Events	Tim Todd	0487 xxx xxx
Mechanical rides	Spin Around	Alvie Marks	0528 xxx xxx
Fire extinguishers	Bramfords	David Door	0428 xxx xxx
Security	Secure Event	Jane Nece	0452 xxx xxx
Shipping containers	Ships Australia	Doug Poon	0428 xxx xxx
First aid	St John Ambulance	Jess Lance	0425 xxx xxx

FOOD VENDORS			
NAME OF BUSINESS	LOCATION ON SITE MAP	NAME	PHONE NO.
Sammy's Sausages	FV1	Sam Snake	0428 xxx xxx
Jane's Juices	FV2	Jane Hare	0452 xxx xxx
Laurie's Lollies	FV3	Laurie Lake	0428 xxx xxx
Bill's Bar and Bistro	FV3	Bill Lion	0428 xxx xxx

Visit the site for more information:

http://www.geelongaustralia.com.au/events/planning/eventplanning/article/item/
8cdc2778104484a.aspx

Events Planning Guide:

Section 1: How to apply for an event (reproduced here)
Section 2: Developing an Event Plan
Section 3: Event risk management and planning
Section 4: Event emergency management and planning
Section 5: Other useful event planning information

Tools and templates for events:

These resources include:
· Event Application Form
· Event Risk Assessment
· Indemnity Form
· Application to Close a Road
· Division 2 Occupancy Permit (POPE)
Application for Siting Approval - Prescribed Temporary Structures

GLOSSARY

A

accreditation Process of issuing access to specific event zones or areas.

action plan Indicates the specific tasks to be undertaken, by whom and when; ongoing improvement is also part of action planning.

audience Anyone watching 'the show', including spectators and conference delegates.

B

back of house In the event context, the operations area, which includes kitchens, stores and so on.

banquet event order (BEO) Specifies the client's specifications and the event booking details.

borders Materials used to mask the upper portion of the stage area, such as fabric or canvas; also known as a valance curtain.

break-even point The point at which there is enough income from an event to meet expenses.

budget A financial plan or forecast; an estimate of income and expenditure.

C

commercial venue Venue that charges for hire or offers event packages, usually designed for the purpose of staging events.

conference Gatherings focused on information-sharing and education, most commonly of a business or academic nature.

congress Gathering that includes representatives from different groups; for example, the National Congress of Australia's First People.

consideration For an agreement to be binding, something of value must change hands, usually money but could include goods or services.

context for risk Depending on the nature of the event, indoor or outdoor, a different context is presented, with specific risks; the weather, for example, can change the risk context very quickly.

contingency plan Developed to respond to potential risk situations.

contracts Agreement concerning an independent contractor's labour or skills whereby payment is made on the basis of hourly or daily rates; or relating to an independent contractor achieving a result where payment is made on the basis of a fixed fee.

convention Large-scale gathering with the intention of reaching agreement on an issue, generally of a political nature.

critical path Determines the minimum time needed to complete a project.

customers In relation to events, includes spectators, visitors, ticket holders, delegates and media.

cyclorama Curved white screen at the back of the stage, used for light projections.

D

deliverables Project deliverables can be tangible, such as an operations manual, or intangible, such as completion of security briefings.

dietary preferences Lifestyle-related food choices, such as a low-sugar or low-fat diet.

digital marketing Marketing using digital channels, including social media and apps.

duty of care Legal obligation of a person or organisation to avoid acts or omissions that could foreseeably harm others.

E

event coordinator Organises all aspects of an event for a client.

event program The line-up of speakers or entertainers at an event.

expenses Money spent or costs incurred in an organisation's efforts to generate revenue, representing the cost of doing business.

experiential marketing Active participation in a marketing initiative.

external customers Users of the end product or service of an organisation.

extrinsic (external) motivator Where behaviour is driven by an external tangible reward such as a bonus or public recognition.

F

facility Alternative term used for an event location, particularly in North America.

financial report Shows an organisation's financial status; may be done at the end of an accounting period.

food allergies Physical reactions to certain foods; in some cases, such as peanuts, these can be life-threatening.

formal contract A deed, or a contract under seal.

front of house In the event context, the area where customers are served.

G

greenfield site Site that has no buildings or other infrastructure, and where all equipment needs to be brought in.

H

hallmark events Designed to gain prominence in the tourism market, helping with destination branding and marketing.

hazard Anything that has the potential to harm people.

I

income Generally in the form of sales but can also include sponsorships, donations and commissions.

indemnity Exemption from liability for damages.

individualism/collectivism Hofstede's second value dimension, highlighting the difference between individuality and conformity to group norms.

induction The embedding of individuals in the workplace with the aim of allowing them to 'settle in'.

initiation Project initiation is the first stage in the project management life cycle and involves defining objectives, scope, purpose and deliverables.

intellectual property Intangible property such as copyright, designs, patents, trademarks and trade secrets.

internal customers Another department or service provider working to deliver the final product or service to the external customer.

intrinsic (internal) motivator Where behaviour is driven by internal rewards such as satisfaction or a sense of achievement.

K

key performance indicators (KPIs) Indicators that help to define and measure progress towards organisational goals.

L

line of sight Audience view of the stage.

M

major events Regular or one-off events that generate significant economic, social and cultural benefits, and so are often supported by governments.

MC Master of ceremonies.

mega events Large-scale, internationally broadcast events of global interest, with significant economic impacts.

MICE Meetings, incentives, conferences and exhibitions.

minor events Smaller-scale events generally involving domestic or local audiences.

multiplier effect Describes how money spent by event organisers and visitors circulates through the economy.

O

organisers Includes the event manager, event producer, management team and/or committee giving oversight to the event.

orientation A new employee's introduction to the organisation.

P

PCBU Persons conducting a business or undertaking.

PCO Professional conference organiser.

performance appraisal Formal process for providing performance feedback.

performers Includes dancers and singers, but in the broader sense refers to anyone in 'the show' – on stage (speakers) or on the field (athletes).

policy Statement of intention, such as to be environmentally sustainable.

power distance First of Hofstede's value dimensions, indicating the extent to which a society accepts differences in power and authority.

precinct Covers a large area that includes several venues (e.g. Commonwealth Games precinct).

procedure Steps involved in implementing a policy, such as separating waste streams.

R

religious requirements Halal and kosher food are prepared with religious requirements in mind, excluding prohibited ingredients or using specific preparation methods.

return on investment (ROI) Return on an investment in financial terms.

return on objectives (ROO) Return on objectives such as brand recognition.

revenue Sales revenues reflect income from sales of goods or services.

RFID Radio frequency identification chip or transponder.

rigging System of lines, blocks and counterweights that enable the crew to move stage equipment such as lights and special effects.

risk Effect of foreseeable uncertainties on objectives – simply, things going wrong.

risk management Involves forecasting and evaluating risks in order to minimise their impact.

risk management process Has five main steps: establish context, identify risks, analyse and evaluate them, then treat the risks; review and consultation are also part of the process.

risk treatment Development of ways to modify or reduce risk.

S

set All objects on the stage.

simple contract Agreement made between two or more parties, generally supported by a document expressing that agreement in writing but which can be made orally.

site Generally an oudoor space with limited infrastructure.

stage manager Organises the production.

stakeholders May include internal and external customers, organising committees, funding bodies, regulatory authorities and other government authorities.

storyboard A collection of graphical items used to illustrate creative designs.

supplier Provides event goods (e.g. floral arrangements) and services (e.g. audiovisual set-up).

T

talent Speakers, actors, entertainers – anyone who is part of delivering the production.

trade show A trade show is designed to sell products, mainly to retailers.

traveller A curtain that moves along a track.

triple bottom line Economic, social and environmental impacts.

U

utilities Utilities include supplies of water and electricity.

V

value in kind (VIK) Also known as 'contra', occurs when a sponsor provides goods/services in exchange for sponsorship rights. In similar situations involving government or community groups, contribution is also given a monetary value and shown in the budget.

vendor Generally supplies direct to the customer, such as a hot dog vendor or concession.

venue Generally refers to a built structure where an event takes place.

venue coordinator Works for the venue to manage the event from booking through to payment.

W

work breakdown structure (WBS) Involves organising key tasks into logical sections or clusters.

Y

yield management Variable pricing strategy based on historical data and consumer trends in order to maximise revenue.

INDEX

B